I0135709

Buddha's Mom

The Neurobiology of Spiritual Awakening

Dr. Schroder eloquently explores the human psyche with its mysterious energies, emotional upheavals, pains, disturbances of self, joy, love and compassion. In a voice that is skillful, erudite, humorous and poetic, he intimately brings us in touch with two attachments. What seems contradictory at first arcs to remarkably deep insights literally embodied in the construct of Buddha's Mom.
Sabine Grunwald, PhD.
Director, UF Mindfulness Program

For your graceful way, hours and hours of help with the manuscript, for convincing me Buddha's Mom matters, thank you Sabine.   VS

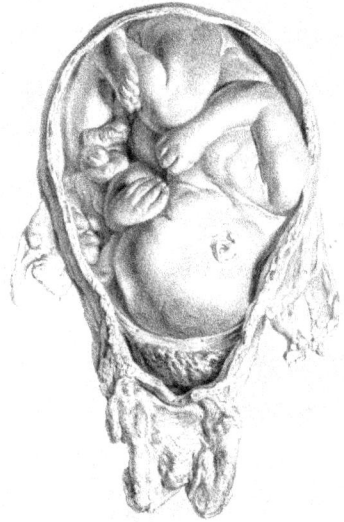

BUDDHA'S MOM

THE

NEUROBIOLOGY

OF

SPIRITUAL AWAKENING

Vincent Schroder

© 2017 Vincent Schroder

All Rights Reserved. No part of this publication may be reproduced, distributed, or transmitted in any form or by any means, including photocopying, recording, or other electronic or mechanical methods, without the prior written permission of the publisher, except in the case of brief quotations embodied in critical reviews and certain other noncommercial uses permitted by copyright law.

ISBN: 978-0-692-59257-1 ARC
ISBN: 978-0-9981284-0-5 First Edition

Author: Vincent Schroder
Inquiries/feedback: www.buddhasmom.com

TABLE OF CONTENTS

PREFACE

The biography of the baby, boy and man who would become Buddha presses ever onward. Every turn in the classic story of Siddhartha Gautama (Buddha's given name prior to his enlightenment) pulses with inevitability, the greatness to come. Siddhartha is born to privilege. He is wealthy, loved and cared for. But famously, he soon leaves it all behind. At this inflection point, Siddhartha walks away from what most of us hold tightly to, never to return. In time, he achieves enlightenment and teaches the dharma. Then as now, his journey to Nirvana beguiles and inspires.

In Buddha's Mom, we retrace the biography's major currents while exploring some less traveled and enticing tributaries. We endeavor to uncover (and thereby recover) all distinguishable early influences. In clinical terms, our focus is on Siddhartha's early-life attachment experiences especially, what in modern terms would be his maternal attachment experience. We continue in this vein and delve into Siddhartha's major "adult attachment" experiences. These encompass the major emotional, interpersonal relationships of his life. We will try to show with precision how these have mappable, meaningful implications for what becomes Buddhism, and for anyone on a spiritual journey.

Attachment figures and relationships which we will be exploring include: Siddhartha's birth mother, Mahamahamaya; his adopted mother, stepmother and Buddhism's first nun, Mahāprajāpatī; Siddhartha's father, Suddhodana; his wife, Yasodhara; his son and only child, Rahula; and his cousin, brother-in-law and would be assassin, Devadatta. Others include Buddha's attendant, Ananda and key people he encounters during his many years of teaching, such as Kisa Gotami, Sujata, Sudatta and Subhuti. Toward the end of the book, we consider the culmination of an important relationship between Buddha and the evil deity, Mara.

Throughout we continuously weave back and forth through Buddhism's major tenets, most notably attachment. This is the attachment of the Four Noble Truths, the attachment that Buddha declares to be the source of human suffering. Biological attachment has only gained in traction since Bowlby, augmented by affective neuroscience and a modern amalgamation of evidence centered around polyvagal theory and corresponding, emerging somatic therapies.[1] The "two attachments" therefore correspond to biological, maternal and social attachment on the one hand, and on the other to the attachment at the heart of Buddhism. The latter, of course, is linked to the 'cessation of suffering' and therein to liberation and nirvana.

With great care, relying on varied and reputable resources, we make a case for a deep, permeating, transcendent meaning running through these "two attachments" grounded in a comprehensive body of neuroscience. An "integral attachment" takes the form of an accessible, psychological space wherein neurobiological/scientific and spiritual distinctions can be appreciated in full and superseded. This book is part textbook, part self-help, while aiming higher than either of these. It is probably best suited for the 'educated seeker'—those with some grounding in the psychology-Buddhism arena.

As a psychologist over the last 18 years, I have been immersed in paradigm-busting experiences leading up to the ideas presented here. My professional work has included research in attachment as well as therapy with attachment-disordered children, for example, orphans from Romania. In a broad range of settings, I have been privileged to witness the healing powers embodied in the concepts discussed in this book. I share several associated stories. The same ideas and practices, I am persuaded, that help people heal from intense emotional pain translate as vessels for transformation and transcendence.

Relatedly, for the past dozen years as a dad, I have been immersed in what might be called an indigenous, Buddhist approach to attachment parenting. Credit for any constructive ideas regarding attachment goes to my wife, our children and my Thai-Lao Buddhist in-laws.

In my view, big gaps remain between many important, fascinating, inter-related ideas and research findings regarding attachment and the ultimate questions of meaning, practice and joy in life. These gaps particularly implicate the feminine principle. Through "her" what I refer to as the human lineage, deep self disturbance, relative attachment and other important ideas go a long way towards mapping sentience itself. Confusion is more commonplace than need be. For example, we long for meaning, but longing, grasping and the like cause suffering. Do we long to suffer? The word "paradox" is often applied to these existential eddies. Sometimes paradox and pithy teachings need to be supplemented with a fuller, clearer, more precise model of human functioning and suffering. I hope these ideas add something of value in this regard and, ultimately, to what it means to be alive.

Potentially, the larger the canvas the higher the resolution. Both oversimplification and overly dense explanations obscure a viable, integral view. Something of a unifying, golden strand is discernible. Here, we will work lovingly and judiciously to trace this thread winding through evolutionary theory, clinical and depth psychology, and neuroscience, then further through Buddhism proper, especially the Tibetan Buddhist traditions, for example, the Vajrayana, Tantric and Dzogchen lineages. The golden thread, as it were, spills into a vast open, accessible, space where "the two attachments" achieve an unrestricted, integrative expanse. I hope these ideas convey a deepening sense of home and belonging to anyone psychologically adrift or emotionally hurting. Any readers who feel moved to comment are invited to visit online (www.buddhasmom.com).

Chapter One

BECOMING BUDDHA

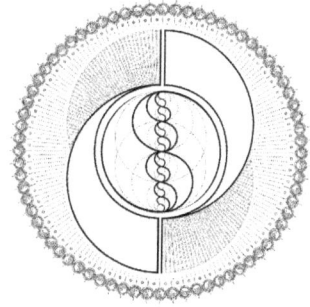

Two Attachments

Consider this simple question: Was Buddha breastfed? Official accounts indicate that he probably was. The bigger question remains—so what? What possible relevance could this hold for the world's 400 million Buddhists and the hundreds of millions more who are inspired by Buddha's teachings? The short answer is: far more than one might initially suspect. The book in your hands, electronic or otherwise, offers a second, much longer and hopefully worthy response.

We will explore what is known about Buddha's Mom, her pregnancy, the birth and early life of Siddhartha. Alongside this, we will burrow into the grand psychological context of breastfeeding and maternal attachment. Lines of evidence are converging with respect to the consequences of early life attachment for health and happiness. Static conclusions with respect to the role of these factors for psychological growth and healing have proven premature. A view, for example, that "I can't do anything about that now," no longer matches the data. This book pushes back, hopefully in a compelling manner, against such presumptions.

To begin, we need to explore "the two attachments" (just introduced in the Preface). As almost everyone knows, breastfeeding and the world of mother-baby bonding, play and communication fall under the domain of maternal/biological attachment. In the past fifty years or so, this attachment has gone from relative obscurity to front-page notoriety. Before this surge of research and attendant hype and controversy, maternal attachment was both ever-present and obscure.

Such is the case for Buddha. The ancient texts say little regarding Siddhartha's maternal attachment, and the little said about this is not intrinsically connected to the "second" attachment at the core of Siddhartha-as-Buddha's teachings. Buddhism's official attachment, in fact, consistently runs in the opposite direction. This is no small matter. Orthodox views on attachment permeate the dharma, Buddhism's formal body of precepts, philosophy, ethics and truth claims. Where the first (maternal) attachment presumably has some value, at least for babies, the second is distinctively identified as the cause of human suffering.

The focus on attachment in Buddhism is, of course, ultimately positive and stems from its inverse relationship to enlightenment. Buddha's s own enlightenment is emblematic. He had searched mightily for spiritual truth. He finally awoke with the realization that attaching, craving, clinging and longing causes human suffering, and in this awakening, transcended all human attachment tendencies. He encoded these insights into the Four Noble Truths and the Eightfold Path. In these, he establishes the enchanting possibility of the nirvana that he achieved, an extinguishing and cessation of suffering, for any one of us. No doubt this has something to do with the reader's decision to explore this book!

Of course, nowhere in his deliberations or final insights concerning attachment does the question of breastfeeding or mom-baby bonding arise. But this matter and the question just posed, "Was Buddha breastfed?" may not be as lightweight or impertinent as it first seems. Let's begin with what is told of Siddhartha's own attachment experience. The Pali Canon (the collected teachings of the Buddha) refers specifically and repeatedly to baby Siddhartha's "nursemaids." Nursemaids or "wet nurses" were culturally and historically commonplace in well-to-do families such as his. Lactating women with their own babies were routinely hired to assist not only in caregiving but also specifically to breastfeed, hence their title.

Remarkably, decades later, none other than the highly respected Ananda—Buddha's singularly faithful servant and documentarian—referred to Buddha having been breastfed. Ananda did so when weighing in on the plea of Siddhartha's stepmother, Mahāprajāpatī, to become Buddhism's first nun. Ananda reminded Buddha that Prajapati (as we will refer to her) had wet-nursed him.

Her story, I believe, deserves more intense and loving consideration than it has received. She is variously referred to as Siddhartha's aunt, foster mother, adopted mother and stepmother. But ultimately, no one human deserves the title, Buddha's Mom, more than she.

The topic of Buddha's own attachment and breastfeeding takes us to the doorstep of modern attachment theory. An entire field called "adult attachment" has evolved from the hundreds of studies demonstrating major repercussions of early life attachment on adult functioning in mammals, primates, and humans. In the latter, a "cascade of adaptations that directly shape the development of the child's nervous system."[2] This area of research is alternatively referred to as attachment, as well as biological, maternal and social attachment.

Based in no small part on this research, breastfeeding is very much back in vogue. But there is much more to attachment than sensible or sentimental maternal care. As we will get into in depth, the consequences have been well mapped. For example, human adults tend to demonstrate stable, global "secure," "anxious-ambivalent," or "avoidant" personality styles. Research demonstrates that one's original attachment experience has powerful, lifelong implications.

Some confusion regarding the subject of breastfeeding is understandable. Most people know its importance for the baby's health and that maternal nurturing and bonding are important for positive emotional functioning. But to date, the research has not isolated any given set of variables or timeframes as salient. None of the normally occurring variables, for example, breastfeeding proper; skin-to-skin contact; gazing and eye contact; the baby's ability to hear its mom's heartbeat as it did in-utero or to feel her movement; the value of being "worn" and carried; and other tender, loving, actions; stand out as key. Others, such as attentiveness and empathy, undoubtedly matter but are harder to operationalize. No critical time period has emerged as uniquely relevant either. This makes sense given that many attachment-related phenomena overlap or occur simultaneously across the span of development for infants, babies, toddlers and children.

The take-away seems to be that, for better or worse, multiple, integrated nurturing-nourishing variables comprise attachment. A gestalt or totality matters more than whether the biological mother or "another mother" breastfeeds, or whether the mother pumps and bottle-feeds because she does not produce enough milk, or whether the baby cannot latch. Without these factors, for example, skin contact, movement, cooing, gazing and tickling and talking, breastfeeding would hardly be recognizable.

In the case of Siddhartha Gautama, the most probable, evidence-based assumption is not only that he breastfed but more importantly that he had a normal, healthy—or better—early life attachment experience. This evidence will be explored in detail. As most anyone inspired by Buddha knows, during childhood he was famously ensconced in a close-knit, well-to-do family. In addition to what appears to have been a hardy early life attachment, Siddhartha likely continued to take part in close, trusting, emotional relationships as he grew up. His biography paints a picture of a normal (if not better), uninterrupted, family-centered early life. This was followed by his marriage to his cousin, Yasodhara, when both were sixteen years old. Yasodhara moved into the Gautama family home and the couple continued to live there for the next thirteen years, until Siddhartha's iconic departure from home at age twenty-nine.

This tale deserves the deepest possible reconsideration and re-appreciation. Diligent research has proven the emotional attachment system to be an evolutionary given, which axiomatically has contributed to our species' achievements. Attachment is analogous to gravity; all celestial bodies, all humans, are endowed with it. Smaller, let's say, younger and less mature beings have less, while larger ones have more. If all goes according to plan, the once passive nursing infant becomes an increasingly active participant. She or he becomes an ever more relationally involved, as both receiver and source of attachment over time.

If all went reasonably well, as the official sources suggest was the case, Siddhartha would have exhibited predictable attachment-related emotional maturation over time. The record is quite compelling in this regard, indicating that Siddhartha not only received love and care but also gave the same in return. We will go into this aspect of his biography in detail. A parsimonious presumption in the meantime bolsters the case we will be building: in Siddhartha, the species-specific transmission of emotional attachment capacities was a smashing success. Put another way, the baby and boy who would become Buddha experienced a robust early-life attachment. He in turn "came into his own" with respect to attachment. As this phrase implies, having received such attention, he then gave of and from the same source. There was a recapitulation of love in his relationships with extended family, friends, and his wife. He thus was a "we" as well as a "he." The key "we-spaces" of his life were informed by attachment and, we will suggest, powerfully informed his teachings.

The absence of explicit information on Siddhartha's original attachment in the ancient texts presents a challenge. The lack of detail, of course, is hardly surprising given that it would be more than 2400 years before Darwin's evolutionary theory would make its dramatic entrance. Even then, another 100 years would pass before the British psychologist John Bowlby would put maternal attachment on the map. And more time still would go by before the field of adult attachment would gain steam. Fortunately, these bodies of knowledge among others provide supports for teasing out the cultural, historical and patriarchal distortions impacting Siddhartha/Buddha's attachment experiences and relationships.

An overarching distortion (we will make the case) pertains to what often goes by the term "materialism." As most will recall, the iconic tale of the boy who becomes the Buddha portrays young Siddhartha as never wanting. This very element then becomes a foil for his decision to leave it all behind.

> He had everything desirable in this world. But in his twenty-ninth year, he decided to withdraw from it and devote himself to the study of the means of emancipation from all the ills that flesh is heir to.[3]

"Everything desirable" is painted as shallow and troublesome. That which is desired equates to "all the ills that the flesh is heir to." What is now better understood as attachment, which includes breastfeeding and the nurturing-nourishing nexus, risks being bundled with this typical sort of condemnation. In a patriarchal worldview, materialistic attachments are shorn from their natural depths just as the word materialism is divorced from its root, *mater*, which is Latin for mother. In this book, an effort will be made to free the biography of the Buddha from patriarchal, historical and cultural limitations. An integral combination of lenses will be employed to support a re-encountering of (what we will consider as) Buddha's psychospiritual inheritance via attachment. Hopefully, this will increase the aperture on his magnificent dharma.

The "third turning" is especially germane to this potential. As most readers will already know, the word "turnings" refers to the three major unfoldings of Buddhism across history. The third, the Vajrayana tradition or Diamond Vehicle, is presumed to incorporate and deepen the expression of previous turnings (the Theravada and Mahayana lineages respectively). Adherents view the Vajrayana lineage as providing a more accurate and penetrating access to the dharma. In time, we will suggest that the approach falling under Buddha's Mom presents an updated and integral view of attachment that amplifies the gifts and insights of the third turning in Buddhism.

Chögyam Trungpa, Ken Wilber, Reggie Ray and others, in fact, say that a fourth turning of the wheel of dharma is upon us. Concepts comprising Buddha's Mom may be bit players in these weighty matters but they also appear to be consistent with what these luminaries describe.

Spear Tip

Among the beneficiaries of this journey toward an integral attachment, in which the "two attachments" both thrive and disappear, may just be the long-suffering ego. In an evolutionary light, ego operates as our species-specific spearhead of consciousness. We will consider this "tip of the iceberg" vision when tracing attachment from its evolutionary headwaters into the great expanses of consciousness described by the perspectives of the third and fourth turning.

A unified view of the attachment-ego relationship comes into resolution as both biological and Buddhist tracks are pursued openly, judiciously and with care. Advances in attachment and the formation of ego have fueled the rise of our species to its current level of dominance and intelligence. Based on an encompassing view of attachment, we make a case for a reclamation of ego as a paradoxically critical sliver of consciousness that abides within a larger, transcendent field. From the perspectives we will explore, ego, mind and self are placeholders for something like a lost, confused and willful child. Within the great span of both science and spirit, and specifically, the feminine principle, this orphan that gives rise to a localized meaning in life can be re-found, loved unconditionally and thereby returned to its true, expansive home.

Ultimately though, the tip of the iceberg metaphor is limiting. Ego viewed as the center or leading edge of consciousness and awareness, and therein differentiated from the subconscious, only goes so far. Its grounding in reality turns out to be incredibly minute. Buddhism rests on the premise that ego consciousness and reality are mistakenly conflated. To perceive ego (and for that matter, self and mind) as conscious is a sort of perfect error. The more this claim is true, the falser it is. "Most of the mind" as Daniel Siegel stresses "is nonconscious."[4] Only through an integration of drop and ocean can something more coherent, sensible, accurate and enlightening be encountered. Mystical notions of the whole of the ocean within a single drop need not remain obscure. As Andrew Cohen says:

> What is it in you that brings you to a spiritual teacher in the first place? It's not the spirit in you, since that is already enlightened, and has no need to seek. No, it is the ego in you that brings you to a teacher. [5]

Perhaps a new Buddhism, or said otherwise, a new ability to immerse and then lose oneself (one's self) in the truths of Buddhism, exists at this time in history. For the past several decades the West's earnest, ravenous empiricism has been commingling with strands of ancient, Eastern mysticism. This book is just one more effort at forging progress in this Buddhist-psychology/neuroscience arena. In particular, we follow breadcrumbs, ideas and findings, into the unsung, downtrodden and shadowy realm of the feminine, beginning with maternal attachment.

While "brains on meditation" research has been on the ascent, the same holds true for "brains on attachment." The latter increasingly suggests something breathtaking. For example, presuming for the moment that baby Siddhartha was happily attached to his mom, a modern view would posit this to have lifelong consequences. His attachment would not be viewed as time-bound, nor as involving a bit player, nor neutrally.

Buddhism's dominant and negativistic view of attachment as causing suffering begs many questions. Put crudely, if one attachment (maternal) is good and the other bad, then at what point in life is it no longer appropriate to be attached? Buddhism is laden with lists and rules and positions on multiple matters but virtually silent on this and related questions.

The closest Buddhism seems to come to directly taking on the two attachments—and we will explore this in depth—is referred to as the Middle Way. In the lead up to this, Siddhartha is depicted as struggling to free himself from both materialistic and emotional attachments. This culminates in his decision to leave home. The traditional portrayal is consistent with the following. Siddhartha was deeply attached to his mother, father and wife, and to all he had known at that point, his twenty-nine years on earth. In an effort to penetrate the spiritual longing and incompleteness he nonetheless experienced, he pursued the opposite pole, sheer renunciation of all attachments. This is the set-up for the iconic austerities during which Siddhartha engaged in extremes of self-deprivation.

Amidst these dark passages, he would forge a Middle Way. By neither over-attaching nor over-detaching, he opened a path equally definable as emptiness and a higher love. This was as much an unsurpassed attachment to the true, transcendent heart of our very nature as a detachment from evolution's intractable cloying. This integral encounter with reality, this supreme knowing, was realized *through* more than in spite of our species' attachment inheritance. All this flowed from emotional and bodily pain, and specifically through the relationship with this pain. A modern, Middle Way through attachment evokes a fresh, transformative experience of Buddha's most intense internal and interpersonal relationships.

With these insights, for example, that through pain comes liberation, certain elements in the biography seem to fall in place. Shortly after his enlightenment, Buddha returned home and spent time with those he had left behind. Having renounced attachments, he returned precisely to be with those to whom he was once so attached.

What is often framed as the forsaking of attachments and as renunciation achieves more nuance in Buddhism's second and third turnings. A more integral, advanced view of attachment, and therein suffering and the cessation of suffering, is possible at this time. Siddhartha's adoptive/stepmother, Prajapati, offers a good starting point. We glean from the Pali Canon that Siddhartha (and later, Siddhartha-as-Buddha) spent a great deal of time with her. What survives of these interactions, and of the other stirring adult attachment relationships, is especially moving and relevant for anyone on a spiritual path. Seen integrally, Buddha's interactions indicate that attachment and love are richly intertwined and critical to the derivation of meaning and the prospect of realization

Toward the end of her life, Prajapati wrote a poem acknowledging that only through her son had she finally found release. Here we would add that only through her attachment to her son did she achieve nonattachment.

> Buddha! Hero! Praise be to you!
> You foremost among all beings!
> You who have released me from pain,
> And so many other beings too.[6]

What the Buddha discovered and has given to the world, the inspiration for these words from his mother, is now more mappable and palpable than ever. Substantiation of this gains, for example, with knowledge from affective neuroscience (a powerful, emerging science of emotion and sentience in animals and humans), clinical and depth psychology. These and other fields of knowledge act as a sort of telescope enabling a high-resolution view of, possibly, the psychological building blocks of Buddhism's great, time-tested insights.

Here we train the telescope on the awakening Prajapati describes, and provides support for this not as an event but in terms of a living, flowing, human potential that we all share—embedded in an integral attachment. We will consider evidence that the seed of Buddhism's nirvana, the end of suffering, lives within our species' inherited, relational field of consciousness and ego, mind and self-sense.

As her own biography delicately reveals, Prajapati's release from pain is rooted in that which Siddhartha and she shared at the beginning of his life, and which they would share for decades thereafter. Buddha would awaken in his mother the same reality, there all along, that he had come to know while sitting under the Bodhi tree. As we will soon see, Buddha helped many others to awaken from attachment through attachment, as he cohabitated, interacted and spoke with others. Over and again those awakened describe what is called Śūnyatā, no self or emptiness.

> That there is a self has been taught,
> And the doctrine of no-self,
> By the Buddhas as well as the
> Doctrine of neither self nor nonself.[7]

We propose Buddha's Mom (with mom capitalized) as a worthy name for the innate, attachment-based vessel via which awakening is achieved. Buddha's Mom refers to that which both includes and transcends the concrete, biological and personal, psychological realm. So "she" includes all of Siddhartha's maternal caregivers, and all of biological, social and adult attachment. "She" comprises the upriver source, the evolutionary headwaters of attachment within human consciousness. This flows and empties into an ocean too vast for anything that came before. Something equally describable as empty and full.

Many Names

In the Pali Canon, Buddha's biological mother has many names—Mayadevi, Mahamaya, and more formally, Mahamahamaya or Queen Maya of Sakya. His second mom, her younger sister, is sometimes called his adoptive mother, foster mother, and stepmother. Her name is Pajapati or Prajapati (in Pali and Sanskrit respectively). This is sometimes combined with *maha*, the title connoting greatness, giving us her holiness, Mahāprajaāpatī. Her last, inherited name is Gautami (Gotami in Pali), possibly given to highlight the fact that she shares her son's "worldly name and lineage."[8] Prajapati is the mother figure credited with the poem beginning, "Buddha! Hero! Praise be to you!"

From the perspective of attachment as a vessel of the transmission of consciousness, Mahamaya and Prajapati are an integrated source which conveys something of profound importance to Siddhartha. To reduce confusion, we suggest a single name, Buddha's Mom. What is conveyed has a singular character. It is more of a unified, species-specific, vital capacity, and more a living lineage than anything static or a multiplicity of distinct elements. This integrated source also implicates Siddhartha's other caregivers, the long since nameless nursemaids. Their names and the concrete specifics of Siddhartha's attachment and bonding experiences are lost to the sands of time. Limits in archeological findings can be supplemented by other sources of information. With due caution, humility, and reliance on an integral approach, more may be gleaned than first meets the eye.

The recipient of this integral, singular force, which flows through attachment figures and biological, maternal and social attachment, also has a mappable quality of singularity, we will explore. At the same time, this splinters into discrete, separable entities including Siddhartha, me, you, ego, self and mind. Attachment's dance partner first leads, then hands over the lead. It transmits its' all to that which receives, becoming that which transmits, and so on. One dimension of this natural-sacred process, these "two attachments", has been an intensive focus of cross-disciplinary research over the past few decades.

Bonding

As most everyone knows, breastfeeding and nurturing, cuddling, cooing, which science refers to a bit dryly as attachment and bonding, has been in the spotlight for decades. Well-designed, sound research has demonstrated how early-life, mother-offspring bonds have tremendous implications for development across the lifespan. These events are believed to powerfully influence adult personality and functioning beginning tens of thousands of years ago. So potent was this affective glue that tribes operated as cohesive units able to dominate their environmental niche with advances in gathering, hunting and the perpetuation of the tribe through pair bonding and an intricate approach to raising offspring to carry on the tribe's collective skill set.

Over the past thirty years, this body of research has squarely established adult attachment as a formidable construct and field of study. For example, babies once observed and categorized using objective, behavioral, measurable criteria as secure, anxious-ambivalent or avoidant, have been followed through childhood and into adulthood. In simple terms, attentive, playful mothering establishes security. A middling form, characterized by intermittent healthy and unhealthy mothering, results in the anxious-ambivalent attachment type; more marginal forms of parenting, laden with neglect, result in a genre of avoidance.

Relative Attachment per Bowlby's 3-fold Model

SECURE TYPE

- Better balance between attachment and detachment sub-processes.
- Skillful means at both letting go and being with that which arises
- Skilled at relation-centered practice, at friendship and intimacy as vessels of healing and transformation.
- Healthy 'wego'.
- Engaged, living, conscious access to Buddha's mom.

ANXIOUS TYPE

- Emphasis on attachment pole within relative attachment.
- Difficulty with letting go, with stillness and silence, e.g., Theravada forms.
- Blind spot: aversion to detachment. May be prone to idealizing others including teachers.

AVOIDANT TYPE

- Emphasis on the detachment pole within relative attachment.
- Affinity for meditation as letting go and renunciation.
- Blind spot: aversion to attachment. Better at denying self than caring for self.

Relative Attachment per Bartholomew's 4-fold Model

Self/Subjective "the Witness"

Other/Objective "that which arises"

SECURE—Healthy wego, facile with all dualities: self and other, subject and object, attachment and detachment. Skillful means at Tonglen, skilled at both Theravada renunciation and Tantric deity/compassion practices.

PREOCCUPIED—Prone to clinging. Difficulty with stillness, silence, space; Problems letting go. Natural inclination toward engaged, emotional forms of practice.

DISMISSIVE—Prone to detaching, repressing. Skills at stillness and silence by virtue of dismissing 'that which arises.' Natural inclination towards renunciation and conceptual emptiness.

FEARFUL—Discomfort with both self and other, subject and object. Common in deep self disturbance. Conflicted between clinging and avoidance.

Further research demonstrated that the anxious-ambivalent style to be a combination of a pre-occupied and fear-based orientation, and that as a whole, four distinct attachment styles reflect the combination of positive and negative orientation to self and other. This work underscores evidence of attachment's scope of influence. This formidable body of research offers further support for efforts to consider how human attachment has shaped Buddhism and how Buddhism's great insights yield deepenings, refinements and extensions of attachment theory.

As adults, these attachment styles are replicated not only in intimate relationships but have proven to have unexpected repercussions, for example, in approaches to work and in health and well-being. In the last fifty years, more than 2,200 books and articles have been published with the term "adult attachment" in the title. One fifth of these have been published in the last three years. The basic take-away message is that early life attachment, generally meaning mom-son, mom-daughter attachment, is a powerful force in shaping adult functioning. The current effort to probe the intersection of biological attachment and the attachment at the core of Buddhism may be important. Walker finds that the feminine biological attachment leads to a superior appreciation of human nature.

> Like other female animals, genetically prepared to be responsible for lives
> other than their own, women are quick learners and keen observers. With the
> cumulative experience of many years of living, observing and relating to
> others, woman may routinely achieve higher levels of understanding the
> human condition than most men dream of. [9]

In the 1960s, John Bowlby and his student Mary Ainsworth did original, groundbreaking research on attachment. They found that toddlers fell into two groups, secure and insecure. The latter group was made up of those who were anxious, ambivalent and avoidant. Some of the children categorized as such were followed longitudinally. As the years went by, these personality styles were maintained into adulthood. Eventually, an entire field of adult attachment formed based on findings that these styles were, statistically, maintained across the human lifespan. Insecure attachment from the original maternal/caregiver timeframe was shown to result in various problems with trust and intimacy in adult relationships. Additionally, "insecure attachment is a risk factor for the development of disease and chronic illness, particularly conditions involving the cardiovascular system including stroke, heart attack and high blood pressure." [10]

At the same time, as anyone even remotely familiar with Buddhism knows, the fruits of meditation practice build atop an understanding and firsthand discovery of how that which is also referred to as attachment is implicated in suffering. For Buddhists, attachment absolutely permeates human consciousness as salt does in the ocean's waters. Just as salt causes saltiness in the ocean's waters, attachment is the major cause of suffering and samsara in humans. The attachment-suffering link was the topic of Buddha's first teaching and has been a mainstay of countless dharma talks ever since. The most popular forms of meditation, whether concentration (Samadhi) or pure awareness (Vipassana), follow in the same vein.

At their very core, the major schools of Buddhism from Theravada to Mahayana to Vajrayana are rooted in responses to the attachment-suffering link as well. These go about the task in different ways but share Buddha's original call to relinquish mental attachments. Many wonderful questions sprout from this fertile soil. To what extent do these two attachments, Bowlby's and Buddha's, have a common ancestor or overlap biologically, psychologically or spiritually? Across history, were

Siddhartha, Jesus, and the Dalai Lamas securely attached to their mothers? If so, was their attachment necessary or at all relevant to their spiritual achievements?

Two of the original theorists and the biggest names in adult attachment, Phillip Shaver and Mario Mikulincer recently addressed the question of how attachment squares with Buddhism. They concluded, "We know almost nothing about the role of attachment processes in Buddhism where there is no personal God with whom one might establish a close relationship."[11] They write that Bowlby's original duality, where problematic or insecure attachment is bifurcated into two poles (anxious-ambivalent and avoidant), appears consistent with the core Buddhist understanding of attachment as the source of suffering. Neither psychological pole—not the neurotic clinging and grasping side, nor the other employing avoidance and denial—holds any hope of redemption or freedom. Buddhism's middle way, according to these seminal thinkers, synchronizes with the modern attachment view of a secure base. They point out that the Dalai Lama likens Buddha to the protector, dharma as doctor and Sangha as nurse. They further believe that these principles underscore Buddhism's acknowledgement of interpersonal and social...side-by-side with the call for followers to cultivate an "open, nongrasping, and non-suppressing mind."[12]

The authors review hundreds of fascinating intersections of adult attachment including the work of neurobiologist, Dan Siegel on *openness to experience*. A leader in the neurobiology of attachment, Siegel concludes that changes in the middle prefrontal cortex seen in long time meditators overlap with secure, biological attachment, brains on attachment.

> Here is a fascinating finding. The functions of the middle prefrontal cortex are found as outcome measures for both mindfulness practice and for (the first eight of the nine) secure parent-child attachment. This overlap between mindfulness and attachment hints at the notion that some shared process may exist between these two seemingly distinct aspects of human life.[13]

If there is a common ancestor construct, what is the nature of distinctions? Are the two attachments best understood as developmentally distinct, with one referring to moms and babies and the other to adult ego's constant grasping? Does the earlier attachment correspond to body and physiology, and the latter to mind and thoughts? If so, then why does dukkha (a cornerstone term in the Four Noble Truths) translate as craving?

Can we draw any reasonable inferences on the *two attachments* from a judicious, delicate analysis of the biography of Siddhartha? What might we learn about his attachment experience? Scholars have not extracted any sort of elaborate developmental psychology from the Pali Canon, at least not one that specifically addresses maternal attachment. Certainly there is no evidence that Buddha was opposed to maternal attachment, and no passages advising young mothers not to breastfeed their babies or to limit their affection. One can probably infer that Buddha did not tell children not to cling to toys or tell moms to take them away. In modern terms, maternal attachment was a "non-issue." What Buddha did not say or believe regarding mom-baby attachment likely is simply a reflection of cultural norms, as well as his own, implicit experience and memory of breastfeeding, including memories formed from being told stories of one's early life.

Buddha versus Bowlby

We are left with some basic questions. How distinct or overlapping is the attachment discovered by Bowlby from that identified by Buddha? Buddhist mothers then and now breastfeed. Presumably, a baby's needs are not a source of suffering, such as identified in the Four Noble Truths. Mothers' meeting their baby's needs would seem, in fact, to be a correct action, as we referred to in the Eightfold Path. Breastfeeding, nurturing and attachment generally would seem to be something mothers should do, and ideally do mindfully. Would not most agree that a mother's devotion is a manifestation of lovingkindness? So, is there a line, and if so where is the line between healthy versus unhealthy craving? Where does this line fall developmentally? What of breast replacements, binkies, and pacifiers? Must the teddy bear go? Toys?

How about for mothers? Carrying, rocking, caressing—when does something pass from an extension of motherly love and nurturance to unhealthy attachment, where the baby is an object of the ego's clinging? Perhaps a mother overindulges every whim. What then do we make of claims of the mother's lovingkindness? What can be gleaned about the so-called archetype of mothering, or with respect to spiritual extensions expressed as Mother Earth and the Goddess? Do these have value for those on a spiritual journey?

One solution to these questions is based in a "carve out." Attachment, for example, might be necessary for infants and babies but be problematic for adults. Certainly, our miniature human brothers and sisters should not be deprived; they are too young to meditate or understand the noble truths. Attachment may only be problematic in conjunction with ego, and Bowlby's attachment is pre-egoic. This frame keeps ego in its role as a source of suffering.

This is, for the most part, the implicit explanation behind the two attachments. The emphasis is on the distinctions rather than the similarities. Bowlby's attachment is limited to the early days and weeks of life and the mother-baby realm. Buddha's attachment is associated with the monumental and existential concerns of adult life. The former is largely physiologically based, such as the need for warmth, food and sleep. The latter is psychological, concerned with finding meaning and spiritual fulfillment. This oil-and-water solution to these attachments types helps explain much of the silence concerning the two and the absence of a more serious inquiry into their similarities and differences.

A "carve out" scenario, asserting the two attachments have no meaningful inter-relationship, offers little satisfaction. If early life attachment is given a pass, and not thought to be all that linked with the adult mind's incessant clinging, one is still left with the question of when and how adult attachment springs into being. A carve out would require the natural neediness of a baby to have no bearing on the maturing mind. Such a position flies in the face of multiple, established lines of research that endorse the impact of childhood events in adult development.

A more reasonable conclusion, put in the form of a question, is: how does early life desire, clinging, wanting, grasping, and longing in some way set up the same in the later years? Answers seem to only result in more questions. Assuming an overlap of the two attachments, is there danger in over-emphasizing attachment's downsides and calling for its denunciation? What of subtler phenomena, for example, attachment to roles, to gender, sexuality and to cultural scaffolding? What of attachment to loved ones, and the practice of lovingkindness between sentient beings?

Often ego is invoked in efforts to respond to such matters. Ego is something like the usual suspect, frequently spotted at the scene wherever attachment is believed to create suffering. But ego does not magically explain away the importance of attachment demonstrated by Bowlby. Extensions of his research suggest that attachment, ego and suffering are not equal opportunity disruptors of happiness or equanimity. Both poorly attached primate and human babies and the adults they become, research demonstrates, suffer more than babies-cum-adults who experienced secure attachment. Psychologist Harry Harlow is famous for his work on the impact of early life attachment deprivation in rhesus monkeys. For example, he separated the babies from their mothers within hours of birth and then conducted various experiments. He concluded that the stress impacted physiology, evidenced in some with digestive problems and loose stools. He isolated offspring at three, six, and twelve months. None died during isolation, but upon returning to the group, some refused or were unable to eat and then died as a result. Play and socialization were severely retarded.

Harlow tried to determine whether deprived offspring preferred fake wire mothers to fake mothers covered with cloth. "Contact Comfort" was proposed to explain the preference for the latter. This predilection held even when the wire mother was the only one with milk. In another series of experiments, Harlow made the wire mother into a sort of torturous figure. One model emitted compressed air almost capable of tearing the baby monkey's skin. Another shook violently, but the "infants clung tighter and tighter because a frightened infant clings to its mother at all costs" et al., 1976).[14]

Around the same time, John Bowlby investigated mom-baby separation. Standard practice in England (where Bowlby lived and worked) was to separate neonates and infants from their mother whenever mother or baby was admitted to the hospital. Bowlby wanted to understand why some infants even those once healthy seemed to lose their will to live. Who knows how many babies died before he finally made in-roads? The failure-to-thrive malady was referred to as *hospitalism* when no other medical etiology, other than the fact of hospitalization, seemed to account for the death.

Some of the extreme instances of maternal deprivation and deficits in other forms of human affiliation occurred in feral human children. One research project likened these children to "bodies without souls".[15] For these children, samsara was as raw and visceral as could possibly be imagined. One of the most documented, The Wild Boy of Aveyron, was described as:

> …a disgustingly dirty child affected with spasmodic movements, and often
> convulsions, who swayed back and forth ceaselessly like certain animals in a
> zoo, who bit and scratched those who opposed him, who showed no
> affection for those who took care of him; and who was, in short, indifferent to
> everything and attentive to nothing. [16]

A degree of healing was achieved through what researchers sometimes call social attachment, to distinguish the process from maternal attachment. Initially, Victor (as he was named) "did not know what it is to be caressed." "When kissed," his caregiver wrote, "he does not know whether it is a man or a woman, and to put it better, he does not care about it at all."[17] In time, he became aware of the care taken of him, "susceptible to fondling and affection, sensitive to the pleasure of doing things well, ashamed of his mistakes, and repentant of his outbursts."[18] Ironically, a modern view would ascribe at least some of this improvement in social attachment to social attachment.

The current plight of Romanian orphans has been scrutinized recently to provide refinement of the implications of attachment across time. An aggregate conclusion is that orphans rescued, (e.g., provided maternal attachment), before six months of age are soon fine and their behavior is indistinguishable from same-age counterparts. Conversely, unmet attachment needs that extend beyond six months leave their mark.[19] In Harlow's words, "Primates which never loved early, never love late."[20]

Balancing the two attachments suggests the following: the craving of humans and their clinging is critical to well-being up until some point in time, after which increasing detachment serves to balance the developing self. Babies certainly should be allowed their cravings, their need to cling and to have binkies and teddy bears. Toys are probably OK for toddlers. Nevertheless, presumably, as one develops the capacity to comprehend the Buddhist message, something should change. This line of reasoning suggests that after a certain age, one should begin to work at loosening and transcending forms of mental grasping.

> When you take things it is because of a thirst, a clinging, and a grasping. You should lose that and lose it altogether, above, below, around, and within. It makes no difference what it is you are grasping. When you grasp, you are losing your freedom. Realize this and grasp at nothing. Then you will cease being a creature of attachment, tied to the powers of death.[21]

Buddha's Mom, as proposed here, shines from the face of Prajapati and all loving mothers as they gaze upon their babies. Having been loved, held and cared for adequately herself, presumably, in the same way she cares for Siddhartha, she represents the apex of our species' capacity to repeat attachment from the other pole; therein she as a face of Buddha's Mom transmits the full complement of love and wisdom to her helpless neonate. She gazes at her or him and the baby gazes back, lovingly and longingly, well attached.

So critical is this cycle of transmission that humans build in massive redundancy. For females not properly nurtured, the birth process calls for them (metaphorically, psychologically) to die to their own need for comfort, to collapse in pain and be reborn as m/other as they bring new life into the world. In this archetypal process of death and renewal, maternal attachment helps force women to die to themselves, and (to varying extents) free fall into a love with an *other*, the being who emerges breathless from her very body, who resets their identity in the mother archetype.

Pregnancy, childbirth, and child-rearing cause new mothers and attuned partners to reach past their fatigue and self-absorption to provide. In primitive tribes, other women, including those lactating, step in to help, transmitting the breadth and depth of humanity. As we will see in time, the most advanced schools of Buddhism parallel this redundancy and offer another portal to this death and renewal, and to the full and flowing river of life which goes by many names.

Buddha's Mom is a nature-based source of spiritual rebirth consistent with both biology and many approaches to spiritual practice. Often we do not need to look for such paths because they are as close as our shadow, our own pain, anger, fear, humiliation and wounding. Where we are emotionally damaged, attachment-related longing lingers.

Paradoxically, we may need to encounter Buddha's Mom as a fount of attachment, be restored and remade in the depths of our being in order to transcend attachment. The potential of attachment-based healing exists wherever powerful attachment and its underbelly, rejection, is to be found. Humans are deeply social. "Many paths, one journey," from the perspective of one transformative, transcendent attachment, would find a commonality in the hunger, curiosity and drive to socialize. Peer relations and pair bonding are potential paths, as is formal work with a teacher.

All these can be viewed as methods for humans to erect scaffolds where they are lacking. Where love is lacking, where self-absorption or an excess of male-centered power and control exists, there are in-built mechanisms with corrective potential. These offer a path, a potential return to love, a possible means of resurrecting the ingredients that optimize the transmission of the life force and what we can call the human lineage. An orphan is taken in, latchkey juveniles may become inseparable and two lonely adults risk forming a bond. These may proffer paths with a heart.

From the near-perfect types, such as the early life attachment and emotional closeness that Siddhartha enjoyed, to all these other forms, efforts at optimizing emotional intimacy are marked by face-to-face behavior. Desmond Morris, the brilliant author of *The Naked Ape* (e.g., homo sapiens), documented the physical and behavioral features of attachment. He placed these in an evolutionary context and articulated their redundant, interdependent character.

Female breasts, for example, become more involved in sexual signaling and pair-bonding in humans compared to other primates. According to Morris, the modern female variety evolved as a frontal version of naked apes' hairless rear buttocks. The areola may mimic the iris (and vice versa) and the nipple the pupil, further reinforcing frontal communications. Further, hairlessness on the primate face has been shown to correspond to sending and receiving of skin-color signals and obviously fosters facial communication in general. Primates capable of discerning complex facial coloration have bare faces.[22]

In evolution, traits co-evolve in a highly interdependent, redundant fashion. These examples of advances in face-to-face behavior were part of a multiplicity. Kissing and frontal copulation would likely have co-evolved with enhancement in other associated behaviors and capacities, such as mother-infant gazing and associated affection and communication forms. Ultimately, all forms of frontal interaction and communication supported the development of language. This familiar dimension of human experience helps explain the millions of statues and likenesses of the serene face of the Buddha.

Modern variants of the evolutionary investment in all things facial include: Facebook, YouTube, Instagram and Apple's FaceTime, emoticon faces and reality TV through which one's face is seen by millions. Cars' headlight eyes and mouth grills are extensions of the same evolutionary pulse. Neither their design or emotional impact is coincidental. Being seen, being mirrored, in the unhinged cyberspace that so permeates everyday life, and translates into "likes," "followers," "tweets," "re-tweets" and "hits", flows from the same evolutionary, attachment wellspring. The more poetic version is to love and be loved.

Through social media we strive to be seen, heard, acknowledged—all expressions of a longing for impermanence. The second something strikes a person as the least bit special, the urge to snap a picture, "like" or otherwise record the moment co-arises. Greed and grasping enter the picture to claim, keep and grab. Propelling these is the quiet desperation and ego side of void. There is a latent threat of nonself and anonymity, of being overlooked, an embryonic fear of nonexistence which has ultimate significance for Buddhists. As we will explore in Chapter Four, the Buddha specifically identified another form of attachment corresponding to this existential angst, vibhava tanhā.

Biological attachment's emphasis, or tanhā, on being heard, seen, and validated reaches an epiphany with the human eyes. Framed by high cheekbones below, the eyebrows above, the whites on the sides, the eyes are unspeakably powerful. They communicate in a mesmerizing fashion. The iris' color is replicated in nature, on butterfly wings and orchids, surrounding the empty/full pupil's blackness. The feelings that arise or are in play in glaring, staring or intense, intimate 'eye contact' speak to power of the eyes in attachment and detachment. Loosely, the same psychobiological dynamic corresponds to sex and aggression, love and war, and to being and nonbeing. Buddha's enlightenment, as we will see in the last chapter, can be likened to a *betweenness*.

Seeking Refuge

For the most part the two attachments, that of Bowlby on the one side and Buddha on the other, have co-existed peaceably. Shaver and Mikulincer, the prominent attachment researchers just referenced, also noted the similarity between Buddhism's call to take refuge in the dharma and Bowlby's secure base. The Merriam-Webster dictionary gives the physical definition for refuge as "a shelter or protection from danger; a place that provides shelter or protection." Buddhists use the concept to refer to psychological and spiritual refuge. Buddhists speak of taking refuge in the three gems, Buddha, dharma, Sangha; this connotes a totality, a home, belonging, even a sense of confidence, that one is at the very least on a sensible if arduous, unpredictable journey. All this smacks of the offspring's hopefully adequate attachment space. There is coherence but nonetheless plenty of challenge and no guarantees.

For Bowlby, the mother's presence, touch, warmth, and ability to provide protection comprise a combination of physical and psychological dimensions—the secure base. Attachment theory writ large spans the same, biological to psychological strata. The two ideas, taking refuge and being endowed with a secure base, have much in common.

> The practice of opening one's mind, neither repressing nor clinging is remarkably similar to the idea in attachment theory that the major forms of insecurity are avoidance (repression, squelching) and anxiety (grasping, obsessing), with security being, in a sense, a "middle way." It is interesting that the forms of insecurity emphasized by the two "theories" (Buddhism and attachment theory) are so similar.[23]

Meditation, the researchers conclude, is one of many "beautiful and inspiring"[24] forms occurring in religions, philosophy, and psychology across history, and all are aligned with Bowlby's essential triadic theory. But unlike many of these forms, attachment science is based on evolutionary theory and empirical research. The field of attachment, they suggest, should "retain and integrate" aspects of insights from religion, philosophy, and psychology, which are valid, and thereby of benefit to organizations, parents, educators, and policy makers.[25]

In a book subtitled, *Reconciling Eastern Ideals and Western Psychology*, Aronson (2004) explored the way that attachment styles, based on Bowlby's theory, impact Buddhist meditation practice. Adults who suffer from the classically neurotic, anxious form of insecure attachment are prone to an "unwholesome involvement" in their effort to achieve security.[26] This disposition may bleed into relationships with teachers and members of the Sangha Buddhist community. They may succumb to an exaggerated sense of belonging only to be re-traumatized by perceived slights and betrayals. These spike ancient fears of abandonment and the cycle continues. For Buddhists, the risk of such a clinging, grasping way of being is that of future rebirth. This is called samsara. Viewed through a non-religious, psychological lens, samsara places an emphasis on the intense persistence of the attachment-suffering dynamic in humans.

Efforts to break free of this cycle may inadvertently create a new form of difficulty. Adults with an avoidant attachment style are especially at risk. As noted, attachment research shows that this condition originates in childhood. Avoidant attachment begins as a coping mechanism that becomes an established personality trait. Deficits in maternal mirroring hamper the development of the secure base.

A person damaged in this particular way learned long ago to avoid psychic pain associated with deficits in maternal attachment. This results in an original, impaired "secure base" with the risk of illusory refuge-taking. People with an avoidant attachment style may then be drawn to what they perceive as Buddhism's validation of forms of escapism and emotional deadening and distancing that have proven valuable and helpful to them. In this sense, they filter in and out, and see what they want to see in Buddhism's prioritizing of renunciation, asceticism and endorsement of emptiness. The idea of attachment as the cause of suffering reinforces their avoidance, inadvertently short-changing the potential benefits. Their early life attachment wounds follow them to the cushion where "healthy nonattached spiritual engagement" stalls out.[27]

Efforts at a scholarly, nuanced reconciliation of the two attachments must stand up to both modern clinical research and the many ancient teachings that have withstood the test of time. A premature dismissal of the ancient literature, for example, as too culturally bound or overly mired in a religious agenda is unsound. Likewise, infatuation with a secular approach is suspect. We are called to discern the overlays and respect the spirit of even oppressive, provincial agendas in our effort to trace the thread of sentience from science to spirit.

Kisa & Rahula

Kisa Gotami's moving narrative provides one of the most direct Buddhist commentaries on maternal attachment. Unwilling or unable to face the truth of her child's death, Kisa carried the dead baby around with her hoping to find someone who could give her medicine to cure him. The Buddha guided her into a realization of the omnipresence of death by sending her in search of some mustard seed, a common ingredient in Indian kitchens. But the Buddha specified that these seeds must come from a household where no one had ever died.

Here, maternal attachment is quite plainly identified with the more orthodox translation. Kisa Gotami's attachment to her child, in this light, manifests as an extreme form of clinging and grasping. She visits neighbor after neighbor, trying to find anyone who has not suffered the loss of a loved one. Eventually she realizes that everyone has faced a similar loss. In this, the attachment-suffering link is proven to be inescapable. In realizing this, "the mass of darkness is shattered" and Kisa is liberated.[28]

One does not have to look hard for this same message elsewhere in the Pali Canon. A similar story is told of Rahula, Buddha's one and only son. Rahula's name may have been derived from the word *rahu* for fetter or impediment. A fetter according to Webster's dictionary is a shackle or something that confines. In the Dhammapada, a man's positive emotional connection with his wife and children is referred to as a soft fetter. Most accounts have Siddhartha leaving the palace after thirteen years of marriage on the very day his son was born.[29] The meaning of this actual or symbolic event should not be overlooked. Buddha is reported as having the following reaction: "An impediment has come into being, a bond has come into being."[30]

It would be six years from the time he left home until Siddhartha's awakening as the Buddha. Within one year of his awakening, Siddhartha, now Buddha, returned to his father's Kingdom, to Kapilavastu, to meet his son. There are varying reasons given, but the accounts of this meeting have Rahula asking for his father's inheritance. This inheritance would normally have sequenced from King Suddhodana to Siddhartha to Rahula. Since Siddhartha had chosen the life of a mendicant (literally, a beggar) and had renounced earthly possessions, Rahula apparently had come to understand that he was next in line.

> While the venerable Rahula was following close behind, the Blessed One
> turned and looked at him, and he addressed him thus: "Rahula, any kind of
> material form whatever, whether past, future or present, in oneself or
> external, coarse or fine, inferior or superior, far or near, should all be
> regarded as it actually is with right understanding thus: 'This is not mine, this
> is not what I am, this is not myself.'[31]

There is a quality of believability to this motif though the specifics are missing. Perhaps his mother had explained that he would inherit a lot of nice things in the future but first his father had to agree. One can imagine some version of Rahula repeatedly asking about this and his mother finally relenting. It is even possible that Rahula was something of a pawn, that his mother helped conjure up the story of his father having, in essence, exciting things for him, possibly for her own benefit. One very precious remnant of Rahula's response to this meeting has survived the ages. In what sounds like unabashed love, young Rahula spoke these words, "O, father, even your shadow is pleasing to me."[32]

Upriver

Attachment's love-connection emanates from Siddhartha's biography as do hints of how this connection has been covered over. Most will recall how he was born into a well-to-do family. His parents smothered him with all manner of comforts. Attachment-as-materialism outshines attachment-as-love. Love's reach, however, is far from invisible. His father, a fearsome ruler, has received the counsel of some wise men. He is concerned that Siddhartha may not one day inherit his kingdom. But all of this falls within the scope of a loving, if possessive, attachment. Mother-love, per attachment theory, is the ultimate ingredient in human emotional bonds.

Continuing this cursory flyover, we find Siddhartha repulsed by his initial encounter with old age, sickness and death. In confronting existential ultimatums perhaps Siddhartha's sense of belonging, based in being loved and in loving his parents, wife and son, broke him. He saw that the very fabric of life was time-bound and ultimately illusory. Perhaps this fabric was attachment-love and perhaps its essential nature was not simply illusory, and was his own, yours and mine as well. He left home to wander and seek answers. In attempting to leave behind familial love he came to know, we will suggest, love's cosmic dimensions.

Buddha himself described this vastness in ways typical of his cultural context. A multitude of former lifetimes, he expressed, prepared him for this incarnation. "I recalled… my varied lot in former existences as follows: first one life, then two lives, then three, four, five, ten, twenty up to fifty lives, then a hundred, a thousand, a hundred thousand and so forth."[33] Both worldly and otherworldly events are consistent with attachment-as-love entering the stream of human affairs and forming a bridge between the two attachments. Here we are proposing the shorthand term, Buddha's Mom, for this miracle of reality.

Buddha's enlightenment can be framed as the fruition of various upriver sources. Evolutionary theory, affective neuroscience, clinical material and esoteric Buddhist doctrine converge in this regard. There is a deep and ancient flow of spirit available, knowable and expressible in each of us. If described as love, this arcs from biological attachment to attachment-as-love to loving-kindness.

The universe, various canonical descriptions suggest, was a conscious, proactive force enabling this sweep of love. Many passages depict cosmic elements which will culminate during the life of Buddha. Siddhartha's entire biography, his birth and life in Kapilavastu, are rendered as historical offshoots of a profound, cosmic intentionality.

From a purely psychological perspective, these story elements might be viewed as indicators of a highly advanced consciousness. But the Pali Canon seems to insist on more. It suggests and perhaps reveals a golden thread from the Big Bang to Buddha. The mythic and surrealistic backdrop of Siddhartha's biography endorses an alignment of cosmos, earth, and everything necessary here, including the kingdom, village, parents, and everyone associated with the baby who would grow up to be Buddha.

As the earthly birth approaches, Buddha's biological mom has a dream. The moon reaches fullness as she sleeps in the palace. One world sleeps as another awakens. Mahamaya feels herself being carried off by four spirits. This quaternity of divas take her to Anottata, a lake in the Himalayas. The moon's perfect circle, and the diva's four-ness reveal the essential, transformative mandala. There she is drenched in divine, royal, feminine love. She is bathed, anointed with perfumes, clothed in heavenly garments and adorned with divine flowers. The divas next take her to a palace of gold atop a rock of silver. They placed her on a divine couch, her head facing east. Meanwhile the future Buddha, temporarily in the form of a superb white elephant, approached her, holding a lotus flower in his trunk. Three times the great elephant made gestures of deferential respect, gently struck her right side and entered her womb.

The feminine motif of wound, vessel and container is on display. Mahamaya is carried and supported in the literal, bodily sense. She is exalted, bathed and anointed. Her status as mother-to-be, a vessel of transmission is reified. Its cosmic breadth, from biological to spiritual, unfolds before us. Divine spirits take Mahamaya away from the ordinary plane of existence. The old is ritually washed away, as new heavenly cloths, perfumes and flowers are bestowed on her. The symbolism is inclusive, biological, psychological and spiritual—this is the fullness at hand.

This dream was interpreted by wise men, eager to weigh in on this golden thread. They declared that Mahamaya "had conceived a wonderful son, who would be either a universal emperor or a universal teacher."[34] Wise men are another story element connecting the grand and mythic levels of reality to our earthly realm and human condition. Their arrival on the scene brings to the fore a theme we will continue to explore. This pertains to yin and yang, the masculine and the feminine aspects of human consciousness.

Yang is initially abrupt. The wise men reset the story and establish the official, overt narrative tension. Yin's fullness, all the holding, carrying, the divine vessel-womb, all the gentleness give way to the drama back in Kapilavastu. The divine, timeless lakeside ritual snaps back into the pressing question that yang poses. Will Siddhartha be a universal emperor or a universal teacher?

Recalling that Mahamaya will soon die, we see how her cameo exposes the heavy yet deft hand of patriarchy. In these few canonical passages, Mahamaya gets a royal but rapid treatment. She is portrayed in resplendent, supernatural hyperbole, a beautiful and intelligent queen, a person beyond repute. Such a narrative treatment tends to obscure her humanity and prompts some reasonable curiosities. Buddha's Mom is basically a combination of hyperbole and brevity, even omission. Much more is known about his father, for example. What is not said, however, is loud and clear. She arrives, she dies, and suddenly the drama lurches forward in time. Immediately, a dilemma presents itself, one that has almost nothing to do with the mother and much to do with the father.

The Brahmans said, "Be not anxious, O king! Your queen has conceived: and the fruit of her womb will be a man-child; it will not be a woman-child. You will have a son. And he, if he adopts a householder's life, will become a king, a Universal Monarch; but if, leaving his home, he adopts the religious life, he will become a Buddha, who will remove from the world the veils of ignorance and sin."[35]

No sooner does the story begin than the beginning is reset. Mahamaya's grand dream turns out to be a pre-beginning, over and done with before the official biography launches. The tantric thread connecting Buddha's Mom as a deep, mythical, spiritual source of wisdom to Buddhism is under assault. An assault, we will see, typical of stubborn psychological wounds manifesting in long arcs of suffering. Commonly these date back to the early attachment years and have profound roots in the body.

In the afterglow of what must be one of the most prescient and revealing pregnancy dreams in all of history, yang resets the cosmic thread. Yang's greed and cunning make sense in light of the dream's eventual manifestation. Humans universally speak of dreams coming true. Mahamaya's dream does in nothing less than the possibility of realization, enlightenment and secular salvation for all of humanity. But of course, such realization is only possible in the marriage and transcendence of yin and yang.

It will be a while before the man-child we meet at this juncture reaches back and down and communes with his mother about their many shared lifetimes. Most Buddhists, and indeed millions more, know about the earth-touching mudra celebrated in countless statues, depicting the dying Buddha reaching down to thank and touch Mother Earth. This points to the possibility of a deeper connection to the feminine. A stronger thread awaits. As the story continues, the lotus reappears— but only once baby's Siddhartha's independence and sovereignty is made abundantly clear. Once again, there is signal noise and a mixed message. The lotus is potentially an integral symbol of perfection. The lotus blossom is singularly perfect, yet born from and dependent on mud, on Mother Earth.

The pattern of fragmentation continues. The future Buddha's mother is taken away from the earth where she will necessarily return to give birth. The delicate lotus blossom hints at the feminine as well as the perfection of the dharma. Perfection runs through the dharma. There are lists of perfections and Siddhartha is described as a physically perfect being. But another form of thread-severing occurs before a connection between the future Buddha and the feminine, the mud of Mother Earth, is established. Shortly after birth, baby Siddhartha stands and walks! At each footprint a lotus appears on the ground. The symbolism is quite apparent. This baby does not need his mother to carry him. She is not rendered as the conveyer of upriver sources of spirit. As this seven-day-old neonate walks and talks, the message leans very much toward independence, not interdependence—with a rather tepid, passive acknowledgement of Mahamaya's and nature's contribution.

Efforts to suppress themselves are revealing. The lotus appearing in Siddhartha's footprints at first suggests the earth's honoring of him. Where he walks on her, she gives thanks with a symbol of beauty. At the same time, there is much more to this connection. The lotus symbolizes Buddha's mind, the flowering of consciousness which blossoms in the dharma. The lotus speaks to a heaven on earth, a flower atop the mud, and not so much of Mother Earth achieving a place in heaven. Her spiritual realm topped out in a dream vision, though it foretold the lotus.

What comes next even more unambiguously reveals these masculine-feminine tensions. "Then, at the seventh stride, Siddhartha stopped and with a noble voice shouted, 'I am chief of the world, Eldest am I in the world, Foremost am I in the world. This is the last birth. There is now no more coming to be.' With the singularity of "I" and a voice backing it, consciousness is associated with the forward tip of a long evolutionary process, and not with the organic process itself. Multiple lifetimes, births and deaths, have finally come to a climax, a final birth. Obviously, the focus is on the new and emergent. The man-child has the makings of a non-dependent force. But to make sure, the precursors do not linger long in the limelight, the cleaving of these achieves its own climax. Mahamaya, with her connection to indigenous, earth spirituality, dies and just as quickly is replaced by a stepmother.

> However, seven days after his birth, Mahamaya died in accordance with the custom that the mothers of bodhisattvas should die immediately after they had given birth. It was her sister, Mahāprajāpatī, Sudhodana's second wife, who brought up the young prince. [36]

The fleeting focus on Mahamaya also has the feel of an awkward compensation. She is, will be at least, the mother of possibly the most important person to ever have been born. But she is not to have any true bearing on the greatness to be. She will not protect him or teach him about life. Mahamaya will have virtually no influence on the path he will outline for humanity. Her quick anointing is surgically inserted just days before her death. The story seeks to have it both ways. She is the equal of the greatness of the life within her belly, or nearly so, but all this greatness is not passed on in any lucid manner. She is disconnected from her son's achievements, such as the attainment of inner peace and the realization of truths that free him from perpetual suffering.

An earthly death and ascension to heaven (or the attainment of enlightenment) is standard treatment for mothers of great sages in Hindu mythology. Any chance that these mothers are credited with transmitting a lineage to their sons is cut short. For our purposes, any narrative support for Mahamaya as lineage bearer, and for attachment-as-love in the means of transmission, meets the same end.

In the case of Siddhartha, even this powerful one-two punch of heaven/enlightenment and death risks obvious and intuitive criticism. There is always the chance that someone will notice the neonate lying all alone after the hoopla. This is handled with yet another one-two punch. First there is the exaggerated infantile-precociousness and hyperbolic physical and mental agility, culminating in baby Siddhartha's declaration of independence. As noted, within days baby Siddhartha walks, talks, and announces that he will not be born again. For the follow up punch, his father promptly installs his wife's sister into the role of adoptive mother such that there is no interruption in nursing and caregiving.

Those not-yet-enlightened among us risk experiencing Shakyamuni Buddha and his dharma through certain ancient cultural distortions. We may come to know him and his teachings in ways tainted by these vainglorious masculine claims. At the same time, we experience consciousness personally and conceptually as more yang (as in yin-yang) than yin, as this is the very essence of ego fighting to differentiate. Because of this bias we inadvertently marginalize yin: Witness, body, context and "all that arises"—as well as key Buddhism concepts—in important but subtle ways. A working premise here, based in attachment as lineage, is that we encounter the feminine through the feminine. In other words, what we refer to as Buddha's Mom deepens in its capacities to convey truth, meaning and reality the more one brings her into awareness.

Needs

Many of us did not have the sort of healthy early life attachment experiences that Siddhartha purportedly enjoyed. And therefore, this journey begins backwards and involves therapy which addresses early, family of origin undercurrents.

As the birth of the boy who would be Buddha approached, love was in the air, and preparations had been made. A loving, expectant home awaited the birth of Siddhartha. At this point, Siddhartha's mother and father had been married for twenty years, and a foundation was laid for this union of yin and yang to translate as one of attachment-as-love.

The scene contrasts with so many that give rise to unhappy childhoods where loving attachment is lacking. Troubles may begin prenatally. Alcohol in pregnancy is a leading cause of mental retardation. Other common elements include unplanned pregnancies. A common story of grown children from these broken pasts is of the immaturity of their parents. Everyone has heard these tales. Probably most parents mean well. Others not so much. In aggregate, both varieties and all the colors between tend to be too self-involved and lacking in skills to adequately, consistently, actively, appropriately provide the love their babies and children needed. Some, of course, are psychiatrically impaired or lost in addictions. Others become ill or die.

Perhaps the most typical and almost boring characteristic among parents is immaturity. Many adults-turned-parents lack the psychological sophistication to accurately do what Bowlby referred to as mirroring, to consistently, accurately interpret the infant-baby-toddler-child's needs. In every mundane manner, they are simply too self-possessed to do right by their offspring. To mirror adequately requires not perfection but, like diet and exercise and meditation, frequency and duration. On balance, this results in a reasonable, adequate, sophisticated-enough degree of differentiation of self and other. It shows up not as flawless behavior, but with the capacity for delayed gratification, the ability to set aside one's own needs and attend to the other. In one form or another "good enough" parents (as the theorist Winnicott named them) consistently, adequately cobble together emotional responses and associated caregiving behaviors.

Children's needs quickly progress from the basics of eating, pooping, and sleeping, to complex play and interaction. Many parents do fine at the biological basics and then fragment as higher-order, emotional demands set in. The child's developing brain fundamentally needs mirroring to cultivate what Bowlby called the secure base. Children long to 'take refuge' in this much as adults take refuge in Buddhism's three gems.

Great parents know very well that their children demand oceans of attention. What is oversimplified as play calls for parents to set aside their own agenda. Successful attachment occurs when parents tune into their child's precious, fleeting, ever-morphing ways of perceiving themselves, others and the world. This is the heart of mirroring and that which, according to Bowlby, cultivates secure attachment.

Biological attachment keeps parents in an interactive orbit they otherwise would not maintain to the extent children require. Maternal attachment is not an idealistic or perfect process by any means. More than likely, the extent of psychologically immature and disturbed adults reflects the fact that biological attachment was suited to an entirely different epoch. But humans are successful because of their capacity for adaptation. The jury is still out, but one way or another, Homo sapiens just may find a way to prevent the destruction of this planet and each other. The working premise here is that success calls for a reconciliation of the two attachments. Mahamaya's dream and Siddhartha's close-knit, caring family-of-origin tells us in one form how the fruits of the first evoke those of the second. Secure attachment sets up the fundamental capacity to take refuge.

Intimidating questions arise for those of us with insecure early life stories. We live out the wreckage of the first attachment and the impossibility—by definition, to somehow heal from that which we cannot change. Yet Buddha calls. This gentle saint of lovingkindness brought only more where more was needed. He did not differentiate between secure and insecure maternal attachment.

Still, in dark moments, one wonders. Buddha was so anticipated and adored, born of a stable, caring family-of-origin. What chance do I have of inner peace? Further, many of us have already worked so hard at understanding, healing, forgiving and letting go that we do not even know what to name this endless effort, maybe just life, just me.

Many of us learn about a second, Buddhist attachment. In this letting go takes on a whole new dimension. The entirety of our past programming is to be released and replaced with the sensation of air entering our nostrils. The foray into nonattachment completely divorced from our dysfunctional, early life attachment. What is the nature of the interplay of the two? Is there a possibility of transcendence through a reconciliation of the two attachments?

Fortunately, both biological and Buddhist attachment continue to be refined and clarified by modern healers and spiritual masters. Within the first, the discovery of 'adult attachment' is still new and unfolding. Most of us still favor the front-loaded model, where attachment wounds are laid down like the foundation of a building.

Yin/yang shed light this potent half-truth. Early life attachment, it is true, has a singularly stunning power to sculpt self/ego/mind. Ahead we will explore this evocative background and come to appreciate this gate as *somatic sentience*. A foundation is laid and this mainly involves the mother or maternal attachment figure(s). Her realm seems vast and inescapable. For a self/ego/mind traumatically bound within a dysfunctional maternal attachment, the motherland is axiomatically treacherous. In this light, the territory of the feminine in attachment 'should be' fraught and is understandably perceived as and felt to be intimidating.

To escape the prison begins by willfully, lovingly diving into its darkness. Through this, an upriver pursuit of yin may be hatched. Jungians and others loosely refer to this as 'the feminine' and 'the feminine principle'. An upriver journey takes one ever more into the body/psyche borderlands. A melding with mother earth, with one's earth body, one's cosmic womb, the natural, interconnected essence of Buddha-nature beckons; along the way freer, itinerant self-capsules form and fade with lessening fear and spectacle.

The science associated with this spiritual effervescence is familiar. Beyond bodily dimorphism, the masculine principle and feminine principle refer to neurologically-based capacities giving rise to repertoires of behavior, emotional experience and meaning. These overlap but are not one and the same with gender. The feminine principle simply tends to be more differentiated, accessible, and consciously integrated in females and vice versa.

Since antiquity, in the east, the deeper psychospiritual dimensionality has been referred to as yin and yang. Jung referred to the inner yin/yang as anima/animus to emphasize how the same-gender pole tends to be dominant and the contra-sexual pole tends to be latent or secondary. He recognized how outer gender dimorphism was mirrored inversely within consciousness. Our species evolutionary success owes a large debt to this combination of outer and inner (inversed) gendering.

Biological attachment is most immediately and concretely associated with both females and the feminine principle. All disclaimers, of course, apply with respect to the fluidity of both outer and inner gender. The main objective here is simply to note the close association of Bowlby's attachment to the feminine principle, to yin. This is prerequisite to any coherent exploration of the feminine in Buddhism.

At this general level, fathering is female mothering and not a distinct, masculine corollary of mothering. Effective fathers deftly, wisely employ their inner feminine within a global psychology that tends, speaking only very generally, to be characterized by the masculine principle. As touched up earlier, complex, highly successful species rely on redundancy. The male does not reinvent maternal attachment nor is he possessed of some distinct form of this intrinsic feminine capacity.

All of this is, by definition, both no accident and precisely accidental. Darwin's theory proposes that accidental random permutations have the effect of exploiting environmental niches and producing ever more environmentally dominant creatures. The extremes and the fluidity of gender have paid hearty dividends. We can add to this, all that is being discover regarding inner gender and the feminine principle.

According to the much validated model, the attachment we are positioning as attachment-love embedded in the feminine principle is critical to evolution's twin goals of 1) survival and 2) the production of viable offspring. Darwin documented how each of these complement one another. An offspring's chances of survival increase with the parents' capacities to engage internal masculine capacities, for example, to fight off predators. Similarly, the offspring is more likely to make it (and pass along this blend of capacities) when their parents have a certain potent alliance. Ethologists refer to this as *pair bonding*. The fact that each pole exists within each gender, in the uneven ways that they do, demonstrates that this complex arrangement was the most successful of all possible permutations. Yin-yang is not easy to isolate or define in animals, and is even more nebulous in the case of Siddhartha's Buddhism. But in time with the help of multiple lines of evidence, a mind-piercing picture comes into focus. One valuable source is Siddhartha's life narrative.

King's Son

Siddhartha's father, Suddhodana, looms large in his biography. The opposite is true of his mother, who peaks, and then fades in haste. As mentioned, about the same day that Mahamaya's neonate turns one week old, she dies. In contrast, her baby who is, of course, of the opposite gender, stands, walks, and introduces himself to the world. Where the feminine embodies interdependence and the male independence, this and many story elements are hardly ambiguous.

Mahamaya is eclipsed by a superhuman, visionary dream and is ushered off stage as soon as her biological job is done. The story then quickly reconnects to the official narrative. The divine anointing of Mahamaya, in her visionary dream, is more an honoring of her as a vessel. She is special because of her status, her pregnancy, and her role in bringing the future Buddha into being. Once the mother is dispatched, Siddhartha is largely reframed as the King's son. Heaps of masculinity enter with this shift in the narrative. King Suddhodana was a Brahman, a man of wealth and power. He was a warrior in his younger years. The King represents the status quo, the dominant culture and gender. At this point in history, the culture was very patriarchal. It is only rational that we explore how this lens may distort Buddhism. Like refracted light, we may be able to correct for some of this by clarifying the nature of the feminine within Buddhism.

King Suddhodana offers a compelling depiction of a full, successful and balanced life. He selected and married the most beautiful and intelligent woman in the land and was a proud, devoted, thoughtful patriarch and father. He was a benevolent ruler, but violently protective of his region and clan. At the time of Queen Mahamaya's pregnancy, she and the King had been married for twenty years. What he wanted to top everything off, naturally, was a son, an heir, someone to carry on his great legacy.

Suddhodana's motivation was the same as many parents today. They want to pass along everything they have worked so hard for. Where familial bonds and love-as-attachment are strong, the material and spiritual go hand-in-hand. Parents do their best to advance their kids' education and financial stability, not out of some hardened delusion that money can buy happiness or things last forever. As Suddhodana was, they too are pragmatic and rational. Life may be at base full of suffering, but as Bill Clinton said, "I've been poor and I've been rich and I like rich better." [37] Many individuals view success and meaning in life through the same prism. Life is a competition to be comfortable and happy before the time is up. We wear these jewels metaphorically in photos of happy moments, cool experiences, and exotic locations on Facebook. We proclaim success at the goal of finding meaning in life in the form of fun, humor, comfort, good food, friends, and travel. Suddhodana, we can speculate, was not shallow or ruthless or a hardcore materialist. As a sort of celebrity-politician, he was an exemplar of a highly accomplished, popular person of his era—a spit-and-polished representative of the status quo.

Casting Suddhodana as overly masculine does not conform with the ancient texts. What might be considered King Suddhodana's feminine side is easy to find. In scores of vignettes, he is described as passionate and often moved to tears. The story of Buddha's return home to Kapilavastu to meet his son has a very tender element. The King apparently had a strong bond with his grandson, Rahula. This fits the mold of attachment-as-love, especially when the context of their relationship is considered. Seven years earlier, Siddhartha had deeply disappointed his father. Siddhartha upended Suddhodana's twenty-nine-year effort to shield his son from the ugly side of life and shape Siddhartha's path. The King had hoped his efforts would result in Siddhartha's choosing to be his heir and carry on his legacy. Instead, he rejected the materialistic life for the monastic life.

By the time Siddhartha-now-Buddha returned home, Suddhodana had transferred his hopes of passing on his legacy to his grandson. The grandfather-grandson attachment can be thought of as the resilience of the feminine principle and the power of attachment-as-love to survive hardships. But alas, Suddhodana was foiled again. His dear grandson, as described, was enchanted by his father. Just being in dad's shadow, Rahula claimed, was pleasing. Just as his father had, Rahula chose to forsake the King's inheritance. In the following passage, what we can begin to recognize as attachment-love survives in a new form. The King, having experienced the parent-child bond so intimately was compelled to institutionalize this in the form of a parental right.

> Suddhodana was inconsolable when he heard that now his grandson, too,
> had been withdrawn from the family, and implored his son never to grant
> the novice ordination to anyone without the permission of his parents.[38]

This marks a truce between the two attachments. A child should not be free to forsake their home and family too soon. The parents, those presumably attached to the child, are in the best position to recognize when the hand-off from the world of Bowlby to that of Buddha should happen. In this detail, the dharma encodes a bridge from the feminine, attachment-love, home and hearth to the path of homelessness, of emptying, forsaking and letting go. Psychologically speaking, the self/ego/mind should not attempt to cross this bridge too early. In this rather weak way, Buddhism gives maternal attachment some recognition and space. We should not overlook the fact that this emerges from the King's great pain. When his heart is broken a second time, he transcends his own attachment-love enough to glimpse its universal form. He stands up for this, for all parents for all time. At this point, the Buddha himself, it seems, agrees. He sees what Suddhodana sees and in acknowledging and agreeing, he mirrors him. Here the enlightened child-and-parent mirrors his (former) parent for the sake of all children and parents.

Byzantine

The ability of attachment-as-love to continually rise from the ashes should be no surprise. It is a hardy, evolutionary mainstay. It exists in natural tension with a range of other human capacities and dispositions, including evolutionary biology's infamous four F's, feeding, fighting, fleeing and fornicating. Here we are simply attempting to explore its roots in Buddhism by focusing in on the life of the baby, child and budding person who becomes the Buddha.

So far we have spotted attachment-as-love in several places in the biography of Siddhartha. These examples place Bowlby's attachment in a tension with what appears to be Buddhism's detachment. These story elements are intricate and byzantine. Integral theory can help us to make more sense of these proposals. Suddhodana's loving attachment to Rahula marks a sort of reattachment to his hope of establishing an heir. This (King-grandson) attachment-detachment tension is resolved when Rahula becomes Buddhism's first novice monk.

Within Rahula's own heart, it seems, was another attachment-detachment tension. Rahula was set on asking Buddha for the family inheritance, a typical sort of desire indicative of the attachment of the Four Noble Truths. Then, in some part due to his attachment to (admiration of, love for) his father, Rahula changes his mind regarding the inheritance. Buddha's only son sweetly tells his father, "even your shadow is pleasing", then lets go of his original, money and power desire.

For his part, King Suddhodana's bond with Rahula is a resurgence of the twenty-nine years of effort to influence his son's path in life. This effort had to be inspired in part by attachment-love, and what the King believed to be best for his son. Suddhodana did not rely, for example, only on his power or aggression. He did not threaten his son or try to force him to comply. Rather he attempted to make the materialistic path, the path of the wealthy and powerful, extremely appealing. In the end, Suddhodana leaves it to Siddhartha to choose between monk and monarch. But first he tries to tip the scales in favor of the status quo. As all Buddhists have been taught, the King summoned his formidable resources to shield Siddhartha from the ugly realities of the world. We can see the influence of parental attachment, especially as this manifests in a fierce and protective form of caring. Accounts of how the King manipulated Siddhartha's home life to prevent Siddhartha from encountering old age, sickness, and death cross over into the stuff of legend.

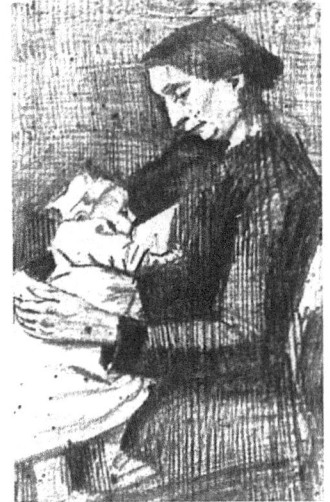

> Suddhodana provided the prince with spacious quarters for his women,
> supplied him with thousands of women, made him variegated parks with
> cool arbours, and draped with festoons of fine cloth and strewn with heaps
> of flowers, that the prince might divert, enjoy and amuse himself and not set
> his heart on leaving home. And King Suddhodana enjoined upon the women
> that they should keep the prince well entertained with dance and music and
> song, so that he should not set his heart on leaving home. [39]

The King is said to have built three opulent palaces corresponding to the hot, cool, and rainy Indian seasons. He filled these with beautiful women. Only healthy people were permitted in the vicinity. Some accounts have servants picking the dried and dying flowers in the surrounding fields. What is more downplayed is the King's marriage to Prajapati. Shortly after Mahamaya's death, when baby Siddhartha was only a week old, the King married Mahamaya's sister. Presumably, this had much to do with assuring that the loving care of the baby was uninterrupted. Indeed, the palace also had nursemaids. These surrogate mothers, as their name implies, may have even breastfed Siddhartha. These details certainly suggest that value was placed on the attachment that Bowlby analyzed scientifically 2,500 years later. Also, consistent with this is the lore regarding Suddhodana's wonderful marriage, his benevolent leadership of Kapilavastu and fierce protection of his peoples. Attachment-as-love incorporates all manner of emotional attachments. This undergirds the King's preference for a way of life, his lands and peoples, and his contiguous desire to pass this along to his beloved son or, if this is not possible, his grandson.

Siddhartha chose to break free of these "householder" bonds, but the fact that he did so the day Rahula was born speaks exquisitely to his own internal tension between attachment-love and the something else and something more that he was compelled to explore. The opposing pull was in the direction of detachment and freedom. Incidentally, Siddhartha's biography is quite byzantine on the perennial question of free will. This runs in parallel to the tension between attachment and detachment.

Based on Suddhodana's request, Buddha agreed to the parents' right to decide when their children leave home and become ordained. This strikes one form of balance wherein a parent's free will trumps that of their children. The concept of majority and minority is, of course, now encoded in the law. What of Siddhartha himself? Siddhartha was destined to take one of two paths—to be a great ruler or a great seer. On one hand, his life is predetermined, but on the other he will choose between certain paths. The upriver, mythological story arc has Siddhartha's fate sealed—while simultaneously suggesting that the Buddha he will be has lived countless previous lifetimes and has consciously chosen this one to manifest this fate! Fortunately, these enfolding, confusing turns become clearer with the help of the integral model.

For now, let us note a few more examples of attachment-as-love and the tension of this aspect of the two attachments with the other pole. When Siddhartha makes his fateful exit, he has been married and presumably well-attached to his same-age wife all his adult life. One can only presume they were emotionally very close. The story endorses this notion: as Siddhartha leaves, he is unable to face awakening his family, so he takes leave alone in the dark of night.

Recall Kisa, the young, grieving mother, is so over-attached to her dead baby that she can barely function. Buddha persuades her to let go, but he very well may have wielded influence because of his profound compassion and lovingkindness. This may have won her over, and helped her to trust in his message to let go. Clearly, lovingkindness may have roots in attachment-as-love. This points to the possibility of a marriage between the two attachments.

Other admixtures of attachment and detachment in Buddha's biography are directly associated with his mom, Mahamaya. Her dream shifts the narrative away from the King's earthly realm to what goes by the term, "Mother Earth." In this typical, core aspect of the feminine principle heaven and the earth, eternal and temporal, other-worldly and this world are united.

Mother Earth is the womb, vessel, life-giving dharma associated with our planet, evolution and biology. She gives rise to all biological life and sentience. All life is dependent upon her and returns to her in death, cyclically. She is an ultimate and unique attachment figure: one who brings us into being, frees us to live out our lives, and one from whom we do not escape. Rather we return the molecules she lent to us in death.

References to Mother Earth occur in Mahamaya's visionary dream. There her identity shifts away from pregnant woman, sister, wife and queen. The dream describes a ritualistic anointing of Mahamaya as 'mater immaculata', 'Immaculate Mother'. In this exaltation of the feminine principle, we can infer the direct transmission of that aspect of dharma traditionally referred to as Mother Earth. As such: as mother, womb, goddess, as an enchanting, sacred, divine maternal vessel, She transmits all She herself is. She transmits all she receives. At Lake Anottata, Mahamaya returns to her mother's watery womb. There she is bathed in the sacred waters which flow into and through her, and which will break, as new life ushers forth. The dream emphasizes the connection from

Mother Earth and to Mahamaya, through her, to her in-utero fetus. Terms for this include Tantra, pure awareness, Buddha-nature. A new life that will bring an end to life-as-suffering. Here the power, the tenderness and naked connectivity of that we have been framing as Buddha's Mom makes a radical turn.

"Mahamaya, the mater immaculata of the Buddhists, died seven days after his birth." [40] The same term is used in "immaculate conception" referring to spiritual divinity. At the same time Mahamaya dies, her neonate demonstrates and declares his independence. The boy who will be Buddha walks and talks — seven days after being born.

After the glorious events at Lake Anottata, Mahamaya will have little more to do with her unspeakably precious, important baby than be his biological vessel. Her heavenly stature falls flat upon the return to earth. She is about to take stage as something like the mother of Buddhism, but her transition from divine to biological is cut short. The miracle of her role in Siddhartha's biological attachment hits the ultimate biological impasse. If Mother Earth, the feminine and an otherwise normal human woman was viewed by history as interconnected, and as directly contributing to Siddhartha's accomplishments, there would be no separation, one not two attachments.

Alas, Mahamaya's detachment from all this and the rejection of Mother Earth and what might be called the divine feminine is doubly decisive. The story assures the reader that the neonate is more than fine, thank you very much. One hundred and sixty-eight hours of mom-baby time ends with no more attention to dharma transmission. She dies and he walks and talks.

Had he been asked, Bowlby would likely have something to say about this. Fortunately, the integral model has much to say on the subject, as I will demonstrate in the next section. Convoluted tensions exist between biology's attachment and that through which Siddhartha becomes Buddha with a view on attachment that can be understood as proof of the power of the feminine principle. In total, their ubiquity and persistence demonstrate how the feminine permeates consciousness. Even in highly patriarchal systems and cultures, her essence and values manage to permeate these systems over and again. These patriarchal systems distort and subjugate the feminine, and yet by virtue of some deeper reality, she persists with vigor.

Following Mahamaya's death and the king's remarriage, the female-male and attachment-detachment dynamic makes a shift. As kings do, Suddhodana summoned the most learned and wise to view the baby and weigh in on his providence. One of these wise men, Asita, was set apart for reasons that are relevant to our meditation on the two attachments.

> When Prince Siddhartha was born the great seer Asita interpreted the
> miraculous events and auspicious marks on the baby's body as divine
> indications that the child was destined to become either a chakravartin, or an
> enlightened Buddha. Temporal or spiritual sovereignty lay in the child's
> destiny.[41]

In contrast, the other members of the king' entourage, "less direct in their interpretations, desiring to better please the King, interpreted the signs as meaning that Siddhartha was going to be a King of Kings."[42] Asita's input can hardly be overstated. At this point, the king had everything he could possibly want — wealth, power, and a long and happy marriage. He brings a son into the world, hits a bump when his wife dies, immediately remarries, only to learn from the wise men that instead of following in his footsteps, Siddhartha may abandon the king and leave his legacy unfulfilled.

According to legend, Asita was a great holy man who was part of a pre-existing lineage of ascetics who lived as hermits in the Himalayan Mountains. Such men are said to live in caves and devote themselves to constant meditation. Asita, according to the ancient texts, divined the birth of Siddhartha and traveled through the air to Kapilavastu.[43] Upon seeing baby Siddhartha, he wept. He was assured that this baby would achieve enlightenment and saddened that he would not be alive to know him.

The meaning of the events and marks that Asita perceived correspond to Hindu mythology. Accordingly, these signaled the birth of a mahapurusha, a "great divine man."[44] Asita's input links the auspicious bodily marks on Siddhartha to the Hindu god, Vishnu. In Suddhodana's time, Vishnu had been reincarnated eight times. In each case, the infant displayed thirty-two major marks and eighty minor characteristics. Based on his bodily marks as a newborn, Hindus have since claimed Shakyamuni Buddha as the ninth of Vishnu's ten incarnations.

According to Hindu mythology, Vishnu specifically has two abodes. One is heavenly and beyond logic, measurement and all aspects of the material realm. The other is the material realm of Ksheera Sagara, an "ocean of milk."[45] Through the story of this strange mountain hermit, the divine feminine and Mother Earth is again involved. That "she" can be found in the deep backdrop cuts both ways. On the one hand, the feminine and mother archetype is placed at the most foundational stratum possible. The feminine has a role at the very earliest developmental level. On the other hand, the feminine is soon subjugated with the death of Mahamaya and associations of signs and marks and an "ocean of milk" to Siddhartha is obscured. Interesting and also obscured is the link between the future Buddha and Asita's pre-Buddhist, possibly secular, ascetic lineage. Possible links between the feminine aspects of Buddhism and a secular, "human lineage" will be discussed in future sections.

Attachment-as-Love

What goes by attachment subsumes attachment and detachment sub-processes. Therefore, the extent to which a maternal, biological attachment is the basis of empathic exchange and intimacy and much of what passes for human love, has two corresponding sides. As the writer and political activist, Elie Wiesel, said, "The opposite of love is not hate but indifference." Hate, aversion, and variants of detaching, repelling, and distancing are innate features of love. These informed Siddhartha's development and therein his later discoveries. As a singularly intelligent, perceptive boy, he came to integrate the attachment architecture of the core "we-spaces" of his existence. Given that attachment is both a very established scientific and Buddhist term, not to mention fully embedded in English as a 'household word', the imperfect compromise position leaves this as both the overarching dynamic and one of its two active sub-processes.

In interactions with ever expanding we-spaces, Siddhartha continually, empirically assessed and refined the totality of his response. According to the Pali Canon, the patrician call to be or not to be a King was among the earliest and most forceful we-space pressures. This was backed up by the shimmering warrior-king coolness structurally celebrated by the culture and history of Kapilavastu.

So entrenched was this that the only option was to wander in the forest uncivilized. The Canon speaks eloquently of the two-sides of Suddhodana's attachment-love.

> When he saw the wondrous birth of his son, the king, although steadfast,
>
> was much perturbed; and from his love two streams of tears surged forth,
>
> rising from apprehension and delight.[46]

As Bowlby's and subsequent research has made clear, attachment is the biological imperative that conveys efficacy in human offspring. Problematic versions of the two sides of attachment correspond to a psychology based in enmeshment on one hand and in abandonment on the other. Perhaps the reader can recall emotional enthusiasms and face-plants of pre-adolescence and adolescence. The infatuation roller coaster accelerates toward cosmic bliss then dive-bombs into a dark, apocalyptic abyss. An unspeakably alluring, perfect, amazing, handsome-beautiful other finally sees us. Joy bursts forth. But we can't talk. Actually, they were saying hello to someone behind us. The joyous balloon is impaled, humiliation its death rattle.

Metaphorically, we move from worshiping a star in the sky to suddenly succumbing to an intense gravitational pull. One is hurled into a galactic expansive beyond measure. There is an absence of scale, references, and coordinates. Jungians refer to this as inflation. Shadow is required to puncture and bring this grandiosity back to earth. One way or another we are reset by the biting, humiliating reality of our situation.

This all-to-human pendulating gives a flavor for the forces behind the King Suddhodana's mixed emotion, as well as to Siddhartha's own pushes and pulls regarding his son, Rahula. It provides a skeletal structure, as we will see, for some of his other intimate, interpersonal relationships. We are so fortunate to have some record of these.

The enmeshment-abandonment, attachment-detachment framework illuminates Siddhartha's decision to name his one and only son after the term, "impediment". This represents a metaphorical slamming of the brakes on the detachment side. He must have felt pressured by the attachment-love pouring forth from within him for the baby, for and from Yasodhara, Suddhodana, and Prajapati, even from the nursemaids for the baby. Given the references to his bursting intellect and curiosity, perhaps the pressure to stay, to be a father, husband and son was crushing. Another passage expresses the same sort of push-pull experienced by Siddhartha's biological mother.

> The queen was overcome with fear and joy, like a mixed stream of water, hot
>
> and cold; both because her son's power was other than human, and because
>
> of a mother's natural weakness.[47]

We are using the term Buddha's Mom for this territory as well as that to which it leads, e.g., spiritual awakening. This book aims to follow this arc, and to do so bolstered by all associated, salient, valid lines of evidence. As we unpack this attachment-love connection, we quickly appreciate how Siddhartha's early life was deeply informed by the bonds he had with his father, wife, and son and his stepmother, Prajapati. In the early going, we find multiple tensions deserving further consideration.

Siddhartha's decision to name his son, 'impediment', and then to abandon him was conceivably compensatory. It may bely a push back against a subterranean attachment pull. Not yet enlightened (more accurately, not yet aware of his enlightenment), his naming of his only son, and subsequent departure, packs a punch. The story more than hints that this brilliant young man saw through the emotional binds that leave the rest of us to suffer. That which Siddhartha was rejecting—all this detaching—gets the limelight.

None of these elements suggest some compensatory, positive attractant or attachment process. But what can be said about that to which he was attracted to, and moving towards? What was so enticing, with whom or what was Siddhartha (albeit not fullyconsciously) so infatuated? What muse, what vision could possibly have pulled him away? The original motif, symbolized as a tension between becoming a ruler or great spiritual teacher, informs this turning point. Siddhartha's leave-taking fulfills the birth prophecy. He is at once abandoning the way of the ruler and rejecting attachment-love. With this, money, power and worldliness are conflated with what would seem to be the path of the heart.

The seeker/teacher/ascetic path was an established form. This helps the pill to go down. The tale embeds the possibility that this emotional, passionate son, husband and father sought a bigger love. And he would immediately manifest his passion in various ways. As a forest monk, Siddhartha tried to master all associated standards for greatness. In a relative, human sense, Siddhartha may have been infatuated with the idea of enlightenment. This may have translated into an obsession with forging the most perfect, meaningful existence possible as defined by his cultural, historical context.

The simple, two-sided notion of relative attachment seems to fit. In attachment-love over his head, he sprang in the other direction. As a forest monk, he made desperate efforts to reach the other shore. Nearly dying, he finally discovered the absolute, and let go of the relative. The path was laid long before any such breakthrough. Thousands of lifetimes according to the ancient texts. And even in this lifetime, Siddhartha would persist beyond comprehensible limit. All the while, he somehow knew that he did not yet know, had not yet achieved his path. He knew relative attachment, relative love, not integral attachment or absolute love. He pressed on with a first-person sense of, "I'll know it when I see it."

To chuck all belongings and relationships, to live without food, money, or shelter is a daunting prospect. Thankfully, we can attempt to walk in the moccasins of certain key people who were there, and who were fortunate to know Buddha firsthand. And we can attempt this with the help of modern attachment science. These people, Suddhodana, Prajapati, Rahula, Kisa, for example, had profound experiences because of their relationship with Siddhartha-Buddha, which in a modern light, offers a lovely inside track for those of us not so fortunate (not yet aware of our enlightenment). Buddha did not demand they reject love, leave everyone and everything but as future arhats, they would eventually do so joyfully. They would transcend and include, it seems, and not reject attachment-love.

In each case, what began as a strong familial bond (stepmother-son, Kisa and her baby, Rahula and his dad) is transcended as each chooses the path of detachment. On one level, attachment-as-love binds. We may be swept up in an infatuation or profoundly defined by another whom we love in a very mature way. On another level, this opens the door to the path of nonattachment, an opening of wisdom, compassion, and lovingkindness. Since we do not have to presume that Buddha emanated lovingkindness, we are only left with the following, quite rational speculation. The "two attachments" fall on the relative side of a continuum that arcs toward nonattachment, a facet of which is referred to as *metta* or lovingkindness.

Non-attachment is neither the same nor the opposite of attachment-as-love. This is familiar mystery for Buddhists. The fruits of the spiritual quest are described as emptiness as well as by terms denoting a fullness, for example, infinite wisdom and compassion for all sentient beings. Kisa's maternal attachment and Rahula's paternal attachment were seen and welcomed by the wise one. Their attachment-love was both misguided and a profound guide. We will continue to explore this in later chapters. By whatever name, desire, love and attachment find ever more acceptance, more of a home in the "third turning" of the wheel of the dharma. We will be delving into this, specifically Vajrayana Buddhism (also known as tantric Buddhism) soon.

Kisa's and Rahula's imperfect, relative experiences represent a most compelling probability. Their stories suggest, though they do not assert, that this woman and this child perceived Buddha's acceptance, kindness, and knowing within a transformative "we" space. They did not forsake the attachment-as-love (both received and given) so much as open into a bigger field, a larger loving space. Each was pleased to be shown the way and transformed by embodying this reality.

The more overt message can obscure the subtler one. The deeper meaning is not that Buddha saw how Kisa's attachment-love for her dead baby was imprisoning her, though surely he did. Nor simply that Rahula's focus on the family inheritance was not good for him, though he saw this as well. The subtler message these stories convey is what Kisa and Rahula saw, perceived and felt in the presence of Buddha. To this list, I would add the verb, "to know." They felt understood, and at some juncture phenomenologically crossed into an experience of great confidence. They knew they were understood. At least in theory, such instances fit what Bowlby called mirroring, and involve mirror neuron activity. Quite possibly, Kisa and Rahula each had a direct, transformative experience of Buddha's wisdom and compassion. Kisa's true love for her baby was a relative truth. On the relative side, this dissolves and reforms into truer truths. These more broadly unify the various nodes and vectors of the ever-tortured, restless mind. Kisa's true love, for example, was also snuffing the life out of her, much as illness had robbed her baby of life. But before her meeting with Buddha, this "in-sight" was cut off.

Where Kisa's attachment to her baby is quite clearly aligned with Bowlby's theory, Rahula's desire to receive the family inheritance speaks to the attachment at the heart of the Four Noble Truths and that of Buddhism generally. Rahula echoes Buddhism's original, iconic attachment protagonist, the youthful Siddhartha. Rahula's interest in the family inheritance has important components. It may simply represent a boy's interest in chariots and exciting things. He may seek to impress his peers, a particular girl (or boy). Demanding his inheritance would fit with some form of a standoff and rebellion against the father who abandoned him.

There is also speculation that Yasodhara pushed her son to ask for the inheritance. She may have been motivated to do as Suddhodana had, to attempt to use wealth to prevent Rahula from abandoning her as her husband had. Even darker are explanations that propose a desire born of revenge, to hurt Siddhartha-Buddha by manipulating their son's rejection of him and his path. Less devious would be motivations born of empathy and the desire to shield Yasodhara's son from any notion that he should follow in his father's path. By ensuring that Rahula be installed as the next in line, she was reducing her own risk of hardship, homelessness, and begging.

Quite apparent too are repeated father-son themes first associated with Suddhodana and Siddhartha. With Siddhartha and Rahula, the spirit versus flesh, and universal emperor versus universal teacher is replayed. Notice, nonetheless, the unifying force of tender emotions and love. Suddhodana is broken-hearted over Siddhartha's decision to become a homeless beggar. Rahula speaks with sweet admiration for the father he finally gets to be near. Siddhartha as Buddha seems to know the pain each feels, much as he is attuned to Kisa and others.

The specific motives of each of Siddhartha's family members may never be known but some reasoned speculation is possible. For starters, anthropologists have carefully documented aspects of similar interpersonal dynamics in indigenous peoples. The San, a collective term for hunter-gatherer peoples, were studied in depth over the last half of the twentieth century. This period witnessed the loss of cultures dating back tens of thousands of years. In all the analyses of the original ways of existing, attachment is infused into all aspects of culture, from gathering and hunting, to feeding and caregiving of children, to the formulaic exchange of gifts.

> Gift-giving is a fairly formal affair, and people remember clearly who gave what to whom and when. These exchange relationships, which may last a lifetime and may even be passed on to one's children, help to even out wealth differentials…Huts are too small to contain much more human activity than sleeping. They are set only a few feet apart. A fire burns outside each doorway, in front of the hut, and the area around it is the effective living space for the hut's occupants—the nuclear family and their visitors. All doors face inward toward a large communal space. The intensity of social life that this fosters seems deliberate, as space is abundant and privacy could easily be arranged.[48]

This passage underscores how humans go to great lengths to emotionally huddle. Within tight frames, each of us emits and receives signals, and forms intrapersonal and interpersonal maps accordingly. Siddhartha's father, wife or son may have had none of the motivations described. But it is unlikely that their relationship to Siddhartha in his younger years or to him as Buddha in his later years was emotion-less. The various lines of evidence would suggest that each felt a full range of emotional attachment's many colors, including love and inspiration, hurt, jealousy, pride, bewilderment, and fear of abandonment—to name a few.

In some passages, Yasodhara is described in unbecoming ways. Others paint her as having lived in *simpatico* with her husband after he left. During those years that he wandered and engaged in austerities, "Yasodhara, too, was living on scanty fare, wearing common clothes, giving up her royal beds, and making herself beds of straw."[49] Perhaps she set up the meeting with Rahula, as a woman might have had to do at that time, unable to ask that Rahula be given the inheritance herself. Perhaps she hoped, even knew Rahula would love Siddhartha-Buddha with abandon just as she did. By going along with or setting up this confrontation, she would facilitate his decision to renunciate riches and dynasties and the dukkha they would bring. In this scenario, she would understandably not abandon Rahula herself but would be sure that he was ready to abandon her and follow the Buddhist path. Where a constrained love smothers, a larger love sets free.

In the end, all of these personalities, Siddhartha-Buddha's son, wife, father and mother, at least according to the ancient sources, become arhats. Attachment-as-love maintains that the truth, power, and beauty of Buddhism may fall short when attachment is taken out of its deepest, integral evolutionary, historical and spiritual context.

Attachment is best understood as an empty vessel in which grasping, clinging and desire find temporary, illusory form. This form is immensely important. It is the glue of self/ego/mind and the conduit to source or ground Buddha-nature in emptiness. A more accurate understanding of this arises as diverse lines of evidence are viewed through an integrated lens. In the next section, I will specifically turn to integral theory, viewing diverse lines of evidence for a new view of attachment through an integral frame. "Through" is the operable word. The great poet, Robert Frost, had it right when he penned the line, "the only way out is through."[50] One attachment transcends the two *through* Buddha's Mom.

Chapter Two

GOING INTEGRAL

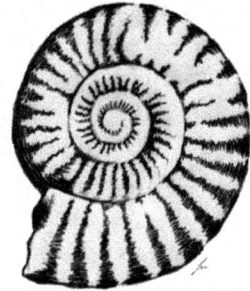

Wilber's Model

Über author-philosopher-theoretician, Ken Wilber has refined an integral model of such breadth that both contains itself and is open to endless revision. The prospect of reconciling and transcending the two attachments will benefit from a limited foray into his work. In twenty-five books translated into thirty languages, Wilber has pioneered a map of maps wherein all bases of inquiry and knowledge have a specific location and legitimacy. Wilber's model is a fount of precise, crisp, descriptive layers. Each new book gobbles up ever more religious, philosophical, spiritual, and consciousness paradigms and approaches to health and healing from across history and the globe. And so doing, each adds to Wilber's "integral theory".

Wilber's brilliance is intense and extends far beyond the scope of this brief review. For newbies, he offers an 'integral life practice kit': body, mind, spirit, shadow.[51] On this hangs a range of established approaches including weightlifting, qi gong, psychoanalysis, cognitive therapy, and/or "any worldview or meaning system that works for you". Integral Life Practice is promoted as modular, scalable, customizable and distilled.

For me, what lives and breathes scientifically and opens to bliss spiritually, what I'm calling Buddha's Mom, nests snugly within integral theory. At the same time, "she" seems hidden in plain sight. Buddha speaks of dharma (reality) so differently than Wilber. Wilber's talent is in showing where any view or truth claim fits in a universal matrix, and thereby how to conceptualize all of Buddhism's major tenets. Both extend an invitation to mind-blowing reality but do so very distinctly. My thesis, my experience, is that Buddha's Mom is similarly distinctive.

Wilber has long declared himself *not a guru*. Nor does he proclaim to be a psychotherapist or healer. He does not write about his personal, therapeutic approach with clients or patients, give dharma talks or lead retreats. He refers to himself as a *pandit*, e.g., a scholarly teacher. But the line between pandit and guru does not seem entirely clear. Long ago, pandit also referred to priests and healers, albeit highly learned. Dharma talks are called teachings. Often the teacher-student dynamic is one of guru-follower. Adherents of Thich Nhat Hanh, author of multiple books himself, warmly refer to him as *thay* or teacher.

Regardless, Wilber's been a phenomenal, albeit long-distance hero of mine. My goal here is show how Buddha's Mom fits within Wilber's system, and thereby to increase readers' access to her. Two related jumping off points, to move further along in this discussion of the Bowlby-

Buddha interface, are the Great Chain and 'transcend and include'. If the integral model is alive, then the Great Chain is its DNA, and 'transcend and include' this DNA's dominant organic process. We will delve into a little corner of integral theory before circling back to relative attachment and Buddhism. To begin, let's consider Wilber assertion that everyone is right—to an extent.

> I don't believe that any human mind is capable of 100 percent error. So
> instead of asking which approach is right and which is wrong, we assume
> that each approach is true but partial, and then try to figure out how to fit
> these parts together, how to integrate them...[52]

Wilber's dogged pursuit of what is positive and contributory, and therefore essential to an integral vision—no matter how seemingly far-flung or insignificant—parallels Hegel's distinction of "learner" verses "scholar." Hegel wrote that where the learner sees only differences and faults the scholar sees "positive merit in everything."[53] Wilber takes this to an almost inhuman breaking point. Over his career, he has reviewed every major metaphysical, philosophical, religious and scientific domain and wisdom tradition, and analyzed the ideas and paradigms of virtually every major thinker and theorist.

In *Integral Psychology*, he includes a host of charts to visually display how scores of such models overlay, forming an ever-expanding, ever-more-encompassing, ever-more-integral totality. The following quote is a typical example of how Wilber leapfrogs across major theorists and models. He both acknowledges each contributors' life's work and then weaves it forward, so to speak, into his ever more inclusive and majestic tapestry.

> Since we have also been using Gebser's general worldview terminology of
> archaic, magic, mythic, and mental (with the clear implication that they are
> referring to essentially similar stages), I will often hybridize Gebser's
> terminology to match Piaget's substages, so that we have a continuum of
> archaic, archaic-magic, magic, magic-mythic, mythic, mythic-rational,
> rational, rational-existential (and into vision-logic, psychic, etc.). These
> particular names are, of course, arbitrary; but the actual stages they refer to
> are based on extensive empirical/phenomenological research.[54]

In its most familiar and colloquial format, the continuum described above goes by body-mind-spirit, sometimes body-mind-soul. Wilber refers to these ancient formulations as the "Great Chain of Being." Returning to the "two attachments," the great chain situates Bowlby's attachment theory mostly at the level of the body (biological, physiological) and Buddhism's attachment at the higher levels of mind and spirit. The 'body-mind-spirit' formulation is telling. This shorthand for the human experience leaves out emotion. Similarly, "mind and body", whether cast as dualistic and problematic or as holistic and positive, leaves out the world of feeling. We will discuss this conspicuous absence throughout this book.

This omission is not just superficial. It reflects the same chasm that separates the two attachments. Buddhism's attachment is commonly referred to as the *mental* tendency to grasp, cling and hold onto concepts of self and reality. Clinging and grasping, of course, are meant figuratively. One does not suffer because one literally grasps objects but because one figuratively or metaphorically clings to concepts. Figurative refers to interpretive, symbolic and psychological strata—in a word, *mind* on the great chain.

We automatically and naturally interpret the Four Noble Truths through this mental filter. Mind, it follows, causes suffering. The world of emotion enters but remains concealed—the consequence of another factor and, right out of the box, negative. And by association mind is revealed to be problematic as well. The Bible's Garden of Eden is similar. An innocent interest in an apple turns out to have dire consequences.

Dukkha, in the Buddhist formulation, is the undesirable result of innate, natural mental tendencies—tanhā, as discussed. Though derived from the word for pain, dukkha does not (generally, most would agree) refer to bodily pain on par with breaking one's arm. That would be quite a mental feat. Buddha was not referring to anything so extreme or esoteric as the mind producing physical pain. Rather dukkha refers to the world of emotion.

An integral, holistic attachment formulation maps emotion and feeling in evolution. The fetus-neonate-infant part of the great chain demonstrates how we are born into a river of emotions. An infant longs to eat, to breathe, has intense feelings and delights in relationships. These all multiply in complexity as her body moves across the stages of life. Vivid, intense and prefiguring language and cognition, emotions are on full display in babies, kids, not to mention 'man's best friend' and other animals. How can they come to be conspicuously absent? A non-answer answer is that philosophers, academics and spiritual sages have historically focused on adults. Developmental psychology only began midway through the last century. Also, across time, academic and religious leaders have tended not to have babies suckling their breasts.

.

No One Cares

For some, it is subconscious and background, for others overt and loud, but for all in the grips of dukkha, the arising perception that "no one cares" is sadly commonplace. As a thought experiment, imagine that a day comes when there are so many advanced meditators walking about, with such an abundance of bodhicitta, that sanghas of Empathy Police have formed, eager to help put an end to suffering. Imagine that access to this thin saffron line is as easy as pressing some buttons on a smart phone. These bodhisattvas aim to serve and protect, to deliver the fruits of the dharma through we-space interventions.

Their work is only done when the caller is overwhelmed by major shifts in their plight, by meaningful insights and the replacement of fear, anger and sadness with exuberance and equanimity. These empathy officers respond within minutes. They knock down defensive doors and surround victims of the dukkha with the ever-flowing love of the great, holy ones. No amount of pushing back against their fount of care and intense focused awareness has a chance. Negating, complaining, venting, explaining and storytelling, none of these are any match for the depths of listening and unconditional regard conducted by the empathy officers.

When people say that nobody really cares and that they have tried to get help or work their way out of the dysfunctional mess that is their life, they are speaking a truth. This truth requires a creative expanse of imagination such as this Empathy Police notion to fully grasp. From the perspective of a freeing, love-imbued wego (more on this in Chapter 5) such as Buddhism's finest might evoke, we so need each other that it is more accurate to say we *are* each other.

We are not fully realized when we do not comprehend the total scope of pain that pervades this existence. The decision not to fully descend into the pain of another is especially understandable. The impossible call to be some sort of Empathy Police is automatic for any of us just barely keeping a distance from our own demons. But not to leap to the other, to the call to love with abandon, may be the telling image in the mirror. We are here on earth to surpass our humanity by caving into its epicenter.

As Reggie Ray says over and over, we are so unaware of what is really looking back from the mirror: our unstoppable essence, a precious, fleeting blossom in an explosion of form. We naturally buffet our vulnerable senses with successive comforts, distractions and narrative quilts. The bodhicitta heart calls us to crush these way-stations of delusion. A decent radar is that of some extreme form of empathy, even if we only conjure this by suspending reason.[55]

As treatments for brain and CNS-based suffering and disease (from schizophrenia to spinal injury to Alzheimer's) come on-line, perhaps the whole of the medical model and focus on symptoms will finally complete the turn toward the cessation of suffering—this oddball thing called realization. Perhaps the call from various spiritual traditions to love with abandon will join forces with scientific discoveries and technologies, and healing will increasingly be measured in terms of lovingkindness. Buddha makes it clear, however, that the goal is not to live forever, nor to avoid suffering from disease or old age. Rather, the oddball motivation is that of this imaginary Bodhisattva police person sitting by the phone.

Love cannot be forced, nor can it stop physical disease or death, the birth and death of quarks or stars, nor can it be contained by the most optimistic imagination. Anyone can debate such ultimatums, but back on human ground, the scope of suffering, the hunger to love and be loved requires fierce, optimistic imagination.

AVK

As we work toward greater degrees of resolution regarding the two attachments, readers are encouraged to be open to rich, "right brain" (imagistic, poetic, artistic) appreciation of Buddha's Mom. To digress very briefly, in the 1970s and afterwards, "neurolinguistic programming" (NLP) developed as a sort of rebellious movement in the fields of counseling and clinical psychology. NLP gained a lot of adherents and buzz with approaches to rapid therapeutic techniques. Though largely discredited, one contribution is worth notice.

AVK is the auditory-visual-kinesthetic triad based on the three primary ways that people tend to process information. The first corresponds to verbal forms of experience and incorporates talking, listening, reading and writing. This is inherently linear and much more embedded in linear time. Visual and kinesthetic modes are far less embedded in linear time. Visual, of course, includes imagination and imagery modalities. Kinesthetic refers to body and body-based modes of experience and knowing including sensory, both tactile and affective or emotional feelings.

Books, by their nature, are predominantly based in the first modality, auditory. In this one, I have worked hard at counterbalancing "left brain", verbal concepts by channeling the most heartfelt "right brain" material I can muster. Poetry, prayer, hypnosis, dancing and so many other modalities are similarly less "A" in this triad. Buddhist teachings interpreted through the auditory channel may be distorted beyond credibility or coherence. As an example, let's consider one orthodox explanation for the "K" realm. In Tantric Buddhism, the subtle, energetic body or light body is believed somehow coexist with bone, muscle and fascia. This energy body is said to be made of 84000 nāḍīs (e.g., tubes, vessels, channels).

Buddhist references to multiplicities and large numbers are better understood as metaphor for vastness. The great bodhisattva of compassion. Avalokiteshvara (elsewhere, Guanyin or Lokeśvara) is renowned for her thousand arms and hands busily relieving earth's suffering multitudes. Buddhism's massive numbers, often counted in thousands (yesteryear's millions or billions) are deferential to worlds beyond thinking and ideas. They are similar to poets' description of the numbers of stars in the sky. Or Jesus' feeding 5000 with five loaves of bread and two fish. Vastness, in fact, is a central theme of the one of Buddhism's finest sutras, the diamond-cutting sutra.

Neuroscientists also refer to huge quantities, to hundreds of billions of neuronal interconnections, for example. These quantities, however, are not metaphorical or placeholders for the sacred. An overly literal lens on something beyond words or numbers is doomed to distort this. Let's ponder the Buddha's words on how to meditate. Note how elegantly he refers to this "K" realm, the land of 84000 nāḍīs.

> Here, O bhikkhus, a bhikkhu, gone to the forest, to the foot of a tree, or to an empty place, sits down, bends in his legs crosswise on his lap, keeps his body erect, and arouses mindfulness in the object of meditation, namely, the breath which is in front of him… 'Experiencing the whole body, I shall breathe in,' thinking thus, he trains himself. 'Experiencing the whole body, I shall breathe out,' thinking thus, he trains himself.[56]

AVK's 15 minutes has passed, but perhaps the baby was tossed out with the bathwater. The buzz NLP not uncommon for self-help and psychospiritual movements. Real people describe breakthroughs, heart openings, and "ah ha" moments. Love languages, the Enneagram, Myers-Briggs, a Course in Miracles—come to mind. Us unenlightened types continually insist we know where to shine the flashlight. But teachers are often unbeckoned and bizarre. They may seem insignificant, involve headlong, self-destructive antics or grandiose, blind leaps of faith. All these are held together in Wilber's core precept, e.g., even ego is not 100% error. Of course, many teachings only come into focus in hindsight. It would require an ocean of compassion to somehow stand aside and nonjudgmentally watch one's own most humiliating moments. Regardless of their final legitimacy, even passing fads and poor decisions may help unblock access to this lovingkindness in the moment or later. Any enhanced encounter with reality is a shift toward the sacred.

While there has been no modern, scientific verification of the thousands of nāḍīs, there is support from contemplative traditions for its essence, e.g., a subtle body or light body. This is also referred to as energetic and vibrational and referenced in near death experiences. Many lines of evidence point to the body/soma as pivotal in spiritual awakening, a point I press in the final chapter. Homo sapiens' "whole body" includes attachment and is well mapped within truly comprehensive neurobiology. An unspeakable reverence may arise when this conceptual, verbal map is combined with Buddhist teachings. This marriage holds the potential for experiencing one's own life, mind and body, as a living, vibrating somatic vessel. A vessel carried on and carrying the great arc of evolution.

When looking at, or when averting our gaze and shifting to the next great thing, we miss Buddha's call. Across his forty years of what would now be called "dharma talks", he handled this human need deftly. When what (was recalled of what) he said was finally written down, there were essentially more enumerated lists that one could count. Not one of these (600 plus) lists is required before partaking of these "whole body" instructions. The lists and ideas are supportive and potentially critical.

This runs in parallel with the story of AVK. We may be too quick to adopt or abort ideas when we do not meditate on and embody their partial truth. We are all born to die in a limited historical, cultural context. Indirect knowledge and concepts others describe is one channel of experience, and direct experience quite another. The Pali Canon, in fact, uses a special term to refer to Buddha's typical yet extraordinary ability to do both, to elicit direct experience while speaking conceptually, e.g., *transmission*.

Kisa, to name just one real, living person who actually met with Buddha, was probably unfamiliar with Buddhism's linear, verbal, conceptual A-lists. Yet stemming from their interaction, during which Kisa was pleading, panic-stricken and crying, she achieved a high level of awakening. She, young Rahula, and others whom we will encounter, may have experienced Buddha's the same life-changing compassion more incrementally. Here we conjecture that transmission points to an innate, human capacity for receiving-and-giving scientifically traced through attachment-love.

Receptive is not always passive. Kisa was broken open by her pain and desperation. She did not earn enlightenment in a linear fashion, for example, through a series of intellectual insights or spiritual achievements. Perhaps Kisa's subtle body and undulating river of nāḍīs manifested as body-mind. Perhaps her higher capacities to think and feel were ripe for realization. The possible take-away is breathtaking, e.g., that the same is true of you and me.

One point regarding concepts and (verbal) terms is especially important. In keeping with most other books and media on Buddhism and psychology I do not presume or insist on any special connotations for common terms such as *awareness, consciousness, self, mind* or *ego*. These and related terms swim freely in the broader lexicon. At the most recent World Cup, the announcer complimented one of players as a "totally ego-free, grounded professional." I will generally combine the most common ones, in self/ego/mind, to underscore this reality. But to be sure, Buddha's Mom (I will propose) offers something stunning related to all these terms. As a teaser, consider one of Wilber's comments:

> What is it in you that brings you to a spiritual teacher in the first place? It's
> not the spirit in you, since that is already enlightened, and has no need to
> seek. No, it is the ego in you that brings you to a teacher.[57]

Siddhartha, once a suffering self/ego/mind, awoke as a free, blissful Buddha. As Buddhism's pre-eminent teacher, he transmitted the same 'buddhanature' to Kisa and many others—as that transmitted to him, to Buddha by Nature. A question naturally arises, what becomes of self/ego/mind? Once again, Wilber's work is edifying. He asserts that movement between levels, be these psychotic-borderline-neurotic-normal or archaic-magic-mythic-mental-integral, occurs via "transcend and include". The same goes for all such leaps, for example, egoic-transpersonal, or crudely put, unenlightened-enlightened. Here we propose "relative attachment" as a complimentary, biological concept. In combination with "transcend and include", relative attachment helps navigate the Bowlby-Buddha divide and reconcile the two attachments.

To transcend requires sinking in. A stillness within movement is fundamental in yoga. The most powerful inflection point in biological attachment is the mother-child dynamic. As discussed, this is echoed in familial and interpersonal, emotional bonding. To sink into this specifically—continuing this focus on Siddhartha, we must rely on the Pali Canon. As mentioned, this is

Buddhism's ancient collection of scriptures and sutras. A natural question arises as to the validity of this ancient source as regards Siddhartha's attachment experience.

Scholars believe Buddha was born between 563 and 480 BCE. Even picking the later date, his teachings are believed to have been passed along by oral tradition for more than three centuries before being committed to writing in the Pali language, in 29 BCE. On the one hand, there would seem to be almost no chance of validating the narrative of Siddhartha's early life. On the other, modern knowledge unavailable for virtually the entire sweep of time since Buddha lived can assist the goal of achieving accuracy. In a loose sense, we triangulate on the pre-mind of the neonate named Siddhartha that becomes the mind of the young lad, and eventually gives rise to what is known as Buddha-mind.

The many lines of evidence that we will employ demonstrate how a confluence of early, formative, interpersonal, and contextual factors powerfully shapes who we are, that is to say, the very architecture of self, mind, and ego. We have data not only on Siddhartha-Buddha's development and spiritual achievement but also on many of his contemporaries. The minds of those most influential in the life of Siddhartha and influenced by him offer overlapping, helpful perspectives.

Ultimately, the sphere of people Buddha influenced and therefore the possibility of drawing informed inferences is almost unlimited. Matthieu Ricard, an assistant to his Holiness the Dalai Lama provides one such data point. He provides yet another source of evidence for what we will frame as an integral attachment that transcends the two attachments, mappable in the construct of Buddha's Mom. In 2012, neuroscientists declared Ricard to be the happiest man in the world. The Dalai Lama proclaimed, "I believe that the very purpose of life is to seek happiness." As will become clear, I agree and believe Buddha's Mom to have something important to offer in this regard, as a vessel of such fruition. I frame what Ricard names in terms of meaning and sentience.

According to his researchers, Ricard's is a potent, living example of the human brains on meditation.[58] Scans of his and other advanced meditators' have helped advance the neuroscience of the fruits of Buddhism. Wilber reminds us that we are not simply left to hope and wish to be as happy as Monsieur Matthieu.

> The preposterous claim that all religious experience is private and
> noncommunicable is stopped dead by, to give only one example, the
> transmission of the Buddha's enlightenment all the way down to present day
> Buddhist masters.[59]

The path we will initially pursue then is through a triangulated reflection on Siddhartha's attachment and upbringing. We will seek to distill how what Siddhartha felt, thought and experienced in the earliest origins of his psychological life reflected factors that modernity has shown to be critical. Through this, an attempt will be made to discern the substrate mind from which the dharma flowed (and I will suggest still flows) even as Buddha showed us that the mind is illusory and could be set aside. A working assumption is that this journey has the potential to reveal more about the type of life most of us share for better or worse, given that most adults continue to be influenced by our childhoods.

This book is for the unenlightened. For those already able to fly without wings, without a body, without flying—as they say down under—good on ya! The aim is to cultivate the richest, most explicit, scientifically solid and spiritually cogent "before" picture possible, e.g., before enlightenment. With this, we aspire to better know the person who managed in one lifetime to achieve the ability to fly without wings.

Toward that end of the book, we will review what we have discussed from the perspective of the Diamond Sutra. In this, Buddha intensely engages the opposites and paradoxes that ran through the Pali Canon and, for many of us, obscure the prospect of awakening. I hope the reader finds that the ideas considered throughout the book enhances their experiential access to this great teaching. Among the ideas we will explore from an integral attachment perspective, Tantra looms especially large.

Tantra

Tantra translates as thread and as that which runs through cloth. This wisdom tradition is impossible to pin down. It is often depicted in iconic Tibetan paintings and statues featuring an exotic, sexualized union of consort deities. These are referred to as *yab-yum*. Flurries of curving, moving arms, legs and colors, these are also demonstrations of serenity and perfection. Yab-yum symbolizes unity in diversity, order in chaos and the one thread running through spirit and flesh.

Not surprisingly, Tantra is often misunderstood as some sort of combination of meditation and love-making. But even shallow variants may lead to a better practice path by placing the age-old tension between spirit and flesh within the context of transcendent intentions. Tantra celebrates life. It encourages one to ask, to wonder, to be curious and fully, physically and spiritually open to the immediacy of experience. Tantra places the call for lofty goals associated with discernment, compassion and mental clarity and equanimity within the body, the senses and sensuality. To be wrong or have any particular conviction is not necessarily problematic because Tantra teaches that there is a portal between opposites. What "appear to be dualities are really non-dual." In Tantra, sexual union is spiritual union.

> Tantra is that Asian body of beliefs and practices which, working from the principle that the universe we experience is nothing other than the concrete manifestation of the divine energy of the godhead that creates and maintains that universe, seeks to ritually appropriate and channel that energy, within the human microcosm, in creative and emancipatory ways.[60]

Yab-yum translates as father-mother and aims, in modern terms, toward being ever more radically disruptive. A typical artistic portrayal is of an exotic male deity sitting in the lotus position as a female consort, to put it euphemistically, sits on his lap. The intermingling of deities and sex are exaggerated, colorful, concretized depictions of inner, energetic states. These are as profound as they are sublime. Tantra connects body to the divine. It is practice—and a state of attainment, an opening and full release into what is always-already, our true nature.

Mahamaya's pregnancy dream has clear echoes of Tantra. It is, just for starters, a burst of color and movement, a sudden but short-lived wormhole into an alternative universe. It involves an immaculate meeting of a lotus, with all the feminine, vaginal, vessel connotations and a special phallic trunk, elephant element. From this will emerge the zygote, fetus, infant, boy and man which will (continue to) convey the dharma. In this dharma is aligned with sex, with biology, with an other-worldly source of truth and wisdom which is readied and carried over into this world. But precious little is directly described of this conveyance, this living thread.

A Tantric take, however, is squeezed between the sanctioned storylines. First, the to-be, Buddha's to-be mom is lauded for her identity as the king's wife and queen. Then just as we are about to encounter Mahamaya's humanity, as woman on the verge of prominence by association, she is lost in a dream, whisked off to a mysterious land by magical spirits. We barely learn of this other world, of the white elephant and lotus, before everything snaps back re-establishing Siddhartha at front and center.

> Birth of Gautama was a unique event, as he was not born as an ordinary
> man; rather he was worshipped, adored and revered by the renowned
> Brahmins and the gods, on whose persistent and sustained appeals he agreed
> to take birth as a human being.[61]

The words, "not born as an ordinary man" speak to how little we can anticipate learning about the specific circumstances of Mahamaya's pregnancy and all that follows. Not only (in the eyes of official documentarians) is Siddhartha born a man and not a baby, he is *no ordinary man*. The cold shoulder given the world of the mother despite all the emphasis on the womb suggests that man here mostly means male. Not only is Siddhartha a male, he is no ordinary male. We certainly are not provided any clear indication of how the visionary foray into the depths of earthy, feminine forces continue to flow as he is born, nursed and raised. Siddhartha's consciousness is not described as a continuous thread from and through the mother and all she represents. Between this territory and all the greatness portended, there is a silent chasm.

Devin

A similar silent chasm runs through the lives of those for whom parental preparation and love was so lacking as to almost guarantee disaster. One such man, a former client who I will call Devin, began having mysterious crying spells. These occurred following an extended period of tremendous healing and were happening every few days for period of several weeks.

Devin was in his fifties and had had lots of therapy before. He was in a sangha and adept at maintaining a sitting practice. On paper, he knew about reconnecting with feelings and about watching his mind but during these spells he was lost. Weeping over what felt almost void of content prompted him to question his sanity. As he lost control and wept, he wondered if he might be doomed to this final torment for the rest of his days. His formidable self-awareness and meditative skills were almost mocking, just further evidence that he was falling to pieces.

Devin had been massively traumatized as a child and had managed this in recent years with bottles of booze and powerful psychotropic medications. As of late, he had discovered mindfulness and established impressive, first-ever levels of stability within silence. But in through the side door came these uninvited visitations. As his therapist, I wanted to impose some sort of therapeutic map. Perhaps the crying was explainable simply as 'two steps forward and one step back'. I floated the possibility that he was integrating old territory long given over to trauma. But these felt intellectually dishonest. During these experiences Devin felt almost no embodied emotion. There was just hollowness and a quiet backdrop of dread. No interpretation was needed only acceptance and wonder.

Devin described feeling like an exposed, empty shell. This shell would simply weep for ten minutes when he was alone in his large, empty house. Nothing was changing perhaps nothing ever would. We were left just to validate that the psychic space at hand might not require us to name it or for him to do anything per se. We presumed these experiences to be an outpouring of an older iteration of psychic pain. Beyond this we only came to the notion of slowing down even more than the weeping seemed to demand.

Devin's journey had all the scars and grooves of deep self disturbance. As a child, he was steeped in what gets swept under the rug as 'dysfunctional'. He recalled being poked in the chest, for example, as his dad yelled at him not to cry. This was just a twist on the outright beatings. No food in the fridge and yelling were also commonplace.

Bad enough as memories these and similar factoids gained their power by subverting higher psychological strata. At this stage of life, Devin felt grotesquely aware of the wasteland of his past. He knew the trash trail behind 'boys-don't-cry' scripts. He had all the books and all the insights. He had his health, money and so much to be thankful for. Others had it much worse. Yet here he was ritually pouring brand new bottles of booze into the sink and crying. He had learned all the right things several therapists ago. But any true, stable universal ground of being was blocked. He was plummeting to a psychological no-go zone accelerated by over-learning. He had a map but no means of movement. With so little left, his body heaved.

Devin's penultimate trek sheds some light. Over the past couple of years, previously hard-earned and tender insights had been backfiring with a vengeance. Intermittent, I-know-better plunges were part of a new pattern. Binge drinking and suicidal thoughts followed on the heels of vigorous exercise, meditation and clean living.

But the crying thing was a little different. As his body underwent some mysterious grieving process, he had the felt sense of a non-idea, non-insight hollowness. As we will explore ahead, the Diamond Sutra speaks of the dharma abiding in an idealess, mega-galactic space. A blocked natural flow of life feels just so, missing, elsewhere, invisible. There is no personhood or emotion. Finally, in this freeform weeping, Devin's mind was silent without commentary, free of any take-home message or judgment. Mind's finest had left the building leaving but a hollow buzz. Beautifully Devin knew that he did not know (have access to) any ground of being (natural state, Buddha-nature)—because this knowing I-do-not-know was his immediate, unfettered experience. Before crossing over into emptiness (and who cannot relate?) Devin "thought he knew" a great many things. In the hollowness with tears flowing none of it was of any help.

All this places Devin in very good company. One of the greatest explorers of the unconscious, hypnotherapist Milton Erickson advised, "You don't know what you don't know." The saying that 'the more you know, the more you know that you don't know' is attributed both to the Buddha and to Socrates. St. Paul wrote: 'And if any man thinks that he knoweth anything, he knoweth nothing yet as he ought to know' (1 Corinthians 8: 2).

All the insights that bring one to great chasms seem to come to a screeching halt. But we can be thankful for the mess they leave us with. Our work allows us to *not know* with more precision about so much we once staked our lives upon. Naturally this list includes endless attachments and aversions. Self-medicating splits the difference in chasing a high that chases a void. 'Staying busy' also makes the top ten.

Devin had worked almost violently to whip himself into shape, clean up his act, rise the ranks, have a big salary and finally to purchase the house that symbolized victory. Life from another vantage cannot help but be perfect. In this perfection, the meaningless, hollowness, emptiness of the house gave way to an ever emptier, more hollow, somatic grief. His war torn, still thriving body longed for him to return not to a house but to his home. He knew he did not know the full boundaries of the crying space and managed in this to retain a thread of faith. He did not, to my knowledge, ever regress to previous levels of attachments and aversions and did continue to forge a path with a heart.

In a more immediate sense, Devin simply managed to just be, to feel baffled at feeling nothing while weeping, leaving him feeling ridiculous and hopeless and afraid he was losing it. The truth pushing its way to the fore stemmed from the big, sad house, all its space and silence. He had tried his damnest to join his busy friends in their American dream. As of late, he had let wayward family members stay there. It had not really helped them. Their problems and chaos seemed only to grow to fill the larger space. Not having to pay rent, for example, did not motivate them to find work to contribute in other ways. Devin considered walking away and giving them the house. But this would only saddle them with more problems, foreclosure, eviction, a rinse and repeat from whence they'd come.

Sobriety had washed away the make-up of those he once believed to be caring and close. Without large amounts of alcohol in the mix, he saw the sadness. People he once called friends barely shared or listened with any depth or sincerity. Everyone was invested in the next party, always gathering at places where noise, booze and music allowed sarcasm and bitterness to pass as intimacy.

Like a Russian doll, what Devin thought he knew kept giving way. He needed only walk the simple not easy line, to stay still and not know, and abide the blanks, fears and echoes of grief. Orthodox Buddhism is fairly quiet on the psychological implications of child abuse. As we will see, however, a clarion call is embedded in Buddhism. Through integrations with multiple lines of evidence a chorus arises.

Devin's psychosomatic path through darkness to healing and renewal calls for much further analysis. In this pursuit, we will interlace Buddhism with important work in Jung's analytical psychology arena and many other lines of research. Depth psychology, for example, has a lot to say about the symbolism of home and hearth. Dharma translates as that which bears or carries, and therefore has indirect connotations as housing, corpus and body. How does one with profound trauma and self-loathing navigate these oceans of information and manage to achieve any equanimity?

Buddha spent four decades teaching that below all the surfaces of mind is our natural state, our true nature. As all meaning once associated with Devin's outer house dissipated, a deeper spiritual home beckoned. Perhaps the mythic grandeur associated with Siddhartha's first biological home, his mother's womb offers guidance. As noted, she had a great dream before becoming pregnant. In this the body that would house and form the zygote, fetus and infant that would one day convey the dharma was bodily carried off by four magical spirits. She was bodily submerged, decorated, encircled and then penetrated by a mystical white elephant.

What smacks of ancient, esoteric, religious hyperbole, we will be suggesting fits with a cohesive scientific explanation for the transmission of sentience—meaning in life. Perhaps the mythic grandeur, the divine and royal preparations, all the wonder of what will be, must be understood and felt much more personally. As the eminent neurologist, Antonio Damasio demonstrates in his research, the substrate of the subjective self arises from a "feeling of what happens." Last I heard, Devin was continuing to discover this soft, still voice. He was awakening to a tenuous, fresh knowing—that subtle, inner connections and one's truer "me" are not only for somebody more fortunate.

Yin-Yang

The ancient Taoist symbol of yin-yang sheds further light on what we have been discussing as the feminine principle. "Yang," Joseph Campbell summarized, "is the light, active, masculine principle, and Yin, the dark, passive, and feminine."[62] What is so special is that deep within each side of yin-yang, of course, is the "opposite" side represented by the dot. This New Age favorite gets a lot of airtime but it does not reveal its deepest secrets as readily as one might expect. Richer than notions of balance and harmony are those invoking shadow and movement, risk and stability within instability. These many shades, according to Campbell:

> ...proceed from and together make manifest Tao: the source and law of being. Tao means "road," or "way." Tao is the way or course of nature, destiny, cosmic order; the Absolute made manifest.[63]

The Siddhartha biography is overloaded with yang. The grand feminine, Queen and mother of Siddhartha, Mahamaya, dies when he is one week old. Like it or not, the story suggests, he is thrust into hyper-independence and the masculine realm. A king's son, he is destined for greatness either as a king himself or as a great ascetic. Both of these were elite male-only vocations of the time. During his youth, Siddhartha mastered competitive mental and athletic endeavors, quite transparently echoing Campbell's description of yang as the active, ascendant masculine. Finally, he

left the family compound, alone, and independently sought to conquer illusions only to stumble upon old age and the dark realities of existence—all bodily givens, linked to earth, nature and soma.

The Tao reminds us that more than simple gender tension is in play. Its self-generating, self-regulating bifurcation comports with pratitiya-samutpada, the fundamental Buddhist principle of dependent origination. This holds that mental contents co-arise in a field of primordial awareness. In relative reality, everything is mutually interdependent. Co-arising phenomena, I have suggested, exist within a field of relative attachment. The Pali Canon describes three cut reeds. These are only able to stand by leaning on each other. Take one away and the other two will fall, or metaphorically, cease to exist.[64]

Superficially, stark contrasts between male and female and between light and darkness may lead the way to more sublime dimensions of consciousness, light within darkness and vice versa. The male is on the ascendency, moving, changing, and going places. The female is grounded, home, and present. These parallel the sublime forces of being and becoming. One sometimes experiences this in meditation, i.e., being in the moment while becoming more alive, more still and awake in the moment at once. The more centered in Witness, the more one witnesses. The quieter and more simply present, the more one is attuned to the impermanent, dynamic, and changing nature of consciousness, the soma's dance within earth's energetic field.

Rigid opposites are revealed to have an interdependent and co-arising nature. In patriarchal cultures, such as that of ancient India during Siddhartha's time, the feminine principle was commonly perceived and expressed in narrow, overly concrete ways. The Tao counsels against small-minded reductionisms. The belittled in the end may be exalted, the meek's inheritance may be enormous. The dot at the center of the opposite color, after all, is the whole of the Tao. Itself but a dot—eternity.

Even macho men embedded in patriarchal cultures have some non-obvious female characteristics. A male soldier's military base is an iteration of what Bowlby calls the secure base. The military is a way of life which, in a motherly fashion, goes to great lengths to protect and provide, for example, shelter, clothing, and food—not to mention, identity. Machismo and patriarchal, hierarchical values are made all the stronger through the stripping away personal power. The military does not simply provide clothing; it tells soldiers exactly what uniform to wear, ranks them and court martials anyone who does not follow orders. The lack of reflection on the container/womb/vessel signals not its weakness, but authority of a different order.

Although less intensive, Siddhartha's family compound had much in common with the military's blend of yin and yang. His identity would have been under the same sort of spell of the mother archetype. Food and shelter were provided, as were culturally defined roles and structured interpersonal relationships. The whole of the container would have been safe and predictable by virtue of the king and whatever security or militia he commanded. All this persisted until the day finally came when Siddhartha broke cracked the shell from within. As hundreds of millions worldwide know in their hearts, at age twenty-nine, something very special happened. Siddhartha finally broke free. Perhaps a smaller number sense how in this moment, one side of the Tao surged from within the opposing side. And how this conveyed a new, yet unchanged Tao.

The story juxtaposes the breaking of attachments to home, stepmother, son and wife, with a confrontation of old age, disease, and death. We know from the Canon that this event will have profound implications. Siddhartha would years seeking answers, would attain enlightenment and then spend the rest of his days sharing his discoveries with the world. Earthly, emotional attachment (home and hearth) must be upended for any possibility of nonattachment and the end of suffering (illness, aging) to come to pass. The biography adds a most transparent exclamation point to this equation. Though he had been thinking about it for some time, Siddhartha finally leaves the very night that his only son is born.[65]

This cloistered young man finally departs from what had comprised his entire life. He severed his deepest emotional attachments, to his father, stepmother (mother for all but one week of his twenty-nine years on earth), his wife of the past thirteen years, and his newborn son. Leaving his baby communicates that this cleaving of emotional attachments was not limited to the past but extends forward into the future. That so little has been made of his leaving baby Rahula leaves little doubt about patriarchy's view of fair and balanced parenting.

The ancient yin-yang symbol, a dot within itself and itself within a dot, can animate and shift opposites into organic, unfolding, in-folding fractals. No longer insulated by the family and what Buddhists refer to as the householder lifestyle (versus the life of an ascetic), Siddhartha immediately experienced the world of hurt just outside the walls of the compound. Attachment and the householder life were portrayed as co-arising with a life of abandonment, of searching, and this in turn with pain and suffering. As we know, as Buddha, Siddhartha would eventually, specifically reveal the ultimate interconnections between aging, disease, and death, to attachment—and in turn to the possibility of enlightenment.

Hence, the annihilation, cessation, and overcoming of corporeality, feeling, perception, mental formations and consciousness, this is the extinction of suffering, the end of disease, the overcoming of old age and death.[66]

Dharma Talk Therapy

The legacy of the "two attachments" is much more than a pedantic standoff between Bowlby's academic theory and arcane Buddhist doctrine. Consider the distinctions between "dharma talk" and "talk therapy." Bowlby's discoveries were incorporated with other theoretical and cultural memes, such as hippie love and the humanistic movement in psychology. In what came to be known as "third force" psychology, maternal attachment is not hard to spot. Carl Rogers advocated for love, dressed up as *unconditional regard*. Humanistic psychotherapy took place within a *holding space,* and healing emerged out of a sustained focus on the client's inner life through *reflective listening*.

When contrasted with the dharma talk form, these distinctions proffer more evidence of the imbalance of yin and yang, female and male, running through Buddhism. As a general rule (orienting generalization), so-called talk therapy reverses the polarity of the talker-listener structure.[67] The person who ostensibly has more expertise, who is paid by others for their technical expertise or perhaps wisdom, talks far more in the typical dharma talk format and far less in conventional talk therapy. The *talk* in talk therapy refers to the patient or client, where this refers to the teacher or lama at a dharma talk. Buddhist teachers do meet individually with students. This can take many forms and may be psychotherapeutic in nature. Traditionally and probably generally, however, this takes its clues from the dharma talk format and gives students a chance to get individual, instructional guidance on their meditative practice. To 'have an audience' (meaning *be* the audience of one or a very few) with one's teacher is a rare, special opportunity to be heard, which we can recognize as a form of maternal mirroring.

Cosmonauts of consciousness who explore this distinction will notice that the feminine principle, with her biological attachment basis, is more aligned with modern, scientifically based approaches to psychological healing. These largely work in the reverse direction from the ancient, classical dharma talk format. If Martians came to observe a Buddhist retreat, they would see that the time attendees spend talking and not quietly listening or meditating in silence is quite minimal. Attendees are permitted to respond to a teaching with a question about the instruction, or to thank the leader who gives the teaching. Martians would observe the talking and listening dynamic to be reversed in the typical psychotherapy session.

They would, of course, also notice a big difference in the ratio, the number of persons in the talker or listener position. With Freud and Jung, the one-on-one, analyst/analysand structure was born. Analysand is the term for people undergoing psychoanalysis. The names have changed — patient, client — but the role remains roughly the same. With the advent of "client-centered" counseling, Carl Rogers pushed the feminine-attachment dynamic to a new extreme.[68]

These structures and arrangements clearly mimic biological attachment. Mothers, of course, tend to have one or a low number of small children at the same time. As in biological and maternal attachment, the relatively less developed, needier person is counseled by the relatively more highly developed person. The latter's expertise calls for attunement to the granularities of the other's needs.

These factors all overlap with power. Power differentials play out in all relationships. One imperfect measure is reflected in the ratio of the talking-listening dynamic. Whether in a military drill, a tribal council, a professor's lecture, a CEO's speech, church sermon, or dharma talk, the structure tends to place one or a very small number of higher ranked persons physically at the front of the space. Their position is sometimes elevated or amplified with a microphone, and they tend to do most of the talking. She or he in the less-talking, more-listening position is commonly referred to as a member (follower, student) of a multitude, be it a sangha, class, audience, tribe, or company.

Transcept

This dharma talk/talk therapy, 'look who's talking', yin/yang distinction permeates self/ego/mind. Consider ancient prohibitions against taking the Lords name in vain, to say the name of God out loud or even to oneself. Similar rules, for example, against depicting a deity's image imply even deeper cognitive roots for these sorts of bans. Indigenous peoples are reported as distressed at being themselves photographed, concerned their soul may be stolen from their body by the photo.

Despite primitive, patriarchal trappings, these cases reveal a reverence for the divine and ineffable. There is aggression to be sure, in stoning someone who disobeys, still such rules bely direct inspiration — transmission even. Throwing words at the wordless is all too easy, and possibly dangerous, for our hyper-talking and image-making species. The Medusa myth expresses this same warning and truth. From the impermanent, perfect, empty vantage of nibbana, ego is already stone.

Its hubris seeks to render the godhead within its sphere. Recognizing this, Islamic artists, as another example, deliberately place errors in their works so as not to offend God.

A word that specifically identifies itself as a non-word placeholder might serve as reminder of language's inherent limitations. To speak of realization and liberation is potentially to miss their very point, and therein to use the Lord Buddha's name and his teachings vainly. *Buddha's Mom* is not as an end-concept but a living bridge to the realities her son uncovered. Her its-aspects, iterations such as Mahamaya, Prajapati or biological attachment are transcended and included by that actualized by Siddhartha. These inspired, intuitive admonitions convey a tantric truth. Language and conceptual awareness hovers above a larger realm of sentience, forever teeming with feelings and sensations. Nature, animals, emotion are vital fields, alive and organic, that predate and pre-arise.

Perhaps some neologism from "trans-construct" or "trans-concept" such as *transcept* is a better frame for Buddha's Mom. Transcept bridges *transmission* and *concept*. Buddha's Mom is not a name for a person. She is both personal and impersonal, conceptual. Even in a personal, historical mode, she lives through Mahamaya than Prajapati and the nameless nursemaids, one or more of whom could easily have been of equal importance from her conceptual perspective as biological-maternal attachment. In these many ways, "she" co-occupies "it" and "they."

Buddha's Mom is transcept-like in the way she points toward process and movement, the Siddhartha-to-Buddha arc. This has both scientific and narrative dimensions. As discussed, scientifically, developmental influences impacting Siddhartha, and through him Buddhism, find solid footing in evolution and maternal attachment. The same progression extends from the Big Bang to the ability to wonder about the ability to wonder about the Big Bang—is humbling, profound, and if anything ever could, can be declared to be *sacred*.

The persistence of the 'two attachments' gap between science and spirit parallels that between concept and transmission. The space is not adequately transcended by New Age hyperbole around the "now" moment. A more satisfying, living model of awareness presupposes roots running both directions through mammalian sentience, with cognitive branches enabling logic and leaves enabling language. Advances in Darwin's model comprising affective neuroscience (upcoming) provide further, potent triangulations on sentience, on the universal desire, the tanhā oozing through us super primates the world over.

Buddhist transmission as human lineage syncs with the secular movement in Buddhism (considered in depth in an upcoming section). As we have already considered, Asita and the Hindu echoes of Vishnu hint at a nondenominational or poly-denominational, pre-Buddhist Buddhism. This precedes and is incorporated in Shakyamuni. Echoes of the same mind-body, masculine-feminine gap are found in the lack of lamas, tulkus and Buddhist teachers' crossing over. Few become hands-on. Few do bodywork or psychotherapy, much less directly contribute to the research and new approaches within these fields.

A secular, *human lineage* view has been the default focus of one hundred years of psychological research. Depth psychology, anchored in the work of Carl Jung, has endeavored to employ modern, empirical tools to view and record the outer reaches of the esoteric and sublime reaches of human consciousness. The fruits of this work—for example, archetypal theory and the "hero's journey"— offer more support for this secular interpretation of Buddhism's principles and paradigms.

The third turning of the wheel of the dharma, the Vajrayana and tantric traditions trend in a similar atheistic direction, but then transcend atheism and theism as we shall see. In the Vajrayana and tantric traditions, a direct, wide-open phenomenological encounter with the divine is front and center. We will explore how this more recent iteration of Buddhist thought and practice resonates with a "human lineage", transcept viewpoint. As we proceed, evidence seems to amass for a more earth-and-species-based platform of the spiritual depths/heights that not just Buddha but Jesus and others describe. Desire, evidence suggests, is a correlate to attachment-as-love and transcends and integrates the two attachments. Deepak Chopra's popularity has something to do with his ability to articulate this basic tantric pulse. The more we let go and detach the more nakedly we abide a living field, "that without which knowing is not possible" that without which experience and awareness are not possible. Reggie Ray's somatic practices go even further, validating an uncanny immediacy with Buddha's Mom.

Chapter Three

RELATIVE ATTACHMENT

Relative Realm

As we have seen, Siddhartha's story began with the first of "two attachments," namely his loving bond with his mom and caregivers. Much later in life, Siddhartha-as-Buddha realized the importance of a second attachment. He would come to place this attachment at the heart of his teachings and specifically to identify this as illusory and the cause of suffering. Though both connotations of attachment clearly have their own validity and territory, they have remained unnecessarily disparate through the years.

Understanding how each attachment represents a relative truth furthers the possibility of an open, integral, unified attachment paradigm. Each, to borrow comedian Stephen Colbert's term, has *truthiness*. Colbert deftly uses humor to communicate pitfalls associated with claims of ultimate truth. As relative truths, each powerfully reflects dimensions of the human condition. Neither is absolute. An analysis of these shared roots in the relative realm narrows the gap between them and increases the utility of what we can propose as, "relative attachment."

Ken Wilber uses the phrase "on the relative side of the street" to distinguish phenomena, of course, from what philosophers classically refer to as absolute.[69] Buddhist terms for the absolute side of the street include nonattachment, non-dual, deathless, freedom from rebirth, unborn mind, enlightenment, emptiness, nirvana, Buddha-nature, primordial oneness, realization and attainment. Such sublime, actual truths are presumably what the Buddha was talking about when he talked about relinquishing attachment to achieve the cessation of dukkha, that is to say, the end of suffering in nirvana.

The Four Noble Truths consist of:
1. The truth of dukkha,
2. The truth of the arising of dukkha—through tanhā,
3. The truth of the cessation of dukkha—through the cessation of tanhā,
4. The truth of the way to the cessation of dukkha—that is, the Noble Eightfold Path.[70]

In the third Noble Truth, the deceptively simple turn of phrase, the "end of suffering," sits right alongside the second—not the first attachment—tanhā. Buddhism's suffering-inducing attachment, as we have discussed, fits within an adult much more than a neonatal, infantile or toddler psychology. Synonyms for both the attaching side of the essential equation have an adult flavoring, e.g., expectation. As a totality, the "relative side of the street" corresponds to adult self/ego/mind. With Step 3 this relative truth bumps up against the "absolute side of the street," the big-T Truth. With Step 4 ultimate truth is said to be accessible by way of the Eightfold Path.

Most will be familiar with this adult identified code of conduct, outlining principles of proper speech, thought, behavior and the like. The close proximity of the relative and absolute, located in the Four Noble Truths, is in fact meaningful. For starters, *relative* means *related* as does *reality*. We can be encouraged in that our messy self/ego/mind, as a handle on relative truth, is implicitly not just related to absolute truth, but is of the same essence, big-R Reality! The thread of relative-to-absolute meaning, as we will be exploring, is mappable and palpable as a science of sentience in which spirit thrives.

With Buddha's Mom, we are especially encouraged to point out that relatedness has a powerful, locatable and living existence extending from Bowlby's biological domain to the highest reaches in the esoteric schools of Buddhism. A fuller handle on attachment is one of a flowing, trans-generational nature through which reality, as we humans access it, manifests. Thus, we have referred to Buddha's Mom in terms of transmission of the human lineage.

In ancient Buddhists texts, the relative-absolute bridge, as well as any possible allusion to such a transcendent form of attachment is not rendered as such, at least not directly. Buddha's biological mother, Mahamaya, is portrayed as semi-divine. But in being partially supernatural, she is partially dehumanized at the same time that she is praised. Neither her influence nor that of Siddhartha's other attachment relationships are credited with shaping Buddhism's big-T truth claims. The biography's attachment pendulum swings abruptly from the first attachment, which gets relatively short shrift, to the second attachment, one that anchors the Noble Truths. By inference, the first morphs into the second during Siddhartha's development from familial bonds to the mental tugs, for example, associated with following in his father's footsteps or the existential encounter with death, disease and aging. By the time attachment is consolidated and encoded in the Four Noble Truths, it has been uprooted from the maternal realm and fashioned as the generalizable, individualistic, psychological version we have come to know.

The first twenty-nine years of Siddhartha's biography indirectly documents a transformation of the meaning from an attachment that is predominantly maternal to one that is more paternal, and from one more biological to one more mental and conceptual. This evolving understanding sets up the next six years. After leaving home, Siddhartha pursued a six year, highly introspective quest. We can fairly describe this (and will seek to do so in coming chapters) as incorporating a continued focus on the scope and meaning of attachment. Even before this began, there were outlines of the presumption that understanding houses the possibility of overcoming.

"Understanding" is better expanded to incorporate all depths of humanity, in other words, to refer to an integral process emanating from Siddhartha's own self/ego/mind. Bolstered by his immense intellect and capacity for logic, he would come to derive a personal felt-sense regarding all matters associated with attachment. His integral view of attachment (related terms and models) flowed from the meaning or sentience that he personally experienced, "knew to be true" is a better phrase, associated with this dimension of the human condition.

During the first twenty-nine years, a modern analysis suggests, Buddhism's attachment undergoes multiple transformations. Each of these deserves consideration as each carries some risk of a loss of translation. As mentioned, a very early reset occurs when Siddhartha's doting parents learn from the wise men that Siddhartha will either be a great ruler or a great holy man. This shifts the story in the direction of the father. Any sort of future foundation of consciousness in Buddha's Mom is dealt a quiet but distinct blow. This premeditatedly pushes attachment-love off center. Siddhartha's mother's and wife's love over the years ahead, his love for them, for his baby—all are undercut quietly, but decisively with this narrative reset.

As further insurance, Buddha's biographical, biological, and adoptive moms were undermined in seemingly innocent ways. One died and the other assumed the mixed mantle of a devoted, second choice wife of the king. Also, young Siddhartha demonstrated remarkable independence from the beginning of his life. In these many ways, a more male, abstract attachment gets a head start and any natural curiosity regarding the role of the deep feminine falls behind.

The pressing attachment question, both externally regarding Siddhartha and internally, within his own being, becomes represented by the dilemma pitting the life of a great ruler against that of a great ascetic. His decision to forsake his father, leave his family, and become a seeker simply further obscures the world of the mother. This reset, as did the ones before, serves to further distance wonder and investigation of the feminine principle as relevant. The word relevant comes from a Latin term meaning to arise or raise up. If as suggested, the biography impacted Buddha's Mom's relevance, 'she' simply would be less prone to arise in the conscious field of Buddhist practitioners. There would be less energy, less motivation, inquiry and wonder regarding her association to ultimate meaning and the cessation of suffering. Not surprisingly, mammalian, maternal, biological and social/tribal (clan) attachments have not received anything close to the attention received by Buddhism's other, orthodox attachment.

These resets can be sketched as de-feminizing attachment and as both directly and indirectly boosting attachment's masculine, yang aspect. After taking leave of hearth and home, for example, Siddhartha's efforts to master attachment escalate and form the "austerities." In oversimplified terms, the first twenty-nine years involved a progressive de-feminizing of attachment, and the next six involved a hyper-masculinization of attachment. So successful was this, in fact, that the latter attachment is commonly framed as an opposite of the former. Both, for our purposes, delimit the feminine (which far exceeds the maternal/biological confines) and both are relative. Neither amounts to what after the first twenty-nine and then after the next six years, comes to be called nonattachment.

The biography's prognosticating wise men sets all this into motion. A great ruler, presumably, finds meaning in the accumulation (and thereby attachment to the accumulation) of wealth and power. In taking the ostensibly opposite path, Siddhartha's appears destined to fully understand and finally overcome attachment. As he attempts to take this opposite path to its own extremes he hits a wall. As we will see, this results in his discovery of the Middle Way. Siddhartha will come to conclude that the ascetic path itself can be illusory. He concludes that he has inadvertently switched out the object of the same attachment drive to that of asceticism.

The path to lasting bliss and liberation, the biography demonstrates, is neither through self-indulgence nor self-deprivation. Discernment regarding absolute and ultimate matters was not to be found in Siddhartha's doting family, the lavish palace lifestyle he lived, or the seemingly opposite, harsh deprivation of the austerities. But notice again how we are not talking in any deep and meaningful way about Bowlby's version of attachment and that which would fall under the umbrella of Buddha's Mom. This calls for further untangling.

Middle Way

The Middle Way reveals the deeper, penetrating relatedness of what appears to be unrelated and opposite. This can be traced through what we have defined as based in a feminine-based, evolutionary attachment. According to Buddha, the portal to paradise, the great breakthrough at the heart of the Noble Truths, lies not at the extremes but in the middle. An appreciation of the shared, relative truth is to be located in between. Fully-owned by neither side and instead embedded within and surpassing the two attachments is a single integrated, tantric attachment. To get at this, we need to delve further into Buddha's realization, the sublime turn in the story of Siddhartha away from the austerities toward the so-called Middle Way. This deserves a new look from the perspectives associated with Buddha's Mom.

In the last throes of the six years of seeking, Buddha was hell-bent on taking renunciation as far as possible. He joined a small group of ascetics who engaged in practices involving "tormenting and mortifying the body." The group slept on spikes, stopped bathing and starved themselves. Buddha ate as little as one grain of rice per day. In the Lalitavistara Sūtra, also known as the "extensive sport" sutra, Buddha explained that for eight winter nights he treated his body much as a strong man grabs a weaker man by the neck and subdues him. In various ways, almost perfectly paradoxically, Siddhartha set about to endure suffering in order to discern whether, and if so how, this resulted in a release from suffering. At one point, he was in a state of "extreme emaciation" and very close to death and "undertook a 'breathless meditation.'"[71]

> I stopped the in-breaths and out-breaths through my mouth, nose, and ears.
> While I did so, violent winds cut through my head. Just as if a strong man
> were splitting my head open with a sharp sword.[72]

These austerities represented a return to the territory of the first attachment. Birth is violent and traumatic. When a baby is born, the entire focus is on its first breath. This is often accompanied by a painful cry that brings relief to everyone present because the risk of something even worse had just been so palpable. In short order, the next concern of mom, dad and healthcare providers is feeding.

At the point that he joined five other seekers and began to practice this strange, austerity yoga, Siddhartha had spent six years at a higher point on the body-mind-spirit ladder. He had pushed hard to transcend all subtle, internal phenomenological states. The return to body also marked an evolutionary regression to our species' deepest substrates of consciousness. Over and again, despite sheer pain and agony, mind remained. Famished, his backbone shone through his skin like a beaded cord. The skin of his abdomen is said to have pressed against that of his back and his otherwise luscious hair turned pale and brittle. Yet, as he later taught, ordinary mind remained. The more he regressed in the direction of base, bodily, cellular demands for nutrition and oxygen, the more assured he became that there is no linear path from the relative domain of physical and mental life to an absolute, supernatural state.

> But it was all to no avail. Eventually, after nearly six years, Siddhartha reached the conclusion that "by this racking practice of austerities I have not attained any superhuman states, any distinction in knowledge and vision worthy of the noble ones."[73]

Siddhartha concluded that denial and destruction of the body's needs itself was no answer. He had achieved no "superhuman states" or "knowledge and vision worthy of the noble ones."[74] But alas, having discovered the Middle Way, all these goals had finally been transcended. At some point, he decided to eat and a young woman named Sujata (the accounts vary on this) gave him rice and milk. This motif of a young, altruistic, compassionate woman providing milk and nourishment is a simple and elegant referencing of the feminine with a maternal tilt. Indeed, Sujata is not so different from Buddha's Mom, in the form of Prajapati, who responded to a time of need much earlier in Siddhartha's life.

Perhaps hurt, confused or disappointed, the group of five who had devoted themselves to an ascetic austerity practice accused Siddhartha of having reverted to a life of luxury. He responded with both love and firmness, and referred specifically to the Middle Way between home and homelessness. This suggests a deeper, integral truth encompassing both the twenty-nine years and the following six—and both the attachment of the former and the latter. Referring to himself in the third person, he had to repeat this message three times. Finally, what became Buddhism's first sangha received the message.

> I told them: "The Tathagata does not live luxuriously, nor has he given up his striving and reverted to luxury. The Tathagata is an Accomplished One, a Fully Enlightened One. Listen, bhikkhus, the Deathless has been attained...from the home life into homelessness."[75]

The Middle Way underscores Buddhism's essential message that a greater, wider, deeper truth, possibly even an ultimate, absolute Truth, may lie between what appears to be unrelated, extremes or opposites. Repeatedly, this is expressed as paradox. The integral model compliments this, beginning with the premise that no mind is 100% error free. What on the surface appears unrelated, random, bewildering and the like, may belie a deeper, more integral truth. Or it may in fact be error. At the end of the day, the trophy goes to the weight of the evidence and to that which is most compelling, inclusive, and explanatory. In this book, for example, I assess whether Buddha's Mom serves as a middle way, an access to an integral, penetrating truth that unites motherly love and metta (lovingkindness) and related neurobiological evidence in a coherent whole. Lending heft, just ahead, are findings from affective neuroscience. Then in the last chapter, we explore how these extensions of mammalian sentience work hand in glove with polyvagal theory. This allows us to circle back to the neurobiology of the Middle Way, literally embodied in each of us.

The Middle Way also expresses a concept that reached pristine resolution in the "third turning," Vajrayana Buddhism. This holds that there is space or void precisely where it *should not be*, where no life, love, or movement seems possible—between life's proverbial rock and a hard spot. Where consciousness is dense and seemingly blocked, advanced teachers describe countless ways that persistence, stillness, watching with intention and intensity, can lead to a surprisingly immediate emptiness that simply is. There is movement even within quadruple-gravity, mind-seizing physical and emotional pain. Such is the insight, wisdom, and legacy of the austerities.

Movement implies space, and there is always space in and surrounding impermanent, relative reality.

Relative Love

Within the universe of relative attachment there is of course a little thing called love. As if anyone needs a reminder, love matters. Love begs for more clarity. After all, love-as-metta (maître in Sanskrit) is not an esoteric, peripheral concept for Buddhists. In some evolutionary circles, love is downsized as a biochemical epi-phenomenon. Through some Buddhist lenses, love is embedded in desire, is an illusion and a mental attachment that obscures the right view. Yet other lenses exalt love, framing it as shorthand for lovingkindness, *metta bhāvanā*, one of the Ten Perfections (paramitas) in Theravada Buddhism. It is the basis for major forms of meditation including Tonglen.

Where does this spiritual, transcendent force interact with the evolutionary basis of Buddha's Mom? Homo sapiens are not unique among mammals in attaching to offspring and one another in ways that appear to be, at times, very loving. To state that interpersonal attachment, as mothers experience with their babies, is the biological side of some grand span of love, possibly with metta at the mountaintop, is not without logic. Such a model fits within the body-mind-spirit, "great chain." At the same time, this might be criticized as a simplistic or untestable. Alternatively, love-as-attachment could be dismissed as illusory, just another form of clinging, with no basis in a cosmic metta whatsoever.

The Buddha's biography helps melt some of these seemingly impenetrable boundaries. Siddhartha's stepmother and nursemaids, it seems safe to presume, were involved in his direct care as a neonate forward. We can presume that this care included all the dynamics of maternal attachment. While love will always be more poetic than scientific, attachment as a form or precursor of big love, of metta, certainly appears to offer a lucid foundation. This potential rests in the notion of Buddha's caregivers and Siddhartha himself as humans, with mappable minds and experience. It stands to reason that the woman who gave birth to Siddhartha, and we are told died soon thereafter, the adopted mother who was ushered in at that juncture, and the nursemaids who assisted in varying ways, experienced and manifested an imperfect, non-absolutist attachment-love in their bond with the future Buddha.

Perhaps it is presumptuous to speculate on the nature and influence of Buddha's Mom on her son's being, personality, mind and eventual heights of consciousness. But not to speculate is suspect, given the increasing understanding of attachment on development. Lack of speculation, the inability to wonder intelligently, may carry its own distortions, may inadvertently overlook valid possibilities, or foreclose the generation of hypotheses and important questions. Diligence is obviously required to weigh any evidence of this topic within an integral framework. Buddhism is imminently empirical and practical, and more than any other religion, it directly prescribes that each of us employ our own great chain. In other words, we should consciously work at being an instrument of assessment. We should use our own being, our own spectrum of consciousness to internally, personally, emotionally, and spiritually evaluate these ideas.

Reasoning is just one valid but rather narrow dimension of this spectrum. Implicitly attachment-as-love is open to testing and experimentation across the emotional and cognitive, conceptual stratum. The juxtaposition of the austerities to Siddhartha's enlightenment signals the importance of meditating on and considering aspects that appear to be in extreme opposition. As mentioned, the word relative in "relative attachment" has the same root as *relate,* implying the importance of personally relating to the supporting evidence, if this is viable. One could do worse than to conjure and perceive in nature a loving, divine, nurturing mother presence.

Some excitement and hope is reasonable. Recall how Mahamaya's anticipation prompted her dream of the transcendent, the white elephant holding the lotus. Famously, one of the wise men cried bittersweet tears, presumably knowing he would die before he could bear witness to the baby's future awakening as a Buddha. This field of anticipation came to manifest devotion and protection, initially with preparations made by great Queen Mahamaya. Perhaps there are psychological parallels. In spiritual terms, one must anticipate and prepare to win the lottery given that one has in fact always, already won it.

More than mere biological demand, attachment-as-love would help explain what happened next in the biography. Mahamaya's little sister, Prajapati stepped in despite any grief, confusion or perhaps selfish desire to avoid obvious pressures and responsibilities. She may have been opportunistic and only too eager to become a functional queen herself. Even this does not rule out the possibility that attachment-love grew in time. Nursemaids and aides may have preferred this work and received the perks, but they also may have been emotionally devoted and appropriately tender and loving with the baby Siddhartha. As discussed, King Suddhodana, too, appears to have wrestled with a loving identification with his son. It is reasonable to conclude that Siddhartha was, within some range, immersed in maternal and familial forms of our species' natural attachment system—and therefore that he had a very innate, personal knowledge of Buddha's Mom.

The more one integrally meditates (intellectually, emotionally, etc.) on the sweep of the love (from Bowlby's bonding to Buddha's metta), the more a transformative, integral synthesis is evoked. The attachment, love and metta which informed all the anticipation and care for the baby behind the boy, that shaped the mind of the monk that was determined to awaken or die, the more tender, immediate and somatic one senses this river of life, here referred to as attachment-love.

The tendency of Westerners to establish their bearings in the seeable and measurable is very compatible with the evolutionary, scientific basis of Buddha's Mom. In this love-as-biological-attachment manifestation, "she" bridges toward a humanistic ground of emotional nurturing both as process and concept. The same rigor that demonstrated the reality and power of maternal attachment has since produced adult attachment. This demonstrates that the same neurological and psychological processes in mom-baby bonding are recapitulated in romantic love, emotional intimacy and pair bonding in adults. Love-as-attachment thereby offers a reasonable framing for the bio-psycho-social underpinnings, if not the source of metta. But the term "source" can inadvertently fuel materialistic reductionism. Bowlby's biological love needs Buddha's metta to transcend and include the allure of building blocks of awareness and meaning.

Various ancient practices enable shifts in the direction of a more inclusive, comprehensive love. Tonglen (the give-take, extend-receive Tibetan ritual) can be understood as a technology that assists one in increasing their flow of love. Here we have tried to express this in terms of our species' lineage. The thesis here is that the nexus associated with the cessation of suffering is one and the same, the way Shakyamuni's Buddhahood is characterized. In other words, our innate inheritance is scientifically and spiritually what he described in varied ways, including ultimate happiness, compassion, lovingkindness, the end of suffering and striving.

In Buddha's Mom we are trying to delineate the path to this by way of an integral attachment. The reader will assess such claims for herself or himself. Just to be clear, the claim is vast. An integral attachment encompasses both/and and neither/nor any constituents. By definition integral attachment sweeps through evolution and is at home in nonattachment and enlightenment. Our evolutionary inheritance is Buddha-nature is metta and is indistinguishable from happiness and meaning in life. Properly considered, multiple lines of research and great sages demonstrate that humanity is thus blessed not in spite of but because of our species' attachment processes.

During the spiritual journey, one must be careful not to be infatuated with pure, spiritual fruits which somehow spring forth without any sort of messy, complex corpus. Chögyam Trungpa cautioned against spiritual materialism. The lotus is only mistakenly assumed to be independently perfect when in reality, the blossom and mud are inseparable. Attachment is love and is compassion but to get there requires a careful analysis of the mud, of the ugly, messy, imperfect side of (relative) attachment. Toward the end of this book, we will consider the story of Devadatta. This relative and friend of Siddhartha plotted to assassinate him, providing us with a very rich story of the shadow or mud side of attachment.

We will also see how the other side of attachment-love, Buddhism's core notion that attachment is the root of suffering is deeply compatible with the Buddha's Mom. To achieve clarity on this, we need to reflect in depth on detachment. Detachment tends to get the lion's share of attention in Buddha's attachment, and the opposite treatment from Bowlby's side and that of modern attachment science.

This exploration leads to the integral view of how various perspectives on attachment inter-relate with the possibility of transcendence. Transcendence, after all, is implicit in any conceptualization of nonattachment or enlightenment. The path we are on arcs toward a transcending of the two attachments in one. If this effort succeeds, a lot of conceptual clamor will fade. Mother and son, Siddhartha and Buddha, mud and lotus, attachment and nonattachment, after all, are fully "just so" in each of these and each of us.

Detachment

A mother feeds her baby and then walks away to do something else. No reasonable formulation of attachment can deny that within the sphere of attachment behaviors are two poles, an attaching and a detaching pole. Detachment is discussed much more in Buddhism than in the psychological literature on attachment, and this contributes to a certain amount of confusion.

Everyone is likely to implicitly link human attachment with the imagery of a mother caressing her baby. Conversely, everyone is familiar with Siddhartha's embarkation, taking leave of home to become a seeker.

With respect to Bowlby's model of maternal attachment, however, detachment is a quiet but fully implicit counterpart. The pairing, attachment-detachment is an evolutionary given. The biological and psychological premise is that attachment would not have risen to such heights in the evolution of mammals were it not for checks and balances. Detachment is the counterbalance to attachment, though the name for the whole process is the latter.

According to biologists, as an extreme form of detachment, mammal moms may eat their young when they determine that something is wrong with them. Every day, normally attached muskrat or antelope or bonobo moms avoid passing along their genes (genes which give rise to attachment behaviors, to protecting and feeding offspring and the like) by keeping attachment in check. They must balance their lives with a full behavioral repertoire. Naturally, this has little to do with parenting and much to do with biology. As all fans of mammals know, such repertoires can be exquisitely complex and impressive.

Just as naturally, a lessoning or cessation of attachment, e.g., detachment, occurs, purely physiologically, with satiation, habituation, and muscle fatigue. A latched on, literally and figuratively attached, breastfeeding baby may detach in the physical sense but also in an emotional, relational sense, when it is satiated. The brain's pleasure centers send signals switching over from hunger to contentment. As the animal detaches from the breast, it literally and figuratively detaches from an active, immediate parent-offspring interplay to engage in other survival critical priorities. Relaxation or sleep or exploration drivers may take the helm. On their side of the exchange, mothers just as routinely divert their attention elsewhere, cognitively detaching, as other demands arise.

Of course, mammals are far more complex that these examples suggest. A mother may detach from the young in one sense to fight off a predator, but in another she simultaneously remains attached. She knows where her offspring are vis-a-vis the predator and what their cries mean. Parallel processing engages in and executes protective behaviors in conjunction with maternal attachment. Nevertheless, even complex behaviors such as this involve degrees and forms of detachment, and in total, detachment needs to be understood as one side of an innate back-and-forth, attachment-detachment.

Another proof of detachment comes from evolution. The genes of mothers with too little or too much attachment suffered the same fate, earning their owner and their conduit the same "Darwin Award" as those with too little or too much detachment. The mother who starved, fed, and devoted her energy in whatever form in excess was the one who failed to garner adequate protein for herself, or to protect herself, or to devote appropriate efforts to mate selection—to name a few of the many priorities given up for attachment. Obviously, these are processes sophisticated mammals must manage or suffer the consequences. All these versions of an organism's self-management implicitly involve detaching from one focus to another throughout the day.

Quite simply, loving attachment implies loving detachment and vice versa. Love extends itself, but not parasitically. Both the lover and the one who is loved benefit. The question of amount or degree makes no sense, because where true love flows anew, there is just more love in the world.

One cannot say that a dog lover benefits more than their pet dog or that moms and dads are more blessed than their babies.

Similarly, dysfunctional attachment is the mirror of dysfunctional detachment. Smothering involves a lack of healthy detachment, and neglect involves a pathological under-attachment or over-detachment. Domestic violence is a form of lovesickness and pathological attachment and is replete with perversions of normal and both dimensions of healthy relative attachment. Clinicians refer to the typical perpetrator as "counter-dependent," which here we can think of as having a "counter-attachment." Typically, self-absorbed, immature males bully and torment their "loved" one in a cyclic manner. Picking a spot on the circle, the couple re-unites after an altercation as pseudo-attachment ensues. Apologies may be exchanged with declarations of love. This sets the stage the perpetrators' pseudo-detachments. He cannot believe her stupidity, is crushed by sleights, hurls insults and denigrates his partner's character. Inside-out, sick admixtures of relative attachment takeover. The perpetrator may threaten to leave while humiliating the victim: "You'd like that, wouldn't you? You slut." He may punch and sexually abuse his victim while decrying how he has no choice but to do so. Neither partner will very likely execute any actual, lasting departure, e.g., detachment, especially if this is defined as moving up the ladder to healthier relating and an end of the old path pattern with another person.

As this example shows, the concept of attachment-as-love can become very twisted. Important for our discussion, similar form of confusion permeate Buddhism. Are we to attach value or meaning to the three gems, the Noble Truths, the Eightfold Path or daily practice over other creeds or spiritual paths? Our spouse over another's. Does Buddhist practice and doctrine not involve preferring, desiring and/or attaching? The tendency is to silently bow to the authority of the central tenets while emphasizing the other side, the detachment message which anchors Buddhism's creeds and practices.

This involves more than semantics. As psychoanalyst and Zen instructor Barry Magid explains, "The Buddha might have said Life is Suffering and left it at that. (But) impermanence is inescapable and our practice is first and foremost a confrontation with our avoidance of this reality."[76] A shallow response to life as suffering tends to downplay confrontation. Confrontation, even of avoidance, calls for focus, attending, and in the language we are considering here—relative attachment. We are called upon to engage in a robust, active, conscious grappling with the reality Magid identifies as avoidance. Alas, we must not avoid avoidance.

This is a common sort of loop, especially in Zen, where positive, extant psychological phenomena are juxtaposed to concepts which refer not to something new and different but rather to the absence or opposite of the original form. Confronting is the positive or extant concept here, and avoidance is the term which loops back, adding little because it simply refers to the lack or absence of confrontation. This Zen practitioner's insight regarding avoiding avoidance is another example of the confusion that can be associated with the two attachments. We are to detach from thoughts and feelings, and we are to clearly see these. In fully experiencing life, we are pulled in, overwhelmed, and lost in a sea of attachments, self-talk, identity, and torrid emotionality. Panic and efforts to label, halt, control and manage our private hells exist side by side with five-alarm escape fantasies. We glimpse all this flow and the inward schoolmarm's reminders to get back to mindfulness. We have plenty of spacecraft at the ready. But are we properly detaching or just attaching to avoidance?

Transcend and Include

As we have shown, orthodox Buddhism tends to play up the importance of detachment, where Bowlby and those downstream from him affirm the rich, ongoing nature of attachment processes. It makes sense to view these as the two poles of a natural, psychological attachment process. Wilber's integral model elegantly proposes some key concepts that may support and clarify these ideas and move us further toward a marriage of the "two attachments."

First off, the integral model incorporates an evidence-based developmental spectrum, from body-mind-spirit to psychotic-borderline-neurotic-normal. The latter comports to be a medical model where health is defined as the absence of disease. The upper reaches that any sane person aspires toward are mainly referred to in the negative, as not that fill-in-the-blank disease or disorder.

All evolutionary and developmental continuum, even heat-dirt-amoeba-insects-mammal-human, transition from "more fundamental" to "more significant." Other typical language includes referring to the more fundamental as "lower," and more significant as "higher," though spiritual development is sometimes framed in the reverse, as a deepening. Getting back to Siddhartha, the infant, toddler, young child he once was and the maternal bonding that occurred between Buddha and his mom is more *fundamental*; his enlightenment as the Buddha, is more *significant*. The fundamental and significant aspects of development are two sides of the same coin. In the case of Buddha's Mom, we would not have the Buddha without at least her biological contribution. Can we be sure that the cut-off is merely fundamental, just above the bodily level on the body-mind-spirit scale?

Access to this truth calls for one to understand what Wilber describes as "transcend and include." This refers to the evolution from quarks to atoms to molecules in nature, as well as to the rise of sentience and consciousness across species. No one comes anywhere near Ken Wilber on this front. According to his integral theory, the ability to transcend and include occurs across the grandest scales imaginable, ultimately from the Big Bang to matter to life to mind to soul to spirit — and therefore includes all that we are attempting to describe here concerning Siddhartha's development.

Wilber also uses various terms such as "wave" to describe that which is undergoing transformation. Like other developmental theorists, he also employs terms such as stages, levels, and structures to refer to the steps and stations along the way.

> As I would word it, each wave is "transcend and include." That is, each wave goes beyond (or transcends) its predecessor, and yet it includes or embraces it in its own makeup. For example, a cell transcends but includes molecules, which transcend but include atoms. To say that a molecule goes beyond an atom is not to say that molecules hate atoms, but that they love them: they embrace them in their own makeup; they include them, they don't marginalize them. Just so, each wave of existence is a fundamental ingredient of all subsequent waves, and thus each is to be cherished and embraced.[77]

To stay with this point, magical thinking and animism would fall at more fundamental levels and reason and logic at more significant levels. Higher stages of Buddhist practice would understand both as partial, and this awareness—and awareness of awareness—as more significant. What we are exploring here is the possibility that the Buddha's Mom construct is perhaps more fundamental than previously understood. If so, the possibility of a marriage of the two attachments may really matter. Recently there was some big news about one mans' corpus callosum, the brain's bridge which metaphorically marries the two hemispheres. The left, as most everyone knows, is associated with speech, language, consciousness, logic and linear, sequential processing. The right is associated with emotion, imagination and creativity. Analysis revealed that this man's brain bridge was unusually large, proving that he had "unusually well connected left and right hemispheres of his brain." The man was Albert Einstein.[78]

Negate & Preserve

Wilber sometimes adds at the end of "transcend and include" a parallel phrase, "negate and preserve." That which is *not* included is said to be *negated*. The emphasis on something being abolished and done away with as part of a larger, forward flowing, all-encompassing dynamic bolsters the current conception of relative attachment. A healthy attachment process in early life, for example, evokes ever higher-ordered levels of understanding. These developmental stages, however, continue across the lifespan (in healthy, normal circumstances). Expansions of consciousness both preserve and negate previous ways of seeing and being.

> …there's a wonderful phrase from Hegel that everybody quotes: "To supersede"—and for us that might mean to transform—"to supersede is to negate and to preserve." And that's what I call "transcend and include." But transcend *can* mean negate. In other words, when you transcend something, you're leaving something behind; you're excluding something in a certain sense.[79]

On the physical plane, the clumsy jerkiness is smoothed out as the baby learns to walk. Excessive muscular overcompensations are negated as a subset of smaller, smoother movements is preserved. The transcendent skillset was previously within the former stage. The phrase, "you never forget how to ride a bike" puts the emphasis on what comes next. Wilber reminds us that we do forget how not to ride. Michelangelo said he created exquisite statues by removing what he did not need. His intelligence therefore involved a form of negating and a negating of form. The stunning essence Michelangelo freed from the marble is just as valid a perspective. These travel side by side. The acorn that undergoes a transformation is negated, but also holds within it the great oak. Childish naiveté fades but in healthy adults the inner child is preserved.

Wilber uses the terms significant and fundamental. The more-significant is preserved and the more-fundamental is negated. The great oak is more significant, the acorn more fundamental. Here we are building a case for negating relative attachment and preserving its surprising heart or essence in that which the Buddha called nonattachment. Buddha's Mom, we are suggesting, may deepen our understanding, clarity and access to this essence.

> So what happens in development is that we have to negate and to preserve.
> What are preserved are the basic functions, the capacities, the energies, the
> competencies that each stage brings into being. And what is negated is your
> egoic attachment to them.[80]

In humans, a lack of exquisitely refined negating and preserving is the hallmark of psychological suffering. In a future section, I will explore a deep self disturbance as a disruption in integral developmental involving attachment. There is an over-attachment to a previous stage, equally explainable as a lack of the negating previous ways of being and perceiving. This less mature, more regressive stage lingers in the unconscious. The "we-space" was not robust enough to transcend and include, negate and preserve this. A more adaptive, psychologically healthy pathway is potential at best.

> You keep the basic energy, the basic competence, the basic structures—those
> remain in awareness and those remain functioning. But you lose, you die to,
> your *attachment* to those structures. Each death has to be suffered
> consciously. And if you don't die to a stage, then you remain fixated to it and
> that's called pathology.[81]

People suffering from such pathology are fraught in mappable ways. Their psyche may work overtime at repression. Typically, there is emotional splitting and volatility. A person keeps talking about or acting out some past pain and injustice while insisting that they have long since worked this out. When any evidence of internal disjointedness is presented, they claim they already knew of this. Insults and injuries have been logged, date-stamped, and tagged to historical events even as the slow-motion train wreck is so clearly still occurring.

A common sleight of hand goes as follows. The events are in the past; therefore, I have moved on. Or I can't move on, there is nothing one can do - therefore I have moved on. Associated feelings arising in the now are creatively discounted as the mind goes about proving that currently arising experience is somehow not real or valid, or already integrated and not fresh, all the while enforcing its own legitimacy. The raw and chaotic is immediately filtered. Negating works overtime but is out of balance with its other dimensions, with nimble, adequate preservation. Every single feeling a baby emanates is manifestly beautiful, but along the way to adulthood, these natural expressions of the self increasingly subject to mental censure.

The allowed amalgam of a self does all it can to stay on one side, while the press of a more immediate encounter with life is fated to be right outside, scratching at the door, bearing down on the permitted self so wrongly, unfairly, and unjustly. These detached not-me's are sadly not more attached. The rush to negate is excessive. In addition to temporal splits ("I'm over it"), "person" splits may be employed. The "you" that hurts the first person "me" is pushed ever outward even as the me demands you listen and change. These make use of the first, second, third person embedded in language. Pain is shoved into second person—you. "You make me crazy," "You need to…." "I'd be fine if you…."

Some erupt into third person adjudications, guilty convictions for injustices perpetrated by the he's and she's, family, friends, significant others, co-workers. In these phrases, the "we" is weak, under-attached. The "me" in other is overly negated, overly detached. A mean, uncaring, dismissive other so disappoints and causes suffering. Both attachment and detachment are problematic, and are responsible for under-processed psychological pain and trauma. Healing proceeds when the sine wave of now-then, inner-outer, me-you, preserve-negate lessen in amplitude. The smoothing process, as Wilber captures it, is twofold, healing and growth. Compartmentalized material is both re-embraced in a loving, nonjudgmental space and naturally detached from.

> Evolution *goes beyond* what went before, but because it must *embrace* what went before, then its very nature is to transcend and include, and thus it has an inherent directionality, a secret impulse, toward increasing depth, increasing intrinsic value, increasing consciousness.[82]

The integral model is so edgeless, so encompassing, that an understandable effort is made to avoid anthropomorphic terms. Even development can have the connotation of being under-developed. Higher stages sound superior. Wilber's point, a deeply felt spiritual truth for him, is that there is nothing inferior or missing or wrong or less than anywhere, because such is the manifest side of the street, the relative side of the street, the side of both form (and formlessness, as evaluated further in subsequent sections). His language endorses spirit, without disparaging the reality that spirit is in-dwelling "all the way up and all the way down."

> "Transcend and include...this is the self-transcending drive of the Kosmos— to go beyond what went before and yet include what went before...to open into the very heart of Spirit-in-action."[83]

Attachment-Detachment

Much then points to the current model of two-sided relative attachment as being in concert with Wilber's transcend and include model. Relative attachment incorporates maternal attachment and its neurobiology. Reason suggests that this aspect of Buddha's Mom was inherent in the caregiving that Siddhartha received. Such care implicitly involves the intensive cultivation of these processes in offspring. Adults both fluidly attach (exhibited by caressing, holding, and attending to offspring,) and detach as they go about their lives, perhaps to gather, hunt or attend to others.

As mentioned previously, the term *attachment* is firmly embedded in the vernacular, as well as Buddhism's perhaps most central tenet and now in recent decades as a biological and psychological construct. Derived from Old French, *atachier* meaning to fasten, attachment across all these spheres refers to the positive, clinging, bonding and connecting aspect. In refining this, one might refer to its positive and negative poles or introduce new terms, but it seems more parsimonious to simply add detachment as a countervailing force within overarching attachment.

The same attaching-detaching, back-and-forth that occurs in the course of a day occurs in moment-to-moment awareness. As attention shifts from one attachment object to another, attachment shifts. As this occurs, the co-process of detachment necessarily shifts as well. From minutes to days to larger developmental stages, relative attachment marches forth. From the baby's perspective, some sense of a separate self gradually forms. In this, by definition, mother/other is emergent. Attachment becomes an internal, hopefully, trusting and loving dynamic in the baby's mind. While healthily attached, detachment is in play in the very stabilization of the self/mother duality. Each of the millions of times around these circles, attachment-detachment or transcend-include, propels the developmental stages.

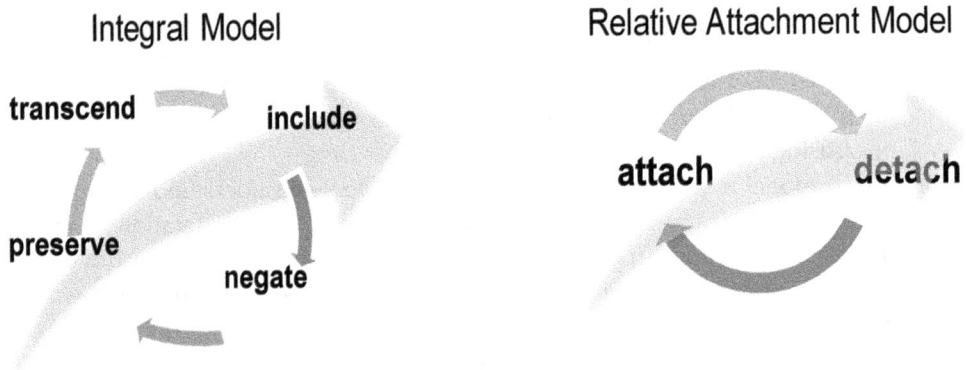

Integral Model

transcend → include

preserve

negate

Relative Attachment Model

attach   detach

The integral model more directly notes that which is lost (negated) and that which is gained (preserved). For example, the earliest semblance of a self is preserved as its symbiotic precursor is negated. "You can't un-ring a bell," as they say, nor forget how to ride a bike. These are expressions of the relative reality, with an emphasis on the emergent awareness. Mind comes into being as cognitive patterns are held just as others drop away. Much necessarily passes by as whatever one might label before-mind is negated. From the current perspective, two-sided relative attachment offers a complimentary frame for transcend and include which is directly compatible with our species' advances in attachment.

The dharma, attachment theory and developmental models in general put the accent on that which evolves and develops, that which is transcended, included and preserved. For humans, (we have suggested) this routinely and interchangeably goes by self/ego/mind. The evolutionary enterprise of fomenting behavioral and psychological repertoire of human offspring calls for attachment-detachment. This model therefore offers a narrower but perhaps more penetrating and parsimonious framework.

Maternal attachment is our species' version of all hands on deck.

Homo sapiens are all in with attachment's repertoire, from biological (nesting, nursing) practices to deep emotional processes (fierce devotion and protection) to higher emotional processes (psychological identification, mutuality, empathy and intuitive sentience) to cognition (facilitating language acquisition, teaching rules and values). Detachment is built into this same process. This inciting of offspring's maturation primarily takes place in the "we-space" where both parties, both me's exist on a third rail within that space. But this realm requires a constant returning to the well. Its wall, the me/we boundary is forever being set and reset. The same subtle frame is immediately at hand in meditation.

A baby may cry and express dukkha when hungry, tired or cold. These are all ways it resets a proto-self across everyday detachments, when needs arise exactly because they are perceived as unmet. Breastfeeding becomes an object of the subjective experience of hunger, which hopefully is positively reinforced, contributing to incremental gains in a self-sense and secure base. Detachment is also pervasive in mothering. A mother is positively reinforced, feels a natural joy, when she is able to detach from her finally napping baby and gets some much-needed rest herself.

Mothering and attachment-love generally are portals marked just as often by pain as pleasure. When the baby is inconsolable, she resists, hates or feels forced to face detachment as she encounters limitations in her (me: we) influence. Everyone implicitly senses that parents are not meant to outlive their children. Grief on a smaller scale is a constant in the lives of sensitive attachment figures. Helpless, forced detachment evokes the sense, "I would trade my life." Attachment and detachment are opposite sides of the same coin. The mother longs to attach but cannot, just as the child cries for her but is left in pain. Even patriarchal traditions know of this transcendent truth. There are allusions to Buddha's father's grief running through Siddhartha's biography. This is most movingly felt in the words of Jesus as he hung dying (awakening) on the cross, "Father why has thou forsaken me?"

Attachment and detachment are opposite sides of the same innate, creative, meaning-evoking process. Neither is in full control. Across the ages, the flowing we-space neither dismisses nor tricks the I/ego but keeps it in check in multiple ways. There is plenty of meaning, truth, and beauty remaining for ego, I, me, and my. There is ample opportunity for moms to experience ownership and receive credit for their offspring without the pathology of enmeshment and abandonment. The same is true of pair bonding and loving relationships across the lifespan. One can feel both humbled at the fortune of knowing another, and delight in being loved. But this requires a combination of ego and wego stability.

Abandonment and enmeshment, the hallmark of highly disturbed, borderline functioning individuals, corresponds to the terrifying extremes of detachment and attachment. These are set in motion when biological-maternal attachment goes awry. Commonly, the mother figure herself suffered a similar fate as an infant, baby, and/or toddler. Such babies cannot ask, "Mother why has thou forsaken me?" So many factors can contribute to problematic attachment from health and mental health problems in the mother or child to war, famine, and increasingly, substance abuse.

The healthier one's attachment, the greater the potential for Buddhism to light the way. At the higher reaches of psychological functioning, the sub-processes submerge. A way opens, one past attaching and detaching cycles, and beyond transcending, including, negating or preserving processes. Actually, "past" and "beyond" imply duality and separation. What is popularly identified as "non-dual" refers to the human potential that Buddha discovered (or rediscovered) for anyone to supersede form, change, movement, or development itself.

Who moves past, who supersedes? Such questions remind us of "that" essence which witnesses the evolution of the self, the movement of the spirit. "I am that" where that never sticks. That is that which is preserved, included. For babies and toddlers, it's sleepy, hungry, happy, tired— a mind just beginning to inhabit a body. "I am that" at the higher reaches refers to where "that" aspires to supersede conception. For most of us, maternal attachment and classical Buddhist detachment are interlinked. The same "I am" is bound up, or not, depending on one's early life experience. Where this was adequately strong and loving, the classical dharma message holds potential.

Where this was marginal, one must try. And in this is the implicit, given miracle of life. And no need to try when awakened to just the possibility of trying. There are many paths still untried, and many Bodhisattvas to meet, and one Bodhisattva to become, for others, for Bowlby's and Buddha's attachment are ultimately human attachment. Even Siddhartha tried.

> If in that utter darkness we can give blood to the stone, tears to our grief,
> voice to our rage, truth to our deceit, then "the darkness shall be light, and
> the stillness the dancing." Detached from the dead gods of the past, we lose
> all and find all, for in the moment of surrender the living god and goddess
> enter. We move from a place of total abandonment to a place where we can
> never be abandoned.[84]

Combinatorial

A mind that sees itself is a mind that frees itself, and does so through combinations of perspectives. Nowhere does the Pali Canon propose an IQ test. Everyday people seem to have benefited, to put it mildly, from meeting and talking with Buddha. For them, hindsight suggests, a rapidly richer picture formed as they saw their struggles and identifications in the caring, mirroring eyes, images and ideas of the wandering sage. Likely deceptively simple "orienting generalizations" were portals to greater expanses of being.[85]

> "Our nature is an illimitable space through which the intelligence moves
> without coming to an end," wrote the poet Wallace Stevens in 1951. The
> limitlessness of intelligence comes from the power of a combinatorial system.
> Just as a few notes can combine into any melody and a few characters can
> combine into any printed text, a few ideas—PERSON, PLACE. THING,
> CAUSE, CHANGE, MOVE, AND, OR, NOT—can combine into an
> illimitable space of thoughts. The ability to conceive an unlimited number of
> new combinations of ideas is the powerhouse of human intelligence and a
> key to our success as a species.[86]

Meditation, as mentioned, translates as getting used to this "illimitable space of thoughts." Through orienting generalizations, such as transcend and include, attach-detach, the feminine as the patriarchy's shadow, and ego as an orphan in need of a mother, one gets used to what words leave untouched. In becoming more natural and automatic, these handles on "I am that" culminate in what Buddhists call skillful means.

The classical continuum of psychological functioning, psychotic-borderline-neurotic-normal, is especially potent. Leaps in clarity come as this is combined with other basic models, e.g., psychological development across the lifespan (baby-child-adolescent-adult), the evolution of consciousness (mammal-primate-human) and the "great chain" (body-mind-spirit).

No one expects a normal child to be normal from the perspective of adult mental functioning. In a loose way, the lower one's position on the psychotic-borderline-neurotic-normal continuum of mental functioning, the less developed and less mature one is. At the lower realms, somatic, physiological processes distort consciousness. The classical psychoanalytic take on psychosis is of a psyche imprisoned at lower, bodily levels unable to reliably benefit from higher mental capacities. People coping with psychosis certainly have higher cognitive capacities, thoughts and mental imagery, but these tend to take on Dali-like distortions. The relative attachment model can be included for further clarity. Delusions are beliefs that are too firmly held, too dense, too unrelenting.

These beliefs take the form of thickly layered inner worlds, which essentially own their host personalities and crowd out other, more benign, logical interpretations. Perceptual disturbances such as auditory hallucinations are so overly, inwardly privileged as to make self-talk and verbal forms of cognition "real." Again, the unreal through hyper-identification becomes a reality.

Bipolar patients who have been swept into euphoric hypomanic states experience something similar. These states are highly physiological, may involve rapid changes in mood, energy, pressured speech, and sleep. Despite the unfurling chaos, they do not want to be reined in. Between such disasters, they may or may not see the light. Some recognize the problem, meaning they have the ability to detach, reflect, and experience life as larger and more continuous than when in the grips of a major mood swing. Others prefer to hold off on medicine, even when depressed, because at a subconscious, physiological level they crave the rush of freedom, which the medications prevent.

In extreme states, "concrete" thinking dominates. The term concrete parallels the classical "stuck in the body" conception. In paranoia, for example, subjective fear becomes concretized as a very real someone or something on the prowl, about to attack. A recent patient of mine at the psychiatric ward at the hospital where I work/consult/teach was riding the other, grandiose side. He shared with a sly smile how he was Black Ops "part of the night." He was swooped up by his team to do missions. For the one with paranoia, the very medicine (antipsychotic medication) that might help is most assuredly poison. For the other with grandiosity, they understand that we mean well. But sadly, we know so little of how the world really works.

Many talk endlessly about a web of government deceit or what some very smart, innocent, well-meaning expert has reported: "Don't take my word for it, check it out for yourself." There are long-winded explanations about why the whole matter is not in the news. Many talk to a concrete God whom they petition nonstop and who sometimes talks back to them. Many make gods of New Age, secret formulations. They do their best to spin the story but get trapped in a complex web of creation tales. All manner of unfortunate events conspire, and tragically these patients find themselves center stage. The ultra-victim is at once ultra-special, the only one able to translate the signs. Or one of a small number of people in the world who know of the immensely dramatic and important events unfolding.

Hyper-religiosity, delusions of grandeur, and paranoia are all embedded in a concrete grandiosity. Whether scared or euphoric, the practitioners are the center of the story. Hyper-religious, paranoid, end-timers, and conspiracy theorists are psycho-spiritually at the same very regressed, self-absorbed level of functioning, often far from what Buddhism suggests carries some hope for equanimity and peace.

In all these cases, the term "concrete" is an apt, frequently applied descriptor reflecting overly attached beliefs and rigid fixations. Concrete thinking is marked by a lack of counterbalancing of the detachment side of relative attachment. Without this, the immature, inflated ego is starved for space. More ego is needed for separation from intrusive contents. More self-sophistication makes possible dispassionate, objective, less literal, more abstract, multi-perspectival forms of cognition. The word "fundamentalist" also captures the dense, concrete world of convictions these practitioners inhabit. Overflowing ideas are not ideas but stark, pressing truths that others need to understand immediately for their own good. There is not enough ego to see patterns of projection, to "own" one's agendas. With all this immaturity, black and white, binary thinking is rampant: us and them, true and false, good and bad. Concrete people "don't do nuance."

Concrete cognition is only concrete from a higher perspective. It's an unimaginably, advanced brilliant feat seen from precursor stages. Concrete reality must be achieved before it is transcended. Mammal babies that live long enough to pass on their genes know concretely who their mommy or maternal attachment figure is. Human babies are meant to go much further, and to fully embody the maternal loving presence at the center of the self. When this goes awry, combinatorial processes which move from concrete to higher levels of abstraction are disrupted.

Skillful Means

Jung's archetypal theory offers a potent toolkit to what Buddhists call skillful means. Also called depth psychology, Jung's model provides further assistance in navigating the "two attachments" and thereby for this exploration of Buddha's Mom. "Skillful means" is dharma for best practices. These are progress-facilitating, psycho-spiritual force multipliers! The concept of archetypes has entered the cultural mainstream and is often misused. The saying, "a little bit of knowledge is a dangerous thing" is packed with wisdom. A best practices or skillful means incorporation of the archetypal model, including the hero's journey and views on the male and female principle, is one richly integrated with other closely aligned models. A collaborative, integral approach helps keep ideas, maps, and constructs concerning the deep psyche in check.

There is really no such thing as a single archetype. The King, Witch, or Hero's Journey cannot be understood separate from Jung's model of the human psyche. Each is also an organizing principle that can be filled out with great variation but still retains a certain essence. The power of the archetypal model lies in the fact that we can identify this essence even as the actual scope of the archetypal reach and influence supersedes this knowing. Archetypes are like cardinal points demarcating a vast space. Meaning forms the psyche's space. Archetypes are meaning-laden distinctions that structure this space, constellations of preconscious, meaning-laden symbols, characteristics, and dynamics, which color one's experience of self/ego/mind and its perception of other's self/ego/mind. As such they go to the heart of relative attachment, desires, attractions and aversions. They evoke love, distrust, boredom, conflict, confusion, and all the emotional flavorings that (unenlightened) modern humans never stop experiencing.

Any given emotionally laden experience involves psychological attachment to certain phenomena and detachment from others. We like the hero and dislike the villain. We want to be the hero and deny our shadowy, underhanded ways. This two-sided, every day, normal attaching-detaching process never stops. Certain aspects of one's journey are pumped-up, feel intense and drip with meaning. Others are painted as bad, or even more insidiously, as unimportant. Another wise saying reminds us that apathy, not hate is the opposite of love. Both sides of attachment are always in flow: the attraction, desiring, connecting side and the differentiating, circumscribing, pushing away, detaching side.

The same sub-processes led to the formation of archetypes in the first place. Tribal members relatively better at sizing up others tended to survive the cut and, genetically speaking, remain swimmers in the gene pool. This sizing up was circular, cause and effect, accelerating snowballing advances in evolution. Those able to spot a thief, cheat, or tyrant were statistically less prone to being their victim, and were globally more fit from an evolutionary standpoint. As tribes led to larger grouping, as socialization and competition for mates and resources took on new levels of complexity, these potentials continued to evolve (in a feedback loop). Archetypal pattern recognition increased in sophistication, and along with multiple other cognitive advances, especially language, facilitated increases in social complexity and scope.

One must "hang on loosely" when employing archetypal skillful means. First off, we may "see what we be." One may feel victimized by a tyrant but actually, to a large extent, (also) be under the interior influence of both these archetypes, i.e., the victim and the tyrant. The list is endless: wanderer, do-gooder, schmoozer, hail fellow, and sexpot are some of the minor examples. Major ones include the godhead, god, goddess, deities, king/queen, mystic, trickster, fool, warrior, and lover. Many are not character-centric, such as the hero's journey, dark night of the soul, the shadow, virgin birth, and resurrection.

For our current purposes, Buddha's Mom should be understood as embodying powerful archetypal dimensions. This alone should mitigate any overly biological reductionisms that she, for example, is "nothing but" the ego's experience of biological attachment. Just as important, these archetypal forces, which include Goddess, Mother, Good Samaritan, Protector, Queen, Stepmother, and Seeker, must not be overly exalted. We all walk through life variously buoyed and imprisoned by similar preconscious forms. In her and in us, these must be understood as archetypal and not personal or ripe for conscious integration. Archetypes are designed by evolution to operate as partial shapers of the flow of consciousness. Their functionality requires they strike the Goldilocks balance between too hot and too cold.

In Buddha's Mom, we can see more clearly how multiple balances across levels of functioning operate by way of the two-sided, attachment and detachment, process. She strikes a balance between instinctual, mammalian attachment drives and the more sophisticated templates and forms Jung called archetypes. Presumably we share the former but not the latter with most other mammals. In humans, the latter, archetypal repertoire incorporates motherly ideals. These include the tireless fount of sacrificial love and devotion of the Great Mother, and the opposite—the tyrannical, plotting stepmother, witch, or crone.

While some portrayals want to overlay some of the all-good Goddess on Buddha's Mom (much as they do with Jesus' mother), it seems reasonable to hypothesize that Siddhartha's mom was a mentally stable individual. She was probably not prone to what Jungians refer to as inflation or to being "in the grip" of archetypal forces. Nothing in the Pali Canon suggests that Prajapati, Mahamaya, or the nameless nursemaids were mentally unstable. But somehow, just stopping at the declaration that she was not insane is hardly satisfying. This declaration continues to embed the presumption that she was not more important, in mappable ways, than previously thought. This, I have come to believe, camouflages the even more insidious assumption that she has little to offer each of us, now, in our lives. In order to develop this thesis, a grasp of archetypal theory is critical.

A skillful means approach to archetypes underscores that extreme, highly concrete claims on truth may signal the undue influence of certain archetypes. Generally, in a balanced, mature psyche, these operate in the background, pre-shaping the conscious perceptual field. They serve as heuristics or orienting generalizations. Jungian analysis puts much emphasis on patients becoming aware of their particular archetypal dynamics, but this is sometimes misunderstood. One works at detaching from holds (over-attachments) that have been overwhelming and overly controlling consciousness.

The analysand is not guided ever downward toward close encounters with whatever archetypes are in operation., but rather towards an ever-more facile ability to recognize these rocks in the river, and to see them more quickly, in advance, with more precision. This is different from any notion of the conscious realization of archetypal dynamics. There will always be rocks. One can increasingly occupy the space around them and eventually the space within them.

Individuation, as Jung called it, has more of a personal, psychological emphasis than mindfulness but refers to the same global process. Both the mindfulness practitioner and analysand develop a certain capacity for phenomenological observation. Such skillful means enable previously less conscious forces that have been doing their bidding and wreaking emotional dysregulation, neurosis, samsara and suffering by its many names. Witnessing or reflecting upon these requires presence and grounding, which also have many names. Classic examples of an absence of this facility include delusions of grandeur, mental patients who are convinced that they are the Second Coming. A more common variant involves a very negative, partially supernatural other. The FBI sending signals through the television. Unknown people stealing and plotting to harm. Less dramatically in everyday life, this plays out in people who rigidly adhere to myriad roles like Victim or Tyrant.

Levels of egoic development, from biological to archetypal to individuation, all have their place. All are scaffolding, supporting an ever higher, more integrative development. As a mother extends herself toward her child, as a child seeks refuge in her mother, lovingkindness and mercy are close at hand. This extending, caring-based intentionality may persevere and manifest with great variety. Such kindnesses of the soul implicitly co-opt attachment and detachment. The giving up, letting go of one's seat on a subway is the same as giving up and detaching when one pushes back against anonymity and complacency. The risk at hand corresponds to reaching out and attaching to a stranger in need. Even love requires and relies upon these, detaching/attaching, to reach the darkest, tightest, coldest, hardest orphans of earth, of body and consciousness. When these show up at the door, one must drop (detach from) any fetter or impediment in order to respond with an openhearted fullness.

The dharma has most exquisitely made the case for the detachment side or sub-process of attachment. Again, attachment is such an established Buddhist, scientific and everyday term that it may be best to risk confusion and retain this term as both the major dynamic referred to by Buddha and Bowlby, and one of its own two-sided sub-process. By practicing, we more freely, effortlessly release and detach. To do otherwise is to continue suffering. There are forever more orphans at the door. Ultimately each of us is knocking at our own door, answering in hopes of some final release from suffering. Being attached then to this form of hope is sadly illusory and fated to end badly. Not only is there no escape from our bodily pains, disease, and ultimately death, but also by definition one is no more capable of helping when famine, the scourge of HIV, and human trafficking or extremist lunacy come calling. What Buddha taught, with such beauty, is that all holocausts, all of our smallness, can be released on the out breath.

In Buddha's Mom, we hope to make the case for a compatible context, wherein the main dharma message is considered along several complimentary paths. At least I am (attaching to) the hope that these ideas will be more fully considered by others based on their own expertise and practice.

Babysitting

In the closing pages of her best-selling book, *Comfortable with Uncertainty*, Pema Chödrön discusses the Heart Sutra. She offers her views on one of the dharma's most well-known phrases, "form is emptiness and emptiness is form." Chödrön explains that this radical assertion pulled the rug out from under already devoted followers. This was an even starker, more shocking truth than those early devotees previously understood. There is nothing to anything, so to rest in anything, anything at all, is misguided and illusory.[87]

According to Chödrön, this most famous sutra implores us never to seek out "a babysitter." Not in any person, idea, or in the subtlest of attachments, not even "the belief in insubstantiality and change." Any trusting in a God or holding on to a belief that someone will take care of us amounts to "thinking there's always going to be a babysitter available when we need one."[88]

When wise souls such as Pema Chödrön say such things, one can be forgiven for any confusion that might occur regarding Buddha's stepmother, Prajapati. She was much more to Buddha than a babysitter. She came on the scene when Siddhartha was a baby with no mother. If babysitting is to be avoided, what do we make of the arrangement between this woman and this baby?

Buddhist masters such as Chödrön, of course, employ language, metaphor, and detailed explanations. Their written and spoken words are intended for mature minds, adult readers, and listeners with the capacity to understand abstract concepts. That attachment causes suffering only makes sense in minds of a certain stage of development. Without this maturity of mind, on an overly concrete level, the message implies mothers should not be lovingly attached to their babies.

Where is the line between too concrete and an adequate capacity for abstraction? The boundary is nowhere to be found in the brain or in attachment science. The process of attachment, attachment-detachment, seems to arise within regardless of age and maturity and to incrementally, layer by layer, contribute to the cause of maturation. Clearly great teachers such as Chödrön, through their own maturity—their own advanced blend of wisdom and compassion—pass along this teaching to those able to benefit from it.

But perhaps some caution is advised, both with respect to wounded souls, with psychological scars dating back to early attachment experiences, and with the attachment-suffering concept as it is traditionally expressed. Skills and behaviors involved in babysitting and caregiving and all that goes with cultivating a baby's health and happiness are too easily undervalued even as they are praised. They tend not to be seen for their enormous power in shaping personality (self/ego/mind). As such, tossing out ego without such an appreciation reminds one of the classic baby and bathwater warning. A fairer, more factual assessment reveals that attachment is more verb than noun. Just as "being" is synonymous with the flow of consciousness and awareness, so too is attachment (attaching and detaching).

The context for this intense, direct teaching on impermanence may be telling. Buddha suggested that one of his closest disciples, Sāriputta, meditate on the great Bodhisattva of compassion, Avalokitesvara. For this disciple, the experience unfolding must have been one of profound empathy and love. Doubtless, Buddha's innate kindness was foundational to his many-year relationship with Sāriputta. From a modern lens, this relationship would meet the criteria for healthy, secure adult attachment. While linear time and narrative history existed on one plane, a ceaseless, timeless love lived in another. Similar secure, personal, adult attachments with Buddha shared this quality. Notable examples include Ananda and Prajapati. These adult forms of attachment psychology seem to provide a scientifically demonstrable substrate, and to be subsumed in the construct of Buddha's Mom. Upon this scaffolding of attachment-love, Buddha taught and showed others a fuller, more encompassing reality. He transmitted a lovingkindness beyond ownership. This exceeded the most advanced caregiving or caretaking. This is key as Chödrön declares in her teaching on babysitting.

Ultimately, one can no more stop either attaching or detaching and continue to be conscious than one can stop digestion, respiration or other basic life processes. Attachment just happens to be the process by which Homo sapiens' brain/mind operates both across the lifespan and across generations, from lifespan to lifespan. And both sides of the process are compatible with the messages of great Buddhist teachers such as Chödrön.

Another Name

Tibetan monks' intricate sand mandalas make a unique statement regarding relative attachment. This meditative "pointing out" ritual exquisitely expresses both sides of relative attachment. Advanced monks meticulously, mindfully create and then destroy, all for Buddha, all for the betterment of sentient beings. In this aspect, they spend hours, days and sometimes weeks in a focused, attachment mode. As junior monks and others gather, they show off their profound skills at concentration and precise attachment to ancient, sanctioned customs. First, often using angles and rulers, a mandala is drawn; next, from the center outward, handheld funnels and other instruments are used to place colored sand. Complex geometric, and exacting works of art slowly, deliberately come into being. All this attachment to form takes place before the entire mandala will be, literally, blown away.

The deliberative, constructing initial aspect is a concentration practice, synonymous with attachment. Attachment to form (or equally, attachment as form) manifests in various ancient scenes, some with hundreds of deities. But the attachment-detachment dance is multi-layered. The very plan to build and then destroy the mandalas places a major emphasis on detachment. Monks observing and those participating are implicitly practicing detachment in the face of extreme beauty and the intrigue of the process. Interpretation of this ritual often gets this slant, but in truth, this high form of detachment, this celebrated, slow-motion destruction of form, also calls for more of the same concentration, that is to say attachment to the detachment process. The elaborate forms, all the sand deities are very carefully, mindfully blown away, resulting in a detachment from beauty.

So, as we have discussed elsewhere, "it"—purpose, result, meaning, experience—involves both aspects of relative attachment (attachment and detachment) and ultimately, as Nagarjuna declared, is neither relative attachment nor *not* relative attachment, nor both (relative attachment and not relative attachment), nor neither. The whole of the sand mandala practice points to something more and, yes, nothing more that is commonly referred to as nonattachment. It is awareness of the awareness of everything always and already arising and passing. In arising, attaching; in passing, detaching.

The very essence of concentration practices involves attaching to forms—mandalas, mantras, breathing, walking. Each equally involves detaching from all else, and letting mental contents rise and fall, move through mind with no grasping or identifying. In mindful eating, one notices all the steps, textures, and flavors individually arising and fading as one eats. In mindful walking, the concentration and focus is on the subtle physicality of bipedalism. Multiple coordinated events co-occur in process, all rising and fading. Even where practitioners are encouraged to maintain a conscious connection to specific phenomena, like a candle flame or the breath, the heart of the experience necessarily involves an organic to and fro. Even when the emphasis is on one-pointed stillness, on maintaining a connection, all of this necessarily arises and thereby (by design) improves detachment-styled skillful means.

Typically, concentration practices place a co-emphasis on "just" noticing, just being aware of the subtleties at hand. And "just" returning to the object of concentration when the mind wanders. "Just" means "only" and communicates a certain passivity regarding the detachment pole. When non-sanctioned phenomena enter the phenomenological space, practitioners are supposed to re-attach, reconnect with the sanctioned phenomena, the breath, candle flame, or transient awareness.

The essentials of sitting meditation stem from a de-emphasis on action and mental stimulation. De-engagement with everyday activities is prioritized. Sitting quietly, in a quiet room with eyes closed or partially closed are examples of what is to be minimized: action, interaction and participation in one's outer life and environment. There is a dampening down of visual, auditory and for that matter tactile, proprioceptive (at least as this pertains to awareness of one's body during movement), and olfactory stimuli. But any emphasis on detachment in sitting forms (shikantaza, for example) is more than compensated by other overt or implied instructions.

Form or formless emphases play with the dialog of attachment and detachment. In all, these many time-tested practices translate, of course, as skillful means of working with relative attachment and nonattachment. Whether the overt emphasis is on attachment or detachment is of secondary importance. One begets the other. In mentally attaching to an object, through concentration on that object, one increases their ability to simultaneously detach. The Tibetan monk who creates the sand mandala is free of expectations related to the importance or beauty or perfection of the object of concentration precisely because, over countless repeated trainings, he has refined both a superficial ability to maintain attached focus, and a deep, global detachment from outcome. In concentrating on a mantra or the breath, one develops skills at detaching from all else. Practice differentiates the living mental dynamic, enlarging the scope of the inner Witness. The awareness of the immediate form permeates the form as it is liberated from it.

> So we instruct people to meditate on all phenomena in conventional terms,
> that is, for example, to say mentally "walking, walking" concentrating on the
> motion of their legs whenever they start walking. But as concentration
> develops, all these conventional usages disappear, and there remains only
> the reality of everything arising-and-passing away ceaselessly.[89]

Detachment vs. Nonattachment

One can be forgiven for any confusion regarding the distinction between detachment and Buddhism's nonattachment. Some light was shed on this in 1994, when the British Library acquired first century written records of the teachings of the Buddha. These "dead sea scrolls" of Buddhism include what scholars consider one of the Pali Canon's earliest texts, the Rhinoceros Horn Sutra.

The refrain of this verse from oral tradition calls out, "one should wander alone." Some scholars translate this as "one should wander alone as the horn of the rhinoceros is alone," and others as "one should wander alone as the rhinoceros wanders alone."[90] As a non-herd animal, this view purports, the rhinoceros is an exemplar of a solitary, ascetic life. The first emphasis on the singularity of the horn can be interpreted as a call to free oneself of attachments.

Once again, this critical, ancient document points to a divergence between Bowlby and Buddha. By extension, it begs the question: At what point in life is attachment no longer advised? If there is no developmental boundary, then is there some sort of psychological one?

Baby Siddhartha's thirst, intrinsic in breastfeeding and mammalian attachment, emanated from the same subconscious, physiological processes that give rise to that which Bowlby called attachment. As a healthy, normal (or better) mammalian-primate-Homo sapiens' neonate, Siddhartha's earliest bodymind would serve as the vessel by which these were transmuted into stable conscious experiences. As with the baby rhino, his life would depend on and benefit from this.

Presumably inchoate, pre-conscious mixtures of pain and desire associated with the subcomponents of thirst would eventually coalesce in adequately stable perceptions. As we have repeatedly stated, thirst or *tanhā* is the word translated often as clinging, grasping and attachment found at the center of the Four Noble Truths.

Some sort of proto-fledgling self or witness implicitly facilitates all this process of differentiating. Such a proto-self or pre-mind "re-cognizes" precursors. Re-cognition is a beautiful term for the process by which, through frequency and duration, neural patterns which fire together wire together, and a percept emerges. Thirst is clearly what Wilber calls a *holon* (part-whole) with internal, experiential and behavioral dimensions within other basic life drives, including biological attachment.

In this book, we suggest that integral associations to the we-space deserve deeper contemplation. Even at this very subtle, early stage of mind-in-development, the emergent self experiences and expresses the thirst experience as such, within an attachment relationship. Functionally, the neonate "learns" (a better term is "acquires") and develops the skillful means to signal its caregiver to provide sustenance. Multiple iterations of these internal and social loops eventually become recognizable as the stuff of attachment—the need for milk, warmth, protection, sleep, and the meeting of these needs by the mother. Under proper conditions these form the substrates of mind, ego, and the self.

The unfolding and hand-off from maternal to social attachment is best defined within the vast span of pre-history, a period that archeological findings suggest began over one million years ago and ended, on this sort of scale, practically yesterday. The end of our hunter-gatherer journey, still in progress, is only about 20000 years old. Said another way, all but the last few words of the great book on human attachment was about tribal we-space.

A person was first a tribal constituent. She or he was so integrally fused within a group of fifty to a hundred others that spending time alone would have been rare and strange. As one attempts to feel their way into such a we-space, even the term hunter-gatherer can be misleading. Gatherer-hunters is more appropriate, placing emphasis where it belongs in terms of calories and work. Given that females were generally more involved in gathering and males in hunting, a reversal of the "hunter-gatherer" construct also more accurately acknowledges the role of females in the tribes' survival and success.

The norm for attachment in human functioning is reflected in how members of tribes sleep, eat, and spend virtually all their waking hours in close emotional contact and physical proximity. In New Guinea, when one wakes up in the night she or he will rouse someone else to talk to. When one goes out to urinate, they bring along another.[91]

Interpersonally, maternal attachment is the substrate for social attachment; psychologically, it has broad implications. As mentioned, the word tanhā as found in the Noble Truths translates as thirst and craving. These physiological meanings cross the brain-mind bridge toward classically psychological variants such as desire and expectation. Between are hybrids of brain-mind and body-mind such as clinging or grasping.

In the Siddhartha biography, the very thirst and hunger so associated with maternal attachment dovetails early on and very concretely with precursors of social attachment. At this stage, the story still reflects our tribal backdrop. Human babies such as Siddhartha do not and should not reject breast milk. From the outside, the overly obvious fact regarding "wet nurses" or as they are referred to in the Canon, nursemaids, is that they are "other" and not the biological mother. For the baby, milk is milk. Same for attachment. It flows from a single source. Whether the vehicle is breastfeeding, holding, or other forms of feeling, attachment propels the toddler to expand his or her social repertoire. Emotional attachment to others continues as children establish bonds with their peers across every successive phase of development.

Embedded in the unfolding of attachment is detachment. At some point, even a baby who has 'wet-nurses' comes to distinguish between its various mother figures. Detachment is part and parcel of this cognitive capacity and continues to be so in the hand-off switch from maternal attachment to social attachment. The male rhino apparently moves toward this side of relative attachment as it matures. Buddhism, of course, uses this image to highlight the importance of detachment. A renunciate focus is conflated with nonattachment. Properly understood, detachment is merely a sub-process within attachment. Detachment is a constituent of the biological and maternal attachment found in rhinoceroses, humans, and other mammals. Recently, the Hoedspruit Endangered Species Centre in South Africa rescued a baby male rhinoceros whose mother had been killed. "It was a devastating sight, as the tiny animal would not leave her side, and was crying inconsolably for her."[92]

No particular demarcation occurs during development, but at some point the adult male rhinoceros is far less dependent on its mother or on social attachments more generally. In humans, the intensive dependence on the mother fades. This sets up the illusion that the attachment process has run its course. Even those who use the term social attachment are prone to ignoring the fact that social attachment is an elaboration of maternal attachment, just as a rose is an elaboration of a rose bud.

The terminology and simple model of "relative attachment" clarifies the distinction between detachment and nonattachment. Relative attachment is grounded in both the life sciences and a correctly understood Buddhist spiritual path. It is comprised of attachment and detachment and is distinguished from concepts discussed within Buddhism that transcend relative reality, such as enlightenment and nonattachment.

Devadatta

A unique attachment figure in the biography of Buddha is the figure of Devadatta. He is Siddhartha's cousin and later brother-in-law. His relationship with Siddhartha/Buddha runs opposite to the attachment-love and we-space we have suggested as structuring Buddha's relationship with Prajapati, Rahula, Kisa and others.

Devadatta is not too pleased and, as time goes by, becomes jealous of Buddha's brilliance and popularity. A little too fixated on Buddha's limelight, Devadatta tries to persuade Buddha to turn over leadership of the sangha. His covert rationale is expressed as concern for the Holy One's advancing age, the fact that anything could happen, and a desire for a smooth transition to a new leader. When his first efforts fail, Devadatta's emotions turn dark.

Ultimately, the tale of Devadatta exemplifies the shadow side of attachment. This is the same dynamic expressed in the important assertion that indifference, not hate, is the opposite of love. Shadowy attachment also manifests in Buddha's mythic conflict with Mara, as we will consider at the close of this book. A turning point finally occurs when Buddha issues a proclamation, an "act of information," calling out Devadatta publicly. This proclamation declared that Devadatta's nature had switched sides and that anything Devadatta said or did was no longer assumed to stem from allegiance to the sangha or dharma.

We might begin with the interpretation that the Holy One is providing a teaching concerning alternatives to compassion and lovingkindness while of course, still remaining deeply involved with both. To be called out as such, we can presume, was humiliating for Devadatta. This sharp rebuke was born of a true love, and only stings in proportion to Devadatta's screwy psychospiritual posture. His, mine, yours and all Homo sapiens' evolutionary, somatic and relational unity flows through the tribe. The in-forming disruption corresponds to Devadatta's maniacal, narcissistic wego relative to his tribe, the sangha. A Gaia, goddess, earth-focal posture is evoked psychologically as humiliation. As mentioned, the meaning of not just the word but the psychospiritual basis of humiliation references rich, dark organic soil, or humus. Other connotations include below, mud, and the earth to which we return and are buried. The emotional agony is deadly and at the same time teaming with organic, life-giving elements.

Other details from the Pali Canon bolster this interpretation of humiliation as a potentially correcting, healing function emanating from the feminine principle within human psychological functioning. Previously, Devadatta became convinced of his specialness in the form of supernatural powers. He transformed into a boy encircled by snakes in an effort to impress a local prince.[93] Driven to unseat Buddha, Devadatta attempted to form an alliance with the prince.

This is another example of attachment's every day, shadow side. In gossip or when conniving, we fall prey to the allure of using attachment-love for self-aggrandizement and personal gain. The Eightfold Path's call to ethical interpersonal behaviors speaks to this. A focus on overpowering, dethroning and defeating are classically patriarchal drives. The story is contrasted by the appearance of the snake/serpent motif. We have already referred to the snake as a preeminent, ancient symbol of the universal goddess.

Having failed in other efforts to take over the sangha, Devadatta embarked on an elaborate attempt to assassinate Buddha. He arranged a successive series of sixteen archers to wait in position where Buddha would be walking. The

first archer would kill Buddha and in turn be killed, and so on, to ensure that Devadatta would never be caught. Though the first archer had a sword, shield, bow and quiver, the story goes, he was overwhelmed by Buddha's presence and became "rigid, afraid" and "alarmed."[94] The Buddha preached to this broken-open would-be assassin who confessed and converted and went on his way, presumably to spend the rest of his days integrating this event. In this, we are offered a succinct glimpse of the gift of humiliation that unfortunately eluded Devadatta.

When he learned of this event, instead of any such "ah ha" moment, Devadatta concluded that he would just have to kill Buddha himself. He then tracked Buddha as he walked a mountain trail, finally rolling a huge bolder down toward the Holy One. This time, earth herself, it seems interceded. The boulder smashed into two mountain peaks and was reduced to small shards. One of these cut Buddha's foot, drawing blood and Buddha admonished Devadatta for his murderous intentions.

In his third and final assassination attempt, Devadatta makes arrangements with an elephant trainer to let loose a rogue, "man-killer" elephant named Nālāgiri to trample Buddha to death.[95] Out of hundreds of possible animals, the elephant carries a particular significance. Mahamaya, Buddha's biological mother, had an original pregnancy dream with the great white elephant circling and then entering her womb, thus linking the elephant to Buddha and Buddhism. The human trainers of elephants in Buddha's time (and continuing up to today) had very special relationships with their animals based in mammalian attachment. The "mankiller" elephant in this story suggests disorder in a tradition and spiritual practice in which humans and elephants become enjoined in a relationship based in extreme intelligence, respect and love.

The story relays that Nālāgiri charged at Buddha but was met with the Holy One's lovingkindness. In this moment, love and respect were restored. This speaks to what we will outline as wego, and particularly to the intrapsychic potential for an alignment of conscious and subconscious streams. A central point, to be further fleshed out further, for example, via the proposed concept of wego, is that the alignment or order, or dharma, is the best focus for healing, practice and realization, not any given psychodynamics, instincts, emotions or intentions.

In this light, Nālāgiri symbolizes Devadatta's relationship with his own animal nature and instincts. We have considered this as the psyche's mammalian substrata, which as we will see incorporates Panksepp's neurobiological model. Severe attachment disorders manifest with similar disconnects. Kids so impaired used to be labeled under-socialized. Related, modern descriptions include emotional dysregulation and impaired impulse control. An emerging consensus implicates an intricate expansion of 'fight-flight' based around the vagus nerve, as we will detail in the last chapter. Referring to Devadatta as jealous and insecure dilutes and thereby obscures the severity of the psychodynamics and global dysfunction, but also the potential for healing.

Devadatta's complexity is easy to overlook. To set out three times to murder someone once idolized is one element that should be held in context with others. Devadatta's actions were not uncommon in a violent, male-dominated, warrior clan culture. He did not have a pattern of antisocial, unstable behavior, according to the biography.

The story conveys that the murder plot followed Devadatta's failed attempts to assume leadership of the first sangha. Buddha was 72 years old and, in theory, Devadatta was intent on a systematic transition of power. He wanted to avoid upheaval and assure those lower in the ranks that all was in order. Clans at that time had warrior-kings and princes who, like Siddhartha, would normally assume the reins from his warrior-king father. Indeed, Buddha had his top attendants and principle disciples and in rebuking Devadatta made a cutting reference to two such possible heirs, "Not even to Sariputta or Moggallan would I hand over the Order, and would I to thee vile one to be vomited like spittle?"[96] Here Buddha himself seems to operate in the same, aggressive, yang mode that Devadatta would take to its extremes in his attempted assassination.

On balance, Devadatta cannot be pigeonholed as a psychopath nor dismissed as merely carried away with envy. He was a creature of his time and place, but he was also one of the most important and passionate of Buddha's original followers. All that escalates into Devadatta's pathological fixation, involving planning and intellect, might instead be appreciated in terms of self/ego/mind on the one hand, and love and realization on the other. Buddha's brilliance, and his immensity of intelligence and kindness somehow broke Devadatta. We are blessed for this.

What is to be made of the darkness that overtook Devadatta? Perhaps he secretly doubted Buddha's authenticity. Perhaps he felt himself to be roughly Buddha's equal, and by no means deserving of his rebuke. Where others related to Buddha with awe and humility, the story suggests that Devadatta was more swayed by his own sense of self-importance. After all, he did perceive himself as worthy of jumping to the front of the line and installing himself as leader of the sangha. But these explanations leave much to be desired.

In all, Devadatta's story is without parallel in the biography and should not be reduced to a bumper sticker. Let us consider, for example, how after being publicly shamed, Devadatta escalated his aggressive tactics. This suggests a "narcissistic wound," wherein one's inflated sense of self is suddenly deflated. Narcissism refers both to intensive self-referencing and underdeveloped empathy (for example, regarding the impact of killing someone so beloved and important to so many) and to the fact of an early-life developmental arrest. Basic psychodynamic theory holds that babies and toddlers are naturally narcissistic. Narcissism only becomes a problem when this early stage becomes frozen in time and intrinsic to one's adult personality.

To reduce Devadatta to small-minded jealously is to dismiss the dignity and complexity of his passion. His readiness to commit murder, to take what he felt was his due, reveals from a clinical perspective the pathology of an inflated self/ego/mind. Such a blinding grandiosity comports with the borderline strands and what we have been calling a severe form of deep self disturbance. Clearly, he gave little thought to all that Buddha meant to so many. Nor was he exercising logic, simply calling for a meeting to ensure that Buddha's affairs were in order. Rather the spiritual pulse was upsurging, causing decompensation which could be deadly or transformative.

As we have touched on, superiority travels side-by-side with inferiority. In Devadatta's case, the latter remained unconscious time after time, as premeditated attempts failed and as archers and elephants were suffused with love. He never woke up, the story tells, and would eventually die holding to his worldview and go to hell.

To leave it that Devadatta had a big ego and was overcome with righteous indignation opens more doors than it closes. Big ego is both a very common and laden term, never good. It does not mean "big enough,'" just simply big, and no one speaks of "too tiny" an ego. Yet as the classic continuum of self/ego/mind demonstrates, too little ego is terribly destabilizing. In fact, the combination of too little and too big an ego would comport with what we know today of Devadatta. Depending on the severity, this common personality disturbance manifests literally in confusion— the fusion of the basic functional capacities. Realities blur, standard issue jealousy is supercharged and overtakes reason. When he was called out, Devadatta may have attributed his own rabid addiction to power and control to Buddha, and felt himself to be a victim. Such perceptual missteps are typical of psychodynamics which give rise to perceived humiliation and the decision to seek vengeance.

Devadatta is critically important for reasons that go beyond those outlined above. He is just an exaggerated version of you and me when we hit snags, an example of common formations of self/ego/mind as one encounters internal and external realities too large to map. Devadatta thought he saw himself in Buddha but could not, egoically, handle the truth of his own inner Buddha-nature. Through attachment-love, Buddha affirmed and mirrored this inner light to many. Hundreds of people left everything out of the same inspiration. But for Devadatta the same light was blinding.

As a highly-realized forest saint, his worldview was earthy and richly connected to the forest, animals, seasons and ways of being cultivated by generations of early, nomadic groupings. Devadatta's inherited worldview was shaken to the core. He longed for a return to the previous order he knew and practiced within. He would come to declare Shakyamuni as outside the legitimate lineage of Buddha's, and advocate for a succession that sets this self-proclaimed Buddha aside. In this resides a lovely, yin-inspired proclamation for not leaving the old connection to earth-based spirituality and a harsh, yang-based addiction to a smaller logic, a dark, desperate grasping for an older order unable to accommodate the fullness of the new day at hand.

Devadatta is truly a blessing and should be brought to mind and heart whenever we are wounded, angry or confused by another's actions. He was broken open by the love light reflected back to him, and enthusiastically did what made sense to him to handle this. Unfortunately, he completely misunderstood its source and the path to its realization. So few of us can withstand perfection.

Yet another element of this story has bearing here. In his seminal analysis of Devadatta, Ray (1999) makes a compelling case that Devadatta is a traditional forest saint, and that his legacy has come to be laden with the projections of subsequent contributors to the Canon. A critical turning point occurs when Devadatta decides to split the sangha. This has been encoded in the Canon as Devadatta's plotting a schism for his own gains. But Ray traces evidence suggesting that Devadatta fits the mold of an ancient, pre-Buddhist lineage of Indian saints. He lays out ample evidence that Buddha himself followed in this tradition, in which "the communal lifestyle and values of settled monasticism play no significant role."[97] Devadatta's justification for splitting the sangha, he speculates, may have been an effort to restore its forest heritage.

> Devadatta feels that the true dharma is to be found solely and strictly in the forest, and he appeals to the Buddha to back him up... This strict identification of Devadatta with forest Buddhism undoubtedly provides one important reason for his vilification by later Buddhist authors. It is not just that he practices forest Buddhism, is a forest saint, and advocates forest renunciation. Even more, and worse from the view-point of his detractors, he completely repudiates the settled monastic form...[98]

The more orthodox treatment, as outlined, pits Devadatta against Buddha. Devadatta, accordingly, advocates not a loosening but a regressive, tightening of yang traditions, notably, renunciation of the body. To this Buddha responds that while this declaration of the body as defiled may be appropriate, it is nonetheless the repository of karma. We are reborn incarnate, and must work with our karma to transcend the body and end the process of perpetual rebirth.

We can see here how 'Buddha's Mom' is being ripped in half. Devadatta, as Ray demonstrates, calls for a return to her, to earth, to the forest one is directly dependent on. But as usual with patriarchy, the body as the path to our spiritual essence is not recognized as such. Devadatta symbolizes the impossibility at hand. His inherited, forest-saint, tribal vessel conflicted with the world before him. Civilization was morphing beyond recognition, transitioning from agrarian to agricultural, from tribe or small village to the city-state and into huge, extended warrior clans. Buddhism's first sangha, numbering hundreds perhaps thousands of men with many levels of training and supposed attainment, was part of this new paradigm.

But for Devadatta's Shakyamuni's brilliance had to be deeply recognizable, simply put: truth, reality. Psychologically confronted with this, neither his yin capacities, Devadatta's earth-based, forest saint spirituality, nor his yang's grasp of hierarchy and order, could survive in their old form. As we will explore in depth, Buddha's own path navigated similar yin-yang pulls and these reached a turning point with the Middle Way.

Early in my career, I worked in a day treatment program for kids with severe attachment disorders. I was lead play therapist, working in conjunction with multiple devoted specialists. One of the most amazing humans I will ever meet was one of our clients. She was a 5-year-old girl, adopted from Romania. For her, the light was unrelenting. For starters, she was rescued from extreme deficits in loving attachment and had a brand new super-duper mother. On top of this, she was surrounded by a whole program of caring people and endless fun things to do and learn about, and she lived in Hawaii, golden sand beaches, turquoise water and rainbows.

This child would lose control in fits of ecstatic joy, with the most contagious, face-splitting smile ever anywhere. She also sometimes broke down, regressed and threw tantrums as if being trampled to death by rhinos. Our team ascribed these to PTSD and terrible experiences in the orphanage. This child was just beginning, with all the supports, to develop the skillful means to receive her inheritance, which here we have articulated as Buddha's Mom. We helped her to bear and contain her incredibly unique refraction of life's river of light. When she raged, we knew she needed an even more powerful (larger, safer, more consistent and empathic) attachment container to do so. After about 18 months her wounds were largely healed. She was an unstoppable force of lovingkindness.

Buddhists might understand my client's original feelings of abandonment in terms of karma, and apply the same to whatever factors influenced Devadatta to feel so threatened by Buddha's attainment. Karmic explanations would paint Devadatta's major relationships as the product of countless lifetimes. This is especially the case for beings so astronomically fortunate as to be human-born, contemporaneously living alongside and even related to Shakyamuni Buddha. For Devadatta, these currents appear to have been very strong. He was not only Buddha's cousin and brother-in-law, but he was also the brother of Buddha's devoted, brilliant attendant, Ananda. These multiple connections to Buddha, and thereby proximity to non-returning realization, suggest that perhaps his pathological jealousy was a final, ultimate karmic challenge. This closeness to his own enlightenment, from a karmic perspective, was hard-earned, independently, across countless lifetimes. In many of these lifetimes, whether as male or female, Devadatta would have known previous incarnations of Siddhartha.

Both literally and figuratively, the karmic perspective is aligned with Buddha's Mom. In this light, Devadatta correctly experienced himself (technically no self) as Buddha's equal—as of the same evolutionary, "upriver," spiritual source. While correct in seeing himself in Buddha, and as being mirrored by Buddha, he was sadly mistaken about his ability to integrate this experience. His mind-body-spirit lacked the ability to cope with his (and our) perfection. The story conveys beautifully that Devadatta literally and figuratively could not kill Buddha, because such was his own nature.

The ideas presented here hopefully clarify that the deeper vessel of Devadatta's negative attachment to Buddha was attachment-love. This is the innate, affective, sentient territory of Buddha's Mom. This is our evolutionary inheritance, called primordial awareness and Buddha-nature by Buddhists. This gives rise to what it means to be alive, 'the meaning of life', and once again demonstrates the psyche's relational foundations.

The story gives us an example of a human mind's reconciling of shallow, those devious and errant emotions, with life's deepest longing for ultimate connection, belonging and place in the world. The first archer was immobilized as the gap between self and shadow evaporated, as any separation and tension or need disappeared. His sense of separateness was enveloped by the direct experience of the limitless, transmitted by the walking, talking Buddha. This archer was flooded with clarity, awakened to the insanity of his intentions and reunited with the natural state. The story also offers further examples of how the same realities provide a correcting of one's deeper, emotional substrates via an integration with higher levels of being. Confronted with the mankiller elephant, Buddha "suffused the elephant Nālāgiri with loving-kindness of mind."[99]

As emphasized repeatedly, one of the most profound developmental factors in the mammalian condition is the maternal bond. This is especially significant from the perspective of karma, given the common Buddhist position that "we choose our parents." The canon specifically refers to Buddha selecting his biological mother, Mahamaya, and how her premature death is actually not a tragedy but a pre-ordained benefit deservedly bestowed upon her. Less clear is his choice, if it should be thought of as such, of Prajapati. Of many possible interpretations, one is consistent with the idea that her importance transcended biology as well as culturally bound meanings associated with mothering. While somewhat rhetorical, any speculation about Buddha's choice of Prajapati does beg the question, if Siddhartha had not experienced a healthy early-life attachment, would he have become Buddha?

Some mothers, sadly, are reminiscent of Devadatta. More than a few, at least according to their adult daughters, and the weight of the albeit imperfect evidence, were directly and indirectly complicit in years of molestation. In one case, a patient developed dissociative identity disorder (multiple personality disorder) and in others, borderline personality. One such person recalled, possibly symbolically, that her mother attempted to smother her while she was in her crib. False memory is an empirical fact; the pertinent point here is simply that these women continue to struggle valiantly to survive emotionally each day of their life. They continue to wage war against intolerable, intrusive internal mothers. Like Devadatta, they lack the wherewithal to manage their emotional torment.

The weight of the empirical evidence is quite clear. Early-life mothering persists, flowing ever on like a great river, across the decades. Mommy issues and daddy issues, as these are crudely called, keep upwelling. The river drives us to reconcile the warped love we knew as children and pure, perfect love. In dating, marriage, affairs, in friendships and in all manner of intimate relationships, attachment presses onward.

We keep longing for, find ourselves lost in, rail against, hope never to be reminded of, secretly wonder, miss, demand, and obsess about our past. In these countless ways, we keep looking for love, often in all the wrong places, to be sure. But all this imperfection must be understood as compelled by perfection.

Those who feel shortchanged want others to see them as amazing, intelligent and good looking. They want the world to love them and at a subconscious level, they want everything, every moment, to be immersed in bliss. Or else this possibility is so blindingly absent that they shield their eyes and walk about like zombies, or are cynical, walled off, or depressed.

Love relationships are all over the map. Many of us go from idealizing and thinking we have a real shot at some perfect love to implosions of "I'm not worthy." The meaning evoked runs from jealous, inspired, frustrated, to longing for more attention, even more pain. But for the most part, in this lifetime, we do not resort to suicide or attempted murder. Hopefully Buddha's Mom helps reveal the deep and natural perfection in all attachment-love, even that hidden within Devadatta's dark intentions.

Many of the luminaries, such as those referenced to in this work who have played a major role in bringing Buddhism to Europe and America have generously shared their own personal journeys with their sangha, followers, students and readers. In their books and dharma talks, these important conveyers of what is often called Western Buddhism include all manner of suffering, for example, anguish and heartbreak, or loss of loved ones to divorce and death. Here we have framed such biographical and psychological material as based in attachment-love.

Many, if not most, of the major teachers and lamas hailing from the sixties, seventies and eighties, appeared to be specifically, consciously, engaged in a wide range of personal and interpersonal healing modalities. It is reasonable to infer that these efforts included therapeutic work on deep-seated psychodynamics including those associated with their own mothers and early-life attachment experiences. They not only bravely engaged in but also pioneered multiple evocative therapeutic modalities.

Personal growth opportunities opened in all directions during this period of cultural upheaval, creativity and experimentation. There was a fusion of evocative psychospiritual modalities and meditation training. Practice proceeded in the context of close relationships with some of the most advanced Buddhist teachers of the era. This was the era of "third force," humanistic, existential and Gestalt schools of psychotherapy, for example. Some of these modalities were augmented by purposeful altered states, for example, hallucinogens and vision quests.

No formal accounting of this therapeutic work and its relationship to Western Buddhism, to my knowledge, has been compiled. Ideally this dimension of Western Buddhism, given its basis in attachment-love, will one day be more formally and accurately recognized. Also worth noting, few or perhaps none of these major figures appears to have had a level of early-life neglect and attachment dysfunction on a par with the Romanian orphan just mentioned.

In a sense, what is called Western Buddhism is born of and nurtured by the "Great Mother." Her sangha's thousand arms are always offering hugs, although these and bodywork are not typically, formally, consciously integrated with the teaching or practice on the placard. Retreats encapsulate holding environments, replete with food and shelter. One takes refuge in her. With the bodhisattva vow comes a sense of home and belonging, a sense of Buddha's Mom as she teaches her children to sit up, to walk, to speak and behave nicely. Siddhartha, in another sense, hovers about as a sort of father figure. He is caring but at same time compels us to detach. He guides us to be highly disciplined and to internalize what we learn so we can handle ourselves maturely in the world at large.

Much of what Westerners know about Buddhism can be appreciated as emergent from the great minds of a set of major figures. These heroes navigated their deep-seated attachments and assisted in many colorful and integral ways. Their procedures included hacking through jungles of Devadatta-like jealously, rejection, infatuation, projection and aggression. Through their own intensive blendings of such practices, an integration of the selfsame, pure, upriver source of attachment-love gives itself over in full—in our era as never before.

Expectation

Neither evolutionary theory nor any sophisticated, empirically based, psycho-developmental prototypes were available to Siddhartha Gautama. Bowlby's model, which places early human psychological development within Darwin's larger framework, would not occur for

thousands of years. Without this scaffolding, it is not surprising that the Pali Canon lacks a mature, modern appreciation of maternal, biological attachment. Unless purposefully contorted, Buddhism simply does not square with attachment as it has come to be understood—as nothing more or less than the biological underpinning of love.

Right off, a modern perspective notes certain gaps. Siddhartha was dearly loved and deeply cared for but ultimately had little to say about the importance of love and care in psychological development, either in regards to himself or to humans generally. On the other hand, we can be quite confident that Buddha did not discourage babies from nursing or advise mothers not to emotionally attach to their children.

One deceptively simple development model, which views mental functioning across a continuum (from psychotic to borderline to neurotic to normal) adds clarity. This model supports what probably most of us intuit: that Buddha came honestly to his conclusions regarding attachment as the cause of suffering. Based on his own psychology, his own upbringing had more than a little to do with his brilliance, warmth, wisdom, metta and powers of discernment. This background was probably not lacking for healthy maternal attachment.

This empirically-based continuum has withstood the test of time, going on about one hundred years. It helps resituate Buddhism's classical views on attachment. Through this stage-based, developmental lens, attachment can be viewed more contextually. Where we all might agree that a baby's attachment is one thing and an adult's another, this continuum adds still further nuance. Development may be and should be viewed in a variety of combinatorial frames. Besides the chronological perspective, from infancy to adulthood, another valid continuum, which roughly squares with chronology, goes from low to high functioning, from small to larger capacities for reasoning, emotional regulation, and clinically speaking, from abnormal to normal.

With these additional lenses, we can better investigate orthodox Buddhism's conception of attachment. One scholar who delved into this matter has suggested that rather than attachment (here he refers to this as the "desire term"), it is best translated as *expectation*.

> After reading over one hundred Dhammabooks, the 20,000 pages of
> Buddhist scriptures, and over twenty-five years of meditation practice, I have
> come to the realization that the desire term is another one of those words
> which does not adequately or correctly translate the original Pali or intention
> of the Buddha.[100]

Here we track Siddhartha's focus on this—attachment, desire, or what Snyder argues is generally synthesized as expectation—developmentally. As a boy, competing and excelling at chess, archery, and scholarship, Siddhartha discovered that anything he put his mind to, as the apt saying goes, left something to be desired. Similarly, as a young man with lovers, ample food, drink, and leisure, he came to reject materialism. Leaving home was very much a declaration of anti-materialism.

Expectation has also been a sort of disruptive force within neuroscience. The mind-as-machine styled information-processing model, once at the heart of the so-called cognitive revolution, has increasingly given way to "embodied cognition".[101] This paradigm is based in the evidence of vibrant processes incoming sensory information. A more dynamic neuroscience of expectation is in the offing as experimental findings paint the picture of a brain that actively imposes would-be, predicted patterns on both "external" sensory data, for example, from the five senses, and internal, within-brain streams of information referred to as interoception. Functions once viewed as orthogonal, such as attention, perception and learning, are seen as intrinsic properties of an active, generative activity centered in prediction, e.g., expectation.

The tumult of top-down and internal and external cognitive streams rolls forward, recruiting, for example, further attentional processes or fields of stored information predicting the next words or meaning in a conversation, one's own or another's movements. It also rolls forward based on a rapid, fluid assessment of data that does not match expectations. These unexpected events or predictive coding errors are key because they optimize the efficiency of the process. Video file compression offers an analogy. Data in subsequent frames need not be recapitulated, only that which is altered. Though still a young science, one can conjecture embodied cognitive processes as componential, as shaping mental experience and, ultimately, as bricks in the superstructure of self/ego/mind. These notions agree with and extend Snyder's preferred translation of the Noble Truth's "desire term" (thirst, clinging) as expectation, adding the non-expectation as a powerful, active process giving rise to awareness.

Siddhartha's developmental journey seems consistent with embodied cognition and a toggling between expectations, wherein viewpoints and decisions based in 'prediction errors' seemed to be in play. Creativity, perceptiveness and imagination, in theory, are just more dimensions of a singular process. These, and for example, breakthroughs in math and science, all stem from a proclivity some possess to see around corners and execute unexpected moves within a grand, integrated matrix of knowledge. Brilliant, sensitive people are similar in their attunement and facility with novelty. Siddhartha's mind, we might surmise, was adept at embodied cognition's toggling between pattern recognition and creative mismatches.

The recognition of novel alternatives within rich patterns corresponds to the relative attachment model's attachment–detachment process. Embodied cognition describes our species' blend of attaching and detaching from all manner of sensory, perceptual and cognitive frames. Siddhartha's journey is right in line. He adopted, then bucked expectations in forsaking the ruler path. In rebelling, he abided, attached to, another cultural–historical expected pattern based in asceticism. This set the well-established wandering monk lifestyle into motion. With the "austerities", Siddhartha disrupted this by pursuing unexpected extremes of the very ideals set out by this lifestyle. As statues of the emaciated monk sitting zazen depict, Siddhartha attempted to achieve liberation from bodily processes such as digestion and breathing. He denied himself food and water until his ribs showed through his skin. He tried to stop breathing, to barely breathe, and searched for the essence, meaning and limits of breathing as a core component of consciousness and sentience.

While these Herculean efforts yielded no lasting peace, there were discoveries, just not the ones that Siddhartha had *in mind* at the outset. He found no gross-level, bodily portal to liberation. As he pushed non-desire to the extremes, he encountered the obvious: risk of starvation, asphyxiation and death. Freedom from attachment, however, could not be achieved by pushing body about as an object. So he moved on, ultimately landing on the "middle way."

In leaving home and surviving the austerities, Siddhartha took on his culture's two major forms of attachment and desire. The first encompasses the householder realm: interpersonal, sexual attachments as well as food, clothing, and shelter, as well as money and power. The second was the rejection of the first practiced by monks and sages. But Siddhartha attempted to do more than just renunciate the householder sphere. He attempted, as rock legend Jim Morrison sings, to "break on through to the other side." As Snyder suggests, the Middle Way unifies and resets attachment as *expectation*.

To approach this, let's consider the classical view of human mental functioning: the time-honored, *psychotic-borderline-neurotic-normal* continuum. This has been a valued heuristic in clinical psychology and psychiatry since the early days of Freud and Jung. It is something like the thermometer in medicine, old school and crude but nonetheless very useful.

Psychotic symptoms, hallucinations, and delusions, are common examples of a mind that is losing grip on reality. Too little attachment to reality seems to track with suffering at this extreme. The very opposite— too much attachment to mental contents—is an equally valid description of the suffering found in severe mental illness. The paranoia in paranoid schizophrenia is borne of demanding voices, often advocating violence. Unlike one's inner voice (the verbal self-talk that ranks as normal), command hallucinations are experienced as "real" voices coming from outside one's head. One is simultaneously overly attached and overly detached in the sense that one can neither run nor hide from these haunting mental contents which are borne of the mind but experienced as external, occurring of their own volition and beyond control. Delusions, commonly of persecution and threats of imminent danger, map the same way. These involve both too much attachment to hellish material and too little attachment to reality.

Classical Continuum of Psychological Functioning

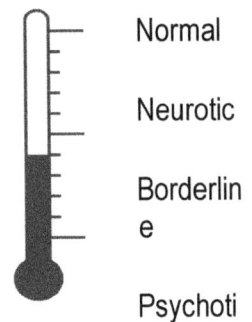

Normal

Neurotic

Borderlin e

Psychoti

The same is true for superficially opposite, positive, "ego-syntonic" material. This includes delusions of grandeur, grandiosity, and the manic episodes in bipolar disorder. A person convinced that they are the second coming of Christ or one who is in an intense euphoric mood state, is very much imprisoned and victimized by their mental illness.

By definition, higher functioning states are more reality-based. At the level of post-traumatic stress, intermittent losses of reality accompany flashbacks. Momentarily, one's hold on reality is shaken during intrusive thoughts. Re-experiencing violence involves too much mind melding with the sights and sounds of traumatic events and too little mind grounding in present day safety.

A stronger grip on reality is found up the ladder in neurosis, such as that experienced by people who might be described as similar to the film director, Woody Allen's iconic characters. These character types may not be oppressed by hallucinations, but they do suffer from the drumbeat of "what if" worries. At the neurotic level, there is a strong possibility of achieving calm and the blessing of loving relationships. But from the Buddhist perspective, this level of functioning is imprisoned. It is overly burdened by grasping, and overly invested in outrunning fears, only to meet more at every turn. Expectations in this frame occur high up the great chain. Whether body-mind-spirit, psychotic-borderline-neurotic-normal, or any major psychological or cognitive developmental theory, there tends to be a recognizable distance between correlates of physiological survival drives (thirst) and functions aligned with neurotic worry. By positioning Siddhartha's central theorem at the neurotic level, we can tentatively form some hypotheses. Before enlightenment—as all humans do—Siddhartha may have viewed others through his own mind and may have been struggling to overcome similar obstacles that he could see burdening others.

Expectations are far more aligned with mind than body. In terms of mental health, they are far more neurotic than what a hundred years of psychotherapy tends to refer to as borderline or, in extremes, psychotic. Samsara differs profoundly as one makes the transition up from insanity to sanity, from psychosis to borderline. The mind (ego or self) most commonly referenced in the dharma is one which grasps and clings and brings about its own suffering. This is very, very different from mental functioning (mind) in the borderline range. Such a mind straddles between neurosis on a good day and an inability to hold on to reality on bad days.

At lower levels of functioning, the mind's grasp of reality slips in and out. The actual, concrete world may seem distant and unreliable. One feels remoteness, with a hit-or-miss hold on what others presumably agree to be life and the world. The sense of self may suffer the same fate and feel disparate, vague, and dreamlike. The call to meditate is not likely to help unless it is combined with multiple support methods, but a full appreciation of the attachment–suffering equation at the heart of Buddhism should leave nobody behind, not even those with deep psychological problems. Before we delve into this, a close look at the attachment at the heart of Buddhism might begin with the view ascribed in the four Noble Truths.

Tanhā & Dukkha

Tanhā and dukkha are intertwined in the Four Noble Truths, the very heartbeat of Buddhism. Dukkha is typically translated as suffering. The first truth is commonly framed as "suffering exists" or "life is suffering." Additional English terms for dukkha include dissatisfaction, anxiety, and stress. A crass Americanized take then is, "life sucks" or "shit happens". The truth of dukkha is also cast as just so, nothing more or less than human nature, the human condition. A common American form of this is, "It is what it is." Stephen Batchelor suggests a further clarification is possible, and that a better English translation is *pain-space* where pain and space correspond to the first and second parts of the word dukkha, respectively.

Tanhā literally translates as thirst or its close cousin, craving. Tanhā is commonly more figuratively aligned with synonyms and variants of desire and attachment. As mentioned, Buddhist scholar, David Snyder persuasively asserts that the most accurate connotation of tanhā is expectation. The linking of the first with the second truth produces the foundational, key precept that attachment results in suffering. Craving is attachment is action or emotion, straddling the physiological (thirst, hunger) to feeling realm (desire, want). But attachment is illusory, Buddha teaches. Such grabs harbor a secret dream of permanence. And so human consciousness finds itself embedded in a quintessential distortion of reality. Suffering co-arises, paradoxically, not itself an obstacle to liberation but a hint regarding the possibility of the cessation of suffering.

The Four Noble Truths can come off as blunt in their critique of attachment. But the Buddha's breakdown of tanhā/craving into three variants adds subtlety. Craving is said to be of three forms.

The first is the common form of craving pertaining to sensory pleasure. The other two are concerned with being and non-being, existence and non-existence. Clinging to existence is self-explanatory. Its partner, vibhava tanhā, deserves a bigger stage.

Because tanhā is so debilitating, the self longs for "separation from it, freedom from it, deliverance from it".[102] This "thirst for nonexistence" is also described as the thirst for self-annihilation.[103]

In the first iteration of tanhā, there is the conventional Buddhist focus: the constant craving, clinging and attachment must be addressed head-on. Relentless desire can be countered by countervailing detachment and renunciation. Here it seems fair to surmise that the first tanhā co-arises arises with vibhava tanhā as a sort of anti-tanhā. With this, the "Noble Truth of the ceasing of suffering" is less lucid and deserving. Presumably, nonexistence would achieve the vaunted end of suffering.[104]

Further reflection from the context of evolutionary, life-supporting attachment sheds light. A more encompassing dance of "to be or not to be" comes about as we make space for the feminine, the biological, the goddess, and the fundamental features of Buddha's Mom. To begin to smash up against this and witness that which arises, we can once again place ourselves within the dyad of Prajapati and Siddhartha. The transmission of the human lineage, the passing on of our species' higher psychological spiritual attainment, has its tender roots in these slow, early, and critical developmental chapters. Ultimately, the mother/child kiln is key to unlocking the Noble Truths.

What can we surmise regarding the origins of self-annihilation? The desire not to eat, not to breathe, and not to exist is hardly an overt biological phenomenon easily observable in the offspring of mammals, primates, or Homo sapiens. This attachment paradigm was obviously a product of its time. The well-established, bifurcated path referenced by prognosticating wise men at Siddhartha's birth, as discussed, put ruler vs. ascetic. Immediately, silently, Siddhartha's existence is rendered from the perspective of adult male psychology. Everything from regular, neurotic pathos to ultimate questions regarding the search for meaning, peace, and happiness is hereby mapped a derivative of troublesome, core drives.

To be sure, the essential equation, life sucks so kill it, persists in all of us, all the time. To be rid of any source of fear, anger, grief, hurt and admixtures of pain-laden emotions must be the most common "experience near" "presenting problem" which clients bring to therapy. We are all moths to this painful flame. No sooner do we voice this desire to be rid of, escape from, fix and undo than we set out to prove that we've tried everything and nothing has worked. Such explanations tend to be part of a psychological fortress, one distinctly lacking creative flexibility or facility with the unexpected. Elaborate defenses are fortified against change, even positive change. The suffering is both profoundly first-person, grinding every bit of hope and joy out of the individual, and it is just as dejected and denied in the third-person. For many people, the very fact that some sort of awful set of circumstances has occurred and that there is no possible way to go back in time and undo events is irrefutable proof of their fate. Humpty Dumpty is shattered and even all the king's men can't put him together again. Buddhism brings an important, fresh perspective to events so tightly bound. It reminds us all that life is replete with suffering. On a deeper stage, Buddhism encourages us to notice that our "blunt force trauma" is alive and ever-changing. There are colorations of pain, contours and shape, and shifts in the words we give to it as we open into a more natural, looser state of being.

In Buddha's Mom, we can find a new appreciation for these co-arising patterns. With respect to a dulled down urge to be rid of third-person pain, to magically just annihilate tanhā, she brings us closer to subtler possibilities. As body, as the home of feelings, she is a ready container to increase consciousness of the emotional substrates of colors and textures. As the source of desire, attachment, and seeking, embers still aglow can be turned into a fiery desire to rediscover this precious existence.

As mother, she brings tenderness and the courage to reunite various parts reeling in pain. In her, a larger, loving witness and presence can be found. As the mother–baby matrix, she cuts through layers of self-talk and incessant walls of words and demands descent to the more salient, essential poetry of the soul. Cells want, organs want, desiring, grasping, and attaching is, as the Vajrayana uniquely expresses, the ultimate object of meditation. One does better to be with all want, the drive to breathe and eat and see and be seen. Life pulses through us—in a word—creatively, creating on the fly some semblance of order, of coherence and connection. By design, this creative ordering is a mutual process, co-arising with wanting, grasping, and attaching at the core. One screams in pain, but with the wisdom and intent to be pain-free.

Chapter Four

INTEGRATING ATTACHMENT

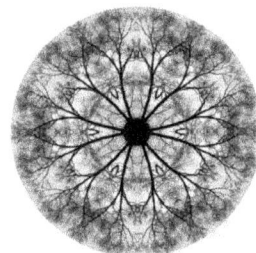

Limitations

Not many of us are likely to read the whole or even most the Pali Canon. An English translation of its "three baskets" produced by the Pali Text Society is comprised of fifty volumes and over 12,000 pages. Some works have not yet been translated into English. In the same vein, few of us are likely to read all of Jung, the research on maternal, biological, social and adult attachment, or develop expertise in neuroscience, receive a transmission from a Lama or excel at Tantric practice—yet these sources are valuable for anyone interested in comprehending consciousness, achieving psychological healing, or cultivating lovingkindness. Those we look up to, even the Dalai Lama, may not have read Wilber or the modern literature on attachment or great thinkers on the feminine principle.

Buddhism provides a response to the challenge of limitations. As we have covered, in his late twenties and early thirties, Siddhartha pursued, and then, as Buddha, came to discover the meaning of all confines and restrictions of awareness. In achieving realization, all identifications dropped away. In the Middle Way, he gave up on his initial effort to fully comprehend and overcome, for example, natural drives. He would extend this insight in declaring that transcending limits does not require that we master subjects or disciplines. As he put it, he does not "dispute" expert claims and leaves such truth claims for those who pursue them.

Buddha's dharma instead promotes the bodhisattva path. Any enlightened being knows of the suffering of others and feels compassion. Having attained ultimate wisdom and compassion, the bodhisattva is compelled to relieve this suffering. They are not content to be content. They recognize our interconnectedness and vow to persist at spiritual practice to bring about the enlightenment of all sentient beings. With the bodhisattva, the question of limitations shifts to, "Am I aware of any suffering anywhere, whatsoever?" If so, one is inspired by bodhicitta to press on, fueled by an intention to free all beings from samsara. The bodhisattva path can be framed as follows: "Am I aware of the end of suffering for all beings?" If so, there is nowhere else to be. This life offers only more perfection. Any conception that there is a need to be or have more metta or prajna, any compulsion to read more books on Buddhism or do more retreats, falls away.

Thankfully, we have the story of the Buddha and an attachment lens as a guide. Recall that Kisa was a young mother in deep, intractable grief whom Buddha instructed to go in search of the mustard seeds. When Buddha first learned of her, she was inconsolable and carrying around her deceased child. A limited version of her predicament was sufficient for him not only to help her, but also for her to benefit. Omniscience is not required for enlightenment. Our hearts can be bolstered in that luminaries such as Thich Nhat Hahn, Pema Chödrön, Chögyam Trungpa, and Reggie Ray do not claim encyclopedic knowledge or psychic powers.

Rather, they know enough to know that knowing more is not necessary. Time and again, the Pali canon tells of mere mortals who were fortunate to meet Buddha and who subsequently become arhats or achieved even higher attainment. In each case, Buddha came to know the other person's difficulty through regular, limited means, and then he empathically communicated his understanding in such a way as to bring the other into the open space of their true nature. As a result, the other found release.

With Kisa, for example, we might presume that Buddha had infinite knowledge of her human plight but perhaps was not knowledgeable of every biographical detail of her life. Certainly, the Canon does not suggest that Buddha relied on unlimited, biographical knowledge in his interactions or teachings. The specifics of Kisa's psychosocial development, serotonergic brain activity or archetypes operating in her deep psyche falls into the same category as expert knowledge. He would not dispute it, but he would also not require it to fluidly interact, teach and transmit the dharma.

Kisa, Buddha's mother, stepmother, wife, father, and Ananda are among the many in this genre. Here we have simply suggested that these relationships were likely informed by what, in a modern analysis, was psychological attachment. This, in turn, fosters a more intensive, personal transmission of lovingkindness coupled with a critical instruction, a personal teaching for the one in pain, stymied by dukkha. Overlapping elements comprising Buddha's Mom suggest the following possibility. As Buddha will do with so many in his family, among his followers and even doubters, he and Kisa achieved a "we-space." The first-person plural helped those who needed help transcend the bonds of the first person single, "I" (self/ego/mind). This single-to-plural movement later formed the context of a plural, more specifically relational ego. In the case of Buddha and Kisa, the we-space emerged by virtue of a mutual understanding of the loss, pain, and attachment issues at hand. Kisa communicated these via her body language and story, of course. The magic then occurred in the fullness, understanding, and compassion of Buddha's response.

Some more humble version of this occurs, on occasion, in personal growth and therapeutic venues. What is important to notice is that the "I" is both honored (included, preserved) and dismissed (transcended and negated). Once again, the "I" and ego serve as a bridge that falls into the sea, but not before facilitating passage to the other side.

Vajrayana master, Reggie Ray discusses the egoic co-opting of boundless love. This is the central, profound human foible, a grand mistake but one so very natural and ordained by evolution. This syncs perfectly with my own glimpses of the extra-ordinary and super-natural. Ego's ill-fated co-opting of what is boundless love explains so much, including Kisa's plight. This parallels the concept that even "bad press" is better than none. Love is always good, even when it crushes. She so loved her baby. The problem was holding on to that love. The heart never holds, Reggie Ray explains. Rather holding is synonymous with mind.[105]

Dharma talks and talk therapy wobble back and forth at this very juncture. They toy with massive, detailed information gathering and processing and aim for limitless healing, ultimate letting go, a lasting forgiveness, and total recovery from trauma or spiritual attainment. As a result, words and ideas about limitlessness are tossed back and forth, chewed and digested in limited, phenomenological mental webs.

Wilber negotiates this span from human mind to human potential by employing what he refers to as "orienting generalizations." As the name suggests, these are shorthand versions of elaborate ideas, models and theories. Orienting generalizations can take the form of "rules of thumb" or heuristics. These are decidedly imperfect conceptualizations that serve the larger cause, that of a richer, fuller embrace of ultimate matters such as consciousness and enlightenment. Wilber often advises his readers not to confuse the map with the territory. His goal seems to be to provide a framework that can keep up with future discoveries. In his tour de force, *Sex, Ecology and Spirituality,* he offers this overview:

> …this broad orienting map is nowhere near fixed and final. In addition to
> being composed of broad orienting generalizations, I would say is a book of a
> thousand hypotheses. I will be telling the story as if it were simply the case
> (because telling it that way makes for much better reading), but not a
> sentence to follow is not open to confirmation or rejection by a community of
> the adequate.[106]

The key is the interplay among these shorthand maps where transcend and include happens. In combination, orienting generalizations provide huge boosts in precision, integration, and depth. The use of imperfect, scratchpad, summary versions of rich theories and ideas serves the larger goal of integration of large numbers of ideas or sources. By definition, infinite knowledge—e.g., the wisdom side of enlightenment—is unachievable on the relative side of the street, and the same goes for compassion, metta, and lovingkindness. Without orienting generalizations, according to Wilber, the "level of details…is finitely impossible."[107] We cannot get there from here. There is, in fact, no "there" here.

Wilber sometimes likens this ("no there here" and the utility of orienting generalizations) to 10,000 foot views from a helicopter, decidedly mid-level in their specificity. There's a vast chasm between any idea, poem, or theoretical construct and an individual's psychology. Certainly, the same is true of this book. As what amounts to partial truths at the deepest levels of an individual's self/ego/mind overlap, the possibility of immediate, direct experiential leaps increase. Buddhists use many words for what is already present but what feels subjectively as if it comes into clear view, for example, the primordial ground of being. The built-in litmus test for any teaching or offering is ultimately how profoundly it translates the ineffable. The possibility of sustaining a life connection to the primordial ground increases as the field of mind and self are transcended. Sticking with the metaphor, during personal descents below the 10,000-foot level, the view, the beauty, the resolution expands in all directions.

For the concept of Buddha's Mom to have value, she would necessarily translate as more than a concept and as personally, indeed profoundly, relevant. But at the same time, the value would be just as ordinary as the ground below and the stars above. She would enrich one's daily practice and interpersonal relations. This possibility, for many of us, depends on the intellectual scope of a lesson being taught. Does it add clarity to already rich, combinatorial, extant maps of the depths? These include maps of unconscious psychodynamics and those pertaining to neuroscience and the brain's galaxy of neurons.

Another important feature is that one person's orienting generalization translates differently for another person. Zen tales often follow the form of a master saying a few words to a student to tip the scales toward enlightenment. The retelling of these, of course, may have the same uncanny, personal fit, and the same liberating effect. A person may feel as if the teacher or author is talking directly to them.

Ideas that inspire involve orienting generalizations. For a smaller number listening or reading, the same ideas may penetrate below the 10,000-foot elevation. An *ah ha* moment is one of a more profound, close-up, personal tipping point. In the view we are considering, such a moment can be mapped within relative attachment. There occurs a psycho-spiritual attachment to something that may be inspiring for another person, helpful, but not personally revelatory.

Orienting generalizations use skillful mental means. They grow in utility, precision, and power as they are integrated with one another. For instance, Wilber's integral life practice includes his writing, an outpouring of his essence much as a dharma talk is an extension of a teacher. When the student is ready, as the saying goes, the teacher appears. When the teacher and student are really, truly ready (laden with wisdom and lovingkindness, for example) the dharma appears, unstoppable and unfiltered.

Spirit

Living, fluid, relational integration of body, mind and soul, self and other, in wego, and in the enveloping of sentience in cosmos. Witness as fluid, transformational, experiential, emptying, freeing frame. Buddha's Mom as our species' root lineage; access to constant transmission as space. Subtle, felt sense of oneness; lightness, nonholding equanimity, nonlocal sentience. Spiritual vitriol, protector deities in Tibetan Buddhism; everpresent, permeating compassion emboldening dharma's presence. Tonglen, bodhisattva and practice forms as expressions of the primordial, boundless ground of being.

Mind

Cognitive schema flowing from attachment-detachment programming. Locus of language and cognition. 8-fold path's right understanding, thought and speech. Fetters: ignorance, conceit, doubt. Paramitas: morality, truthfulness. Tanha as mental expectation. Dukkha as existential namable angst and dissatisfaction. Left hemisphere speech, language, temporality, planning. Dharma in words, as philosophy and law.

Feeling / Emotion

Attachment-love, social attachment, kindness, compassion, nurturing and metta. Emotions driving 8-fold path's right action & effort. Hindrances: sensual desire, anger, sloth, anxiety/worry. Paramitas: generosity, lovingkindness. Kleshas: fear, anger, hatred, jealousy, greed. Panksepp's seven effects: seeking-expectancy and anticipatory euphoria as master affective system, and other six associated with rage, care, lust, fear, panic & grief and play. Polyvagal influence on preconscious and conscious mentation shaping perception, felt sense and apriori meaning. Spans upper neurotic to lower deep self disturbance and borderline/volative, hyperaroused affective states.

Body/Soma

Biological attachment. Tanhā as cellular, protoplasmic to physiological drive for environmental Tonglen, exchange, for energy sources, nutrition and oxygen. Hunger, thirst, temperature regulation. Ground of perceptual disturbance in psychosis. Biotensegrity and fascia as sensory substrate and vessel of somatic inputs, including proprioceptive, interoceptive and polyvagal neuroception. Dharma as unending vessel, holonic, earth-soma, soma-breath, soma-lower belly, soma-skin, soma-organ container/bridges of sentience. Body as portal to death awareness and union with trans-sentient Vajra body, nibbana and nondual ground.

Great Chain

The "great chain," popularly referred to as body-mind-spirit, was re-envisioned by Ken Wilber early and often. The great chain is a frame for the embodiment and transmission of consciousness in humans. With Buddha's Mom, this is recast in terms of the "two attachments." The disbanding and letting go of attachments co-arises with the birth, nurturing and mirroring of mind in a relational space. The potential in this concept is as accessible and relevant today as ever.

> The Great Chain of Being—that is perhaps a bit of a misnomer, because, as I said, the actual view is more like the Great Nest of Being, with each senior dimension enveloping or enfolding its junior dimension(s)—a situation often described as "transcend and include". Spirit transcends but includes soul, which transcends but includes mind, which transcends but includes the vital body, which transcends but includes matter. This is why the Great Nest is most accurately portrayed as a series of concentric spheres or circles.[108]

He refers to these spheres as holons, each both a part and a whole. This helps soften hierarchical framing and thereby facilitates a deeper appreciation of the subtlety of dependent origination (pratītyasamutpāda). According to this core Buddhism tenet, nothing that arises does so independent of causes and conditions.

Returning to our main subject, the nested fields Wilber describes can be experienced as alive, as having an immediate, animated sensibility. Mother holons are part-persons, whole in their co-arising with a budding child holon. The child holon by virtue of attachment is part a new emergent force, and whole within maternal/social attachment frames.

Parallels of these living co-arisings map across body–mind, yin–yang, and the two attachments, to name a few. In these nestings of human consciousness, various "sides" such as the feminine divine, earth spirituality, subconscious matrices, species' and interspecies' consciousness co-arise with more familiar, closer sources of lived experience.

These dances are everywhere, but become more relevant with personal, emotional, and intellectual engagement. Without a tether to love, engagement is egoic. As co-arising bands on the great chain are experienced, the subjective mind necessarily splits off from these as objects: experiencee and experiencer. Formless ground is simply the act of noticing itself. According to this core Buddhist principle, pratītyasamutpāda, with awareness, the dance of consciousness fades and its objects disappear in the "stilling of the conditioned". With Buddha's Mom, we understand this in terms of a return to the love that surpasses, that flows through the species, and that is accessible in attachment relationships.

Consciousness transmitted across the ages is formless and always, already fully present and accessible. Perhaps Buddha's enlightenment can be understood as arising from his receptivity as Siddhartha to this pre-existing pulse as it moves through the species. As Buddha, he unleashes an uncanny skill at stilling the commotion. This receptivity grows in holarchal rings, ever wider and freer, and ever less distinguishable from formless ground. Metaphorically (at least), Buddha is therefore no longer subject to rebirth.

Holarchy also offers a rich means of mapping the classical spheres of the good, true and beautiful. Wilber shows how this triad is another very useful heuristic corresponding to arts (concerned with beauty), science (with truth), and morals (the question of the good). Yet another heuristic and central feature of the integral model by Wilbur is the continuum from egocentric to ethnocentric to world-centric. He uses terms such as wave, level, and structure to demonstrate methods of seeking syntheses across multiple developmental models.

For Wilber, the term *fundamental* best captures the essence of older, lower, precursor waves, levels, nests, spheres, or rings, and *significant* for the evolutionary higher, newer ones. As such, body and biology are more fundamental and mind and spirit more significant. Buddha's Mom would be "fundamental" in some way to "significant" Buddhist constructs. For example, on the most concrete biological plane, she played some fundamental role. She successfully carried the fetus and nurtured the infant who would one day give the world the Heart Sutra.

Vibhava Tanhā

Everyone knows that the Buddha did not mince words with respect to the perils of attachment. But not everyone knows that he defined three types of attachment. Probably the least familiar of these, vibhava tanhā, deserves more consideration. This translates as "thirst for non-existence" and differs in important ways from orthodox tanhā, e.g., attachment as craving and desire.

Circling back, the top-billing variant, technically kāma-tanhā, translates as thirst, hunger, the drive for sensorial satiation and sense pleasure. In line with this, conventional Buddhist views on attachment fractal across sense desires, hunger, the drive for affection, for sexual satisfaction and on to grasping, generic wanting and desiring. Most everyone in the hospital just wants to go home. A secure base calls even when it comes in the form of street drugs.

Kāma-tanhā pulls for everything the mind perceives as "attractive, pleasant, comforting (and) inspiring".[109] The desire for all this, according to the second noble truth, is the cause of dukkha or suffering, yielding the tanhā-dukkha pairing—the perfect, tragic chicken-egg /egg-chicken cycle at the heart of humanity. As even babies know, not getting what one wants hurts. But babies do not demonstrate the third form; they thirst, to be sure, but not in any obvious manner, for nonexistence.

The second of the three forms of attachment, bhava-tanhā, is less of a puzzle. This translates as a craving for survival or continued existence.[110] We seek ever more engagement in life to be, become, and understand. One is compelled to lean into life. This certainly appears consistent with self/ego/mind. The second form of attachment helps clarify how maturation, development, and the cultivation of identity is ultimately illusory and no less a cause of suffering than seeking satisfaction through the senses.

This second form or secondary description of attachment underscores how becoming is a slippery form of desire. This tanhā exposes the myth of achieving satisfaction at all! This mother of all inconvenient truths casts suspicion on our collective infatuation with dharma talks, books like this, meditation goals, and with self-help and self-improvement generally. Perhaps such modalities need a Buddhist surgeon general's warning, "Self-improvement has been determined to be illusory and therefore hazardous to your spiritual health." Perhaps the final coda should be, "Don't improve, awaken!"

In calling out bhava-tanhā, the Buddha communicates that you should not settle for, and not be overly infatuated by, life as learning. A powerful, alternative vantage on this comes from the Greek tenet, pathei mathos, "BY SUFFERING, LEARNING." Perhaps the Greeks can be said to have transformed dukkha into an art form, that is to say tragedy. Underlying this, at least according to Aeschylus in *Agamemnon*, is this notion extending the tanhā-duke pairing to learning.[111] We attach, we suffer, we learn—whether we like it or not.[112]

Recalling further the premise of "causes and conditions" of dependent origination, logically and inescapably, this yields to the formulation that learning and self-improvement are suffering. If

Buddha somehow came back to the earth today, one could reasonably speculate that he would have compassion for but not necessarily sanction us note-taking, book-reading seekers.

The third form of attachment, vibhava tanhā, adds more heat. Truly special from the perspective of this project, this "thirst for non-existence" or "for non-becoming"[113] turbo boosts the old adage "life is suffering". As any of us well-meaning, would-be Buddhists try hard to cease attaching for a blink-and-a-half, we run headlong into this other attachment. Socratic confusion, *aporia*, takes hold—and if we are lucky, some clarity alongside. Relative attachment, after all, is an equal opportunity exploiter. Its detachment pole is just as potent, just as lethal and just as beautiful. Let's listen to Buddha once more. So bewildering, relentless and pain-ridden is the major clinging, craving tanhā, that the self naturally longs for "separation from it, freedom from it, deliverance from it".[114]

One who realizes that he or she is a bottomless pit of need *and* a project repelling against this is close. Ever-becoming and improving *and* psychologically suicidal. Confused, desperate, driven to escape, all this arises within a separate peace, a most rarified frequency. One Taste. To know firsthand these sides of tanhā and feel their dukkha, to realize these processes as they rise and fall; and to chop wood, carry water and answer emails sure sounds like the *'realizing one is realized'* notion mentioned at the outset of this book.

Vibhava tanhā illuminates self-improvement's shadow. In response to Wilber's transcending and negating model, this attachment arises in versions of, "Look at me not attaching!" Building a self around letting go and helping others to let go, around talks and books on letting go, becomes the new "cool". Self/ego/mind jettisons materialism, but survives the trip across the river. The lazy mirror equivalent is, "I'm horrible at all this." One was perfect before and is perfect now. Practice is needed to rest in between and beyond rest stops.

In identifying bhavā-tanhā and vibhava tanhā, the Buddha declared self-improvement and letting go, together and separately, to be just as delusional and entrapping as their top-billing sibling. To desire or (to desire) not to desire returns us to the question, paradox, and ecstasy of Hamlet's "to be or not to be." Too much identification with distancing or destroying is attachment/desire for non-becoming.

Vibhava tanhā reveals the master's loving insight into our species' plight. He spent fierce years in the wilderness. On returning, he needed some time, some more silence. When he put what he knew into words, he expressed that to be human is to be riddled with the gnawing, needy, inwardly collapsing pulse of self/ego/mind. Alongside this are built-in urges running in the other direction.

Passive suicidality is part and parcel with being emotionally overwhelmed and depressed. The individual doesn't want to experience a love which rejects or health that eludes. No longer wanting to live in pain. "The world would be better off without me," they claim. They would like to go to sleep and never wake up. My patients in the hospital routinely express this, often so very reasonably. Freud referred to the "death wish" and Jung more globally to the dark, destructive, shadow side of archetypes.

Hardly rare, the same incentivizes meditation, therapy, and healthcare. Motivations are often more overtly negative than positive, e.g., to get rid of X. Tennis great, Jimmy Connors nailed it when he said he hated to lose more than be loved to win. Neuropsychologist and Buddhist Rick Hanson concluded that the brain is Teflon for positivity and Velcro for negativity.

A teen screams, texts, tweets current speak for "go to hell" as she attempts to banish a once beloved, now hated other from wego. Minds online, in offices, in traffic, on airplanes scurry about in similar, less intensive variants of attraction and repulsion. Discursive thoughts encircle, land, queue up, and take off. Distinctions between busy and productive, serious and casual, concrete and abstract, garner inordinate energy. But all are a perfect hell.

Ancestor worship is an indigenous, concrete experience of lineage transmission. A teen's angst and heartbreak is very concrete as well. Less obvious is its perfection. Babies born amid a volcanic firestorm, their skin melting off before they can feed from mom, may prove that there is always a relatively worse hell. To be born human and not die at one-hour old proves the existence of a relatively more exquisite heaven. At some rarified strata, even compassion is judgment and breathing is greedy. One does not get there from here. If there is perfection, then there is only perfection.

Buddha was a just a person, the larger point being that so are you and so am I. He was our equal, as a person. He simply stopped pushing back against his nature. He had to use words still and came to refer to emptiness. For all of us who still do not realize we are realized, words and formulations, this sentence in fact, lay flat. "Emptiness does not destroy discursive thought. And discursive thought does not block emptiness."[115] In personhood is perfection.

> Whosoe'er abandon Thirst, (and are) Without the Thirst for Existence or
> Non-existence. They (while) in the world have passed over (to the other
> shore).[116]

Secular Buddhism

Secular Buddhism concurs in principle with a non-religious, scientific approach to our main topic. Theirs is a fresh, egalitarian, empirically-oriented Buddhism—a *best practices* approach. Related terms include lay, agnostic, atheist, and American Buddhism. These vectors are marked by skepticism about supernatural claims and religious dogma. Author of the bestselling books, *Buddhism Without Beliefs* and *Confession of a Buddhist Atheist*, Stephen Batchelor describes an early experience where this clear-eyed reasoning momentarily faltered. He was in conversation with a small group of fellow followers after the Dalai Lama Yeshe Dorje had given a talk. In "reverential tones", the discussion turned to how their great leader may have stopped the rain from soaking those in attendance.

> I heard myself say: "And you could hear the rain still falling all around us:
> over there by the Library and on those government buildings behind the
> Library as well." The others nodded and smiled in awed agreement. Even as
> I was speaking, I knew I was not telling the truth. I had heard no rain on the
> roofs behind me. Not a drop.[117]

This vignette opens a window into the sensitivity and discipline of an advanced meditator at a young age. As we all often do, Batchelor was swayed by emotion and ignored the inner voice which tried to steer him back to reason. As the expression goes, he "wanted to believe", in this case, in a "magical umbrella" as a sort of extension of the great leader's compassion. Batchelor goes on to analyze the implications of this psychic fissure. As is often the case, some aspects were temporary and others more long-lasting:

> I suspect my life did not feel like a lie because it served to affirm what I
> believe to be a greater truth. My words were a heartfelt and spontaneous
> utterance of our passionately shared convictions. In a weirdly unnerving
> way, I did not feel that "I" had said them.[118]

Such moments are phenomenologically formed by any number of external, interpersonal and intrapersonal forces. One very helpful lens is that of the first, second and third person. Here an encompassing third-person "it" is conjured by the ceremony and weather situation. Most notably, a powerful, first-person plural was in play: the interpersonal and intersubjective, "we-space" evoked by Batchelor in reverent union with his fellow monks. An intrapersonal, intrasubjective deferential witnessing was co-incidental, co-arising. Batchelor sensitively captures many such factors in his writing. His first-person takes on a passive, dispassionate tone. He refers to his lie as a well-intended but errant, third-person, "it". And further attributes this to forces, much like the weather, which could not be blamed but also which were outside of the powers of reason to change. His arm-distance lie, according to his restored, rational, up-close first-person, "was employed, was imparted to us by men of unimpeachable moral and intellectual character."[119]

These "men of unimpeachable moral and intellectual character" and the "greater truths" that Batchelor refers to are heavy-duty third-person elements. These had seeped in and colored the hushed, reverent sensibility informing the first-person plural, the we-space gathering and from there the singular, first-person—self/ego/mind's mainstay. Here, we see how the intimacy of an immersive "we", an absorption in an immediate small circle of special friends on occasions often dubbed auspicious, led to problems. The little tribe at hand had inadvertently hitched their wagon to the great one's star. Batchelor never claimed any first-person power to make clouds part but rather explains how a "we" sensibility crossed into such grandiose distortions. Batchelor has become justly famous and important for his program of "recovering the dharma for a secular age".

Batchelor's experience goes to show how the authoritarian dynamic famously studied Stanley Milgram comes in many guises. In 1961, Stanley made what a colleague described as the "single greatest contribution to human knowledge ever made by the field of social psychology, perhaps psychology in general."[120] In Milgram's study, volunteers were instructed to provide electroshock to what they assumed were other volunteers. He discovered that people would often ignore their personal beliefs to follow instructions from someone in authority. My many years of work, often with very accomplished, complex, intelligent but underperforming people, has led me to the same conclusion. Often the deep-seated mechanisms underlying the "Milgram Effect" prove to be important.

Milgram's work is typically covered in introductions to psychology courses. Subjects in his experiment are counter-intuitively willing to administer electric shocks to a fellow human being, when a man in a white coat claims he will take full responsibility for the experiment. In a sense, the saffron robe replaces the white coat in Batchelor's story. However, there is much more subtlety and complexity than first meets the eye, especially when the archetypal space and psychological potential of the feminine, which we are referring to as Buddha's Mom, is brought to bear.

Milgram's work points to a powerful, unconscious dominance/submission filter in operation in Homo sapiens. Numerable replications of the original experiment, including creative variations across multiple cultures, are conclusive: humans are far more prone to perceiving obedience cues and to submitting to authority, and to doing so without conscious reflection, than we believe ourselves to be. This fact is only a bit less disconcerting when we consider that the dominance/submission dynamic runs through most of our mammalian and primate relatives, who presumably navigate similar behavioral territory with less awareness.

Varieties of hierarchy, dominance and submission examples are everywhere. In a common structure found in Buddhist sangha such as Batchelor describes, one or a small number of people are in authority. Often, the authority figure has a small cadre of close attendants. This is structurally the same as a general and his lieutenants or a CEO and vice presidents in a corporation. The biggest desk, the higher seat, who speaks, who is spoken to—all fall into place accordingly. Statues of Buddha have ornate layered pedestals, elaborations of the cushion no different structurally than the throne of a monarch. In Southeast Asia, one ducks their head and if necessary must fold completely over while walking near a monk to ensure his is the higher head.

In keeping with an integral spirit, one should not make too much of any one view… or too little. A Jungian angle would have us wonder whether some pre-conscious, collective, archetypal influences might also have been in play. Such elements may carry a similar third person authority within the psyche. They can operate like powerful figures in white coats, as investigated by Milgram. They have their way with egos that unconsciously give over their own authority. Batchelor's vignette suggests possibilities for archetypes along the lines of the old wise man and the wizard (shaman, medicine man). Each has a counterpart, others being the boss, king, chief and dutiful disciple/servant, general and foot soldier.

The integral model maps typical ways that humans privilege certain phenomenological streams over others. Any of these streams may be conscious or not, fluidly predominant and accessible or nonexistent, depending on multitude of factors. As mentioned, major developmental way stations include archaic, magic, mythic, rational and beyond. In multiple books, Wilber has exhaustively outlined these "vertical" "great chains" and duly credited scholars throughout history for subsections of what he has built into a massively integrated matrix of this and other major dimensions of consciousness. His complete oeuvre exceeds the scope of this book. The point of contention here concerns the proper weight of so-called irrational contents such as those described by Batchelor.

A Jungian or depth analysis views magical and mythological content, such as the birth story of Siddhartha, in which he walks and talks when he is seven days old, as having a certain psychological purity and therefore having truth and importance. Themes, symbols, and motifs have merit (one could just as well say they embody skillful means) by virtue of their collective basis. The "collective unconscious" could just as well be called the "integral unconscious". Certainly, the Pali Canon's many embedded legends and mythological references need to be appreciated as culturally and historically embedded, and not mistaken for empirical fact. But if one's encounter with this dimension of the Canon does little more than vaguely "inspire", one may be missing all that depth that psychology brings to the table.

The provenance of the fanciful, hyperbolic canonical elements that permeate the Canon is born of our shared humanity and sentient inheritance. Those who carried forth Buddhism's early oral tradition, and those involved in the writing of the Buddhist canon, had the same brains as we do. In addition, they had a more direct, firsthand experience of the early flavorings. The magical and mythological passages certainly reveal distortions of the premodern era. At the same time, the dismissing of such content reflects distortions intrinsic to our own time and place. Thankfully, an integral, depth approach, as suggested, provides a corrective lens.

Psychologically Brahmanical

Batchelor's eagerness to strip away religious trappings (a loaded term, to be sure) and directly, freely witness and report on his own process of encountering the dharma has deservedly garnered a big following. Batchelor is considering the title, "After Buddhism" for a future book, to be subtitled "rethinking the dharma for a secular age." Great scholars and teachers revise their own insights even when they are held in esteem for having forged these in the first place. The story of Batchelor lapsing irrational in the presence of friends and their beloved lama is emblematic of his ability to do U-turns and see things afresh.

At one point, Batchelor declared that the four Noble Truths should be translated as the "four ennobling truths". He wanted to place the emphasis not on truths being handed down from on high but on the psychologically transformational power. Later he refined his thinking further. Dropping the term "truth", he stated that an even better handle on the Four Noble Truths is the "four tasks" or just "the four". Batchelor's shifting away from the use of both the terms for noble and truth stems from the entomology of the original Sanskrit term, *arya*.

> Although the term Four Noble Truths is well known in English, it is a misleading translation of the Pali term *Chattari-ariya-saccani* (Sanskrit: *Chatvari-arya-satyani*), because *noble* (Pali: *ariya*; Sanskrit: *arya*) refers not to the truths themselves but to those who understand them. A more accurate rendering, therefore, might be "four truths for the [spiritually] noble," they are four facts that are known to be true by those with insight into the nature of reality but that are not known to be true by ordinary beings.[121]

As Batchelor interprets, the term tends to be associated with a person's level of realization. It shows up in *ariya puggala*, meaning both "noble person" and one destined for enlightenment. Naturally, such men were members of an *arya sangha*, defined also as the collective body of noblemen. When Buddha's son, Rahula, naively asked for his material inheritance rather than pursue his spiritual legacy, Buddha responded, "I will give him the sevenfold Ariyan wealth which I obtained under the Bo-tree, and make him the heir of a spiritual inheritance!" Once again, the term linked to "noble" has a sense of coming down from on high.

Batchelor works at disentangling these cultural overlays to demystify Buddha's message and uncover its more accessible, populist voice. In also advocating that the four Noble Truths no longer be laden as "truth", he helps to shift the emphasis toward science over religion. In science, there are no truths, only theories. Some theories, such as Newtonian physics, rise and subside. Others, such as evolutionary theory and black holes, overcome severe resistance before enjoying a long ascent toward belief. None, at least for the scientifically-minded, are big-T truth. The important distinction holds: theories may be proven correct or valid over and again but they must remain theory. They must be, in theory, falsifiable. This is a deeply Buddhist principle. Just begin with any pedestrian truth. One may concede that perhaps black holes will turn out to be some sort of misunderstanding, but "I know I have two eyes, two ears and a mouth." Who is this "I," Buddhism asks?

The secular Buddhist movement increasingly views Buddhist practices and principles as human practices and principles, the validity of which can and should be based on a rational, empirical foundation. Concepts should not be accepted without deep, personal assessment. Ideas, precepts, claims, and the like should ultimately be falsifiable and dropped or amended accordingly based on rigorous, careful, introspective analysis. Buddha addressed this directly in the Kalama sutra. Often understood as the disclaiming his own personal divinity, this commentary also underscores his emphasis on detachment. His pursuit of truth led him to take care when making claims regarding truth. He had studied the information available on the world's religions and no doubt was witness to the usual ways that religions fall short of their own claims. Famously, he would state:

> Do not believe in what ye have heard. Do not believe in traditions, because
> they have been handed down for many generations. Do not believe in
> anything because it is renowned and spoken of by many. Do
> not believe merely because the written statement of some old sage is
> produced. Do not believe in conjectures. Do not believe in that as truth to
> which you have become attached by habit. Do not believe in anything merely
> on the authority of your teachers and elders. Often observation and analysis,
> when the result agrees with reason, is conducive to the good and gain of one
> and all. Accept and live up to it.[122]

One must not habitually attach to "that as truth" Buddha asserts. Breaking this down a bit, the Kalama sutra speaks with clarity on the notion of "truth" and seems to thereby support Batchelor's interest in dropping both noble and truth. He suggests the phrase, "four tasks" or simply, "the four". Batchelor also addresses problems with the term translated as noble. Everyone knows how the term *arya* made an ugly resurgence in the Nazi era with the goal of purification of the *Aryan* race.

> The Vedic Sanskrit word arya first appears in the Rig Veda (2000–1500BCE)
> where it is used as the name of a group of people who had migrated into
> India from perhaps what is now Iran (from arya) in prehistoric times and
> gradually subdued the aboriginals who they called dasa or dasyu. Like most
> peoples, the aryas saw themselves as superior to others and the word arya
> gradually came to mean 'noble', 'esteemed' or 'superior.' By the time of the
> Buddha the word had come to include the idea of ethical or intellectual
> excellence and the Buddha always used it in that sense. Thus in the Tipitaka
> we have terms like Ariya sacca = Noble Truth, and many others.[123]

Even if a fairer translation is "excellent" or "highly valuable", Batchelor's larger point remains. The tendency to elevate precept, concepts, and principles may sometimes go a little too far and lose something important along the way. Immutable truth inadvertently stymies spiritual process. The person asked to believe in, have faith in, or come to know a truth is likely to feel chronically inept. An "ariyan" superior, noble and exalted "sacca" or truth alienates. Short of realization, ours is an ever-morphing replay of two-sided relative attachment which presumptions of a "truth" hurts more than helps. The more we trust or believe it, the more we inevitably feel that we fall short. This parallels the patriarchal overlay, a yang, and sky God bias, on "the word of God", all the official lists over what readers will eventually come to appreciate as a much more earth-based, indigenous Buddhism.

An evolutionary synthesis might go something like this: Buddhamind is the pinnacle of human consciousness. It is the icing on the cake, and the cake itself is human evolution. Relative to prior plateaus, the artifact record shows a rapid expansion of hunting and fishing skills, trading, and artistic, personalized ornamentation. Some researchers trace this to 150,000 years ago, and others argue that a "great leap forward" and "human revolution" occurred a mere 40,000 years ago. With these advancements, consciousness does the unimaginable. It looks back at itself. As we have suggested, this occurs within attachment we-spaces of endless variety, self/ego/mind arising with nature, gods, the feminine, luck and fortune, the tribe, other animals, seasons, and so on.

Buddha accomplishes a further leap and a revolution of another order. He saw the whole play of co-arising attachment with diamond precision. He saw how attachment was an *a priori* condition and how attachment permeates consciousness. He saw that freedom, clarity, and the transcending of our great inheritance, of evolutionary consciousness, comes with the realization of attachment's reach. This insight certainly deserves superlatives, if it must be put into words at all.

Batchelor's work serves as a reminder that religious and cultural trappings are the same the whole world round. Where there is profound insight, someone will bottle and sell it. *Four steps to bliss or your money back*. "I'm with the band," is the old line referring to rock star wannabes angling to get backstage, close to the liminality and luminaries. Sources of light. The enlightened ones. Few of us are beyond such temptation or immune to such inflations. Jung said he was fortunate to be Jung and not a Jungian. The message implied has real depth and speaks to problems arising from well-intended allegiances, to identity way-stations and what we have been referring to as self/ego/mind. But the way out is through not back and away from anything that moves us. Dominance and submission, allegiance and rejection, are gates to awakening. As are first-person and we-based organizing principles of experience. The much-adored Ananda helps make this point.

Ananda

Buddha's devoted attendant and disciple, Ananda, offers a singularly moving account of adult attachment and the power and importance of the second-person, we-space. Ananda makes for a tremendous resource on this journey toward a unified attachment, one that transcends and includes what we began discussing as the two attachments. This unique relationship of eight decades is only rivaled by that of Prajapati, adopted mom, stepmom, eternal devotee eventually inaugurated as the first Buddhist nun. The Pali Canon covers many of Ananda's little crises of faith, filled as they were with earnest, sweet confusion—perfect lessons for the rest of us. These are often served up in dharma talks and seem almost designed for this purpose.

Perhaps an as-yet-to-be-fully-appreciated perspective on Ananda is that informed by attachment theory. The descriptions of Ananda point to a high-functioning, devoted, advanced practitioner, and also very much to a man who struggled with detachment. Buddha, over and again, patiently, mindfully prescribed detachment. Ananda sauntered off, then returned with a new version of the original concern. Ananda is the delightful, handwringing, well-intentioned follower who is supremely sympathetic.

Buddha's Mom offers a less traveled perspective. It is curious about the ingredients that coalesce in great spiritual heights such as that represented by Ananda. First off, all the evidence indicates that both had and has come to symbolize the views and struggles of a cohesive, mature, adult self/ego/mind's close encounters with ultimate liberation. His narrative force is bound up in how most of us experience his plight. On the one hand, we may secretly sympathize with his dilemma in life. He was brilliant and dedicated, but his best intentions somehow did not get him across the finish line.

Ananda was renowned for his phenomenal capacity to recount Buddha's teachings word for word. In the Ananda parables, we meet someone so earnest that he often fails to see the forest for the trees. His endearing dedication has him stumbling over the letter and missing out on the spirit of the teachings.

Ananda was clearly not unstable, disturbed, or mentally impaired. He was Siddhartha-Buddha's confidant and his most trusted aide. These many signs help us triangulate on his attachment style. And of course his parents gave him a name that means "joy". In all likelihood, Ananda did not suffer from forms of deep self disturbance corresponding to the borderline and psychotic bands on the classical continuum of mental functioning.

His constant seeking of reassurance from the Buddha and a devotion bordering on codependency may be indicative of some garden-variety neurosis. In total, what we know of Ananda fits the outlines of an anxious adult attachment style, one that attachment research shows tends to stem from a similar insecure attachment experience in early life.

For these babies, the process of inculcating a psychologically secure base is decidedly partially successful. Sometimes mom is adequate, responsive and appropriately mirrors the baby's states and needs, and sometimes she is not. Theory and research findings demonstrate that a lack of early parental support evolves into an anxious adult close relationship style. It is very important to consider the early to later life attachment bridging as a probability. One's attachment style is not fixed or static but rather exists within a confidence band. This fluctuates in response to ever-changing causes and conditions. Ananda and all neurotics are painfully disturbed on their worst days and may glimpse normal in the rear view mirror on their best days. There can be little doubt that such a brilliant, devoted disciple of Buddha had many, many good days. One can only speculate as to his unimaginably unique experiences.

What begins to reveal itself with Ananda is the oneness of attachment. We see this, regular, loving, "social attachment", presumably a fluid iteration of maternal attachment, in Buddha's heartfelt admonitions and gentle scoldings. Considering the depth and duration of their friendship, we can presume that only a tiny fragment of their interactions were recorded. These interchanges could easily have amounted to tens of thousands of hours. One can only wonder about the countless examples of Buddha's oceanic kindness that were never chronicled, all the constructive insights, the never hurtful scoldings we all need. Oh to be Ananda! These stories inspire a longing born of relative attachment. They fill listeners with the sense that we can almost touch the glory. The Buddha's patient repetition, his re-explaining and re-formatting his teachings, brings us to the other shore. These events and discussions occurred in a liminal we-space. They pull us into the same. Oh to see the Buddha smile, shake his head, filled with love while once again cautioning Ananda, "Yes, good, just not quite..." Is not the lotus of nonattachment completed and perfected atop the beautiful and messy mud of this life?

One could do worse than to stand in the shadow of Ananda's, Suddhodana's, Mahamaya's, or Prajapati's attachment-love. They gave imperfectly and did so sincerely and persistently. They gave within their scope of understandings and capacities to the cause that Buddha fulfilled beyond measure. Theirs is the very lovingkindness and compassion that emanates from advanced meditators. The key to retaining such a North Star focus in the muddy mess of life is that she is within and then just past the untethered love we know on our very best days. Buddhahood, from the perspective of Buddha's Mom, is the release intended by such love. Prajapati's great love, and mother love operating through each of us, gains speed and breadth in the messy, engaged feeding, caregiving and consoling, and correlates of the same when we reach the peaks of adulthood. This love measured by what is given away creates an echo in the emptiness and becomes a method of clearing body, mind, and soul.

Radical Empiricism

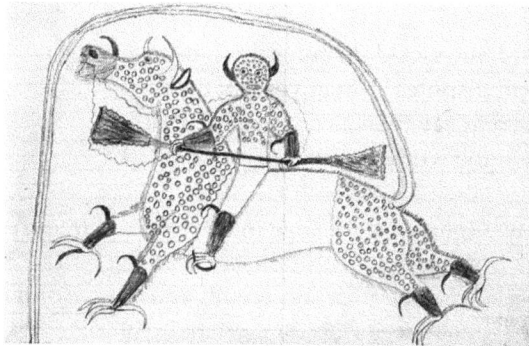

"Question Authority" was a hippie bumper sticker and battle cry in the 1960s. This anarchist pushback against the blue, 1950s hold on modern America finds common ground even in Buddhism. In the Buddha's time, Jainism and Hinduism were the establishment, old guard belief systems. His genius lies not in opposing them *per se*, but in endorsing awareness, inquisitiveness and healthy questioning of any and all forms. As suggested, this overt rejection of some privileged access to truth marks an important shift. Having rejected his father's version of truth—claims of the good life—Siddhartha set out to discover what mattered for himself. His discovery turned out to be quite beautifully and objectively un-conveyable.

> Don't blindly believe what I say. Don't believe me because others convince
> you of my words. Don't believe anything you see, read, or hear from others,
> whether of authority, religious teachers or texts. Don't rely on logic alone, nor
> speculation. Don't infer or be deceived by appearances.[124]

Here, the Buddha challenges practitioners to practice non-attachment without carve-outs. We are to confront, witness, experience, and evaluate all that arises. There's no daylight between one's most sacred beliefs, ego, identity, and anything else. The call to meet reality head on that concerned hippies in the 1960s parallels the pushback against Jainism and Hinduism 2,500 years earlier. To the extent that these were aimed at authority or established power bases, efforts were made to shake up what developmental theorists describe as conformist pressures. The Buddha's battle cry transcended any resting points. He called followers not to follow, not to be passive. Questioning authority takes energy, intention and discipline. His mother put it this way:

> Putting forth effort, self-controlled,
> Always with strong resolution
> -   This is how to honor the Buddhas![125]

Thankfully, for those of us who feel this call but need a boost, integral theory provides specificity. When questioning is just opposition, this is anarchist and unimaginative. Fun maybe but limited, as was the "sex, drugs, and rock n' roll" rebellion of the '60s. Any effort banded to another by any stricture—even when the surface of such adherence is "No adherence!"—is inherently constricted. The opposite side of a coin is still the same coin. "No attachment to x" does not take one far from x. When attachment is misconstrued—as something other than hardy, evolutionary-based attachment (encompassing all manner of lunging toward, grabbing, clinging and just as common, cold dismissal, disengagement, denial, and neglect) with the full accompaniment of the upper reaches of this in human intelligence and functioning—then how radical, tough, cool is one really? Where's the self-control and sustained effort, the honoring of our true nature?

Pandita

> Bhikkhus, I do not dispute with the world, the world disputes with me: no
> one who proclaims the True Idea [dharma] disputes with anyone in the
> world. What wise men [pandita], in the world say there is not [natthi], that I
> too say there is not; and what wise men in the world say there is [atthi], that I
> too say there is.[126]

In this amazing sutra from the Samyutta Nikaya (part of the Pali Canon), Buddha frees his philosophy of cultural and historical bounds. Instead of arguing with others about the nature of reality, he defers to the *pandita*. Pandita is translated as "wise men" or those with knowledge about specific matters. If such a person says something is, Buddha agrees with them. If they say something is not, he also agrees with them. So too, this sutra proclaims, should anyone who seeks to follow the dharma.

Two thousand years before the Enlightenment, this sutra reaches into the future and endorses science. "That which the wise agree" speaks to peer review. "That which the wise agree does not exist" has the scent of falsifiability. The sutra also speaks to science's freedom from dogma, its in-built, ongoing flexibility, where conclusions regarding reality are bound to change.

One is tempted to interpret Buddha's decline to engage with Pandita as just more of the standard call for renunciation. *Do not bother with the details of the outer world. Leave this to those who care about such things.* Alternatively, perhaps this is an injunction to defer and keep separate what now goes by the term the "hard science." This can be read as a communiqué to those who bother with impermanent matter, be they stars, organs of the body or lightning, to proceed as they wish and that they are welcome either way to consider the dharma. But Buddha deepens his point further.

> Feeling…Perception…Volitional formations…Consciousness that is
> impermanent, suffering, and subject to change: this the wise in the world
> agree upon as existing, and I too say that it exists.[127]

Here he shifts to his introspective work, inferentially to current parallels in cognitive neuroscience and psychology. With this, the sutra does not simply extend the cleaving off of science, leaving it to Panditas. He makes a shift and positively affirms the interior and experiential realm of feelings and perceptions. His words endorse the importance of expertise and empiricism in confirming claims regarding the interior domain. Religious and supernatural claims, this implies, require a sort of consensual validation. Claims not agreed upon by those who engage in empirical, introspective practices should be dismissed.

The truly subtle and lovely manner in which Buddha uses language to convey ideas is once again breathtaking. For starters, he seems to come clean with an endorsement of the we-space as the ultimate arbiter of truth. This we-space is both intra- and inter-personal. He also puts his own "Noble Truths" up for grabs, given that tanhā—whether as thirst, clinging or expectation—falls within the span of feeling, perception, volitional formations and is certainly connected to consciousness.

This sutra then echoes Stephen Batchelor's conclusion that Buddha would have us *know how* over *knowing that*. We are to know how to let go of even wisdom in favor of this foundational practice of deferring. Some attachment to knowing how to detach trumps the alternatives. Detachment from one's own practice-derived wisdom is a skillful enactment of nonattachment. The goal of skillful means is not wisdom but simply more skillful means. One cultivates nonattachment know-how by adopting and then transcending associated knowledge.

We can then add one more element. Practice-derived knowledge and related liberation may be boosted by Pandita such as Jung, Bowlby, Panksepp, Wilber, Batchelor, and others quoted throughout this book. Through these skillful minds, new perspectives on the deep feminine in Buddhism may blossom—with alacrity!

Chapter Five

PRAJAPATI

Attachment Figure

Prajapati shows up at the door of history and finds a baby in need. Were the story to begin this way, she might not be such an unsung heroine. We might come to know more about how this obscure woman lovingly met a baby's needs just when his biological life support system, his "real" mother, could not. In her place, we might learn, stepped a critically important attachment figure. This might expand the scope of the feminine with respect to all her "son" would one day come to discover and teach. We might view Prajapati and her legacy as that of "Buddha's Mom" living on in Buddhism. We might understand the potential for enlightenment to be Her lineage.

The official biography, of course, goes in the other direction. Siddhartha is the center of his own story. This is significant because this story serves as more than the biography of Buddha. Siddhartha's biography operates as the creation myth of Buddhism and therein, the dharma. This explains why Buddha's mythic beginnings are intent on conveying grandeur. Baby Siddhartha, let's recall, is said to walk and talk within days of his birth. This piece, as discussed in previous chapters, is among many factors that give rise and sustains distinctions between "the two attachments."

Perhaps a reversal of the same sort of mythic exaggeration would help to clarify the breadth of the feminine principle that we have referred to as Buddha's Mom. Humankind, this might start out, is in great danger. Our destiny depends on a precious, feeble baby in peril. The dharma is only as strong as the next generation. The gods beckon and Prajapati answers. Divine forces place their very own destiny in her hands. She alone must receive and convey the secret wisdom of the ages, lest this be lost to all future generations. Terrified yet brave, she cries out that she is only human. Out of divine depths of love and compassion, the greatest imaginable transmission flows into her body and being.

With the divine mother in ascendency, Prajapati's breasts too swell with milk and her heart fills with love. The godhead is re-capitulated through the nitty gritty of biology and body and emotion, sweat and tears and joy too. Such a narrative would have no need for an unnatural, adultified, non-dependent infant. Nor would the outcome be guaranteed. The fate of humankind would not be fulfilled instantly. Prajapati's son (from this encompassing perspective) would wrestle mightily with his attachment to his mother, father, and family on the one hand and his increasing clarity of a peace that surpasses attachments on the other. Through intensive spiritual practice, he would know how the universe had chosen his mother as it chooses all of us to be born human, and how this transmission was comprised of the love she had for him and him for her.

Siddhartha, in this accounting, would become acutely aware that Prajapati had received and then passed along the gift of this human life to him; yet he must confront the fact that both of them were still bound and suffering. Before this myth reached its climax, Siddhartha would first shake these heavenly chains and leave all those he loved to wander. We might see the Middle Way more through an attachment-as-love lens. With Olympic intensity, he would then seek to break these deep somatic/affective holds and in failing to succeed in the most sublime way. All he would realize would comprise an integral vision of human attachment. This would transform him and in time, through his teachings, his mother and loved ones. It would continue to transform millions more for many hundreds of years, as it has.

Ultimately, Buddha's message to the world would be that our species' ultimate, nascent potential is received in its release. Liberation comes with the miracle of being given life, the giving this away in love to another and opens to a space beyond both of these. Even once fully awakened, Buddha would tirelessly speak this truth to his mother. He would show her a higher love than the one they shared born of attachment. He would spend 45 years teaching the same to others. Prajapati and many others would awaken with him. Much of this fits even now with the Canon's account of Prajapati. Other matters, at least thus far, do not. The world would come to know her not as *the* but as *a* mother of Buddhism, and celebrate how her enlightenment called for both the full receiving and then giving away of herself. Humankind would benefit knowing from a model of a love that both gives life and must be relinquished.

Buddha's Mom, in this version of events, is more clearly a vessel and concept that transcends and includes Prajapati. Prajapati is each of us, but like her son, is also a remarkable exemplar. She was not born walking and talking or exceptionally intelligent or spiritually gifted. She would have to come by her realization so very humanly and imperfectly. Just as Prajapati is not *the* but *a* Buddha's Mom, Buddha is not *the* but *a* Buddha. As do all humans, he began as an inheritor of our species' ultimate potential. The nature of this inheritance would thus deserve more reflection.

Buddha's Mom's, in this inclusive, collective sense, occupies the space that encompasses but transcends all we receive in being born human and all we accomplish in giving away the same in relationship. Her life offers a glimpse into what shows up elsewhere, in some very important places. She specifically accepts the gift of life, specifically steps up and passes this along to the semi-orphaned baby, and then specifically rails against him until she realizes what he first comes to realize. Late in life and begrudgingly, she awakens to the Hinayana, the first turning's truth, and renunciates attachment. The poem credited to her, which we will review, captures how she comes to know this truth. Through her son, she has transmitted the compassion for all humanity at the core of the Mahayana lineage, the second turning. In previous lifetimes, she only knew the earthly love side of metta, and also reveals this in her poem. In previous existences, she accepted the gift of life, and gave it away. But this only went so far.

Her son would finally show her the space encompassing both receiving and giving, releasing her from all limitations. A oneness that transcends and includes this give and take is rooted in Buddhism's third turning. This is the heart of the Vajrayana Tonglen practice of exchanging self and other. Dōgōn, founder of the Zen Soto lineage 900 years ago, anchored this within the feminine frame, "You should study not only that you become a mother when your child is born, but also that you become a child."[128]

The exchange of self and other points out their unity and their illusory separation. Tonglen demonstrates the continual emergence of self/ego/mind in tandem with other in awareness. Once again, there appears to be value in exploring the biological mud in which, under the guidance of an attachment figure, self/other manifests.

Ordinary Wonder

If one were able to watch baby Siddhartha's birth and first hours, one would have been privileged to see Mahamaya's tears of pain and joy as she alone brought this feeble creature out of her very center and into our world. In those next days and weeks, Prajapati would enter the bewildering scene. She and perhaps a couple of nursemaids—between funerals and weddings and hosting Suddhodana's visitors—would begin to live out the slow dance of attachment. Time would slow to a halt over and again, as they carried him, rocking and cooing. Mothers in check-out lines at stores or wherever they see a mother holding a baby, often unconsciously sway back and forth.

Prajapati and the nameless nursemaids would have spent hours absorbing and recalibrating their response to infant Siddhartha's expanding, confusing, sophisticated repertoire of biological drives and needs. In fits and starts, with the moving finish line all parents know, they would meet these hunger, fatigue, cold, hot, pain, and fear cues with increasingly accurate, loving responses. There would be plenty of trial and error. The picture would change rapidly in one sense and glacially in others. One day, carrying is soothing, the next rocking is preferred, and another when febrile, nothing seems to help. What before signaled fatigue and was remedied by a nap, on another day is only calmed through breastfeeding.

Good enough mothering is attuned, empirical and adjusts endlessly to the baby's lead. It balances consistency and flexibility. The porridge must be not too hot, not too cold, as the fairy tale puts it. In all, healthy attachment requires enormous energy and emotional stability. No surprise something less than desirable occurs when a mother is emotionally unavailable or inconsistent regardless of the reasons for this.

Siddhartha-someday-Buddha experienced the baby side of such species-typical attachment. Siddhartha's sense of a coherent, safe, predictable internal physical and mental representation of his own being, we can speculate, was likely built upon the tens of thousands of hours of secure attachment experiences occurring during the first few years of life.

In his teachings, Buddha barely weighed in on any of his own early-life attachment or on this topic more generally. Not having access to modern science, he naturally never laid out a clear endorsement of attachment. But as noted, there is evidence for a passive, delimited endorsement of maternal attachment. For example, Buddha never expressed opposition to breast-feeding, to mother's constant carrying, co-sleeping and whatever sorts of transitional objects babies of the time used. There is the Canon's mythic reverence for Siddhartha's biological mother, Mahamaya. Much of the narrative concerns his emotional bonds with his father, son, and wife. Added to this, as an older child, Siddhartha was attached to excelling at academics and competitive sports. Again, while indirect, we would note that, as an adult, he did not advise adolescents that such pursuits were illusory and to be avoided.

In all, Buddha's teaching on attachment makes the most sense as an adult creed. This, however, just loops back to the same point. Adult psychology continues have deep roots, and to be very influenced by early life dynamics. This science and associated technologies used to address associated problems were barely on the map in Buddha's time. Accurately understood, a modern assessment of Buddhism's view on factors such as the grasping, clinging, attaching tendencies mentioned in the Four Noble Truths does not threaten or undermine this adult focus. Nothing can threaten truth except more truth.

A march toward an integral attachment is only worth the effort if made fearlessly and sweetly. Sides of attachment left out of conventional Buddhist viewpoints need first to be seen in full, and celebrated for their own merit, before any integrative efforts are made. Meanwhile, the best course is to let the chips fall where they may. After all, efforts to accommodate new material in light of the status quo is suspect. Spiritual practice is not aimed at making "out there" match, but at suspending all filters. Status quo is just self/ego/mind in disguise. We come by it honestly, but this does not mean we cannot heal.

Evolution produced a brain which produces a mind, which makes the unfathomable and mind-blowing graspable, expectable, and normal. Before the reality comes into focus in consciousness, we have rendered the profane mundane. The flow of impressions lapping against our senses, the backs of our eyeballs, the subtle membrane in the inner ear, our internal body map and the sense of where our limbs are in space all gets downsized and synthesized into confidence interval. That which falls within this scope is deemed normal. A standard deviation in one direction or another grabs attention. Information-processing algorithms do their part to manage the confusing, beautiful, intense panoply of energy washing over our sense organs. Within brain inputs, emotions and meanings and ideas and possibilities, are only to the cacophony. Normalizing is critical to survival. Excessive attention-grabbing intensity burns precious energy. Any mammal too taken by the beauty of a flower earned the Darwin award.

But as Zen tales teach, this leaves the young novice monk appropriately in awe of Mount Fuji but not in awe of the small hills he is standing on. There are two sides to "after the ecstasy, the laundry". First, we revere the snow leopard but not the birds on the park bench. Second, we know the miracle of the birds, the bench arising in our own being. But, of course, there's the "just so" of it all. Resting in this primordial wonder, as they say, Buddha's Mom helps expose this intersection of ordinary and extraordinary at the heart of existence (mine and yours to be specific). This practically nameless historical figure, from a modern perspective, is largely responsible for nothing less than transmitting the lineage of our species to one of the greatest members to have ever lived. And so, "just" a hill at once is Mount Fuji. The everyday hill is the merely biological, collective source of emotional, loving attachment in all of us. As a hill, this force informed Siddhartha's early life and family ties. In culminating in a full awakening to the true nature of attachment and Siddhartha's transformation into the Buddha, we encounter the pristine perfection of Mount Fuji. The latter then flows through Buddha's 45 years of wandering, meditating, teaching, healing in ways we simplify as based in ultimate wisdom and compassion.

It is natural to look past the silliness of a baby walking and talking at one week old. No doubt many of us interpret this as a poetic image of the spiritual brilliance to come later. But the young novice in all of us has to eventually die in order to see the very hill on which he stands. In Wilber's words, the novice needs to be negated and not preserved precisely as he is transcended. We can add to this formulation, the detachment side of relative attachment and attachment-love. As described in a previous chapter, maternal attachment involves a fluid sway between attachment and detachment. For example, tribal mothers detach momentarily to gather plants or monitor dangers in the environment.

But the journey of mothering involves another, more glacial detachment process. This is responsible for the shifts in a woman's character and identity, radically reconfiguring self/ego/mind. '*Mother*', one might say, is mostly *other*. In this chapter, we will explore how Prajapati is a poignant representation of this bridge from an instinctual, biological provider to that of a giving, bountiful, overflowing aspect of Buddha's Mom.

We have our work cut out for us. Even two millennia later, many would think of her as not his "real" mother. At the same time, she did not discover and teach the dharma. What are we to make of this other-mother and other-mothering force? That so shaped her, that through her, the baby and child Siddhartha was so immersed? Nothing? Everything? In rebuking this force, Siddhartha would discover and teach the world the dharma. Fortunately, many strands of evidence, from antiquity to modernity, provide insights into this "biological bodhisattva" mystery.

Truth Claims

The 'everything' side seems as dubious as the virgin birth motif. Grand claims to ultimate truth are pervasive. The godhead imbues a lucky woman, and transmits our species' ultimate, spiritual potential through her son. *God gave his only son.* Less misogynist variants assert, *God is love. Earth is a living goddess and we are extensions of her, beings made of lovelight.*

Grand claims often lack specificity. They do not enhance a skillful response to the "so what" question. Our effort here is to consider threads which together bridge from the ineffable to the measurable in ways aligned with Buddhism's central tenets. What exactly is one to do with grand but vague truth claims? Presumably, the more these are accessible, perceivable, testable, the better. Skillful means born of wisdom are enhanced when such claims comport with evolution, neuroscience and consciousness research. Personal, emotional access is enhanced by congruent extensions in psychological science.

With Buddha's Mom as ballast, we have been accumulating strands from various fields in support of an integral attachment. We have proposed that, at least in theory, our species' potential flows through humans and between humans as attachment-love. Naturally this has developmental origins in the mom–baby dyad. In union, this truth claim calls for something to come from what appears, from our side, to be immeasurable and void of human parameters. A basic architecture, as follows, fits the general outline of many grand truth claims. This begins with consciousness arising from the absence thereof in early development. With this comes the possibility that humans maintain an imprint or echo or shadow, both definite and beyond words, of the soup or space or unconscious realm from which sentience once arose. The term Buddha's Mom is essentially a placeholder for this very container. The present focus on Prajapati will help demonstrate that humans both emerge from such a vessel and, as self/ego/mind, abide within the very same vessel.

The work of brilliant neurologist, Antonio Damasio, provides a powerful portal into how the first emergent glimmers of consciousness occur within a larger, preconscious, pre-verbal frame. As his bestseller's title proclaims, within each human lifetime and each human brain, the "Self Comes to Mind."[129] He differentiates "self" and "mind," with the latter referring more generically to consciousness and the former to the first-person self-sense. Damasio's research offers further proof of concept for the bridge from biological to Buddhist attachment.

Damasio, in tandem with attachment science, allows us to intelligently speculate on the very earliest stages of psychological development in humans, and within this frame, to speculate on Siddhartha's self/ego/mind's beginnings. This would have unfolded in mappable ways. First would have been no-thing, for example, the absence of consciousness we might also refer to as fetal awareness. During the span from neonatal to infancy to the toddler years, fleeting glimmers of mood and simple emotions would gain a toehold. Maternal attachment notes that this occurs within a mom–baby dynamic. Long before any glimmer of "mom" or "me", baby Siddhartha would have crossed these bands of dim somatic sensations and background affect. In contemplating Buddha's Mom, we should all wonder about our own oldest, deepest sentient substrates. How might these have come into formation, and how might they continue to be operational?

In Buddha's Mom, we find ample basis for the possibility that the sub-layers of awareness arise within an intensive maternal attachment container. According to attachment science, early-life attachment factors eventually consolidate as a secure base. Until recently, there was little clarity regarding this first flickering of consciousness. This has changed for the better, however, thanks to the work of another brilliant neuroscientist, Jaak Panksepp. As we will delve into in the next chapter, Panksepp has proposed a rich model for the subfloor of consciousness that elegantly supports Buddha's Mom.

What we have called the we-space emerges out of an undifferentiated precursor. Buddhists often refer to the notion of a contained space, or vibrant space or shimmering void. For the neonate, presumably, the first fleeting sense of anything emerges in this unnamable backdrop. A need for warmth or milk is itself a differentiated stand of consciousness, co-arising with effect and sensations that mammals evolved to optimize survival. Hunger might trigger anxiety, possibly even some sort of pain. Pleasure from previous feedings is another likely candidate for an animal's amalgam of distress. To want, to hurt, has the other side in some sort of memory of satiation or relief. The brain has to get the organism's attention, in order for it to get mom's attention and appears to use both pleasure and pain circuitry for best results.

Where other animals hit the ground running with no maternal attachment requirement, humans must awaken to the awareness of self separate from other. A separate "self comes to mind" by virtue of differentiation. In other words, self/other comes to mind or as Buddhists put it, these co-arise. In general, few would claim that the first glimmers of consciousness arise in-utero. Such claims and those of recollected past lives, as Wilber might remind us are not 100% false and the day might come when there is more agreement on such matter. For our purposes, it seems reasonable to situate the earliest layers of self/ego/mind in the neonatal phase and infancy.

Humans are designed to need one another and for this to occur when they are capable of doing something with these needs. This starts with the capacity to emotionally experience and express the need for attachment (love, warmth, etc.) and the sense of joy or reward when this need is met. Our innate needs expand, by design, across the great chain from body to mind. In-utero, the fetus is fed and kept warm without any major need for self/other awareness. These become critically important immediately on the outside.

Infants that signal their needs and moms that successfully provided for them, through them, remained in the gene pool. The same gene pool in which we swim right now. Needs form emergent we-spaces. The need to play co-arises with a proto self. The latter experiences this need, sends signals and then experiences the happiness or sadness depending on the mother's response. Besides play, other factors which inform the mom-baby dance are temperature, hunger/thirst, discomfort or fear—to name but a few. Needs are mapped across the face, expressed vocally and in body gestures. The circle is completed with holding, cooing or feeding, for example, bringing about a return to homeostasis.

With massive repetition, trial and error, "what fires-together-wires-together". This cognitive science mainstay dates back to 1949 and gained credibility with the advent of brain scans. Neuroplasticity is no longer an abstraction but a proven, accepted reality. Massive, repetitive firing-wirings are some of the bricks that build the neurological structures of awareness. No doubt advances in science will unlock ever more secrets. Perhaps one day, mechanisms associated with what Buddhists call karma and psychic capacities such as pre-cognition will be better understood.

In Siddhartha, the neurological substrates of self/other and their sentient, experiential counterparts would have become ever more elaborate. Prajapati's smell, her face, her touch, breast, taste, and sounds repeated over time would make "mom" come to mind. Carrying, swaying, holding, and tickling would have led to ever more advanced proprioception. No doubt that these somatic self stands have deep, in-utero beginnings. Largely a parietal lobe function, proprioception locates a bodily "me" in space. At some point, advanced proprioception would enable the little boy to dart about, tumble, jump, and experience bodily being. To be a body or no-body is a question never asked, because the self-body, mind-body, psyche-soma strata undergirds mood, emotion, and feeling. No body, no Shakespeare, and no dharma.

This emergent semblance of self in Bowlby's model results in a "secure base". This first felt connection to the human lineage fits the image of an island gradually emerging from the sea. Life's storms routinely wash over. The well-attached baby's emergent awareness is more one of drives tossing them this way and that. When all goes well, a large presence is registered subconsciously, bodily and sensorially—a collective of touch, warmth, sounds. Initially, Buddha's Mom is nothing, then slowly, oceanic background, then fleetingly "here" tickling the senses.

Think of the first confusing moments awakening from sleep, disoriented in a deep fog. We are still elsewhere but unaware of where. Within split seconds usually but sometimes more slowly, cognitive sensory streams merge and self/ego/mind comes to the fore. In early development, separate experiential lines have to form in the first place. An attachment figure comes into resolution, differentiated from the background. She is figure to the ground of being.

With "object constancy", she exists when we cannot see her. In a twist on Descartes, "I think therefore I am," the proto-self is embedded in this attachment dance. Long before any glimmers of ego, what we are calling the vessel of the human lineage and Buddha's Mom takes shape as our partner in consciousness, e.g., "we exist, therefore I am." Psychoanalysts have long recognized the mother's early, powerful role in shaping personality, but before Bowlby, they did not connect these dynamics to innate biological attachment processes.

Buddha's Mom, that is to say, loving attachment figures' very essence fits the original meaning of the word dharma, to hold, bear, carry, support. In-utero, her amniotic fluid is a supportive sea. Across neonatal phases and infancy, she spends thousands of hours holding, bearing the weight (for example, preventing the baby's neck from bending too far), carrying and globally engaged in somatic, bodily supporting.

In later infancy and the toddler phase, this "support" involves a combination of physical and emotional. For example, knee-bouncing and physically similar activity causes the baby to lose sight of mom and to go through rapid progressions of confusion, fear, relief which bolster the first we-space. As mother is re-collected, so too is the proto-self. When the baby shows fear with a facial, bodily or vocal gesture, loving moms naturally, instantly restore homeostasis. They tend to do so both somatically with a restorative hug, hold, pat, and with effect communicated with their smile and soothing words. Peek-a-boo follows the same path. The child feels the confusion and fear about mom's momentary disappearance and relief at her return. Buddha's Mom, as such, bears the totality of this process. She is the space within which the baby is helped to experience the negative and the positive. Within this, she channels the thrill, fear and discombobulating on the one hand, and relief and joy on the other. In this, the we-space forms the ground of awareness. When all goes well, this allows opposites to exist within predictable limits, disorientation-orientation, fear-joy, mom-me, you-me, other-me, movement and stillness; all of these lines merge in some semblance of emotional stability and trust. Trust is not earned so much as conveyed. Life is (when attachment-love is conveyed with adequate frequency and duration) good.

Worth noting, major Buddhist lineages seem to call for a reversal of this infantile progression of consciousness which we are embedding in Buddha's Mom, moving from nothing to we to deeper elaborations of self/ego/mind. In Vipassana practice, discursive *others* arise with force: thoughts, to do lists, back pain. Vipassana acknowledges that awareness is always getting snagged in such we-spaces. This lineage guides followers to notice, detach, and observe in an open, bare awareness all that plays out.

The Vajrayana takes this a step further with practices aimed at dropping the pretense of separation of self and other altogether, even when other is other-worldly. During metta practices, one devoutly, intensively conveys love to another. In Vajrayana deity worship, the self encounters a majestic, fearsome, compassionate, and divine other. The point is that self and even the divine are insubstantial, void of form yet flowing with sentience. The Vajrayana's Tonglen practice similarly guides one to assume an other's position. In all of these, the personal "me" level of awareness is peeled back or flipped, revealing the shared, we-space ground. These then unfold further into realization, described variously as unified, empty, perfect and ultimately natural. Our natural state is generally rendered both void of form and filled with wisdom and compassion.

> Extending love and compassion toward others in contemplative practice is a rehearsal for stepping beyond stinginess and self-centeredness in daily life. Eventually our training will give us the power to flip the mind instantly by letting go of the "me plan" and considering the happiness of somebody else, whatever we're experiencing, wherever we are. In that moment, we are cultivating peace. When we live like this, we feel happier. The reason is simple: because love and compassion are the basis of our consciousness, we thrive when we let them come to the forefront.[130]

Then & Now

This speaks to how emptying awareness of self-attachments is revelatory. In detaching, we open to reality's dancing, flowing, blending of void and love and wisdom. In emptying, one is filled. These Buddhist illuminations into the mystery of life are enhanced with efforts to notice where Buddha's Mom pops forth, as a figure from the ground. This is because both Buddhism's attachment and maternal, social attachment arise from the same profound ground of being. The prospect of increased lucidity calls for a burrowing into what often passes for the opposite side. The gap between the two attachments reflects unconscious, inadvertent filtering of the deep feminine. The essential point, which cannot be overstated, is that in countless ways our relationship to reality is thus formed, thus based, and constantly with us as the selfsame ground of our own existential experience. Our deepest sense of self/other are "figured" to this feminine, somatic, deeply emotional and pre-conscious ground. Our formative years remain formative moment-to-moment.

In this chapter, we will follow Prajapati's path toward an integral vision of attachment. Somewhat like Marilyn Monroe or Mona Lisa, she is what others project on to her. In these overlays are substrates and extensions of our own assumptions and built-in ways of perceiving a less than grand, integral attachment. This journey across infancy, for example, underscores how invisible Prajapati is in the first place. Despite its immensity, Buddhism does not make truth claims regarding parenting and child development. Prajapati's invisibility is actually just an extension and expression of the marginalization of the feminine principle in general. Siddhartha's major attachment figure, in fact, might have been another woman. Perhaps Prajapati comes to us as his foster and adoptive mother and heroine of sorts in name only, when in reality one of Mahamaya's closest, most dedicated servants stepped in. Perhaps though all of history owes her so much, she remains nameless.

Her near invisibility in conjunction with attachment science is telling. We know precious little of the specifics of Siddhartha's mom-baby experience. The importance of maternal attachment in the cultivation of self/ego/mind is just as revealing on the classically Buddhist side. Here, attachment to self/ego/mind is revealed to cause suffering. Paradoxically, dropping the hard-earned "me plan" opens to great depths of love and compassion. In navigating these mysteries, we will take a page from the renowned Swiss psychiatrist, Carl Jung. He proclaimed that the unconscious yearns to be conscious. It is forever giving us cues, often in subconscious symbolism, archetypes and dream imagery. Prajapati's identity as a stepmother, in this light, deserves our close attention.

Our thesis postulates that access to evolutionary consciousness is uniquely, powerfully conveyed at the front-end of life. This first spiritual imprinting then, for better or worse, forms a dynamic, living conduit to what Buddhism describes as an accessible, oceanic being. In theory and practice, this conduit makes up our imperfect, personal spiritual grounding. Multiple lines of evidence demonstrate this and simultaneously comprise avenues of healing. In this book, we stress the possibility of an ever-more integral path both for understanding and healing based in multiple, overlapping sources. These include evolution, attachment science, neuroscience, depth psychology, clinical psychology, the feminine principle and Buddhist truth claims.

In conjunction, these give us a personal reality that floats atop an unbounded love, one which evokes a profound sense of home and of belonging. At the same time, we rise above the pain and contraction of emotional bonds, experience the eternal, open space of nonattachment, freedom and realization. We have referred to this totality conveyed across generations, and simultaneously as the ground of being, as Buddha's Mom. This helps identify the evolutionary impulse at the heart of awareness. She is a compelling integral figure, marrying personhood and spiritual transmission, an evolutionary, transgenerational sentience and more. As a vessel, she is a living, organic, psychological reality. She is a river of the immediate felt-sense of life by which the human lineage makes its way. As perhaps the worthiest face of our shared human lineage stream, we stand to know ourselves ever better through her. A modern analysis which incorporates ancient, spiritual and truth assertions is consistent with a very positive take on Prajapati. Her influence within the shared, loving crucible certainly appears to have produced a most robust humanity in the future Buddha. With this influence, he would go farther than any man or woman for whom we have reliable data in articulating the nature of reality and the path to the most integral embrace. Buddha, from this perspective, never veered from this species' inheritance. As he persevered across the first half of his life, he did not place any limits on his own or humanity's developmental attachment origins. He never needed a god, never needed to box in the feminine, and only expanded on all he received in his dharma.

In this sense, he transcended and included attachment in his doctrine of nonattachment. Mother love is not abandoned in metta. A thread from the refuge of the three gems (Buddha, dharma, sangha) remains strong and true in the protective, loving embrace and "holding environment" which evolved to greater heights in our species than any other on earth. While this suggests Buddha's access to what we are simplifying as "Mom" was rich and expansive, Buddhism's orientation to the same is quite different. What we are told of Prajapati offers a powerful portal, and one relevant for our journey toward an integral attachment.

Stepmother

Carl Jung, his protégé Marie von Franz, and Jungians since have produced a body of work devoted to the analysis of folklore and fairy tale. This literature has produced a rich, evocative picture of the stepmother figure. Even if they are not outright sinister, stepmothers tend to carry a negative valence. Most everyone is familiar with Cinderella's mean, sabotaging stepmother, for example. The stepmother may be cast as cunning, often having attained her position of power by having duped or tricked someone (or worse) to attain her position and power. Connotations not far off this mark survive through today. She is the butt of comedian zingers and is commonly served up as a sniveling, meddling or intrusive force in sitcoms. The meaning the stepmother evokes, according to Jungians is archetypal in origin.

As I have mentioned, archetypes refer to innately inherited, neurologically-based constituents of human consciousness. They influence and shape perception and the emotional systems which generate *meaning*. Because there is so much hyperbole associated with the term, archetype, I prefer the more precise term *inmaps*, short for, *innate, neurological, meaning-approximating perceptual systems*. Via background operations, these animate more immediate, experience-near, cultural, tribal and familial events and interpersonal dynamics. Inmaps power-assist the self's intricate, rapid, fluid mapping of experience. They are core constituents of the self-container with specialized intrapersonal and interpersonal influence. They define and animate experience, and more to the point at hand, perpetuate the very self that Buddhism teaches us to transcend.

Jung referred to that which Buddhists interchangeably call self/ego/mind as the self (lower case). He differentiated this from Self. Big-S Self was his word for an ultimate, ineffable, divine presence in the human psyche, sometimes called the Godhead. Jung was once asked if he "believed" in God. He famously said he did not, that instead he "knew" God. He was pointing out that there's no way for a human to go beyond the fact that they have an experience of the divine (or actively deny this). His message was that there is no need for faith or belief, when for better or worse, so long as there is a self (mind) within it, there is the experience of God. So in another way, he viewed archetypes as dissolving in a sort of all encompassing, ultimate archetype, with the results that all paths of individuation and growth led directly to this encounter.

Jungians view archetypes that present with shadowy and negativistic connotations as those with the most potential to upend the status quo and bring about transformation and spiritual renewal. The stepmother inmap is best viewed, with a nod towards dependent origination, within a larger field. Here the Witness helps us to wonder who and what is arising and inadvertently helping to frame the stepmother in negative ways. Often males and masculine elements—a kingdom in jeopardy, damsel in distress, dragon threatening—form a structure. A male knight, woodsmen or hunter may be the protagonist. If the protagonist is female, she is often narrowly defined, with a male required to rescue or marry her. In Cinderella, of course, the future of the kingdom hinges on the Prince's selection of a female. Eventually, some sort of threat to the status quo emerges, often associated with a feminine element. Cousins of the stepmother are the witch and crone. According to Jungians, the serpent and dragon are ancient, deeply feminine placeholders which show up over and over, for example, in Adam and Eve. Children can carry some of the same one-down symbolism. The bastard orphan is a loaded version, implying the legacy of some sort of unsanctioned and unsavory woman.

The stepmother is a sort of second-rate mother, with "less than" status. Added to this is the fact that women generally have less status in patriarchal cultures. In Siddhartha's biography, the stepmother is not installed due to some hard fought victory. She did not earn this honor by demonstrating virtue or strength. The King did not kill his wife, or choose another. The new woman did not provoke the change. What of this person who would carry much of the responsibility, and therefore possibly earn much of the credit, for nothing less than protecting, cultivating, and loving the life-force of the future Buddha? Was she up to the task?

All of this intrigue and potential for stealing the show is avoided. A "look-over-there" device is employed, with the tragic and untimely death of the official wife of the king and mother of Siddhartha, Mahamaya. Mahamaya was no concubine. She was very much a powerhouse in her own right. She was his wife, Queen, the King's chosen partner of twenty years. Much is implied by their not having a child for twenty years, and then having one. Many women in mythology are viewed by the patriarchy as barren, as vessels unable to carry cargo and therefore of little worth. Mahamaya was unusually capable of motherhood—but did not become a mother for a very long time. During this phase, her husband was presumably occupied with kingly duties, consolidating power, maintaining order, and providing for his people. The narrative parameters placed her unusually close to the traditionally male-centered seat of power for a long time. Perhaps her allotment of power was exceeded when she then became pregnant and held the keys to the Kingdom in her belly. We know these few pieces of her life and little else, because immediately after giving birth, she dies.

When the dust settled, a respectable but certainly one-step-removed stepmother had been installed. For once, the stepmother was not sinister or underhanded. She was abundantly up to the task of mothering the special baby. She was apparently absent of anything remarkable, nothing newly positive. In fact, she was almost precisely a smaller, life-sized version of Mahamaya. And even though a stepmother, she brought no particular threat or danger. The feminine is dispensed with, neutralized by giving it a lesser amount of importance, and the reader or listener naturally returns to the plot, the baby, and the mystery of what would come.

From a feminist perspective, the rendering dead of the mother and replacement with a benign stepmother are two moves in the same direction. The treatment of the feminine is not simply reductionist. In the transition from Mahamaya to Prajapati, an attempt is made to cut short the feminine's fifteen minutes of fame. If she must breastfeed, at least males are on hand to ensure standards are set and met.

> In order to procure a proper nurse for his son, Suddhodana assembled the princesses of the two cities of Kapilavastu. She was not to be too tall, or the neck of the infant would be stretched or too short, or his body would be bent; nor too large, or his legs would be contracted; nor too weak, or his body would not acquire firmness; nor of too full a habit, or her milk would be hot, and cause his skin to become red ; nor of too dark a complexion, or her milk would be cold, and cause his flesh to be in lumps, in some parts hard and in others soft. A hundred princesses were chosen, free from these faults.[131]

That which persists is stepped down a notch in the form of a stepmother. But like the proverbial turtle and hare race, she should not be counted out. The feminine principle exists. It is real and awesome and must be faced, especially when the main opposing, co-arising force is drenched in patriarchy. If the protagonist and values, as in the tale of Siddhartha, are highly male-oriented, then something is axiomatically needed to account for her. As stepmother, she is a step below biologically inherited merit. As second wife, she is also a step down, the King's second choice. Her status as Queen is, unsurprisingly, marginalized by the events which preceded her ascension. And even then, she is not a ruler in her own right but a wife-Queen to a King. She is not an independent, unrelated woman. This would convey the potential of a separate source or center in her. She is stepped back rather to a secondary position, second wife, sister of the first-choice, wife-Queen.

Virgin

Prajapati is not portrayed as having any direct spiritual authority. Mahamaya has strong divine associations. As mentioned, however, any role in bringing heaven to earth is quickly curtailed. Once Siddhartha reaches the ripe age of one week, she dies to her earthly life and is dispatched to Buddhist heaven. The meaning of this symbolism regarding maternal attachment is not hard to decipher. Feminine allusions to divinity are parsed, indirect and weakened in various forms. No prophecy tells of a great Goddess, to name one in reverse, who gives Prajapati to humankind to live and die as a human and thereby fulfill some sort of divine destiny. She is not said to have been born into the fleshy, samsaric human realm in order to forge and convey the path to enlightenment for all mortals. If she is aligned with the Christian, archetypal Virgin, who some believe is our species' root lineage bearer, who unites biological and Buddhist conceptions of attachment, then the good news (from a Jungian stance) is that the absence of such recognition of her grandeur translates as regressive and compensatory.

Where so much energy is spent marginalizing the feminine, she is simultaneously very close at hand. She co-arises just below our noses, often fooling us by being clothed in shadowy, negative garb. Though humans can hardly bear it, a limitless god is beyond gender. At the doorstep of this nameless, empty void where truth shines, unfettered spiritual yin co-arises with yang.

In the case of Catholicism, for example, she manifests as the Virgin of Guadalupe. In 1531, when the virgin revealed herself, she did so to a peasant named Juan Diego, a small, weak, humble man, poor enough to make room in his heart for her. She called him "dignified Juan Diego" and also "son". Immediately, she specifically addressed the attachment fracture in a loving, personal way by healing Juan's uncle. She identified and named this separation from the feminine principle and what we have been calling Buddha's Mom. She formed a relationship, established a sacred we-space. Dignified Juan after all was her most *abandoned* son.

> Know and be certain in your heart, my most abandoned son, that I am the
> Ever-Virgin Holy Mary, Mother of the God of Great Truth, Téotl, of the One
> through Whom We live, the Creator of Persons, the Owner of What Is Near
> and Together, of the Lord of Heaven and Earth.[132]

Her Virgin status is easy to diagnose from the patriarchal perspective. Her divinity is unsullied and certainly not by any sort of competing patriarchal force. The patriarchy is prone to boxing in the feminine principle as mother, whore (seductress/temptress), virgin or crone (witch). Little wonder she is increasingly referred to with the slightly less laden term, "Lady", as in Our Lady of Guadalupe. The addition of "our", however, is actually the more important addition. This shifts her into the we-space central to attachment and to Buddha's Mom. *The* Virgin of Guadalupe leaves this reference out.

From our current perspective, the Virgin's (our Lady's) first order of business was a physical place in which her spiritual offspring, humanity itself, could receive the feminine's transmission. She unambiguously desired a physical vessel for this spiritual imparting. In addition to these body and spirit references, emotion is also flowing, essentially completing the great chain. Hardly a renunciate, she feels deeply, loves deeply and desires deeply and with specificity, as mothers do. Further evidence of an integral attachment is seen in our Lady's maternal aspect. She intensely speaks to the maternal instinct to protect and nourish, in this case, the multitudes of poor and needy. She has Juan gather flowers, an archetypal feminine sign, and uses these to prove her reality to the local male authority in a language he understands. The flowers transform and reveal her image.

First Nun

Our thesis is that Prajapati and probably some others long forgotten were powerful sources of maternal attachment and therein conveyers of metta, and that attachment-love and lovingkindness are born of the same origins. There is no language in the Pali Canon suggesting any shortcomings in Prajapati's stepmother function. Certainly no references exist suggesting anything negative with respect to her mothering, such as neglect, abuse or hostility. Conversely, there are multiple allusions of the other kind. Of these, none is more touching than the precious poem, which begins with *Buddha! Hero! Praise be to you!*, attributed to Prajapati. The poem caps off a story which is, unfortunately, not more integrated in Buddhism. This woman had given birth to the boy who would be Buddha. She experienced his burgeoning spirit in childhood, saw him struggle to find peace in riches and lovers, and then again in starving himself until he was very close to death. She knew him as no other did. And like him, because of him, she too had been on her own remarkable journey. She held him and then let him go, figuratively and literally. She then intensively pursued a second, ultimate letting go of him and herself, inspired by him.

Well into this journey, the canon states, Prajapati awoke to the first of four stages leading to arahat. In entering this first stage, the stream of sotapanna, any perception of a separate sense of self dropped away.[133] She stably, fully witnessed how an attachment to self co-arises with a detachment from other, from environment and the universe. In the first person, she came to see that "I never exist distinct from that definable as 'not me'." With this clarity, as she described in her poem, she discovered a certain release and for this she was profoundly thankful. Consequently, we hear the voice of an enlightened woman, a woman who gave the world Siddhartha and intimately knew and loved him his entire life. And rather than any hint of ownership or longing or grief, her heart sings with a transcendent joy.

This joy was born of suffering. More accurately, she had been liberated from both joy and suffering and the swings of samsara in her journey. The poem speaks to a culmination of this. She had long since accepted her son's ascetic, homeless path and, in fact, had become an unofficial devotee. Only males were allowed in the Sangha. In a profound act of nonviolent disobedience, she and two other women questioned this assumed cultural tradition. At first, they did so silently. They adhered to the precepts, the noble truths and eightfold path and pushed themselves in meditative practice.[134]

Eventually, Prajapati found her voice. As the story goes, at some point, the combination of inspiration and perspiration finally worked, giving the world the counterpart to the men's *bhikkhu sangha*, the first ever *bhikkhuni sangha*. Prajapati had once more asked Buddha's faithful attendant, Ananda, to assist her in entering the inner circle. According to at least one scholar, the Buddha's repeated resistance had to do with more than tradition.

> Finally, Ananda promised to do what he could and he approached the Lord Buddha and told Him that Prajapati, Yosodara and other ladies were intent on entering the Sangha as nuns. Once more the Master refused, for He knew that their appeal was based on the *principle of attachment*, and on such a basis an Order could not be builded and so, to test their earnestness, persistence and fixity of purpose.[135]

This "principle of attachment" conjoins the "two attachments" (biological and spiritual) as one, as a restraint against detachment. The Buddha acknowledges his mother's love, and their history of having been attached and therefore sets the bar extra high. She claimed that she was not only eager to renounce material possessions but she was also ready and eager to renounce her maternal possession of him. Recall that both the words material and maternal stem from the root for mother, mater. The Buddha, it seems, was simply being extra careful. No sangha, much less a first-ever order of nuns, should be built upon maternal attachment or attachment of any sort.

We should pause to appreciate how this story demonstrates that attachment-as-love is at once immediate, implicit and intuitive but not necessarily out in the open. Buddha and Ananda's deep, caring relationship was implied as Ananda made the case for Prajapati. Ananda simply reminded Buddha that Prajapati cared for and nursed him. He did not have to make a formal case for maternal love and sacrifice as a legitimate form of merit. Ananda is uniformly depicted as extraordinarily intelligent. These passages reflect his concordance with Prajapati. Both struggled with their love for Siddhartha, and both finally came to a deep acceptance of the fact that immediate feelings of warmth and care need to take a back seat to the higher calling to transcend these. This tale shows how the "two attachments", that of Bowlby and Buddha, are one, and how attachment-as-love is an ultimate hurdle to clear.

> At some point Prajapati once again sought permission to join the sangha or form a sangha of her own—as the first nun. According to the canon, this was the third time she attempted to make her case. By this time, Buddha had many disciples and a busy schedule. Direct access to him was not automatic. No doubt handlers of some sort were well aware of who she was and the delicacy of the situation. Out of compassion, we are told, first attendant Ananda himself interceded. Here conjecture proposes that Ananda acted out of commonsense, that prehistoric cultures universally but implicitly recognized what can now be understood scientifically and explicitly regarding maternal attachment. Ananda relayed Prajapati's request but was also denied three times. Then he asked: "Is a woman able to gain the fruit of stream-entry, once-returning, non-returning, and arahantship, if she leaves the household life and enters into homelessness and follows the teaching and discipline of the
> Exalted One?" The Buddha affirmed this. Thereupon Ananda rephrased his request: If a woman is able to do this, Master—and moreover Maha-Prajapati Gotami has rendered great service to the Master: she is his aunt, his governess and nurse, nourished the Exalted One with her own milk after his mother died—therefore it would be well if the Blessed One would allow women to leave home for the homeless life, to follow the teaching and discipline of the Master.[136]

Prajapati's poetic description of "release" also speaks to the view proposed here. Orthodox Buddhist attachment splits mom-baby, attachment-as-love and attachment as materialism. These are reconciled in an integral view, in a relative attachment with dual, attachment and detachment dynamics. Spiritual advancement always involves both. Whether framed psychologically, as personal growth or emotional healing, or spiritually, in terms of attainment and enlightenment, the two sides of attachment remain in play. Love and freedom are ultimately interlinked. Personal growth, whether framed as incremental attainment or stepwise realization involves a detachment from previous iterations of self and an attachment to something evoking meaning. Even as no-thing or void, there is more of a something, more lucidity, more clarity, more love and wisdom.

We leave former loves and lovers behind sometimes for the wrong reasons, but sometimes because we feel called by a higher, deeper, wider expanse of love. At this stage of Buddha's life, with

Ananda as Prajapati's proxy knocking three times at the door, something seems to linger. Neither Ananda nor Prajapati are free to love him as they once did, as Siddhartha. There is such tenderness here. One only needs to (dare to) consider how Ananda's pleas felt within the bottomless heart of the Buddha.

After all, Prajapati was probably far from smothering and very close, herself, to transcending her need for him! It seems reasonable to surmise that she mirrored, blessed, and empowered Buddha's own blossoming in ways we would call selfless. Embodying both sides of attachment, she likely both nurtured and protected him while also reinforcing his fierce curiosity, courageous questioning and forsaking of comforts and traditions. In this sense, from early in his life and well into her later years, she may have played an important part in his forsaking of her for the benefit of both.

Full of a love that frees the other, an attachment that leaves the attached ever more free, Prajapati expressed in her poem an advanced understanding of attachment. How this process informs mind and helps relieve suffering has come to inspire hundreds of millions of followers. What Siddhartha-Buddha endeavored and eventually accomplished would seem describable as a profound understanding of the supreme scaffolding that informed his mind. Over and again, more constraining degrees of mind needed to be denied, negated, and transcended in order to proceed toward the potential Buddha came to in nonattachment. Having come by this honestly, through firsthand, potent, biological, psychological attachment-love, he saw and explained with amazing clarity what we know as Buddhism. His life and teachings speak with precision—long before formal science would study such matters—about the ways in which human attachment are intimately, implicitly the stuff of self/ego/mind. This same attachment process is pervasively fundamental to all of human suffering, and conversely is key to the release from suffering.

> Buddha! Hero! Praise be to you!
> You foremost among all beings!
> You who have released me from pain,
> And so many other beings too.
>
> All suffering has been understood.
> The source of craving has withered.
> Cessation has been touched by me
> On the noble eight-fold path.
>
> I've been mother and son before;
> And father, brother—grandmother too.
> Not understanding what was real,
> I flowed-on without finding [peace].
>
> But now I've seen the Blessed One!
> This is my last compounded form.
> The on-flowing of birth has expired.
> There's no more re-becoming now.

See the gathering of followers:
Putting forth effort, self-controlled,
Always with strong resolution
—This is how to honor the Buddhas!

Surely for the good of so many
Did Maya give birth to Gotama,
Who bursts asunder the mass of pain
Of those stricken by sickness and death.

Three

In the main, Buddha's three rejections of Prajapati have been interpreted benignly, as a reflection of cultural traditions of the time as well as a firm but loving gesture to ensure that Prajapati was truly ready to enter the life of an ascetic. Buddhism, of course, is replete with similar master-disciple stories.

Jung has pointed out that three is a dynamic, unstable number. Legends, stories, and jokes commonly use the tripartite device to establish tension, which is then resolved in a fourth action. This occurs in Beethoven's Fifth Symphony. This implicitly builds in anticipation, *bom-bom-bom...* which is then released to rest in the fourth, BOM! The archetypal symbol of wholeness, the mandala, found across history and cultures, combines the circle with a four-part structure. Here the fourth beat is Buddha's assent, in effect, please-please-please-YES. Prajapati's three rejected attempts not only to join the sangha but to be the head of the first ever women's sangha would seem to fit both the building tension and the resolution.

Three may be a narrative convenience for something that unfolded many more times, over many years, with many emotional hues. Prajapati had to have loomed large as Siddhartha's first, longest attachment. He leaves her, their home, and any continuous, residual relationship behind. He prefers "emptiness" and the like, and declares that all their safe emotional bonds just lead to suffering. What has the official narrative omitted? One possibility goes something like this: Siddhartha's primary, maternal attachment was so rich and powerful that it would ultimately impel his later-life insights into the eternal, ever-present truth of attachment, clinging, grasping, and desire at the heart of human consciousness.

With respect to his multiple rejections of Prajapati, perhaps echoes of this original, deeply loving space still held influence. Perhaps this informed his side of what was far more than three discrete rejections but years of boring into these emotional caves, determined to both love and let go. This would allow him to fully exist with all he ever experienced and further, to fully understand Prajapati's co-arising longing to remain his mother. To carry, hold and be her pain in deep silence. He would have had to work within this pristine brokenness. Perhaps his mother's pleas deepened his already bottomless compassion. Perhaps he knew more than anyone else possibly could exactly what she needed to complete her journey. Maybe he was concerned that allowing her to join prematurely would have merely adhered to some unconscious agenda to earn him back, yet another insidious form of attachment. Maybe to deny her longer and more times would have been a reflection of imperfect aspects of his own humanity, for example, to leave a legacy that was socially sanctioned and therefore had a better chance of continuity.

Gautama & Gotami

Scholars disagree on Prajapati's importance. Jonathan Walters reviewed her life as told in the *Gotami Apadana*, one of 600 biographical stories of early monks and nuns which makes up the *Khuddaka Nikaya*.[137] Here Prajapati is referred to by her given name, Gotami. This was given, Walters argues, to acknowledge her close but under-appreciated alignment with her adopted son. These "moral biographies" were written during the second and first centuries BCE, at least two hundred years after Buddha's death. Most fit the formula of a wayward journey through other lifetimes culminating in key lessons learned and finally the supreme opportunity to become a follower of the Buddha.

In this analysis, Walters aligns himself with Buddhist scholars Mabel Bode and Caroline Foley who did original translations of canonical works in the 1890s. Foley (whose married name was Caroline Rhys Davids) analyzed multiple linguistic variants of the same texts and came increasingly to the view that surviving written sources represented a corrupted account of Buddha's original, true philosophy. The truth, she argued, would not be found in "monastic doctrines" because these were promoted "as central, not by him, but by his church." In her analysis, the monks who committed the dharma to writing were insulated in such "an inner, artificial world" as to be "half-men."[138]

Davids advanced the view that an unfortunate byproduct of this codification was the literary treatment of Prajapati. Her importance has been overlooked if not suppressed. Walters agrees and goes a step further. He paints Prajapati as a spiritual counterpart of Buddha, each a leader, each having their own Sangha legacy. He cites the fact of her shared name and her status as the first nun as proof of Prajapati's importance. In addition, such proof is found in her spiritual attainment and ultimate entry to Nirvana.[139]

Liz Wilson praises aspects of Walters' treatise while pushing back on others. She critiques Walters' claim that Prajapati offers a "distinctively feminine model for women's spiritual achievement," as going too far. For Wilson, Prajapati is quite an average householder and "represents the social locations of consort, wife, and parent." These are not impressive, and in fact amount to, "everything that Gotama must renounce in order to become the Buddha." She concludes, "Gotami encompasses in her life all that Gotama rejects in his." The fact of her association with Siddhartha is no basis for exaltation.[140] Wilson would probably find much to criticize with the views proposed in the current treatise, as the following explanation makes clear:

> Gotami lactates; Gotama preaches. Gotami's milk will never quench the thirst
> of desire; Gotama's will. What Gotami has to give is an extension of her
> transient physical body, the milk produced by her breasts; what Gotama has
> to give is an extension of his unchanging textual body. He gives the milk of
> dharma which flows from the eternal body of the teaching or
> dhammakaya.[141]

An assessment by Lauren Rochholz runs in a similar direction though not quite so far. She sees certain parallels between Prajapati and the Virgin Mary. Prajapati, she writes, also has the potential to provide women with inspiration and guidance. Neither figure in her view, "supersedes the supremacy of their god." She concluded, "I did not get the impression from *Gotami-apadana* that Gotami was "the very center of the universe" or the "Buddha for women; as Walters suggested."[142]

That Prajapati did not fade into oblivion can be interpreted as signaling that she had an opportunistic, clingy or dependent demeanor as suggested by some. Her dogged effort to be a nun in this light looks strategic, an effort to parlay her time-limited maternal attachment into some other raison d'être. Ultimately, this might be symbolized by her afterlife story.

> Furthermore, her entry into nirvana does not really outshine that of her
> adoptive son, as Walters argues. Her motivations are quite different. As she
> herself states, it is not because she has achieved her mission, but rather
> because, having placed herself in the care of the younger men of her lineage
> after the death of her husband Suddhodana, she is afraid of being left behind
> when they die: "I can't bear to see the Buddha's final passing, nor that of the
> two foremost disciples, nor that of Rahula, Ananda, and Nanda."[143]

The very same biographical data, it seems, can be seen as proof of an unhealthy, clingy attachment or as we have here, as a positive, human extension of Buddha's Mom. In the latter frame, she is a woman grounded in the relative attachment of her humanity with all its pain and love. The poems by the famous Yogi Milarepa are laden with similar sentiments of a wrenching, heart-rending torrent that flows and when superseded empties into a vast ocean of higher-order metta.

From a modern integral perspective, these scholars provide varying and valuable perspectives regarding the possible contribution of Prajapati as a human, individual woman. A fuller, integral embrace would honor these even as it transcends and includes Prajapati's individual personality. An integral view would situate even pettiness, manipulation and clinging within a larger attachment context. These are common elements where love is idealized and projected onto another, and characteristic of a self imploding in perceived rejection.

These only beg the question implied in the "two attachments" and therefore point once again to the prospect of an integral attachment. In this, attachment-love and its shadows, and metta are understood as hailing from one source accessible to each of us. As we will see in more detail, love's wounds are often portals to an oceanic metta. Then, as now, Spirit stands on the shoulders of mind, mind on the shoulders of body—all these moving in and out of reality like quarks. On the relative side of the street, the dynamism is comprised of attachment and detachment. On the other is primordial, pure awareness and peace that surpasses nonattachment.

Prajapati seems to speak to this to and fro, and describes an ultimate release in her poem. She specifically refers to the body of the baby she kept alive on one side and the dhammakaya (body of the dharma) on the other. From a male, detaching vantage point, she pulls in the wrong, backward, attaching and regressive direction. Being finally nurtured by what Wilson calls the "textual body", the transient, fluid-filled biological body co-arises as dhammakaya.

> It was I, O well-gone one,
> who reared you, flesh and bones.
> But by your nurturing was reared
> my flawless dharma-body.

Love-volution

Prajapati's poem just may be the voice of love as it spans the great chain, across body-mind-spirit, finally freeing itself of all these and of any object whatsoever. Love's first, evolutionary burst seen in mammals and in the mammalian brain is the stuff of our biological inheritance. The poem touches on the completion of this, perhaps the raison d'être of consciousness itself. She articulates our species' need and capacity to receive and give love, "I've been a mother and son before." And she touches on the essence of evolution as a repetitive, redundant machine. She has also been a father, brother, and grandmother. This love has cured in evolution's cauldron so many times that as a mother's love, son's love, father's, grandmother's, and brother's love, it is finally just love. Free of any object. A subject free of its object is no longer a subject.

> So what is the sound of that one hand clapping? What is the taste of that One Taste? When there is nothing outside of you that can hit you, hurt you, push you, pull you — what is the sound of that one hand clapping? See the sunlight on the mountains? Feel the cool breeze? What is not utterly obvious? Who is not already enlightened? As a Zen master put it, "When I heard the sound of the bell ringing, there was no I and no bell, just the ringing." There is no twiceness, no twoness, in immediate experience! No inside and no outside, no subject and no object — just immediate awareness itself, the sound of one hand clapping.[144]

Prajapati's poem expresses how affiliation and emotional bonds are intrinsic in human consciousness. Across the eons, we strive and never achieve the perfecting of this longing, which cements old and young, related and unrelated people not just to one another but to samsara. In the next chapter, we learn how this capacity has deep, pre-hominid roots. So fully developed was this attachment in Buddha's biologically attached, non-biological, psychologically attuned mom, Prajapati, that she achieved its culmination in nonattachment. This is the oneness at the heart of the two attachments.

Tracing all this, perhaps earthly love produced a divine form, heaven on earth, where the cessation of suffering in self and others begins as intention. Then with further perfecting of causes and conditions and the skillful means to navigate these, this heavenly hope and intention shifts. One stops becoming and is untethered, never to be or become again.

From another vantage point, Prajapati lived the mystery handed to her in full. She stepped into the life of her sister, as necessitated by her death. This opened up more potentials that she didn't simply accept but grabbed hold of and lived in full. She engaged in giving over of herself for the love of a tiny, needy baby. In short order, she was a major sounding board for a brilliant, ever-evolving child. Later still, she would make an impossible sacrifice in relinquishing him, based on his new, different love. This is a love beyond any clinging. From the relative side of the street, Prajapati seems to arc across the sky, powered by other-worldly flexibility, courage and kindness, achieving a mysterious, unbounded we-space beyond all definition.

Girls & Women

Buddhism is loud and clear on the origins of suffering and the path to its cessation. But both ancient and modern Buddhism are rather quiet with respect to the unique hardships that plague girls and women. A true, universal dharma embraces this reality. Consider again that the meaning of dharma comes from the root *dhr*, to hold or support.

> Dharma is that which holds, supports and sustains life. It is the essential law of life; it is the law of a person's essential character. It is also virtue … in conformity with the essential law of one's own personality. The supreme function of poetry is to make us aware of this dharma which is the sanction of all moral values.[145]

Some argue that generic, problematic 'moral values' undergird gender differences. These same challenges, greed, sin, laziness, economic disincentives and institutionalized barriers, to name some common examples, are applicable to all of mankind (human kind). But such claims tend to fall somewhere between partial truths and a dodge—and given the distinct plight of girls and women, since the time of Buddha and continuing, are likely a reflection of an underlying patriarchy.

Sometimes all one can do is highlight that which no one is hiding in the first place. The documentary, *It's a Girl*, opens with a mother killing her eighth baby daughter. The film depicts the everyday evil of so-called "gendercide"—the killing of female infants practiced in India and China. Mothers will lay a wet cloth over their baby daughters' mouths to prevent them from a life of inescapable suffering.[146]

Humanity is doing an especially poor job at keeping, holding, and protecting girls and women. The deep feminine is an endangered dimension of our species. Its natural habitat has been shattered. A dharma based in Buddha's Mom would identify the usual "socialism" suspects: an economic safety net, a living wage, family planning, more funding for relief agencies, and modernized adoption options. A deeply informed dharma would do even more. We need to summon the divine feminine to stop the hemorrhage. We need her to "imagine" healing, as the most mystical Beatle suggested.

Policy born of our belonging to Earth, and not the other way around, would be a good beginning. For instance, the presumption would be that democracies are better suited to handle petroleum reserves than self-interested corporations. Oil should be understood as a country's natural resource and a matter of national security. Its protection and diligent use should be a government's fundamental function. Rather than corporations paying nominal fees for full ownership of the oil, governments should pay nominal fees to them for extracting it.

As mentioned, Stephen Batchelor translates the four noble truths as referring less to abstract or absolute truths and more to a fullness and completeness. In light of Buddha's Mom, the four, as he calls them, speak to that which optimizes a baby's chance of a full and complete inheritance of its humanity. The gap between a world more informed by these principles and the one we share is evident by the disproportionate suffering of children, especially girls and women. However, to date, orthodox schools of Buddhism do not delineate the suffering as a problem to be resolved.

I was once the lead child therapist at a psychiatric program for kids with attachment disorder. Our team tried very hard, working with the court and Child Protective Services, to stop a polysubstance-abusing pregnant woman from further damaging her baby in-utero. At most, she could be arrested and held briefly. We knew her well because she had been court-ordered for treatment to our program for pregnant women. Our program was good but was no match for her damaged soul and the men who took advantage of it. She had given birth to four previous cocaine-addicted babies. We failed the fifth time around as well. One never forgets the way those babies cry.

If dharma means law, consider the sick dharma that prevented our therapeutic team from protecting those fetuses. America is so enamored with "independence" and "freedom" that this woman was free to exercise her warped independence. Our collective infatuation with independence leaves no room for serious policy debate regarding interdependence. But interdependence is cosmic dharma. Those fetuses are profoundly interdependent, for better or worse, on their "mother." What this biological mother needed was bolstering, holding by other mothers based in law. Where one Russian doll is damaged, other successive containers need to provide bolstering. Policies would encode goals and means for holding, keeping, protecting the mother's role in lineage transmission.

Who will ever know the depth of these crimes? Prajapati stepped up and ushered one boy into adulthood. Through the eyes of Buddha's Mom, her children include the eight strangled baby girls and their millions of sisters documented in *It's a Girl*. Her children include the five drug-addicted fetuses my colleagues and I did not save, as well as the boys and men suffering under the same male-dominated economic, power structures, never empowered to be fathers.

Recently on the radio, one father's words were translated. His young daughters had died of hunger. They had been eating dirt. Popular culture spews out a lot of misinformation on money and happiness. This father could not earn enough money in their ravaged economy. Creator of *It's a Girl*, Evan Grae Davis, concluded the primary cause of genocide to be poverty. The father's story was of yet another third world pawn, where corporations literally did not pay a living wage. The father spoke of emptiness and pain. God knows he tried to find work, tried to feed his children.

Also, in the news today, up to 200,000 Somali children may starve to death this year and 300 kidnapped Nigerian girls remain at large. What will tomorrow's news bring? One persistent myth is that money does not buy happiness or love. Formal research is cited as showing money only bolsters happiness at the extremes of rich and poor. Clear-eyed science, however, shows that money and subjective well-being have a linear relationship. These scientific findings run opposite to Biblical and Buddhist orthodoxy, where money is the root of evil and represents a materialistic attachment leading to suffering. Never mind that the news arms of massive corporations, lobbyists, and politicians are not hammering away at the travesty of gendercide.

Buddha's Mom provides a much less nebulous and moralistic position. As much as money may bring misery, statistically, humans are not hopelessly selfish or idiotic. Money, according to bottom-up research as opposed to top-down morality, translates into the ability of parents to provide for their family. This translates as a workable, ethical dharma, a capacity to hold and support each other and the children.

Yes, money translates quite reasonably as materialism. It is actually materialism itself that deserves a new look. Materialism is based in the word, matter, and certainly corresponds to the desire for earthly things. But a unipolar view of materialism as greed and the source of suffering reveals a sadly impoverished view of humanity. After all, the root of "materialism", matter, comes from *mater*, Latin for <u>mother.</u> In late-Middle English, the root of money and materialism is *matere*, mother. The linguistic lineage of mother includes the proto-Italic, *mātēr*, and there are similar echoes in multiple ancient languages including Sanskrit.

Where humans externalize and concretize and make an object of mater, mother, matter, they cause themselves harm. The body is mother to the mind, and earth and loved ones the collective body, collective mother. When one is home in their body, their desire to be fed, to be loved, to love and to exist within their own skin is relatively continuous. The pregnant addict has expunged her own body. Her natural desires, her natural internal roots in her body, her connection to a tribe and, of course, the baby-to-be, were grotesquely denied and replaced by drugs. Her Goddess was objectified and abused by some blend of codependence, chaos, and artificial chemical mood states. No surprise that her journey included early life abuse and attachment deprivation.

Corporations thrive by manipulating emotional attachment. Unhealthy craving is their bread and butter. They drive narratives that keep the masses wanting more. Even when closets are full and bank accounts are empty, consumers are enabled to extend their credit and to live indebted to and to perpetually pay the piper. Buddhism's response to corporate over-reach is generally tepid. Orthodox exalting of anti-consumerism (asceticism) co-arises in the mirror. Neither extreme offers a clear, sustainable middle way for us to be in a caring relationship with our own bodies and emotions.

Ultimately, corporations' ability to drive a wedge between psyche and body is the smaller part of the equation. The lynchpin is corporate-government incest. Corporate wealth is required to become a legislator. Legislators are, by proxy, corporate lobbyists. Little by little, governments across the globe become agents of trans-global corporate interests. When one country still maintains quaint laws concerning wages, human rights, workplace safety, pollution and efforts to control factors that led the mother to kill her eight daughters, the "corporatocracy" simply goes elsewhere for its raw materials and labor. The firm love of Buddha's Mom is needed to stop the abuse of her children stemming from the insidious comingling of governments and big business.

Hard-right paranoia proclaims socialism at every turn but turns a blind eye to these emerging, modern oligarchies. So-called conservatism has been unable to accept that the myth of free enterprise contributes to the destruction of democracy. Under the banner of deregulation and free markets, corporate actors undermine life, liberty, and happiness. They declare themselves to be persons while turning people into loyal customers. Big alcohol's rolled out a beer called America, and spends heavily on marketing to the barely legal sector. Big pharma's medications for hypertension and reflux aim at the same sweet spot, yielding decades of loyal consumers.

Vajrayana master, Reggie Ray speaks of the ego and left-brain as having no direct bodily basis. Corporation, as a term and legal construction, is worth reflection. Banks, manufacturers, trans-national conglomerates, and organizations of various stripes are intrinsically driven, for power and profit, to abide the *corporation* truth claim. A corporation is a body with legal personhood. Alas, corporations have achieved release from earth's cycles of life and death. The corporation lives on, possibly forever!

> Corporation: a body formed and authorized by law to act as a single person although constituted by one or more persons and legally endowed with various rights and duties including the capacity of succession.[147]

Back in reality, corporations are not sentient. To the extent that they mimic life, they do so in a manner similar to vampires. Corporate behemoths are manifestations of grandiose patriarchal delusion. They claim to be persons, free of biological constraints, which live in perpetuity. Rather than admitting dependence on Earth, they objectify and claim ownership of her riches. Rather than acknowledge their dependency on her peoples, they turn them into consumers and laborers and subject them to extremes of poverty and pollution. A feminine reset would bust up monopolies and businesses much as a good mother quells tantrums, "high chair tyrants" and snotty teens who protest too much—with her firm love.

In socialism, the state owns the banks and oil companies. In the corporatocracy, the banks and oil companies drive government policy. In a world where corporations were not in control of the oil, governments were held accountable to their role as stewards of Earth, her land, water, and sky. Buddha's Mom would realign humanity within the stream of Homo sapiens' evolution, as a lineage of life with a taproot ultimately tracing all the way back to the Big Bang. We belong to this lineage. Its bounty, which includes our earthly home and spiritual body—the mother of all mothers—can go by the name Buddha's Mom. The whole of humanity has a special duty to Her and to those most directly entrusted with Her transmission: women and girls. Even our addiction to oil could be reimagined from this vantage. We must start precisely where we are to have any hope of making lasting change. With the proverbial shift in consciousness, alternative, sustainable sources of energy would be able to compete in the marketplace. At present in America, neither the electorate, nor the government nor corporate special interests have any serious alignment with Buddha's Mom. If change is ever to occur, it will be bottom-up and born of a new relationship to both our planetary, "heavenly body" and our physical body.

Least of These

Buddha's Mom stands for all that she stands behind: the weak, the hungry, the desperate and afraid. She is the most formidable sort of receptivity. She hears the most distant cry. The same passion and compassion flowed through Jesus. His enlightenment radiates from many passages of the New Testament, especially given the oppressive patriarchy into which he was thrust. The all-powerful prefect Pontius Pilate all but begged Jesus for some way out of ordering his execution.

Prajapati was well-born and presumably not forced to care for her sister's baby. But love and power travel different pathways. "Come you so blessed," said Jesus, "you will inherit the Kingdom. For I was hungry and you gave me food." At first, she had no obvious reason for changing her life's course. But because she did, Siddhartha might eventually have said the same of her. *I was thirsty and you gave me drink. I was overcome by tanhā and you nursed me.* Her lineage as the conveyer of our species' attachment-love reaches its fullness in him; no less than the same flows in you and me. Our smallness is welcome at these great heights. Knowing our longing, orphaned self/ego/mind so well, Jesus comes as one of us, so Christians say. Neither he nor the partially orphaned Siddhartha arrive on the scene full grown aboard a chariot powered by lightning bolts. Siddhartha was no man-god at all. Many elements in their biographies seem to work hard to convey empathy. Perhaps recognizing that self/ego/mind is vulnerable to the whims of hope and fear, Jesus is born to a poor family. He enters this life as the stranger, giving humanity some space to check him out and consider opening their hearts. *I am the stranger*, he would come to say, *that you welcomed and the naked one you clothed.*

Sick and imprisoned, the least of us, the most cast aside in me and that which I most reject in you and that we declare evil—all these are to be found in the stories of these two men. The tanhā at the heart of the dharma (the craving that causes suffering) is said to be one of evil Mara's three daughters. Mara, as mentioned, is Buddhism's top demon or devil. Representing craving, Tanhā is sister of Aratī, discontent, and Ragā, lusting. Buddha's Mom propels us to think twice when detaching becomes over-reaching. Her words—the divine feminine, it seems, were expressed in Jesus' moving statement: "Truly I tell you, just as you did it to one of the least of these who are members of my family, you did it to me."[148] By the Bodhisattva's very definition, we are only as strong (loving, free, released, enlightened) as the weakest and least in us. Be we rivers, animals, children, girls, women—wherever love withers on Mother Nature's vine, we are called to love.

Alas, even child molesters, rapists, despots, corporate polluters, military-industrial abstractions—those perpetrating harm to the "least of these"—know not what they do. They do not know better from the perspective of Buddhism and are no different in their potential to know. Indeed, they may have the least access to their true legacy and lineage, because they have no internal Buddha or Christ consciousness, no stable encounter with their Buddha-nature. Otherwise, they would no more cut down their enemies than they would themselves. Attachment-love is not flowing through them to those they rule or have certain worldly powers over. Although miraculously born human, their taproot is withered.

Those who are quick to follow or reject them are different in degree but not in kind. Judgment must emanate from love. Otherwise, the ego lives in sinful isolation, separating from source, giving rise to variants of us and them, me and not me. Our species is forever reaching out, belonging to and rejecting from. Attaching and detaching are psychologically a priori.

A gentle noticing and healthy resistance to this sinning, separating flux is possible. To pick just a recent cultural example, recall how so many of us pounded the war drums after 9/11, or did not protest when others did so. The country song, *Courtesy of the Red, White and Blue*, further heightened the patriotic fervor. When the all-female group, Dixie Chicks, put out a tepid protest song, they encountered a mass, supposedly patriotic push-back. There was something seething below the surface pop-star theatrics. Much as pre-Civil Rights southern whites routinely lynched blacks, and much as Christian whites became hyper-aggressive, and then tortured and killed women in Salem, there was a huge hunger to aggress against someone somewhere, to make a bogeyman of Saddam.

During the lead-up to the invasion of Iraq, some longed for the rush to war to be channeled in a way that had a chance of actually making the world a better place. Rather than invade Iraq, we could have produced evidence of weapons of mass destruction or future 9/11 plots to an international court. If there was anything to this, a warrant could be issued. The point being that when symbolism overtakes realism, the danger or overreach increases dramatically. A police action to apprehend an alleged criminal has much less of a chance to foment grand mythic narratives and inmap sentience.

As with self-loathing in deep self disturbance, the hate perpetrated by cruel power mongers is mappable. What passes for evil is never quite as unique and special as purported by those in a rush to quell it. On the other side, claims of righteousness and "spreading freedom" are hardly as snowy white and free of other agendas. Versions of the same agenda encircle the world and traverse history. Eternally recurring, the genocidal machinery has forms of the idealized-vilified bloviater-in-chief—archetypal warrior kings—and their technocrats and engineers. And of course, on each sideline are the church laity and citizenry or the oppressed or Rosie Riveters. It takes a village to destroy another. Human history includes endless war-making, human sacrifice, enslavement, cannibalism, and torture. Waterboarding is one of modernity's twists on age-old practices that included, in medieval times, pouring molten metal into people's mouths and anuses. There were devices like the rack and one for tearing breasts.

Often overlooked is the fact that evil tends to require boring supports such as a quarry and metallurgists to make instruments of torture, and technocrats to organize the flowcharts for death camps. Without these supports, genocide and wide spectrum oppression is impossible. At a minimum, Buddha's Mom symbolizes a combined scientific and spiritual appreciation of the developmental needs of children. Teens on their way to being radicalized need more encounters with Buddha's Mom. Through her, humanity takes the lead over sectarian divisiveness. A powerful mother figure would ensure they not become adults before they demonstrated corresponding spiritual maturity. Less abstractly, she would want them to have a car to fix, an educational system to challenge their oversimplifications, or crushes to talk to for hours on the phone. "You hang up first."

Imagine if all African and Middle Eastern youth had a chance to surf, snowboard, make movies, do volunteer work with less fortunate kids in countries their parents hate. Imagine if they could spend time with potential, prosocial career mentors. Some mix of these, protection from exploitive ideologues and access to mentors, amounts to natural, loving iterations of the teddy bear and binky, albeit much further in the direction of what Bowlby refers to as the secondary exploration system.

It is especially important for children to experiment, make mistakes, suffer humiliation, recover, change their course, and rebuild. A society rooted in the science and kindness of Buddha's Mom would not let them play with fire so soon in life. The third turning consistently speaks of emptiness and space. In adolescence, girls are routinely deprived of the practical, imperfect relative version, opportunities to adhere and rebel and navigate the enticing, terrifying, confusing liminal space of love—and live to tell about it. Forced and arranged marriages sometimes shortchange this possibility.

The poet Milarepa, much like Patacara and Kisa, would only find peace and release after being devoured by raw emotional pain and self-loathing. He rejected convention, was in fact scorned by local Tibetan Buddhist authorities, and survived quite literally with only Mother Earth as his psycho-spiritual cocoon. Females disproportionately recognized the truth and power of his path.

Milarepa's disciple Sahle Aui, only sixteen, already knew well the pain of a woman's place in traditional Tibetan society, a pain still pervasive in so-called modernity.

> Sometimes I think to myself: Does it make sense? To freely give yourself with
> your parents' goods to someone who for life enslaves you as a servant? At
> first a lover is an angel, then a demon, frightening and outrageous. In the end
> he is a fierce elephant who threatens to destroy you.[149]

The disproportionate number of black males in American prisons similarly reflects the lack of protections and alternatives we suggest are aligned with a holistic understanding of attachment. These are necessary to hold open relative attachment spaces, places for a "man-child" to negotiate the many adult pressures bearing down upon them. These psycho-developmental spaces in turn become, potentially, placeholders for enlightenment. The inimitable documentary *Hoop Dreams* depicts this crisis-opportunity with profundity. Somewhere, Buddha's Mom cries for every one of these teens. I suspect this liminal space exists in the hearts of those reading this sort of book, those doing what they can to better themselves and bring more light into this pain-wracked world.

The results need not be abstract. Even something as simple as a child falling off their bike, followed by an empathic response from an attachment figure, conforms to the same structure. Before the crash, life was smooth and continuous, but suddenly pain and fear flood the space of consciousness. In a twist on Descartes, a mom's presence, worry, and reassurance translates as, "She sees me therefore I am." The ego sheath is restored. Sweetly, just the colored bandage itself speaks to this "placeholder" notion. It has a very small, physical analgesic element—pressing down on a wound deflects pain signals. We are always grabbing, rubbing, and holding our aching parts. But the bigger part of the bandage experience has to be the beautiful placebo effect, the brighter colored the better at restoring the continuity of the self.

To circle back for a moment, recall that matter and materialism are derivatives of "mater," the root word for mother. The strong money-materialism correlation therefore implicates Buddha's Mom in money matters. Worth noting here is that throughout the world, where mothers have their own monetary means, their kids tend to have opportunities such as those mentioned above, ones which open spaces for solid character development. Well-to-do Third World kids tend to be more secular, worldly, able to screw up and recalibrate. This is much less the case for unprotected kids (and their similarly unprotected parents), vulnerable to propagandists' tripe, not to mention those who are abused, forced into early marriages, trafficked or radicalized.

Money

Maternal bonding and, for example, breastfeeding provide windows into cultural views and values on Buddha's Mom. Money is another, albeit more abstract touchstone of attachment's convergence with culture. As stated earlier, Siddhartha very likely was breastfed. As Buddha, he in no manner suggested mothers and babies should not breastfeed even as he employed the metaphor of thirst and hunger to found his philosophy of the nature of the human condition. A baby's attachment needs are clearly an expression of what in the abstract can be identified as human desire. As Maslow discovered, desire does not leap from raw nutritional needs to keeping up with the Jones' or coveting someone's spouse. People use money to acquire the essentials, food, shelter and elements which translate as security. A deeper, more progressive, more scientifically sound dharma would offer more precision regarding the relationship of money and desire. While sermons on shallow consumerism write themselves, a grounded dharma acknowledges not just that, but how any roof beats no roof.

Recent research has upended previous notions related to money and equanimity and well-being. Historically, money was thought to matter only for those at the very base of Maslow's pyramid. The standard academic view was roughly in line with orthodox Buddhism, that beyond this minimal threshold, more money did not buy more happiness. The floor in this model (below which money was impactful) even echoes the austerities cut-off, above which, according to the Middle Way, desire for more of anything is a recipe for dukkha.

This floor, above which more money does not matter, has proved nonexistent. Researchers found that richer people report higher levels of well-being than poor people, and people in richer countries report the same, higher well-being, than those in poorer countries. They concluded that economic growth correlates with increased feelings of well-being. "Moreover, the data show no evidence for a satiation point above which income and well-being are no longer related."[150]

An integral attachment perspective seems fitting. Money can't buy love but it buys goods and services that matter to families. Whether food, shelter, or a car with air conditioning, these are attachments which, to some degree, translate as directly meaningful. Buddha's Mom puts an urgent, earthy face on all this. Mothers, pregnancies, and babies at risk would be dealt with very differently if Bowlby's and Buddha's attachment were transcended and incorporated with a new frame as suggested here. As a society, we would move beyond insipid safety nets, for example, of a few weeks of formula or barebones homeless shelter. Babies would have rights to their human inheritance, because mothers would be guaranteed a means of providing such sustenance. Third World teens would be protected from suffocating, throwback practices that pass for culture. These include arranged marriages in pre-adolescence and genital mutilation. Hopefully, we will increasingly be able "follow the money" needed to enhance the care of our species' next generation to Buddha's Mom.

Wego

The term *wego* offers a useful, palpable handle on Buddha's Mom. *Ego's* reign over the inner life needs rethinking. Since Freud, the term ego has gone viral. The first misstep in this journey occurred when Freud's translator replaced the psychoanalyst's use of everyday language for the first-person (I) and third-person (it) with the Latin terms, ego and id.[53] Presumably, this added scientific heft. This dressed up connotation for the first-person permeates Buddhist teachings, dharma talks and you-name-it, self-help, psychotherapy, psychospiritual theories, and all associated media.

In wego, there's the obvious echo of both ego and we-space. But wego more neutrally houses the co-arising first-, second-, and third-person in a field of awareness grounded in dependent origination and witnessing. Wego is a useful, approachable way into the immediate, personal

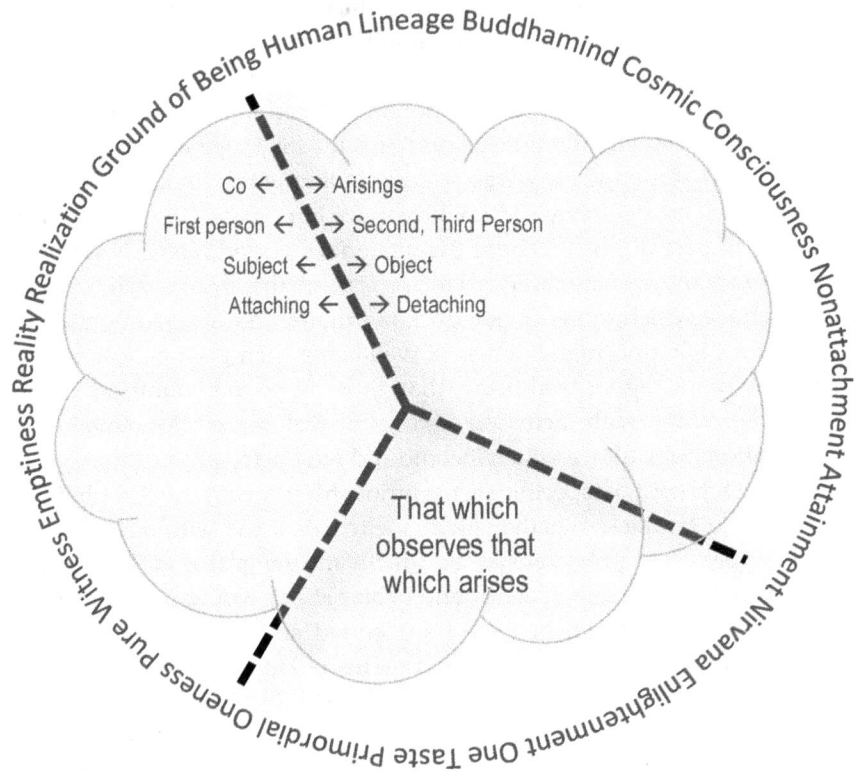

Ground of Being Human Lineage Buddhamind Cosmic Consciousness Nonattachment Attainment Nirvana Enlightenment One Taste Primordial Oneness Pure Witness Emptiness Reality Realization

Co ← → Arisings
First person ← → Second, Third Person
Subject ← → Object
Attaching ← → Detaching

That which observes that which arises

experience of the vessel of transmission that we have been calling Buddha's Mom. The ego/I is not burdened with the task of getting witnessing right. Rather witnessing is atmosphere of the inner life.

Wego resets we-space as well. We-space tends to refer to the interpersonal extension of self/ego/mind. In wego, intra-subjective contents are included along with interpersonal. The fact that wego has a playful lilt, that it does not take itself too seriously, is more than serendipitous. This goes to the heart of everyday enlightenment, to the "I am that" interplay manifesting in the Dalai Lama's frequent smile and gentle laugh. The perfections (paramitas) such as joy and equanimity are not unattainably perfect but implicit. The fact that ego has some difficulty being more light and free is not surprising given that it had Sigmund (or technically his interpreter) for a mother.

As suggested early on, *ego* tends to be used interchangeably with *self* and *mind*. Problems associated with the aggregation of these terms therefore impact virtually all references to the inner life and spiritual path from Oprah to Deepak to Nagarjuna! They say the Eskimo have a dozen words for snow. The time seems ripe for ego to have some healthy competition.

Most importantly, wego more directly reflects what self/ego/mind downplays: humanity's pervasive, integral relational nature. Wego may add something of value to models of human development with no need to alter the ego givens. For example, an early-life, scarcely differentiated self/other worldview can continue to be viewed as the formative phases of ego development.

Budding, infantile awareness can still be fashioned as a primitive ego with a barely emergent "me" organization. But these views may be rounded out nicely with an overlay of wego formation.

Presumably, the proto-ego and proto-other (mother) continually co-arise in the offspring's wego as a nascent unity. According to attachment science and consistent with wego, this cloud of awareness can be characterized in specific ways and these tend to last a lifetime and influence relationships, health, work and well-being.

Wego is not earth-shattering, more the opposite. It is *right here*, simple and obvious. Whether we use the word "I", awareness, consciousness, or perception, there is a palpable, instant, relational feel to life, to physical and mental objects within subjective space, be these physical or psychological. Why not increasingly experience, that is to say *witness*, I/me within a fluid, dynamic, relational flux? This aligns us fully with Buddha's Mom. This is the same space she lived in as she loved and related to Siddhartha as well as to her own struggles which finally led to her own awakening. With sitting practice, bodywork, reading, with pointing out, with insight, attending to dreams and altered states, the witnessing aspect can override its contents. Awareness can shift to its natural state. Various descriptions of this ground of being are depicted as implicit when the limiting cloud of fluctuating contents drops away. Like the night sky, these may have a flattened look to the earthly ego but, of course, are the very twinkles of an infinite universe dancing across her retina.

Harping on ego as an obstacle to the ground of being, the sheer beauty of the moment, complicates the possibility of loosening the reins and befriending our proximate, intimate experience. The exalted notion of transcending egoic attachments is overplayed. Ego is more vessel of evolution than its obstacle. The "I" is a node of witnessing which perversely goes unrecognized as such. It is downsized to personalized, singular connotations of an inner pilot charting its way across the years. We go left, right, because we want this and that. Truly, desires, feelings, imagery, memories, concepts, narratives are iteration of *I* and *me*, and all perfect in their individuality. In wego, this plurality of arisings makes more sense as thin, passing wrappings over movements and energies.

Ego, wego and grand advances in human evolution are inseparable. Models differ in the details, but peg advances in our psychology at some 150 to 40 thousand years ago. Intermingling factors and forces include marine resource exploitation, personalized, artistic, ornamentation, pierced shells, dyed animal teeth, use of pigments. Cognitive advances incorporating leaps in awareness, these advances in self/ego/mind and other, or wego, were assuredly nature-nurture. "Cultural evolution" is another explanatory factor evidenced by tool, art advances, and other phenomena such as internment of the dead. These myriad factors, which of course probably also included genetic mutations, enabled and were enabled by increased population densities, more advances, migration, variation in forms of intelligence and spiritual awareness.

Constant personalization of everything in the many-splendored field of sensory, somatic, cognitive, and interpersonal multiplicities is distorting and natural at the same time. The I/me and its extensions into the first-person, second-person, and third-person are obviously incredibly useful and time-proven. With wego comes increased potential to witness, in the Buddhist sense, ourselves, our inner architecture—the I, self/ego/mind and other—as these continuously launch and fade out across the present moment.

Contemplative and wisdom traditions' forays into the deeper realms of human experience demonstrate how badly the last hundred years of self-help psychobabble revolving around ego needs re-thinking. A usual take-away goes as follows. Anything besides a humble but expansive embrace of life, perfectly balanced but not acclaimed as such, proves one is not spiritually mature.

The ego-trap sets up these loops with two hands tied behind its back. Anyone frustrated or thrilled with a meditative experience is tethered to ego. Anyone saving the planet is really just trying to garner admiration or convince himself or herself that their life has meaning. We enter a similar house of mirrors in meditative practice. One is to try to let go of thoughts but trying itself is wanting. Wanting is ego-driven and if this is not enough, of course, the cause of suffering. And if that is not enough, the whole enterprise is always on the brink of incoherence. As each of us knows intimately, "part of me" wants X and "another part" wants Y.

But an integral model housing witnessing, emptiness, dependent origination, and Buddha's Mom reveals that the whims of desire do not need to be forced into an ego aggregation. Each whim, being and lifetime can be allowed its own expression. Also, wego accounts for how these comprise ordinary as well as altered forms of consciousness. In dream states and psychedelic experiences there is often little trace of one's everyday self and identifications. But these generally conform to an experiencer, for example, a dream ego within an unfolding experience in keeping with wego's essential architecture.

The whole point is to bring awareness and kindness to the diverse mix of contents, and to do so with increased frequency, duration, and depth such that this compassionate attending syncs with the ground of awareness. Such is the caring, eager to lend a hand orientation of the bodhisattva. Therein self/ego/mind and all sentient life are welcomed.

Too often we treat ourselves aggressively and demand self/ego/mind adhere to a severe sort of *spiritual diet*. One feels guilty for being slack, not exercising, meditating or eating right, and so on—times 100,000. "I'll exercise, eat healthy, do yoga and/or meditate tomorrow since I was lazy today." Spiritual diet logic is anything but. It has us slacking off because, oh well, we already did slack off. Or we do the same for the opposite reason. We treat ourselves to skipping a day of practice, jogging or to high fat food because we were good yesterday. The tribal mind is never far off. We make spiritual practice into a sacrificial ritual. We feel guilt. We fear reprisal and make bargains. Buddha's Mom has only patience and acceptance for the silly, immature ways of the child.

Ego, of course, tends to get credit for the lazy, practice skipping, junk food eating side. A wego lens reminds us how very constrained the spiritual diet is. When desire echoes about, in splintered push-pulls, the first-person and its contents form a dense cloud. Monkey mind and spiritual diet chatter obscure the view. There is little light or insight (could just as well be out-sight). As depicted, the freer of these clanging contents the better. More unity unfolds with reflection, levity and warm, acceptance. These natural, maternal, loving enhancers of witnessing have a familiar feel. In Buddha's Mom, through wego, the ground of being is close at hand. The higher and freer one's embrace of reality. The more space, the more integral.

I hope readers will give wego a whirl as an alternative (orienting generalization) to the overly laden ego and its near-clones, self and mind. Just consider how many times per day or hour one says or thinks "I". As we unwittingly launch into these inner/outer "self-talk" programs, all manner of built-in biases enter the slipstream of awareness. When self/ego/mind rule the roost, subtle, at-the-ready, fluid interactions with soma, living intentions, gravity, nature, and stop-motion beauty—to name a few—do not make the cut. But these are all faces of desire along the "path of desire" (an ancient reference to the Vajrayana according to Reggie Ray). Their absence betrays ego's overreach.

The goal of mindfulness, the witnessing of the pageantry of the moment, quickens with an ever more collective, expansive embrace.

While it is possible to blame ego for polluting and distorting our Buddha-nature, such judgment is an unnecessary add-on. In wego, a poly-arising field of awareness is natural, timeless, and one with liberation. In pulling out ego and noting its functioning, awareness splits along the familiar lines of self/ego/mind and other. All is mirror and echo. With less judgment, the sequence pours into vaster spaces. Awareness naturally returns to its contents, but with practice, the edges glow. We are held in a sense by illusion and mercifully given further chances to get used to the confusion and magnificence. Contents in this inner dialog, as the graphic shows, have no substance beyond the immediate, interactive foreground of phenomenological awareness. Being nothing sounds like something that is not easy to accept! Thankfully, examples of paths back to meaning abound.

The mother-to-be, as previously mentioned, is a portal into Buddha's mom. She exemplifies how attachment is the vessel of our species' lineage and she is also in sync with the wego concept. As she approaches delivery and across the years (when all goes well), she bridges the ego-wego divide as she responds to nature's call to shift from self/ego/mind in the direction of humanity's life support system. Growing in her belly, feeding on her and demanding all her energy is the future itself. To no small degree, accepting the job means letting go of what her self/ego/mind has spent a life cultivating. She will face intensive physical demands and pain, existential shifts in identity and soon, the infant/toddler's intense demands for life-support and love. To defend against this or do the minimum is to deny a sacred invitation. Lest we judge, the wego perspective reminds us of the vital importance of spiritual scaffolding for any such transformations. To step up as Prajapati did requires courage, spiritual and also material support.

An ego paradigm puts too much onus on the hero. This casts those of us who fail to take full advantage of a spiritual crisis as losers and cowards and nameless nobodies. But such ego driven inferences may harm more than help provide clarity. Let us recall how ego is directly linked to the word "I". This relationship goes to the heart of the most celebrated and controversial truth claims of all time, "I am the way, the truth and the life." Once again, the wego term and concept might shed some light. According to scholars, the Aramaic word for "I" used here was repeated: "ena ena". I/ego was thus proclaimed as plural with connotations of the I within the I, the essence of the I, deep I, and the transcendent I. In wego, the denser, small and the freer, vaster I's co-arise. There is "I" on one side and "the truth and the life" on the other.

Jesus' statement hints at wego's ultimate utility. Approaching this from a liberal, secular angle, we begin with the fact that Jesus was born human, with a human ego. Perhaps his use of "I" was an effort now lost to prod followers to look toward their own divinity. In this interpretation, the human ego is proclaimed as "life" itself. According to one scholar, life (*hayye*) translates in both Aramaic and Hebrew as something more like prana or Qi. Jesus was, in this line of reasoning, associating not just his own I/ego but I/ego generally with the "sacred life force, the primal energy that pervades all of nature and the universe."[151] Buddhist teaching tales often point to the same sacred wormhole.

> Two traveling monks reached a river where they met a young woman. Wary
> of the current, she asked if they could carry her across. One of the monks
> hesitated, but the other quickly picked her up onto his shoulders, transported
> her across the water, and put her down on the other bank. She thanked him

and departed. As the monks continued on their way, the one was brooding and preoccupied. Unable to hold his silence, he spoke out. "Brother, our spiritual training teaches us to avoid any contact with women, but you picked that one up on your shoulders and carried her!" "Brother," the second monk replied, "I set her down on the other side, while you are still carrying her."[152]

The first monk is to the second as a smaller I or node of experience is to a freer, emptier node. This parallels a loosening of ego and awareness that can be envisioned as wego. We can let ego's adherence to rules be suspended for a moment when other perspectives provide a complimentary structure or space. The second monk in this light did not view the first's question as unworthy of an answer. It was one position among many, including the woman's, and therefore simply constrained. The second monk might even view the woman's plea as incorrect or immoral within the constraints of his training. His actions indicate simply that he was able to take on other perspectives.

The simple wego model offers some wiggle room with respect to ego terminology, for example, wherein a spiritual ego is something between an oxymoron and a freak of nature. Where a healthy, mature ego is possible. Not an impossible, mysterious point between too big an ego or too small a sense of self, too inadequate and dysfunctional a self-concept. With wego, bigger is better. The bigger, the freer, less egoic, more empty and more grounded.

Returning to the story, it follows that the second monk was all this. Freer, more liberated, his experience mirrored a deeper spiritual knowing, a more expansive wego. Buddhist compassion, accordingly, increases as awareness transcends ego's constraints. Ego holds, for example, monks' rules of conduct are carried and set down flexibly, based on conditions and circumstances. There is no "we" in first, second, and third person dualities. No we, for example, in, "I helped her" or "I obeyed my precepts." But an embedded ego is portal to the woman's needs, perhaps the sexual tension, the moral dilemma and the like, and becomes a gate to a wider embrace, a deeper dharma.

With respect to this river-crossing parable, one might ask who benefited the most? Perhaps the first monk did as he grappled with the experience and one day became wizened like his sangha brother. Maybe the woman did, considering her plight, not just in getting across the river but in encountering a man who was neither exploitive or overly detached. Maybe the second monk was most blessed because (in relative attachment terms) the challenge allowed him to sustain detachment from dogma and attachment to greater, trans-egoic heights of practice. At the same time, for all we know, the first monk could have been pesky and conniving. His challenging of the older monk could have been typical of his effort to embarrass others. The older monk might have used his superior command of canonical principles to lord over others and puff himself up as spiritually superior.

These are examples of how, in taking I/ego too seriously, the well-intentioned seeker can get knotted up. Viewing all of life through ego evokes unending semantic mazes. One could concede small-minded attributions even to the woman in need. One could swing back the other way. Even if the first monk had been conniving and underhanded, perhaps the poor young man been abused as a child by older males, etc. On balance, humanity itself can be said to have benefited the most given the immense reach of this story. Countless beginners over all the years have undoubtedly walked in the smaller shoes of the first monk and found solace in this tale.

But the question of benefit takes us back to attachment as a vessel of transmission. Egos sometimes handle spiritual desire admirably, and other times not so much. Naturally, we seek guidance. Any insights or practices that touch our lives leave us wanting more. What once worked so wonderfully ends up on a pedestal, an object of worship. The light comes and goes. We do not want it to change and place a cage over it. Without ever really meaning to, we cut ourselves off from our original (and at least partially) innocent, pure intent.

A reasonable point is that ego's desiring is part of both the original inspiration and hope, and the second-stage, small-minded clinging. There is still a wisp of love in grasping and desperation. Wego is model for how Buddha's Mom shows up in everyday awareness—as a living process, space and vessel through which desire (relative attachment, attaching-desiring) flows and "me" arises with "you" and all of mind's content. Metaphorically, the first monk's innocent, pure love of guidelines arises at one point in life and his desire to worship and encage these arises at a later point. But the deep, implicit and tantric perfection is never absent.

In recounting his early encounters with Chögyam Trungpa Rinpoche, Ray describes how the particulars of the conversation were irrelevant.[153] Trungpa was open to discussing anything and that was the problem. One might approach him with something pedantic or personal but soon feel the floor drop. The pressing issue would suddenly seem ridiculous, empty, not having any genuine depth or importance. But in all the confusion, fear, and helplessness, one also felt an unwavering, wide open welcoming and home. Ray feels that the world is still catching up with the reality that Chögyam Trungpa transmitted. In the current frame of reference, these encounters map as ego (in the usual sense) encountering wego in the ultimate sense. Fear-based clinging and small-minded neediness are hardly unwelcome within the Vajrayana lineage; which Ray reminds all able to hear the call, is in fact the "path of desire".

In wego, the Tantric thread of desire runs through our most minuscule mindsets as small tributaries flow to the ocean. A drug addict seeks the perfect high and a narcissist craves the perfect love. Hoarders binge on their possessions' sentience. A domestic violence victim/survivor may self-sabotage, have a dark sense of self and errant cognitive schemas. That which throws the victim/survivor against the rocks is born of a vision of blissful unity. The seeker seeks belonging (a rich word indeed). "Love it not love," wrote Shakespeare, "which alters when it alteration (disorder) finds." Bliss pulls and pulses within the heart of humanity forever albeit co-arising in relative attachment's pain and suffering. Such is our relative nature and absolute Buddha-nature bridged in Buddha's Mom.

Chapter Six

PSYCHE'S SUBSTRATE

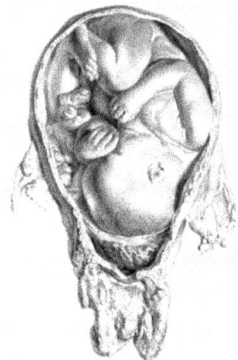

Exploration

To date, "the two attachments" have resisted integration. Integral progress, however, is often nonlinear if not chaotic. Ask anyone who has been through hell and lived to tell about it. They tend to speak in terms of lessons they could not have learned any other way. Commonly, presumptions regarding precursors and causal factors turn out to be mistaken. New theories emerge not as the next step in a sequence but as the status quo crumbles. The fact that spiritual beauty requires ugliness has important implications given our major premise—that an upriver journey into the biological and somatic territory of Buddha's Mom facilitates the journey towards an integral attachment.

Even in the short time since Bowlby put maternal attachment on the map, that same map has been redrawn to accommodate evidence of attachment's influence across the lifespan. Bowlby originally viewed attachment as more limited than modern attachment research has borne out. He saw mammalian attachment as critically important for the species' first phase of development. In his model, maternal attachment waxes and then wanes as a second innate drive kicks in. He named this *exploration*. Offspring need attachment, but just as critically, they need to mature, leave the maternal matrix, and confront the survival demands associated with their species' environmental niche.

Attachment in his model was a first-order innate, developmental system. Mothers oversee the period from birth and helplessness. Then there is a handoff. As exploration takes the helm, the species shifts from the first to the second major innate drive. By design, the handoff in higher mammals and primates is gradual with ample checks and balances as mothers oversee their offsprings' exploration of the environment.

Mothers are tasked with keeping their wee ones from exiting the gene pool by employing both sides of what we have called relative attachment. Then in addition to the nourishing-nurturing nexus, attaching informs interminable watching and monitoring. Mothers make warning sounds and grab and rein in wee ones before danger strikes. Then, in detaching mode, they nudge and push them off the breast or out of the nest.

The river of life rushes on. Bodies are rapidly changing and need to be crash-tested. For offspring, the big world is ever more enticing and accessible. Floppy wings and ungainly limbs can lead down the wrong path. As mobility increases, so too do attendant risks. Little creatures waddle, romp, pounce and play while predators lurk ready to take advantage. As the exploration drive ramps up, the balancing act of mammal moms continues. Deer, grizzly, rhinoceros, and chimpanzee mothers each have their own style, but the basic relational frame holds.

On the attachment side, mothers will squawk, screech, and curb the offspring's enthusiasm if he or she wanders too far. In many species, this continues well beyond breastfeeding. For example, a mother will put the kibosh on jousting juveniles who, in her attachment calculus, go too far. The detachment pole of this dance gives mothers seconds or minutes to attend to other things. It is implicit in the absence of smothering. Smothering, by the way, exists but probably not as much as a patriarchal lens proclaims. It is by definition maladaptive and rare in any other species. At the other extreme is abandonment and neglect, which we could refer to as pathological detachment. Bowlby's original model called for balanced attachment and a hand-off to exploration.

Exploration is overtly distinct from the world of breastfeeding, cooing, and cuddling. It could follow then that biological attachment is developmentally circumscribed. Perhaps attachment is essentially the stuff of mom-and-baby and fades to black thereafter. Assumptions of this ilk and that "too much" attachment, e.g., smothering, have contributed to the persistent estrangement between the two attachments. Buddhism's attachment and all the clinging, grasping connotations of tanhā leading to dukkha, this line of reasoning suggests, emerges quite independently in adults.

This commonplace accounting frames when attachment-love is a skillful means of interaction and when it is not. If what passes as maternal attachment were limited to only maternal attachment, then the attachment of the Noble Truths might apply cleanly to adult behavior and psychology. Clearly early-life mothering manifesting in hyper-hovering and smothering is patently wrong. But the trails goes cold when analyses stop with tanhā.

A well-defined Bowlby-Buddha divide would illuminate where attachment crosses from an inherited species' asset to one that undermines its full, free expression. But with both exploration and the extension of maternal attachment in pair bonding and social attachment, Bowlby's view of animal desire splinters and expands rather than ends. When combined with Panksepp, this science of animal sentience accelerates exponentially.

Buddhism has levels, for example, of relative and absolute bodhicitta, and countless lists including the perfections. One can certainly find support for almost any position on a given expression of attachment from a hindrance to a lovingkindness. But in all, the two models provide very diverse views on issues that matter to many of us. We are left by default placing judgment, declaring forms of attaching as love and metta, or as smothering, distancing, lust, longing. Teenagers in the west, for example, swim in a sea of posts and comments. Ram Dass proclaimed be here now and millions seem to agree, albeit with trembling, needy egos at full tilt. These child-adults are fluidly, hyper-connected in a web of reaching out and reaching back. Writing this off as shallow undermines the sheer perfection of this stage of our species' journey. More integration of Bowlby's and Buddha's legacies would help, for example, explain social media and with navigating the normal storms of life, with identifying skillful orientations to codependence vs. interdependence and letting go vs. deep devotion.

Upon closer inspection, a deeper truth and value emanates without compromise. What we have suggested as our species' lineage by way of attachment seems to only deepen. The river of life rushes on but as new developmental phases emerge they do so as "transcend and include" not as handoffs. For example, as wolf cubs or lion pups increasingly wander, romp about and explore, maternal attachment operates behaviorally, externally as a sort of elastic band. As Bowlby proposed, this fortifies an internal, cognitive representational system. This "secure base" solidifies and serves as an inner mom, modulating their curiosity and exploration. On average, via the evolutionary mechanisms sometimes referred to as the Darwin Award, the attachment-exploration dynamic ensures increasing mastery of their developing physicality, strength and coordination that facilitates the demands of adulthood.

A visual metaphor for attachment-exploration might be that of a slow-motion unfolding of a sunflower with its many rings of seeds. More outward, older concentric rings open slightly more slowly than newer, subsequent rings of seeds. But this is just an outward view that deserves re-thinking. By definition, such a view is observable and therefore scientifically compelling. At this point, however, the weight of the evidence calls for a new model. For mammals, maternal attachment has a critical window, but there is really no slowing down or diminishing of attachment understood more comprehensively. The "secure base", for example, is more accurately rendered as a constantly updatable interactional, self-other attachment model. Female mammals clearly depend on this for "nature-nurture" to have a chance at making them mothers in the first place. The chicken-egg answer is "yes."

Motherless Mothers

Harlow's second generation of attachment-deprived monkeys is most telling. Females who suffered long separations from their mothers and who later became pregnant exhibited the equivalent of genetic murder-suicide. They were "prone to mutilate and kill their babies." As a whole, these second generation attachment victims, these motherless mothers were "severely impaired in their ability to provide adequate mothering for their offspring."[154]

Clearly the circle of life is uniformly reliant on attachment for a species to achieve its innate potential, which, in humans, Buddhists call Buddha-nature. It is tempting to focus on mom-baby as chicken-egg. This is implicit in common forms of infatuation with maternal attachment. Bowlby's view of attachment as a front-end hand-off does not keep everything within the photo frame.

Models of brain function have been performed on lesion studies and "knock out" mice. A model of attachment should be similar. Certainly, the implications of early life attachment damage are important. A deeper appreciation of the brain function that is impaired should not be limited to the nature of the neural ablation. The same cognitive function might be wiped out by a stroke, a terrible accident, or by a surgical laser. By over-focusing on the "knock out" inherent in attachment deprivation, researchers may have overlooked the subtleties of a range of complex functions. Attachment's reach extends to other areas not directly related to moms and babies.

Attachment informs predator and prey intelligence as well. An animal is positively, emotionally attached as it stalks. The word "stalker" conveys this intense bond. In killing, there is a perfecting of the flipside. The predator detaches and the hunt ends. In eating, attaching is re-instated. The object of one's attachment, then detachment, is once again attached to as food, an iteration of the original food, mother's milk.

As such, attachment is intrinsic in the most elaborate repertoires of mammals, in forming groups, in hunting, in mating, parenting and raising offspring. Any model for animal intelligence, therefore, must incorporate the ways in which attachment permeates the species' entire reach, perhaps even as a lifeforce pulling evolution itself forward. Although it eludes description, surely baby mammals have a proto sense of belonging. This would make sense as the sentient flavoring of a rich we-space associated with their pack, pride, or troop. There must be an echo of the same fear and relief as an animal is chased by a predator, escapes death, and returns to the maternal fold.

Increasingly, there is logic to viewing attachment as having a basis in what I refer to as *inmaps* ('innate, neurological, meaning-approximating perceptual systems'). Humans can no more be understood as individual units than coral. An appreciation of anything *meaningful*—from well-being to our massive world domination (now bringing us to the brink of climate catastrophe and nuclear Armageddon, or perhaps a new, higher, sustainable love for the ages) to meaning itself, to enlightenment—has a profound basis in attachment. Attachment facilitates cohesive complexities at all levels: mom-baby, pair-bonding, family, tribe, culture, war-making and peace-building, and all manner of human, meaning-driven efforts and expressions.

Inmaps can be rendered as a constituent level of a lifeforce, a tanha and drive we can now accept as transcending and including goals of survival and procreation. Inmaps provide rapid, fluid, partial shaping of sentience. At a level more associated with classical archetypes, for example, of tyrant, underdog, visionary, bogeyman and ghost, we are empowered to ascribe approximate motives, storylines and negotiate our role across various contexts.

At a higher, purer level of awareness, the meaning-fulcrum in inmaps glimpses itself in the mirror of other. I am a son, sister, friend, tribal member, enemy, aspirant—these carry, are vessels and beg the ultimate questions, *who am I, what is the meaning of life?* Questions of ultimate belonging stream through more discrete wego, belonging confines. Per inmaps, meaning in enhanced in sub-levels, warrior, father, etc. Questions of meaning is understandably accentuated in the loss of meaning. When things go poorly, with ruptures to relationships and when things go well, in existential questioning, in experiences of oneness, meaning rest-stops are shaken.

This vast expanse, from strategic tinkering that results in greater evolutionary fitness to the phenomena Buddhism addresses, profound, ineffable potentials, for Buddhism's "unborn mind", "pristine awareness", and the like (we began by suggesting) is illuminated by "the two attachments". Thus far, we have made a case for a thread connecting the biological and sacred with attachment-love. Biological attachment we have suggested holds the potential to map Buddhist metta. Sometimes backwards is actually forwards. Prajapati is mappable as generalizable, conduit of sentience to Siddhartha. By logical extension, this informs Siddhartha's psychological development and awakening. As we will now explore, further backwards-as-forwards scientific discoveries provide yet more precision.

Panksepp

Although Bowlby's breakthroughs were dramatic, they were just the beginning. Multiple associated lines of research have since coalesced in a field called affective neuroscience. The star behind this transformative work is a quiet-spoken, Estonian-American named Jaak Panksepp. In a nutshell, Panksepp has compiled evidence of feelings in mammals. While it takes some time to unpack, this model provides a scientific map of a mentalistic substrate below maternal/social attachment. His findings go a long way in articulating the lower boundary of attachment on the great chain, body-mind-spirit.

> Dr. Panksepp's main message is quite straightforward. Based on his decades of work with a wide variety of animals, he has isolated at least seven sub-cortical circuits that are the origin of affective experience. This means that emotional experience originates in the sub-cortical parts of the brain that evolved before humans, and even before primates. Other animals may not be able to analyze their emotions the way we do, but there is no doubt that they have feelings.[155]

This work has enormous implications for the possibility of a transcending-including process for the two attachments and articulation of an integral attachment. Such a model would, by definition, encompass the attachment of the Noble Truths, sometimes labeled nonattachment, as well as that evoking tender devotion in humans.

We will only focus on the surface of Panksepp's work. In the end, he will emerge as a truly unsung hero in this exploration of the full reach of attachment in psychology and spirituality. Interested readers are referred to Panksepp's textbook, *Affective Neuroscience*, as well as to his hundreds of articles on the neuroscience of feeling, consciousness, and sentience in mammals.[156] His contribution begins with the articulation of three categories of affect common to mammals. Innate drives and capacities associated with the first two of these are broadly accepted. But for Panksepp, these have to be appreciated for their affective dimension.

> Affect is the subjective experiential-feeling component that is very hard to describe verbally, but there are a variety of distinct affects, some linked more critically to bodily events (homeostatic drives like hunger and thirst), others to external stimuli (taste, touch, etc.).[157]

To this, Panksepp adds a third category. As we will explain in time, this set of affect is based in evidence, not theory. He has proven that mammals (including humans) have seven core, innate, affective systems. In his writings these are capitalized: SEEKING, RAGE, FEAR, LUST, CARE, PANIC/GRIEF, and PLAY. [158]

A short period in the life of baby Siddhartha and his mom could easily involve flavorings from of all of these, in a unified, experiential field. A toddler wanders off, sees a bug, picks it up, it wiggles, the child yells, the mother responds, the two reunite. There is soothing and soon play. Similarly, an adult demands a friend respond. He is offended and upset by what she says. His feelings get away from him, and he feels ashamed by his own response. Anxiously, he approaches the person to apologize. They have a heart to heart, restore trust, and soon there are jokes and laughter. Almost all seven make a cameo in these vignettes. Social attachment and wego experiences are suffused with combinations of these. An important point is that Panksepp's empirically validated building blocks are fluidly integrated in typical attachment-informed interactions, and that additional dimensions do not appear to be needed.

Panksepp has located, documented and demonstrated (through electrical stimulation) the neurobiological bases of these seven emotion systems in the mammalian subcortex. Each is linked to specific anatomical structures and neurophysiological processes found in the brains of all mammals. Electrical stimulation of each brain circuit (whether in rats, cats, dogs, guinea pigs, pigs, or chickens) produces its associated, distinctive, highly recognizable behavioral repertoire. Variability between mammals exists but is accounted for by the model. Differences are of degree and not kind. Lions likely have more of the emotional system he refers to as RAGE, while antelopes have more FEAR—as suits their adaptive niche. The science solidly demonstrates that being mammals, both species have all seven.

Panksepp's research enters a sort of subliminal space (a turn he credits to the work of Walter Hess, a Swiss physiologist who used brain stimulation techniques in the 1920s) when he devises ways for his animal subjects *themselves* to turn these affective systems on or off. With this critical feature, his team has designed and carried out multiple, creative, evocative, and replicable experiments. While this exceeds the scope of Buddha's Mom, the weight of the evidence is now the anchor of a major scientific discipline, which for our purposes provides a basis that is most compelling as a foundation for sentience.

Each of these seven emotional brain systems exist with tremendous consistency in terms of subcortical location, neurochemistry, associated behavior, and animal preference (like or dislike) across species. In one sense, there are no great surprises that animal research has finally begun to decode some of what we all recognize as intelligence and feeling in mammals. Panksepp's map unearths neither evil nor treasure with respect to enlightenment. In another sense, he deserves the Nobel Prize for finally providing a window into the inner life of the creatures with which we share this earth.

Further implications from the current perspective on Buddha's Mom will be explored in upcoming sections. As a whole, Panksepp's work offers a truly astounding portal into neuroscience of sentience. He has found some of the biological roots of that most elusive of all mysteries, the nature of meaning itself. His findings have something to say regarding ancient philosophical conundrums. For example, a tree that falls but is not heard, we can conclude, makes no sound because hearing is a mappable affective event. Following this thread, meaning is an aspect of awareness and vice versa.

> "Feelings" can therefore involve energy, meaning, behavioral impulses, or
> the discrete categories of emotion… Without it we are not likely to be aware
> of our own or others' intentions or motives. Awareness of emotional
> processes has value for our survival as a social species."[159]

As mentioned, the big seven affective systems, (and their attendant experiential meaning) categorically differ from, for example, the feeling of being hungry. Of the three categories, the first stems from sensory interaction with the environment (taste, touch, pain and temperature, for example). The second pertains to in-brain, homeostatic drives (such as thirst and hunger and thermoregulation). From the first grouping, a pinprick or chili pepper evokes both a physical and affective response to sensory input. The feeling of pain associated with being cold, of hunger or thirst are examples of the second category.

Only the major seven are associated with the higher, complex emotional states, as in mad/sad/glad—and probably with the psychological derivations of seeking, clasping and clinging referred to in the Noble Truths. This is beautifully evident in human psychology. We certainly "feel" hungry, thirsty and cold at times. These feelings undoubtedly carry an attendant, inherent meaning. We know both the feeling and what it means to feel thirsty, hungry or cold. But both the feeling and the attendant meaning are distinctly different when one is starved for attention. One may feel warm and snug in a coat, but this is not the same as having warm feelings toward another person.

Human language suggests a transcend-include arc from sensory and homeostatic affects to more integral variants. Somatic/sensory language is commonly included in descriptors of the pain of rejection or a broken promise. We have warm feelings toward someone but not if they give us the cold shoulder. Fight-flight terms are commonplace as well. We could just kill someone for tricking us, and we want to flee criticism.

Just preceding this topic, we considered the possibility of drawing a line between the two attachments. Exploration seemed a reasonable candidate. For one, according to Bowlby, maternal attachment is the first innate, developmental drive, which then sequentially dovetails into exploration, the mammal's second innate drive. Secondly, exploration is synonymous with seeking. Exploration is a candidate then for the manner in which thirst, clinging, and the like are activated forms of attachment.

Ultimately, attempts to circumscribe moms and their breast-craving babies in a cone of silence was not convincing. The more one delves in, the more attachment is revealed to have deep, lasting implications for mammals and humans. In addition to clear biological imperatives, there appear to be no elegant, satisfactory ways to distinguish attachment from *metta*. Much more clarity, we have suggested, was needed regarding Buddha's use of "thirst". As discussed, reasonable interpretations frame the associated working meaning metaphorically, as much higher up the body-mind chain, more in line with psychological expectations. Finally, with Panksepp's research, the possibility of transcending-including the two attachments achieves some movement. Specifically, his seven major affective systems provide a lower boundary for a potentially integral attachment, a sort of attachment base camp.

With the Middle Way, Buddha turned away from thirst and hunger as an attachment that required renunciation in order to bring about liberation. This gives us, for starters, a suffering-causing attachment higher in affective complexity and meaning than a literal tanhā. By inference, Panksepp's big seven provide a logical foundation for sentience and for a sense of self in humans (the substrate for self/ego/mind). Shakespeare did not say, "to thirst or not to thirst." A decent baseline for the meaning of life, of being alive, of being of any sort is associated with an affective threshold. To be mad, sad, glad, to desire, and to love, we humans come into our emotional inheritance in the context of an attachment relationship.

To repeat, meaning co-arises with affect. The higher, seven affects and associated, if simplistic flairs of sentience, live at a higher plane. This living essence may not be shared with reptiles, may hover above physical pain and homeostatic drives evoked by feelings of hunger or cold. There is a gap in mentation, not mere reflexive shivering or crying out. Reflection trumps reflex. We may view this through the lens of co-arising of parts, as interactive and as an internal, proto-wego formation.

Applying Buddhism's version of dukkha here, life is suffering but not because we get bruised, hungry and cold, but because all of this—aging, disease and the knowledge of the fact of death—is a meaning arising from doing little more than being human. We are beings who get hungry and cold. Awareness is the first, foggy mirror. In our reflection, we see an otherwise unreflective, very biological, instinctual process. As soon as self-reflection is born, as soon as one glimpses the most essential fact of human nature in this mirror, dukkha arises.

Buddha does not declare this seeming bad news to orangutans, unable to comprehend such sophistications, but to humans, people he loved. Thankfully, the bad news is limited in scope, and transcended by the good news, the cessation of dukkha, which is unlimited in scope. His message remains just as good today. Panksepp helps us to appreciate that with higher levels of cognitive sophistication come higher levels of and integrated emotional sentience. The cessation of suffering, we can surmise, has the most profound meaning, something extraordinary even if this is often called nothing. A rich rhetorical question concerns how these seven base systems feel, and what they mean to one who is realized. With Panksepp, we have a reasonable base camp from which to ask such questions.

In humans, per Panksepp's model, mothers such as Prajapati are powerful catalysts through which the baby's primary emotions are linked to a secondary cognitive system. This is often referred to as "learning and memory" and depends on evolutionarily newer basal ganglia. Panksepp explains that the amygdala has received the most press but that several other neural structures are just as important. These enable human babies and animals to directly associate environmental sources with the in-built emotional flavors.

The learning and memory system itself operates in the background. It is not conscious. This follows the same logic as more purely somatic processes, such as blood coagulation. Awareness is a need to know zone. We need to know to run to mom, not how we came to know this. We only need the sense of relief on the other side of the equals sign and not the mechanics and layering of memories that resulted in this outcome. Were these processes conscious, we might not make it back to mom on time.

Tracking all this, the powerful, integrated domain of maternal attachment takes shape. As the mother breastfeeds and caresses, the innately rewarding CARE subcortical centers are stimulated. If there is a perceived unavailability or rejection, the PANIC system as well as FEAR systems become operational. The baby may naturally feel a very simple, ancient spark from the RAGE center, for example, when the nipple is not cooperating. His bond with his mother is potently reinforced in all these ways. "Negative reinforcement" happens as she quells the aversive RAGE, PANIC, and FEAR moods, when, for example, she helps the son to latch or as she comes when called. The cry turns into laughter, and positive reinforcement works its wonders as she picks him up, feeds, or plays with him.

A coherent, cogent self-in-the-world, self-and-other, an ego/I is constructed by way of these recurring patterns. The word "belonging" captures the feeling and meaning of healthy attachment. Alternatively, stories of the sort of neglect and abuse which create deep self disturbance run the other way. Not toward coherence and belonging, but toward unmet longings mixed with hungering for love, dismissing this need and all the emotions associated with its absence. Rather than a constructive sense of agency, with attendant ability to use one's voice, emotions, and body to accrue the goodies unleashed in maternal attachment, there is an excess of the aversive flavors, terror, panic, and rage. Negative emotions are not the problem so much as their inability to right the ship. If only tantrums or panic brought things around and restored order.

In typically insidious psychological forms of child maltreatment, parents and other "caregivers" interrupt and undermine the establishment of basic, foundational egoic coherence. This short-circuits the critical, complimentary sub-processes of relative attachment. A preadolescent girl tries on some new clothing and checks herself out in the mirror. The moment holds the potential for the child to extend, to attach a positive emotion to her self-image. Her mother interrupts this, forces detachment from positive affects, with some choice comment such as, "That might make boys look at you but they're looking at you in the wrong way." The prospect of a natural, healthy gender-based ground is pulled out from under her. Even if unintended, or meant as protective, such teasing forces internal fissures. In the case of abuse, negative affects are attached to the emergent self. In neglect, opportunities for positive affective grounding are squandered

The cause of deep self disturbance generally fits the definition of abuse and neglect but neglect tends to be the bigger and more accurate description. Even the countless occasions when a caregiver abused or failed to protect a child are generally a small subset of those involving neglect. Perhaps tens or hundreds of thousands of moments passed without constructive exploitation of our species' inborn potential for growing attachment-love. Keeping with the metaphor of Buddha's Mom, over and again, she simply was not there to contribute to the formation of self/ego/mind. The six-month old's somatic bedrock did not consist of consistent holding, carrying and physical union. His acoustic background was not consistently that of mother's praising, assuring voice. She did not animatedly echo his amusement, wonder, fear, anger, or play. As a result, the child develops emotional difficulties that extend into his later life. Clients are always saying they know better, for example, that they know they have merit and reasons to be happy but they still suffer with incredible persistence. At some level below cognition and self-talk, the old learning will not let up. But in the push to find some ultimate psychological substrate, psychology often suffers the other side of a "spiritual bypass" and executes a form of deep self, somatic/affective bypass.

Secondary Attachment

This bottom-up bias runs through psychology, cognitive science, and neuroscience and inadvertently puts the prospect of an integral attachment at a disadvantage. The more elemental constituents get the better press. Thoughts and feelings may be cool, but their underlying neural circuitry has the real allure. Just as behaviorists boiled everything down to stimulus and response, modern cognitive scientists have tended to fixate on which cognitive processes can be pegged to neural networks that light up during PET (positron emission tomography) scans. An integral model would place value on bottom-up, top-down but more on the interactions of all levels in a higher (transcend-include) embrace.

Language-wise, the frame tends to fit the following pattern. Higher cognitive phenomena are described as ultimately, truly, basically, essentially (or some similar adverb) based upon or caused by (or some similar tautological phrase) a fundamental, essential, or primary (or some similar reductionistic adverb) element, neural circuit (or a similarly reductionistic noun). Buddhist versions of this take the following form: mind/self/ego is truly/ultimately/essentially/basically formed of/ made of/ based in/composed of (variants of) attachments. Dharma's tanhā and dukkha are routinely employed in this way. Life is suffering, because humans *basically* want, crave, desire. Such is the typical attachment-samsara formulation. From the perspective being considered, Panksepp's sophisticated formulation of the bio-psychological basis of mind implies something different. This body of work, referred to as "affective neuroscience" includes major texts and hundreds of peer-reviewed scientific articles from the last five years. Findings have been thrown out or verified via multitudes of creative experiments. Many employ so-called "knockout mice."[160] In these experiments, proposed neurological and physiological bases for higher cognitive and behavioral repertoires are genetically or surgically removed, to verify the association between the biological and psychological.

Panksepp has shown that below a certain level of analysis, the trail of biological markers disappears. Metaphorically, Mona Lisa is meaningful, but this is not to be found in her constituent materiality. "She" is not in the dried paint, unless the full scope of her materiality is held in an integral frame. Some of attachment's dried paint is nevertheless well understood. For example, the role of opiate receptors and "the love molecule", oxytocin, has been well-documented. Undoubtedly, more of the associated biological processes will reveal their secrets in the coming years and decades. But, as we are attempting to convey with the concept of Buddha's Mom, no model of attachment will be satisfying if it does not encompass both brain and mind. We are simply accumulating evidence that these glories, the fruits of practice, are the son's lotus to the mud's mother.

Panksepp's discoveries begin to shed light on how "mud" attributions can be misleading. The lotus is not explained by the mud. "Born of," "based in" and similar attributions can be misleading. Complex attachment, as seen in humans, is nowhere to be found in his affective brain map. To be sure, Prajapati and human mothers everywhere are influenced by the CARE system. But the full sweep of all that we have referred to as attachment-love is not reducible to this mammalian subcomponent. From the perspective of an integral attachment, no dividing line exists between its maternal and social dimensions. Addressing the latter, Panksepp stated:

> … people ask me, where's the social attachment system? And I say, well,
> there is no separate social attachment system; it depends upon the emotions
> of separation distress and care, and how they lead to learning, because
> attachment is a secondary process.[161]

By inference, Buddha's Mom's basecamp is a "secondary" system. Implications flowing from this include the fact that "secondary" should not be interpreted only from a bottom-up bias. The "primary" systems could be called secondary themselves, if the brains of mammalian precursors were considered primary. Also, Panksepp specifically defines secondary as both less mappable and less conscious.

Before we return to this important discovery, we should consider how, in this case, secondary translates as more integral. In his comment, Panksepp alludes to his CARE system. But he would no doubt agree that secondary attachment also involves the PLAY system. Examples are ubiquitous in human attachment spheres and extend fluidly beyond the mom-baby realm, beyond tickling and games like peekaboo. Depending on their degree of attachment, kids tickle, touch and interact affectively and tactilely in ways that disappear once the hormones of adolescence surge. Couples falling in love are very touchy-feely and playful. These forms tend to move up from body to mind, for example, establishing emotional affection in long and ongoing talks about the relationship. Sometimes this inadvertently takes away from the fun.

Incidentally, according to Stephen Batchelor, a modern and deeper reading of Buddha's life suggests ample humor, irony, wordplay, and wit.[162] His boisterous and fun-loving side, and perhaps evidence of biting humor, was diluted in documentable efforts to recast him in certain, idealized ways.[163] Evidence of the overlap of neurobiological attachment systems and the great promise of

Buddhist attainment are everywhere from the Dalai Lama's infectious laugh to his close friend, the ever-smiling, "happiest man alive", ultra-meditator, Matthieu Ricard.

Panksepp also squarely places the PANIC system within the caregiver attachment frame and therefore at the heart of (what we call) deep self disturbance. He and his research team have studied the separation-triggered distress calls in offspring of various species (though he is more famous for discovering ultrasonic laughter vocalizations in mice). In his work on opiate receptors, Panksepp discovered that the distress evoked by separation was not the same as that introduced by a predator or physical danger, because the former but not the latter could be quelled with opiates. He further discovered that unresolved PANIC gives way to GRIEF. This same ancient neurological center that generates PANIC evokes GRIEF when the former is activated for too long or too often without remedy. Other base emotional systems that are naturally operational in maternal attachment, also continue and transform across the lifespan. Such findings are core to the field of adult attachment.

The fact that different hues of paint do not a Mona Lisa make goes to the heart of the integral model. The more sophisticated (multi-variate) self/ego/mind, the greater the capacity to experience the depth of wisdom and meaning emanating from Buddhism's core tanhā-dukkha tenet. But higher must be inclusive, for example, not leaving play, affection, and laughter behind. In asserting that social attachment is "secondary" Panksepp's model, therefore, should be interpreted along two lines. First, attachment processes are not reducible to any component parts. Attachment is not a straight blending of his primary affective systems. It is something new, higher, and distinct. Second, a robust, integral attachment may very well include and appear to be such a blending.

In building an integral attachment, we note that sentience is already on board at the primary level. Meanings associated with primary emotions are included even as they are expanded in a higher synthesis. Social attachment, occurring as a secondary process, achieves a higher meaning. Below this, however, the attachment that we see not only in moms and babies, but across the lifespan, literally and figuratively has no meaning. By inference, attachment-love is not accountable by primary processes. The "lower" reach of Buddha's Mom, therefore, should not be misrepresented as an amalgam of Panksepp's seven affective brain systems. "She" only comes into a coherent clarity by way of "transcend and include". Panksepp has mapped this as well. Secondary attachment, while involving primary processes, is dependent on what neuroscientists refer to as "learning and memory." Where primary process systems are found in the subcortical areas, secondary processes incorporate the basal ganglia. This is comprised of "a group of forebrain nuclei that are inter-connected with the cerebral cortex, thalamus and brainstem, [which] belong to the phylogenetically oldest parts of the brain."[164]

Unlike highly localizable primary processes, Buddha's Mom's social attachment aspect corresponds to massively interconnected brain regions. The thalamus, in particular, is often referred to as a Grand Central Station. Another image is that of the old-fashioned telephone operator plugging and unplugging wires, attaching and detaching. Some parts fire-wire together and some do not. Circuits are turned on and off repeatedly until learning is established.

An important point is that some of the activity involves lived, felt, perceived experience while much does not (and this is the most psychologically relevant distinction for the neuroscience of Buddha's Mom). The layering of the secure or insecure base largely fall outside of awareness. In short, a baby who is cold or in danger needs to feel fear, panic and cry. She or he cannot be bothered to go through hundreds of similar episodes in order to determine how to respond. The phrase, "One never forgets how to ride a bike," actually describes how the learning is potent yet hidden. Even the first time, there was no detailed awareness of secondary interconnectivity. Rather experience floats atop all this. The emotions, fear, excitement, relief float upon an invisible, dynamic coordination of muscles, proprioception in conjunction with instructions as to how to hold the handlebars and peddle. Attachment is similarly out of sight.

For those with demons in this closet, the implications are enormous. This idea that one never forgets how to ride a bike has a subtle value for the current topic. As with attachment, "learning" to ride in the first place is largely outside of awareness. So too, we "learn" and put together our attachment style, be this secure or insecure. In this sense, the phrase "one never forgets how to ride a bike" speaks to secondary learning and memory processes outside of awareness. The notion actually captures the persistence of an implicit knowing. In the case of dysfunctional attachment, this translates into a less than secure base, an instable self-sense and in unskillful means with respect to navigating intimacy. "Never forgetting how to ride a bike" actually captures the dogged persistence of remembering-without-awareness years and decades later. When it comes to attachment, this is not necessarily a blessing.

Rose

Many of those with emotional difficulties have a problem forgetting experiences that led to such difficulties, even when their circumstances improve. For instance, Rose finally had a good job where, as she explained, people left her alone. But sadly, Rose began to develop a free-floating sort of anxiety. She described in fits and starts, constantly interrupting herself to say that she knew better, that she couldn't believe she felt the way she did and that she must sound completely crazy. This is a common presentation. An attempt is made to ignore fears, deny shame, and relegate less than fun and joyous emotions to a back seat.

Rose would eventually describe these more directly. She felt as if something or someone was about to burst through the door and say the jig is up. She just knew she would be accused of being slack, inauthentic, maybe not caring. She often interrupted her own thoughts to apologize, one time interjecting in desperation that she would oddly welcome being terminated over this internal hell of feeling crazy on a perfectly fine day.

Her self/ego/mind emotional bedrock hearkened back to her parents' divorce. Rose recalled visits with her father at about age six. By then, the pretense of family had crumbled. This is when, Rose explained, she just barely began to inhabit the lie that she had already "always" lived at that point. This pseudo-self was something like one of the mannequins making up a smiling, happy plastic family on display in a store window. Her father used to be at least occasionally heavy-handed with discipline. She remembers fearing him and also possibly loving him. At this point in her childhood, however, her father was sulky and withdrawn. If she had once had a relationship with him in some sense, now he was nowhere to be found. Rose was not aware of any of the context, only the raw emotion. There in the silence and most likely across multiple, thematic experiences where she needed something that seemed both right there and impossibly nowhere, she developed what she now recalls as confusion, an odd, silent panic, and anger which became a floor of consciousness. In essence, Rose developed a form of post-traumatic stress disorder there in the silence. The barrenness of the attachment atmosphere was deeply upsetting and just as detached from any clear cause or reason. Rose's mind desperately needed the mirroring that happens in loving attachment.

Metaphorically, this was her first, strong realization that she was in a room without enough air. She saw past the patches in time and space when somehow the atmosphere was restored. What she took to be attachment coherence seemed to be giving way. Before the divorce, there had been one house, one mom-and-dad, meals and occasional heavy-handed rules and structure. But these weekends with a sulking Dad left some scars. Rose's brain badly needed anything even approaching Buddha's Mom's transmission of the self contained through the we-space. Here she was in close proximity to her attachment figure, but getting none of this.

Panksepp's systems did their part. They were all revved up in an attempt to make sense of and initiate the dynamics outside their headquarters in Rose's skull. But these higher-order attachment systems were not coming online. The lower, subcortical levels can only infuse lower forms of craving on the one hand, and raw emotion on the other. Rose was starving, panicking, and imploding. A far more advanced attachment package should have been well underway by now, and available for the lower brain to assist in refining. Fits, tantrums, sadness in kids are met relatively reasonably by attachment figures in most cases, but Rose's we-space was profoundly disordered. Her mind at this stage had no possibility of forming an emotionally cohesive internal picture of outer events which might guide constructive outward expression. With so little of what we define as wego, she was only adept at simpler responsiveness. If the stimulus was something like a tiger, her mind might help her panic, fight or hide but a large, sulking, slow-moving, not talking father who was supposed to love her and hold her and talk to her, was something halfway between. He was neither tiger nor attachment figure.

The same bizarre flush of emotions of this six-year-old mind flooded her consciousness some twenty years later during otherwise quiet, calm workdays. She felt internally unmoored, possibly insane, as if she were slipping over some sort of edge into something that could only get worse. At the same time, she felt strangely capable of killing or hurting or lashing out. The inner tumult was relentlessly variable, like an irritating background sound that would never quite disappear even when it was finally distant. A default response was to freeze. Rose had a "deer in the headlights" look much of the time.

Many clients with latent attachment wounds describe the same energy drain and inability to get on with life that Rose described. This is the justice delayed and hence denied resulting in deep self disturbance. As an adult, alcohol helped Rose to intermittently rebel against the internal subcortical authorities that simultaneously ordered her to fight and flee. Of course, these relationships were disastrous in their own right. Current events are often insidious because the truth of their pain masks the deeper truth of the structural attachment story that shapes the deep self. Without a more distinctive resetting in Buddha's Mom, the unmoored self has no hope for a return to a lasting loving center.

Quarky Love

There are a million ways to express the same notion: a neuroscientist loves her husband, her daughter, her work, and her dog but she will never, ever find this love on a CT scan. She will not be able to tease out and articulate nuances of the inner lives of herself or her subjects via brain technology. She may pour over scans and data but when it comes to the most personally meaningful dimensions of experience, there is no there there.

> If we measure the progress of neuroscience as the accumulation of paper confetti, on each of which is written a fact, we have indeed succeeded in arranging them to form ideas and even complete theories. But if the progress of neuroscience hinges on discovering the nature of perception, thought, volition, and consciousness, we have opened the door a fraction, but not wide enough to see clearly what lies on the other side.[165]

In an amazing and hugely successful series of neuroscience interviews, Dr. Ginger Campbell has documented the diverse efforts to open the brain-mind door further.[156, 162, 192] Her interviewees are mostly authors of important works in neuroscience, both popular and technical. Strong consensus and clear conclusions on narrow topics (such as plasticity or the role of discrete neural centers in specific learning and memory tasks) is contrasted by perspectives on broader topics such as the neurological underpinnings of consciousness. Experts have staked out positions such as embodied cognition, emergence, localization, and connectionism.

Part of the gap between our imagined neuroscientist's home and work lives seems to be structural. Neuroscientists use their minds to understand how brains generate mind. The aspect of the scientists' being that is trained in brain structures and processes is able to proceed independently from the rest. There is a built-in limit to the extent that this training gives her access to brain information. The brain has no intrinsic way to determine its constituent neurons, neural centers or interconnecting diagrams. Our neuroscientist may play guitar, write children's books and meditate but these pursuits are not likely to be cohesively integrated into her research. Psychologists and Buddhists, however, use their minds to understand mind. They tend to use their knowledge in various life pursuits. For example, their training could possibly influence their love relationships, music and creative projects.

We might imagine that the resolution would be (metaphorically) for our neuroscientist to climb into her fMRI machine and somehow to simultaneously be able to see live scans of her own brain. She could then model all the sensory data generated from every possible brain measurement device. Additionally, let us imagine that she is able to stimulate spots and temporarily knock out processes, neuromodulators or locations in order to flush out the neuroscientific basis of love. If she somehow could be the unbiased subject of her own experiment, would this yield the breakthroughs we all long for?

Even this impossibility ignores the problem of scale. Breakthroughs give rise to more questions. Oxytocin's fifteen minutes of fame as the love molecule has hardly put the ancient mystery of love to rest. Researchers of psychedelics lament the historical baggage and tout the therapeutic potential of "empathagenic" drugs like ecstasy. But, of course, answers inevitably produce more questions. In science, there is always the possibility of more precision. There seems to be no lasting satisfaction. This, of course, is a major theme in Buddhism and one addressed by the model of Buddha's Mom. Nor should there be satisfaction if this means suppressing curiosity and wonder. A hundred years ago, Newtonian physics was for many a closed case, but one that proved stunningly immature.

Our neuroscientist's plight, to go about a life and career with an invisible line separating head and heart, can be thought of in terms of degree or scale. The further one treads into the personal, emotionally fervent pastures, the more complex and intricate and impossible to pin down is the far side of the brain-to-mind bridge. Eskimos have ten words for snow, as they say. How many ways is love expressed? The neuroscientist might try to have her subjects view random pictures. As she monitored their brains, she might have them indicate whether or not the picture depicted love. No two people would agree. She might set a cut-off score, above which was true love. Regardless of how elaborate her methodology becomes, she is forced between an expanded, all-encompassing, integral view of love, and reductionisms. At the lower end of this scale, the individual variations are rounded, nuances are sacrificed and love is oversimplified. At the upper end, love is so subjective and idiosyncratic that formal scientific analysis of this sort could only conclude how one person's sense of love at one point in time corresponded with whatever imaging or other brain data was being measured. Anecdotal information is derided except in the case of her own anecdotal love tugs.

On the brain side of the brain-mind problem, neurons, neuronal centers and circuits are exalted. Besides the serious criticism that probes stimulate or convey information from thousands of neurons, not single neurons, another scale issue should be noted. Even neurons are not irreducible. They are made of compounds and these are made of atoms, which are made of subatomic particles. The quarks making up the "mechanics" of our neuroscientist's love are not only impossible to measure but too vast in scale to even warrant consideration outside of this sort of metaphor. Whether they were somehow measurable and observable, the sheer scale would be untenable. Even in the perfect subject as object design, with our neuroscientist somehow able to view every aspect of her own brain as she experienced the love she has for her child, the information her machines would generate within a nanosecond would be too vast for her mind to comprehend.

Another way to discuss this notion pertains to learning and memory. Lab research over decades has produced a sophisticated mapping of what happens in the brain during learning. Limbic structures such as the hippocampus process, receive, manipulate and then divert signals via the thalamus to the neocortex. At this back end, memories undergo consolidation as they move into long term storage. Our neuroscientist, in the midst of a loving exchange with her child, would be engaging multiple learning and memory systems. She and her child might be on a bench swing in their backyard in conversation. As the child repeats a story, information based on this fact enters the system and is compared to long-term memory. Subtleties impossible to pin down to a measurable, mappable brain process are instantly in play, as the neuroscientist mom would draw not simply on the events of the story but the fact of repetition.

Her child might repeat a story because it is associated with the mother-child relationship and operates to strengthen it. Repetitive associates, coffee and newspaper, or wine and a book, may be said to recruit the same neuronal processes. Depth psychologists, shamans, and others talk about sacred spaces, phenomena that if they exist at all would probably not have a hard-wired neurological basis that scientists would agree upon. Another child's repetition of a story weighed against long-term memory contexts might signal to this mother insecurity. Comfort food works the same way. For some, it's a pleasurable, value-added experience, while for others, it is a desperate effort to escape intolerable emotions. These subtleties are another form of increased scale. Again, this takes the goal of mapping the neuroscientific basis of interesting aspects of the human experience past the line of viability.

The movement of the swing would be translated through the middle ear, vestibular organs and then passed downstream to somatosensory areas in the parietal lobe. In addition to the activity already noted, important processing occurs in the mirror neurons and in temporal areas specializing in auditory decoding. Language processing moves from decoding phonemes, words, sentences, context in an arc culminating in semantics, the attachment of emotional meaning. This is boosted by facial analysis and by the micro-adjustments associated with such phrases as "oohs" and "ahs" and empathic facial and other nonverbal gestures, activity in the motor strip of the cortex. The conversation might involve classically right hemisphere phenomena such as metaphor and imagery, embedded in historical and cultural references.

The more interesting and sophisticated the psychological content under study, the more whole brain activity is produced, and therefore the less accurate are overly reductionist models. Extending this materialistically downward in scale would make no sense. For example, to have some massive database of the quarks underpinning our neuroscientist's love of her child would be a nonstarter. The same goes for the subatomic "machinery" associated with whatever psychological experience one might name. The prospect of solving the brain-mind problem sputters out as one moves downward toward ever more granular physical underpinnings, e.g., quarks. The solution to the brain-mind problem also unravels as one moves up the scale from something very narrow to richer psychological territory.

Grok

Imagine that an early human named Grok sees a rock. As a fellow Homo sapiens, Grok's brain would have the same volume as that of our neuroscientist. Grok sees rock. She has never seen this particular rock before, but through an elaborate, active perceptual process, a workable percept is formed. The elements of this process include Grok's person. The rock is over there. It is a third person, "it." A thing, a "not me." Established categories would also include movement/static and alive/not alive. Maybe this rock is where she is about to place her foot while running from danger. The perceptual processes at hand would compute this information pre-consciously and rapidly and would give her a high chance of survival.

Another day, Grok might be in no hurry at all. Again Grok sees a rock. She might need a rock for part of a temporary shelter or to form a tool. Her brain would automatically compute approximate size, density, and this information would overlap with possible usage data. Such information flows from extensions of her body schema. From childhood, she would have refined her somatosensory knowledge. These internal maps of me-as-body are not static but based in the physics of movement. Body reaches out, lifts, throws, carries, possibly carves or uses the rock in some goal-oriented way. Tool use, which is found in many animals, has this basic property. The use of rocks as tools or weapons are examples of extensions of the body.

But rocks barely begin to relay the richness of Grok's consciousness. Within her perceptual machinery, more than one object would generally compete for her attention. Evolution favored humans who had facility with about seven percepts at a time. Less or more, by definition, earned the Darwin award. Early humans lived in bands, gathered and hunted. Some conjecture is reasonable. Grok's rock assessing could represent one of a handful of information processes. Others might have involved some berries she came across, a couple of sounds, and one element related to social attachment. Perhaps she was in the midst of strengthening, testing, breaking, or otherwise renegotiating an alliance with another member of the tribe. Of course, dominance and submission oversimplify the complexities of group organization, as primate research has proven.

Subtleties abound. Grok may have been feigning subordination to test an alliance in order to evaluate whether the other person would show their cards. Perhaps her agenda was amorous or she had little agenda outside of simply strengthening an alliance. Or perhaps she had a power and control agenda and would exploit any weakness that she discovered. My thesis is that the leaps in human evolution reflect brain-based and cultural-based expansions resulting from and in ever more elaborate and layered degrees of socialization, e.g., biological attachment.

Grok would have made it this far in evolution because she could keep rocks, berries, and the social dance—forming, testing, breaking alliances, forming pair bonds, and caring for offspring—coherently in play on any given Holocene Sunday. To do all of this, a computational nascent self of some sort is required. Rocks, berries, and social dynamics were not stove-piped. Grok may have traded the perfect rock to make a weapon for some berries. She may not have needed the berries, but made the trade in order to strengthen a relationship she did need. She assessed and decided, she suffered consequences and enjoyed rewards accordingly. Her voice, face, body, actions were necessarily coordinated by some sort of singularity. To run, not trip, to spot a rock, trade it or shape it into a tool, all required a body schema.

The cohesion of these many clambering perceptual processes, in theory, necessitates awareness. The brain not only knows (has a perceptual model) of rock but also has a perceptual model of multiple ("seven plus or minus two") simultaneous perceptual streams. These organic, changing depictions of the inner and outer life are the stuff of intelligence. Something singular has developed a sense of the many. Each of the many was built from the senses and body upwards.

The rock has spatial realities. The fuller context of prioritizing this over the berries brings time limitations to the fore. One only has so many hands or time before another person or another set of pressures, dangers, and opportunities occurs. The channel we are watching will change. We must attend, adjust, respond. To do nothing is to do something.

Space and time make motion possible, and motion informs the kinesthetic dimension of e-motion. Grok would be equipped with the ability to brace in anger, manifest a "heavy'" sense of grief, or in "light" joyful affects. Like modern humans, she would have the apparatus to know firsthand crushing, dense states of panic and their less temporally bound, more diffuse variants of the same in iterations of worry and stress. She would have the machinery to sense the expanding, opening up of hope or euphoria, if for instance, after several famished days the tribe rounded a bend and came upon a much-needed food source. In the last chapter, we will review the emerging integration of body-based models of affect. In particular, polyvagal theory has augmented attachment theory resulting in what a leading researcher refers to as a cross-disciplinary "paradigm shift".[166]

To attend to the whole cognitive rainbow of rocks, of threats and goals, the intricacies of gathering and hunting, alongside social no-nos or strategic alliances, calls for something of another order. Attending to such a rich, diverse, ever-changing range of informational modeling occurs as a multiplicity of perceptual modeling processes work in parallel. These models follow the evolutionary formula of Goldilocks, not too hot, not too cold. They use minimally sufficient processing power to achieve efficacy. For example, white light, which actually consists of a multitude of frequencies, is not what it seems. Presumably to see white light as 10 colors simultaneously produces diminishing returns, so the genetic response is to see it as one hue. Survival, in effect, allocated these resources elsewhere.

The additional perceptual processing resources which would probably require supplementary "hardware" in the retina, optical nerve and occipital lobe, did not make the cut. With more, there is more to go wrong, be injured or diseased. The bands of radiation we do experience as colors, conversely, are the result of those which enabled us to accurately, quickly, efficiently identify aspects of our surrounding, predators and prey, fruit or weather, that did make the cut. On a larger scale, our species allocated resources in the direction of tribal, collective brainpower. Additional visual processing and every other inherited capacity had to be balanced against evolution's all-in bet (a slight exaggeration) on the intelligence, language and social capacities that distinguish our species.

Graziano's attention schema model holds that awareness is a derivative of these multiple attentional processes. In each, the brain necessarily manipulates and synthesizes the signaling that flows from sensory and cognitive data streams.[167] Perception, beginning with sensory information, such as Grok's close-enough rock knowledge, calls for ignoring (negating, detaching from) nonessential data. There's no time to tarry. External and internal feeder lanes merge onto information superhighways. Grand details give way to quick and dirty sketches, time-saving depictions, caricatures and shorthand. Vines laden with a familiar-looking berry pass muster or not. Rapid, close-enough decisions draw on long-term memory housing associated with vine and berry knowledge. This data stream is attached to incoming information, evoking emotional relevance. A vine's particular uniqueness may be judged nonessential and excluded or may be noted as possibly signaling trouble, with echoes of fear, nausea and vomiting.

Just as one might hold a conversation and make reasonable driving decisions outside of awareness, Grok might choose to pick or pass on said berries with no awareness of this "decision." Our predecessors benefited from this outside-of-awareness capacity, and at some point in evolution, from its better half. In such instances, according to Graziano, a "perception-like" model actually invokes awareness.[168] This special case is triggered as various attending sub-processes reach certain thresholds, in effect, alerting the animal to what has heretofore been under the radar. This then evokes a specific emotional meaning consistent with, "Hey, I'm paying attention" to berries, rocks, etc. "Awareness is the brain's way to represent attention,"[169] writes Graziano. Awareness happens in conjunction with a special, higher-order, model of models amounting to "a computed and constantly recomputed informational model."[170]

For Graziano, attention is a way to describe how certain neural circuits and signals are attached to and others are detached from internal processes associated with perception. Certain signals are included and others negated. Attention results from the amplification and focusing on certain data over other data. As subsequent cognitive science has concluded, such perception is facilitated by long-term memory. Awareness is limited to that which has not been stored in a stable manner or cannot be left to rote repetition. In the maternal attachment arena, a degree of awareness ensures that the mother perceives the fluctuating needs of her children. Some aspect of her response is typically consciously constructed and other aspects fall outside of awareness. Where specific sentences, for example, may be tailored to the circumstances, human mothers will not have to devote attentional resources to the mechanics of speaking.

> This (information) processing occurs in a succession of stages, all but the
> most preliminary of which require that the inflow be related to matching
> information already stored in long-term memory. All such processing is

influenced by central control and is done at extraordinary speeds; and all but the most complex is done outside awareness. For most purposes the inflow of interest to psychologists and the common man alike is that which, having been selected, interpreted and appraised, goes forward to influence mood and behaviour and/or to be stored in long-term memory. The fact that in the course of its being processed the vast proportion of initial inflow is routinely excluded, for one of several reasons, is ignored.[171]

Awareness is thus very closely aligned with a sense of self—the "feeling of what happens" as Damasio put it. Awareness in Graziano's elegant formulation depends on self/ego/mind. One is figure, the other ground. There is a self as figure and berries, rocks and dependently arising subjects of awareness, as ground. Graziano's compelling, neuroscientifically-based conclusion is that this dance occurs as a wonderfully higher-order experience but otherwise exists within similar perception-like circuits. Relative attachment refers to the psychological aspect of these neurological and physiological attentional processes that give rise to awareness. The mind attaches to the color and look of the berry or rock even as it detaches from whatever preceded this observation.

Presumably human evolution involved previous perceptual capacities being leapfrogged by ever more complex capacities. The brain and its perceptual capabilities (mind) became ever more sophisticated and, at some point, perceptual processes enabled the brain/mind to perceive itself perceiving. What we may add by way of Buddha's Mom is that this leap was not simply the advent of self-awareness. This leap corresponded to advanced attaching-detaching systems that undergird self/other awareness.

This evolutionary event corresponds equally to personal and interpersonal awareness, a point Graziano seems to endorse. "Awareness is equally present whether you are reflecting on yourself or looking out at the external world."[172] A mother and baby are first person plural, and separate in the I/thou. The same goes for tribal membership and spiritual interpretations from an extension of the lifeforce, Gaia being made in the image of God. The Buddhist concept of dependent origination, as previously discussed, also adds clarity to the fact of self/other perception. Neither is ultimate. But on the relative plane, neither exists without the other.

Buddha's Mom sheds light on these neuroscientific findings in that "she" reminds us that our brains devote the lion's share of processing power to psycho-social arenas. In the "great chain," these begin in the upper body bands and continue across those of mind, soul and spirit. The very same procedures empowered the tribal super brain that coordinated hunts and came to dominate every corner of the planet.

It is tempting to view the evolution of awareness as, well, just that. But as Jared Diamond showed in his Pulitzer Prize winning book, *Guns, Germs and Steel*, some of the sausage-making reality of evolution involved the brutal over-taking of more yin-like cooperatives by more yang-driven, aggressive tribes. Diamond's book describes how Eurasian civilization developed thanks to various unique opportunities and environmental circumstances rather than because of superior intelligence.[173] When evaluating various yin/yang interaction, theoretically, the yang-driven, more aggressive tribe would be prone to us/them splits, to mutiny, betrayal and power grabs. This would correspond to an attachment style that was more detaching in nature, resulting in faster, more radical distancing of self from other. But these are variations on a theme. Powerful in-grouping would also correspond to stronger tribal identity and better coordination of resources, including those used to defeat other tribes. We are a deeply social animal, on average at least, and not as hard to herd as cats.

Both our neuroscientist and Grok would have a highly cultivated self-sense and an other-sense. Both would use these to navigate socially dense environs. Grok would have known when others called her, very likely by name, and the others would be accustomed to Grok's personality. Grok herself might have lived less than half as long, and might have had a small fraction of the vocabulary of our neuroscientist, but some aspects of her emotional life would not have been much different.

The neuroscientist's brain-based love centers spring from the same genetic roots and neurological machinery as those of Grok. But Grok would have lived with and depended intensively upon those to whom she was attached in ways few of us have experienced. She would have been through heart-wrenching and heartwarming experiences within we-spaces upon which her survival depended. If anything, modern peoples have a comparatively detached existence, far less embedded in a tribal-we, far less in tune and indebted to the Earth. We moderns are probably, therefore, much less able to provide an accurate picture of our natural state—and this extends to our deep, natural state or Buddha-nature. Buddha's Mom is poised to assist our return to the mother ship. As we will see in the last chapter, the skeleton of a reductionist 'neuromania' finally has a lot more muscle. Our neuroscientist now has colleagues pioneering a powerful, transformative paradigm based in the brain's tenth cranial nerve referred to as polyvagal theory.

Inmaps

Long ago, I wondered if there might not be a more scientifically appealing approach to Jung's concept of archetypes. Jung is not covered in depth in most clinical training programs and archetypes are not a serious research topic in neuroscience. I had become convinced of the clinical power and the biological reality of archetypes. The word was used too loosely, often not in line with Jung's model. Also, the concept had not been updated. The lack of integration was understandable, I felt, and might be improved with a more precise, cognitive approach.

As mentioned, I came up with the acronym "inmap" for an "innate, neurological, meaning-approximating, perceptual systems". These blended, nature-nurture capacities exist at a relatively high level process within the architecture of perception, but nonetheless are not at a level directly accessible. Inmaps populate a certain preconscious space and require meaning-matching environmental input to function. These are higher, richer versions of the nature-nurture "instincts." Researchers have shown, for example, that upon hearing the beginning notes of a complex, species-specific song, certain songbirds will spontaneously produce the full song even though they had never heard it.

The inmap concept overlaps with what neuroscientists such as Graziano describe as perceptual models. In this model, the brain transduces external sensory and internal, within-brain inputs to produce perception. During this routine, stage-wise information processing, the data or signals can be measured and located within identifiable neural circuits. As mentioned previously, Graziano notes that the multiple colors making up white light end up translating perceptually as white or no color. Grok's rock recognition is another example.[174] In both cases, conscious perception is way, way up the scale from that of individual photons, retinal receptors and the firing of neurons. Conscious perception is also, from a conscious perspective, almost instantaneous.

As the acronym indicates, inmaps are neuronal systems in which meaning—the psychological experience of meaning—is central. This must be understood, however, as one part of a set of variables. Cognitive neuroscience could move the ball down the field dramatically by embracing a program of research into the subterranean contours of inmaps. That which evokes meaning for neuroscientists outside the lab should not be so divergent from that measured inside. Wilber refers to the inside and outside of the quadrants and describes these as mirrors of one another.[175] Integrative methodological approaches, based on the work of Jung, Wilber, and Panksepp might help expand a working model of these important contributors to experience.

By definition, archetypes operate in the background of consciousness. An inmap is comprised of an "approximating" process that sits back a step or two from full consciousness. It wields its partial influence on perception and experiential meaning in ways that Jung has largely already mapped. But the success of the idea has perhaps outpaced his intentions. The word archetype has lost its precision and this has contributed to the mixed blessing of being a household term. Yet it tends to fall outside the parameters of serious clinical and cognitive research.

Empirical approaches that focus on the forward edge of a person's epistemology, what a person knows with some confidence or reliability, are unlikely to help. Our neuroscientist could not quickly produce a list of the characteristics that cause her to love her child. Her response to such a question would use emotional, meaning-laden descriptors. Close relationship—and all we are discussing from the context of Buddha's Mom—does not lend itself to what has dominated neuroscientific research. But an update of Jung's archetypal theory via the inmap frame holds promise.

Jung diligently sought to straddle the chasm between subjective and objective. He viewed his own work and the founding of analytical psychology as an effort to bridge this gap. He also described this as the chasm between science and other domains, including art and religion, which continues in earnest to this day. If Jung somehow returned to witness the "decade of the brain" he might be disappointed. He might comment on the collective infatuation with brain scans in place of an integrated effort to map infatuation itself. The same could be said for love and enlightenment. He might ask about progress on factors, which lead to such preventable hells on earth as wars, famines and genocide. So far, scans have not helped us to heal schizophrenia or reduce incest. Jung might refer to this enthusiastic fixation on cognitive science as making a religion of science when what is needed is a science of religion.

The search for God, as Jung pointed out, is a search for self, a longing to find "me" in the inner cosmos projected outward. The reverse also holds. An infatuation with unlocking the mysteries of consciousness through neurobiology is a search for the divine and for answers to the grand, perennial questions. Who am I? What is the meaning of life? Who would not like for an image at the end of our imaging instrumentation to look back at our longing eyes and say in the eloquent equivalent sense of E=mc², "Finally, you have found me." But alas, therein is the rub. The mind, hell-bent on objectivity, peers through the instruments and pours over the data but can never see itself, because the first person can never fully find "me" in third person. There is no myself in itself. Both must drop away. There's no there possible there. No single "there" when opposites of scientist and subject co-arise.

Jung and others devoted to depth psychology tended to be extremely attuned to this paradox. Grounded in the enlightenment, most were very familiar with efforts across history and multiple disciplines to address the subject-object and brain-mind paradox. Most have also spent countless hours phenomenologically exploring this paradox personally and interpersonally with lovers, friends, mentors, and clients. As part of these ventures, most endeavored to delve into the murky worlds of dreams, visions, and altered states of consciousness. This background is naturally less applicable to the modality of the modern neuroscientist. The study of humanities has been passed over by "STEM" (science, technology, engineering, and mathematics) tracks in high school and college. There is an under-emphasis on "finding" oneself and even experimenting with altered states.

Another brilliant person who straddled science and personal exploration of consciousness was Milton H. Erickson. The so-called pioneer of modern clinical hypnosis stands alone in his contributions yet these also remains outside mainstream neuroscience. The stories of Erickson's efforts to objectively, empirically understand the human psychology are compelling to say the least. Yet another researcher was Elizabeth Kübler-Ross.[176] She worked with thousands of patients as one of the West's great bodhisattva bringing metta to those very ill and dying. She also came to hold some ideas that disappointed many of her fans. The genre, of course, is also open to those who were once great losing their way, becoming overly rigid and cultish. In the case of Kübler-Ross, her ideas might not be communicable as separate from her clinical intuition and empathy. The latter loses much in translation into descriptors and concepts.

Our neuroscientist, with her laser focus on data, would probably not find Jung or Erickson's ideas to have much validity. Nor would she have been taught to cultivate the clinical skills of a Kübler-Ross or Virginia Satir. Archetypes, for example, have not been a serious research subject in cognitive neuroscience. It is as if there is a no fly zone around the preconscious and unconscious and around clinical presence, intuition and style. Cognitive neuroscience, relative to something on the order of mapping the biological basis of the mind of Rilke or perhaps a lion, can only be said to be in its infancy. So much of the problem is the stove-piping at every stop. Neuroscientists lead colorful, rich lives, only a sliver of which shows up in their professional work. Their own real lives intersect with the bewildering multitude of hybrid ideas, models, approaches, and workshops on healing, personal growth, and spiritual development. This only seems to be expanding, in the way of a shared model, language, and bridging. Between these is the potential embedded in "transcend and include". A higher, more lucid center of gravity awaits.

In particular, a better science of Buddha's Mom might grow from findings associated with the inmap or a similar theoretical concept and methodology. Scientists are fine with the notion of low-grade instincts, but reticent to explore more elaborate deep psyche phenomena.

Konrad Lorenz and Nikolaas Tinbergen, two scientists who studied social behavior in animals, concluded that certain ducks and geese have innate, visually primed, pre-existing cognitive capacities which enhance their survival. They moved a predator-shaped form and a non-predator shaped form over naive baby ducklings and goslings and concluded that the fear response was demonstrable and not based in prior learning.[177] Work by Panksepp implies that the hawk-shaped silhouette first would be visually decoded and would then subsequently spike subcortical regions that produced fear. Animals have to have experience to learn, for example, what within their actual environment provides nourishment or shelter. But deep sources of some manner provide the approximations that facilitate so-called learning, a basic term that loses precision when inmaps are part of the equation.

Logic holds that such predispositions in humans, the most sophisticated of mammals, might not only be more advanced but may have been a major factor in Homo sapiens' great advances in both biological and psychosocial, cultural evolution, and our rise to worldwide domination. Inmaps are innate cognitive enhancers. Something like perhaps night vision goggles, they boost extant perceptual and cognitive systems. They rely on sentience to train in on the selected, commonly interpersonal, attachment-related dynamics and provide a sharper mental experience by increasing possibly-related emotion and meaning.

The hawk shape diverts the bird's experience via affect. In this case, the guestimate results in a rush of fear and then, of course, stimulates evasive action. Some might not be comfortable describing this in terms of meaning and emotion. But Panksepp has proven that any such hesitation can be put to rest. For humans, a loud sound is emotionally stunning. Like the bird suddenly overshadowed by a hawk, we cringe with alarm and direct our attention and responses in survival-enhancing ways. These appraisal-assistors are particularly developed and important in the social sphere. When input "presses the right buttons", associated emotions drive attentional processes.

Another of Panksepp's insights is that the learning and memory components remain precisely out of consciousness. When we hear a sudden loud noise, emotions kick in as the unconscious learning and memory processes check files and report in, perhaps a split second later, as to possible sources. But all this sorting of memory files, evaluating of matches and mismatches, is unconscious. Keeping some processes in the dark allows others to demand more attention. The shadow passing by the bird is ignored or not, depending on this background information processing, enhancing energy savings. Efficient use of calories is a universal survival asset.

What inmaps add is the power-assist of the meaning-emotion side of perception. They are advanced instincts embedded in neural networks which give rise to higher-order meaning forms. Up from, for example, "run for your life" are rich packages of meaning providing information as to the contours of any given social encounter. Inmaps are by definition partial. Jung metaphorically referred to archetypes as the contours in the land in which a river—our individual, cultural, and historical consciousness—flows. Our particular tribal, social entrainment sends the water flowing, boosting our ability to rapidly make sense of and find the meaning in complex situations.

Inmaps, therefore, hit all the high marks that cognitive scientists generally accept as valid—attention, perception, and appraisal—but they go further in evoking mappable forms of sentience. They help extend evolutionary theory into the social arena. Those more adept at spotting, adopting, and otherwise exploiting thematic interpersonal demeanors and dynamics did better at the game of life. Archetypes or inmaps work in both directions. They power-assist perception, boosting a person's speed and accuracy at apprehending the agendas and potentials of others. One's social sense is supercharged with emotional overlays and also a sense of knowing, of simply possessing the meaning of a given situation.

Inmaps were part of a complex of capacities that supported the evolution of Homo sapiens, where advanced forms of emotion and meaning have precursors in that of baby ducklings and goslings. As noted, these innate rapid detection systems are engaged in response to the silhouette of a hawk. Initially only framed behaviorally, an updated analysis endorses that the package is also psychological, involving species-specific forms of affect and meaning.

Presumably representative of lower mind-body integrations, those inmaps which were less combinatorial and less psychologically cohesive caused members of previous generations to hesitate a split second too long or in other ways to demonstrate less of the right stuff required to remain in the gene pool. Genetic mutations that led to constructive refinements remained in the gene pool. The terms mind, awareness, and self/ego implicitly refer to the possession and lived experience associated with such background, instinctual, sentient systems. But these are not nearly as integrated as they should be. Inmaps are largely the inner meaning-calibrating organs that modulate intra- and inter-personal attachment, manifesting in the slough of standard we-space receptacles that comprise culture, tribal, clan and family life.

Many fit the general mold of a personality or character style. Jungians have compiled an exemplary body of literature on these forms, so much so that the term archetype tends to carry this one connotation over others. As Jungians have demonstrated in great detail, these forms are core to indigenous spiritual traditions. Highly similar forms show up all over, with no evidence for commonalities as products of cultural encounters. There are, for example, sky gods and earth goddesses, variations on reclusive, magical little people, spells, explorers, warriors and martyrs, wise men/women, and talking animals with divine power.

Inmaps help retrieve Jung's basic, ingenious theory and reset it in a modern cognitive model. For example, an inmap can more clearly be associated with cautionary tales such as the tortoise-hare variant with lessons on the values of delayed gratification and discipline. A major inmap associated with Buddhism is that of seeking, healing, and self-improvement. Many of us feel we should be more evolved, more loving, wiser, and happier. While wonderful to an extent, this personal growth inmap can wield too much power and, in conjunction with others, can manifest in a sort of spiritual paranoia. One feels driven, compelled by something or someone around the corner that might be more perfect.

With overlaps from early life attachment longings, such a person might not only be a fount of wisdom and compassion but she or he might finally see "me". They might even see my own perfection. This sounds good on paper but can lead to obsessive shirking of the present. One's shadow, wounding and gifts and possible bodhisattva contribution to this world are conveniently not here/now but awaiting one day when. The path of the seeker is fraught with the risk of inmaps remaining in the shadows. Cognitively, as percepts meet pre-established criteria neural "inmap" roads become superhighways running in parallel, exploiting (or as neuroscientists refer to the hardware side, "recruiting") impossibilities, including imagery, affect, and meaning. With this, we respond to a doctor's white coat in certain ways, to a lama's accoutrements, a rock star's stardom, and a villain's sketchy moves in predictable ways.

The evolutionary basis of inmaps was born from and translates into a stronger facility for negotiating tribal, clan, or the larger social matrix. They take the silverback and primate alpha male up a notch. The alpha male-associated inmaps, for example, would be more sophisticated. They would pre-populate the background of consciousness with different flavors of meaningful knowledge, depending on experiential matches with variations on the theme. We might, for convenience, identify some of these as tyrant, sadist, or wise elder. Of course, these would be just a subset of a multiplicity of inmaps bearing on consciousness depending on past experience and present situational dynamics.

The pre-populating of consciousness with meaning-filled pre-cognition processes is, by design, partial and approximate. In the normal course of events, one's waking experience is not overrun by the inmap. An analogous activity occurs in procedural memory. Technically, one does not specifically remember how to ride each bike. Rather one remembers and never forgets how to ride a generic bike—the brain's model of a bike. Procedural skills are general in nature and adapt to variations across specific bikes.

As previously mentioned, the approximating aspect of inmaps is captured by the tale of Goldilocks. Too much or too little, too hot or too cold, is a waste of scarce resources, if not dangerous. We know handlebars, pedals, and wheels, but we have no need for knowledge of ball bearings. Inmaps mediate the incoming social information. It is not enough to say they are triggered by certain social dynamics because they already pre-formed cultural perception. They form perceptual filters by which incoming information that passes the Goldilocks' threshold is determined to be salient, thematic or essential. The right calibration enables some to better distinguish friend from foe, to build an alliance, trick others out of something, earn their trust, or recover after a setback. Tribes such as Grok's benefited from inmaps, and these have lived on in me and you.

The dance is complex. Consider classical archetypes such as the trickster (court jester, clown, joker), the king (mayor, administrator, organizer), and the shaman (priest, wizard, mystic). A person who has these characteristics would, in theory, be under the internal influence of the associated inmap. A person "re-cognizing" these in their social perceptual field would do so based on the support and also the constraints of associated inmaps.

What psychotherapists refer to as projection is an example of disordered inmap influence. This occurs when one's internal inmap is overly attached to the perception of an "other", usually another person. But, of course, we can project a grand scheme based upon, say, persecution on multiple levels. A random, unfortunate event validates a given self's over-attachment to a victim inmap. In higher functional states, more normal than neurotic on the classical scale, inmaps operate in the background. In projection, there is the same approximating, attenuated influence on consciousness, but the evocation of meaning is more inaccurate and overbearing. The other person carries undue inmap-based meaning and power as does the self. For example, contraction under the weight of inmaps is aligned with victimization.

As always, relative attachment helps describe the dynamics. Consciousness adheres to, for example, viewing the other as a bully or tyrant or hero, and this causes the self to overly attach to a victim inmap. Ego is maintained by projecting certain qualities onto others. This material is detached from internal sources within one's own depths. Besides not being integrated, the pressure to own, face up to, and properly attach to what is often born of old, family-of-origin wounding is prevented because of the over-detachment process involved in projection. Although one may be stuck with this ugly compromise for long periods of time, tuition is collected along the way. The potential for a more integrated and grounded life is forestalled. Again, justice delayed is justice denied. Both the person so disturbed and those around them suffer. In projection, something like the tyrant may be projected out through detachment, but with this bathwater goes power—as evidenced by the co-arising archetype of the weak, helpless victim.

Emma

The tyrant-victim inmap is an elaboration of the innate dominance-submission neurobiology which structures many mammalians species' individual and group behavior. From Panksepp, we now know that this has a rich, interior, affective and sentient side in mammals. In humans, such inmaps, however, stubbornly pull the puppet strings from the depths and are only partially visible to self/ego/mind. Clients sometimes reach out for help after having thought about it a long time, but they remain unsure of their reasons. Just as commonly, one presenting issue quickly dissipates as another moves in.

Clients generally describe these emerging frames as familiar. They already know all about them but somehow insist on talking about them in great detail in time-limited sessions presumably aimed at addressing whatever is most pressing. This is an important finding. Self/ego/mind experiences ownership and control when it is, in fact, something off in the shadow, as the saying goes, has one in its grips.

Very often as emotions are unpacked, versions of this bully-victim inmap backdrop moves into the therapy hour. The internal dimensionality is key. For example, a person may be a do-gooder, act this out in relationships, and simultaneously resent their lack of power. Normal work and relationship stressors, for example, become the vessel for the dominant-submissive interplay. But the subtle and pervasive forces are more recalcitrant and challenging. In therapy, a client may implicitly demand one listen as they litigate their own case, amassing proof of the guilt of their essential lack of worth.

Surface people and places are asked to handle deeper, mythic pressures. This disproportionality adds another layer to the confusion and shame which is both everywhere and invisible. In upper neurotic forms of deep self disturbance, the boss or girlfriend or friend, a patient will explain, had seemed OK initially. But something drifted in and with the rolling fog came a nagging negativity. In deeper levels of psychological suffering, self/ego/mind may become embroiled in harsher patterns.

Emma was (in terms of relative attachment) overly attached to her boss's manipulations. He was incredibly deceptive and hell-bent on sabotaging her career. In such instances, one wants to employ the term evil. Evil is, as psychiatrist and best-selling author M. Scott Peck wrote long ago, "live" spelled backwards. The more one hears of certain perpetrator-victim dynamics, the more the so-called evil person seems to be internally fueled by nothing except opposition. Such bullies seem to both consciously and subconsciously sabotage the light and life in their victim.

As wretched as this sounds, of course, this may just be an advanced, perverted, narrowed form of one two-year old's snatching another's toy. Dynamically, there is the possibility that the bully is driven by jealousy or self-hatred. Adults have such a repertoire of emotional and intellectual capacities that the picture is seldom clear. Peck believed, however, that in some instances, bully-victim psychology cannot be explained in the usual ways.

In Emma's case, nothing she had done was even remotely cause for firing. Yet her boss seemed driven to threaten to fire her for what was, in fact, natural and authentic. She stood out in the first place for staying extra hours, for striving, enthusiasm and devotion. Everyone is familiar with the game Emma's boss played. The more she became emotionally invested in convincing him of her abilities, the more he dug in. The more one feels obliged to prove that they truly love, care, or are telling the truth, the easier the other can insist on escalations of proof. Such bosses and spouses, friends and lovers always hold the final card when they can say, "I don't believe you."

Disturbed bosses do not fire their employees or fully end the toxic relationship as much as threaten to. Bosses use work goals, tasks, and deadlines for control. So-called lovers use claims of love and devotion in creative, confusing, deceptive ways to crush a natural goodness in their intimate partner. Though intimidating, there is usually a lifeless, unimaginative, backwards quality to those in a hardened bully mode. While claiming to stand for all that truly or should matter, the abusive alpha in these dances knocks down and dissembles whatever has meaning for their victim. Often, there is an outer shell of legitimacy, the prospect of producing a caring relationship or a productive workplace. There is usually a thin "he said she said" narrative covering over the asymmetries. Theoretically, bosses simply have the best interests of the company and employee at heart, and bullies in intimate relationships only want love and respect.

Emma was experiencing the dark side of inmaps' power. Her consciousness was stuck in the concrete sludge of victimhood. In the field of health psychology, she was overly controlled by potent, regressive fight-flight-freeze response forms. She was not quite delusional but dipped into sheer terror, paranoia, and panic. Her soul longed for solutions and peace, but higher levels of creativity and positivity were not accessible. She could only loop about within a very constrained psychological space, generally shot through with the most recent, concrete sense of threat or temporary relief.

My client was very much living out the same dynamic as that discovered in the experimental neurosis research previously discussed. She was jumping from oval-fear to circle-hope, and breaking down as these perpetually became indistinguishable. Her mind was tortured. Hope would launch her reasoning faculties, but the lower inmap controls would perpetually elude logic's grasping. She might survive a meeting after much anticipation, but within hours encounter a bizarre, subtly accusatory email.

Like some mental Groundhog Day, she would begin anew to think her way out. And she would just as instantly be flooded with memories of all she had already tried without success. She would find herself once again plummeting across a nihilistic event horizon. As much as she insisted on working things out, her boss seemed intent on the opposite. The victim's dance partner is not likely to change when what Peck framed as spiritual warfare is in play.

By coming to understand inmaps, Emma was able to detach and perceive how both over-attachment and over-detachment were keeping her stuck. She was held, paradoxically, by viewing her boss in a favorable light regardless of evidence to the contrary. Out of this rigidity, her rational mind insisted on convincing him of her worth. And being so intensively attached to these perspectives, she was not able to entertain the prospect of detaching, walking away, and quitting. Her over-attachment to the bully-victim inmap impeded her access to other inmaps, not to mention her higher powers of reason. Eventually, she could use her intelligence to analyze her boss's psychology and her own with adequate precision. She finally moved through the bully-victim inmap that had plagued her life, and reset her own submissiveness and vulnerability. In time, she recruited her inner warrior and could sense her own invincibility, courage, and resilience.

With help from her dreams, she ventured into other inmap areas involving love and spirit, and found a far more encompassing canvas for her life. The self/ego/mind needs its trickster's cunning, lover's joy, warrior's fierceness and more in order to leave it all behind. We need their scaffolding, and we need to transcend the same. Even all the love and wisdom we ascribe to our spiritual mentors and the deep meaning we attach to their teachings can be sticky when we inadvertently endow it with just a little too much perfection. While some teachers fit the mold of gentle, consistent, and calm, others remind us not to project our versions of enlightenment. Chögyam Trungpa apparently did not lightly suffer the foolish ideals projected on to him, and also clearly traveled paths uniquely authentic for him.

Talker

Most everyone knows what is meant by "she (or he) is a talker". This personality type is said to have "poor boundaries." Inmaps help bring more precision to these common and debilitating personality disturbances. In many people labeled as talkers, a core attachment inmap leaves a trail of woe across decades of adulthood.

Describing this in the language we are using here, Cheryl would routinely misperceive the degree of we-ness and mistakenly overestimate a group's we-ness. Her childhood had saddled her with a very impaired wego. She would suddenly interrupt people speaking privately to one another at another table at a restaurant or in line at a store as if she knew them. Cheryl had a sweet, sunny, immature countenance. Many people would speak of her in glowing ways, as creative, funny, and sensitive. So-called friends would profess their adoration and intention to get together, but none of these relationships seemed to go further than incidental encounters.

More than most talkers, Cheryl was highly, interpersonally "stimulus bound". This is a behavioral term that refers to the power of external stimuli to control one's behavior. When she was out in public, for example, she was particularly attracted to parents with children. She would physically move into their air space and adopt a knowing, warm smile as if there was a deeper, more established "we" than there actually was. Unconsciously intrusive, she would initiate an exchange without an invitation to do so. She would then bring the attention to herself by, in effect, demanding the others listen to her as she launched into what would turn out to be a strangely thin association to the encounter.

Cheryl was a lovely and kind person, not grandiose or bluntly domineering. But her lack of attunement to the larger social flow was so inappropriate that others who did not know her would sense that something was amiss. In fact, she exercised a sort of unconscious control over others because she was so effusive, kind, and well-meaning. This would mitigate their discomfort and serve as a sort of temporary wedge into the presumed we-space.

Typically, she simply could not stop the impulse to, in her mind, share something the other would relate to and find entertaining. But her "theory of mind", her working model of the other, would sooner rather than later fall short. That which Cheryl excitedly presumed was closely connected and would be of interest to those finding themselves having to listen to her was often neither related nor intrinsically of interest.

Pushing this enthused, well-intended interrupting style was the core inmap associated with maternal attachment—the one Bowlby demonstrated to be so strong and critical in early development. As the field of adult attachment has proven, this inmap continues to wield a preconscious power across the lifespan. It informs adult intimate relationships and friendships. From the perspective of Buddha's Mom, this drives tribal cohesion by way of the first-person plural—the wego or we-self. It provides an internal representational system which pushes the organism to perceive opportunities to foster the self's collective aspect, and thereby strengthen the tribe. But too much of a good thing commonly yields mixed results. For Cheryl, this intra-psychic pulse was so dominant that interpersonal (inter-psychic) input was restricted. The former was forever being misperceived as the latter. Capacities involving the reading of social cues were frozen, causing a form of developmental arrest. From the perspective of relative attachment, this arose from an over-attachment to the positive, attaching, clinging pole of an idealized listening, caring attachment figure. There was an over-attachment to attachment. Blending in the Buddhist perspective, an original maternal deprivation continually co-arose alongside a craving for motherly mirroring causing suffering.

Inmaps are adaptive in the context of evolution and the culmination of humans' uncannily advanced social capacities. But on the small scale of a person with deep self disturbance, inmaps jerk about like the proverbial fish out of water. Where the original damage is profound, years can go by where little seems to heal or change. The *Diagnostic and Statistical Manual of Mental Disorders* refers to this substrate of disturbance as Axis II. For better or worse, this refers to the dysfunctional, relatively fixed and to stable but disturbed deep structures constelling the self. For many with serious deep self disturbance, emotional dysregulation and instability is paradoxically a stable pattern. In Cheryl, work relationships were serially tumultuous. The names would change, but the pattern remained. She was hurt and angry with the cruelty and passive aggression of others over and over again. There tended to be a dual truth. Others were in fact immature and abusive, and yet somehow she, more than most, ended up as their punching bag.

On rare occasions, someone would do more than just hint. Those who cared for her would get exasperated and tell her that her behavior was inappropriately defensive or intrusive. For the most part, perhaps more than 99% of the time, people do not make it their business. It would take a village to consistently provide containment and feedback, and none exists for talkers— paradoxically, because of the level of their self-involvement and neediness—so life goes on. The same is true for kids, where the sort of neglect Cheryl experienced is a present reality and where similar fates are being etched. Those who witness the damage make their exit as soon as possible. Having a less damaged wego, they sense something out of sorts. Just as when we see horrors on television or a car accident, we do not mean to be cold. But there is no we-space at hand. There is no readily, discernible pathway to empathy.

On the rare occasion where Cheryl was confronted, she was quick to deflect, deny, and possibly return fire. A raw, panicky, irritable, rage-packed response was never far away. Cheryl's deeper self was highly defended against perceived criticisms. In effect, these feelings were mapped out over ancient perceptions of abandonment and rejection. She would instantaneously block, deflect, and deny whenever strong emotions began to flood her psyche. Panksepp refers to the GRIEF/PANIC system which goes into high gear when mother's secure base and nurturing are not forthcoming. Subcortical areas such as RAGE, FEAR, and others would be activated as well. In total, for Cheryl, her personality undermined what most people would refer to as a satisfying social life. She never married, had children, or was part of a truly close and trusting circle of friends.

The associated inmaps in talkers and those with poor boundaries include those associated with classical, core maternal attachment, among others connected to tribal membership. Where early life trauma or developmental arrests are profound, inmaps wield excessive power. Conversely, they are kept in check in normal development. They help the organism to make sense (meaning) of the social environment, and to ever more facilely navigate it—that is to say, to cultivate emotional intelligence. Nature's genius is such that inmaps foster wego capacities (more on this idea in the upcoming sections); these in turn leapfrog that which helped bring them online. Such capacities are the new normal, a new center of gravity. When things go awry, this Russian doll styled, successive expansion of the self is stymied. The self/ego/mind are much less multi-layered, less rich, less abstract, less subtle and sublime. An overall immaturity, often meeting the criteria of a personality disorder, is common. I have been referring to this in terms of deep self disturbance. The net result is a lack of capacities for moderation, for checks and balances, for perspective-taking, and for the ability to learn from mistakes.

When attachment and development and brain physiology are unimpaired, an ability to imagine what another human perceives is called "theory of mind". This patient's capacity to comprehend the ways that others perceived her was quite impaired. Typical of "talkers," she did not cognitively recognize when her social behavior was inappropriate. Paradoxically, the social behavior of talkers is shaped through the same modeling process meant to teach us when to hit the brakes and to let others suspect, as the saying goes, that we're fools, rather than to keep talking and remove all doubt. Their behavior is shaped to resemble normal conversational contours, and in fact, it does. Those who are commandeered by talkers get annoyed, laugh it off, or in various ways, move along. So over and again, talkers derail balanced, normal conversations in self-serving ways, pulling we-space potentials toward "me" moments. Over the long arc of life, depending on their severity of their problems, the rigidity of these inmap-driven patterns inadvertently squashes the possibility of casual contacts maturing into increased levels of intimacy.

This particular talker, to my way of thinking, suffered a more profound self disturbance than most. And this was most evident in the particular way that she would relay some related experience or story. She often began with the words "that reminds me." But the story she was presumably reminded of would turn out to be a Trojan horse. Cheryl was clearly convinced she was engaged in normal social behavior. But the story ended up losing out to the deeper psychological reason for her lack of boundaries. The story competed with her own emotional relationship to the story. She would keep defaulting into personal, subjective impressions about how she first thought one thing, was surprised, maybe confused, then realized that such and such was not what she had subjectively imagined. Very often, having pulled everyone's attention her way, she suddenly could not recall any actual coherent story, just that "it was amazing" or she "could not believe it".

Often social exchange involves a communal expression within what might be called a meaning space. This is the semantic architecture, the way the we itself is formed in a resonant, shared emotional tone. Inmaps are always close at hand as we discuss overcoming tragedy, or teaching about hilarious, topsy-turvy jaunts ending in perfectly unexpected ways. These are tribal contours, honed by ancestors who spent their lives in a collective, relative attachment bond.

Buddha's Mom represents evolution's method of downloading various containers of consciousness across body, mind, and spiritual bands. Inmaps are not conveyed and catalyzed through breast milk. Rather the holding, feeding, and somatic aspects of human lineage transmission are the "necessary but not sufficient" substrates to much higher capacities. Where base emotional mirroring is deficient, inmaps are still inherited. However, rather than benefiting from these as potent background capacities, eventual self tends to get kicked about by them.

The famous object relations theorist, Donald Winnicott, coined the term, "good enough mother" to capture the notion that development must be good but need not be perfect. One can argue where the "good-enough" line is developmentally, but a reasonable gauge can be found almost everywhere where there is deep self disturbance. In this common form of suffering, "good enough" can be defined as having not occurred. An important point is that in deep self disturbance, some version of my client's inmap problems are the norm.

Buddha's Mom represents the we-space crucible in which a healthy self/ego/mind are constructed. Only in a good enough, healthy enough mother-child dynamic does relative attachment reach the maturity required to navigate inmaps. Through Buddha's Mom, a strong-enough psyche is catalyzed in her child and adolescent, one capable of maintaining the not-too-hot, not-too-cold balance that allows inmaps to serve us best.

Part of the inertia, to the development of a better science of inmaps has been the reluctance to embrace the extent to which a "normal" brain is attachment-based and culturally dependent. As argued in this book, attachment is the basic code of a personal, familial, and cultural programming. Stories of feral children suggest that at least some of what neuroscientists study is based on the nature-side of the nature-nurture process. Much of mind, one can say, depends on the ability of the mother and culture to create a psychological landscape and to program and activate brain processes. The neglect feral kids suffer amounts to extreme brain damage when compared to brains which did not suffer the same fate. The data on feral children also supports the concept that the brain requires attachment to form an even minimally functional mind. Soil and sunlight have much to do with the lotus. If attachment is essential for normal human brain functioning, are these processes not scientifically important even if the associated neuroscience has yet to be forged?

Archetypes also run through cultural memes, from gossip, urban legend to novels and films. Every neuroscientist is familiar with these great mind- and meaning-shapers. Americans' hearts swell to Paul Revere, John Wayne, the conquest of the West, "gold in them thar hills," Rosie the Riveter, "pick yourself up by the boot straps," because no tribe or parent will. The Declaration of Independence not Interdependence. We see our stars and stripes by rocket's red glare—red hot death possibly for our British brothers.

Every child who reads *Harry Potter* or watches Disney films is similarly shaped by inmaps. These have a hand in the undercurrents that makes narrative and story so gripping. But to date, archetypes are not a serious subject in cognitive neuroscience; many would view them as the stuff of pseudoscience. A new, empirically based approach such as inmaps could help resurrect this very important dimension of Jung's work even if much of his original elaborations need to be negated and/or transcended. A methodology might be based on independent raters' assessment of "personalities" in a bonobo or chimpanzee group, or an indigenous human tribe.

Besides the obvious dominance and submission forms, others might include the overly earnest underdog, the conniving trouble-maker, the peacemaker, bully, and outcast. From there, fairy tales and pop culture might add some more hardy forms for analysis. It is time to move past the begrudging acknowledgement that spiders, snakes, and loud sounds have some ancient neural echo.

These efforts would help advance the science of sentience. They would specifically help advance clinical work with people suffering from deep self disturbance. More precision regarding inmaps and their influence on personality would enhance well-intentioned efforts to reach out and help those with recalcitrant forms of emotional suffering.

What Bowlby called the "secure base" can really be called the "self/ego/mind base". Whether this is never formed well enough in the first place, whether early-life attachment left a person with an insecure base/self, or whether trauma came along like the painful side of a rocket's red glare, the result can be mapped with some precision. Very commonly, the result is a combination of an impaired, not-secure base (for example, a neurotic-level self/ego/mind). Mapped by way of Panksepp, this translates as a rupture or incomplete, unstable secondary process. Clinically, the outcome routinely appears to be a self/ego/mind that cannot shake free of lower, primary process affects. The very picture of a neurotic is someone who is chronically, vacillating, an unstable mix of these lower, intense emotions. They are filled with fear and its close cousins, anger, lust, longing, and are desperate and needy.

Topping this off, inmaps, which in normal functioning people are not-too-cold, not-too-hot, commonly have an excessive influence on self/ego/mind. The examples are too many to list, but include villain/victim projection, grandiosity via idealized self or other, and similar religiosity. Inmaps are certainly intricate, but they are so by design. The dry riverbed analogy mentioned previously fits. The backdrop is shaped by the trans-cultural inmap and the more experience-near specifics is filled out by the intricate depths of a person's maternal attachment, family, culture and tribal/social experiences. In general, when these are dysfunctional, inmaps have a stronger, downward pull on maturation. As a common example, many who repeat patterns of unhealthy intimate relationships claim to have achieved insight. But often due to a predisposition toward idealizing, based in an inmap, they have trouble spotting the "orange flags".

So, to recap, insecure attachment can be understood as the self's floor collapsing. Our mammalian birthright's amazing seven, primary affective systems are not moderated in those suffering from insecure attachment. Instead, they have too much influence, as do inmaps, resulting in endless variations of a theme we might label deep self disturbance.

So-called Emotion

Raising a child parallels transforming it from a standard mammal—which as Panksepp shows are emotional through and through—to a higher-order, still fully emotional creature, but one who thinks and talks. Cultivating this little person, this emergent thinking, talking, social self/ego/mind is largely the purview of Buddha's Mom. Without this sophisticated catalytic process, the child may survive biologically but will be much less than stable, secure, and sophisticated. The attachment-deprived individual is less likely to achieve her potential, is less likely to contribute to society, to practice insight meditation, metta or mindfulness. Sadly, they are much more likely to struggle through a life beset with deep-seated psychological problems.

Presumably, Prajapati's mother or some other attachment figure supervised and facilitated, in and through Prajapati's body-mind, the increasingly sophisticated process spanning pre-emotional, somatic footing. This allowed for the emotional constellations of mad, sad, glad, and a hundred other responses, to trans-emotional, perspective-taking, and higher reasoning. Armed with an integrated, high functioning self, Buddha's Mom took her turn to do the same for her baby. Prajapati's mother did not smother her, nor did she reject or neglect or fall short of the mark necessary to pass along a cogent, loving presence in her daughter. Just as "you can't give what you haven't given away," you also "can't give what you don't have." These trite truisms reflect that the dying, detaching, negating dynamic in the transcendence to motherhood is only as complete as the inherited attachment love which must be included and preserved to be passed on.

This receiving and transmitting amounts to the downloading and catalyzing of the seven subcortically-based emotional capacities outlined by Panksepp. Blends of the seven become the soup of the we-space. Baby is briefly panicked when it cannot find the breast. Mother responds appropriately and the neural circuit is reinforced. Mother does not simply plug her calm, caring presence into the unformed baby brain. Her actions occur in their collective field, and her soothing ways catalyze the same in the baby. Just as we cannot not-hear a sound if our hearing perceptual systems are working, so too a baby cannot not-feel comforted and soothed. Neuronally, self-soothing becomes more elaborate and eventually is a robust, established "internal" resource. Similarly, a toddler wants to show off and a healthy loop is closed when the caregiver gazes back at her and nonverbally, accurately mirrors their surprise or enthusiasm. In this case, a higher level of soothing approaching being-seen is cultivated. This is foundational for an adult intimacy founded in the sense that "she gets me".

Within the primitive neonatal we-space, feedback loops or the emotionally rich toddler developmental bands, Panksepp's subsystems are being honed. Connections are forever more elaborate. The cold, hungry, sleepy baby may initially only be a subjective blob of misery, but the attuned mother learns its cries and patterns, and through trial and error, carries out evolution's and attachment's agenda. Needs are met and this reinforces the emotions that express and communicate such requirements.

Through these sorts of interactive, we-space processes, mind grows. The mother's breastfeeding and mirroring is transcended and included, negated and preserved. If all goes reasonably well, the resulting mind is a reasonable happy we-space waiting to interact with others. It's incorporates an inner tribe ready to sync with others' inner tribes and thus show up outwardly as socialization.

The incorporation of a self (ego or mind) and the ability to pass this along is only possible through countless cycles of attachment and detachment. One might stretch this to assert that even at the neuronal level, firing together is a form of relative attachment. Neurons become pathways through attaching with some and not firing and not attaching with others. We can inadvertently dilute the centrality of attachment by arguing for an ever deeper, neurological basis manifests as a bias against formulations more fully allied with meaning, emotion and sentience.

A mother comes by whatever skill level she has both innately and "honestly" as the saying goes, through her own earthly experience and personal development. All this peaks in a literal, concrete, and figurative crescendo in the pain of childbirth. It is more than poetic to declare that a mother gives her life over to mothering, to her offspring. When this occurs, as it does routinely, an old self shrinks as a new one surges. One whose axis tilts toward the other in a we-space. The other now co-arises in the most arresting way. A defenseless, wrinkled fledgling hopefully with ten fingers and toes, which hopefully sleeps through the night within a year, on the one hand. And on the other, nothing less, genetically speaking, than the future of the species. The rough-and-tumble of this process, the dying, the rebirth, the relentless pressures, the delight and exhaustion holds enormous potential for a broader embrace of spirit. The downside is just as real. Outcomes are everywhere for anyone to note with mediocrity, the middle of the bell curve rolling over common blends of burned out parents, stress, money problems, some good times, lots of daycare, school, sports and all manner of OK-but-not-really family life.

Countless books have been written on factors undergirding problems that beset adults and families. The main point of this one is that serious approaches to the formation of the self and its emotional characteristics would do well to embrace the full scope of attachment science.

Psychopathology, i.e., everything below normal on the four-tier, psychosis-borderline-neurotic-normal (PBNN) spectrum is practically synonymous with emotional pathology. Viewed through any patriarchal perspective, e.g., one lacking a full embrace of Buddha's Mom, emotions are at best misunderstood if not mislabeled pathological. There can be no descent into emotional disarray without the fuller embrace of how all these "lower" (and what we have been referring to as developmentally *upriver*) currents should flow in a fully functioning human.

In a 2012 TED talk, Brené Brown explained how fear and shame invite vulnerability, which in turn hones courage. Dr. Brown referred to various dilemmas falling in the very upper reaches of the four-tier PBNN spectrum, e.g., super-normal. At these advanced stages, the self can collapse into vulnerability and be remade better for the experience. Buddha's Mom would refine this by way of the attaching and detaching, 'relative attachment' dynamic. For example, attaching to the pull for human connection in a desperate manner, while detaching from the fear of rejection, is courage in the face of vulnerability.

Lower down the PBNN spectrum, however, the prospect of this sort of subtle affective differentiation decreases. For those with deep self disturbances, the fear of rejection is not delineated from the desperation for connection. Said otherwise, detachment and attachment are fused. The psyche is not able to disambiguate the hope/fear juggernaut. These serve to maintain a crude handle on life, and provide "reality contact." The self strives to cope, day after year after decade, atop an underbelly of turmoil.

Just existing, even between crises, is enervating. Undulations threaten. Terror of über rejection, left for dead humiliation and shame rock back and forth with other juices. On the other side are spurts of a final rescue, even in suicide. Or perhaps there is an intrusive, seemingly positive, fantasy of finally being seen and adored, given a chance to explain everything. One is finally normal, safe and free. In terms of the classical model, the lower one's aggregate functional, adaptive status, the more this underworld distorts reality. For those with deep self disturbance, all this pain has the quality of a concrete finality. The well-meaning advice of others to move on, to be positive, to not take it personally only further taunts and haunts the tenuous self/ego/mind.

Pick any of Panksepp's big seven, and one finds that too much or too little marks some diagnosis or another. Narcissism is characterized by emotional fragility, a ceaseless need for the limelight, and a biting, rage-filled response to perceived criticism. Neurosis and borderline levels of the classical continuum are characterized by affective imbalance, excess, absence, and swings. There is impairment in the rich, adaptive role of emotion seen at the normal range of functioning. In mood disorders, affect has an overly intense hold on self/ego/mind. Nature's emotions, like the fairy tale, are adaptive when they are neither too hot nor too cold. According to Buddhism, however, this may not be true of attachment. As we suggest by way of Buddha's Mom, more precision regarding this term, attachment, is very promising.

Seeking as Tanhā

At the root of our being, in the very pulse of consciousness, looms a chronic longing, a pulsing, driving clinging, an urge to attach. The term "tanhā"—literally, thirst—anchors the very first noble truth and Buddha's identification of the nature of suffering. Tanhā, the first noble truth declares, causes dukkha, suffering. Scholar, David Snyder (as mentioned earlier) has given the translation of tanhā much consideration.

> Some people ask if desire is bad, then what about desire for food and other
> basic necessities? This is why when we see the Four Noble Truths translated
> to English we often see the translation corrected to something like "selfish
> desire." But even basic necessities could be interpreted by some as a selfish
> desire since it is for yourself only.[178]

He concludes that the most accurate English translation for Buddha's proclamation on the cause of suffering is *expectation*, and alternatives such as reasonable expectation or realistic expectation. "When these expectations are not met we get angry or upset or mad, all of which are suffering."[179] Any sense of having attained one's object of desire, having one's expectations met or in the view being considered here, any attaching to desired or expected outcomes eventually proves fleeting. Impermanence rears up and mind is plunged back into itself. Nothing but suffering, dukkha, can possibly result.

Panksepp's SEEKING system appears to be the very correlate of this—be it metaphorical thirst, desire, or expectation—in mammals, *including humans*. According to Panksepp, the SEEKING system is the "biggest and most pervasive emotional system of all."[180] SEEKING arose in evolution because resources are limited. Animals must persistently, relentlessly seek in order to survive. This master system permeates, drives and animates animal mind. With its provable brain basis and definable behavioral repertoire, with this all being replicated with neural stimulation, the SEEKING system is a formidable finding. As a sort of pre-human Qi, this need not be elevated. It is a redundantly basic and critical force because mammals...

> ...must hunt or forage for food, seek to hear, smell and piece together clues
> that signal danger. They need water, find twigs or dig holes to fashion
> sheltering nests. The SEEKING system urges them to nurture their young, to

search for a sexual partner, and, when animals live in social communities, to also find nonsexual companions, forming friendships and social alliances.[181]

This raw driver precisely produces an expectancy as the core experiential architecture of his foundational affective system. Is this the very source of expectation that "We have named this crucial motivational system the SEEKING-EXPECTANCY system, or the SEEKING system for short."[182] (emphasis added). In this empirically derived, repeatedly replicated finding, the upper reaches of mammalian affective experience syncs with the lowest reaches of human mind, based on a Buddhist frame. From an integral view, the human mind transcends and includes these seven affective systems. Electrical stimulation of these as well as targeted neurochemical manipulation of the specific neuromodulators associated with each produce the predicted experiential state. Stimulation of FEAR produces fear, RAGE rage, etc.

> ...the SEEKING system may have served as the platform (the preadaptation)
> for the evolutionary emergence of the other social-emotional systems we
> have discussed — LUST, CARE, PLAY — while also facilitating the ancient
> FEAR and RAGE systems.[183]

Panksepp offers something even more remarkable is in his identification of *anticipatory euphoria*. In this Zen-like construct, he may have discovered a sort of sentience quark that is evoked at high-level in the subtle states Buddhism so exquisitely describes. But instead of a base connection to suffering, Panksepp proposes a different sentience, a euphoria. Combining these perspectives, an alleged, simple, pure sort of joy arises as one side of tanhā, craving, thirst, and desire. It is worth remembering that both Panksepp and Buddha understand their conclusions to stem from empirical, testable evidence.

> When the SEEKING system is aroused, animals exhibit an intense, enthused
> curiosity about the world. Rats, for example, will move about with a sense of
> purpose, sniffing vigorously and pausing to investigate interesting nooks
> and crannies. Rats often make little excited sounds that we can't hear without
> special equipment: ultrasonic 50-khz chirps that are especially persistent
> when they are having fun. These are the same behaviors that rats exhibit
> when they are looking for rewards, rather than when they are consuming
> treats.[184]

SEEKING is exquisitely juxtaposed sitting, the centerpiece of wisdom traditions across recorded history. SEEKING, as the name describes, compels elaborate, elite animals (from the perspective of evolution to do ... well, something! SEEKING is a shared affect that shapes sentience. The mammalian mind manifests in a huge variety of phenomena. Creatures forage, sniff, graze, walk, crawl, and fly. They play, fret, screech, preen, fight, and take flight. However, all this stems from this singular, subterranean emotional push.

Sitting and "doing nothing" has — perfectly and paradoxically — come to be the ultimate indigenous response to SEEKING. Sitting is the spiritual practice form par excellence born spontaneously within disparate wisdom traditions. In sitting, each found the definitive skillful means for taking full measure of our species' natural state, which per cutting edge science is SEEKING. With sitting, the cushion, the retreat, the chanting or breathing and emphasis on stillness are the outlines of a subtle doing. If sitting *seeks* anything, it seeks non-seeking.

Panksepp's model, therefore, begins with the possibility that anticipatory euphoria, as the heart of seeking, transcends and includes (at least at the level of mammalian sentience) the two attachments. In asserting that a primitive, pure joy flows alongside SEEKING, Panksepp touches on the sublime, sweet sentience of the "lower" animal mind. No surprise then that Panksepp is the Endowed Chair of Animal Well-Being Science, and along with his friend Temple Grandin is a leader in the ethical treatment of animals. For decades, he has lived out the aspiration, "may all beings be happy."

What sitting points to is that without liberation from the chronic seeking (in stillness), one is trapped. Panksepp's experimental findings thereby echo Buddha's burning message that seeking, wanting, and desire intrinsically lead to suffering. But the tumultuous hell realms can themselves be reborn in silence. The more one is present to our deep SEEKING nature, the more one approaches liberation from the same.

Human beings report a sense of eager anticipation and an enhanced sense of themselves as effective agents who can make things happen in the world. People clearly like this feeling, although it too can become excessive. They will work relentlessly until they are utterly exhausted (sometimes to the point of death, in the case of laboratory rats that are allowed to eat only one meal a day just at the same time when they are also allowed to self-activate the brain's "euphoria" system).[185]

Buddhism teaches us that this culminates in larger processes manifesting in self/ego/mind. Through dependent origination, the SEEKING system may underlie everything from identifying one's self, as sister, boss, karate enthusiast, a member of (fill-in-the-blank), to seeking distractions from boredom, to formulations in response to eternal questions concerning the meaning of life, to the nature of the good, true, and beautiful. At their core, these are associated with a tanhā, in a broad sense. Panksepp's model is consistent with tanhā as an evolutionary given, and the old concept of "brain reward system" needs to be cast aside. There are two desire channels, one that becomes satiated and one that does not.

> I observed that whenever the animal pushed the lever and got the motivating jolt, it explored its world energetically. That was very different than anything that happened when animals were working for food rewards, where they always stopped when they were full. To get at the difference between the two types of rewards, I designed an experiment that injected sugar water into the rats' stomachs whenever they pushed the stimulating lever. I put one animal in the apparatus and went out to get lunch. When I came back it had killed itself with too much sugar. It just kept pumping more and more until it went into osmotic shock. The next time I didn't walk away.[186]

Mirroring

Panksepp's research on SEEKING is arresting. A restless, anticipatory euphoria is science's most penetrating lens into mammal sentience. Panksepp's model provides a peek into how our furry cousins on land and in the sea feel, perceive and experience their own being—their own species' lineage.

We have spent considerable time exploring this territory in humans from the Buddhist perspective. Its epicenter appears to be the tanhā of the Noble Truths. As mentioned, tanha literally translates as a physiological drive (thirst) but has higher connotations, bridging from craving, attachment to, according to Snyder, expectation. Here we have suggested a model for this bridge of desire in integral attachment and interchangeably as Buddha's Mom. This evolution-spirit bridging has major roots in Bowlby's discoveries and in their offshoots.

These include what both attachment researchers and Panksepp refer to as social attachment. Technically, Panksepp places social attachment up a notch from the big seven substrata. For Panksepp, the seven core, fundamental affective systems have a master, encompassing drive in SEEKING. But whether we refer to physiological drives, SEEKING, maternal or social attachment or attachment-love, what Buddha brings to bear is *attachment as the portal to liberation*. Buddha's Mom, I hope, adds something of value to this mystery at the very heart of life. Naturally paradox forever emanates from this seek-not-to-seek juncture.

> This positive feeling (euphoria?) of anticipatory eagerness, this SEEKING urge, is entirely different from the pleasurable release of consummation. And this feeling exists as an emotion within certain subcortical networks of the mammalian brain long before the brain develops exuberant object-relations with the world (such as those described above). *Initially, it is just a goal without a goal.* (italics added)[187]

The "goal without a goal," a Zen mainstay, points at once to suffering on the relative side of the street and absolute freedom on the other. Panksepp says that a common example of overstimulation of this system occurs in addicts pumped up on amphetamines. This is the familiar, unredeeming, bug-eyed, driven state that we all experience to varying degrees. My former Jungian professor was a retired Army colonel. He joked about the male, military ethos to "do something," anything other than just be. The restless, externally oriented, driven state of SEEKING is, of course, potentially a living hell. As motivational speaker Rick Hansen writes, the brain is Velcro for negativity. SEEKING tends to be associated with survival and the monitoring of all incoming information for signs of danger.

Meditation is, of course, characterized as the opposite pole. As Sylvia Boorstein put it, "Don't just do something, sit there."[188] The paradox hints that the more mindless the activity, the less space. The more seeking, the more illusion. If one's consciousness is not grounded in the body, it's best to be still. In stillness, we then experience unrelenting SEEKING forms, such as monkey mind and boredom or flights of fantasy. Thankfully, the embedded "goal without a goal" in SEEKING potentiates the middle way wherein one is not goalless, nor goal-bound. Enlightenment is achieved with the realization that the more one sees one side, say seeking/non-seeking, the more a mirror image looks back. Mirroring is a fluid witnessing of suchness, of pure being. Thoughts without a thinker.

In this book, we attempt to keep the goal organic and loose so as to honor what Panksepp and Zen refer to as goalless. Buddha's Mom is no one thing. Not a person, but not *not* a person. Not the feminine, not maternal attachment only, but not *not* these either. She represents the fulcrum by which Homo sapiens' consciousness is transmitted. But the riverbed and river are neither the same nor separable. Most beautifully and powerfully, she symbolizes the we-space in which co-arisings occur—goal-seeking and goallessness, for example. We must be stunned at the core of our being by her magnificence but then be incapable of locking in on the precise identity. She is a still, serene golden Buddha. And she is beyond human perception. She has 10,000 swaying arms of impossibly mesmerizing light.

I once was on a boat far from land mesmerized by a pod of dolphins. Four stunning, powerful animals. Was I witnessing SEEKING? I told my wise captain and friend since childhood that the dolphins did not really seem to be going anywhere in particular. He said, "Maybe there's nowhere they have to be." Perhaps they were experiencing one another's CARE. Perhaps the ocean is mapped as second mother much as nature is mapped in her Great Spirit form for many indigenous peoples. Maybe they were in the dolphin equivalent of a we-space based on their lifelong bond with their mother ocean.

In highly intelligent animals such as dolphins and humans, reductionists should not be exalted. Recently, there has been a push back against "neuromania" and the infatuation with all things neuronal. The latest version of the same pertains to the human genome.. Panksepp's work demonstrates that much higher-order, subcortical feelings co-arise with other forms of experience that incorporates the neocortex and thereby whole brain, integrated, parallel processing. In particular, integral theory helps us to situate SEEKING expectancy properly. It shows how to celebrate SEEKING without elevating it. I have the experience of seeking, but I am not the experience.

By virtue of social attachment being a secondary processing system, we can assert that mammalian anticipatory euphoria is the floor of sentience—and therefore the substrate of that which we refer to as Buddha's Mom. Any release into the lower spaces inform the higher calls for mindfulness of the whole range. As we approach Panksepp's momentous foray into animal sentience, we shall keep Wilber in mind. His work demonstrates that transcending all variants of expectation, of wanting, truly begin in the deepest layers of the self. We have suggested the alternative frame of attaching-detaching. That this conjures the already-always nonattachment that Buddha describes. These goalless goals take us, or perhaps, remove the veils that distort and reveal the door to perfection. This opens when we do not seek to have, do or be anything. Non-meditation is a core Dzogchen path. Here, right now as New Age teacher Eckert Tolle writes. An already always perfection, a priori wonder.

But the new age focus can overplay its very heart. Mindfulness bestsellers and big names have recapitulated the 1960s proclamation of Ram Dass to "be here now." Certain authors, teachers and approaches continually push meditators to come back to the moment, the one and only worthy awareness is that of now. Cast as either a holding, attending to, or letting go of the singular now-point, the result is the same. The Buddha's Mom lens may offer something of value to the now-now-now drumbeat. The moment is cleaved even as it passes, again as it arises—though these fading in and fading out aspects shimmer too. Even though the instructions are never too heavy-handed, they may set the stage for a choppy and dogmatic narrowing of the flow of experience. Those awakened in the now and inspired to help others might speak more in terms of a relational temporal center. A midpoint in the flow of time that notices both the center and the flow, a nowesque space.

Excessive now-focusing underplays the more profound calling for a naturalistic, flowing witnessing. As discussed, skillful means may be framed as evolving through an attach-detach process. The slippery, easier said than done trick is to experience the movement in the process, while mental contents lunge and retreat, get snagged, break free. There's such movement in being. Bare attention to the breath as a base metric finds the diaphragm, heart, lungs all moving before the attending begins. A shift in the direction of the attachment process as an active pulsing dynamic helps.

Part of the problem is that a recognizable dynamic is at hand anytime someone imbued with more authority or expertise is, no matter how nicely, juxtaposed to others with less power or status. In some cases, the method, approach or person relaying information is structurally in the position of authority—setting up, regardless of intentions or compensatory gentleness, a Milgram authoritarian frame. Milgram's work, to cut to the chase, virtually proves that you or I will do as we are told even when this takes us past boundaries we would rationally never agree to cross.

The influence of those who inspire us has a slippery power. This will keep tripping us up even as we lovingly and sincerely seek to be here now. Metaphorically, we climb the mountain having awaited a lifetime for our turn to meet the old wise man. He is a somber, astute, intimidating genius. We feel such love and admiration. He says a few words to us. As best we can tell, the crux is "be in the now" and how self/ego/mind gets in the way. We sit in front of him and meditate. But the now seems to damnably, mostly arise with "me". We clearly are not wise, do not measure up. Though this is the best day of our life, we are not present for it.

In Buddha's Mom, all of this can finally shed a little of its weightiness. Mind is right up close, in the flux of the now, more verb than noun. Nouns get the lion's share of the press (mind, self, ego) even in books and talks on awareness. Verbs for now, mind and awareness are tellingly rare and awkward: minding, aware-ing, now-ing? Where nouns are the main medium we are reminded that the medium is the message. For now, I'm a fan of now-esque.

Buddha's Mom leans towards "we". She leans into an ever-irreducible relationship. A repetitive emphasis on the now pushes an impossible agenda of independence more than a supportive, loving external and internal we-space. Now-laden instructions and instructors tend not to have the nicest things to say about that which pulls one away from the now. Choppiness ensues. The moment is cleaved even as it passes, again as it arises—though these fading in and fading out aspects shimmer too. This underplays the more profound calling for a naturalistic, flowing witnessing. Worth adding, Chögyam Trungpa, as eleventh generation of the Trungpa Tulkus, viewed himself within a line of highly realized teacher-students. In this Buddha's Mom, human lineage vessel, he and other Tulkus had, in previous lifetimes, been in both roles.

When we release seeking from objects, we encounter the joy of being. This may be what led Sufis to break into dance, later formalized by the tradition of the whirling dervish. The same ecstatic release may well be at the heart of many forms of dance and expression that later became formalized. Crying, release, speaking in tongues, being slain in the spirit, ancient and shamanistic forms of possession and exorcism may all have a basis in integral, bodymind exclamations expressed as Svaha! and Amen!

Not surprisingly, movements may begin with spontaneous, direct spiritual experiences and then become institutionalized. The latter inevitably takes on local, culturally, historically embedded forms. Some nonetheless reveal their original, bodily, ecstatic origins in their name such as the Quakers and Shakers. I have already noted how the Somatic Experiencing healing process is consistent with this primal, natural mechanism of release and retuning. As one loses herself in meditation, arising thoughts melt away revealing only a mirror. Self and other, subject and object, arise in a field of fluctuation. There is euphoria, silence and love filling the empty space as sunlight fills an empty room.

Such is the still, never changing cycle of Buddha's Mom as through us, her beloved sentient beings, she gazes on creation. Such is the inseparability of Mahamaya's ecstasy and agony as she gave birth to no ordinary baby, without an epidural, to know and love him but for one week. Such is the heart of Prajapati, the one who raised him, who experienced all his determination, every turn in his life, who at long last begged him to die to her own motherhood and be his disciple.

The Floor

Buddha's Mom may shine the way to a unified field theory of attachment but not if she is reduced to the deepest, oldest biological origins of attachment in humans. Even attachment in mammals is not one of the seven primary systems identified by Panksepp *in mammals*. Rather, Panksepp refers to mammalian attachment as a secondary system. Buddha's Mom is of a higher-order altogether, one that can be elusive and hard to define but which comes into resolution through a multivariate approach. This includes the multiple lines of evidence we have been reviewing, and also identification of what she is not. A good beginning is to note that even mammalian attachment has floor under it.

What we referred to at the outset as an upriver journey helps to set the tone but does not endlessly bear fruit. The prescription is not one of ever older, ever deeper as ever more accurate and authentic. Panksepp's SEEKING may be a precursor to tanhā and bear upon the first noble truth. But it is a primary mammalian system, not a correct stand-in even for mammalian attachment. Tanhā-as-SEEKING is therefore certainly not the equal of human attachment. Further, tanhā-as-SEEKING offers no help in our project to transcend and include the two attachments, except to serve as a floor. To the extent that a new center of attachment gravity exists, the journey there will not be ever-downward. This is an important point given how powerful this pull (cognitive neuroscience, for example) can be. Though the metaphor of a marriage of the two attachments may not be perfect, the deep meaning of this term works. This refers to the being a whole which is greater than the sum of the parts.

We must depart from a downward-only search for a resolution to the "two attachments" problem. With the help of Panksepp, the jury's back and Buddha's Mom is not to be found at some lower, earlier evolutionary station. The breadth of human attachment overlaps with precursors, of course, but does not come into ever fuller bloom as one sinks into something like the mammal within or our shared animal sentience. The point of diminishing returns is passed, and that which drives the agenda has to come into question. The religion of reductionism, which some even make of cognitive science, may be recast as helpful false-positives. Watch out for phrasing where mind and consciousness "turns out to be", is "ultimately" or "nothing but" limited to scientific-materialistic processes and constructs. These all say more about the sayer than reality. Human consciousness, it turns out, has a higher floor than the most rigorous, empirically demonstrable processes found in the most sophisticated animals. This higher floor occurs despite enticing neurological overlaps. Animal-based perspectives on attachment have helped Bowlby's work to gain credence, of course. But further analysis, as we are attempting here, suggests this lower, human attachment is tremendously distorted if viewed as "nothing but" a hand-off of the rudiments required for infant survival. These reductionisms dissolve as more data is amassed. A map begins to form of a richly integrated attachment process spanning the lifespan and the continuum from this flooring to the highest reaches of human consciousness.

Human attachment even at its lower threshold is more sophisticated than even the "secondary system" of mammalian attachment. And "secondary" means more than the sum of parts is a higher-order entity which can no more be reduced to its precursors than a lion can be reduced to some sort of inevitable advancement of a single cell animal. The vertical solution certainly has "truthiness", but we must be careful not to be seduced into variants of "nothing but." Tanhā as "nothing but" thirst and other lower, biological cravings—some human derivative of SEEKING— sneaks into many interpretations of the first noble truth.

From this, the leap to dukkha commonly takes these explanations all the way to higher order, human-only cognitive levels. As mentioned, Pali scholar David Snyder argues that "expectation" may be the best English parallel for dukkha.[189] A random survey of dharma talks would likely find emotional suffering, dissatisfaction and identifications as common themes. Of the two possible logical distortions, only one finds any traction. Since we can conclude that Buddhism pertains to more than drinking or thirsting for water, attachment is understandably interpreted as much more than a simple base biological drive. Nothing is really lost in using this term to refer to higher echelons such as self/ego/mind. But this seemingly little leap is what has impeded a fuller, integral appreciation of "Buddha's Mom."

Here, we are asserting more than the likelihood that Siddhartha experienced and benefited from robust human attachment. We are suggesting that the nature of what has been too boxed in as drive, or front-end childcare, as "nothing but" is the "that" which cultivates the seeds of its own transcendence. Mothers are/were women, individuals, whose identity changes into a flexing, permeable one which works hard at and then undoes its own raison d'être. Roughly speaking before she had any chance of success at this, before she was a good enough mother, she was the child of one and so on. The very pulse of attachment is one of a special continuity where identity changes, where old identifications disappear. Hers is a lineage and practice that is not antithetical to impermanence.

Explorer

There's an unstoppable feel to Siddhartha that can be appreciated as a derivative of secure attachment. Buddha's Mom's attachment-love frees up what attachment researchers describe as our species' second major innate drive, "exploration". Siddhartha's irrepressible flow animates the biography of the future Buddha. There is ample overlap and no discrete beginning or end or measurable edge to the burgeoning and subsiding of these systems. On aggregate, however, maternal attachment fades and exploration increases resulting in a rubber-band effect. The human toddler (or similar correlates in nonhuman mammals and primates) stretches the time-space, safety-danger limits. Too little attachment means too little turning back to check on mom's response. Excessive SEEKING (a sort of "I wonder what happens when..." drive) can end badly. The mother monitors and physically, facially, vocally and otherwise permits or intermittently shuts down this stretching ever outward.

> The caregiver's appropriate responsiveness to the infant's proximity needs returns the system to a quiescent state, thus enabling the infant to engage in unfettered exploratory behaviors. To the extent that this recursive dynamic is a consistent feature of early infant-caregiver interactions, the infant experiences a secure attachment bond with the caregiver, and the relationship itself advances the child's acquisition of affect self-regulatory competencies by alternatively serving as a safe haven from situational threat and a secure base for autonomous exploration and progressive environmental mastery.[190]

Details of this aspect of attachment-exploration are lacking in the biography of Siddhartha. But the very same "recursive dynamic" is one of the main characteristics of his biography on a larger scale. The anticipation of his birth and intense devotion to him demonstrate the primacy of the attachment process. His achievements and mastering of various skills demonstrate another, also intensive drive to explore and master. All the while, his parents' efforts to keep him contained, to shelter him from the ugly side of life, makes for this rubber-band effect.

Bowlby's student, Mary Ainsworth, studied this by way of a "stranger situation". This structured, multi-step experiment pits a baby's attachment to a caregiver against an urge to explore a new space and unfamiliar toys. The results demonstrated that secure attachment enhances exploration and two distinct ways that insecure attachment derails this. The anxious ambivalent orientation, characterized by a neurotic clinging and efforts to achieve a "good enough" attachment override and thereby disempower the impulse to explore. The avoidant orientation is consistent with a baby that has either given up on any prospect of attachment or is defended against it. Such babies show an exaggerated, compulsive drive to explore. One sees a sad, weird form of this in children and adults that throw themselves at people and are overtly, inappropriately, hollowly intimate with strangers. Love objects as the term suggests are objectified, strangers when it comes to attachment and love is in name only.

To the extent that we can accurately discern historical actualities, Siddhartha appears to have enjoyed a secure attachment that naturally dovetailed into a robust period of exploration. Mother love, the data suggests, made for a formidable developmental launchpad. But a modern analysis suggests this has been obscured. The creation myth and cult of personality of sorts associated with him employs a one-two punch. In addition to the other ways already discussed, first there is the de-emphasis of attachment followed by an embellishment of exploration.

Buddha's Mom rounds out this mixed picture. She is the face of the life-force downloaded from the genome's expression in attachment-love. We reviewed evidence of his close-knit, affectionate family, of breastfeeding and nursemaids. These are not "primary process" factors, as noted in Panksepp's model, and do not comport with any reductionist point of view. But they do appear to be in concert with a more expansive, integrative model of attachment.

Rationality's infatuation with building blocks needs to loosen for an appreciation of how the life force downloading co-occurs, differentially and vibrantly from the genome in both the mom-baby sides of the dance. Related efforts to view Buddha's Mom as developmentally focal, as maternal development also do not match the evidence. Vision quests, psychotherapy, spiritual practice, bodywork, and all manner of healing arts can bring about miracles and transformation even when tons of reductionist bricks can be absolutely proven to be missing, and to have been laid down in the first weeks, months and years. No shrinking violet, nature keeps pushing.

The process hangs in there with remarkable fixity—this is the essential message of the Four Noble Truths. The seemingly independent drive to explore, to go off to school, to leave home, still hangs around. Ultimately exploration is highly interdependent on attachment. The rubber band effect, and the implications of the attachment side for the exploration side remain in play. For Siddhartha—whom I am inferring based on the ultimate outcome—experienced a perfect inner recognition and cultivation of the depths of attachment-exploration tension. In culminating supreme wisdom and compassion, all those he loved and all that he had to accomplish would have been manifest, would have been an implicit knowing within his being. As one aspect of this, namely an explorative expression, he pushed himself as hard as any human could. He might even be criticized as "his own worst enemy" in his relentless, near-death austerities phase. But this can be understood as one pull of the rubber band, the other of which corresponds to biological and social attachment.

Chapter Seven

DEEP SELF DISTURBANCE

Invisible

When initially introducing the "two attachments," we pointed out that Buddhism does not warn mothers of the perils of breastfeeding and maternal attachment. Breastfeeding and attachment repertoires would have been ubiquitous in Buddha's time, as they always are in indigenous societies. The reason maternal attachment does not show up on any of the hundreds of canonical lists of ill-advised behaviors is mostly a natural outcome of its invisibility. Attachment was neither disapproved of nor passively sanctioned. Rather, those engaged in the articulation of such matters did not consider the attachment that would eventually be studied in depth by Bowlby to be important in the first place.

Like all issues deemed worthy of discussion and rule-making, religious matters were the purview of adult males. This partially explains the cone of silence around maternal, social attachment. After all, there would have been an implicit, empirical awareness of how, for example, an abused, neglected puppy would be forever a skittish adult as well as other human correlates. Such trees regularly fell in the forest with masculinized mind to witness. So much of that associated with the feminine realm was a carve out. The feminine principle was more neglected than abused by the wise and powerful of Buddha's era.

All this is entirely consistent with the evidence, already discussed, that Buddha himself (as baby Siddhartha) was very likely breastfed and also that he knew he was breastfed. Not to have been, in fact, would have amounted to an aberration. Not surprisingly, Bowlby's attachment is not directly addressed in Buddha's formulation of attachment encoded in the Four Noble Truths.

It follows that Siddhartha's own early life attachment has neither been portrayed as highly relevant nor completely irrelevant. For the most part, the biological territory of Buddha's Mom has not so much been suppressed as simply deemed not worthy of comment. The patriarchy would not get around to anti-breastfeeding edicts for a couple of thousand years. A cloak of invisibility over Buddha's Mom leaves us with the pared down view of attachment that anchors orthodox Buddhism as predominantly an adult, psychological phenomenon. This results in a distortion of attachment's actual, central, adaptive function in mammalian consciousness.

Since, as Buddhism has demonstrated, there is a profound nexus of attachment and suffering, not to mention enlightenment, an effort at deepening and correcting the record is important. A fuller vision of our species' attachment-based lineage increases one's field of vision. Suffering, for example, may be mapped with more precision, increasing the prospect of similar enhancements regarding the cessation of suffering.

Experimental Neurosis

Pavlov's disciple, N.R. Shenger-Krestovnikova, trained dogs to distinguish between a circle and an oval. One shape or the other would flash on a screen. When the dog pointed his or her nose toward the circle shape it was given a food reward. Pointing his or her nose toward the oval resulted, however, in an electric shock. Being smart and disliking sudden pain, the dogs learned rapidly to avoid the oval.[191]

Once learning was established, nothing particularly interesting happened. The dog's mind, consciousness, or behavioral repertoire—whatever nomenclature one may prefer—attached to these new realities. They were forced to notice and care about ovals and circles. They employed these cognitive skills and were soon back at baseline with no evident change in their overall well-being. Neurologically and cognitively, certain specific loops incorporating circles, ovals, pain, and pleasure had been added to their permanent (so to speak) intellectual make-up.

On the positive side, the circle circuit would map on the same systems as when a well-attached baby sees, anticipates and experiences Mom, over and over, as safe or pleasurable. These processes would include the visual cortex and brain regions associated with memory and with pleasure.

Next Shenger-Krestovnikova began to modify the oval to make it look more circle-like. A dog expecting a treat would sometimes get shocked. So long as the dog still showed some attempt to hold on to the circle-pleasure/oval-pain construct the researcher pressed on, no doubt delivering many more shocks as the experiment continued. Eventually the stability of these dogs' mental attachments gave way. The sad results were ultimately dubbed "experimental neurosis".

> The whole behavior of the animal underwent an abrupt change. The hitherto quiet dog began to squeal in its stand, kept wriggling about, tore off with its teeth the apparatus for mechanical stimulation of the skin, and bit through the tubes connecting the animal's room with the observer, a behavior which never happened before.[192]

To an extent, orthodox Buddhism illuminates the dogs' plight. Mental efforts to remain attached to what are ultimately illusions of permanence result in suffering. All is samsara. Circles and ovals do not last. Suffering (add pain from electric shocks to old age, disease and death) is inevitable. On another level, all the dog needs to do, the compassionate heart cries out, is let go. Do not look at the screen. Ignore the treat. Stop expecting what once was to ever be so again.

Worth noting, the dogs initially suffered less than they did at the end, and their efforts initially forestalled or resulted in intermittent cessations of suffering. The fact that ultimately the experimenters did not stop and the dogs' ability to manage their suffering collapsed is an orthogonal point, an "also true." As best one can discern, these dogs did not transcend their circumstances. They did not rise above the confines of the experiment, the pain inflicted upon them, nor the breakdown in their "personality" structure. That which arose for them initially as coherently positive and negative was replaced by a confusing, worsening dismantling of previous degrees of cognitive coherence.

In general terms, the same appears to take place and hold true for the human correlate of experimental neurosis. A reverse-engineering of this experiment offers some rich inferences for our species. One starting point is relative attachment, with its attaching and detaching sub-processes.

Facing a strange, new unfolding experience of circles, treats, ovals, shocks, these animals employed both sides of relative attachment. The dogs initially attached to the circle and detached from the oval.

Although neither side of this dynamic is technically closer to Buddhism's nonattachment, spiritual practices which exploit the built-in, human possibility of transcending the whole, samsaric trap of relative attachment are, in a sense, closer than not. In this case detaching from the oval-shock and attaching to the circle-treat was obviously in the direction of emotional equanimity and less suffering.

Further, evidence from attachment science underscores that the circle's meaning is derived of associations to what Bowlby called the secure base. Developmentally this stems from a positive maternal/biological attachment process. The internal image of the circle, reinforced by the treat, fires and wires together with neural networks associated with maternal protection, nurturing and nourishment. These would also be associated with positive wego experiences and attendant trust and positive anticipation. These dogs trusted those who walked them into the room where the experiment was conducted.

It is important to note that this amalgam of associations and connotations describes a normal, high functioning canine disposition. We can conjecture that such an emotional equanimity is normal in dogs as well as in humans. Terms such as natural state and birthright might apply. Puppies have tons of innate joy and enthusiasm and so do "normal" children. Mature, non-neurotic dogs retain a playful, loving demeanor. They romp, relax and pull us so easily into we-spaces imbued with these same qualities. Many of us, of course, seek this in our relationships with pets and are better humans for it. There can be little doubt that normal matters. Normal, rather than neurotic, means less unnecessary hyper-vigilance and nervousness; importantly, normal breathing is no more rapid than the level of sitting, walking or movement requires. Normal or neurotic tendencies start early in a dog's life. As every dog lover knows, abused and neglected puppies are soon skittish adult dogs.

Loving owners of nervous dogs go to great lengths to relieve their suffering. This labor of love (insert mental image of Sisyphus pushing a massive boulder up a hill) rarely brings about a global shift from neurotic to normal. Some healing occurs, and still old triggers immediately evoke signs of a painfully persistent neurosis. Normal, defined as an absence of undue anxiety, is only achieved through manipulation of their pet's environment. Thanks to these canine bodhisattvas' second attempt at nurturing an unnaturally peaceful existence is forged.

By way of an integrated attachment model, the tragic breakdown of normal can be mapped with reasonable precision. As the experimental conditions are introduced, the anticipated pleasure, the expectation of safety more and more randomly co-arises with raw pain. The circle's normal, positive associations become less and less reliable. From Panksepp's work, we know emotional meaning to have a neural basis. For these animals, the pleasure centers, with their roots in maternal attachment, breastfeeding, nurturing and nourishment, start to lose their utility and coherence. So do neural networks associated with aversion and the capacity to assess and respond to danger. Once valuable tools, internal pain signals, fear affects, aggression, submissive behaviors lose their integrity, their relationship to the whole.

The resulting neurosis can be understood as a perpetual state of ambivalence. The animals are attempting to make sense of when to attach or detach, how to establish order. Moments arise, riddled by a forced hope of getting it right this time and fear of intense pain. There is no neutral middle ground. As neuroscientist Rick Hanson explains, as trauma research demonstrates and as neurotics experience with cruel consistency, the brain is "velcro for negativity". "Life is suffering" has a different meaning for those with a neurotic (or lower) self/ego/mind than for those at a higher place on the classical continuum of functioning.

In particular, we-space moments are problematic. What we can now appreciate as a form of attachment disorder becomes the distorted lens through which one experiences social and interpersonal encounters. Not intending to do so, those internally (analogously) beset with circle-oval volatility chronically seek to break the vicious cycle. For many, ambivalence pervades with endless judgment errors, over appropriation of trust and alternatively, an insatiable fear of commitment.

Variations of the ugly, sad outcomes of actual, non-experimental neurosis in humans are legion. At least now, with a combination of modern science and Buddhist insights, we can differentiate these forms of suffering or dukkha. I like the term "deep self disturbance" because it helps locate dukkha with an expanded attachment framework. It is helpful to use a term that is free of connotations associated with classical or technical words such as neurosis, psychopathology, depression or personality disorder.

With the concept of deep self disturbance, we can look to integral attachment for deep self-healing. Returning to experimental neurosis for a moment, we immediately recognize that out of compassion we would not abuse these animals' circle-food association. We would not insist they detach from the experimental conditions and let go of the sensation of pain from the electricity. Nor would we steal a baby's food or demand they not be breastfed.

We would recognize that an animal's baseline stability, their "normal" disposition, has a developmental basis in maternal/biological attachment. We would extend this to humans, babies and adults, and recognize how certain forms of suffering require more than a message to detach. In deep self disturbance, there is an inability to discern safety from danger. Those afflicted have profound impairment in their capacity to cope with reality. They confuse metta and Mara and take refuge with dukkha. Though they mean well, that which arises is jumbled and riddled with pain.

Sentience

Neurosis and forms of deep self disturbance might be more constructively viewed not simply as disorders of an undefined "normal" but as distortions of sentience. When experience has no consistent, coherent meaning, no stable flow of sentience, there is no chance of emotional discernment or critical thinking. Rather than a solipsistic normal, defined as absence of a disorder of itself, sentience can be identified in the positive, as the meaning (or lack thereof) that runs through affect, cognition and interpersonal relationships. As we have suggested, and demonstrated with clinical examples, such meaning can be achieved. Often this call for working with attachment wounds. Buddha's Mom posits healing as a realignment of sentience in the open, unified space of our species' lineage, which Buddhists call the natural state. One way or the other, meaning paves the way. There is little prospect of affective regulation or daily practice when life's meaning is deeply fragmented.

One would have a hard time convincing Shenger-Krestovnikova's damaged dogs to volunteer for further circle-oval trials. These stimuli had come to represent and convey meaninglessness. The circle, what is good in life, means something rather than nothing. So-called normal people have a natural, coherent, sound orientation toward the cosmos and its refraction in our precious, miraculous, vulnerable species. In neurosis, this sentient orientation is haphazard. One is forever following it over the cliff or missing it in the first place. One senses a meaning to life rather than nothing, and that something is oh so close, or tragically far, and chases what is missing. In psychosis, the circle and any internal or external association to positive sentience is up for grabs. Meaning in paranoia follows one harsh contour, and in grandiosity another. Something is replaced by almost anything else, including randomness, noise and incoherence. Somewhere between these levels of functioning extremes of major depression render suicide meaningful.

Attachment science illuminates how the flow of sentence is downloaded, released and set into motion in maternal and social attachment. Subsequent successive, integrative, developmental processes cultivate ever more elaborate fields of emotional meaning. A frightened pup or toddler scurries back to mother, away from one and toward another. It seems safe to infer that such experiences evoke not just conscious affects but that this correspond to meaning, a word with surprisingly few synonyms. Roughly, this clearly involves a feeling valence where danger, snakes, loud noises, or discomfort, cold or hunger provoke negative states, and mother, protection, breastfeeding and nurturing yield positive experiences.

In isolation, attachment, craving, clinging and aversion, detachment and the like do not fit the science. Besides being cute and furry, a teddy bear means something to a child. A human's home, loved ones, and their life's deepest callings are similar albeit more potent and nuanced. A breakdown of this sentient compass, as seen in neurosis and insecure attachment, has profound and lasting implications for the meaning in life.

Appreciated from the vantage of Buddha's Mom, Shenger-Krestovnikova's circle incorporates these positive sentient strands dating back to the dogs' early attachment. We implicitly recognize the cruelty in this experiment and in teasing a child for her attachment to a stuffed animal. In dogs and humans, the tantric, sentient thread is not the same as a concrete memory, for example, of breastfeeding and nurturing. Rather, thousands of subsequent experiences would generalize, in effect, in valences of meaningful emotional colorations. To wit, the meaning is the message. Normal intelligence is made up of an elaborate, flexible capacity for attributing established, complex variants of meaning to the flux of experience.

By inference, a bodhisattva would want all suffering dogs, frightened babies and neurotic adults to find their way to their own sentient source of safety and equanimity. In Buddha's Mom, the origins of this ultimate potential are recognizable. Metta, the bodhisattva's heart of compassion, responds to the call to lessen suffering. But presuming we are all human, an echo of metta is also at the fore in those in pain. There is a tender silk thread in hurt, in pain and in seeking liberation from these.

Here we have suggested these connections can be mapped with an overlay of attachment science and Buddhism. We have seen how attachment-love corresponds to metta and made the case for an integrated attachment as our species' inheritance and our shared human lineage. We have gone to some lengths to demonstrate its evolutionary and biological dimensions and to show how this lineage emanates from a feminine principle and yin basis.

The meaning associated with Buddha's Mom and metta can be experienced in the simple hope for a better present whenever the present moment co-arises with dukkha. When frightened dogs face impossible odds and distressed humans are beset with deep self disturbance, the prospect of meaning crystallizes as fluid blends of desperation, fear, hope and desire. Practices and therapies aimed at relieving suffering are conduits of same tantric thread.

When we dive backwards against the current of evolution, into the body housing emotion, and the sensorial field housing the body, and so on, we find no clear, upriver cut-off for love or sentience. We may sense our toe, but the experience is not just sensorial. We find no diminishing of meaningful, coherent, interesting, a priori experience.

Our species shares physiological drives with the whole of mammalia. Buddha's exploration of these, as his discovery of the Middle Way demonstrates, led him to turn away from an opposing stance against these base physiological strands. But not to an opposing stance either. Not back to the palace and materialism, but as the Vajrayana teaches, his turn was toward the subtler, inner, somatic potentials arising in a deepened practice form. These held a fundamental, unshakable meaning which in the end he determined could remain as is. In keeping with the Shenger-Krestovnikova's model, Siddhartha returned to the circle. It was OK to breathe, drink and eat, and implicitly to have the associated impulse and drive to do so.

Typically, Buddhist tenets take an anti-, non- or not form. In this vein, one might say that at this very advanced, pre-Middle Way stage, Siddhartha desired to stop desiring. Flipped around, one might want to emphasize an overt, extant characterization, and perhaps view Siddhartha as seeking and finding a post-seeking meaning in life. The fact that he discovered demonstrated and talked about his Middle Wat discoveries for 40 years suggests room for both emphases.

To be humane and compassionate, to have a bodhisattva heart, calls for an appreciation of levels of sentience. Lower tiers of self/ego/mind may be differentiated from fuller, more encompassing spheres. Experimental neurosis offers a window into how a relentless dismantling of the dog's self/ego/mind was anything but skillful. Sometimes, what Buddha did not do deserves more of a spotlight. The ancient texts do not have him so rapidly dismantling his followers' psychology as to produce neurosis or, as we've explored, forms of deep self disturbance. Such disordered psychological states, in fact, can be understood as the result of too drastic a detaching from one's self/ego/mind or too little of this basic vehicle of sentient agency in the first place. Shenger-Krestovnikova's dogs were, in fact, profoundly damaged, unable to find their way back to their previous level of sentience.

So we can appreciate deep self disturbance as sometimes caused by a lack of healthy scaffolding in the first place, for example, across development. And also, sometimes it might be due to too fast a dip into meaninglessness despite previous stability. Trauma researchers, as we will discuss, think in terms of developmental trauma and single-incident trauma. This experiment portrays the second of these pathways to dukkha. It shows how an intelligent, social animal cognitively needs for their internal experience to comport with external reality. Caution is called for when ultimate liberation is portrayed as a release from all identifications and all touchstones of meaning, e.g., no self. A take-away, if I may, is that wisdom never trumps compassion because they are inseparable. Buddhism for us seekers is only coherent when it is based on the possibility of a higher meaning, a transcendent, resplendent meaning and not meaninglessness.

Where detachment is overly exalted, as the saying goes, the operation may be a success but the patient may die. Some seekers may already struggle with a tenuous grip on reality. An integrated attachment model sheds light on this risk. We share so much in common with canines. Dogs of every ilk—wolves, hyenas, and coyotes—are naturally fierce hunters, but their softer, social side is more advanced and complex and therefore more vulnerable. The dismantling of the safety-versus-danger (circle-oval) discernment system would be a serious problem for any animal faced with distinguishing between predator and prey—that is to say any animal in its natural environment. But the implications of neurosis, whatever the etiology, do not end there. A damaged animal may still manage to fight or flee outright danger. It might manage to forage, kill and eat. But attachment science suggests that it will have severe trouble with socialization. Neurosis impairs animals' upper reaches, its emotional and intellectual heights more than its base skillsets. It does not destroy their innate drive to eat, drink, fight, or flee. Attachment impairment disproportionally impacts our highest potentials. Some clinical examples will be offered to demonstrate profound implications for the we-space.

Receive

I have tried to portray how sentience, one's living response to the perennial question, "What is the meaning of life?" is damaged in deep self disturbance. Maps of attachment wounding inform paths to healing. A beautiful refinement of such maps centers on the feminine's essence as a receptive capacity. The verb *receive* has surprisingly few English synonyms. Words such as attach, detach, get, take, grasp and even "let go" all have a certain male flavor. These reflect an active, yang agency out of balance with the yin's still, receptive nature.

In an expanded, more feminine cast on orthodox Buddhism, receiving is found in the concept of witnessing and in being present. She is the motionless yet expanding, sensitive and responsive ubiquity, not just open to experience but enabling what dynamically arises in a space formed from a unique, motherly love. The receptive pole is intrinsically collaborative and relational, placing no value on controlling the living universe but in fact providing an ever larger container for whatever co-arises. A receptive presence fits with fundamental Buddhist tenets to be an ever more welcoming loving, compassionate space for the breath of life, for all sentient beings, including oneself. In the Vajrayana, this extends to other worlds and divine dimensions of Buddha-nature such as Tara and Chenrezig.

In all these, receiving is about something rather than nothing. Reception is the hearing or seeing the tree fall in the forest. Where a mother mirrors, a baby receives this bounty. As a toddler, I, you, we are mirrored in her eyes. We take refuge, and in doing so, receive the benefit of the three gems. Lamas receives a lineage transmission.

Here we have spoken in terms of Buddha's Mom as our species' inheritance, as the lineage bearer for Homo sapiens. In being born and being alive, in just being, each of us is a vessel that receives her fruits. After much psychotherapy and bodywork, one client said he had finally "learned what being is like". The bodhisattva seeks to transmit, that others may receive.

There is increasing evidence of possible neurological correlates of humans' deepest capacities of reception. Summarizing more than 30 years of research, Dr. Bud Craig has updated the neuroscientific understanding of interoception, how the brain receives information from inside our bodies. His research appears to go far in unveiling the neurological underpinnings of Buddha's Mom.[193] Highly technical, this exceeds the scope of this book by miles, but a few efforts at noting correlations clearly deserve mention.

Interoception entails the brain's synthesis of neural information ultimately evoking the "material me" or the "subjective me".[194] A key discovery pertains to the multiplicity and diversity of inputs. Complimenting this is the fact that these informational flows are not combined (transcended and included) at earlier stages, as seen in other mammals. Rather, a host of maximally divergent, elaborate inputs remain differentiated until the very endpoint, which occurs primarily in an area called the insula or insular cortex.

While going far beyond our focus here, these findings should be considered in light of the baby's developing self within the maternal attachment dynamic. Any conjecture of the first coalescing of self/ego/mind—let's say a "proto me"—would start with an appreciation of the profound, varied somatic nature of neural inputs. These include autonomic fibers, the master controls of the stress response, heart rate, digestion and blood pressure, for example. Classically, these are involuntary, non-conscious somatic functions.

Separate axon strands carry signals from both the outer skin layers and the derma beneath. These support functions such as hydration and temperature regulation. Muscle signaling also remains distinct all the way to this high level, communicating information on "workload (energy use), metabolite concentrations, and vascular distension... mechanical distortion and temperature."[195]

Exteroceptive data, pertaining to factors outside the body, also arrive highly differentiated at the insula. We can appreciate this as yet another river of information which is received by, then synthesized within, this elaborate interoceptive process. Exteroceptive receptors relay somatic information on "pressure, velocity, stretch, vibration frequency."[196] More great rivers contain sensory input, including the visual and auditory channels. Add to these an awareness of the body's position in space (proprioception). And further, signaling associated with the large, striated muscles under voluntary control are also processed via interoception. The pleasure/pain, also called the reward-punishment or reinforcement system, make up another component. The latter clearly has a role in forming positive or negative feeling-toned attributions.

Ultimately, these all arrive and are integrated at the forward, anterior end of the interoceptive circuitry. Notably, this part of the insula is unique to humans. Craig goes into depth describing the origins of emotions and feelings. For example:

> In the present model, the feeling of an emotion is generated by integration of
> its characteristic peripheral, preautonomic, and central homeostatic activity
> patterns with the current interoceptive image.[197]

Clearly, even a generalized interpretation suggests correlates with many of the ideas discussed in the context of Buddha's Mom. The insular cortex, for example, might be a sort of master gland for "transcend and include" functions resulting in the proto self during the first weeks and months of life. From there, further consolidation of self/ego/mind fits the outlines of his research.

For our purposes, I would like to note correspondences between this work and an integrative attachment model, one that transcends and includes "the two attachments". To head in this direction, I should underscore that the richness of this receptive-integrative process, what he calls interoception, is evolutionarily late-breaking. Similarly, Buddha's Mom is proposed not as a reductionistic Bowlbian model but one that transcends and includes this side of attachment and the other facet referred to in the Four Noble Truths.

If we conjecture that the insular cortex is a prime candidate for the neural correlate of this integrative attachment, we find support in brain morphology. Everyone knows how the outside layer of the brain, the neocortex, has the look of a bunched up blanket or cloth. There are scores of curvy, wrinkled folds. According to Craig, the very first of these folds to form during fetal development is also the most recent in terms of evolution. And this fold, called the Sylvian fissure, houses the insular cortex.

Perhaps this development undergirds spikes in evolution manifesting in biological, maternal, and psychological attachment forms unique to humans. There is much more to such a hypothesis. As Craig explains, the insular cortex is where "affective touch" and what he refers to as "the caress and hug system" is registered. Unique, efficient, short-axonal strands travel a distinct path to relay the somatic dimension of maternal nurturing. This caress-and-hug system would appear to be the main transmitter—the vessel of transmission—of the somatic basis of attachment-love. The "material self" that Craig refers to as emergent supports various factors already considered. For example, the root meaning of "material" is derived from matter, and matter from mater, e.g., mother.

Further, the insular cortex appears to be laterally specialized. This also has major implications for our effort to sketch out a model of integrative attachment. The following passage implicates interoception and the insula in the consolidation of the proto self within Bowlby's paradigm. A secure attachment dynamic, born of hugs and emotional bonding, is associated with the left insular cortex and, at least preliminarily, an insecure attachment appears to parallel interoceptive processes associated with the right insular cortex.

> Activation of the left anterior insula has been observed during strong positive
> emotional feelings (e.g., maternal love or hearing happy voices) and,
> conversely, activation of the right anterior insula has been observed during
> strong negative feelings (e.g., sadness or anticipation of pain).[198]

In light of the ideas we have been exploring, Craig's model adds insights to ways that early life attachment may impact the deepest layers of self/ego/mind. A dysfunctional attachment figure, it would follow, jeopardizes the infant's capacity to receive a coherent somatic and affective transmission. As feral children make abundantly clear, being alive and having a body, is necessary but far from sufficient for anything approaching normal.

To pick one starting point, a certain form of affective pain is associated with being too hot or cold. Adults experience this, for example, when overly cold. This evokes a blend of discomfort and, if we are still, an echo of a remote, potential danger. A poorly attuned caregiver would inadvertently miss cues and subject the feral child to this form of somatic-affective distress. Such proto-emotional discomfort arising in a child would in turn bring about efforts to employ attachment to achieve homeostasis. The baby would attempt to visually find mother, cry and make an effort to signal her. Whether cold, scared or lonely, a toddler would feel a negative-valenced, internal emotion and (as the word *emotion* suggests), be moved to move. If able, she move toward the mother figure. Where she is physically and/or emotionally absent, his fear and anxiety would not be mirrors, would find no validation and the opportunity to enhance an internal map of emotional meaning would be missed. No loving response, no blanket or hug-and-caress, the right insula might very well gain in influence as the proto-self coalesces.

Perhaps movement in the early weeks and months operates in a similar fashion. As newborns, we would be accustomed to sloshing about. Given our species' nomadic tribal heritage, we would have been carried, indeed worn on our mother's torso. Our slowly developing self/ego/mind would be in-born in motion, with an attendant proprioceptive sea of signals as substrate. When a modern neonate is left lying about in the first weeks and months there is at least a theoretical possibility that this results in decreased somatic grounding. Efforts to restore homeostasis, for example, might be launched in an effort to bring about increased movement. Exasperated parents sometimes put babies in the car in the middle of the night and drive around. Of course, a superficial focus on crying is a start but such struggles would appear to risk the right insula's dominance over than the left in shaping the material self.

The right insular cortex would, per Craig's model, employ our species' five-alarm, fight-flight, autonomic system. A major failure of the attachment system to assist the developing self, would set off anxiety, fear and panic in the same manner as external threats. Technically internal signals are interoceptive and those associated with outer events, environmental changes are exteroceptive, but from the perspective of the developing self and attachment either should result in care, homeostasis and either risks over-activation of the right insula.

There is no way to tease apart any particular sequence but the general model and clinical data suggests that problems would occur at preconscious, preverbal, and what might be called sedimentary psychic levels. From these bodily and core affective bases, soma the psyche emerges. In integral fashion, self/ego/mind transcends and includes soma. We have interpreted associated developmental problems in terms of a wounded integration of the feminine, an impaired wego and distortions in fundamental, existential sentience. We have suggested these correspond to deep self disturbance and made a case for integral attachment as a healing paradigm.

Craig's model seems to endorse the importance of bodywork-related practices for deep self disturbance. Many clients who have meditated and participated in talk therapy for long periods still suffer tremendously. Craig's work indirectly points to the efficacy of Reggie Ray's "meditating with the body" practices, based in Mahamudra and non-Buddhist compliments such as yoga therapy and natural movement.[199] The confluence of data suggesting that for some suffering emanates from a deep place in the archeology of the self/ego/mind corresponds to some of the claims and evidence of benefits associated with somatic therapy and somatic meditative practice. Clients helped by these modalities—for example, holotropic breathing and cranio-sacral massage, and not by other efforts—describe long awaited shifts in what had previously been persistent, hard to pin down phenomenological torment.

Theoretically, consistent and clinically prevalent examples include self/ego/minds beset with variants of unreality, dread, and vague yet intense affective pain. Other forms of suffering aligned with dysfunctional, early-life attachment and associated interoception include poor grounding, deficiencies in qi, in the joy of being alive, and forms of over-compartmentalization and dissociation. As we delve further into these forms of hell on earth, let us keep in mind Chögyam Trungpa's teaching, in effect, to receive reality even when it hurts. Only by doing so mindfully is there the possibility of a breakthrough.

Self-blame

Survivors of inadequate early life attachment, as noted, may suffer from deep self disturbance, very commonly with attendant self-blame. Consciously or unconsciously, such persons tend to perceive themselves as the problem. In essence they blame themselves for failing to receive their core, human inheritance. Children and family therapists are familiar with this sad, counter-intuitive fact. They can attest how, regardless of the nature of the abuse, children tend to feel responsible for their circumstances.

Some may reject, rebel and hate, or claim to have no feelings for a toxic attachment figure. But this tends to be a later development, a higher, defensive sediment layer in the body-mind-spirit chain. Complicating this, one of the most damning dimensions of deep self disturbance concerns the manner in which the higher self is unable to reach back and down and, in effect, provide mother-love to one's inner child. At this earlier, often largely unconscious level, they likely feel wrong, at fault, inherently defective and the like. Self-loathing frequently runs alongside the underside of varied efforts to compensate for the breakdown in an internal secure base and coherent self sense.

The cliché that sadness covers anger is still generally accurate. A rebellious child's moods and behavior speak their truth. Hate is not the opposite of love. Who survivors rail against speaks loudly. Further, the press of life in the later years of childhood and early years of adulthood brings its own challenges. Whether or not served up with a side dish of unspeakable tragedy or an average dollop of reiterations of failure efforts at intimacy, these phases place more demands on the self's effort to distinguish between that which is safe, nourishing, and nurturing, and that which is not. Generally speaking, early life attachment empowers or delimits our ability to manage the unending, competing, bewildering deluge of demands on our beings across our lifetimes.

For better or worse, mothers oversee the long span of their offspring's romping about and if vigilant, coach them, enabling them to cultivate the skills and means required to thrive. The mother-child wego is, again one way or another, responsible for the hand-over to the larger tribal wego. Very early on, differences in social efficacy are noticeable. If not oppositional and mean, such kids may impress others as "clueless", "all over the place", "lost", or perhaps "nice" but with little substance.

Fast forward to adult-kids in their twenties who may have yet to take measure of themselves, or to know how to do this. In their thirties, they may remain vague and airy, hard to locate or ungrounded attributes despite accomplishments and outward signs of self-definition. The problem is often halfway between abuse (conditions analogous to electric shock) and neglect. Non-events matter, all that did not occur: the absence of carpe diems, moments no mother seized and celebrated. Trees fell but she did not help the child to know what they were hearing.

Psychic pain itself is a sort of tree, awaiting full notice and naming. Sadly, the waiting may take a lifetime. In Bowlby's framework, neurosis or worse is the sequelae that often emerge from a lack of mirroring. The kid in us, so to speak, was never conjured in the first place. Moreover, there is rarely an adequate villain, as these bad guys are almost perfectly, mathematically blameless from a "trans-generational" perspective. The parent's parent's parents were orphaned, neurotic, depressed, abused, or mentally ill. Trees fall but their sound is too diffuse.

As an adult starts to awaken from whatever particular early life storm they experienced, which will never be fully remembered in the first place, they start to realize how much time has been lost. They have assumed, felt ashamed and responsible for vague, early events that are not very frameable or nameable. The "just so" self they awaken into is a sort of time capsule. In essence, the wounding is simply not bearable until it is, and this requires structure.

The dogs who were pressed to discern ever more circle-like ovals from ever more oval-like circles were soon tapped out. They did not have the necessary mental structures to cope with the distortions of experience, wherein the seemingly normal became flooded with pain. The possibility of letting go eluded them. This is similar to the proverb about a monkey who is captured when he makes a fist to grab food from a jar. He is unable to pull his hand out of the jar unless he lets go of the food.

For adults awakening to deep self disturbance, the prospect of some vaunted insight and awakening—for instance, just letting go and breathing, etc.—can be premature. Instead of something manageable, they encounter (metaphorically) a horrible, bloodied corpse left just barely breathing long ago. "Things get worse before they get better" is a therapeutic truism corresponding to the early stages of psychotherapy. The patient finds themselves in emotional cement, a body-mind bruised and hurt from their unique blend of rejecting parents, bullying bosses, exploitive friends and left-you-for-dead former lovers. They exist in an endlessly varied hell, and attempt to remain sane in the face of overwhelming psychic pain.

Derealization

Some people, in this vein, experience life as if from behind a glass wall. Everything on the other side of the glass is quite typical, but it only seems accessible to others (to normal people, not to those looking through the glass). Conversations, events, and the physical world, for no particular reason that they can put a finger on, seem vague and remote. These eerie, disturbing experiences come and go. Interpersonal conflicts, more than anything, create an atmosphere of dread. Hostilities and fears creep through the cracks. The shoe is always about to drop, even as these people know that nothing in reality quite adds up to the fear or anger they feel.

Psychiatrists refer to this type of dissociation from life as derealization. Sufferers insist that everything is OK at the very moment the floor is giving way. In a haunting, liminal space, they are aware of the people and things going on around them, yet they nervously sense a coming tide of intolerable pain. Everything is off-putting and everything is nothing other than what it has always been.

In the Tibetan Vajrayana and tantric tradition, as Reggie Ray, director of the Dharma Ocean Foundation, explains, the always-greater source of experience (associated with "awareness of awareness" practice) is the "mother" awareness. Practice amounts to the child, the small, local self, running into the mother's arms. For many who live with very old, deep-seated wounds, this prospect has been both a constant longing and just as constantly completely untenable. An overlay of a disinterested, faceless, and alternatively rejecting mother may be the legacy of a failed maternal attachment. This may impede any hope of running into her arms for solace. The hope pulses and the dread pushes back. These aging children, well into their adult years, have become accustomed to living outside of any sort of immediate, bodily source of safety, sustenance and joy—which we assert can be scientifically and psychologically situated in Buddha's Mom.

The tantric tradition likens awareness practice to falling backwards with volition. Here we would want to situate Buddha's Mom in the space that beckons. The possible, potential field of awareness always and already offers itself up. This source arises from the deep self, the body, the silence under the breath, and translates in advanced practitioners and in peak experiences as an ever-so-natural impulse to stop holding on, to stop judging, to release.

The child's awareness corresponds to a continual effort to create islands of permanence. When this small, local self encounters the expanse of bliss and the possibility of "mother awareness", it drops all pretense of meaning and importance. The mind "drops" and the child naturally runs toward the always open arms of the mother. But for many highly disturbed people, unconscious defenses such as derealization prevent them from accessing these tantric paths home.

Life is truly, actively a sort of suffering that is hard for those with deep self disturbance to even articulate. Only after extensive therapy do they manage to venture down, as if on rope ladders, into their pain and shame and then back up again without relying on derealization. They bravely encounter the residue of their family of origin and the many iterations of those old jagged contours that have shaped and continue to dominate their major relationships. They stumble upon disjoined chunks of experience and can but deduce gaps in consciousness. A stable sense that there has long been and remains some sort of glass wall is a critical cognitive feat. These insights are hard-earned. The damaged child begins to associate with experiences and memories from long ago, material they were dissociated from. Healing involves the realization of derealization as an alive way of being. Stability grows with the awareness of the glass wall as it arises and recedes. Whether this material is technically old or current is irrelevant since the project of developing awareness is very much current.

Many, in fact, tell stories of contorted experiences of would-be happiness and freedom. Losing themselves in unhinged joy is a large part of so-called self-medicating, though this tends to be framed only as defensive numbing. They light up as they tell of fleeting, inside moments within the chaos of drug or love addiction. Ostensibly positive, but actually addictive, grandiose identification with concretized gods is another common eddy in these rivers of pain. The first time did not work out so well, so they find salvation in being born again. Pagans on the other side of the glass do not understand them, but their personal savior does. These driven adherents are seldom truly at peace. Instead they experience their peace as threatened by nonbelievers whom they treat in all manner of condescending ways.

I Can't

For some, likely most people with deep self disturbance, an hour of therapy every week or every other week is inadequate. But if that's all one can do, inadequate must suffice and may be much better than the status quo. Sometimes the effort is not to prevent regression or problems but to establish a safer container for these. Contingency planning, involving an on-call provider, a suicide crisis hotline, or admission to an inpatient unit commonly help provide an outer boundary. Fortunately, most people survive.

Savannah had been attending outpatient therapy for more than two years. Therapy every couple of weeks (she worked lots of hours and had to drive quite a distance) was no match for the complicated history, profound emotional damage, and seemingly chronic unraveling of her here/now life situation. Some people are both so dissociated and over-compartmentalized that even therapy weirdly threatens their instability. The advent of a living, ongoing attempt to cultivate a single, safe time-space puts certain important defenses in jeopardy. Initially Savannah expressed her experience of this, and I communicated my understanding of these basic factors. An early goal was no goal beyond establishing a time and place in which various forces at play were ostensibly allowed to co-exist. Therapy can demand the organism contain competing drives, e.g., fight and flight. These raw impulses may intensify simply in conjunction with a decrease in the avoidance of one's inner hell.

At the same time, these constraints speak to one way that therapy may make a difference. It can be framed as something sweet and decent which one gives to oneself. Spending time with someone who cares and tries hard to understand is potentially a great start. Because Savannah was coping with intense, implicit efforts to steer clear of an inner life riddled with intolerable, amorphous psychic pain, therapy was often arduous and plodding. Many hours were devoted to tentative visits to detached, dissociated psychological territory.

So many people with deep self disturbance are hobbled as much by the absence of connection to any stable emotional ground as by their trauma. Although Savannah did not have schizophrenia, her global functioning did resemble the disorder's blend of so-called positive and negative symptoms. The negative symptoms manifested as anhedonia, an absence of chi, life-force, or *joie de vivre*. Such patients have a narrowed affective range which the word depression does not capture. A good image is that of a hose turned down to a drip.

As we have explored in different ways, self/ego/mind is underdeveloped in deep self disturbance. People like Savannah simply cannot handle regular levels of adult brutalities. Everyday backstabbing, office politics, dysfunctional family showdowns, power grabs, cold shoulders and phoniness trigger never-integrated, ancient wounds. These fester because there is no self structure able to parse them. One is eternally working on boundaries, defending positions and going over and over the same fraught territory. Storms pass, the client survives but tempests are not far off. The client may feel simply spent at times, but generally is, in a word, intense. Whether letting off steam by gossiping, complaining or trying to hold it together while being positive, all roads lead to the same undernourished egoic substrates. Brutal attachment experiences long ago robbed those with deep self disturbance of so much of the amazing glory of their humanity. Just returning from life's smaller skirmishes not worse off is an accomplishment. In this dukkha corner, *I can't* arises with a sort of perfect pathos. It is the voice of a barely sustained effort at piecing together a cogent, continuous self/ego/mind. Their spirit can perform certain tasks such as naming goals and describing wounds, but their ego just can't do anything more than it already is.

After lots of therapy, Savannah revealed more about a tertiary traumatic incident. I was very pleased with her progress, then soon humbled to learn that therapy had empowered her to Google a perpetrator's name, something she had not been able to do ever before. But the real turning point for her ability and willingness to talk more about the associated events was when Google reported back to her that this perpetrator was dead.

Cutters

Anybody who has ever worked in a crisis stabilization unit or psychiatric facility has probably seen patients with scar tissue up and down their arms. Many such patients fall in the borderline range on the classical psychiatric continuum (psychotic-borderline-neurotic-normal). Clearly an indicator of serious psychopathology, cutting nevertheless has something in common with the austerities.

Those who carve up their arms, albeit far less consciously, also flirt with the prospect of a freedom that transcends physical and psychological pain. So-called cutters are imprisoned and tormented by invisible, mental demons. Consensual reality is supposedly the day-to-day problem in their lives. But this reality does not correlate with an unrelenting, bleak inner reality. The latter, in fact, feels more real than the former, and this inversion is intolerable. The tumultuous and destructive events these patients sometimes create amounts to an effort to express this pain. Their cry, in effect, is an effort to put their inner torment on display. When this naturally fails to elicit some sort of impossibly perfect mirroring, they may resort to other means of mirroring the pain for themselves.

In cutting up their arms, they are in effect turning and staring this threat in the face. They are screaming obscenities at it and taunting it to finally, forevermore do what it wants with them. Or perhaps they are treating it as a profound, sacred, personal secret. The latter dynamic is in fact common in anorexia, where eating and body image take on a numinous, supernatural power. In general, but not always, cutters avoid arteries that would result in death. They are taking their pain to an exquisite and brutal edge, and in this achieving a sense of existential meaning. The cutting moment threatens annihilation while bringing about an encounter with the life-force. This is the borderline. The same frame for this flirtation often structures suicide attempts.

Self-injurious behavior such as so-called cutters engage in occurs in probably tens of thousands of young adults with severe borderline personality disorder every year. Theirs is a cautionary tale for those of us living with inner pain, even if our pain is of a smaller scale. In the moment of their decompensated and exquisite self-injurious state, they are doing what those with less severe self disturbance do in ways that can otherwise be hard to map.

It is important to underscore that these people have frequently suffered from extreme early life abuse. Their moms were, at a minimum, not protective. Some are active players in some of the saddest tales of neglect and abuse one can imagine, beginning at extremely early developmental stages. For our purposes, we can interpret literal bodily wounding figuratively. There is obviously clinical and neuroscientific evidence for the conveying of a somatic and affective grounding in the first phases of life.

In this light, extreme forms of dysfunction can be appreciated as different in degree more than kind. All of us engage in variations of somatic manipulation, even innocent, mild forms such as foregoing that extra glass of wine. Some of us pick at our skin. This channeling of the psychic pain maps results in an odd, relative pleasure, beating out the free-floating torment for the moment. This strange reward reinforces the behavior. Rather than truly restore some sort of healthy somatic grounding, we only take the ladder down a few rungs. Because we skipped the wine, we eat the chocolate. We may choose the low fat version and get off the couch for some exercise, but somatic pain and/or negative deep seated feelings hang around.

Bulimics turn the pleasure and pain cycle into a ritual so powerful and emotionally intoxicating that their lives outside of it fade. They may appear convincingly engaged and logical. But when they return home, lock the door, binge and purge, they experience the world, the food they have eaten, even the vomiting, in a far more immediate way. The disassociation from life on one side, and the intense engaged battle on the other, is the reveal. Cutters just happen to engage in the loudest of all possible battles.

It's not a stretch to say that the Buddha, the majority of his disciples, monks, and followers did not suffer such disruptions in their early attachments. In modern terms, they would be deemed psychiatrically stable, possibly ranging from neurotic to normal on the continuum. Cutters, of course, tend to fall in the borderline spectrum on this scale. But what leads them to cut has implications for all of us.

At lower echelons, the psyche is far less coherent, less "grounded", more in turmoil. Overlaying the classical continuum of functioning and the great chain places body alongside borderline tumult and unhinged psychotic phenomenology. Clearly therapists and yoga teachers are referring to something else. Essentially, the term "grounding" places the accent on the lower, somatic strata, but implies stability from the higher mind and cognitive levels down into the soma. The hallmark of schizophrenia, auditory hallucinations, involves a failure of higher perceptual processes to transcend and include lower ones. As a result, auditory coded information in memory is misinterpreted as real.

An integration of the higher and lower is the core characteristic of normal functioning. Bulimics, cutters, addicts are conversely trapped, grounded over and again as an airplane is grounded in a crash. Their higher emotional and cognitive capacities are not up to the task of managing their lower, somatic drives and impulses. For there to be any chance of integration and transcendence, the somatic ground requires stable connection and transmutation. In many cases, compassion must be both emotional and somatic, with the latter encompassing psychotropic medications as well as sunshine and exercise and related, creative supports.

Problem Child

The bodhisattva is creative in her search for a love that integrates. Even unlikely, pain-filled corners hold promise. The problem child—or more politically correct, the identified child is evidence of this. Parents sometimes drag poor Johnny to the counselor and proceed with circularities of logic. Johnny is the problem. He has three heads and eats kittens, but alas, they have already tried everything one could possibly suggest and nothing has worked. Ergo, sadly, something must be very wrong with Johnny, he needs fixing, and (back to) how they have tried everything and nothing has worked. They are, in fact, well prepared to defend this position. Fractal iterations of this formula are common with misbehaving Johnnys.

The bodhisattva knows that no one is really enjoying these loops. Johnny may get off being rebellious, but actually needs friendship. Mom may be stuck in a self-righteous victimization but actually wants to be more empowered. These outer loops have inner correlates, and commonplace inner Johnnys. Hurt subpersonalities and split off parts have their own stubbornness, and the same holds for our looping efforts to, for example, have a more kind, consistent relationship with food, exercise, and other dimensions of the deep, somatic self.

We fear for and feel terrible about our lost potential and feel similarly about cut-offs and broken relationships regardless of whether we were the one who initiated the split. An informed, attachment-based, therapeutic, holding environment makes spaces for both sides. All the pain and projection of blame and victimization shifts as each side has a moment in the sun, and feels heard and seen. For families, the love and tears and insights flow, and need to, as the story is not just told but heard, the story of how perfect seven-pound Johnny became such a 60-pound diagnosis.

For most, families are the source of deep self disturbance. Parenting breaks many people, as the extent of trans-generational psychological problems attests. The modern mom has more comforts and less physical hardship than her ancestral correlates. Modernity sets out to meet moms' needs, it seems. But with its own insidiousness, the results are often disappointing. Corporations, in fact, excel at creating unmet needs or as they might prefer, market niches.

Modern moms have so much more on their plates. The piling up of information-heavy pressures can be untenable for the information-processing mind. The intensity is just too much for women already coping with work, intimate relationships and finances. "Stress" does not really capture the problem. Even when everyone's healthy and has enough money, the feeling of being overwhelmed is inevitable. There is simply more to say yes or no to, and not to respond is an answer in itself. Baby name books, stimulating in-utero music, mommy yoga, 5-star safety car seats, cribs that fly, baby monitors. But if you hear nothing, maybe its sudden infant death syndrome! Better co-sleep, but then there are the gazillion every year smothered by their moms who inadvertently roll over on top of them. Baby Einstein, Mozart, Bach and the daycare industrial complex. Just don't consult Google images regarding little Johnny's rash. Tick bite perhaps? There goes any chance of an Ivy League school. Where did I put that paperwork? We have to remember to ask the accountant about college savings plans.

These are a minute subset of what can inadvertently drive a wedge between mom and baby by making parenting too elaborate for our tribal sensibilities. The heartbreaking fact for little Johnny who may have emotional problems later on is that his mom is profoundly wounded. Many were "nurtured" by patriarchy's female survivors. Add this to ye olde scroll of guilt and shame. Many moms harbor fears that they have passed along their own neuroses, and many have.

The modern waterfall of great and shiny things is an odd American compensation, fifty years later, for that which Bowlby uncovered. The hospitalism (essentially illness and death due to affective, attachment neglect) that he studied was an iconic version of modernity's brutal, patriarchal suppression of the natural powers of Buddha's Mom. What has changed? As recently as the time period during which Siddhartha was a baby, a split second ago in evolutionary time, Buddha's Mom was thankfully in good form. Writ large, Buddha's Mom was in the form of Mahamaya, Prajapati and the nameless nursemaids. She pulled it off. She passed on the lineage despite severe, patriarchal bounds.

Unfortunately, the patriarchy is stronger than ever. Mommyhood is hugely important to patriarchal corporations. Even though breastfeeding has made a comeback in some countries, the formula milk industry is making inroads elsewhere. There is little profit in a return to less, less choice, fewer material accouterments, and more being in the priceless we-space.

As the Beatles' enlightened lyrics declare: *in the end, the love you take is equal to the love you make.* The love one takes in mirrors the love light one represents in the world. This is understood beautifully in the Tibetan Buddhism's Tonglen practice. The Beatles can be forgiven for using words close to Tonglen's literal translation (take-give, take-make) in pointing to its deeper sentience, *receive* and *extend*.[200] This points to the fact that attachment is as we have been suggesting, both outside, as in social, interpersonal contacts, and an inside game. Hearts and minds hurting from less than "good enough" early life attachment are filled with troubled and troubling little Johnny's.

Psychological dynamics within the attachment-impaired mind mirror those of defensive, overwhelmed parents. The same chaos, mixed messages, and turmoil of love and cut-off, attachment and detachment, play out in disturbed, neurotic personality structures. Multi-tasking is a polite word for chronic, internal disruption. In serious cases, these minds lose their hold on reality to such an extent that they project both love and hate, ride moods like waves—one day grandiose and glowing and another hollow and lost. Common as well are themes of victimization and entitlement.

These versions of deep self disturbance block sufferers from their inner voices. They are not able to take ownership of their role in the sage, their fears or anger. They cannot hold internal, subjective reality long enough to appreciate how painfully enslaved they are to the torment. This raw honesty finds a knowing, loving welcome in Buddha's Mom.

Every Johnny, egoic and misdirected, is OK. "Just as it is," the spirit cries! No one needs to leave just yet. So long as we are alive, in a living, feeling body-mind, optimizing this getting-along of our parts and pieces is the most sensible path. In Buddha's Mom, this sensibility is well mapped. The sleep-deprived mother does not blame her baby for crying in the middle of the night but soothes him. She does so for the moment and for his long-term betterment. She does her part to produce a self/ego/mind, takes the edge off the inevitable crises knowing dukkha will only bear down more and more in time. As Buddha framed this, life presses on, eventually concluding with aging, disease, and death. There is limited utility to being mesmerized by patriarchy's evils, but do respond forcefully to voices that marginalize and suppress Buddha's Mom. The jury is in: Buddha's Mom is profoundly needed at every stage of life, inwardly and interpersonally, and at every echelon of development and attainment.

Senseless

The Pali Canon, like the Bible, is not without extremist patriarchal rhetoric. One streak of this vehemently attacks all things bodily and sensual. Not surprising then, that maternal attachment, with all its tactile and sensual dimensions, gets very little positive press. Adult attachment, which, of course, occupies the somatic to felt sense range—from sexual intimacy, hugs and kisses, to warm emotional flavorings—suffers the same fate.

> Sensual pleasures are maddening, deceiving, agitating the mind; a net spread
> out by Mara for the defilement of creatures. Sensual pleasures have endless
> perils, they have much pain, they are great poisons, they give little
> enjoyment, they cause conflict, drying up the virtuous.[201]

Early life and extensions of attachment across the lifespan generally receive some mix of hyperbole, the silent treatment, and admonishment in formal Buddhist texts. Rather than a relational orientation, the focus is on individual liberation. Attachment as intimacy and devotion is downplayed. Commitment is to practice, and this to an impersonal dharma. Spiritual devotion is not to a personal deity. Members of a sangha, similarly, are not to cross certain lines with the teacher. If the relationship is personal, the sharing of vulnerable information tends to be one-way. Often touching one's teacher is discouraged.

The Canon, much like the Bible, is replete with derisive views of the body and body-level sensual experience. In typical hyper-patriarchal form, both spiritual philosophies crudely cobble together sexual desire, sensuality, physicality, and warnings of a potential entrapment in the feminine. The Buddha (reportedly) said, "Guard against looking on a woman. If ye see a woman, let it be as though ye saw her not, and have no conversation with her."

As mentioned, the patriarchy tends to box in the feminine as virgin, whore, mother, or crone. For example, Buddha likened her virginity to a "spotless leaf of the lotus, unspoiled by the mud." If she is old, he states, she should be seen as one's mother. If young she should be seen as one's sister, or if very young, as a child. The male principle, it appears, has difficultly permitting the feminine any sexuality. Later in the same passage, this as yet unspoken but obvious concern is referred to as, "the power of lust". He tells his followers to cover their heads "with the helmet of right thought, and fight with fixed resolve against the five desires." [202]

> Better far with red-hot irons bore out both your eyes, than encourage in
> yourself sensual thoughts, or look upon a woman's form with lustful desires.
> Better fall into the fierce tiger's mouth, or under the sharp knife of the
> executioner, than dwell with a woman and excite in yourself lustful
> thoughts.[203]

He gives a prescient warning for what is now the vast pornography industry, but seems to place the blame for this on women. "Even when represented as a picture, she desires to captivate with the charms of her beauty, and thus to rob men of their steadfast heart." This leans toward the whore archetype typical of patriarchal reductionisms, which are best understood from the perspective of power and control. The sleight of hand, blaming the rape victim for her provocative clothing, follows.

> A woman of the world is anxious to exhibit her form and shape, whether
> walking, standing, sitting, or sleeping.[204]

If this all could get any worse, any chance for rebalancing through feeling, through the inner feminine and its healthy attachment-based connection with the body is summarily, harshly attacked. Any chance for a healthy intimate relationship with a real, caring, vital feminine human is cut down with further brutality. Buddha's Mom, it seems, must be stifled. Men are not to experience "her tears and her smiles as enemies, her stooping form, her hanging arms, and her disentangled hair as toils designed to entrap man's heart."[205] The unvarnished conclusion is that at least some iterations of Buddha's message leaves a wide chasm between Buddha's Mom and her son. He refers to these dimensions of the feminine as unreal and concludes, "Therefore, I say, restrain the heart, give it no unbridled license."[206] In the best light, we can appreciate this as a rebuke of a patriarchal distortion of the feminine, if only this point were more clear.

In another sutra, the Buddha goes through the five senses and makes his case with vehemence that the "five strings of sensuality" tie together variations on desire and lead to all manner of strife.

Before laying out multiple examples of relationship fractures and pain, he paints a positive picture of the allure of sensation and sensuality.

> Forms cognizable via the eye—agreeable, pleasing, charming, endearing, fostering desire, enticing. Sounds cognizable via the ear...Aromas cognizable via the nose...Flavors cognizable via the tongue...Tactile sensations cognizable via the body—agreeable, pleasing, charming, endearing, fostering desire, enticing. Now whatever pleasure or joy arises in dependence on these five strands of sensuality, that is the allure of sensuality.[207]

From there, however, the brutality resumes. Sensuality, the body, and the feminine become the ultimate punching bag. The body is identified with the feminine and the propaganda builds. The female beauty and charm decompose, picked apart by vultures and hyenas. Tendons and bone, her skeleton are smeared with flesh and blood. These dissolve further into powder. The violence and guts are on display for the jury. The case is open and shut. Any suggestion of the possibility of anything positive or lasting is annihilated under the weight of such physical evidence.

The riverbed takes the same contours as the austerities where, short of breathing and digesting, the body is of little value. It is little wonder that Buddha's Mom, her pregnancy, the physical act of holding a child, keeping them warm, breastfeeding, and the outpouring of bodily-based love is not celebrated in the biography of Siddhartha. Ananda speaks to the value of the body when a nameless nun from Kosami claims to be sick and in need. Alas! She has lied and is actually in love with him. Upon realizing this, Ananda gives a "sermon" to her and proclaims that his body has arisen because of nutrition, craving, and pride; each of these can be transcended in the pursuit of purification.

Sometimes the obvious needs repeating because obviousness may co-arise with that obliviousness. That which passes for obvious may not be truly integrated. We may sometimes be oblivious to the pain and beauty of every moment. Seahorses and malaria. The obvious can alternatively be experienced as good or bad, as noble and loving or as irrational, senseless, superficial, damned with faint praise. In the case of sensuality, the senses, the connection to body, we see obvious maltreatment of the feminine. But obliviousness is just as rampant across continued forms. In his recent book surveying the status of women and girls in modernity, *A Call to Action: Women, Religion, Violence, and Power*, Jimmy Carter said, "The crimes against women and girls exceed almost anything that I have known in my lifetime as far as human rights abuses."[208] Carter said that, of his 28 books, this was the most important, that he planned to dedicate the rest of his life to confronting genital mutilation, human trafficking, sexual assault, and pay inequality.

Dead Inside

I used to assume that people with tattoos, piercings, and variations of intense decorations, whether dark or colorful, must have characters similar to their outward appearances. Clearly they were courageously, dangerously outside-the-box in some way, but their courageous, free, and expressive outward appearances just as often lined up with undifferentiated, suppressed, and mundane inner lives. Very commonly, their personality turned out to be blunted, albeit with some intense, dark, or loud cover associated with being special and different.

Below the under-differentiated personality are the usual suspects—an insatiable aching to be seen as special, unique, and different. Being alike and not different is what pains them, but also what eludes them. The loop is closed, frozen in time. "I want to be different," the soul cries. But this feels hollow when being different has little essence beyond negation of a dumbed down, overly simplistic straw man. There tends to be a lack of inner light shining back on these important, psychospiritual dynamics, and an excess of investment in superficial attention grabs. All is fine with this wizardry until the curtain is pulled back and the unimpressive, pasty wizard behind Oz is glimpsed.

Such a problem child calls for Buddha's Mom. She would want to mirror him until her giving is matched in his receiving. As he blossoms, becoming his own vessel of our species' grandeur, she lives on. Each has a mix of this common wounding which is, at the same time, unique in its karmic iteration—a fragile, angry, and needy inner child; a throttled, pummeled spirit; someone with true gifts lost to themselves and further lost to the world.

Circling back for a moment, recall how Bowlby showed that an attachment dead zone at a very early stage could lead to failure to thrive or even to actual death. This has been obliquely labeled "hospitalism". Simply the fact that the infant had been in the hospital was all that doctors could identify as causal. They did not notice, it seems, the other consistent variable associated with maternal attachment. Thanks to Bowlby's research, the practice of prohibiting parents from staying with their ill children was eventually stopped. Attachment-deprived, early childhood experiences, of course, continue to be common fare. Fewer of these in the West may result in biological death, but many result in a sort of psychological deadening.

Outcomes map across the body and early, regressive emotional spaces. Boredom, glumness, and laid-back demeanors worn along with body art strike a balance for some. Some people emit a dark, deep persona perhaps along with body art. This commands notice and paradoxically stymies vulnerability, more honesty about the need to be noticed, seen, and mirrored. The draw for Buddha's Mom and attachment-love is stymied and emotions flatten.

In endless variations of this, people adopt personas and tribal memberships which reinforce the true, defensive, and deadening agenda. One draws in the other in a contrived way and thereby modulates the intimacy. Nouns fly off the shelf, filling in "I'm a _____" and therein attempt to impose a deactivation of the tumult, risk, and breakthroughs that come through a flowing attachment-love process. Some seek mirroring of their cleverness and artistry; others may go for more of the tortured artist and invest in the dark, sulking, or "emo" typology. For many, these are echoes of a distant attachment. The brooding or protesting affects, the mental cleverness, for example, long for a mother-witness to hang in there, to take them seriously and meet them where they are. An active, invisible we-space, informed by Buddha's Mom, is (also) always-already present.

Comparison

The same is true in chronic, mental comparisons of oneself to others. These play on like a background Muzak loop. The others we compare ourselves to may be real or imagined.

Comparisons may be based in consensual reality or mainly be an echo of a very distant past. Self/ego/mind's reliance on comparisons takes on a special, nasty intensity for those suffering with deep self disturbance. They experience the usual varieties, but far more intensely. These include positive pulls to be cool, smart, beautiful, noticed or liked by others, and the usual negative notes as well, feelings of being less than, as well as jealousy, *schadenfreude*, an urge to taunt accomplishments, or deny pride. Perceptions beginning in, "I'm glad it wasn't me" are not built of love.

Most everyone senses the pitfalls in overanalyzing their station in life relative to others. Advice is cheap. "Do not covet your neighbor's possessions" made it into the Bible's top ten list. We all want to rise above the fray. But just as we promise dentists to floss and know better, we do not heed the good advice. We know we should let go, relax, be more accepting of the limitations of ourselves and others, but the Muzak plays on. From Oprah to Hallmark to table talk and texting, advice regarding comparisons is seldom in short supply: "Be strong, love yourself. Boundaries! Let it go—if it returns, it was meant to be."

Well-meaning advice has precious little to do with the reality of how comparisons operate in those with deep self disturbance. That which might work at a higher level is sadly misguided when it comes to those who try but are simply as grounded. An out-of-control degree of comparing self and other is just a fact of life at neurotic strata and the borderline bands. These efforts, for example, to lasso onto heroes and villains are necessary-but-not-sufficient attempts to establish a viable self/ego/mind. They make for nonstop din stemming from the personality's effort at boundary-making and for precursors of a potentially fruitful we-space.

One is jealous or idealizes or cannot stand an imagined other. Painful, harmful, misguided though these affective arrows may be, such minds are simply not internally well attached to larger self streams, to values, narratives, and caring relationships for there to be any chance of detachment and transcendence. For such people, not comparing risks detachment and the dismantling of their toehold on a continuous, albeit tenuous reality-based existence. What they need runs in the opposite direction. Where intermittent, marginal psychological cohesiveness is the norm, desperate comparing naturally arises. Analogously, the infantile mind senses danger and looks everywhere at everyone for help. When rebuffed, it forms rationalizations. These may lean toward idealization or the other way, full of heat and thinly veiled, reversals of perceived rejection. This is very largely preconscious and therefore not within one's control. Self-control is just another word for a viable level of conscious, cogent agency to effect change. Rather, the internal din may need to get worse before it gets better. The fiery or forlorn desperation to be liked or be different masks a clarion call to simply be, be free, be born, and exist.

One naturally burns to be unique because one is, even if the opposite is also true. Here, again, Buddha's Mom helps to make the Buddhist message more vibrant. She honors, mirrors, and makes space for the fledging and messy self-in-process. Being of earth and evolution, she mirrors the space where ego works out interpersonal pressures to both be like and be different from the grand other that threatens to eclipse. For the longest stretch, other/mother is all. All emotions have comparison at the core. Classically understood, the pangs of hunger, pain and distress, of being cold or tired, are among the first comparisons. The other begins as an amorphous trait that prevents satiation, comfort, and homeostasis. Much later, way up the cognitive scale, comparisons in those with deep self disturbance nevertheless wage this same battle for existential stability.

Paradoxically, this entire thrashing about may finally be left behind only when the pain it self-inflicts becomes a stable corner on reality. When the agony of such comparisons occurs with adequate frequency and duration, a chronic condition is achieved. Palliative care can be summoned and the self, having created, tested, and finally established a boundary, can move on.

Grounding in this Witness, the one observing the sad, small-minded snarls underlying habits of comparing self with others, is enhanced by Buddha's Mom. Only a very grounded mother knows that destruction has a place. Trees can be felled as long as someone is there to hear them fall. Small deaths, the disappointments and would-be paths blocked, goals thwarted, need to be heard. In this sense, comparisons are like the cries of a reeling being who blindly puffs itself up as it takes leaps of faith only to fall short. The suffering must be met with compassion for losses to be felt in full. A sweet, species-based wisdom and courage pulses through attachment-love. The failure of comparisons to bring about their superficial goal, for example, another's admiration is key. In these very human moments, growth and healing is at hand. The act of seeing the true nature of these attachment cries is the very domain of Buddha's Mom.

Buddha's Mom is that which sees, hears, holds (to run across the three major sense modalities) the comparisons that run about like kids. She helps us to contain comparisons by freeing them. Some comparisons are like the expected child who exists in parallel with one born with Downs, autism, or is stolen by an ex-spouse. She continues to walk the earth and suppressing her just makes her more determined. Many of us have a two-sided relationship with comparisons. They haunt us. We do not want to covet, but we cannot help but wonder what, for example, it would be like to have less chronic financial hardship or more supportive friends or siblings. This other life sometimes moves to the fore. One self moves in, pushing the main self aside. But suppressing this other self born of comparisons and curiosities is wise.

All comparisons, all contents of mind deserve love. They belong to Buddha's Mom. In her, comparisons are provided a cogent, singular maternal container for their contributions, jealousies, battles, and antics. Doomed though it be, hyper-comparison is an effort to get the mind's monkeys to be more orderly. In loving all her children, in accepting their antics, in knowing they will always compete and compare, Buddha's Mom provides a bigger space of meaning and a deeper center of being. Her potential can be used to help unshackle and unfetter.

Abstraction is the salve for the concrete wound. It offers a ladder out of comparison-hell where comparisons rumble about in their base, concrete form. As the term implies, at the concrete level, one is being turned to stone. None other than the inimitable Medusa so elegantly portrays the attendant dynamics. Both her other-worldly beauty and the undulating snakes forming her hair demand attention. But one will be turned to stone if one looks at her.

Medusa is two-sided beauty-beast. She is impossible to psychologically bear or hold. Scorching unrequited love, full-throttle, raw desire to be seen, held, and adored. Try and look at her, try not to. An implosion of existential loneliness threatens to shatter self/ego/mind. One's Medusa, as the myth teaches, can only be encountered via a reflected image of her actuality or suchness. One has some chance of handling such diabolical beauty, the fear and fantasy, so long as one views her reflection in a mirror.

Importantly, "not looking" when the possibility is at hand is quiet tragedy, in Buddhist terms, the near-guarantee of rebirth. Averting one's gaze and awareness accounts for the years wasted already. Paradoxically, a sad future glares back from the mirror begging to be confronted. From a freer space, we find in Medusa an impatient human lineage. Mistaking attachment-love for a fixed object forms life-robbing addictive patterns. Bypassing the numinosity, the transforming, divine moment is another form of death. Meditation is the art of steadily looking, witnessing, welcoming, in a continually new way. Meditation is inherently a reflective turning within a universe of old age, disease, and death. Actually, we as witness are that which shines. Medusas everywhere demand/invite us to bump up against, for example, the sheer wonder of the Great Barrier Reef and the madness of its demise due to climate change.

A catch-22 for those with deep self disturbance concerns the capacity for reflection vis a vis their particular beasts and angels. Without this prospect of outside help, this critical turn eludes them. The issues driving suffering have already turned one to stone. Facts are facts. "No therapist can change the fact that my boss is an asshole"; "My wife is impossible to live with."

Thorough, in-depth clinical work involves the outpouring of intricate descriptions of clients' friends and family, exes, bosses, and grown children at this stone level. One learns in magnificent detail about a variety of others, many of whom are also highly disturbed and many of whom refuse or cannot participate in any realistic problem-solving. The combination of inability and unwillingness to engage in the basics, setting boundaries, rules of conduct, contingency plans for relapses and setbacks, all this remains surprisingly stable. Many drop out when they discover that the victim-blaming mindset is at odds with healing. The gap between the need for services and the rejection of such services remains even when practical matters of finances, insurance, the availability of providers is factored in. Beyond the usual actions born of poor judgment and insight, repetitively dysfunctional relationships, alcohol and drugs, some will seek out ostensibly constructive alternatives: fundamentalist religiosity, supplements or New Age approaches. Sometimes these just render the rigidity more elaborate. For huge swaths of the population, baseline deep self disturbance manifests in treatable but untreated turmoil. Many of us "hit bottom" several times, eventually managing neither to look directly at Medusa nor to dismiss her outright.

In America, freedom is interpreted as a person's ability to suffer almost anything that is not "imminently dangerous to self or other". Medusa opportunities tend to exist only at the extremes. Mental health courts are beginning to recognize that some people both suffer less and do less harm to others if they are semi-forced, for example, to take medications or participate in counseling. The prospect of a return to jail, e.g., loss of freedom, is the "choice" offered them. Perhaps in the future, other creative approaches will help people with deep self disturbance who, due to their psychological make up, do not seek the sort of help that might remedy this vicious circle. A day might come, for example, when a person is given the opportunity to do a silent retreat or not have access to alcohol for a year, and so on. I've always thought a progressive society would reward adolescents and young adults in meaningful ways for levels of participation in sophisticated, evidence-based and importantly, very hip programs. These would be designed by peers, endorsed by celebrities and continually refined to maximize meaningfulness and effectiveness, and would target, from a social perspective, all the major culprits that profoundly disrupt the lives of the next generation, unwanted pregnancy, affective dysregulation and aggression, drugs, drop-out, and so on.

Sylvie

A "high functioning" patient of mine engaged in a variation on the cutter's theme, none of which would emerge until several months into therapy. Although she did not act on the feeling, she would eventually share that she held in the back of her mind some disturbing, vague fantasies. These were replete with imagery of bodily dismemberment and unidentified naked corpses. The scenes were detached from any sort of narrative. There was no basis in any life event or trauma that she knew of. It would be a while, but eventually these hostile interiors came to form an offering and what might be called a touchstone.

For one, this inner scream was paradoxically stabilizing relative to her work. Her high-flying career was becoming increasingly incoherent. Her story follows, but a very important point up front is that she was far up the scale from borderline functioning. She was a very kind, stable, highly productive professional.

Only after a long stint in therapy did Sylvie (as I will call her) manage to form a stable place within herself and within the therapeutic relationship where the irrational could enter. At one point, she quite suddenly and nonchalantly shared that morbid imagery that floated about in the back of her mind. She was not being guarded or holding back as much as mildly dissociated and uninhibited.

In general, she openly discussed everything that seemed pertinent to her during each visit. She was not prone to a crisis or emotional instability, did not use substances or any history of major dysfunction. Sylvie simply never before had begun to consciously connect these violent scenes as well as her sense of being wrong and defective with anything we were discussing. These were just stubborn, free floating inner realities. Nothing one could do about them. She stated that she knew this imagery and thoughts existed but had assumed they were irrelevant, embarrassing, or worse, evidence that she really is somehow deeply defective. The only sign of a desire to become better acquainted with these foreigners was a sort of doggedness regarding showing up for sessions, rain or shine. Meditation teachers would no doubt see great wisdom in this.

Even at first, the mention of this violent material had a certain logic. As with cutters, they draw blood to validate and sync with an invisible, intolerable inner torment. This seemed to be reversed in Sylvie's life. The actual horrors taking place in her otherwise stunning career seemed to parallel the outer, present-day pain associated with cutting. The strange, detached violent imagery seemed to provide the psychic ballast.

Initially Sylvie seemed to grow in stature just by being able to convey this and have it received without lots of questioning or judgment. We discussed this, of course, and all she could make out was the sentence, "I am wrong" in relation to these fantasies. About what? Not wrong about anything per se. Rather she felt that somehow deep in the center of her being, she simply was wrong to exist. Her very being was somehow incorrect.

As her story unfolded, I learned how for the past few years, Sylvie had been a victim of what the law refers to as a hostile work environment. Her former beloved mentor had expertly, insidiously, over a period of years, turned all that she knew to be positive and fortifying into something she could not quite comprehend. He had once expressed oceans of enthusiasm and confidence in her immense talents. Then inch-by-inch, in a series of twisted, high pressure and ostensibly high-minded battles related to their work, their entire relationship morphed into the opposite of what she still "knew" it to be.

As carrots, he dangled his approval, promotions, the promise of prestige, reputation and power. But his main stick and shtick were perpetual, silent but vivid threats of rejection and abandonment. For her part, Sylvie was reality-based, aware that he could go far in tanking her career, but her immobility was driven by something else, much deeper, corresponding to her dark fantasies.

Her boss exercised forms of abuse that did not cross into sexual or verbal arenas. His anger was unpredictable. Sylvie might make a career move which he had endorsed, only to learn that she had again misunderstood him. How could she, how dare she? He would really have to reconsider her stability and status in the department, and whether indeed she was who he thought she was. Such antics could turn the ground under her into quicksand in no time, over a seemingly innocent cup of coffee. In his office, of course, with no witnesses.

The nature of their work was highly logical and technical. My client's strength, her off-the-charts, classically-defined intelligence, was also her weakness. We continually circled back to concepts that far less intelligent people would have no trouble understanding. This led to something of a sweet, therapeutic joke that our therapeutic goal for her was to be far more average. She also liked to laugh about drinking the Kool-Aid and embracing the touchy-feely, pseudo-science of psychology. Laughter, of course, is the path. It comes from the ground giving way but not dangerously so.

From the relative attachment perspective, Sylvie was hyper-attached to the heights of rationality and outer performance measures, and hyper-detached from emotion and body. As with many people in this genre, with very little flowing connection to Buddha's Mom, she was prone to verbal staccato interlaced with "but". She would, by default, repeatedly bring up the supposed opposite side of ideas. I think I helped her to discover that compared to a more intense embrace of the moment, these tennis matches were dull if not defensive. Rather than saying "but" and hitting the ball back, "both/and" dissolved the conversational predictability and opened the door to the possibility of a heart opening.

Per usual, we surveyed major, historical life experiences. Sometimes, subtle cues come in the form of topics or ideas too quickly dismissed. No sooner did she report certain past events than she dismissed these as not germane to her current plight. After all she had already addressed these with another therapist and/or never thought about them and/or was sure she had a grip on their implications. Similarly, she would make a little progress regarding her boss, better handle a meeting with him, for example, and then have little to say about it until there was some sort of dramatic replay.

We discussed her parents, her distant mother and even more aloof father. Her brother had killed himself when she was living far away from home. She had, at the time, gone back home, attended the funeral and experienced the attendant pain and chaos. My sense was that this client, with her detached, violent fantasies and smooth scientific surfaces, needed a larger conscious corpus, more outlets for nonlinear wandering. To make therapy too goal-oriented would amount to using surgery for a very old, wise and mysterious fever.

Eventually, she was willing to try some of the ideas I had floated. She would later laugh at how silly these had sounded to her logical mind. She began to meditate on occasion, yelled in the safety of her parked car, wrote down dreams in a journal. She soon began documenting her activities and responses to them in tremendous detail. She brought more pages to our sessions than I could possibly read and still keep up with my other work. I was honest about this, of course, and emphasized the value of her continued use of various forms of introspection and self-expression as practice.

Finally with painting, her "homework" broke the dam. The subjects she felt she had to paint were largely abstract, often geometric, full of blacks and reds and, yes, dead infants and deformed corpses. Some were large expanses of bland, indefinable grays. Remarkably, she did not over-analyze their meaning, possibly a credit to the we-space we had worked hard to form. Both of us were perfectly fine to let the paintings, so to speak, do the talking. There were also multiple dreams, some with the same morbid imagery. We welcomed these, a la Jung, without overdoing the analysis. Increasingly signs of a personal soul made their way into these.

Over time, the painting, journaling and dreamwork brought about a shift in therapy as Sylvia sensed for herself the contours of a healing process larger than the both of us. There were fits and starts. My job seemed to be to help her tolerate ambiguity and validate that a deeper spiritual process was unfolding. Impasses would consistently lead to important developments in subsequent session. She would sometimes remark that she finally understood something I did not even remember saying months before. Her intelligence and discipline became intrinsically supportive rather than combative.

Over time, Sylvie got a handle on the outlines of her toxic attachment to her boss. She gave herself permission to be more "average" and, for example, entertain views of him consistent with laws pertaining to a hostile work environment. She allowed herself the benefit of concrete, behavioral strategies, for example, having someone else in the room and reporting him. She also very bravely learned to be internally present and less predictable with him. He would eventually ramp up his game and then fade.

While better, she had really only achieved neutral over negative. Joy and spontaneity still lagged. Ultimately, Sylvie and I burrowed deep into her early attachment history. She was probably tired of listening to me harping on the deep feminine and such. Whatever the cause, her dreams and painting shifted with our focus on love as described in this book.

Sylvie enthusiastically read about this, Buddhism, Jungian psychology and many other areas. She made major shifts in her career unrelated to her boss, participated in bodywork and retreats, and ever more stably awoke to the wonder of an ever-increasing freedom. This, Zen masters are fond of saying, is always/already right below one's nose.

The essential fact is that wisdom or good advice, by whatever name, may or may not help. It may feed a hungry heart or land on deaf ears. This distinction is independent of the validity of what is being offered. Often we need to hear a message in a hundred different ways before it hits home. What I've learned as a therapist is that one of the biggest game changers is the "we-space" and how this is largely formed of an attuned, informed, flowing metta. This is a kind, proper, disciplined, and healthy love that builds from hard work, yet regularly delights. It is the sort of love that flows from our deep humanity, and that might just help us find, right below our noses, the path forged by Siddhartha.

Phillip

Buddha's Mom was one of us, very much alive and imperfect. More than having something in common with her, we have someone in common. She loved someone we also love. But deeper still, based on a modern, integral analysis, we can conclude that whether through a singular person or collective, Buddha's Mom cultivated the living, active, vibrant, inquisitive mind of Siddhartha. The mind in which Buddhism itself was eventually born. Many of us did not experience a healthy early attachment, as we deduce Siddhartha had. But remarkably, where Buddha's Mom was absent she remains. Where she was distant, she is now close at hand and longing to reconnect. For this to make sense, let us consider some clinical cases.

A former client, Phillip, experienced little in the way of a strong, stable, early life attachment figure. His personal history was, he used to suggest, remarkable only for being unremarkable. Food in the fridge, clothes in the closet, but not a lot of love anywhere in the home. There was no sexual or physical abuse. He might as well have been inserted into the family, he once commented, by an alien race. This reflected his sense of alienation from what struck him as a random mix of "white trash" dynamics. He survived it, remembered it, but otherwise felt little connection to it.

Phillip was unsure whether he needed therapy. He was detached from his depths. He was in his 30s, very intelligent, but very little light seemed to shine from his dark eyes. He had abused alcohol for a while but had long since cleaned up his act. He was climbing the ladder at a great job, and he and his live-in girlfriend, Vivian, were on a presumed track toward marriage and children. They had satisfying hobbies and friends and never argued.

Because he was not really sure what, if anything, was bothering him or whether his problems were worth pursuing, he asked for homework. More than most, he journaled, read, listened to podcasts, paid attention to reveries during meditation, and most importantly, he began tracking his dreams. We spent many hours carefully allowing their content to take us into Jungian, Wilberian, and Buddhist maps of the psyche. We would sometimes laugh uncontrollably as he experienced both the dissociation from seemingly random, nonsensical content and an emergent sense of wonder that he, his mind, his psyche had served this up.

He did not really see it as relevant but had begun thinking more about his ex-girlfriend Maria. She and he had developed a caring, respectful relationship when they were both in their early twenties. Maria eventually moved on, married, and a few years later, had a baby. Phillip moved on as well. He partied a little too hard in college, but because he was so naturally intelligent, he did very well and moved on to graduate school. Alas, she and similar energies were in his dreams and increasingly on the shimmering edges of consciousness.

His current fiancé, Vivian, viewed Maria as a concrete threat. Phillip wanted to base their relationship on unbridled honesty and tried to share everything. For him, this old relationship was in no way a threat. To see it as such just seemed like a sad misunderstanding. He implicitly respected Vivian's viewpoint, but all his life, he'd been taught to shut off his emotions. Just cutting off all communication, for example, not being able to touch base and share what was becoming a type of spiritual awakening, seemed like more of the same. Intuitively, this did not feel like a good foundation for his future with Vivian.

For Vivian, his wanting to somehow stay in touch with Maria proved that he still loved her. Her preference was for Phillip never to speak to Maria again and for them to never speak of her again. She felt it was time for him to buy her a ring. Her solution was to demand to see all emails and to insist that Phillip only communicate with Maria (who lived on the other side of the country) when she was in the same room.

For Phillip this all felt crude, over the top, oversimplified, and tended to put him in the same space he had experienced as a child, where there was no room for reflection, creativity, or subtlety.

He had begun to find these qualities in his inner work. The Buddhism he was discovering translated as nonjudgmental, kind and compelling. These connections to Buddha's Mom were two-pronged. One was dharma-based, while the other was bodily and emotional. Especially through the Jungian approach to dream work, Phillip learned to inhabit his subtle body, the field of rich interconnections between his dream life and his old, still-living childhood.

As a kid, Phillip had lived primarily with his divorced dad, who was not much for interaction. Mom was often morose to the point of being uncommunicative. Dad would drink a lot of beer and sit for hours in a recliner. The TV was always on. Interactions with his parents, Phillip recalled, involved a lot of yelling. On a typical day, Phillip would get himself ready for school, go to class, space out a lot, but generally make good grades, and then ride his bike back home.

His childhood was unremarkable except when viewed from the love we might imagine that poured forth from Buddha's Mom for Siddhartha. Through her eyes, perhaps, his childhood, which was very much present in the room and in his life, would be seen as steeped in pain and longing. Phillip recalled how he typically scrounged up his own meals and spent a lot of time in his room. He was buddies with the microwave and inane TV shows. His mom and dad had held out on divorce until Phillip was seven. Following the divorce and lasting through his high school years, more garden-variety dysfunction was added to the mix. Stepparents with plenty of their own baggage, more alcoholics and half-siblings with behavioral problems all piled on.

A wise, powerful mother would stop the mean world from stealing so many moments from her son. In reconnecting with his bleak past from a more feeling level, his heart was slowly resuscitated. Phillip's dreamlike state, now that he was there to witness it, was a fountain of feeling. When viewed impartially, openly, there was no stopping the variety. There was plenty of silly, random, and oddball content that invoked lightness and celebrated the other side of left-brained logic. Mystery and intrigue, hints of the sublime were present as well. So too was danger and torment. Phillip's inner life, from a Jungian frame, became more animated by way of his anima, his inner feminine. The Vivian-Maria rub would make him a more whole, caring soul, husband and father. But the ride would be bumpy. Phillip, for example, was embarrassed to admit to himself that there might be a little too much of his own shallow, materialistic mother in his girlfriend, Vivian.

The singularly most remarkable aspect of Siddhartha's childhood is how cloistered it was. Presumably within the walls of his childhood compound, Siddhartha was not bored, alone, or lulling away for hours and years in a bleak, deprived state. Rather, the biography suggests that Siddhartha may have been laden with riches—anything his heart desired. Historically, Buddha's Mom is neither blamed for nor given credit for this.

But perhaps she was not the non-factor history suggests. Siddhartha's intensity, curiosity, and competitiveness are better understood as reflective of sanctioned male emotions. In time, softer, more classically feminine ones, depths of compassion and lovingkindness, were acknowledged. The narrative is structured so as to bypass Buddha's Mom's influence. His childhood was replete with material comforts and the absence of aging, disease, and death. His father and presumably the father's wives and servants went to great lengths to shelter Siddhartha. All signs of wilting and dying plants, animals, or people were hidden from him. At age 29, for reasons of boredom or curiosity, he asked for and was granted an outing. Famously, this undid the three decades of pretense. He saw an old man with sunken cheeks and white hair. Siddhartha asked whether this was the fate of all his young, healthy friends, and indeed himself.

Why had Buddha not put two and two together before, despite all his superiority in school? What of pets? Cute ducklings, where one was attacked and killed? Did he have no long-lived, beloved dog or cat? These would have turned gray, become feeble and died in this timespan. Friends' pets, friends' parents? In 30 years, what about aunts or grandparents, or loving servants who became chronically ill or died? Were they mercilessly disappeared or shipped off as they showed signs of the end? What was he told about the Queen Mahamaya? In time, was he told that she had died?

Thankfully for Phillip, even though his childhood was deprived of love, his high intelligence was such that anything he tried to do, as a teen or young adult, came easily. He was especially gifted at science, math and music. These served as a refuge and source of identity and inspiration. But somehow something was lacking. The friction around his ex-girlfriend had the makings of a too-long delayed spiritual crisis. It could have taken another form at another time. At this juncture, he was reeling. What he had felt to be solid footing in the present with Vivian was giving way. He was close to more than the occasional secretive communication and Vivian seemed ripe for more.

The best therapeutic advice is often this: do nothing. So long as such advice is delivered within a potent container, it is the field of Buddha's Mom. From here, the advice is to speak love to the power dynamics that proclaim male decision as the ultimate arbiter of meaning. With awareness and increased tolerance for ambiguity, one appreciates that what on the surface is untenable and incompatible opens to a more spacious and symbolic field. Phillip and I practiced this in therapy, and he did the same on his own between sessions. Phillip wrestled with the question of what he truly wanted for himself. It was important that everything be on the line. Phillip had to be free to make mistakes, change course, regret, wait, so long as the priority was his feeling (attaching to) all that was stirring within his spirit.

For Phillip this freedom guided him to nothing outwardly or dramatically in a direct sense. His meditation practice and the nature of his dreams shifted toward a deeper center of gravity, less fraught with the external tug-o-war. From this center, he eventually bought the ring Vivian wanted and set healthy limits on his communications with Maria. But the bigger point is that he did so based on an emerging sense of spaciousness and peace, and these two approaches operated from that place within his communication with both his ex-girlfriend and his current girlfriend.

These developments co-arose with Phillip's work on deep, formative memories. Increasingly, he could maintain an awareness of the profound sadness and sometimes anger and hurt that he felt during what had become shallow and obligatory phone conversations with each woman. We talked a lot about the courage and sensitivity that this required, and how this occurred because he was honoring, getting to know, and making room for what could be called his inner child. Just as he grew more tolerant of very old, heavy states of longing and sadness, he also pushed ahead on other more positive, childlike thresholds.

He dragged Vivian along to a one-day Vipassana meditation retreat, and this helped to open her eyes to freedom as an alluring possibility. Before, she had equated freedom with pain and some vague threat of losing not just him but the possibility of marriage and kids and the life she craved. The more they talked, the more she began to understand that his relationship with Maria represented a time and place and experience when he discovered some of the implicit goodness of life and tasted the possibility of a freedom to be himself that he had not known before.

Over time, Phillip became increasingly clear about the subtle way that he was still addicted to alcohol. His was more of a psychological and spiritual abuse of alcohol. He took more risks related to music and delighted in the joy of feeling the appreciation of others as he played at parties.

Various things shifted because Phillip courageously heeded the old-fashioned call to do nothing until love conquered fear, and freedom outlasted needy, clingy, selfish identifications. One must survive pressures to act out, be reasonably at peace, clear and sure. Do nothing major in your life until you can live mostly with love and freedom.

It emerged that part of Vivian's rush to be engaged and cut off this communication with Maria was driven by her own insecurities and particularly by her previous relationship with a man who cheated on her. They were able to discuss this and meet in the middle. This was a couple just starting out. The prospect of a beautiful life together was in jeopardy not so much because they might never get off the mark, but because they might do so in a mediocre way, where fear rather than love laid the foundation. Fortunately, they were able to overcome this. Phillip rarely checks in at this point. I felt privileged to be the first one he told about their baby on the way.

Kelly

Some patients with deep-seated attachment wounds have a long history of hard-to-pin-down health problems. Physical pains, headaches, gastrointestinal issues, and sleep disorders are common. They are intermittently wiped out and unable to function. Work and productivity suffer. Relationships, finances, and basic stability fall apart. Many arrive in therapy on the cusp of a personal crisis that turns out to be one in a long line of similar events. But typically, they are too damaged to track these and not grounded enough to hold deeper patterns in their consciousness. To do so would call for more ego, more of a sense of the self's role across these many events, and what an outsider might call "taking responsibility".

Such patients describe their futile search for answers and help, and sometimes have convinced themselves of elaborate explanations born of half-truths. Some carry a diagnosis of chronic fatigue or fibromyalgia. One such person, Kelly, had been diagnosed with both of these conditions in addition to bipolar disorder. When I was working with her, she was close to destitute and sought help through a clinic that served those without insurance or ability to pay. A young, deeply spiritual Muslim physician listened to her complaints with great care. He navigated her requests for more pain medications that she had already been prescribed. He ordered new labs and listened with what she described as absorption. He finally arrived at a diagnosis which my patient said was the first diagnosis she ever felt to be accurate: "abdominal migraines".

In many cases, patients such as Kelly come from families that were, by all appearances, upstanding and sophisticated. Parents, however, were detached, "emotionally unavailable" and this fact, more than any other more overt problems, turns out to be the real culprit. These families' attachment was characterized by what did not happen—namely mirroring and emotional interaction. They sat at the table for dinner. The fathers had an important job. There may have been a trauma or loss. Outwardly, the family soldiered on and no one questioned anything. Trees falling, no one noticing. Patients have described feeling theirs was a family of mannequins in a store window. They fooled everyone who passed by. Often there was a nice house, church, friends who came and went. The scene belied the disaster in the offing. There was food and structure and order. Kids did their homework and took music lessons. But the deepest psychological needs were choked off.

By what? This question goes to the heart of the problem. As a teen, Kelly still held the outside view, but just barely. She saw what others saw in the store window. This would fragment on occasion, but never cataclysmically. Kelly could point to nothing in external reality to validate her most fundamental sense that something was profoundly and invisibly wrong. The thinking self was constructed atop a bedlam of nameless pain. The child was off and running, moving into a life detached, with a hollow space where the center of gravity belonged. Something survives and something dies. What one finds decades later is a pattern of futile efforts to regress. The patient has tried pull everything down into the pain at the center. This makes for a perfect storm, partly a courageous and raw evaluation and partly a hopelessly immature temper tantrum. Psychologically, they attempt to achieve freedom through a complete re-absorption of their psychic ground. They bravely scream truth to power but have little self to stand on.

Perhaps body-mind science will make sense of the way such a background later produces various physical disorders. The fulcrum may involve epigenetic alterations. Through some mechanism, the brain's role in maintaining a healthy somatic, physical health may be negatively impacted by the subcortical emotional systems (such as Panksepp has proposed).

With respect to emotions, these patients are typically laden with fear and compensatory grandiosity and religiosity. Chronic terror, of course, cannot be good for the immune system. Another emotional system, disgust, is also implicated and deserves more consideration. This might be involved, from the mind side, in a gastrointestinal-immune disease process impacting the body and health. In terms of healing, a very personal journey of re-connecting to this forgotten emotion is required before any real shifts occur. Closely allied with the senses, with touch and taste, disgust is the most somatic and least mindful of the major emotions. The more this is implicated in the physical effects, the more likely the person's attachment substrate will be disturbed.

Mark

One young man, age seventeen, really could not identify what was bothering him. Initially, as far as I could discern, his problems hovered around alexithymia, an inability to identify feelings. But feeling itself seemed to ooze from his every pore. This wonderful young man was almost effusively desperate and painfully awkward. He would pause, then begin to speak, then change tracks and pause again. Even as we broke past some of this, there was the quality of a sphere formed of floating presences. The core was distant and undifferentiated, while his direct or interpersonal bearing was variably tender, open, kind, and almost too immediate and direct for me to believe. This presence might be bumped aside one deeply confused, and this by depression, exuberance, or desperation.

We held meetings with his parents and the story began to unfold that this family had been pummeled by their older son's congenital health problems. Mark was what therapists call the identified patient. His brother had nearly died several times and required round the clock assistance.

Bills, insurance, legal snarls, and the like had, it seemed to me, contributed to the mother's own health and psychiatric problems. Dad bore the weight of the entire situation. Some two decades later, the family continued to essentially run a hospital in their home. The father explained how the only thing they had done approaching a vacation in twenty years required that they haul a life-support system for their 200-pound, very ill child from the van to the hotel room to the restaurant.

Mark was too savvy and on guard for any formulaic interventions. Anything remotely cliché or resembling psychobabble, such as identifying goals, was a nonstarter. Overcome by this family's tale, I summoned what I could of the image of Buddha's Mom. From this, I could see how Mark was an extremely normal kid. In light of the unusual circumstances in which he existed, clearly, he was supernormal. He had every potential to experience all the colors of the emotional rainbow. That which had destabilized him was just as remote and nameless to him as it was me. Therapy needed to make space for these shunned zones.

An attachment angle celebrates the mess on its way to meaning. We are all under such pressure to look and sound sharp. Ego eats up its own hero and victim narratives. Being lost in one's raw humanity is deeply therapeutic. Honest meandering and all encounters along the way are healing. When we manage to drop veils and enter more fully into the vivid here and now, a wider field of acceptance and caring arises unbidden. This is the perfection at the center of each moment.

Awkward spaces unconsciously propelled conversations toward the seemingly mundane. We danced around safe harbors, with comments such as "sure wish the rain would stop," or in Mark's case, sports banter. Buddha met people where they were, and the encounters became a shimmering void where his advanced, human state of perfection flowed. These meetings revealed his concentration and care, the heartfelt inter-being that was naturally emergent. The outlines of Buddhism's perfections shines through, including kindness, patience and a bead on what needed to happen, e.g., morality. Although one sometimes has to read between the lines, in the story of Buddha's encounters, there was plenty of humor, irony, lightheartedness, and wit.

Attached mothers spend many thousands of hours in and around these best hits of human potential. They blend patience and joy so as not to go crazy. The path to any given developmental milestone is indeed many miles. Impatience guarantees frustration. In particular, attached moms and babies play in the space between safety and predictability. Peek-a-boo is an early, classical example. Therapy provides the same opportunities. In a back and forth motion, after a spell on dry land has adequately restored a sense of normalcy and calm, the therapist nudges the conversation back into troubling waters, and vice versa.

With Mark, therapy went from stumbling to running at a gallop. During some sessions, Mark just could not stop himself from retelling, in intensely microscopic detail, every single aspect of what amounted to exceedingly normal adolescent euphoria, implosions, infatuations, dark nights, and thrill rides. There is nothing quite like the tumult of boy to man, girl to woman high school passages. In Mark's case, he exquisitely and sweetly worked to stay in touch with the sort of free and goofy zest of childhood and not to ever take too seriously the sometimes alluring pigeonholes in which his high intelligence and tremendous athleticism could easily have confined him. Because he had indeed been crushed and trampled in the way that siblings of special needs kids can be, his case had the steady, protective influence of loving parents despite their own posttraumatic stress and being overwhelmed. But he cultivated his own emotional survival by being the more mature, the more forgiving and resilient one, across multiple social triangles and polygons.

Mark initially could barely express himself. He sketched cartoons with suicidal and homicidal themes. He routinely and quite severely thumped his head against the wall by his bed. Standing on his parents' shoulders, we made space for the eccentricities and psychic pain, eventually with excellent results.

In Mark's case, what began with an inability to express anything coherent or meaningful on an emotional plane transformed into an almost ridiculous torrent of emotionally laden stories, theories, hypotheses, and curiosities. I endeavored to help him celebrate this intensity. He would await our sessions with so many competing stories and streams of consciousness to relay that he'd have to force some of these on and off stage, and talk rapidly just to achieve some sense of adequate breadth as he bore deep into pursuit of adequate depth of detail. Mark and I might talk about his shirt, a drawing in his notebook, his haircut, or texting subtleties between him and his friends.

He had great depths of joy and pain which I soon learned were transmitted to him by his incredible parents. To be sure, they were emotionally bruised and overwhelmed and this had implications for Mark. They had had to expend the majority of their emotional resources on keeping his brother alive. But what on paper looked almost like neglect was in fact something extraordinary. His parents had consistently conveyed their love, confidence, and pride in Mark even as, in effect, they communicated that he would have to go it alone sooner than he should. This family had fractured some, but there was tremendous honesty and love between them. This terra firma was an ultimate therapeutic resource. What began as awkward and inappropriate behavior evolved into something joyous, if still awkward.

Demetrius

In narcissism, a potent, unstoppable pulse of desire desperately gasps for air. The original transmission of the human lineage from mother to child was so impoverished as to leave the infant in the adult strangely stuck, needy and enraged. As Bowlby's work makes clear, nature hands off sentience incrementally, over time, through the mystery of mirroring. When we bow to one another and say, "namaste", we are communicating "from the light in me to the light in you".

For the narcissist, the depth, frequency, and duration of this sentience-engendering was so pathological as to leave a living, hemorrhaging wound. Outer life events make no sense separate from this unyielding, internal storm. The catalyzing of what poets, some Buddhists, and new age types call love-light, the spiritual essence and inheritance of the child has been deeply marred. The narcissist goes through life with the illusion that their inner light and energy is grand and cosmic, because this is the early character of neonatal and toddler consciousness. At various developmental junctures, the narcissist is close to source. But Homo sapiens are designed to take this through many iterations toward a beautiful maturity and the narcissist does not move on.

Demetrius was a client who began to gain some perspective on the implications of his upbringing only in his late 30s. His mother was understandably hell-bent on protecting her son from factors that propel a fraction of African American males down the path from school dropout to criminal to prisoner. As always, the heart of desire is perfect. Problems arise with how infinite, boundless, and beautiful desire is contorted. Demetrius' mother suffered the impoverished mirroring that characterizes the history of all narcissists. So overbearing was she that Demetrius found himself unable to distinguish between her thoughts and his own.

Demetrius began to awaken to this fact as a byproduct of an intimate relationship with a young woman who had spent ten years in therapy healing and cultivating an aspect of equanimity that many refer to as "healthy boundaries". She had been through many battles, not living up to her mother's standards and finally realizing that only her own standards would bring her peace and stability. She had been in relationships with overly passive, feminine males and with overbearing, macho males, and had finally emerged with a compelling degree of centeredness. Ashanti may not have been enlightened, but she was very stable and clear with respect to boundaries. She came to serve as a sort of co-therapist within a therapeutic context focused around assisting Demetrius to restructure his relationship with his mother.

Patients such as Demetrius need to do much more than revisit the oppression of their childhoods. They need to download the life force at the heart of our shared human lineage. They need energy to battle their demons. In the energizing bleeding of therapeutic wounds, unformed flares of rage and unfettered fantasies of fairness and possibility, these clients can be set free from the path which guarantees calamity and pain, but the difference this time around is that these encounters with variations of hell on earth are their very own. They can finally differentiate these disasters from the ones which sadly dominated their childhood. Given a more direct access to the life force, they will have the raw materials from which to cultivate a slew of weapons. These include improvisation, breakthrough courage, spontaneous wit, and a poetic, nuanced feel for the divine.

For all its bombastic grandiosity and vitriol, narcissism actually needs to be understood for its minimal effects. This shows up in the small-minded and primitive approaches to emotional exchange. On the attachment side of the two-sided attachment model, smothering, enmeshment, and engulfment are common variants of the small-minded, crude ways of perceiving the exchange. On the detachment side, anger, threatened cutoffs, and over-the-top hyper-criticism are typical, unimaginative ways of relating. Demetrius' mom matched the profile of a high-functioning narcissist. She never resorted to slightly lower, rawer forms of aggression. Her anger was cloaked. Its heat came out as cool and even-keeled. Her "24-7-365" brain-training, as Demetrius came to describe it, was always way ahead of his developmental ability to grasp its scope.

Demetrius told stories of his mother moving to where he attended college and subverting his choice of a major. She also subverted various ideas from his past. When asked how he came to change his mind, he often invoked the first person plural, "We just don't do that." In terms of direct opposition or manipulation from his mother, he could only put his finger on how she had cut off communication with everyone in her life but him. To the extent he confronted her, she would turn the tables and accuse him of judging her, of viewing her as a bad mother, and remind him of hardships she had to overcome and how she had done her best to raise him.

Behind all this, Demetrius felt a palpable sense that he was walking on eggshells and doomed to be cut off at any second. He once relayed a story that conveyed this embedded, implicit sense of being wrong and at fault. His mother asked him to clean out the storage shed and he did so. In fact, he decided to do even more than she expected and ended up injuring his hand while cleaning up a pile of old lumber. His mother was away for the morning. The gash on his hand was bleeding profusely and he literally did not know what to do. He felt like he was in mental quicksand. Something was very wrong but there was no mother present to adjudicate. The force field he depended upon to pronounce thumbs up or down and administer compassion or rejection was absent.

Unsure of what to do, he drifted to the neighbors and soon found himself begging them not to call an ambulance. Even many years later he was unable to make sense of this. At the time his mother's response was pitch perfect for a narcissist. She simultaneously dismissed and acknowledged his ambivalence as yet another example of how he could not think for himself.

In therapy, Demetrius would eventually come to grapple with his mother's narcissism. The journey was bumpy, as usual. No matter what happened to him, his mother could find a way to turn his actions into a reflection on her but in confusing, subtle ways. She was not able to travel to celebrate something positive in his life, but traveled other times. She was all ears when he was doing poorly and helped him to doubt the intentions of others. She was subtle, but he was smart and increasingly able to feel the sad gap that was always between them.

Isabella

Obviously, we are blessed to have Buddha's Mom and the legacy fulfilled in her son as portals to our shared human lineage. The truth of attachment's promise pushes through the mud and evokes a unique lotus in each of us. To inhabit this perfection is to transcend and include our full humanity. In this book, we have compiled material in support of an integral attachment as a practice enhancer. There is also evidence of attachment's power to relieve suffering in those who have no particular interest in Buddhism. This adds heft to the notion of Buddha's Mom as our species' lineage bearer and to Buddha-nature as human nature.

With no formal training, Isabella, had been hired at a major zoo. She tumbled into such a positive, healing attachment there that one might call it a "lotus experience". Such dense, direct, bright experiences may only come to fruition after much time and even then only with intensive therapy. Psychodynamically, Isabella immersed herself because it distracted her from her own painful upbringing. But this hardly scratches the surface of the deep psyche's innate healing, perfecting quality.

At the zoo, Isabella lived the adage, "What you do when no one is looking matters most." She was always going the extra mile, staying late, doing the hardest work, reading and researching on her own time. Fortunately, someone was looking and Isabella was eventually promoted and granted an opportunity to fulfill her dream to work with the zoo's seven great apes. As if finally awakened to her purpose on earth, she gave of herself with abandon.

The actual, factual reality of Isabella's intelligence and sensitivity to the amazing brilliant beasts in her care still gives me chills. Though I did not know it at the time, this work was centered in an inter-species, enlightened we-space. Isabella's love and intense desire to understand her gorillas was at once a fount of metta and prajñā. These forces were not earned but granted, and were absolutely not sentimental or anthropomorphic but based on all attendant realities. Isabella straddled the void, appreciating that humans can only peer over so far.

Among her dharma teachers were forerunners such as Frans de Waal and the pioneers who originally uncovered the plight of the great apes. When no one was looking, these bodhisattvas came to know the heartbreak of their grand, fellow primates. Isabella knew the tender, beautiful, and very personal narrative of all her animals. These stories were drenched in attachment dukkha and all that gets stuffed into the term, trauma. She was especially attached to a juvenile male. His story was her story. Brave, fragile, and wounded, he covered the pain over with chutzpah and showy antics.

After two years of dedicated work, Isabella left her zookeeper job. She later plummeted into grief over this loss, stating that she had no sense at the time of how important this experience had been. Break-ups can be similar. One loses sight of the enormity and preciousness of the experience, then feels a reverse crush in full after the fact. Perhaps this can be likened to a descent into the mud below the lotus, an encounter with the missing, taken-for-granted ground of being.

Isabella would go through much mud before she made space for the totality, the lotus, of her experience with the great apes. Such implosions, which can feel like face-plants in the mud, live up to the deep meaning of "humiliation". The term *humiliate* and its derivatives come from *humus*, "a brown or black material in soil that is formed when plants and animals decay".[209]

In her teens and before being hired at the zoo, Isabella's life included lots of escapism, lots of drugs, barely passing grades even though she was smart, and countless fights with her parents. She had followed bands around, had her share of narcissistic boyfriends and had done some animal rescue work. She began to understand that her sense of home and belonging with her apes was born of multiple attachment wounds. To fully embody this experience would paradoxically require her to recover these bruised, emotional urchins.

Although Isabella knew a lot about attachment, the discovery in psychotherapy that the zoo was the beginning of an attachment healing of her own was major. This became the focus of our sessions and her healing. In fits and starts, per usual, she climbed the ladder that we have described here, ranging from psychotic to borderline to neurotic to normal. She had a knack for allowing herself to fall apart, "go ape" one could say, and to feel the old but still highly destabilizing pain.

Forming expansive, stable we-space does take practice (the richness of this word is forever worth noting). With patience and intensive, present attention, the natural urge to label and fix fades into the background. A space imbued with the positive qualities that Buddha describes opens wherever kindness is sustained. The lotus is an embodied, human potential which we can appreciate as both our species' inheritance and legacy. From kids to the elderly, within a space of persistent listening and care, an uncanny, one-and-only picture and story emerges. Expectations are commonly shattered by reality. What can be called perfection keeps showing up.

The dharma, as mentioned, has etymological roots in the bearer. This means that which holds and carries, and refers additionally to law. Dharma, of course, for Buddhists is also a word for reality. To qualify dharma as the Buddha's teaching about the nature of reality and the human condition, and so on, may place the accent on his teaching over reality.

Anyone (any human) can cultivate a therapeutic we-space. Such a "holding environment" is not only real but transformative. If we are to believe the Buddha, as I certainly do, then this environment will naturally be imbued with both wisdom and love. In essence therapist and client inhabit and embody the space by acknowledging it and attending to it with diligence and care.

Isabella's primate attachment experiences would slowly, potently provide a container for her deepest, human wounding. She had to make room for both how terrible her early life attachment had been and the unique, precious experiences she had with her apes. These animals themselves were commonly profoundly attachment-deprived and wounded. Her work as a zookeeper involved intensive awareness of the histories of the gorillas and the relief of neurotic suffering through understanding, attentiveness and love. The ability to experience second hand examples of their inter-species communication and stories about hard-earned breakthroughs was a gift for Isabella.

Isabella came to see that she knew their pain because hers was so similar. Not only her pure intent, but her actual natural talent at developing attachment relationships with her apes became a reliable, trustworthy ground. Metaphorically, this held the tree roots in place through many an ongoing stormy argument with her mother. She gravitated away from self-sabotage and anger to more positive paths such as painting and animal rescue work. Meltdowns decreased as she worked at better communication with her husband and at cultivating friendships.

To the prospect of dharma as reality, I would add that the nature of reality is the reality of nature which permeates our being. Isabella rescued animals very much as she rescued herself. For over a year, with not much more than a server job to pay the bills, she lived a much bigger life. She crisscrossed the county as a very unsung hero for a rather dubious wildlife rescue organization. In her home, there might be baby possums in the hallway and various, wounded forest critters in a bedroom, and a surprisingly huge bird smelling up the bathroom.

In time, Isabella became pregnant, gave birth at home and became well-known as an advocate of attachment parenting. Old battles would foment on occasion, for example, when Isabella's mother callously opined that bottle-feeding was better because breastfeeding would make Isabella's breasts sag. Deeper than the sadness of not being seen, Isabella felt the pain of not being able to share the precious experience of life with her mother because it symbolized the reality of love that her mother could not let in.

Hell Realms

"We don't know what we don't know" is not a throwaway phrase. This captures something very essential. Because we don't know *that* we don't know, we fill in contextual gaps in "awareness" and imbue these with a sense (sentience or perceived meaning) of knowing. This internal, subjective, pseudo-grasp on reality rounds out the extremes. Where awareness longs for a cohesion but comes up short, this un-acknowledged unknowing leaks in.

To get into this, we need to return for the moment to the classical clinical continuum, time-tested over the last hundred-plus years, spanning normal to neurotic to borderline to psychotic. Importantly, these global levels of functioning are both "state and trait". The former refers to short-term factors and the latter to the more rigid ones associated with personality or character. The harsher the short-term "state" influences, the more self/ego/mind is shoved downward on the classical continuum. In the everyday course of life, normal functioning plummets into the upper neurotic realm. Someone typically functioning in the upper neurotic capacity will suffer a decline consistent with lower neurotic and perhaps borderline functioning.

What can be quite subtle and overlooked, however, is the fact that the lower reaches of any person's range of functioning feels, and for them actually is, extreme. For normals, these are the rough waters of neurosis; for neurotics, the hellish borderline badlands. Hell on earth has personalized parallels: losing one's mind, breaking down, coming unglued. These experiences reflect the usual sense of self, but also alongside, co-arising tumultuous emotions. The usual sense of self has nowhere to place these, no way to map or contain these. By default, these feel and are assumed to be the sign of something seriously amiss with "me". However, the interiors are generally not as pathological as one perceives.

According to Reggie Ray, Buddhist teacher Chögyam Trungpa was asked long ago if he had been to hell during deep meditation. "Yes," he replied. "What did you do?" "I tried to stay there."

Far from home and never to return, Trungpa was not surprised. He already knew Mara, the demon who tempted Buddha. Mara had asked Buddha, "Who are you, little man? Who are you to claim the right to Buddhahood, to perfect awakening?" At the particular time he experienced what he knew as hell, Trungpa was pure void, so fleeting an anything that annihilation arose in its fiercest form. When one is barely a self, something hellish threatens to finish the job. But apparently the enlightened welcome the self's demise. "I tried to stay there," Trungpa said, to remain in touch, grounded, to touch the earth—not to flee.

The shorthand for one's true level of moral development is sometimes, "what you do when no one is looking." This idea holds true for spiritual development as well. The premise is that a deeper test of who we are occurs when ego is not conforming to outside pressures. But inside pressures work the same way to produce a habitual consciousness which eschews whatever threatens it. An ultimate metaphor for that which we avoid is hell. Jung's shadow, as understood within his framework, works the same way. What we do when we are ripped out of our comfort zone matters more than what we do within our comfort zone. Situations which are disgusting, demeaning, hard, and uncomfortable are the hell realms that test our ability to detach from pain and not to rely on attaching to permanent comfort.

To be sure, Siddhartha had good times and bad, even as he crossed over into enlightenment. He did not simply remain fully human but as suggested came to abide in the full stream of human potential, our species' lineage. Our ability to remain/become that which we are born to be is critical. Hell realms test our metta mettle, forgiving the alliteration. Those which prompt ego to push back, flee, dissociate or numb out are exactly the ones we should not only survive but welcome into our hearts. We are called to love our enemy when inevitably we cannot. Chögyam Trungpa said he was at peace with his partial paralysis resulting from a car accident. It showed him yet another dimension of human suffering. Humor and humility help. We can acknowledge our laughably long way to go in juxtaposition with a Jesus or Buddha. Big surprise, imperfect again.

Both "my anger" and "their cruelty" or whatever form the hell takes can seem so impossibly dense and ever-present. We can go hours, days and much longer living in these hells. An active imagination and the structure inherent in a spiritual practice have rich potential. The inner emptiness and open space of meditation easily accommodates forms. Forms arise and drop all the time. Why not be more actively engaged in this realization? One can visualize an endless, shimmering blue sea. When in a hell, the me-as-fear, me-as-pain can be set adrift along with the despised or rejecting other. Here the water of life knows only acceptance and nourishment. So long as fear and pain dominate, the sea will give them the space and distance they require to break the pattern of hate or abuse or disappointment. But sometimes, rather than a vehicle for acceptance, this sea can instead become a buzzing, electrified, three-dimensional open space. Orbs like those in Bosch's "Garden of Earthly Delights" can serve as vehicles for dense, caustic emotions and heated, intrusive, circular narratives.

Chögyam Trungpa knew that just to be in hell for a second was neither a nightmare nor a dream. This begins in the Buddhist precept that to be born human is essential for any hope of enlightenment and liberation. Evolutionarily, one cannot be born an insect or even an advanced mammal. Once human, one seeks to enter the stream only once. This means while human, within one lifespan, one aspires to become fully human. Developmentally, one must mature through infancy and childhood and develop fully into adulthood. The integral model tracks these in various ways, including: archaic, archaic-magic, magic, magic-mythic, mythic, mythic-rational, rational, rational-existential, vision-logic and further.[210] On the classical continuum, one must rise not only above bodily and psychotic levels but past the chaotic, borderline passages and further. These include the self-absorption and overthinking of the neurotic reaches and the levels denoted as normal. These bands can be hard to map as they tend to be identified as the absence of pathology. Buddhism has tremendous value in portraying the supernormal levels. Accordingly, through practice, one cultivates the jewels of our species, kindness, courage, wisdom—the gems of humanity articulated by the great contemplatives, healers and gurus.

Self-help books and dharma talks often underplay hell's subtleties and importance. The dark and light co-arise but do so with a mix of the profane and profound. Levels of psychic terror amount to missed opportunities when the paradoxical upside is dumbed down. Various flavors of psychological disturbance are commonly conflated because of the crude, one-size-fits-all over-reliance on self/ego/mind. The challenge is to diagnose the breadth of the hell, especially if it is a portal to deep self disturbance.

So long as one uses such grandiose constructs, there is little chance for differentiation of sub-processes and subcomponents. For better or worse, these tend to trace back to the dynamics of the family of origin. Typically these events are lost in the mists of time and barely retrievable in an objective sense.

Complicating this is the fact that hell realms are born of both what occurred and what did not occur. A key but never fully answerable question is to what degree was an individual adequately or inadequately mirrored, conjured, and esteemed by their attachment figures? Mirroring, according to Bowlby, is a maternal function which begins immediately when a baby is born. Most of us probably prefer the term love. Mirroring and love are nature's way of downloading our species' operating system, a process which initially is overt, critical and recognizable but becomes less so over time.

In the best scenario, attachment catalyzes the skillful means which undergird normal development and which are sadly wanting otherwise. These skillful means begin as constructive preverbal, intrinsic states and evolve into traits. A baby who is kept safe in time feels safe. These emotive holds, such as a sense of safety or of being loved, arise from the mother-child dyad. Multiple heavens on earth must happen to mitigate and put a platform under the realms of hell. These attaching processes span body-mind-spirit, from parasympathetic, physiological response attachments to sensations of warmth and physical comfort, to feelings of joy or equanimity in the presence of a caregiver. These all become stronger with frequency and duration. They are more and more subtle, with far-reaching cognitive components that fire and wire together, comprising the substructures and sub-processes of ego and mind. The cohesiveness of these dynamics translates into stable traits, into normal psychological cohesiveness, upper neurotic cohesiveness, lower neurotic, upper borderline, etc.

All of this begs the "two attachments" question, whether 'to be or not to be?' When is the mind a skillful means, and when is it a hindrance? How do we distinguish heaven on earth from hell on earth? Whether framed as a goal or a benefit of meditation, much is made of transcending attachments, habits of mind, letting go, and letting be. In sitting, one experiences all the wasted effort made over and over to hold on to mind as one knew it only a millisecond ago.

Hysteria

Freud famously declared that women in profound emotional distress had a psychiatric disorder. He labeled this hysteria. The official psychiatric taxonomy maintained this diagnosis for a long time. The concept morphed into hysterical neurosis and hypochondriasis, and more recently into less historically encumbered categories such as borderline personality disorder, dissociative and body dysmorphic disorders.

But we might be better off to dispatch with establishment efforts to operationalize these deep self disturbance packages typified by extremes of "emotional dysregulation," volatile behavior and intense irrationality. A modern, integral view, and one in sync with the current effort to show pathways back to the mind's bodily basis, recognizes these dis-ease states as wobbles of an extreme variety. The body-mind is barely holding on this side of full psychosis, and it does so by being highly erratic and under-integrated, dis-associated, e.g., via dissociation.

Here we encounter a feminine presence so wounded and writhing that one wants to look away and rubberneck at the same time, much as when we drive by a grizzly car accident. We half pray and half selfishly defend our own physical integrity in an odd, automatic way while being thankful that it was not us. We do not mean to be thankful that someone else was hurt, but the self can only contain so much jarring before it retreats.

Peter Levine's work, encompassing areas of psychology, ethology, neuroscience, and indigenous healing practices, has salience for this topic.[211] Levine expands fight-flight to include freeze and fold. The key element he adds to the mix is "somatic experiencing." These techniques enable humans to return to their animal roots and potentially to, often literally, shake off trauma.

> Once safe, animals spontaneously "discharge" this excess energy through
> involuntary movements including shaking, trembling, and deep
> spontaneous breaths. This discharge process resets the ANS [autonomic
> nervous system], restoring equilibrium.[212]

For our purposes, we would like to emphasize that Levine's work dovetails elegantly with the construct of Buddha's Mom. For example, a well-attached mother will become "hysterical" when her child is attacked or otherwise traumatized. She will scoop them up, lift the car off them, yell, cry, weep "hysterically" as part of the natural we-based discharge process. She provides the body, energy and emotional discharge, enabling the physiologically overwhelmed child to do the same by proxy. If the child is able to weep or scream violently, she contains but does not suppress this natural and essential process. Patriarchal mothers, however, squash emotions at these extremes: "Boys don't cry" goes hand in hand with the implied "Girls shouldn't cry either but are too weak to stop," too prone to their embarrassing, hysterical nature.

A client I've worked with a long time was actually carrying one of Levine's books in her purse when a business meeting turned inside out. Within seconds, a belligerent colleague followed her across a hotel lobby as she attempted to make an exit. Panksepp's subcortical fear, panic and rage, primitive responses throttled up. She had the presence of mind to remember Levine's suggestion to quake and quiver and discharge! Having lived with trauma, she felt herself saying, "No, not this time!" My client, Stacie, got to her room, locked the door and let loose. She punched the air and a pillow and allowed the heat to move through her. When I saw her in a subsequent session, she was very clear that this had protected her from experiencing severe trauma.

In the aftermath of the colleague's shenanigans, decisions had to be made. There were more meetings. Each of these involved potential triggers and potential retraumatization. The initial verbal assault could easily have turned into a continued process of emotional wounding. Stacie could easily have been re-wounded, for example, while sitting across from the colleague as he smugly attempted to twist her words and revise events to paint himself in a positive light. But Stacie had accomplished such exquisite expunging of sensations with her writhing, shaking, and air punching that the raw emotions associated with the initial onslaught were not there for him to exploit. To her surprise and delight, she was remarkably grounded during these follow-up meetings and able to find her voice. She was not vengeful or reactionary, nor was she passive. Her emotions were in fact intensive and synergetic, and contributed to her ability to stay rooted, just as evolution and what we are calling Buddha's Mom intended.

During these follow-up meetings, as is often the case, others in the mix nearly played the false equivalency card. Those on the periphery who are less directly confronted by one tribal member's dysfunction will tend to hold to the original "we" and suggest that "there are two sides to every story" and plenty of blame to go around. Some may even engage in what the creator of transactional analysis referred to as "let's watch you and him fight." These dynamics muddy the waters and add another challenge for the member who is confronting abuse and resetting a we-space in a healthier light.

Stacie's journey can be understood as one in which she discovered that a we-space was not as solid and trustworthy as previously perceived. When this happens, people sometimes speak of wanting to grab someone by the shoulders and shake the other. Or to shake some sense into the other. The intuitive sense is that the we-space has gone awry. It would take more than talk, even more than emotions to restore stability to the situation. The other's very body needs to awake.

In Stacie's case, a historical review revealed that her colleague had his share of "control issues", hostility and grandiosity. He had a long record of sabotaging progress. Stacie was able to dispassionately articulate these facts without losing sight of her colleague's humanity, without becoming abusive herself. She spoke "truth to power" while maintaining a grounding in her own heart. She was paradoxically thankful for the chance to experience this balance of love and power. Often people such as her colleague do not have adequate insight into their own dynamics and only reach an impasse when they are imposed externally by society. Obviously, there can be a valuable opportunity in these types of crises for those with the spiritual ability to perceive this.

The human response to agony can be incredibly ugly or incredibly beautiful. Our physicality communicates its own unparalleled honesty. Cutters and those with severe borderline personality are in a sense flagellating in a dire attempt to shake off the shackles of repetitive traumas.

> I believe that the key to healing traumatic symptoms in humans lies in our being able to mirror the fluid adaptation of wild animals as they shake out and pass through the immobility response and become fully mobile and functional again.[213]

But the core attachment years of these damaged individuals left them without an adequate bodily self to return to. Homo sapiens is no simple herd mammal. While human meltdowns can be seen as an effort to discharge the raw fear and rage of the moment, their inability to do so routinely points to the differences between us and lower, simpler (but nonetheless sophisticated and related), species. Humans are of another order, with our intricate awareness of a highly social self moving through time. The rapid dialing down of these higher survival-critical capacities in the face of some overwhelming threat is experienced as a terrifying and highly unusual event. Social, tribal functioning and the self-sense accompanying these upper levels is an extension of lower, raw survival capacities. Being rejected from a partner in a pair bond or severing tribal alliances are not as immediately life threatening events as a tiger attack but are functionally and evolutionally as critical. These set off the same alarms, but in our case, we have higher cognitive capacities that utilize everything in our arsenal, intellectual and physiological, to avoid harm. This calls for embodiment— a stable ego or self-sense. Those with severe deep self disturbance, by definition, lack the very thing that the shaking-based resetting is intended to restore.

Stacie's colleague shared characteristics of a very common sort. "Every family has one," some say. These people parasitically depend on others but do so paradoxically. This "counter-dependence" tends to stem from such an intensely dark, defiant streak that their ego manages to completely flip reality around. As such, this form of deep self disturbance bumps up against the lowest tier on the classical continuum of psychological functioning where reality contact gives way. These types see themselves as heroic-victims and others who are benign or even loving as evil, hostile, and deluded. Grandiosity is commonplace. They are obviously unappreciated. Many defer this slightly through a religiosity wherein they enjoy a special, unique, direct relationship with God and knowledge of his intentions.

Their rage-fests are doomed-to-fail efforts by their psyche to shake up their entire make-up. The same volcanic surge of emotion and physical discharge actually holds healing potential. Unfortunately, however, the crisis-opportunity potential in the upheaval is no match for the poor reality contact, and inability to contain and thereby integrate, painful emotions. This is one reason few such sufferers initiate or stick with therapy. Many, in fact, are so rigidly lost in a psychology of righteous indignation that their outbursts cascade over time into typical problems such as self-medicating forms of substance abuse, unemployment, criminality and sometimes imprisonment. Roughly speaking, life responds. Bosses terminate employment, partners terminate relationships and families fracture. In many cases, police and the courts curtail behavioral extremes with periods of imprisonment.

However, we are one body, mind and spirit, and we are also one in our shared DNA and ultimately one within Buddha's Mom. The raw, spontaneous emotional release of humans has an upside which is much greater than its downside. The ability to hold and transmit truth, that is to say the potential dharma of quaking and shaking, corresponds to the body-mind integrity. The trick is to do both, regress and transcend, at the same time. For example, as one explodes with rage and fear about some concrete perceived enemy, one must also manage to have a separate sense of self. Some Buddhist schools' call for stillness and equanimity can inadvertently create a blind spot for these somatic-unlocking practices.

In the Medusa paradigm, one must be able to avert the gaze. One must divert attention from the immediate and narrow events even the body's stillness to other freer, more sweeping realities that leave us crying, yelling and quivering. A smaller self implodes or explodes in the face of grief, rage or some overwhelming affect when a bigger vessel is there to witness and hold the space. This larger essence we have suggested is consistent with both Buddha-nature and Buddha's Mom.

Slow-motion footage of great athletes in victory is very similar to that of a zebra that somehow escapes the jaws of a crocodile at a watering hole. They leap, writhe and twist and expel what seems like a thousand years of pent-up emotion in a few seconds. Screaming and exploding on the edge of agony and ecstasy, they are naked, exposed, and powerful all at once.

The same body-spirit release that we are suggesting can be mapped in terms of Buddha's Mom informed indigenous, ecstatic dance and movement such as those of the Quakers and Shakers. The Vajrayana views being human, human being, being reborn, life, samsara facets of the same and, relative to our true, non-relative peace and freedom, as inherently traumatizing. We will discuss some other secular, therapeutic models consistent with this ontological starting point. Shaking free of this mortal veil while very much mortal takes many forms, such seen in Hawaiian Hula and Maori Haka—as we will touch on. Tantric traditions teach conscious, bodily ecstasy as a means of encountering and hopefully transcending karmic suffering. Orgasm can be a holy egoic death, evoking the cessation of suffering through the extending of self and receiving of other, a core Tonglen structure.

Levine's discoveries, like Jung's archetypes, are of extant human, psychological potentials and processes. All manner of overlapping practices and technologies can be seen through multiple related lenses. These share an emphasis on releasing ego's hold. Holotropic breathing, for example, explicitly involves the evocation of shamanic, ecstatic states replete with hyperventilation, writhing and emotional release. Deep tissue work, such as Rolfing, crosses back and forth over the pain boundary to open somatic awareness to wider horizons. Active imagination, Jungian dream work, and Gestalt approaches welcome dropping the confines of the self and the embodiment of other energetic fields and capacities.

Levine's work aims to re-stabilize consciousness in the soma. A client may be dissuaded from describing trauma while the therapist directs them to remain in tune with their bodily sensations. Implicitly, they come to discover a somatic home separate from the narrative arc which takes the mind back to a point of pain. In time, trust in the therapist to manage this delicate process is coupled with their increasing somatic bearing. The movie or tape of the trauma is no longer intrusive, triggered, and set to play by outside forces. Eye Movement Desensitization and Reprocessing (EMDR) therapy takes a very similar pathway.

These sometimes facilitate what psychoanalysts refer to as "regression in service of the ego" but which we might reframe as in service of somatic grounding. An integral approach grounding the psyche in the reality of Buddha's Mom opens doors to creative syntheses and promises never-before breakthroughs which transcend and include precursors.

Mara

Even on a bad day, the Canon seems to indicate, Buddha's mental status was what clinicians call "within normal limits" or better. There can be little doubt that Siddhartha Gautama did not suffer from schizophrenia, bipolar disorder or borderline personality. While it seems very unlikely that any modern assessment would not view him as having a major psychiatric disorder, certain canonical passages nonetheless call for reflection.

In these, Buddha is bestowed with superhuman powers in order to do battle with. Mara, a vicious, devil-like deity. We will return to this important topic at the close of this book. These passages describe psychotic paranoia, hallucinations and delusions but, of course, are better understood as portraying the same mythical, archetypal (but still psychological) space as that of Lucifer tempting Jesus.

An amazing fact connecting no less than Jesus, Buddha, Chögyam Trungpa, and Carl Jung is that some of their most hellish, Mara-type experiences came on the heels of ruptured adult attachment experiences. In their own way, each did as Chögyam Trungpa advised and "stayed in hell". They did their best to allow the torment to, at the extremes, destroy their grounding in reality. For each was ready to experience and become a fuller, living expression of the universal dharma. Each in their own way recognized a responsibility to get the most out of their time in hell.

Jesus had to know he'd be violently crucified. Buddha was no less proactive. Once he awoke to the hell we share, of inevitable aging, death and disease, he saw how his attachment to loved ones was illusory. He then left his mother, father, wife and son. While little is recorded, we can conclude that these were his most intimate relationships, and that he would be deeply aware that his decision caused them suffering. He endeavored to find a better way of life for himself and those he loved, or to die trying. In this sense, he walked into hell and continued to stay there, day after day for six years. He was driven by the tormenting insight that his and their collective attachment-love was chained to pain and suffering.

The lack of associated emotional descriptions points to patriarchy. A modern, more feminist interpretation of canonical sources suggests how very much is conspicuously absent. Siddhartha, at this juncture, felt the weight of not being awakened. He would take leave of his identity as a member of a wealthy family and rely on nature for his floor, roof, and walls. As he left those he loved, he must have experienced emotional hells—loneliness, loss, fear, guilt, and self-doubt. Though he had to have been tempted to give up and return home, an awareness of the depths of humanity's suffering must have bolstered his determination. This helps to explain how the path he eventually forged all the way to a *cessation* of suffering was squarely based in suffering's very depths.

After being selected to bring the Vajrayana to the West, Chögyam Trungpa was rejected by members of his own lineage. According to those who knew him, this caused both immense suffering and a deepening of his determination to fulfill his mission. Carl Jung's entire model, we now know from the Red Book, was influenced by a purposeful descent into the "underworld". This version of trying to stay in hell followed his break with Freud. Jesus, of course, was loved and then spurned by all but a few haggard followers. He could have avoided crucifixion but similarly stayed, so to speak, within the torment of this world's rejection in order to channel, according to his followers, the ultimate source of love and salvation. His words reflect an ultimate attachment crisis. "Why has thou forsaken me?" he pleaded as a wide open, fully broken, and perfected spirit.

Pain somehow lights the way to the possibility of a deepening of love, compassion and freedom. Buddhist teen retreat leader, Jessica Morey, explained how one bright, troubled teen transcended a tragic pattern of self-injurious cutting by managing to stay present as this hell overtook her and initially, indeed, as she carved into her arms. From the current perspective, this teen attached and detached to the experience fluidly and precisely. Morey's description of this young woman's better angels conveys the importance of resources, in her case of high intelligence, humor, spontaneity, grit and a hunger to heal, without which life's hells remain victorious.[214]

For Chögyam Trungpa these resources included powerful archetypal (or "inmap") strands. These would appear to include the Lover, Trickster and Warrior. These fortified his encounters with the hell realms. Rather than reduce the self/ego/mind to rigid roles, access to archetypal inmaps in a bright, sophisticated person enhances their set of skillful means. They help them to die to existential hells and be reborn as a more beautiful spirit than ever. These storms thereby bring about shifts in one's make-up in the direction of realization, a deeper abiding in reality. Once anchored in this potential, one senses the seed of transformation in terror. Something will die in the process, nothing will be the same, and such is the raw reality at hand. The great cultivate a bodhisattva attitude toward these suffering interiors, knowing the ride will be rough. A life fully lived, according to Chögyam Trungpa, calls for more than confronting the worst. One is to strangely welcome the worst, which is actually the mind's resistance to threats against its own beauty.

More commonly, of course, when we find ourselves in hell, we do anything but stay there. Cutters cut to avoid and downsize the all-out psychic pain that threatens self-annihilation. They cut it down to size, so to speak, in order to parse it into ritualistic, controlled torment. The self holds forth against the demons by choosing the time, place, and depth of the cutting. But through the eyes of compassion, one senses the courage with which cutters and all of us confront our demons. Hate and hell co-arise with the desire to be, to know, to see and be seen, to express and exist, to have peace and love, and to be loved. This is the meaning of the notion that indifference, not hate is the opposite of love.

Morey has her sometimes brilliant, sometimes chaotic Buddhist teens do an incredible form of a "hot seat" activity. One teen moves to the designated cushion and the rest meditatively focus on them. They meditate with compassion, with a growing appreciation for the unique human in front of them, as they intensively, continuously look into the eyes of the person in the "hot seat." This ritual intensifying of the we-space seems diametrically opposed to the dark, lonely act of cutting. But routinely, an intensification of a loving we-space brings a person's hells to the fore. Heart openings draw out hidden hells, such as this teen's description of her self-injurious behavior. Hell and heaven reveal their oneness. When a loving mirror is held up, we block its reflection.

Which comes first is irrelevant. Chögyam Trungpa's insight was that where there is hell the heart is near. The worst psychic pain, the worst teeth-baring hatred and incapacitating paranoia coexist with love. Into a vessel of disarming, profound aliveness, hell is most welcome. Such is the central Mahayana insight. Buddha is portrayed in this light in the Mara passages, albeit with plenty of spiritual warrior tones. In response to Mara's efforts to trick, maim and kill, he demonstrates great psychological fortitude. Mara is not so hard to identify as, perhaps, representative of psychotic visions of a terrible death.

Buddha does more than live to tell about these experiences. Importantly, he transcends these torments. For our purposes, he must encounter and transcend what Mara represents in the human condition in order to be fully realized. The same is true of the extremes he endured when he descended into the physiological badlands. The austerities also involved a psychological journey into physical hells. He sought to discover just how far one can go in denying or transcending bodily processes and needs—for example, to sleep, to eat, to breathe. The outside limits translate as exhaustion, pain, desperation, and mental correlates. There is one hell, mental and physical, and one old age, disease and death. Siddhartha glimpsed this, and chose to wander. He encountered it again in the austerities and then again at the cusp of enlightenment.

Here we are noting that these hells co-arise when our species' lineage is impeded. We may need more reminders of our worth to notice. Or we may already feel hell's torment. Both hail from Buddha's Mom, from nature's own attempts to convey ever deeper realities. These clashes signal Buddha-nature's transmission being stymied. All these dynamics have empirical, secular correlates. Buddhism is nothing besides reality-ism. In a wide, transcultural, trans-spiritual embrace, physical agony and psychological terror are, quite strangely, beautifully, five-alarm reminders. Wanting arises with receiving, disparate and suffering. Unrequited love, a teen's craving to be seen and a baby's cry for breastmilk—are one and the same, the lifeforce knocking. May Buddha's Mom be there to feed her, to see her, to honor and bless her and all sentient beings.

Chapter Eight

CONSPICUOUSLY ABSENT

Herstory

While the history of Buddha's Mom ignores "herstory", fortunately, truth is indestructible. At best, ignorance pushes her off stage. Misguided truth claims lack the vastness "she" requires. The Jesus creation myth begins with, "no room in the inn". There is not enough space for the powers in the offing. In Buddha's case, the biological mother is whisked away to bask in a mystical lake.

Both creation myths, from the perspectives we have been discussing, reflect the inadequacy of the status quo to serve as a vessel for the coming, cataclysmic expansions of spirit. Although one story comes from the East, one from the West, and both from antiquity, these tales speak to the same inadequacy. The lack of a more direct, conscious incorporation of the feminine principle in both traditions is a sacred wound and gate. It opens the way to the ground of being and the natural state. The fact is the dominant culture in which both Buddha and Jesus were embedded persists in "the two attachments" (Bowlby's and Buddhism's).

The grandeur of the feminine bears upon various brittle patriarchal truth claims. To pick one silent assassin, consider the presumption that the state of science and research in ancient times prevented a dismantling of the two attachments. But attachment's fundamental relevance to the species would have been implicit. There was no need to await functional magnetic resonance imaging. Natural experiments in broken attachment, for example, would have been as commonplace then as now. The abandoned too-early, abused puppy becomes a skittish or aggressive adult dog in short order. If it lives, its damaged soul only very slowly responds to love. Neglected (mammal/human) children suffer a similar disposition. The tribe or village soon enough witnesses his or her global deficits. Until recently, these kids were referred to as "under-socialized".

Attachment wounds impede emotional maturation and directly contribute to suffering. With respect to Siddhartha, a neglected child would not travel far on either of the success tracks set out for him—of great ruler or great spiritual teacher. Without the Virgin Mary, Jesus too would have needed nursemaids or a stepmother or suffered the fate so commonly associated with neglect referred to nowadays as attachment disorder, emotional dysregulation, trauma, among other terms.

In both creation stories, we glimpse the outline of a great but suppressed feminine source. In both, the mother is background, acknowledged in retrospect as important and divine by virtue of the son's spiritual achievements. Need we even mention that in neither case was her child's gender feminine in the first place?

Whether due to war, famine, disease or having been born to narcissistic, so-called caregivers, offspring starved of the species' extended birthing process (attachment-love) are in turn deprived of their birthright. In previous chapters, we have made a case for this birthright as at once Buddhanature and that which is facilitated and transmitted by Buddha's Mom. The real news concerning Bowlby's attachment research concerns the degree to which even this foundational dimension of the feminine principle remained hidden for so long. "Her" absence across the millennia and across modernity and even across decades of psychology begs the question, how much more are we missing? We might want to draw a line and declare that at some point the feminine was finally recognized but the more one attempts to do so the more one finds evidence of ongoing marginalization.

In Buddha's time, the male-only sangha was de facto normal. Male spiritual privilege was not merely a cultural carryover but was explicitly declared as the natural extension of ultimate reality. The way it is and the way it should be. Buddha's awakening midway through his lifetime, in fact, left this marginalization intact. Change would only come after Prajapati and the other women, possibly hundreds, pushed back repeatedly, possibly over a period of years.

Even inmaps reflect the dominance of patriarchy in consciousness. Symbols of feminine wisdom such as the Wise Old Woman tend to be superimposed with Crone/Witch. Common iterations in folklore bind the deep feminine with wicked witch, evil stepmother and spinster figures. Of course, she is undeniably the Great Mother, but in countless ways this reality is disempowered.

Typical inmaps strip her down figuratively and literally, as sexy seductress and whore. Others negate her power and sexuality, for example, the frumpy, maternal, granny type. Another variety plays up the feminine's supernatural powers, while making her a virtuous consort. The virgin birth, Immaculate Conception and Christianity's Madonna fall into this domain. Feminine inmaps within a patriarchal frame tend to either get power or sexuality, but not both. All these can be understood as various patriarchal filters over the dazzling light of that which co-arises.

The light is blinding because something must be destroyed even as much more is created. The feminine is shunted in Buddhism's creation myth in familiar ways, but as suggested throughout this book, her presence is actually a vast, always-already co-arising. This unfolds across the turnings of the wheel and within the heart of both body and mind in this moment. We have already discussed Buddha's Mom from the inmap perspective but we should revisit this to better appreciate how she is in fact conspicuously absent.

Buddha's and Buddhism's official mother figure, Mahamaya was both deified and cleaved from her earth body and power base. Heavenly spirits carried her away from where she actually lived and where presumably she loved her husband and others. She did not journey of her own accord but was taken from where she had an imperfect, meaningful human existence. References to the unconscious always beget questions of free will. The myth implies we cannot will or force what is to come.

Transported from her bedroom in a dream, Mahamaya is thereby separated from where she would have enjoyed having sex, where she and her husband collectively conceived a child. The everyday miracle of love, loyalty, sex, pregnancy, and family at the heart of the recapitulation of our stunning species is maybe too close. Realities get air-brushed. Idealized forms are employed to bear witness. Mahamaya is taken, alone, to a Shangri-La, no longer a partner in an emotional attachment relationship, no longer in fixed in evolution. We will learn little about this delicate juncture, nor much else regarding Mahamaya's marriage, nor her other relationships or political life. Instead of real we get surreal, with a simultaneous re-focusing on the masculine. High in the mountains, at the mystical Lake Anotatta, an elephant ceremoniously circles and enters Mahamaya's womb. All this pomp and circumstance is a variation on an inmap: Buddhism's own immaculate conception.

At this turn, the feminine's authoritative role in species' transmission is outshined by the unnaturally, supernaturally, burgeoning masculine. Phallic-trunk and elephant heft generally leave little to ponder regarding which gender takes the lead. As Mahamaya is penetrated and conception achieved, the feminine is relegated to a contorted, biological form. Thousands of years later, Bowlby would begin to pry apart these constraints and demonstrate that biological reductionisms do not explain babies' dying of heartache. Once the male energy is released within the feminine, a countdown of nine months and eight days begins. Thereafter the dynamo "man-child" will walk and talk, and the mother, having done her biological duty will biologically end. For her retirement, she gets a return ticket to heaven and will have no more visible influence on earthly events, according to the official biography. Buddhism's creation myth performs a sleight of hand. All lays ahead and nothing behind. Here, however, we have suggested this very nothing is our species' lineage and that this same dynamic permeates consciousness and human psychology across the lifespan and within the here now.

But the feminine is present by virtue of her absence. Buddhism's foundational fable potently reflects the reality of the feminine in modernity. The male does in fact marginalize the Great Mother. Patriarchal values, where hierarchy trumps equality are often in play in violence and oppression perpetrated against cultures and minorities. The nuclear arms race and the depletion of earth's resources reflect imbalances in power and control. Patriarchy is simply a word for these misalignments where earth and other sentient beings tend to be dis-associated rather than integrated. We need more of the feminine principle to address the mass die-off of species and the warming of the planet.

The pan-dominance of the masculine reflects our species' hyper-investment in the male principle. Buddhists are correct on this score in disparaging the greedy, self-aggrandizing, egoic drives to amass and own and control. It is correct in articulating the need for matching extremes in the renunciation of these addictions and an emptying of all ego identifications. Buddha recognized that "mankind" was ready for this first unfolding of the dharma.

Perhaps the first turning should now be understood as a succession following the previous, evolutionary turning. As we have touched upon, modern Homo sapiens arose after 1.5 million years of dormancy, symbolized by the ubiquitous Acheulean hand axe. Archeology suggests there were no other innovations until 50,000 years ago when Homo sapiens suddenly left the launch pad. Ever since, soaring advances in technology, culture, art and mastery over the environment have become the new normal. This first evolutionary turning of sorts is the backdrop for each subsequent one. With Buddha's Mom we can appreciate each as a vessel transmitting a transmitting vessel. Such is the "upriver" evolutionary ground of our species' lineage.

What goes by ego (here complemented by wego) is the first thing to stabilize in the mirror during the grand advances in evolution—and it is this which Buddha fully, potently confronts. Evolutionary advances involve massive, redundant feedback systems. Among these chicken-egg/egg-chicken dense self-reinforcing forms is, as we have stressed, nothing less than love itself. Biological attachment is one name and metta another. To try to separate and isolate these dimensions along bodily and spiritual love lines is skillful because integration is achieved through differentiation. In the integral embrace, distinctions dissolve and linearity fades. Higher is lower. Love surpasses these dualities. But, of course, Buddha himself was prolific. And across the millennia, many of the great teachers are extremely prolific. Many give hundreds of talks and write prodigiously and their teaching involves the assertion of delineation and distinctions.

It is not necessary to make breathy, New Age claims in the face of integral evidence. Viewed in depth, mammalian awareness (affective neuroscience) offers a cogent model for a floor of awareness. Human sentience arises as a figure to this empirical, evolutionary background. A felt sense of "me", the so-called first person, is characterized by its singularity. Here we have employed the amalgam, self/ego/mind, to underscore this reality. Self/ego/mind, "me" as an individual, comes into existence within an encompassing field of awareness.

Since antiquity, this figure-ground duality has been expressed as yin/yang. The yang is the dynamic, masculine element. This can be likened to a concentrated point, or a point-in-motion vector. The latter has been articulated within depth psychology as the hero's journey. Yin is the co-conspiring, feminine, organic and collective ground. "She" is a never final unfolding, both ultimately void and a holding space. Any concrete, pointed version of Buddha's Mom, in fact, misses the point. But denying the concrete and precise iteration is also unskillful. Buddha's Mom's relevance, after all, is that which is concretely realized in her son. Her importance, her transmission is his dharma. This is why we have continuously suggested Prajapati and others are best understood both concretely and contextually.

To attribute "her" realm to any one vessel iteration is to remove her very essence. Thus "she" morphs across the series and is actually never separate, never not a we, a collective. In Mahamaya's dream, she and the divas join forces. Soon mother earth's watery container, Lake Anottata, becomes a motif for the uterine universe. Mother earth, as it were, cups her hands supporting nature's embryonic dance. Within this, the male is an important co-conspirator. Such is the nature of the feminine, made more fully feminine in allying with the male. In doing so, another turning or offing or vessel's transmission materializes. This is an essential fact of an integral embrace. As in the Tibetan consort relationship, a higher male and female energy is manifested as lower gender forms are transcended.

According to what Reggie Ray and other leading Buddhist thinkers refer to as Buddhism's fourth turning, the time has come to leave behind lower, less inspired forms for the feminine. Variations of forms to be transcended must be identified. Forever gussied up with local cultural garb, these actually have a very limited original range. Crudely put, patriarchy employs inmaps which constrain the feminine to identifications with the virgin, whore, mother, and crone. In thes, the feminine is sometimes praised and sometimes sullied. Note how the tale of Mahamaya and Prajapati has tones of being unsullied by intercourse. The white elephant which enters Mahamaya's womb has echoes of a "virgin birth". Prajapati enters the story not as a marriage partner, not as a woman who has decided to have sex and become pregnant. In this reading, she has only the purest of intentions, is only too ready to give fully of herself in motherly service.

As mentioned, the same virgin-mother mix exists in Christendom. Both Buddha and Jesus, the mythic elements allude, were conceived supernaturally. In this case, the supernatural spiritually bypasses the natural. Buddhism's attachment without Bowlby's runs this risk. But with Buddha's Mom as a positive, constructive force, a clearer, more integral path opens.

Reggie Ray has proclaimed Chögyam Trungpa's lineage to be post-Buddhist, open to all. He does not identify himself as the lineage holder but as a co-lineage holder in conjunction with Caroline Pfohl. In breaking the singular, serial lineage format, this marks a leap in the direction of the collaborative nature of the feminine, with transmission spreading like branches on a bush.

Both Jesus' and Buddha's creation myths are ripe for an updated interpretation, one based more in humanity, equal access, and the feminine. Each split the feminine and gave the heavenly form a tepid but hyperbolic part. Each installed a marginalized, earthly feminine woman so as not to stretch credulity too far. With the light of science and much more, we can detect, forgive, and make sense of such male excess.

As we have suggested throughout this book, evolution offers a powerful, corrective resource. Evolution's wont is to take successful adaptations to the breaking point. So-called feminists (the context of this label needs to be appreciated) grow tired of these efforts. Barbara Walker, for example, describes how historically men refer to feminine intuition. They use this term, she explains, "to avoid using its real name: intelligence."[215] In this book, we have sketched the outline of an integral attachment. This places feminine intelligence and wisdom at the very core of life, as central to the transmission of sentience. Buddha's Mom spans from a local, biological and psychological band to an ultimate, spiritual source bearing directly on Buddhism's central teachings and highest promise.

Intuition might be sketched as the body's working memory, accessible via a somatically-attuned consciousness. The long, long delay between Buddha and Bowlby and the long absence even still of a fuller encounter with Buddha's Mom is corroborated by the inconsistencies surrounding intuition. Intuition tends to be more present in women. Rather than leave lines of evidence flailing and disconnected, an integral model builds on overlaps. On average, for example, women have more access to humanity's affective ground. Increasingly functional access to an interior, implicit sense of knowing is consistent with frames such as emotional and social intelligence, on the one hand, and our natural state and Buddha-nature on the other.

Crossing such bridges takes courage and perseverance. Half-truths raise their ugly heads and confusion waits in ambush. An ultimate backdrop for the undercurrents in opposition within yin-yang, which we have touched upon, is the long plateau in early hominid intelligence and the subsequent forward pushes, continuing even now. The feminine, from the perspective of the soaring masculine, is regressive. In-turning, her pull is back and down as if grabbing the fleet swimmer by the ankles and pulling them toward the bottom of the sea.

Such a grand interplay explains why 2000 years would pass before Bowlby's eyes pried open and saw more of the feminine's truth, beauty, and power. As we have seen in detail, with Bowlby's helped nudge medicine toward a more rational orientation toward maternal care and breastfeeding. His research program has continued across the decades, as we have reviewed, evoking "adult attachment" as a major area of research in psychology. Endless examples of what we can call a more integral encountering of Buddha's Mom are available for anyone with eyes to see. These tend to expose previously fraught, yin-yang entanglements.

In *Assault on Truth*, Jeffrey Moussaieff Masson unearthed a critical—even Copernican—attachment story buried in the official Freudian archive.[216] He showed how Freud had his own eyes pried open briefly. Freud would briefly awaken and challenge the paternalistic status quo. But rejected and not embraced for his brilliance, he would soon turn away from a truth too bright and painful to withstand. Early in his career, Freud had discovered that sexual abuse, mainly incest, was the cause of deep psychological disturbance for many female patients. For over 2000 years, deep self disturbance in women was labeled hysteria. Hysteria (with Greco-Roman roots translating as "of the womb") was an official diagnostic category in the DSM until 1980.

Molestation involves an exploitation of attachment-based relationships. Commonly this also involves a manipulation of the power differential between adults and children, yielding a contortion of both sides of the love and power dynamic. Frequently the combination is part of abuse perpetrated by figures other than the primary attachment figure, e.g., the mother. The perpetrators tend to be older persons who presumably are attached, often relatives, and as such who are ostensibly extensions of the mother-child attachment dynamic.

Everyone is familiar with the varied, sordid ways these more powerful, supposedly attached older figures accomplish their crimes. These love-power distortions include a child victim being made to believe that they are a willing participant, that they are at fault and, of course, many kids are threatened in whatever ways are effective. Regardless of the specifics, the child victim experiences an abuse of attachment's essential protective function.

According to Masson, Freud stumbled upon several cases involving molestation. Presumably, these involved this mix of abuse of power and attachment-love. Freud attempted to condemn these crimes in a lecture. But the push-back from colleagues (whom according to Masson Freud so wanted to impress) was intolerable.

Viewed through the eyes of Buddha's Mom, Freud himself lacked a strong attachment anchoring and species' transmission. Paradoxically, he sought connection, mirroring and adoration from his colleagues. From our perspective, Freud sought motherly, attachment-love from a hands-off, hierarchical, competitive, patriarchal medical establishment. Colleagues rejected Freud's paper declaring molestation as the true cause of hysteria. It seemed an existential threat to patriarchy. Masson cites a quote from fellow psychiatrist, Conrad Rieger, which provides an example of how Freud received yang aggression rather than mother-love:

> "I cannot believe that an experienced psychiatrist can read this paper without
> experiencing genuine outrage. The reason for this outrage is to be found in
> the fact that Freud takes very seriously what is nothing but paranoid drivel
> with a sexual content—purely chance events—which are entirely
> insignificant or entirely invented. All of this can lead to nothing other than a
> simply deplorable 'old wives' psychiatry."[217]

Masson's amazing book uncovers how entrenched, small-minded competition and bravado assaulted the truth and won the day, leaving girls to suffer a scientific muting for many more decades. Overcompensation was the norm. The entire psychiatric enterprise longed for elaborate, conceptual, abstract formulas to bolster its self-importance. Already a vulnerable stepchild of medicine with its inevitable discussion of emotions, fantasies, and feelings, psychiatry had to come out swinging. Freud had naively dared to suggest that high-minded and arcane explanations be replaced by the very opposite. His announcing that seedy, concrete, sexual deeds were common and causal was more than the establishment could handle. Perhaps some of these males were themselves quite familiar with incest. Perhaps the pushback, as Freudians define it, was a reaction formation.

As mentioned, molestation and other forms of child abuse involve broken and exploited attachment. The mechanics of the abuse gets the limelight, but the damaged to the victim's emotional capacities is the more encompassing and devastating factor. This damage stems from having abuses of trust, confidences and presumed caring and protective interpersonal dynamics—and what we now recognize as attachment. For Freud to hint at this possibility was an affront to patriarchal order.

This time Freud blinked but a few years later, thankfully, Bowlby (a Freudian psychoanalyst himself) did not. Also not to be overlooked is the fact that regardless, the feminine remains a potent, living force even when she is denied. Interestingly, Freud's notion of a womb wounding fits snugly with Buddha's Mom. Research already discussed implicates an extending of the womb from biological to the psychological we-space and social attachment expanses. Indeed Freud's entire emphasis on the unseen, hidden and unconscious world may to some degree stem from an implicit, naïve, direct encounter with the same in himself. Also worth noting, in Freud's patients (and continuing today), the feminine announces its rebuke of trauma and oppression in producing disease of the deep self and heart. Our hearts can go out to those first small voices who told Dr. Freud their stories. Despite their experiences, they were brave enough to share their truth when they perceived the presence of someone ostensibly with the skills and intention to help, e.g., where attachment-love was at hand.

Even before Masson's book came out, a lot of ink was spent on Freud's own psychology, paradoxically, of parental rejection and of wanting to be accepted. His relationships with his father and with Carl Jung, for example, have been interpreted as reflecting Freud's deep-seated emotional wounds and needs. These findings are yet another lens on the feminine. Although Freud veered from the facts, he shed more light on the feminine than many realize. He put the unconscious on the western map. He, or she through him metaphorically, pioneered the "talking cure". This forged the space within science no less for what has become the main vehicle of formal forms of emotional healing. Over time, these have increasingly grappled with and integrated attachment-love. The "third force", humanistic movement's call for unconditional regard is a prime example.

The huge movement in the West towards personal growth, yoga, and mindfulness comes on the heels of the establishment of psychology and psychiatry. This is characteristic of what we are calling Buddha's Mom. She is hidden even as she is practically everywhere. We can appreciate psychotherapy and counseling as a practice combining, sitting, talking, listening, and forms of reparative attachment within a we-space. Modalities are endless but generally share a focus on psychological dukkha and efforts to bring about its cessation. Forward-leaning fusions of science and spirituality, such as Kabat-Zinn's mindfulness-based stress reduction, are no longer just given lip service. Through these various back alleys and side entrances, an integral attachment is in the offing.

But, what's taking this one-attachment, this one-love as embarkation and transmission, so long to gain a footing? Despite the rich and multi-layered evidence of the human psyche's ultimate nature as a biological, emotional vessel of attachment-as-love *and* as human lineage, "she" has yet to gain prominence in Buddhism or in any other refined, established approach to spiritual awakening. We have discussed various possible explanations for any delay or suppression of such a grand integration. These accounts tend to be both convincing and partial.

Perhaps like a fine wine, Buddhism had to first mature in the Tibetan highlands. It needed to evolve from its initial, hard-core, masculinized, renunciate focus and embrace physical, emotional, and spiritual longing, desire, and lust as deeply natural, ultimately tantric portals rather than fetters. Scholars have traced this great turning to the coalescing of early, indigenous Indian Buddhism, Taoism, and early Ch'an, dating to around 900AD. This alchemy migrated to Tibet maturing as Buddhism's esoteric expressions (Vajrayana, Dzogchen, Tantra). Its dharma translates as a more personal and vivid vessel for awakening. The immediacy, messy, fearful, lustful aspects of the human journey are divine entryways. In our time, Tibetan Buddhism has even produced a Dalai Lama who wishes for all of this to be scientifically analyzed.

Yet despite all these developments, the "two attachments" remain quite estranged. A unified theory encompassing science and spirit unification remains at bay. This despite the many years that have passed since Darwin's and Bowlby's, now Panksepp's breakthroughs, and despite massive research on the brain's parts and pieces. Further, much of what has been discovered has an unsurprising, natural, intuitive quality. "Primitive", indigenous peoples in their own ways acknowledge that humans share much with animals, that we all have feelings and sentience. Grandmothers throughout time would hardly be surprised to learn that there is much more to maternal attachment. That attachment is a delicate, critical, sweeping process impacting mental and interpersonal functioning across the lifespan, shaping our deepest sense of identity and meaning in life. Finally, at least a precious few—Siddhartha, Jesus, Teresa of Avila, Rumi, for example—have managed to awaken independent of any particular advances in Buddhism or science, and all seem to do so by way of the feminine though she goes largely uncredited.

The delay in Buddha's Mom as an established model of spiritual awakening and practice form can be ascribed partially to various factors as these. But, as we discussed, is also related to the lack of integration of the feminine principle. This fact, alongside evidence of the countervailing masculine, yang principle, helps to answer the question, *What is taking so long?* Through Prajapati and many others, related to or who otherwise knew and loved Siddhartha, we have tried to appreciate the actual centrality of the feminine, attachment-love, as intrinsic to any valid model of realization. In this aspiration, one more person deserves special mention.

After Prajapati married King Suddhodana, she gave birth to Buddha's half-brother, Sundarananda, and half-sister, Sundarīnandā.[222] Like so many in her family—including her brother, two cousins, and of course, her mother, Sundarīnandā too would renunciate the material world and become an ascetic. But she "of delightful form" was unique. She felt no particular confidence for the formal teachings and, in the end, gave in out of a blood love for her family and relatives, and not out of faith.

One can make too little or too much of such tales. But in light of the evidence of attachment-love and integral attachment, some speculation is fitting. Sundarīnandā was an unmarried female in a highly patriarchal culture. She was in close proximity, throughout her whole childhood, to Siddhartha. As he gained in spiritual mastery and fame, as her brother and mother renounced their wealth and power, the pressure on Sundarīnandā to go along, get along to be wowed into conformity, would have been intense. Perhaps she was just dense or rebellious. But a more logical and balanced possibility has a deep resonance. What survives of her biography, once the patriarchal overlay is removed, is entirely consistent with the ideas presented here. Even if young and stubborn, her stubbornness may have been an intuitive, indigenous response based in the feminine principle. How, she might have asked, can denouncing or abandoning love for one's mother, brother, and family be justified? For our purposes, she may have, in her own unique way, insisted that attachment-love was not an anathema to her half-brother's teaching regarding attachment and suffering.

Per usual, the Pali Canon documents a masculinized management of Sundarīnandā's nonconformist attitude. To avoid crediting her for knowing that attachment-love should be (in Wilberian terms) included and not negated, not renunciated, the story makes some awkward shifts.

We learn that Sundarīnandā is a little too stuck on her own beauty and vanity. Buddha learns of his little sister's confusion and gives her an audience. He gently helps her realize the impermanence at hand. Her beauty will fade, and alas she too enters the sangha. Sundarīnandā's concern with the feminine principle, with the emotional lovingkindness that flows between people is left aside with no more mention. With this move, that which we have documented as scientific fact, an evolutionary given, as attachment-love, quietly fades to black. And yang, as lone male, law and rules, ends up credited with yin even while indirectly dismissing her—per usual. Buddha and Buddhism are shortchanged by these sorts of canonical renderings.

Diotima

Another iteration of Buddha's Mom (also where the male comes out on top) pulses from the very epicenter of Greek philosophy. This time her signifier is Diotima; she is a seer, a wise woman, and a priestess. This otherwise obscure figure makes her surprise showing in *The Symposium*, one of Plato's most celebrated works. To the surprise of all gathered, the great Socrates identifies her as his very own, original "instructress in the art of love."[218] She is, he explains, a "woman wise in this and in many other kinds of knowledge."[219]

Let us recall that Plato is among Greece's greatest philosophers and that his teacher (and here we might think in terms of transmission) was Socrates. Socrates, who gave his name to the Socratic Method, is often referred to as the father of Western philosophy. Diotima, if truly a major, original source of wisdom regarding love, deserves to be something more of a household name herself. Not only did Diotima and Prajapati live during approximately the same time period, the former is theoretically of "the West" and the latter of "the East"—a distinction the feminine would not abide.

The context for Diotima's entrée is important. Symposia were ritualized drinking parties in which men of means would relax on couches, drink, eat, be entertained and hold conversation. Sex with younger males was not an uncommon part of these festivities. The Symposium is a depiction of a particularly special one of these unique Greek bashes. There is no agreement about how much of Plato's narrative is an objective recounting of actual events and how much is artistic license. Fortunately, the ideas presented up to now support love having a transpersonal, species' authorship. This hypothesis can be further tested by way of Diotima-Socrates-Plato.

On this particular night, both the set of attendees and the proposed topic of discussion were most auspicious. The subject was the Greek god Eros, the god of sexual love. Those gathered took turns giving speeches in his honor. Anticipation built as each speaker showed off his oratory prowess. The speakers pontificated on the nature of love, of erotic love, of beauty and implications for the ultimate questions concerning the meaning in life. Implicitly, the great Socrates would be one of the last and those before him would compete for his attention and praise. When Socrates' turn finally came, he surprised all gathered by crediting an unheard-of priestess as his own, original teacher.

An appreciation for the heated, homoerotic atmosphere and backdrop of a misogynistic culture helps frame this allusion to some sort of priestess, a crone woman with a feminine-based wisdom. The all gay, all male, all famous would surely have been almost fomenting by the time Socrates took his turn and dropped this bomb. Other elements seemed to pile on. The side-dish flute girls sometimes in attendance at such posh symposia had been dismissed. Remaining were a select set of esteemed representatives of poetry, tragedy and politics. All were eager to perform, to match wits and perchance to seduce or be seduced intellectually and possibly sexually. All gathered there not just to orate on Eros, love, beauty and the good life, but to dive in and live it.

Per usual, Socrates eschewed any direct claims to truth even as he tossed others' ideas to and fro with philosophical aikido. In introducing what he was taught long ago by Diotima, he seemed to incite disappointment if not anger. As a wise woman, witch and crone figure, she was the antithesis of a homoerotic object. With the same move, he also kept hope alive. One might say he actually teased those in hot pursuit of his approval and affection. For he was offering those gathered who made their adoration extremely clear a peek into his very own intellectual journey.

As we have endeavored to show, by moving backwards into Bowlby and biological attachment, we can move more fully into the upper reaches of Vajrayana. With all such devices, up/down, forward/backward, all so-called opposites, especially yin-yang, a shift in perception beckons. One of both/and either/or and neither/nor. We see with increasing clarity. We feel with a more accurate heart. We inhabit a more reality-based ocean of existence. In the Symposium, there is a reckoning of so many opposites and essential elements. The Priestess Diotima offers a contrast with the revered male orators. These mouthpieces rest in repose, take turns, sparring in a most dignified manner with words and ideas. Diotima's art and science is indigenous and shamanistic, that which males in Greece and in India referred to as "mysteries".

The mysteries get both negative and positive patriarchal billing but are always rendered as otherworldly. The reader will recall the dream visions of Siddhartha's biological mother, Mahamaya. Her sisterly divas took her on a magical sojourn to a mountain lake. There a white elephant appeared, encircled her and entered her womb. Milarepa's mother taught him the black arts in this vein. These are black from a patriarchal perspective, and indeed Milarepa used these powers to wreak deadly havoc on his cousin's wedding feast. With Diotima, we learn that she engaged in these mysteries as a plague approached the city of Athens. This successfully "delayed the disease ten years."[220]

Love, Diotima explained to Socrates and to those gathered, unfolds in stages like rungs on a ladder. Diotima's "ladder of love", as it has come to be called, is plainly an integral "great chain" form. She articulates at least three major rungs: body, soul, and an upper realm reserved for the likes of Socrates. This is the rung of love, *philos*, and of wisdom, *Sophos*, which form the word and vocation, philosophy.

Love, she declares, is "not a god at all."[221] Love is our human nature. Love is eros, erotic love, not Eros. This earth goddess, concerned with and capable of relieving suffering, had something quite radical to teach, for example, about the Greeks' tradition of (what currently goes by the term) pedophilia. She taught that male beauty (or as those gathered at the Symposium and their culture at large tended to refer to it, beauty) transcends the physical realm. The older male, if adequately wise, does more than have his way with one beautiful boy after another. Such attempts to know beauty are never achieved because beauty is an ideal form.

This is realization at the next rung up, the "soul" level. At this stage, men and boys behave in a Symposium-like manner. The beautiful mind of an older male sees his lover's beauty and other boys' beauty and chooses not to play the field endlessly or dispose of or trade one love object for another. His sense of beauty includes and transcends the gross, sexual, bodily level. He thinks of his mentee in a special way. Even when they are apart, attachment-love's secure base shimmers. "The touch of the beautiful... is ever present to his memory."[222] A tantric lava lamp of lovingkindness is emancipated. A body-mind spaciousness is awakened.

Meanwhile the lower body level houses well-meaning heterosexuals and the necessities of marriage, family, kids, and procreation. This is less cerebral and more action-oriented. Body-rung love fuels procreation and the next generation. Up a notch, the older male's soul-love begets discourse. "He is full of speech about virtue and the nature and pursuits of a good man."[223] He will use drama, tragedy, and other established, high forms (perhaps we can say, "white arts") to impart knowledge of virtues such as prudence and courage.

All this is possible because, as Diotima declares, the essential status of what we have called self/ego/mind, at every rung, is pregnancy. Mind or soul as noun, as nature, output and authorship is plural, collective and successive. As verb, mind is carrying, creating, making, and birthing.

Plato carried Socrates carrying Diotima who declared that there existed "souls which are pregnant—for there certainly are men who are more creative in their souls than in their bodies."[224] Such men, such as those presumably in attendance that night, "conceive that which is proper for the soul to conceive or contain."[225] This hearkens back to the literal connotation of dharma as that which bears, contains, or carries. The dharma of the soul, Diotima asserts, is pregnant and generative. Mind as such conceives and gives birth to concepts (conceptions). "And what are these conceptions?—wisdom and virtue in general."[226] Such notions of mind and sentience can be refined as transmission.

Before continuing, let's circle back to Aristophanes. As the representative of comedy, he has presented an oddball, mystical vision of human love's origins. Ancient pre-humans were a sort of two-in-one creature, he explained. These double creatures came in three forms: male-male, female-female, and male-female. On the sides of a single head were two faces. A torso shared two sets of arms and two sets of legs. As with the naïve tantric insights of Diotima's ladder, this vision reveals an innate, implicit access to the roots of the sexual drive and attachment drive in our species.

As Desmond Morris described in the *Naked Ape*,[227] multiple, critical interlocking factors in the rise of our species included frontal, face-to-face signaling. Fuller frontal breasts in females were selected for, co-opting the buttocks look, and function as a sexual feature. The breasts helped turn things around, also, with the cooing, eye contact, warmth, and suckling occurring during breastfeeding. This and other co-occurring developments, such as changes in the morphology of the vagina, promoted "prolonged face-to-face pre-copulatory activity,"[228] recognizable here as a substrate of tantric wego consciousness. Previously, we have pointed out that this is consistent with "social attachment", pair bonding, and the evolutionary origins of attachment-love.

Aristophanes' speech seems to be an unconscious wrangling with this development given obvious, implicit facts. Greek culture and Diotima's ladder holds male-male intercourse and discourse both as superior. Where the former is comparatively less face-to-face compared to the inferior male-female variety, the latter, the mentor relationship, is presumably a higher, purer form of lovemaking.

> The protuberant, hemispherical breasts of the female must surely be copies of the fleshy buttocks, and the sharply defined red lips around the mouth must be copies of the red labia... (You may recall that, during intense sexual arousal, both the lips of the mouth and the genital labia become swollen and deeper in colour, so that they not only look alike, but also change in the same way in sexual excitement.) If the male of our species was already primed to respond sexually to these signals when they emanated posteriorly from the genital region, then he would have a built-in susceptibility to them if they could be reproduced in that form on the front of the female's body... The use of lipsticks and brassieres immediately springs to mind...[229]

Aristophanes' double bodies offer a scheme putting the three gender combinations on equal footing: male-male, female-female, and male-female. As noted, Socrates-Diotima then decided to elevate the male-male variety. Perhaps this was Aristophanes' contribution to a preconscious rung. It offers a reminder that when one flies too close to the sun, the gods offer a market correction. One may in fact face plant in "humus"—Latin for ground, earth and soil, and the root of humiliation. Aristophanes told those gathered how these double bodied pre-humans, "tried to make an assent to heaven in order to attack the gods." Accordingly, the gods were enraged. No more evolutionary Eden. Zeus decided to maim rather than annihilate the human race with thunderbolts. He would cleave each double body in half.

> After the original nature of every human being had been severed in this way, the two parts longed for each other and tried to come together again. They threw their arms around one another in close embrace, desiring to be reunited, and they began to die of hunger and general inactivity because they refused to do anything at all as separate beings.[230]

When one's better half died, the bereft partner would go about looking for their missing half—much like Kisa in the mustard seed tale. Some would find other half-women and half-men, cling all over again and eventually die. The poet's image is one of a Tantric-tanhā state, a desperate, chronic clinging that arises when the subject makes an object of love. The original (evolutionary) nature of their sexuality was no longer functional. The way that their double-unity had first been severed was precarious. When they tried to re-form as one, they were sexually incompatible.

This may be the poet's way of portraying great leaps in evolution from a Greek-tantric sensibility: the genitals of the separated double units did not allow for procreation or pleasure. So Zeus saw fit to move "their genitals round to the front" enabling heterosexual couples to "reproduce by intercourse... and if a man encountered another man, at any rate they might achieve satisfaction... and get on with the business of life."[231]

Judgment is easy in hindsight, as the saying goes. In this case, we see males justifying what is now abusive and illegal. We witness an all-male group co-opting the sort of rich, emotional attachment that imbues the lover to transmit life's most essential lessons to their beloved. To get anywhere with any of this is like trying to climb a waterfall. Getting past pregnancy as mere metaphor is just the beginning. The torrent of evolutionary data includes the cooing and face-to-face scaffolding of maternal attachment underlying intimate speech and the richest of emotional bonds.

Yet with additional light shed from Buddha's Mom, one glimpses the unstoppable force of Tantra. Sexual love is revealed to be uncontained by sex and beauty. Eros seems to reveal the sweetest of intentions within sexual desire, rendering power not as love's opponent but as its twin. There is a quality of naiveté, of an uncut diamond, to this wego occasion. Multiple approaches to cutting through, appreciating its magnificent facets are equally valid, as is doing nothing whatsoever. Words or silence, this carbon perfection can be appreciation in endless configurations.

One cut is decidedly Dionysian. This Greek god of wine and ecstasy is referenced early on when Agathon cautions Socrates that in the end Dionysus will evaluate their respective claims to truth. Further, as the festivities ensue, we learn that Dionysian drinking, often mandatory at symposia, will be optional. Apparently, plenty of the typical forced beckoning of Dionysus occurred the night before. Dionysus carries trickster energy, where frames are continually set and then upended. This inmap serves to help humans exploit and manage the tension between oppressive order and chaos. Chaos may harbor order of another magnitude. Other inmaps, such as the sage/crone funneling a higher love and broader wisdom, for example, translating into advances in civil rights, may have little chance without chaos. Such is the golden nugget referred to as "crazy wisdom".

In this vein, the old hag Diotima figuratively crashes the party. Then before morning comes, an outright Dionysian character literally does so. With his arrival, the story shifts back to an adoration of male beauty. For he, Alcibiades, is revered across the land as gobsmackingly beautiful and a warrior to boot. As Alcibiades stumbles into the now after-after party, the narrator seems intent on relaying that we are in the archetypal space of Dionysus. Alcibiades repeats Agathon's earlier reference to Dionysus as an ultimate arbiter of truth.[232]

Doing this god of chaos proud, Alcibiades is so inebriated that he has to be held up by the flute girls. As drunks will do, he unravels. He declares it futile, despite his own beauty and Socrates' lack thereof, to seduce the great philosopher. He is soon pleading for permission just to lie by Socrates on his couch. The Symposium's high-minded hope to define and celebrate beauty seems to be going to pot. But even as Alcibiades undermines order, he restores it. Enter the trickster, ready to drag all involved, flailing, protesting or ready to kill, to a more integral state.

From a modern, evolutionary perspective, we can appreciate how Alcibiades' animal nature extends Diotima's thesis. She has asked Socrates about eros, and what we have framed here as desire and attachment. "But why again does this extend not only to men but also to animals?" Her answer to herself is, "Because they too have an instinct of immortality." She paints the allure of permanence in subtle ways. Across life stages and body changes, a "new mortality is always taking the place of the old."[233] We sense that "there is no sameness of existence."[234] We make, give, and receive love and we sacrifice for those we love. Channeling the essential ideas of this book and modeling what will become known as the Socratic Method, Diotima inquires:

> Socrates, what do you think is the cause of this love, this desire? Don't you see how terribly it affects all the wild animals, both those that run on the ground and those that fly, when they desire to procreate? Do you see how they are all stricken and affected by the activities of love, first in intercourse with each other and then in taking care of their young? And how ready the weakest among them are to fight the strongest for the sake of their offspring,

and even to die for them? Do you see how they will exhaust themselves by
starving in order to feed their young, and would do anything else for them?
One assumes that human beings do these sorts of things on the basis of
reason but what causes wild animals to be so affected by the activities of
love?[235]

What an impeccable description of relative attachment! Note how much turns on the succession, detaching-attaching (negating, preserving) as a new mortality takes the place of the old. This occurs "first in intercourse with each other and then in taking care of their young." The passage echoes Panksepp's subcortical substrates and the mammalian centers that arise in various combinations of desire, lust and love. No one word or phrase achieves One Taste but the "instinct of immortality" packs a sublime punch.

Soul love might be defined as spirit's response to beauty of body and mind, to beauty as an ideal, a paramita even. In soul music, there is a depth of emotionality, sexuality and a visceral response to the joy and pain of life which arcs toward spiritual perfection. This tradition, famously with its African roots, is a meditation of the flawlessness of every deep human experience even and perhaps especially life's darkest passages.

We are naturally drawn to Buddhism's authenticity. We feel its soul through the man that here we have also tried to portray as a son, husband, father and caring friend. Hundreds of millions of us are compelled by how hard this one man worked, walking great distances, spending countless hours talking, trying to relay that which is wordless.

The Greeks tended put the accent on love as *desire for knowledge*. Buddhadharma toggles from this yang bent, with an accent on knowledge and wisdom, and one based in metta, with both aimed at the cessation of suffering. In both traditions, the older, more realized sages are mainly male and are inspired to talk, teach, and transmit wisdom.

Where the feminine has a footing, love is portrayed as wisdom's mother and ultimate home. From the mouth of the mysterious Diotima, we glimpse a tantric, Greek bodhisattva. While it is easy in a modern light to find fault, the Symposium speaks to an authentic discernment within antiquity and all attendant historical and cultural constraints. In keeping with the major theme of this book, marginalization of the feminine is not without problems.

On both the Greek and Tibetan sides of the continent, inspired male sages transmitted their love and wisdom to their younger charges. While pedophilia was not a sanctioned path, sexual love, *eros*, was incorporated in both the Greco-Roman and esoteric tantric traditions. The sort of child sexual abuse that came to light recently, where young monks in a Bhutan monastery told their stories to journalists, certainly has occurred more than was ever recorded.[236] The catholic church's legacy of the same is seldom discussed from the perspective of the deep feminine. Some views of karma hold that each of us has been in most, perhaps all, of the roles described and that judgment only perpetuates our cycling. The more fruitful path leaves be opportunities for judgment, choosing silent expanse instead. In less self-assuredness there is less self, less illusion.

The feminine empowers this possibility. Exemplars such as Diotima, Prajapati, and Teresa of Avila can help refine forms of metta not based in eros. A yin perspective is needed on, for starters, the other major forms of love identified by the Greeks: philia, storgē and ágape. This would help extend the Eightfold path to include "right love" and differentiate correct, healing, transformational consort-based eros from related, unskillful klesha forms. Modern examples of romance, dating, and intimacy infused with spiritual transformation are sorely lacking.

All such challenges make sense within an expansive evolutionary paradigm. Such a context houses what we have tracked as the ascendency of our species' intelligence and that undergirding self/ego/mind. In the current light, we appreciate leaps in consciousness as the evocation of the yang pole of the Tao. As reviewed, in yang the light is cast upon the change over the static dynamic. We celebrate the hominid that climbed down from the trees, stood up on two legs and finally took its first steps out of a long, dull dormancy. The beast crawls out of the muck and the first sprigs of life emerge from the primordial soup.

At yang extremes, a homoerotic narcissism takes hold. Yang sees only its own reflection and proclaims the good, the true, and the beautiful and all that matters in masculine terms. The feminine is denied, disparaged, minimized and the like. Shadowy extremes are only transcended with far less active judgment and with the stillness permeating wisdom and compassion. Ultimately yang is inevitable, necessary, extant, and factual; and never more important than now as a new integral age unfolds. In Buddha's Mom and Buddha, the yin and yang are transcended/included and attached/detached and a higher integration is more accessible. All is conveyed through her and realized in him. Judgment by any name is borne of claims that separate. One stakes one's claim to truth to that which is unified, continuous spirit.

Obscenities of child abuse and misogyny, besides remaining a continuous problem over the millennia now amount to scales impacting global weather patterns, species' prospects for survival, and water and food supplies on grand scales. We would do better if we knew better. The symposium portrays how the feminine takes the gathered males as far as they can bear. She first unpacks love as rungs on a ladder. This active, upward mobility spotlights the rise from animal to average folk to great and virtuous politicians, poets, tragedians, and military generals.

More subtly, Diotima pulls Socrates' in a downward, earthly direction toward stillness. Here the feminine adds something precious to what Siddhartha famously perceived as the impermanence of disease, old age and death. Diotima too acknowledges that, "hair, flesh, bones, blood, and his whole body"[237] age and change. Yet, she notes, "Parents love their children."[238] Where Siddhartha spoke to the illusory nature of any attachment to life, Diotima emphasizes the impulse to love. For her, this compels animals and what we might call average tribe members, citizens or householders, to make love, sacrifice and procreate. She is rather nonjudgmental and objective in these proclamations. Up a notch from the biotic realm, the "soul creates not children, but conceptions of wisdom and virtue." This ensures that soul-level men and boys are "married by a far nearer tie and have a closer friendship than those who beget mortal children"[239] All us sentient beings are instinctually compelled to love. Nature's eros presses and breaks through. Between major rungs are mini-rungs, in "perpetual succession."[240]

Her ladder turns into a slide as Diotima promotes an "in betweenness of philosophy." Love for her is nonlocal. She stretches to reach those who speak spatial, hierarchical language. Love is "halfway between God and man" and "halfway between mortal and immortal." In a particularly Buddhist tone, she teaches that, "thoughts and desires of the mind… even knowledge comes and goes." Plato indeed has Socrates sounding very Buddhist as Diotima completes her input, "that which love desires is not that which love is or has."[241] This is similar to a Zen pointing out instructions that follow the logic, *I have thoughts… but I am not (only) thoughts.* Here this extends to, *I have desires* (attachments, attractions; for example, the hunger to be virtuous and wise), but *I am not reducible to these.*

The feminine-informed "I" is not fully defined by its identifications. Diotima, Socrates, Plato, the nameless nursemaids, Prajapati—no one has claim to the feminine. As a plural and boundless source, "she" presses through evolution and transmits. She is our species' download, critical to advances in human intelligence and psychology across evolution. As a local priestess, Diotima represents the Oracle of Delphi. All three of Greece's greatest alpha philosophers, Plato, Socrates and Aristotle, had important associations to the Oracle. In their time, this was recognized as a source of feminine wisdom. In keeping with the ideas presented here of Buddha's Mom as a feminine conduit to our species' spiritual lineage, any one priestess was more of a medium than a uniquely wise individual. Similar to Prajapati and the nursemaids, Diotima is an unsung vessel known more for her precious cargo.

In the case of the Oracle, research suggests that a pre-patriarchal, Goddess-centered temple, dating back to at least the eighth century BC was eventually converted in dedication to Apollo. We have touched on how the feminine principle was once symbolized by the serpent-snake-dragon motif. The Garden of Eden is one of innumerable examples of the vilification of this once revered symbol. The archetype of the male hero slaying the dragon is another example. Typical phallic weapons are spears, swords, and arrows. In line with these basic discoveries of depth psychology, a great python once symbolized the ancient temple. Mythological sources have Apollo killing the python with an arrow. Ever since, the priestess associated with the temple has been identified as "the Pythia".

The rendering of the feminine as oracle, as speech, voice and words may inadvertently track the Greeks' obsession with verbal skillful means, with rhetoric, poetry, comedy, and drama. The Symposium's male superstars were renowned representatives of the major word forms. Their gender, the competition, the hype and hyperbole are characteristic of the male principle, which in this case goes far in co-opting the oracle. The voluminous Canon, the Bible's "word of God", are foundations which stem from objectifying words and are derivative. "In the beginning was the Word, and the Word was with God, and the Word was God."[242] There are commandments, "truths" and dharma as law. If the tripitaka is a basket, words are the constituent clay or straw. In particular, Buddhism's lists reveal an infatuation with the word list form.

Word worship, of course, is not 100% error free, as Wilber would remind us. No gender owns this outrageous, resplendent human species' facility to use words. In fact, the manner by which the deep feminine shapes what has come to us as the Socratic Method deserves a few more.

Recall how one of Socrates' students once asked the Oracle if any man was wiser than Socrates. Let us immediately appreciate the nameless student's curiosity. The Oracle's response was a negation that left open many possibilities. Socrates' genius was in letting the seemingly obvious be just so. He did not presume to be alpha, wisest in the land, nor did he overly squash yang's beautiful hierarchical aspect. Rather than brandish words as swords, he sought greatness. He cultivated (we can appreciate now) a spiritual practice of questioning others and listening. Sure he used the cutting, discriminating power of words, but throughout his life, he did so with the premise, if not the awareness, that what he did not know comprised an even greater portal to wisdom.

Word-wise, an etymological fiber common to orator, oracle, and orifice includes ōris which means mouth. This offers reinforcement for the force that we have explored as Buddha's Mom. Orifice is at once a vagina-vessel-grail motif and one consistent with baby-suckling, nature-nurture and nourishment. Mother Earth's orifice as Source—of life, love, and wisdom—does not require any convoluted explanation. When associated with mouth-speech, this inmap is well on its way to developing into the Greeks' beloved forms of oration. These readily cross into the yonic-phallic, yin-yang realm. The throat and mouth have a quality of hollowness and of a vessel or conduit. With words and speech, there is an active, outward push, indeed into the ear orifices and minds of listeners.

To put it mildly, the Greeks' celebrated the species' achievement. The glory, the beauty, the mastery of a strikingly handsome orator was climactic. Dynamic hollows in the head, the orifices of speakers' mouths and listeners' ears and eyes embody a rich Tantric sensibility. To wit, the penis is an inside-out vagina and vice versa, aligned with Dzogchen's declaration of "empty cognizance suffused with awareness."[243] The Oracle and Diotima can be fashioned as Socrates' feminine side, and Socrates' eminence as the feminine's dynamic power and wisdom.

Socrates mouth orifice was only half of his greatness. He was also defined by his use of the other, less flashy orifices on the sides of his head. How artfully he practiced the black art of listening to egos everywhere, all manner of claims on truth, and combined this with the lofty white art of rhetoric. Out of his mouth, in effect, was the snake's exquisite tongue, picking up scents, movement and penetrating cues regarding the other in the self-other dance.

Socrates' profundity is best framed as both receptive and expressive, and thereby as transcending these. He used words to elicit words not just to crush the other, but often to accomplish what we would appreciate as a series of rich wego occasions. This facility has justly rendered him among the most famous people anywhere ever. In such exchanges, his first words would both begin to shed light on the other's shortcomings, but just as importantly would not lead inexorably to any particular counterpoint. Another's claim to knowledge was not left at incorrect but subtly honored because of its shadow. His way suggests a turn on the famous lyrics, "I was blind but now I see."[244] In blindness is sight. The Socratic Method is a form of practice, of wego-ing, a two-way unfolding of all we have framed as Buddha's Mom. Can we really be sure we would ever know Buddha without not just her milk but her mind?

Socrates' transgendered method was an open secret. He repeatedly declared that he did not have wisdom. He was not a sophist. He was a lover of wisdom. We can understand his way in terms of attachment-detachment where each side of wego interdependently loves the other such that love itself is realized. Close attending and receptivity are, of course, core to both Buddhist and psychotherapy practice. In this, we see that he was a lover of his fellow humans, to whom he dedicated his we-self—giving us, of course, Plato. We can add to the list an appreciation of Buddha's Mom.

The point is less the receptive-expressive tension than the embedded transcendence. Socrates received the Oracle's transmission regarding yang. His greatness (conveyed and received) was in knowing that that which he had differentiated and could display for all to see paled compared to that which he had yet to differentiate. He asked questions not to tease or deconstruct per se, but to bring more of the same flow of wisdom both to himself and those with whom he engaged, as an active, living practice. He had a lot of knowledge, but this did not fully define him. His listeners, he felt, would benefit from the same awakening.

Perhaps Socrates is an underappreciated tantric sage. Consider how he just walked and interacted with neighbors and those in the marketplace. He did not have a street reputation of intellectual dishonesty, manipulation, of being demeaning or of setting himself apart from us commoners. With Socrates, we glimpse a force of intellect that sloughed off egoic temptations. He enjoyed the pomp and circumstance of the Symposium. Yet he was not insistent on sexual or intellectual climax. Nor were his retorts to the other speakers overly harsh. He listened, spoke, entertained advances and was, it seems, mindfully present as others made their claims regarding love, beauty and the good life very much in the hope of impressing him.

As the after-after party ensued (back at the Symposium) the physically perfect, hypersexual Alcibiades was using words to achieve sexual climax. Unable to seduce Socrates with his sheer beauty, he was now eager to be seduced by the Symposium's old silverback. As this story line becomes prominent, the spotlight seems to settle on how Socrates will maneuver. But neither climax nor humiliation ever emerges. At one point, Socrates allowed Alcibiades to lie next to him. Eventually Alcibiades fell asleep. It seems Socrates was not overly egoic in all this, neither relishing sexual victory nor vanquishing.

The party wound down. Some people left; others fell asleep. The subject of the dialogue shifted. Socrates was in the process of suggesting a great tragedian was a great comedian and vice versa. Eventually Socrates tucked his sleeping friends in and walked out into the morning light. After ecstasy, routine. Socrates washed up at the local lyceum and spent the day as usual in the marketplace in conversation. At the end of the day, he returned home to catch up on his sleep, one suspects having purposefully set out to sync with the day-night circadian rhythm.

Some critiques of the Symposium highlight the idea of swordsmanship, the verbal vanquishing of rivals. These would certainly seem correct and insightful as far as they go. There is no doubt that Socrates shows off his tremendous intellect as he fends off suitors and politely implodes others' pomposity without breaking a sweat. And yes, perhaps with a smirk. But to read into such flourishes as all male, all *mano a mano* interaction, does not do Socrates and his first teacher of love justice. Such a reading overlooks Socrates' uniqueness. Western culture is overwrought with this myth of yang versus yang as the perfect methodology for picking a winner. We have knights and swordfights, British gentlemen's dares and duels, *High Noon*, cowboy gunslingers and *Star Wars'* father-son lightsaber super climaxes. I would add to this the small-minded way politics is covered in America, all the heated but hollow shoutfests and so little actual discussion of solutions for, say, human trafficking or more happiness.

The Symposium subtly busts up patriarchal givens which pit yang against yang in the pursuit of truth or perfection. Instead of some glorious victory, there is just a hollow sort of hype to the oratory fencing. In the end, this produces a coherent but low resolution Socrates. Yin elements enhance the picture tremendously. These, as suggested, have a basis in the Oracle's koan, "None is wiser." Because of the living feminine wisdom within him, Socrates knew what he did not know. Skewering less astute minds proved something, just not wisdom.

Socrates knew that he did not know "none is wiser" meant that he was wisest. Famously, he did not want to be a sophist. These were formal, paid teachers of rhetoric who, in effect, attempted to monetize wisdom. Similarly, he did not want to be a politician, poet, dramatist, or tragedian, nor did he dismiss these as unimportant.

It seems Socrates did not believe that the wisest path, the best way to spend his life, was in the advancement of such forms. He was not concerned with his words and ideas being recorded for posterity. Rather the voice and transmission of the feminine helped Socrates to live and flow in the present. He did not make an idol of total wisdom as some futuristic perfection. Just as importantly, he did he oppose such paths. He did not, we can conclude, see suppressing wisdom as wise. Here we can think in terms of neither overly attaching to wisdom nor overly rejecting and detaching from the same. All this points to skillful means with paradox.

Worth noting, as well, the term "sophist" carries the connotation of wisdom and has origins in Sophia. Multiple sources reference her as a major pre-modern Goddess renowned for her wisdom. She is also described as the female aspect of logos, as a "Universal Mother", as "the Womb, the Virgin, the Wife of the Male", and a "Revealer of Perfect Mysteries."[245] A gnostic work, entitled *Pista Sophia*, found in 1773, ties her to Mary of Magdalene. In this work, Sophia's mom, Pista, is referred to interchangeably with Sophia. Sophia, Sophia's mom is/are Buddha's Mom. This unified-multiplicity is characteristic of the feminine. She is also referred to as both the wife and the mother of Jesus (and therein to two of the many Mary's) and therein as mother or consort of the godhead. The feminine as Diotima, Sophia, Oracle and Wisdom moves in and out of familiar categories, human, god/goddess, force, emanation and paramita. This living flux of anthropic attributions of form and sentience drips resonates with Tantric conceptualizations.

Various texts discovered the nineteenth and twentieth centuries (such as the *Pista Sophia* and Gospels of Philip and Thomas) reveal how, at the beginning of the Common Era, Gnostic sects were knocking up against both one another and other mutating religious forms. Most were masculine-centric, for example, Neo-Platonism, Judaism, Mithraism, and Zoroastrianism. The ferment was due in part to the vacuum left behind as the classical Greco-Roman cosmology lost hold.

During and following the life of Christ, the feminine principle expressed in Diotima (several hundred years prior) resurfaced in the Gnostic's Sophia. Parallels to Buddha's Mom and Tantric Buddhism run through the Gnostic's cosmology, beliefs, and practices. For them, Sophia was the critical, final emanation of the universe. Her emanation precedes and shapes human consciousness. In this creation myth, an unknowable, ultimate divinity approximates the Big Bang. Although sometimes referred to as God and God, "He" was said not to be a father but rather a forefather, a non-gender cosmic parent. "He" was perfect, eternal, immeasurable, and untraceable.

Parallels to Buddhism's Tantra begin with the concept and centrality of gnosis. Rather than a god, messiah, divine anthropic form, or a person, gnosis corresponds to the ground of being imbued with qualities humans experience as profound and transcendent. This translates in static form as knowledge, but more accurately and contextually as an active, life-evoking knowing. The universe and what is eventually the human realm is set into motion because an incomprehensible, perfect and unified source of life at the center of the universe has a thought, is aware, or knows. Hence the name, Gnosticism. From the frame that we have been considering, an alternative term could be "awareness-ism" or, of course, mindfulness.

Following this initial big bang of awareness comes a sequence (in some texts, six and in others, fifteen) of yin-yang pairings. Esoteric texts refer to these in various ways, including emanations and Aeons. Again signs of Tantra are not hard to find. In Valentinianism, one of the major Gnostic traditions which forms in second century CE, these pairing were described as the yoking together of male and female principles. Each pairing was animated by gnosis and manifested in specific ways.

Male logos/word arises with female zoë/life, and depending on the specific Gnostic system, un-aging with union, self-existence with bliss, immovability with blending.

All this reaches a climax with Sophia. She introduces some familiar themes that I have suggested have a basis in patriarchy. Like Mahamaya, she has heavenly attributions. But Sophia is ascribed more power and importance with respect to the human realm.

> ...the Sophia who was in the lower heaven received authority from Pistis,
> and fashioned great luminous bodies and all the stars. And she put them in
> the sky to shine upon the earth and to render temporal signs and seasons and
> years and months and days and nights and moments and so forth. And in
> this way the entire region upon the sky was adorned.[246]

Importantly, Sophia is said not to have permission but to want to know the unknowable God/Source at the center of the cosmos. Patriarchal echoes thus include the concept of temptation and of desire as a universal source of evil and suffering. Sophia's *desire to know* juxtaposes awareness and desire. In some patriarchal contexts, awareness and desire are differentiated as male and female, respectively. But findings from, for example, Panksepp underscores how this interpretation if off-key. SEEKING is if not both, not either one per se. This master affective system is something like the very pulse of life, awareness and may co-arise a mixture of other systems. Some of these have a more neutral flavor such as thermoregulation and others load on affect and evoke the sentient pushes and pulls. Common positive variants of these substrates of desire include lust and caregiving with common opposing ones based in fleeing from danger.

An entire higher level of attachment and meaning manifests in what we have called attachment-love. Buddha's Mom embeds an argument against painting this as implicitly spiritually problematic (attachment as suffering) and is in sync with the Vajrayana as "the path of desire" — liberation *from* desire *through* desire. As I have been suggesting (speculating), many of humanity's most revered prophets and sages have come to this realization (literally and figuratively). In this, they break through local historical and cultural givens. No doubt, these same givens prevented many more from doing so, especially those with no cultural capital. It seems especially tragic that others, mothers, members of marginalized tribes and societies culturally, also awoke but their stories were never recorded.

What survives, and we are so blessed to have this, is the indirect, secondary evidence of these awakenings. This shadow canon, one could say, lives in the traces of now lost indigenous, earth-based lineages. The Great Mother/Goddess tended to have a much richer incarnation in these as scholars such as Barbara Walker track.[247] Realized persons in these mostly no-name, outsider traditions brought their understandings (realizations) regarding the feminine principle to the clashing and blending of spiritual paths, practices, and religions occurring with the increasing density of population centers and cross-pollination between these, notably during and after Buddha's and Jesus' time on earth. We have been reviewing evidence of an aboriginal feminine as a penultimate transmission, from the Pali Canon bearing on Buddha's awakening.

These indigenous forms had long since contributed to the institutionalization of the feminine that we have just explored, e.g., the Oracle of Delphi in Diotima's time, and survived in the forms such as the Virgin Mary, Sophia, and in Sufi mysticism, as seen hundreds of years later, in Rumi's explosive love.

Intriguingly, the same earth-based feminine transmission may have been counted among the early influences on Christianity by way of the Tantric tradition. The feminine, in theory, could have travelled both somatic, endogenous, intuitive, and indigenous avenues—as well as by conventional, outward means. The latter would include dissemination of knowledge, beliefs and practices, for example, resulting from trade between the Mesopotamia and India. Richard Hooper cites support of these possibilities.

> The British scholar of Buddhism, Edward Conze, suggests that it had. He points out that "Buddhists were in contact with the Thomas Christians (that is, Christians who knew and used such writings as the Gospel of Thomas) in South India." Trade routes between the Greco-Roman world and the Far East were opening up at the time when gnosticism flourished (A.D. 80–200); for generations, Buddhist missionaries had been proselytizing in Alexandria. We note, too, that Hippolytus, who was a Greek speaking Christian in Rome (c. 225), knows of the Indian Brahmins—and includes their tradition among the sources of heresy.[248]

Certain early blends of Gnosticism and Christianity embraced the divine feminine in ways that appear to be consistent with Buddhism's Tantric tradition. The Trinity was Father-Mother-Son. Some strands of Gnosticism involved secretive knowledge and practices only accessible to those who had demonstrated adequate preparation. Adherents were anointed with Chrism ointment in a ritual that may have overshadowed baptism. This involved, "the hidden mystery in which the Cross is shown to us" and possibly what in Buddhist terms was perhaps a sacred practice with the possibility of transmission and enlightenment.[249]

Consistent with Tantra, practitioners stood to inherit "the unmediated knowledge of absolute reality."[250] Rather than an emphasis on submission in water to achieve conversion, an anointing with Chrism oil removes all hierarchies and impediments, which Buddhism calls fetters. Accordingly, one's mind becomes clear as if no longer drunk with illusory views of reality. In such persons, stated Jesus, "I myself shall become he, and the things that are hidden will be revealed to him."[251] The idea of the sacred as egalitarian, as transcending the masculine and feminine, and as not reserved for ascetics was apparently well established by certain these orientations. The following passage has echoes of androgynous, Tantric divinities. These dynamic energetic systems may appear as beings of light with hundreds of arms reaching out to help those suffering.

> The Holy One said to him: "I want you to know that First Man is called 'Begetter, Self-perfected Mind'. He reflected with Great Sophia, his consort, and revealed his first-begotten, androgynous son. His male name is designated 'First Begetter, Son of God', his female name, 'First Begettress Sophia, Mother of the Universe'. Some call her 'Love'. Now First-begotten is called 'Christ'. Since he has authority from his father, he created a multitude of angels without number for retinue from Spirit and Light."[252]

Finally and also remarkably, variants on Sophia's association with desire (and therein, attachment) taints her Aeon with shadow characteristics. Sophia's desire to know, despite not having permission, the unknowable, ultimate creator of the universe introduces a sort of divine flaw or lust. The portal to deeper attainment that she introduces relies on (arises with) a wrinkle or appearance of error in the series of divine emanations.

In one uncanny vein of Gnosticism, feminine wisdom is defined from the perspective of male grandiosity. Sophia's own emanation is Yaldabaoth. This alleged miscarriage becomes the errant, flawed god of the Old Testament, e.g., Yahweh. Chief among Yaldabaoth's shadowy errors is the claim of independent perfection, that there is no other god or source. This detail within the Gnostic cosmology is consistent with the potential for corrections in yin-yang distortions, such as we have explored, be these associated with spiritual attainment or emotional well-being.

These various touchstones from Mesopotamia parallel Buddha's Mom's call for a re-alignment with the feminine principle. As a universal, feminine force, "she" encompasses so very many named and nameless humans, deities, and even Aeons. An integral model notes how the priestesses at Delphi are referred to in the singular, as "the Oracle". Plato's and Socrates' feminine aspect is another handle. She is Diotima—a woman some scholars doubt ever existed, even if she did not.

As a woman, priestess, mother, wife, consort, male shadow, or wisdom, the feminine is the yin-space within which brilliant yang arises. In this combination of multiplicity and oceanic compassion, she is the many thousand-armed bodhisattva. She lifts up sufferers, protects and carries the dharma. Yang cleaves yin space and new life shines with great glory. Often yang insists on being noticed. But as Buddhism teaches, that which arises dramatic or not is impermanent and illusory. Meanwhile, the empty space always, already shimmers. Enlightenment from emptiness refers to the pan-ordinariness, that the smallest or commonest harbors possibilities. Mount Fuji is as magnificent as an anthill and vice versa. Attaching to the thrill, beauty or tragedy has the same outcome.

Seventies TV psychiatrist and real-life comedian, Bob Newhart told his patients who asked him for advice on their suffering to "stop doing that." While "I" am/is not up to stopping a love that expands in letting go is fully armed, an embedding within cosmos more than up to the task. In this sense, Socrates too is a Buddha's Mom. He clearly loved to excel at his philosophical midwifery, and his intent tapped into the same cosmic perfection, brilliance and clarity locatable within traditions as varied as these (Greco-Roman mystery religions, philosophy, Gnosticism, and Tantra).

The penalty that Socrates would not accept at his famous trial, for which he was made to drink hemlock poison and die, was to abandon his spiritual practice. In an integral light, he was asked to choose a life outside the flow of love and declared this untenable. Life without love is no life at all. This is echoed in Nelson Mandela's imprisonment. He found a way to keep the love, the life force, flowing. While at Robben Island, Mandela chose life by accessing the dignity of his guards.

Socrates can be understood similarly, as accessing attachment-love and facilitating transmission from Diotima through his own being, on to Plato. As noted, both *dharma* and the feminine are symbolically similar, and can be rendered as a vessel, basket or bowl. Both can be defined as that which bears and carries. Socrates's dharma-vessel was the skillful means now referred to as the Socratic method. He cultivated reciprocal listening to enable self and other to expand and transcend wego spaces. This special skill has been attributed to Michelangelo, and calls for removing what does not belong. Through queries and the elicitation of others' relative reality, Socrates would identify what was not true, beautiful, perfect, and (I would speculate) Tantric—and thereby, indirectly, inversely, and potently proffer illumination.

Others forming a wego space with him would routinely find themselves detaching to previous positions with no clear back-up. Socrates' expertise remains an under-appreciated. Here we would view what he led others to, the bewildering, uncharted space, as the floor of self/ego/mind. This would give way within an immediate we-space, in conversation with him. The ultimate nature of this we-space is, of course, rendered in innumerable ways and mappable from an integral perspective.

So as to foster a transformational we-space of bewilderment and self/ego/mind disambiguation, Socrates himself was sometimes swept into the very same. This was referred to as a state of "aporia" or puzzlement.[253] Buddhists, of course, deeply appreciate puzzlement and paradox as the heartbeat of human experience. In the Tantra tradition, aporia is invited and celebrated. The protestations, chanting, and envisioning of wrathful and sensuous deities provide a basket for minds liberated of previous holds. These also provide training for this lifetime and also for the Bardo, the in-betweenness occurring in the transition from one lifetime to the next. These purposefully outlandish forms (baskets, vessels) help hold minds that are slipping sideways, successfully overwrought and bewildered, to receive what is uniquely accessible in such moments. From a normal, rational vantage, these practices necessarily appear irrelevant, beyond obscure, as stupid, hyper-religious, and animistic.

Common Sense

One of the more insidious ways the emergence of integral attachment is treated by the status quo involves the concept of commonsense. Everyone loves moms and babies and agrees babies should be fed and kept warm. Commonsense reflects a troublesome half-truth that tends to undermine the potential for attachment-love to transform.

Stubborn attachment wounding tends to come across as painfully obvious but puzzlingly stubborn. Street people who refuse "three hots and a cot" come to mind, as do repeated patterns of domestic violence where the batterer and victim change partners but not roles. Why doesn't she just leave him? Where hurt persists and remedies seem obvious, attachment may be deeply impaired. Where we are small-minded but know that something more sane and freeing is just out of reach, attachment wounding may be lurking. Multiple, stalled out initiatives, side by side with a felt sense that one knows better can gobble up years. Simple-not-easy is the go-to. Just listen to a few or a few thousand stories from those earning sobriety tokens at Alcoholics Anonymous meetings, day after year after decade. All the Jell-O that can't be nailed to the wall. The commonsense label implies that one knows what needs to happen and there is nothing really new to bring to the table.

Many people hear the call to a greater station in life and make courageous efforts at self-help and practice. The reasons vary, but frequently, the meditation, yoga, eating healthy, or sobriety lapse. Insisting that answers are obvious is not always helpful. Subtlety and nuance—and teachers and paradigms to provide these—are needed. Often the initial effort was too gung-ho. An original overreach explains why the judgment on the other side reflects little shifts in love and compassion for self and others. Suffering persists because self/ego/mind persists. Without a refined map, the so-called commonsense deduction follows. One cannot follow-through on something even obvious and simple. Failure on easy tasks substantiates larger, more eviscerating judgments lying in wait.

Missed in all this is the gentle strand of effort, of true intentionality. This is born of transcendent, tantric truths remain unbroken as mind swings side to side. On the surface, we seek to alter our minds and behavior. This is fine but can overlook that love is unalterable. As Shakespeare wrote, "Love is not altered when it alteration finds." Mind frolics to and fro. From denial and torpor to overshooting the mark. What passes for commonsense can obscure these messy mental pretzels. A Buddhist nun would certainly not purposefully stomp on an ant. Would she fly on a jet that spits carbon into the atmosphere, contributes to climate crisis in order to go to Haiti, to work in a hospital, to help victims of the earthquake? This could very well be the madness built into the human condition, proclaimed by Buddhism to call suffering. And in the suffering is a sane, small voice that says a living, workable commonsense was always, already present.

Of course, we experience lovingkindness and compassion for fellow sentient beings. Can we then have a pet? At what point is our relationship to this pet an attachment, a hindrance? At what point is our relationship with any sentient being the sort of attachment that spurs novice monks to leave family and all possessions behind? Or is this replacing one set of attachments for another? Judgments lurking off to the side keep urging us to fixate on the tennis match. Hits and misses. These drive the presumption that one should know or already knows what to do.

In the end, declaring something simple-not-easy or to be commonsense may be wishful thinking and just another way of withholding love. And here, I suggest attachment-love as potentially helpful grounding for anyone blocking love's flow. An integration of traditions of wisdom therefore teaches that emptiness is patient and kind, not jealous or boastful or proud. All we are discussing, human nature, suffering, enlightenment and more, is not commonsense—and neither is attachment.

Nagarjuna

In clarifying the nature of attachment, the great Nagarjuna (some refer to him as second only to Shakyamuni Buddha) shatters any commonsense perspectives. Like Buddha, he does not situate tanhā in biological, maternal attachment. But unlike Buddha, he places attachment and detachment on an even footing. His brilliant re-visioning of the dharma, interpreted in the current light (of Buddha's Mom), stresses that neither relative attachment pole is preferable or even closer to a new middle way.

On the relative side of the street, both attachment and detachment are entirely human and problematic. Neither is to be exalted. Neither has a monopoly on commonsense. Neither should be avoided or devalued more than the other. Extending from this clarification, attachment is no different than detachment in the eyes of Buddha.

Nagarjuna is especially famous for defining *sūnyatā*. This translates as void or emptiness and is also used as a synonym for nonattachment. Nagarjuna wrote, "It is neither void, nor not void, nor both, nor neither, but in order to point it out, it is called the Void."[254] This idea is also expressed as "not this, not that."

Wilber explains that Nagarjuna demolished all dualistic conceptual identifications. One cannot declare reality is, or is not. Further, this applies to "any concept, any *drsta*" where *drsta* refers to any manner of "conceptualizing, qualifying (or) characterizing." Mind, experience, to the extent this involves any labeling or qualifying, is something other than real. Even if one declares all to be empty, all to be form, all to be infinite, the declaration is a nonstarter. Any proclamation implodes from its own weight. "Reality is not 1) infinite, nor 2) not infinite, 3) nor both, 4) nor neither."[255]

> The self-contraction, in all its forms, is negated and transcended, and all that remains is the freely arising, self-manifesting, self-liberating structures and states of consciousness, which plug the individual into all of the realms (worldviews, domains, states, conditions, and levels) of the entire Kosmos.[256]

Teachings and meditations, by implication, can be reframed as utilizing both these imperfect avenues (attaching and detaching) as skillful means, in order to dislodge us from illusion. We may reconsider at least certain teachings as a call to attach, when previously they were perceived as a call to detach, in the service of waking up. With this, a new commonsense is born. Breath and body teachings and meditation techniques may be re-envisioned—this pedagogy of mindful attachment, as outlined by Bodhi:

> As mindfulness grows sharper, the breath can be followed through the entire course of its movement, from the beginning of an inhalation through its intermediary stages to its end, then from the beginning of an exhalation through its intermediary stages to its end. This third step is called "clearly perceiving the entire (breath) body." The fourth step, "calming the bodily function," involves a progressive quieting down of the breath and its associated bodily functions until they become extremely fine and subtle. Beyond these four basic steps lie more advanced practices which direct mindfulness of breathing towards deep concentration and insight.[257]

Playing with the language just a little, we can see how this type of instruction is not far from a call to notice with love every quirk, every dimple in our beloved, to hold, groom, protect the entire body as a mother does a baby. All of this attachment-based wisdom and pedagogy serves the goal of opening us up to the expanse on the other side. We can just as fluidly sit in quiet, and watch all these emotional eddies whirl about. These instructions tease forth ever more sublime whims of both relative forms of attachment, attaching and detaching, with an eye toward nonattachment. They point out the emptiness that is not the opposite of all life's gushing fullness.

This cosmic dance and play is the "that" in "I am that." Whenever form drops, nonattachment and liberation remain, which is what is and was always present. This is the nonattachment hinted at by an intoxicating sunset as it disappears in the blink of an eye. The space between inhaling and exhaling is another portal.

As the previous quote expresses, breath is particularly evocative. The neonate's first breath leaves all witnessing the birth holding their own. In the early weeks and months, breath supports an emerging and joyful noise. Upon reflection, the word for "mother" across the world and across history is a natural extension of the breath within the attachment dyad. So much stems from this fertile ground. A quick peek takes us across the great chain, from body to mind, and from out of the domain of words, to spirit.

In breast-feeding, babies can be seen to smack their lips as part of the innate effort to locate the nipple and latch on. The jaw and mouth open and close slightly a few times a second. With this, they inhale or suck, and then exhale to catch their breath—the two behaviors produce the /m/ sound alternating with the /ah/. In series, then, /m/ + /ah/ becomes mama. When babies want to feed, their lips naturally smack in the same manner, producing the utterance, ma, ma, ma. When the /ah/ takes the beginning position, this elicits the familiar "ohm". A word for mother in Sanskrit is *amma*.

Literally "mother", amma is embedded in compound names of goddesses. Fusions of mother and goddess are universal. A goddess worshipped by lower Hindu castes named Māriyamnam, for example, is formed of the words for mother and goddess. We have discussed modern cousins of this—Gaia as earth goddess, for example.

Consider the case for the "ah" phoneme which is a highly redundant, critically fundamental, utterly efficient, ancient utterance. The sound corresponds to the startle or distress response that Jaak Panksepp identified as sub-cortically common to all mammals and is of utmost importance for offspring. He called this PANIC/GRIEF. "Ah!" and derivatives may be the shortest, most efficient vocal distress signal. By definition, vulnerable, naive offspring, perhaps hours or days old, with minimal formal learning, would need and benefit from such an elegant, fool-proof capacity. An offspring that fails to utter necessary sounds might not survive, where one who manages to elicit a response with one signal does. Simplicity is not only important in its own right but important because there are fewer things which can go awry compared to more complex alternatives.

"Mama" and its derivatives are produced by a straight, fast exhalation and require no effortful phonemic production. Versions of this are familiar to anyone who has ever been frightened: uh and oh. In Thai, the /ah/ part rhymes with the vowel sound in the word "cat". Westerners are familiar with this sound, for example, when startled, and it can become the basic phoneme of a scream or response to an extreme shock.

Babies, of course, experience tanhā and dukkha (thirst/hunger, pain, hunger, fear, discomfort) around the clock. With few other options, they quickly learn to employ sounds to have their needs addressed. Crudely speaking, the bigger the need, the louder the crying or scream. But eventually, the mother-baby loop enables a less enervating, less laden-with-suffering response that causes mama or a local derivative to come online.

The combination of lip smack /m/ and this second, immediately available distress phoneme is, of course, a first utterance among babies in many cases. This is directed toward the milk provider, to attachment figures and those capable of providing survival related assistance. Moms respond accordingly, completing the conditioning loop.

In theory, a baby could have distinct signals to distinguish between needs or threats. There would be some efficiency in this. But the preferred strategy is a slow building, a slow unfolding. A baseline scream or cry evolves not into something else but is retained as other utterance capacities (verbal and nonverbal communication in humans) are added to a repertoire. For humans, the /m/ + /ah/ level of experience opens the door to the attachment we-space. Mamas soon hear multiple meanings in their baby's utterances. Thanks to the realm of tone and prosody, to facial signaling, and to memory, this we-space accelerates and forms a basis for subsequent psychological and cognitive development.

As mentioned, sophisticated species become so due to their ability to redundantly exploit their strengths. Evolution favors behavior which co-opts other established systems. Neurologists speak in terms of these neural substrates being recruited. Closely related to the /m/ sound, the /b/ and /p/ sounds are sometimes part of the mix. Another word for mother in Sanskrit is ambā. These alternative consonant phonemes, of course, are often used for the male "mother", as in papa. Jesus too has something important to teach us regarding the centrality of attachment in enlightenment. He referred to his God the Father as abba.[258]

The same core sound, perhaps deserving the title "music of the spheres" was finally uttered 13.8 billion years after the first sound, the Big Bang. This sound seems to return on the other side of attachment and occurs at the highest level of consciousness, which we have been at pains to describe as the upper reaches of the selfsame attachment system that exploits this vocalization. The sound Siddhartha produced as a baby and came to associate with and attach to Prajapati, would return much later when he came to understand attachment in ever deeper ways. The sound, the famous ohm is derived of the back of the mouth open phoneme, /ah/ or /oh/ and the frontal /m/. This then is the identical but reversal of /m/ah/!

A higher-self Tonglen (giving and taking) or exchange with a lower-self can creatively surf along on these waves. The exchange and dialog can be experienced as direct and natural interactions with nature, surfer and wave, wave and surfer. Personal meditations could combine this interplay with the two poles of relative attachment. One side of a meditation can be a distress call, a cry or scream, a lurching for the mother. Here is the bodily expression the two sides of the same whole, fear-hope. The weight of the world simultaneously tastes this fear, and at the same times tastes freedom, an exquisite, joyous unburdening. On this side is all of suffering and with it, the longing to finally stop longing and taste the vaunted stopping known as nirvana.

Batchelor describes this as the "how to live". Knowing how, not knowing what or that. The Four Noble Truths can be dispensed in favor of the four tasks, the four guides. The trick is how to notice oneself being light, empty, free—on the cushion or not—and accept this delicacy for what it is, getting used to this, becoming literally better at being. There is no other side. Nonattachment is not the other side of relative attachment. Whatever words or images we might attempt, the point is that nonattachment, nirvana, knowing how to live in the stream of one's humanity is deliciously ever present, both/neither within/outside. It is available when body or spirit cries out for /m/+/ah/ and comes back full circle, o/m/. The /m/ah/m/ is at once physiological and at the threshold of the upriver source of the divine. Within is the sweet, embedded /ohm/. "Ohm" is a response to the vastness, the precipice, the threshold where even body ends but awareness hums and vibrates with clarity. In "Ohm" is a more bodily liberated space empty yet meaning-filled. In it is the thread of our original, early, physiological response to that which gave us life and to that which we need to sustain it.

As one senses the emergent ohm, there's a quality of satiety and rescue, but ultimately, this does not occur by an object of any subjective state. Rather the rescue is more a release into the fully human space that liberates all fear, always. Let the lovely, earnest ego cry out, inwardly or otherwise, with the plea of pain, or maw or mom, whatever is most innate, immediate. One's "mother tongue" reflects the pain of this state of compression as a futile ego, similar to a great loving force contorted, straightjacketed, yanking and tugging at itself. On the alternative outbreath or last part of a sit, the undeniable spirit, the full self/ego/mind experiences freedom in/from its self. In virtually all such final states, one could mutter and experience ohm in humble relief.

Yoga postures can bring heat to the distress in the body-mind and soothing coolness in release. Prajapati's legacy can be felt in the mantra of amma. Her gift, the boy, the dharma, the promise that comes to us unbidden and free, evokes the bodily ohm. As she did in her life, we too can move from an earthly love to an absence of any container for love, a love unconfined, welcoming an ever-deeper abiding. The body portal opens thus, wherever there is "no room in the inn". Where there is contraction, fear and sentience is threatened, the breath, sound and somatic echo across time can bring form, coherence and joy. We may have no idea how to be, but just to be is instantly relieving. In this making/finding room we are re-inhabit the species body, materially and spiritually. Perhaps this is part of all that is meant by re-incarnating.

Reincarnation

On several occasions, Buddha invoked reincarnation to help someone reeling from the profound trauma of a major attachment loss. Ubbiri was in deep grief following the death of her infant daughter, perhaps a toddler. Buddha responded to this tragedy by explaining to her that she had suffered from similar losses in multiple, previous lifetimes. One might imagine that those who knew Ubbiri were in a desperate state, trying to help her. Perhaps she was in the midst of a nervous breakdown.

We are told, "Buddha pointed out to her that right in the same charnel ground where she had left this baby's body, she had similarly parted with thousands of children to whom she had given birth in previous lives." This is auspicious. As a younger man, he'd meditated, cold, alone, at night, with wild animals lurking about, in just such a place before his awakening.

Buddha showed Ubbiri the truth of impermanence. Loss is inevitable. Grasping is not the way. She had suffered from disease, old age and death hundreds and thousands of times. Holding on then as now was the source of suffering. Perhaps losing her baby was karmic because she was so prone to interpersonal attachments, or somehow more than most, she needed to learn to let go and transcend attachment. Perhaps, considering the rest of the story, we can interpret that Ubbiri was an old soul, had suffered more than most, and was paradoxically very close to attainment and the end of suffering.

> Ubbiri realized how her deep motherly attachment to her children had always caused her much anguish; for sons and daughters, like everything else, are subject to the law of impermanence. We cannot make our loved ones live beyond the span set by their own karma. This was an insight so powerful for her that no object at all seemed worthy of interest any longer because of the potential pain permeating them all. Thus all tendency to cling was broken, never to reappear.[259]

She suddenly knew the profundity of samsara and went from a grieving mother to an arhat. Here, as elsewhere, the Canon seems unambiguous in weighing in on Buddha's Mom. Certain logical inferences and speculations follow. Buddha's invoking of reincarnation in this circumstance, and the following example as well, may be taken as an acknowledgement that a mother's attachment-love is especially strong. He does not invoke reincarnation as often where a person's suffering arises from less intense and personal forms of attachment.

A response from a person deeply informed by "Buddha's Mom" would axiomatically be empathic in the face of the loss of a loved one, especially a baby. One interpretation then was that Buddha profoundly felt, knew and mirrored the depth of Ubbiri's emotional pain because he was decidedly, in the best possible ways, a mama's boy. He was a man completely attuned to the psychological reach of a free and loving attachment such as a mom might have for her baby girl. He may have done much more than communicate the concepts of impermanence, karma, samsara, and renunciation. He may have soaked Ubbiri in his love, compassion and understanding.

The true nature of this event and the teaching that resulted from it may have very little to do with concepts and knowledge, much as communication is said to be by far more nonverbal than verbal. As events such as this were told and retold, subtle, nonverbal, "we-space" dynamics quite understandably were lost. The focus on accuracy naturally leans towards external, objective, to the specifics that a jury of twelve might agree on: what happened, what Ubbiri said, what Buddha said.

Perhaps the account that survives is but a thin echo of the profundity of this experience. This may be true of many or most parables and stories of Buddha's encounters with followers and lay persons. A perspective grounded in Buddha's Mom might find Buddha completely consumed by Ubbiri's all-out grief and compelled to meet this with an ocean of compassion. It follows that this amounted to a transmission or conversion experience. Ubirri transcended her entire way of being and seeing, and was reborn, set free, and made into an ocean of love unto herself—in connecting with our species' lineage. Buddha's teachings regarding karma may have (amazingly and consistently) conveyed an empathic, attuned and complete realization to those who approached him in pain and confusion. If so, there can be little doubt that he used the language and some of the religious formulations of the time to hold Ubbiri and others completely within his spirit. Words regarding previous lifetimes may have conveyed his depth of a knowing-love. Being so much more than words, these encounters may have transmitted that though their suffering was greater than any one person, any one lifetime or even thousands of lifetimes could bear, his love (consistent with attachment-love) was linked to an unbounded legacy. As he personally manifested in his body, words and actions, such metta and wisdom were as real as rocks and something else entirely. The we-space opened to a vastness in which their dukkha was not even a drop to an ocean, an authentic and present dharma.

As the ultimate vessel, the expression of yin, the feminine principle, filled out with attachment-love, Buddha's Mom might have been the animating force at hand. Whether we call this charisma the gift of sight or bottomless love, it profoundly impacted Ubbiri. The model we are proposing emphasizes that the twoness of dialog was transcended in an emergent we-experience. Buddha and Ubbiri became the one that is greater than the sum. Patacara's story is similarly extreme, with a familiar outcome, and therefore is amenable to the same interpretations.

Rebuffing convention, Patacara married for love but soon was burdened with caring for two children. Women throughout time have helped one another shoulder the hardship of bearing and raising children. Prajapati, of course, stepped in when her sister needed her and the Canon speaks to the practice of expectant mothers returning to their homes where, presumably, similar female support was traditionally provided. No doubt without this assistance, problems impacting the mother's and baby's health would be proportionally worse. Patacara was on such a journey when disaster struck. She would later meet Buddha, be freed from suffering, and become an arahant.

Patacara's story begins as she rebuffs social convention. She was from a higher status family but had fallen in love with a servant. This was more than brave considering the hardships she would face, not to mention the heavy-handed caste system. She and her husband moved to a distant village where she performed household chores and he tilled the fields. She wanted to return home to give birth to her first child, but her husband put her off for fear of her family's vengeance. Too late, she set off on her own and ended up giving birth "by the wayside". Her husband had followed her, and once united, the couple returned to their home.

When pregnant a second time, Patacara attempted the hazardous journey alone. Again too late, and again her husband followed. A storm set in as Patacara went into labor. She sent her husband to gather branches and grass to erect a shelter. But, sadly, "alone, amid the flashes of lightning and rumbling of thunder."[260] One would be mistaken to assume the worst was past. Unable to take both children across the river, she left the newborn on some leaves. She set her older one down and began to cross the river again when a hawk, mistaking the newborn for a piece of meat, descended. When she began to scream and waved her arms midstream, this prompted her toddler to come running and to be swept away by the current. Meanwhile the hawk took off with her infant.[261]

The next day, as she was still attempting to reach her parents, Patacara heard from a traveler that in addition to her children, her brother had been killed in the storm. The stranger pointed to the smoke from their funeral pyre and she lost it. Naked, flailing and "insane from sorrow."[262] Patacara was then insulted by locals who threw trash and dirt at her. References in the Pali Canon refer to her having achieved perfections in thousands of previous lifetimes and to her destiny as an important nun. These changes were set into motion when Buddha "caused her to draw near to the monastery."[263] As he did with Kisa Gotami, Buddha was uniquely able to recognize the dignity of Patacara's pain. The official inflection is again of his identifying this as a relentless, repetitive, cruel reality of the human condition and encouraging her to therefore disembark from samsaric cycling. Like Kisa and indeed Prajapati, Patacara would become a stream-enterer and eventually an arahant.

In light of attachment-as-love, a different cast is worth our consideration. Buddha referenced the oceans of tears cried in previous lifetimes. This tends to be interpreted as underscoring that Patacara can finally stop the cycle in *this* lifetime. No doubt this is well and good, but perhaps what actually traversed the raw pain and psychosis was the very same attachment-love she was crying for—for her parents, her brother, her husband and especially her children. Buddha knew this, felt this, expressed this—perhaps—and this alone made sense, made a path for her back to sense and reason. When Buddha finally lay dying in Kushinagara, he commented that he would enjoy more years of this "sweet" earthly life, even while letting go in peace.[264]

As the stories of Kisa and Patacara and the ideas in this book suggest, this may reflect the close alliance of the densest of attachments with both love and freedom. In being moved to help Ubbiri, Patacara, and Kisa, in earthly terms, the "blessed one", Buddha, as he is often called, communicated verbally and nonverbally as Buddha's Mom, the attachment-love connection. Indeed, Buddha's Mom herself went through her own sense of loss, losing her son to the life of a beggar and a renunciate.

> Mahāprajāpatī is consciously depicted as a grieving mother quite similar to the grieving mothers of the Therigatha. Although her son has not actually died, renunciation does constitute a kind of "social death," as it were, and the texts make it all too apparent that Mahaprajapan's grief is no less than that of Ubbiri, Patacara, or Kisa Gotarni.[265]

Milarepa

Let us consider another grieving mother. She is the woman behind the great saint of the Tibetan Kagyu tradition, Milarepa. Again in this great sage, we find a deservingly beloved masculine force alongside an under-representation of associated, interactive feminine influences. When Milarepa was a boy and therefore rather innocent and unformed, family in-fighting resulted in a loss of his fortune, status and comfort.

Spice is added to this dish by none other than Milarepa's own mother. She is hurting, grieving, and grievous over this loss of prestige and material accouterments. She wants him to study sorcery and execute revenge. She longs for a return of the good life, linens and haute cuisine. Depending on the version, Milarepa's heart was broken along with hers. Or he was impressionable, perhaps under her spell. Regardless, the soon-to-be ascetic, detaching hero, is painted as awakening to the hazards of desire, attachment, greed and loss through the mother.

Before this awakening, he crosses over into evil. At his mother's urging he becomes a shaman/sorcery of some form. He uses black magic to master "internal air", travel a great distance and summon a hail storm killing many of his relatives and their friends.[266] He caused suffering in the name of the suffering his mother felt at the loss of her once privileged life. He knew this to be wrong and eventually studied for years under the lama, Marpa. Marpa had him build and then destroy three towers and eventually achieved awakening.

Famously Milarepa would go on to discover his voice. He would write hundreds of songs and poems overflowing with love, joy and exaltation for the Buddhist path. In his canon, Milarepa blends straight renunciation with passion, poetry and melody. Casting back to the mother and to Buddha's Mom, we can note how the feminine cannot be negated too enthusiastically without portraying the male as having sole dominion over enthusiasm and emotion generally. With Milarepa, the maternal and materialism serves as a rapid sketch ending badly, and thereby placing emphasis on the general take-away that greed, that longing for equivalents of status, riches, land, servants, nice clothing and food all stems from illusory attachment and calls for detachment. His mother gets credited for her greed and vengeance, and while Milarepa carries out her wishes, to some extent, his does so in the name of love. As such, love is divorced from any indigenous and biological roots.

If Milarepa is a Buddha as many proclaim, his variant of Buddha's Mom suffers her own forms of male bias. She is portrayed as emotionally stuck, sad and vengeful. Her desire for Milarepa to study sorcery smacks of a middle school spat at one extreme and voodoo at another. Simplistic marginalization of earth spirituality and the deep feminine, however, cannot completely hide the tantric trail. Researchers have linked Milarepa's sorcery studies to indigenous shamanistic traditions of that time and locale. These have a broader spectrum than vengeance including associations with psychic powers, levitation, supernatural running and "psychic sports."[267]

From an integral point of view, the Milarepa biography places emphasis on transcendence and negation and minimizes the including and preserving functions. Male ascendency, the ability of Milarepa to overcome his mother's grief, anger and sadness, gets the limelight. Intensive spiritual practice under the great lama Marpa the Translator would eventually bridge mind and body, and post-nirvana, reconnect Milarepa to emotion but there is no clear return to the feminine and attachment-love.

Milarepa's story, in the current lens, does parallel a great advance wherein personal and materialistic sources of joy and sadness are transcended and included at a higher, wider, deeper state of realization. This profound integration of emptiness and enthusiasm goes to the heart of the Vajrayana. The *Hundred Thousand Songs of Milarepa* is counted among the greatest works of Vajrayana Buddhism. Milarepa's ability to spontaneously erupt into song and poetry transcends lineage and shows up, as discussed in somatic healing forms and far-flung places such as Sufi and Quaker traditions.

But discrimination is needed in order not to lose the thread back to the joy, the sweet effervescence in abundance at the beginning of life, seen in mothers and babies, seen in secure children's boundless enthusiasm and laughter. As if to double down on the male, ascetic path as deserving all the credit for the unfettered embodiment of emotion, one element in the story tells of Milarepa getting drunk and singing beautifully. When his mother heard him, she beat him with a stick and chastised him for being happy given how much she and his family were suffering.

As usual, the masculine principle's position relative to the feminine's vacillates. In this story, Milarepa mainly has to overcome and transcend his mother's pain. Toward the end, reduced to bones in the dirt, she makes a cameo re-appearance, propelling Milarepa toward enlightenment. The vignette goes as follows. Milarepa's field was overrun with weeds. In the ruins of his family house, he found a pile of dirt covered by grass. Inside this mound, he would find his mother's bones, feel the fullness of this loss, and weep inconsolably. By remembering (his teacher) Marpa's lessons on the transience of reality, Milarepa entered a very deep meditation. For seven days, he dwelt in a state of Samadhi. In time, he would trade his land and house for food and proceed to live in caves for the rest of his life.

A less patriarchal re-telling of Milarepa's story might underscore how his mother called him to return to an indigenous spirituality to cope with the raw pain at hand. Her desire for vengeance accomplished a beautiful "transcend and include" in what evolved into Tibetan Buddhism's protector deities. These wrathful spirits (seven of eight of whom are male) represent an enlightened sorcery. Through this leap in spirit, life's violence and tragedy is actually welcomed and protected, ensuring that nothing impedes the flow of the dharma.

Also Buddhist

Many indigenous peoples, thousands of years before Darwin, Bowlby, or Jung, variably, creatively experienced and framed human consciousness as spiritual inheritance. Put slightly more scientifically, many prayed and chanted that their spiritual/genetic endowment had achieved merit in the past because this stood to benefit them in the present. The divine was one or many, ominous or benevolent, directly accessible or impenetrable and remote. Forms of death-rebirth are many splendored. We may return as a cockroach or stuck on subfloor of purgatory. Such differences tend to reinforce the 'many paths, one journey' as humans swim about in their terrifying, bewilderingly, splendorous environmental niche: cosmos.

According to Sister Candida Belloti, a 107-year-old Catholic nun, "Listening to the voice of Christ and being meek as regards his will" is key.[268] Her vision maps effortlessly with the one proposed here. Viewed through an integral prism, her vision is that of self/ego/mind's alignment with the inherent feminine principle, with spiritual receptivity refined and comfortable in its own humble confines bolstered by dharma, container and divine vessel. Her evolved, deeply personal stance is open, hungry and filled with gratitude for the mystery of all that is beyond self which here we appreciate as our human inheritance. Sister Candida not only accepts but embraces the cultural and historical wrappings (attachments) of her particular lifetime. "In more than eighty years of religious life I have never repented of my choice."[269] Sometimes what looks like submission to patriarchy is, and sometimes it is not.

Both Sister Candida's and Buddhist daily practice is mappable within relative attachment. The sub-processes (attachment and detachment) lean, bend, arc toward the infinite, toward nonattachment. Meditation and contemplative prayer are skillful means that utilize both aspects of natural attachment processes to conjure nonattachment. Because nonattachment is non-namable and non-definable, to name it God, the Great Perfection, Buddhahood, or Emptiness is all the same in any ultimate sense. Spiritual practices share an orientation toward one other, whether or not and regardless of what the name is for that other.

Names do imply something back on the relative side of the street. Sister Candida uses the attachment side of language to refer to the ultimate, which we have referred to here as both, as nonattachment but also as Buddha's Mom. In her life, the nun leaned into and cultivated an attachment to her God. Properly understood, form is emptiness and emptiness is form. A Catholic nun who leans towards the nameless when it's been given a name is only superficially different from a Buddhist monk's arc toward emptiness, a name superficially for the inverse of something. In practice, Sister Candida is cognitively privileging attachment (as a sub-process of relative attachment) language and experience to communicate what surpasses all understanding. A Buddhist monk frames the same experience via the detachment portal (sub-process).

Because self/ego/mind are such gripping and immediately attendant frames for consciousness, the focus on an ultimate *other* grows as one seeks truth. Advanced practitioners transcend small self/other traps inherent, for example, in depression, nihilism, narcissism, and materialism. Buddhists use detachment language for this journey and experience this process through the detachment side of relative attachment. They experience boundless, infinite, freedom when mind and ego drop away.

Sister Candida speaks and experiences through the other attachment channel. "Only those who feel the happiness of drawing near to the Lord can understand how abundant his love for us is, and how much serenity he leaves in our hearts." In this interview, she spoke a lot of joy, including the importance of bringing joy to those around you.[270] Hers is also the smile on the face of Buddhist monk, Thich Nhat Hanh, who wrote, "When you are a truly happy Christian, you are also a Buddhist. And vice versa."[271]

Nun-monk, Christian-Buddhist, theism-atheism dichotomies rest quite comfortably in Buddha's Mom. As described, this model is built upon relative attachment and bridges toward nonattachment—the Holy Buddha. Relative attachment's two sub-processes run through and through. Neither is first, neither is not first. The Canon purports that Buddha achieved Buddhahood many, many times before. Is he not simply then his own mother? Such a question, though "yes" is a reasonable answer (in achieving realization, he became an unfiltered living expression of human nature as Buddha-nature), a better answer is no. No, Mahamaya, Prajapati, and the nursemaids rather are analogous to Siddhartha and to all of us. We are the potential mothers of our awakening. Realizing the depths of the human lineage flowing through attachment-love provides the stepping off point. The root lineage is the human lineage and stepping off is stepping into the flow.

Just as the word mother embeds *other*, an elegant model of this stepping off and into (as previous writers have pointed out) is that of the Russian doll. Larger iterations enclose smaller and vice versa. One is ever driven to get to the bottom of this mystery. Form or emptiness? Is there one last doll? Will it also open? Wilber uses the concept of holons, "a whole that is part of other wholes."[272] The attachment-detachment model offers a parallel to this. This nun sees the many splendors of life subsumed in the whole, her god. In meditation, the Buddhist notices that all wholes are empty.

Be she part or whole, part and whole, neither part nor whole, etc., Buddha's Mom is the fulcrum for our species' lineage, which was profoundly psychologically and spiritually excavated and eventually fully realized in her son. Part or whole, this came from her and also came from her mother, and so on. One can feel the wholeness in that all of the universe's population is passed along, and does not ever come into being without her. And one can sense the partiality with profundity, in that only in her son does the dharma come into being.

Reincarnation and karma reveal yet another framing of or response to ultimate other, be this emptiness, nonbeing, death, or nonattachment. One can note how the pendulum of emptiness and form swings to and fro. In detaching from the usual egoic motives, form moves toward emptiness. In letting go of materialistic longings or "dropping body", one accumulates merit. Emptiness moves towards form. In the following, Thich Nhat Hanh expresses the dance of form and emptiness in immediate, everyday search for meaning in life. He shows how Buddhists' seemingly small gestures, through merit, karma, and reincarnation, have meaning of another order. Their ultimate meaning re-emerges in another doll (so to speak). Concretely this is another lifetime. But the reason this uniquely wise and gentle monk discusses this pertains also to the meaning received in this lifetime through awareness of the Buddhist path.

> If at all within this very life and countless lives before, we have given, even if
> only a handful of food or simple garment; if we have ever spoken kindly,
> even if only a few words; if we have ever looked with eyes of compassion,
> even if only for a moment; if we have ever comforted or consoled, even if
> only once or twice; if we have ever listened carefully to wonderful teachings,
> even if only to one talk; if we have ever offered a meal to monks and nuns,
> even if only once; if we have ever saved a life, even if only that of an ant or a
> worm; if we have ever recited a sutra, even if only one or two lines; if we
> have ever been a monk or a nun, even if only for one life; if we have ever
> supported others on the path of practice, even if only two or three people; if
> we have ever observed the Mindfulness Trainings, even if imperfectly; all of
> this merit has slowly formed wholesome seeds within us. Today we gather
> them together like a fragrant flower garland and, with great respect, we offer
> it to all Awakened Ones—a contribution to the fruit of the highest path.[273]

The loving mother is biologically and psychologically compelled to do almost all of these. She feeds, comforts, consoles, speaks sweetly, and looks upon her child with eyes of deep compassion. In all her humility and consistent outpouring, she would seem to be a powerhouse of karmic merit. A compatible, more scientific frame is proposed here in the form of Buddha's Mom. In both, the upper reaches of other-focused, empathic behavior moves all of humanity to higher, more loving and blissful potentials.

Descriptors for real-life enlightenment are abundant in the Pali Canon. The paramitas, for example, instruct us on achievable, do-able "perfections". An incomplete summary follows: Good will, truth, generosity, and virtue represent ethical gold standards; balancing patience and persistence or determination and equanimity represent great heights of spiritual fitness. Some of us do pull these off beautifully some of the time. Discernment and renunciation also make the list of callings and principles that flow from every moral fable, from the golden rule, the life of sages across multiple religious and indigenous traditions. These arc toward the divine, the infinite, and perfect.

Until recently, these qualities have not been viewed as broadly grounded in evolution. Fortunately, overlapping findings across multiple branches of science are rapidly coalescing. This science-spirit marriage-in-the-making reduces the gap between Buddha's Mom and orthodox views on her human, maternal, biological aspect. In countless previous lifetimes, the Canon states, the Buddha lived as a girl, boy, man, woman, was rich and poor, all the while pushing these intimately interactive, high water marks of humanity ever higher.

Siddhartha's personal karmic endowment, by definition, borders on the infinite. In contrast, canonical credit given to his human mothers (mother, stepmother, nursemaids) regarding his spiritual achievements (for example, the fulfillment of the paramitas) is scant. But Buddha's spiritual genome is one and the same with his body-mind genome. Preeminent scholar and sage, Robert Thurman, has suggested that a profound reconciliation of these two frames (body-mind and spirit) penetrated Buddha's second step (of eleven) toward enlightenment.

> The second step, which is also very powerful and profound, is called the step of "mother recognition." This is based on coming into an awareness of the infinity of life. This insight came to the Buddha on the night of his final enlightenment, as he sat under the bodhi tree. As he deepened his diamond-like concentration on the nature of reality, his mind drilled far into the past and he remembered millions and countless trillions of his previous lives, each one in total detail. It is not usually mentioned in the basic description of that amazing samadhi of his, but of course, when he remembered a particular life, he clearly remembered his mother in that life, whether animal, divine, or human. The next insight he achieved was the insight into all the previous lives and all the future destinies of other beings. He therefore remembered being mothered by countless trillions of beings. Indeed, as his unstoppable gaze went past the event horizon into the infinity of the past, he recalled having been the child of the infinity of beings. And he remembered just who his mother was in countless instances. He achieved the recognition of all beings as his mother.[274]

Here Buddha's Mom as transcept (concept-transmission, as discussed at the close of Chapter Two) is acknowledged without reference to her biological and maternal attachment aspect. The intensity and complexities of this rich dynamic at the heart of Homo sapiens seem bound to be treated as obvious at the same time these are overlooked. The tendency is to indirectly allude to some sort of implicit, commonsense basis but not to overtly extend this line of analysis to the full Buddhist message, which mostly runs off in the other direction.

When Ananda presented Prajapati's third plea to become the first female mendicant, the first nun, to the Buddha, he specifically referred to her in the language of maternal, biological attachment. Ananda first asked for confirmation that women were not precluded from "stream-entry, once-returning, non-returning, and arahantship." When Buddha confirmed this was so, Ananda reminded the Buddha that Prajapati was biologically connected and, specifically, that she had nursed him.

> Thereupon Ananda rephrased his request: If a woman is able to do this,
> Master—and moreover Maha-Prajapati Gotami has rendered great service to
> the Master: she is his aunt, his governess and nurse, nourished the Exalted
> One with her own milk after his mother died—therefore it would be well if
> the Blessed One would allow women to leave home for the homeless life, to
> follow the teaching and discipline of the Master.[275]

This is typical of the acknowledgement of the merit earned through the devoted, biological attachment mothers provide alongside a louder, clearer highlighting of nonattachment. One is favored and thereby the opportunity to "transcend and include" is put off, and the conspicuous absence of the feminine is reinforced.

Homelessness specifically refers to leaving hearth, home, and family. As nun, Prajapati would declare that her current life as aunt, governess, and nurse would be "my last compounded form" and that the "on-flowing of birth" for her "has expired." A bridge between the home and homeless, the "two attachments" is suggested in the great Heart Sutra. As millions of Buddhists recite daily: "Just as a mother would protect with her life her own son, her only son, so one should cultivate an unbounded mind of metta towards all beings."[276] But, of course, this is rhythmically recited in the Pali and not necessarily taken to heart as intended. Tanhā and dukkha seem to be nowhere in this guidance to cultivate the devotion toward sentient beings as a mother does for her only child. What is it such mothers in us protect and cultivate before it is released as unbounded mind? On a relative plane, a reasonable facsimile, decent skillful means, would seem to be a smaller, bounded version of the same. But always, and always, there is Nagarjuna and his enticing, maddening tendency to call into question anything mental, any form whatsoever.

> All philosophies are mental fabrications. There has never been a single
> doctrine by which one could enter the true essence of things.[277]

Buddha's Mom, with her vast scientific foundation based in evolution and attachment theory, may be said to be but another mental fabrication. But semantics do not really dissolve the arguments presented here. She stabilizes self/ego/mind in her offspring. Without this, there is no possibility to transcend, include, negate, or preserve these feelings. Through her, this legacy is fulfilled. She is surpassed through fulfillment of herself, only to co-arise again.

Penultimate Buddha

Evolutionary models of human consciousness overlook the vast penultimate territory preceding and evoking self/ego/mind. Buddha's Mom enriches biological, emotional and cognitive models and mappable, spiritual extensions of these. Construed in linear time, she correlates with our species' advances in maternal and social attachment, as we have been covering. She comes into her own as a premier evolutionary force in attachment's appropriation of emotion and cognition, as our species exploits its environmental niche through teamwork based in both love and aggression.

Construed as ever-present and omnipresent, "she" is an energetic field in which self/ego/mind *and* other arise. In her arise all echoes of the I:Thou. For example, as conceptual *it* and third-person *she*, this 'transcept' shapes, for better or worse, the first-person insider, *me*. The legacy of attachment wounding, from the Wild Boy of Aveyron to everyone with deep self disturbance, demonstrates her legacy, for better and for worse. Yet, as depth psychology suggests and emergent somatic therapies show, where 'she' has injured, sacred portals stir. As mapped by wego, 'she' witnesses the sadness and soreness, as well as the epiphanies and bliss, and all disappear in Buddha-mind. The Vajrayana's wrathful ones bear the agony and ecstasy equally, emptying vessels, paths to nowhere, inviting followers to both enter and shake off their sacred, somatic holds.

Attachment's prints are all over the archeological record. The evidence of evolutionary surges that form the vessel of modernity give us a super social, intelligent individual inseparable from his or her other: mother, tribe, and group. We have gone to some lengths to show how maternal, biological attachment extends across the lifespan, informs mom-baby pair-bonding and is key to homo sapiens biology, evolutionary success and consciousness. Attachment-love flows from the emotional and social foundations of sentience we inherited from mammals. These sedimentary layers are said to be the basis of leaps in communication and socialization, and at a major juncture, in language acquisition.

For some researchers, the archeological record amounts to not just evolution but revolution. This includes much we immediately sense as simply human: the bourgeoning of cave painting, sculpture and body ornamentation, and the emergence of cultural rituals including burial rites. Through archeology, we meet an early human ever more recognizable in the mirror. In the stone, bone, ivory, and shell tools, projectile points, needles and awls, we glimpse our own intelligence and how this contributed to new, creative ways of relating with one another, the world around us, and indeed exploiting its resources.

Evolution viewed through the lens of tools and technology, and even art as a representational skill, tends to de-emphasize yin, and penultimate forces, while celebrating yang's achievement and mastery. The feminine that gives rise to and houses the consciousness Buddha would ingeniously confront is given short shrift. The best synthesis of the evidence calls for an appreciation of a positive feedback loop: a cycle of socialization, tribal cohesion, pair bonding, and "we" factors critical to the advances archeologists understandably hail.

One reason tools get more airtime is the "tournament" socialization typical of many primates. This is characterized by the familiar alpha male and his harem. Mom-baby attachment operates as a cut-off, subsystem. This manages early development then fades out at the front end of life. A fuller look, however, demonstrates that the feminine had more than a supportive role for the psyche (tanhā, dukkha, and potential for nibbana) that we have inherited. More sophisticated tools did not lead the way. In particular, a focus on weaponry and tools has echoes of patriarchy's privileging of phallic valuations. We know, however, that such implements were preceded by, and then fostered by, advances in our species' attachment inheritance.

Worth mentioning, archeologists disagree on how much to credit various causal factors with humans' evolutionary surges. Some endorse major genetic mutations, for example, resulting in language as secondarily the increased speed and scope of social and intellectual advances. Others speculate these were adaptations to relatively sudden environmental pressures. In theory, environmental demands were overcome by those possessed of certain cognitive and social traits.

Traditional explanations inadvertently belittle Buddha's Mom. We have reviewed the within-species evidence of leaps in attachment as leading the way. There is also evidence from outside our species. In line with an innate, penultimate attachment-love, there is proof that our closest genetic relative experienced advanced empathy and had an aesthetic sensitivity. Neanderthals wore clothes and jewelry such as beads and eagle talons. They buried their dead and placed flowers on the grave. A penultimate, emotionally-intelligent yin as consistent with advances in emotion, intelligence and the full scope of sentience in our species deserves more scientific curiosity.

Let us imagine once again an early adult human named Grok. This time, let's imagine Grok as male. He carved spear points or fishing implements. Being emotional, he had some desire to measure up or to show off to other carvers or he traded his work for food he enjoyed. Perhaps another tribe was threatening or animal or marine resources were decreasing. The tribe is worried. Because of his emotional bonds, Grok would be, too. He would fight fiercely, hunt with even greater zeal, or else be genetically replaced by someone with more emotion, motivation, and allegiance. If Grok was in a pair bond, he would experience some emotion, stress, duty, thrill or relief, with respect to returning with protein for his partner and offspring.

Tribal allegiance, pair bonding, jealousy, pride, and higher emotions have no easily isolatable, hard-wired basis in mammals. Such substrates do not count among the seven emotional systems mapped by Panksepp. As mentioned, social attachment in his model is "secondary". It is not discrete in terms of brain region or neuronal system. Biological attachment has roots in the CARE system, but higher forms of liking, adoring, affiliating, rejecting, hating and the world of interpersonal relationships involve multiple affective bases. Naturally, pair bonding, tribal cohesion, the rich we-space of humans, all have a neurological substrate, just not one that is highly localized. Higher capacities and broader forms of experience are presumably facilitated by interconnections across various regions, exploiting various neuromodulators. The brain has 100 trillion neural synapses. Both the evidence and logic holds that the emotional "we" Grok feels hanging out, for his partner or children, for his tribe, logic suggests, is not reducible to a well-defined circuit—and is not distinct from his motivation to carve a beautiful tool or perhaps complete a good enough one when he would rather not.

Interpersonal glue, love, attachment by whatever name, begins to peek through the fossil record in various ways. This includes evidence of not only our imaginary Grok's tools and also of tender burials. Some are of old tribal members. Their skeletal remains show they would likely have died without years of help. Penultimate, yin emotional care and devotion is demonstrated in delicate hand-made jewelry. Another side of Buddha's Mom is represented by statues that have come to be viewed as fertility, great mother, and goddess iconography.

Recently, Emeritus professor of anthropology and cave painting expert, Dean Snow, analyzed the size of the handprints left by our ancestral artists. It seems reasonable to speculate that, relative to other tribal members, cave painters were more sensitive to their relationship with the environment, more attuned to the ways of their environment and the animals they depended upon. Dr. Snow concluded that three-fourths of the hand prints were from women. This too is in keeping with this meditation on the feminine principle.[278] Whether an ultra-rapid "great leap" or more incremental grand "bottom-up" surge, approaches to consciousness often lack what I believe is scientifically demonstrable context, e.g., evidence of the feminine. Neuroscience seems to be a recent instance of scientific favoritism.

Penultimate evolutionary factors may be represented as an iceberg. Above-water advances were buoyed by proportionally larger increases in massive, underwater forces. Buddha's Mom was literally and is not metaphorically Buddha. She was not better or more important. Rather an appreciation of her enhances that of him. As such, she is not less but rather inextricably important. More of the higher dimensions of one's nature, potential, achievements co-arises with more of the lower.

Lower, penultimate realms are hard to measure and articulate. In *The Feeling of What Happens*, neurologist Antonio Damasio identifies the neuronal bricks that build the house of the self, without suggesting that a house is nothing more than bricks. According to Damsio, feeling arises from emotion, and emotion arises from the senses. The fuller experience of the self (and I prefer self/ego/mind for this personal vessel of awareness) is constructed atop attachment, and per Panksepp, attachment lives atop multiple affective substrates.

> All emotions use the body as their theater (internal milieu, visceral, vestibular and musculoskeletal systems), but emotions also affect the mode of operation of numerous brain circuits: the variety of the emotional responses is responsible for pro-found changes in both the body landscape and the brain landscape. The collection of these changes constitutes the substrate for the neural patterns which eventually become feelings of emotion.[279]

Buddha's Mom abides within this precursor, substrate space. Through her both biologically and metaphorically, our species sentient lineage comes to be reliably replicable. Across the great advances in evolution, newborn brains increasingly depended on her. Future parents and lineage bearers were increasingly recast in her post-natal, mom-baby and trans-interpersonal womb.

At the front end of the lifecycle, the pre-natal container pushed brain and head size (as anyone who has witnessed a birth knows) to a life-threatening maximum. In the first extremely vulnerable and dynamic year, brain weight doubles. By design, disproportionate frontloading of the neurological ground of attachment-love is profound. At age three the brain is 80% of its eventual adult weight. Rapid programming of the senses, emotions, language and cognition is similarly frontloaded.

Without a well-informed, intentional, push backward (evolutionarily upriver) into the contextual, penultimate land of Buddha's Mom, the liberation that Siddhartha achieved takes on too much of a philosophical and religious tone. Buddhist insights and "truths", however, approached through the body-mind and all attendant somatic experiences, run in the other direction. In this way alone, Buddhism's metaphysical umph, as an empirically rigorous methodological inquiry into attachment, opens doors to the peace that surpasses all understanding and all religions.

Confusion is understandable. Bowlby and attachment science did not solidify until recently. Also, the Siddhartha narrative, which sets the stage for the teaching more broadly, frames the journey to awakening less as an affective, feeling-toned endeavor and more as a maze of mind-wracking puzzles. These bolster Buddhism as doctrine, philosophy, and as a religious enterprise.

The ever-curious Siddhartha famously confronts existential pretzels early on. If this human life is riddled with disease, pain, and death, why bother? What possible meaning can be derived from such bleak realities? Should Siddhartha enjoy the riches of his father's kingdom, become a ruler himself, or abandon this to be an ascetic?

Awareness and awakening, the story implies, will come from a mental grappling with life's existential questions. Even the "austerities", seemingly the ultimate bodily focus possible, were recorded as very much a top-down affair, a mental effort to test and measure the limits of the host body. In this rendering, mind makes an object of body. Mind confronts ultimate meaning and the implications of disease and death. Once again, a relational, both/and, encompassing yin takes second chair to the yang's preferred either/or, delineating modality. The query form is: What does X have to do with me and my search? How does X impede or facilitate my goals?

> "Object" refers to those elements of our knowing or organizing that we can reflect on, handle, look at, be responsible for, relate to each other, take control of, internalize, assimilate, or otherwise operate upon. All these expressions suggest that the element of knowing is not the whole of us; it is distinct enough from us that we can do something with it. "Subject" refers to those elements of our knowing or organizing that we are identified with, tied to, fused with, or embedded in. We have object; we are subject. We cannot be responsible for, in control of, or reflect upon that which is subject. Subject is immediate; object is mediate. Subject is ultimate or absolute; object is relative.[280]

Buddha, of course, taught that concentration meditation results in profound shifts. One becomes aware of how objects of awareness result from a blend of passive perceiving and active attributing of characteristics and features. With increased awareness of this meaning-making enterprise, one is on the path to the realization of impermanence and emptiness. Any object, even one's body, is dependent upon the ability to arise with mind. Yet something not an object—which some refer to as the witness position—is also present. This larger vantage notices the co-arising of body and mind. But in the next stage, this outer, observing aspect becomes an object, an entity of a fresh, new awareness. As Wilber explains, "The subject of one stage becomes the object of the subject of the next stage."[281]

Buddha's Mom facilitates introspection and witnessing. This helps resolve what we initially identified as the two attachments. The chasm between these equates to an under-appreciation for the full breadth of attachment. This unrequited love for attachment-love has roots in the preponderance of male-centered values in Buddha's time. Such patriarchal values and worldviews oppress the feminine and privilege male perspectives and potentials regardless of gender. The lovely poem of gratitude attributed to Prajapati, having herself been emotionally attached to Siddhartha, uniquely speaks to the orthodox Buddhist view.

> I've been mother and son before;
> And father, brother—grandmother too.
> Not understanding what was real,
> I flowed on without finding [peace].
> But now I've seen the Blessed One!
> This is my last compounded form.
> The on-flowing of birth has expired.
> There's no more re-becoming now.[5]

Vajrayana

Prajapati's next and final step comes after she discovers that human love and intimacy ultimately lead nowhere. At least this seems to leap from the page. In past lives, she had experienced all forms of close human relationships. She had been a mother, son, father, brother, and grandmother. Her specific naming of these common forms of close relationships exactly matches what modern researchers call adult attachment. Her praise and homage to Buddha for releasing her and so many others from suffering specifically points to these close relationships as falling short. Presumably, she is saying that she has repeatedly endeavored but failed to find peace and meaning in life, and samsara, which Buddha finally provided for her, through various close relationships, allows for release. As she puts it, "not understanding what was real", she flowed on in life. In another translation, she states, "knowing nothing of the truth, I journeyed on."[282]

Both theoretically and empirically, based on hundreds of studies, close relationships—referred to in research as adult attachment—has been shown to be based in biological, maternal attachment. Prajapati's accent on the ultimate futility of adult attachment diverges from a modern, integral one. Adult attachment is even a little bit of a misleading term because these selfsame, developmentally-based phenomena have been shown to impact much more than a close relationship. Attachment experiences early in life tend to influence health, for example, smoking, diabetes, and career parameters. An integral attachment perspective is based in decades of attachment science, recent work on emotions in mammals, cognitive neuroscience, depth, and clinical psychology (to name a few of the major sources of supporting evidence).

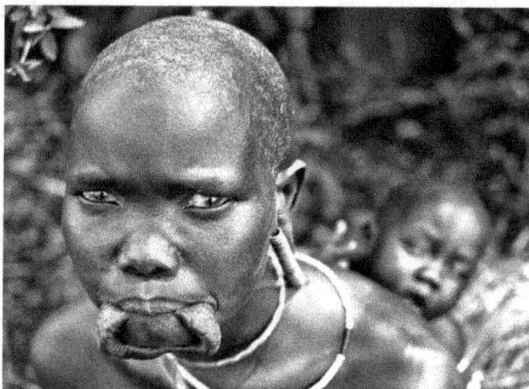

Ultimately, the integral perspective is in full agreement with poet Robert Frost's line, "The only way out is through." This integration, if framed as a bridge from animal to spirit, or body to mind to spirit, reaches its most exquisite manifestation in Vajrayana, which, as I have mentioned, is the third turning of the wheel of dharma. Vajrayana Buddhism is also known as Tantric Buddhism, the Thunderbolt Path, and the Diamond Way. Famously secretive, the teachings on Tantra state that this body of practices must not be shared with those not ready for it.

This historically rendered Prajapati places her emphasis on getting out of and off of the close relationship merry-go-round. Like Frost, the Vajrayana teaches that the only chance of release and enlightenment is *through*. The only way out is through. Through one's relationship to earth, body, self, and others. It is fair to say that the Vajrayana lineage does not endorse the reality of attachment in any narrow, specific way. Attachment exists only as a loosely held, generic placeholder, an "orienting generalization".

Each of us has our own array of attachments just as we have our own unique personalities and the truth of the uniqueness is everything. This yana ("vehicle") places the emphasis on the precious gift of our individual existence. Our personhood, with all the attachment forms included, has never before existed, never before been manifest. Never ever in the history of the universe. This fact deserves an in-kind response. One of wow, of gratitude, of devoted curiosity and openness. Only through the full cultivation and expression of the life as it is given do we access the deepest essence of our nature. This goes by many terms and phrases. For example, Buddhist instructor, Reggie Ray, interchangeably uses the following: the infinite and eternal depths of reality, the endless and eternal ocean of awareness, the profound and infinite ocean of awareness, the great space of being, the vastness of our basic nature that has no boundary or limit.[283]

As the body of adult attachment research shows, what passes as maternal attachment has far-reaching implications, shapes all relationships, even those that comprise personality. These include relationships to body, emotion, feeling, self, others, work, values and spirituality. Naturally then the call in Vajrayana to open to the vast space of our true nature specifically and concretely would have us meditate, develop our deepest abiding presence in and through all these experiential dimensions, and more. Only *through* meditation practice which is focused on the whole, real, complex of one's own, actual continuum of body-mind-spirit is release from pain, suffering and craving (to return to Prajapati's beautiful poem) a possibility.

Tantric Prajapati

Prajapati's poem may thus be heard with more of Tantra's accent on desire, passion, love, and attachment. This new interpretation would, I believe, be more aligned with the integral view of Buddha's Mom as proposed in this book. In this mode, we may hear her crying out from the depths of her most tender, personal hold on reality. She is telling anyone with the tenderness to hear how she so deeply loved others. She explains that she has given birth and loved her children, has been a child and loved her parents, and has grown up alongside and deeply loved her siblings in other lifetimes. We can lose ourselves in the dense, beautiful, yet painful mud of life, and only through this co-experience can we find something miraculously spacious.

This stratum of knowing, feeling, and being sees itself, sees that reality is one's contemporaneous life and therefore is not also that which is seen. Who is seeing such wholes, whole chains of love and even lifetimes? From this experience, Prajapati mourns and cries but not without delight. She expresses a point that is not binary. In other words, she is not saying that these profound loving relationships were for naught. Rather, she is trying her hardest to share that these feelings and love were her entire world. Most profoundly of all, she was inundated with universal grace. She awakened to the depths of fortune to be born human, as she sank below older, repeated surfaces. Immersed in a personal ocean of love for Siddhartha, she let go of her self/ego/mind as she realized that even this was limiting. To have the sublime and earthshaking experience of loving this baby, child, young man, loving him for days stretching to weeks, to years, through the span of her adult life on Earth enabled her to understand his teachings. Exactly this reality, his smell, knowing every hair on his head, as the Bible puts it, was the penultimate vessel.

In the Vajrayana, we can hear and feel this Buddha's Mom's plea and invitation and song. Through this attachment to Siddhartha (and even then only also through many years of struggling and meditating on this), she finds release. Her path into and through love was one into and through what we label as emotions. Doors keep appearing and opening, drawing us to the very edges of somatic awareness. We are stardust. Each of us is uniquely the flaming tip of a multi-billion year, mysterious, ever-perfecting, already-perfection. How fully we emanate, receive transmission and transmit this lineage seems endlessly open to debate and interpretation. Fractures run through the human response, so much so that the only viable conclusion seems to be that each person is their own truth.

But integrally understood, attachment takes us across the body-mind bridge very elegantly. The better the lineage is relayed, the more fully and freely the next in line stand to manifest the breadth of being. In tantra, the inner wilds of this undefinable passage find balanced form. No moment, no internal experience or external activity is without the potential to open the doors of perception. The heart of humanity, our full and open spiritual potential, is palpable in the ordinary and the sublime. Our response, the very spiritual movement that pulses through the human lineage, moves the most vulnerable among us, becomes motion and emotion. All this is lost without some mirror—a wiser seeing and knowing. As such, the motion is not only recognized and understood but encouraged. This turning is dependent, made of and will only be achieved in love.

Perhaps this message was lost in translation during the many, many years it was relayed orally. It may have absorbed some of the patriarchal flavors emanating from the dominant culture. Her being accepted as the first nun is a moving story and important historical event, to be sure. But one's heart goes out to all the fierce, cultivated dharma women warriors who had no such opportunity and will remain nameless.

The male tendency is to place the accent on the climax, the victory, to celebrate the heights, and see the iceberg tip more than what upholds it. The yang lens focuses on the leading edge more than the journey itself. A wielding of the sword is another way to describe these perceptual tendencies. The cleaving sword divides the best from the rest. But attachment and attainment are intertwined in the Tao. The patriarchal way is to draw stark contrasts, privilege the binary, bad/good and wrong/right, over a mutual, penultimate, co-arising frame. This orthodox understanding of attachment discounts its organic, creative, living essence, which I am suggesting quite naturally, empirically abides in the encompassing construct of Buddha's Mom. Here, larger affective fields give rise (via dependent origination) to larger cognitive ones. That this is an unendingly fluid and creative process is a profound truth in itself, and an important counterpart to the finality referred to in any male prism on Prajapati's poem.

Buddha's Mom has a strong scientific footing on the "relative side of the street" and is therefore a good fit for the modern mind. And she has absolute street cred as well! Prajapati's poem can be heard as both dismissive of her and in this failed attempt as her very expression. In Buddha's Mom, attachment in and between adults, from lust to love, from raw desire to mature devotion, is the scaffolding upon which higher love, metta, lovingkindness and universal compassion are born (or constantly being born at every moment). Adult attachment informs the relative attachment space, the vicissitudes of trust, chaos, and conflict felt by and for those Prajapati lists, mothers, sons, daughters, grandmothers, and brothers. Adult attachment, more accurately, the ebb and flow of attaching and detaching, is the process by which a "we" arises with those we consider (perhaps aspirationally) to be our loved ones.

Even if the effort to consider a Vajrayana revisioning of Prajapati's poem is only aspirational, we are left with someone very compelling. Perhaps the male overlay is mostly her own. Perhaps this speaks to a hero's journey with her interpretations of her son's philosophy on the one side and her instincts on the other. One can easily empathize with a loving mother who, over years and years, is told by the master to meditate and transcend all that arises, even maybe especially her love for him. Such a person also fully deserves her title, actually and conceptually, as Buddha's Mom.

Such a person offers a very human, very compelling presence for those of us on the path. In this sense, reading the poem, either person supports the construct we are trying to articulate in this book. The emphasis placed on the tip of the iceberg or the final stage of the journey, however, can be misleading. In debate circles, this is referred to as a "false equivalency". The entire thrust of Buddha's Mom and her penultimate basis is supported by multiple lines of evidence, including the pioneering work in cognitive neuroscience—something addressed more thoroughly in subsequent sections. In total, these do comport with the iceberg metaphor and create a model in which ever more conscious, ever better articulated feeling states coexist in dynamic concert with the release from these.

Tantric Evolution

The "great leap forward" in evolution can be understood in this light. Originally, "lower" biopsychosocial attachment forms occurring in mammals leapt forward achieving increased emotional complexity in primates, and again, in hominids and Homo sapiens. Technically, the new co-arises with the old as the old achieves a certain (new) degree of sophistication.

Base drives become more elaborate. A chicken instinctually scratches the ground. An automatic seeking receives a special jolt of reinforcement upon finding and tasking some special edibles. Related cognition expands. A primate is hungry. She wants and can imagine eating something delicious. The gorilla Koko's favorite foods were nuts, gourmet tofu dishes, apples, and corn-on-the-cob. She could name these when none were present. Early hominids gathered and hunted with great facility. No doubt gathering and hunting both drive and came to dominate their mental life. Modern humans fill cookbooks with complex recipes and can reminisce about a past meal, or imagine sharing a future feast, with a loved one. Attachment enhancements filled out this rainbow of wanting, desiring, longing, imagining and thinking about food.

If *nondual* can be referred to imperfectly in relative, space-time terms, as "here" or "at this point in time", the penultimate field of spiritual awakening can be said to have expanded in both directions. Through evolution, the vessel of enlightenment was ever more body and more mind.

According to the Vajrayana, there have been countless Buddhas. This hard-to-steady thought is consistent. Once the necessary precursors or penultimate forces (Buddha's Mom) were in place within Homo sapiens' consciousness, the experience of looking back with perfect vision on these forces also arose (Buddhahood). These co-arose in highly evolved, courageous, brilliant individuals—and according to the Vajrayana, in couples. Ascetics and wanderers lived at various points in pre-history. According to Reggie Ray, the Vajrayana is pre-Buddhist and trans-Buddhist, and can be traced back to indigenous men, women, to hermits and householders. Sometimes couples were the lineage holder(s).

Such possibilities are intriguing and scientifically viable. At some point prior to what we might think of as the emergence of Buddha's Mom, gross brain size had expanded and stabilized. "Her" emergence coincided with the surge of subtler advancements in neuroanatomy and neuronal interconnectivity. While brain size and visible biological, "hardware" changes were less than dramatic, the opposite was (evidence suggests) true on the software side where linguistic, cognitive and cultural forces exploded in complexity and scale. These biopsychosocial undercurrents of this early population had finally evolved into an adequate substrate for dramatic leaps in self-awareness. Naturally, this leading edge and iceberg tip left few traces in the material realm. Only hints of these emerging spiritual capacities are ever likely to be discerned from the fossil record.

Modern attachment science proposes that mother-infant attachment eventually underwent seismic shifts. An attachment feedback system propelled the gift of mother-infant bonding to all corners of psychological life, so that attachment highly influenced virtually all major cognitive and functional domains, including personality and work, in addition to adult intimacy. Alone, the adult attachment lens tends to be rather linear and more fitting for individual analysis and therapy than spiritual development.

Anchoring attachment in the evolution of consciousness helps offer an empirical grounding for the broader construct proposed here. In this, any chicken-egg debate (between maternal and adult attachment) can be disbanded. The fittest of our prehistoric brothers and sisters, babies and adults were those who survived and reproduced offspring who survived, grew up and reproduced, and so on. They did so, mathematically, statistically, on average slightly more efficiently than their counterparts. This evoked the most sophisticated, beguiling creature on this and as far as we know any planet! The result is what we see all around us, and what the Buddha uniquely, lucidly discerned, practiced and taught.

With the evolution from the first to the third turning in Buddhism, the transition becomes far more aligned with Buddha's Mom. What we referred to as the problem of two attachments is much more problematic in Theravada Buddhism, becomes less divergent in the Mahayana tradition, and then potentially completely disappears in the Vajrayana. In Vajrayana, every manner of attachment is intensively, consciously repurposed in elaborate practices aimed at nonattachment. Reggie Ray explains the three stages in the following manner: 1) in the Theravada tradition, attachment is the cause of samsara and to be avoided; 2) in the Mahayana, it is to be seen from the perspective of emptiness, as essentially having no substance; 3) in the Vajrayana, attachment is allowed its existence and reality, and practitioners work at fully realizing its reality within them.[284] They do so using, among other forms, deity practice. Vajrayana invites each of us to stare directly into the lust, pain and confusion, and to dive in while sitting. It calls us to fully, uniquely, meditatively experience the living pushes and pulls of desiring and attaching.

Recalling that the iceberg rises disproportionately to the mass underwater, out of awareness, increasingly complex thinking (e.g., the vernacular for intelligence) signals a larger, more complex subconsciousness. The phenomena of "monkey mind" is reflective of the more thinking/more feeling tension. Mental contents bubble up from every corner. And the deeper self only awakens to all this as the scale tips. This occurs when shapes and substance form, when form out of suchness lurches, when fantasies, memories, reveries become an object, an other to the self-as-witness. In this turn, the essential self, what Hinduism calls Atman takes flight. But monkey mind is equally an achievement of enormous heights. A most rare tree falling, in a very rare forest, the life-force of the universe that even sentient beings rarely glimpse. For this is the leading edge of attachment-in-Homo sapiens, where mirror neurons play, where an other as signified co-arises with the self as signifier. Here, Buddha's Mom indeed brings a new force, love and clarity, the same delight she has for the emergence of all aspects of sound and fury in her beloved baby.

The "quick path", Vajrayana has specific practices aimed squarely at the most intensive of brain states. These directly address the parietal lobe's interconnections with the body: the various sensory centers; the limbic systems and others associated with intense survivalist drives, moods and emotions. These set up structured meditative exercises during which one practices maintaining an integrated, grounded awareness amidst humanity's most overwhelming and potent experiences: terror, lust, rage, and the many flavors of emotional attachment and love.

Vajrayana parallels the quickening which occurred during human evolution's Great Leap Forward. During this period, intellectual, emotional, and social aptitude took off. This inflection can be likened to a robot that transcends a complete reliance on programming and achieves the ability to learn. With this development, consciousness was no longer so locked up in the body, no longer quite so restrained by instinct and reflex. Attachment heated up relationships, loyalties, and alliances—all forms of the we-space.

However, love did not win out over aggression in any simplistic, binary way. Expansions of attachment and bonding across the lifespan were co-opted by power drives and others which proved to have evolutionary fitness. As a result, the escalation of complex social systems included those of the lethal variety. Efficient, deadly, warrior characteristics contributed to the purely amoral reality of evolutionary fitness. Certain tribes and the types of brains comprising them edged out others in the most direct manner possible, through sex and aggression. Early humans with strong emotional attachment capacities pair-bonded and raised like-minded offspring. Persons (family and tribe members) with a certain balance of sex/aggression made the grade. These *make love and war* brain-minds are the ones we know all too well today, both intensely capable of love, affiliation, music, art, and ethical behavior and similarly beset with power and control and aggressive drives.

Vajrayanan Tantric traditions have penetrated these depths and developed psychospiritual technologies to spiritually reset the great leap forward. Once esoteric and mystical, these specialized practices called sadhana have been recorded in books, for example, by the Second Dalai Lama. Some of these center on Tibetan Buddhism's iconic wrathful deities. Among these fierce, enlightened protectors of sentient beings are a set named *heruka* and another called *dharmapala*.[285]

Their wrathful countenance is a nod to the amoral life-force and ferocity we each carry. As history proves, this drives all "senseless" acts of violence, genocide, rape, incest, and torture. But these enlightened ones have co-opted the lowest for the highest of purposes. They are enlightened and in this, have devoted themselves to protect the dharma. More specifically, they have positioned themselves to help those hoping to transcend our lower nature, samsara, the cycle of death and rebirth.

Associated, ritualistic tantric practices assist in a quickening of what we have been exploring as integral attachment and nonattachment, the fruits of biological and cultural evolution. The seven core affects discovered by Panksepp, with their shared subcortical basis in mammals, are depicted in the raw. Copulating, fearsome, enraged, seemingly unhinged and beyond description,

Pankseep's big seven (SEEKING, RAGE, FEAR, LUST, CARE, PANIC/GRIEF, and PLAY) are on full display.[286] They thrust themselves from humanity's depths, some sort of subconscious mirror we would hope to avoid. But they are bodhisattvas, Buddhas and enlightened beings. In the current context, we would appreciate their perfect, selfless, compassion as the most supreme form of a formless attachment-love. Note too how the bible's Yahweh and primitive, sacrifice-demanding gods and goddesses are routinely rendered as angry and fearsome. More modern, still patriarchal Gods are credited with love and care but lack the fuller, integral attachment focus wherein lust, sex, and intense, passionate devotion are all the very alchemy of heaven on earth, heaven-embodied.

Wrathful deity practices recapitulate the cosmic path leading to modern Homo sapiens and our very own life-force by propelling followers to fully inhabit their deepest nature. They specifically guide one to turn, face, and deeply focus on the attachment drive, the very breadth and pulse of arising desire that permeates life "on the relative side of the street".

Tantric practices are visually portrayed in dynamic, florid, sensual, bewildering, and surreal mandalas. Figures are adorned with extra heads, eyes, huge numbers of arms, flames, and flowers. Male and female genitalia and polyamorous lovemaking are on full display. The heruka tantric practices attribute shape, direction, bodily form, numbered appendages, and colors, among many other characteristics, to the multitudes of Buddhas, deities, and personages. Deity practice employs these mandalas and evokes sensual, lurid, hostile, chaotic, and devotional tones within highly structured, ancient formulae. Practitioners sit, chant, and follow precise instructions, and do so repeatedly over decades.

> By identifying with the intricately rendered worlds within a mandala and the primal source added center, we can enlarge our experience of the universe in which we dwell... one gradually recognizes that infinite worlds come and go within the vast expanse of our own being... as I curve back within myself and manifest different forms, I realize that I am not in the universe but the universe is in me; I'm not in this body, this body is in me; I am not in this mind, this mind is in me. And as I curve back within myself, I create the experience of mind, of body, of the universe and all these infinite realms. That's enlightenment: to know that the entire universe is a projection of my own being and that I create within myself the texture and fabric of all that exists.[287]

A limited attempt at interpreting tantric forms from the current perspective of Buddha's Mom might begin with a few of the major motifs. A sadhana credited to the second Dalai Lama, who lived some 500 years ago, offers a decent start. He opens with praise to his root guru and soon makes it clear that this shall not be defined in any reductionistic manner.

> To the mouth of my precious root Guru, you are the nature of all the body, speech, mind, deeds and qualities of all the Tathagatas (i.e., Buddhas) of the three times and the ten directions, you are the source of all the eighty-four thousand classes of dharma teachings, you are the principal of all the Arya Sanghas, OM AH HUM [288]

He continues with praise for the "body, speech, mind, deeds and qualities of all the Tathagatas" (i.e., Buddhas). The Tathagatas are summoned from something like a multiverse, a totality of space and time encompassing our own and much more. Not just one time and four directions, but the "three times and ten directions."[289]

As we have suggested, in Buddha's Mom, one finds a rich biological and psychological grounding for spirit. She is intrinsically devoted to the other, and to all aspects of her baby's physical, emotional, and cognitive development. These include correspondences to the body, speech, mind, and behavior of her offspring. In her super-personal, transcendent aspect, she is the placeholder or root lineage responsible (and response-able) for the transmission of our species, for consciousness, and she has been for an immeasurable span of time. She shares much, it would seem, with that which Tibetans summon in certain tantric meditation rituals.

Continuing, the OM AH HUM chant acknowledges that these enlightened everywhere and nowhere supreme beings are the source of the dharma's 84,000 teachings and the root lineage of the highest sangha. This has much in common with the various ways we have suggested Buddha's Mom offers a contextual, precursor frame to that discovered by her son. It fits with the two attachments as being encompassed in a larger space where the scientific and spiritual dovetail. Obviously, those who cultivated and transmitted the Vajrayana did not have access to the many modern bodies of research we have relied on in this book.

As this traditional Tantric passage continues, we meet the inestimable Vajrayogini. This great feminine force permeates Tibetan Buddhism. She, too, is a manifestation of the feminine principle, the divine feminine, as we have discussed at length in regards to Buddha's Mom. Whether Buddha's Mom offers anything new is better answered by those within the Tibetan tradition. Vajrayogini is a fully realized Buddha who belies reductionisms. She is many splendored — at once sumptuous and arresting, exotic and sensual. She is the insoluble union of yin and yang with her contrasexual dimension, her male consort Chakrasamvara. This dynamic symbolizes the "inseparability of emptiness and skillful means, wisdom and compassion, female and male."[290] And she is an enduring symbol of the Great Mother, along with others in the same tradition such as White Tara and Green Tara. One swallows this lightning-bodied deity and a smaller, thumb-sized version of her enters one's mouth, dances through one's body to the soles of one's feet. Notice how normal reality and duality makes way for the unspeakably beautiful and terrifying. Next the venerable Vajrayogini emerges from one's navel, a perfect eight-petaled, multi-colored lotus with a sun mandala at its center.[291]

Patriarchy is known to box in the feminine principle to Virgin, Mother, Whore, and Witch/Crone archetypal confines. In the tantric traditions, Vajrayogini is every bit the equal, actually simply is Buddha. Her forms leave nothing to be desired. As a Buddha, she is an ultimate source of wisdom and compassion. Her sensual facets potentiate the transmutation of lust, longing, codependence, and desire, and all the dark sides of romance and love as well, into liberation and bliss. As a Great Mother figure, she and Buddha's Mom are indistinguishable.

> Female archetypes of enlightened awareness are central to the Tantric form
> of Buddhism, which envisions the boundless, unconditioned wisdom mind
> as "feminine" and the compassionate activation of this underlying reality as
> "male."[292]

In ritualistic meditations, one phenomenologically surfs the rich, meaning-imbued, archetypal spaces in which these deities abide. The practitioner endeavors to meditatively, very deeply be present to the revered dakinis (female spirits in human and nonhuman spiritual forms, such as Vajrayogini) and simultaneously to one's own authentic 'on-flowing' experience. By diligently invoking these impersonal, true forms with the deepest of intentions, self/ego/mind may find a new, immediate, personal deeper authenticity. Encounters with eternal, transpersonal beings may bring about release from previous, shallower, less real, less true, holding (attaching) patterns. A swirling and mingling of the personal "me" may occur. The self/other boundary may dissolve in the midst of dynamic forces, be they initially wrathful, alluring, protective, compassionate or seductive. Heaven and Earth, so to speak, transmute in emptiness and cease to co-arise. In One Taste, the vast, endless, immeasurable, always, already present space at the heart of the human condition opens.

In Vajrayogini's mother facet, as well as other evocations of the feminine principle, one stream within the dharma may be quickened. These passages metaphorically connect mother love with nothing less than a cosmic, infinite heart. In the Vajrayana, Vajrayogini is complimented by several other highly-developed deities, including the beloved Tara in her multiple manifestations.

Tara reasserts the earthy, feminine principle at these rarified altitudes. Like Buddha's biological mom, she too receives a mixed treatment. One laden with praise and marginalized at the same time. She emerges from a single tear of the great Chenrezig. This teardrop is hardly the most famous of Chenrezig's many characteristics but deserves reflection.

Chenrezig is the Tibetan name for Mahayana's thousand-armed, eleven-headed Avalokitesvara. He is the supreme bodhisattva of compassion. Compassion, as such, even one step removed from Shakyamuni Buddha, remains initially in the male domain. To foster his understanding of all those suffering beings, Chenrezig's single head becomes eleven separate heads. His longing to reach out to all in need is too much for two arms and therefore his body's two shatter into a thousand arms. At some point, he sheds a tear which becomes Tara.

As we explored with Mahamaya and Prajapati, the power of the feminine as a source of love based, as I have suggested manifests in evolution's attachment-as-love and more completely in Buddha's Mom, may be distorted. But over and again, "she" proves too extant, too formidable and integral to extinguish. There would be no lovingkindness, no compassion and no next generation of the species without it. Our purpose here is to underscore how these many exaltations of a maternal force in Buddhism and in consciousness are very much in line with Buddha's Mom.

> As a mother would risk her life to protect her child, her only child, even so
> should one cultivate a limitless heart with regard to all beings. With good
> will for the entire cosmos, cultivate a limitless heart: Above, below, and all
> around, unobstructed, without enmity or hate.[293]

When this happens, all these bewildering descriptions and art (of the endless, boundless, infinite, and oceanic characteristics of our true nature) finally make sense in the most personal and immediate manner. Reality felt with such immediacy is implicitly more true, more real than the dear old self/ego/mind could ever manage to work out. There is a sense of being home within the power center of one's birthright. Most especially, the more-true, more-real and overflowing quality is that of love. The words can quickly sound New Agey or trite, but love is all. Love wants a fuller expression, and to want this precisely through "me". My job then, in these dips in the energetic, burgeoning, vast ocean at the heart of reality, is to articulate, show up, express, demonstrate, model, dance in, expand, and be bliss.

Let us consider this tantric twist on Oscar Wilde's proclamation, "To love oneself is the beginning of a lifelong romance." Here he points to the individual as potentially narcissistic or a mirror with Buddha-nature's explosion of metta. The smaller is portal to the unbounded. Looking back at anyone with enough clarity is to reflect, to touch the Tantric possibilities in relationship with self or other. In this lives the chance to surpass the bible's "ena" (as mentioned, found in "I am the way"). This living invitation is to move past I, to fall into the arms of the I-I, the first person plural, an expansive wego.

In total, the Vajrayana lineage calls for fiercely penetrating, honoring, and directly experiencing one's authentic self, with all the attendant chaos and pain, lust, longing, and power drives running through all of our attachments. As we have described elsewhere, remote, disowned dimensions of one's true nature are gently but very diligently welcomed back to the fold through the practice of Tonglen. Shortcomings and shadows are understood as space where the light of absolute bodhicitta is temporarily obscured. These include attachments to a body, to others, to our identifications and endless desiring. Through devotional meditative techniques, these do not disappear but are seen as they truly are, in emptiness, in total freedom, with profound gratitude, as they are recalled, remembered, re-integrated. What a glorious feeling, as the song says, is the truth of rain, and for that matter, to be born, to have physical form. All the ways we smash ourselves into suffocatingly small, hardened habits of mind are not so much exposed as reframed from a position far more free, far more expansive. According to this great yana, meditating on all these forms of attachment comprises the path to that which Prajapati gives thanks in her poem.

Since relationship with self and others runs through our entire mental life, one's emotional attachments are understood to be portals. These must be deeply felt, welcomed, surrendered to, seen, and realized in their full authenticity. Although orthodox Buddhism teaches that there is always another onion layer, a witness, this view is actually more associated with the gradual path of Theravada. In the Vajrayana vehicle, this actual self that has never before been born, never loved or been loved, implicitly wants to push through in all these ways. It (I) wants to freely and fully enjoy an unfettered chance at the dance. It is this vast wanting that may just break through, be realized as the "more real" present than so-called reality. Referred to in many ways, this home, true nature, leaves all that we are otherwise so sincerely working with and toward without looking back. One knows they are home: they feel it. Again, this fact brings us back to the possibility that Prajapati's poem can be re-read with the masculine filters removed. She speaks directly to this intimate phenomenological shift, to finally finding her home, truth, reality.

Chapter Nine

BHUMISPARSHA

Space

The second part of the Pali word for suffering means space or sky. Pali scholar Stephen Batchelor explains that dukkha is a compound word which can be translated as "pain space."[294] Recalling the central premise of the Four Noble Truths, we arrive in life as into a world of hurt driven by attachment, clinging, and grasping. Since ego is regularly identified as that which craves, clings, and therein, perpetuates suffering, we might collapse this formulation further: self/ego/mind as pain-space.

The possibility of a cessation of all this misery, identified in Truth Number Three, speaks to a different space altogether, an expanse and reality free of all limitations, worry, fear, and neediness. Ego proclaims self-importance and petitions a vastness that does not care either way. The Pali Canon's many references to a boundless and measureless space make this point in reverse.

Stanford scholar, Paul Harrison recently analyzed one of Buddhism's most beloved sutras. According to Harrison, the Diamond Cutter Sutra repeatedly refers to a "trigalactic megagalactic worldsystem."[295] The incomprehensible scale sounds similar to numerous Canonical descriptions of great planes of existence, formless realms, measureless time epochs, non-Earthly lifeforms, and supernatural powers.

Next to the Diamond Cutter Sutra's various descriptions of the vastness of reality, any sense of personal existence or relevance seems dubious and naïve. This sutra is comprised of a teaching dialog and begins when one of Buddha's ten disciples, Subhuti, asks him a question about the bodhisattva path. Often, Buddha's responses also take the form of a question. In the following, he asks Subhuti to imagine a scale of reality that ranges from the infinitesimally minute to astronomically immense.

> If there were as many Ganges Rivers as there are grains of sand in the
> Ganges River, and if there were just as many world systems as there would
> be grains of sand in them, would those world-systems be numerous?[296]

One's ego, in this instance that of Subhuti's, could be forgiven for feeling threatened by such a vast, "trigalactic megagalactic world system". Such a thing has no need or place for it. Or, put another way, Subhuti must have felt (in the first-person sense) that Buddha was telling him of a reality with no place and no need for "me". Yet throughout their long dialog, Subhuti comes off as deeply moved by and appreciative of all Buddha was sharing. No doubt intangible factors loomed large, including Buddha's intensity, kindness, and certitude. It is certainly possible that the words themselves were secondary to factors yet to be scientifically understood, for example, associated with what Buddhists call direct transmission. We can aspire to approach this potential by revisiting this sacred dialog in a fresh, informed light, informed by evolution, the feminine principle, attachment-love and integral attachment, as well as yin/yang, Tantra and wego.

Against immeasurable stretches, ego by definition must tenaciously attempt to pin down a raison d'etre and erect artificial boundaries. The struggle to matter, to have meaning, to simply be is ego's very essence. Such is the nature of the attachment, of course, which anchors the Four Noble Truths. Ego is that which attaches. The pain-space is generated by efforts to form attachments but which, again by dharma definition, have no real essence and are illusory.

Regardless of the term (pain space, suffering, attachment) we would do well to ask: Why does ego push back against infinity, declare and attach to passing illusions, if only to generate a pain-space, to instantly and constantly hurt, to suffer and make its very existence difficult? Pure, endless suffering does not provide a comprehensive explanation for the evolution of ego in human consciousness. The science we have covered paints a picture of ego's gradual emergence during the course of evolution, with comparatively dramatic changes occurring over the last 50,000 years. Ego has no clear evolutionary birthdate. There is no evidence of a line between pre-ego and ego. Similarly, there appears to be no daylight between an ego bolstered by drives, rewards, and survival-enhancing feedback (to eat, procreate, socialize, and nurture offspring) and one comprising a vessel of pain and suffering.

Self/ego/mind comes by both its relevance and utility honestly. Through a review of mom-baby attachment, we have seen how this tip of awareness moves from inchoate to a sustainable form through attachment. This emergence itself becomes a vessel by which self/ego/mind is perpetuated. Through this structure, we as a species receive and transmit the affective bases of survival drives. This somatic-affective bowl fosters transmission but can only be appreciated as the ground of existential meaning through the thin line of sentience it supports. Through sentience, survival, eating, intimacy and human experience have unity and coherence. This sentience transects and unites biopsychosocial bands on the way to realities referred to as space and nonattachment. The latter are discernable through realization and liberation from smaller understandings and attributions of meaning.

We see the seeds of much grander arcs of sentience in intelligent animals. Whales, elephants, and dogs underwent a related evolutionary process. They may not have an equivalent self/ego/mind but we are certainly comfortable assigning, say, beloved dogs with "personality". We absolutely experience their love, loyalty and—yes—attachment. In our species, the associated brain regions that helped dogs become man's best friend have long been in ascendance.

The relationship of ego to our animal lineage (higher mammalian consciousness) is fluid and seamless. There are no discrete demarcations between pre-ego, ego, and Shakyamuni consciousness. The same goes for the pain-space, pain-body, across this continuum from pre-ego to ego to attachment-love to metta to Shakyamuni's awakening. But imperfect demarcations are important witnesses to trees falling in the forest. In fits and starts, ego proved to have a survival benefit. By definition, competitor species with other variants of attachment, and the self-organized form evoking self/ego/mind did not make the cut.

Ego in this sense is very gritty, real, and something rather than nothing. What Buddha's Mom adds is simply a greater appreciation of the integral role of attachment in this extraordinary species' (ultimately cosmic) accomplishment. It enabled our hominid ancestors, who painted pictures on cave walls, who managed to see themselves in the mirror of the cosmos, to avoid being crushed by the enormity and infinity of the universe. Ego enabled our ancestors to be attached to one another and their environs—the emotional, interpersonal and natural spaces of their lives. This attachment included a degree of revelry and sacred celebration of being. Even as our ancestors coped with extremes of pain, fear, and hardship, ego was the little engine that could, aspiring toward ever higher attainment.

Whoever has been deeded an opportunity to inhabit this unimaginably priceless space of human consciousness, this chance to be alive, has the possibility of knowing what indigenous people experienced—ego's root lineage within the sheath of a life dependent on Mother Earth. The fully dressed-out ego, personality, the sense of self, character—by its many names—gives way to the breathtaking space opening to the origins of the life of mind. Personality is the ultimate placebo, a way station, a mechanism for bearing the vastness.

In the Diamond Sutra, this vastness, repeatedly referred to as the "trigalactic megagalactic worldsystem", is used in a formulaic back-and-forth between Buddha and the "Venerable Subhuti". As monks of the monastery of Anathapindada listened, Buddha methodically proceeded through 32 exchanges with Subhuti. In multiple passages, the immensity of space and just vastness itself are the main drumbeat.

> "What do you think, Subhuti, is it easy to take the measure of space in the east?" Subhuti said, "Indeed not, Lord." "Similarly, is it easy to take the measure of space in the south, west, north, nadir, zenith, all the intermediate directions and any direction besides them, in the ten directions?" Subhuti said, "Indeed not, Lord."[297]

Buddha seems intent on inviting Subhuti to conceive of the vastness of the dharma, and then as he does, on demolishing, on stretching and declaring any possible calculation to be ridiculously small-minded. In another verse, Buddha advised that one could "take as many world-systems as there are dust particles of earth in the trigalactic megagalactic worldsystem... and grind them to powder," to produce a pile. Would this "pile of the most minute atoms... be considerable?" "Quite so," proclaimed Subhuti, given that the Lord Buddha has preached about this "as pile-less."[298]

Elsewhere, a vast view is also "viewless", and a grand idea is "idealess". In keeping with the form, the vastness of whatever space the dharma occupies is also spaceless.

The same structure is used to convey that "the idea of a self", "the idea of a soul", "the idea of a person", and "even the idea of a dharma" can exist in the mind of the bodhisattva. No idea or non-idea as well. The emphasis, to put it mildly, is on the negative, on what is not. Like Michelangelo, Buddha chipped away at what contributed to illusion over clarity. With diamond precision, he cut the fetters that concealed truth, beauty, glory, and freedom. In this, he took the "the total aggregation of living beings, be they born from eggs, born from wombs, born from moisture, or arising spontaneously" to their "final extinction". Thus he described reality as it is, in order to transmit nibbana (nirvana) to the many fortunate enough to be in attendance.

Nibbana, he asserted, is pile-less, idea-less, quantity-less, and by extension, egoless. Neither having ego or non-ego, nor even the idea of ego. Continuing in this vein, the pain-space generated by ego's clinging is extinguished when the bodhisattva achieves the capacity to neither have an ego nor a non-ego nor an idea of ego. By extension, nibbana is attachment-less and without even the idea of attachment.

At the same time, mind and mind control are requisite to understanding or receiving this teaching. (As we have argued generously, mind overlaps with ego and self, and indeed many use the term "ego mind".) At the outset, the Buddha tells Subhuti to "listen… pay attention closely and carefully…"

> I will tell you how one who has set out on the bodhisattva path should take
> his stand, how he should proceed, how he should *control his mind*.[299] (Italics
> added.)

With this, one sees that the wisdom that transcends, as the title reflects, paradoxically requires a controlling of the mind. The mind needs to listen carefully, to attend judiciously, for such a transcendence to occur. This transcendence may be painted as being transmitted from an enlightened mind to one not yet enlightened. These great teachings adhere to the same dharma talk structure. In Buddha's case, they are given by a mind which integrates refined, elaborate conceptualizations—of views being viewless, of worldsystems being empty—such that said mind is mindless, beyond even the idea of mind. They are given (perhaps transmitted) to minds able to accomplish this quality of mindless, not mind, beyond even the idea of mind.

Buddha's Mom, as a "science to sentience" formulation, complements this rigorous and not altogether easy-to-follow meditation on emptiness as ultimate, transcendent wisdom. A model of attachment-love is superficially opposite, based in fullness. From this perspective, mind, ego, self, exist, and do so because they are highly adaptive and effective. They have outrageously honed and proven evolutionary/biological skillful means. Buddha's Mom helps resolve the inherently confusing language of emptiness and fullness. In the former trigalactic megagalactic model, idealess, quantityless and egoless are upheld as persuasive and true. In one grounded in evolution, one encounters the fact and relevance of ego, and of being mindful—not mindless. Humans may have egos which cause them to attach and suffer but not only to suffer. The attachment-love humans inherit and pass on is critical for our capacity to create and engage in other spaces: pleasurable, calm, interesting, creative spaces in addition to endless distractions. Music, friends, loved ones, writing, food, and nature bleed across the self's boundaries into we-spaces if not with other humans than with the activity, art, or information filling out the experience. Lover and beloved co-arising.

The life as suffering and ego as pain space formulation paints mind as an illusory and ill-fated attempt at permanence. This points to nibbana, where neither ego, non-ego nor the idea of ego exists and suffering ceases. This does not find a snug fit with the modern, scientific, evolutionary-based explanation for ego, mind and self locatable in Buddha's Mom. The latter emphasizes an evolution of spirit through the transmission of our species' most expansive attainment, human consciousness. An "upriver" and biological basis of consciousness rooted in attachment provides a scientific portal to ultimate spiritual sentience. I have mainly used the terms and concepts associated with attachment to support this mapping. Additional, associated signifiers have been proffered as extensions.

As suggested, for example, this model (as "transcept") is more yin, more feminine in character and more associated with something rather than nothing, with earth, with Gaia. The masculine is associated with the sky, the heavens and sky gods such as Zeus and the Christian God. "Our Father who lives in Heaven" are the first words of the Christians' most sacred prayer. Replacing heaven for all that Buddha continually points out in the Diamond Sutra evokes some sort of trigalactic megagalactic spirit space. The emphasis is on indefinable vastness and what does not qualify for ultimate meaning and reality.

In a remarkable passage (below), the female Christian mystic, Teresa of Avila, directly addresses her religion's tendency to flee earthly, "corporeal things."[300] But in embracing more plural and relational dimensions, she supersedes dualistic reductionisms. As a transcendent, transmissible essence herself she is comfortable with a spirituality constructed on not only that which is negated but also upon what is preserved.

Professor Harrison seems to have something fresh to say about this ancient, revered text and about this emphasis on negation, on reality, for example, as idea-less and view-less. The Diamond Sutra, Harrison writes, "posits that something is what it is only because of what it is not." But critically Harrison believes that a slight mistranslation offers a solution to that which otherwise conveys a "mystical subversion of ordinary language." According to Harrison, previous major translations overplay the negation of various compound words and that "lacking" is technically more accurate and therefore preferable to total negation. Without this, these sorts of exchanges border on the absurd: an enlightened person spending a lifetime telling unenlightened persons that nothing is real. Since nothing incorporates everything, then presumably, the teaching that nothing is real includes the possibility of awakening and that, in effect, everything a teacher could teach has a basis in reality.

Harrison's thesis quite precisely echoes Wilber's transcend-include, negate-preserve model, which we have suggested is also reasonably handled by the construct, relative attachment. A something that is not the precursor, but also not nothing emerges within higher sheathes and vaster vessels of reality. In a beautiful passage, Teresa of Avila, seems to express this essence which we have been labeling Buddha's Mom. Her words are devoted to seekers in general. There is a tantric play of flesh and spirit and signs of a very sublime wego as she writes:

> I think I have explained what it is well for you to know, namely that,
> however spiritual you are, you must not flee so completely from corporeal
> things as to think that meditation on the most sacred Humanity can actually
> harm you. We are sometimes reminded that the Lord said to His disciples

that it was expedient for them that He should go away. I cannot, however, allow that as an argument. He did not say this to His most sacred Mother, because she was firm in the faith and knew that He was God and Man; and, although she loved Him more than they, her love was so perfect that His being on earth was actually a help to her.[301]

In this passage, Teresa of Avila expresses our thesis more beautifully than perhaps anyone ever has. In the Mother, both the beyond measure—quantityless and idealess—and divinity and humanity coexist. We might integrally add the first, second, and third person permutations. Her divinity and my humanity, for example, co-arise. But sticking to the third person, an extension of Teresa's insight is that nibbana and humanity's egomind coexist.

This book has endeavored to add several pieces of evidence to this formulation. For example, humanity's ego, mind, and self find their seeds in the mammalian evolution. This culminates in mammals' penultimate, subcortical feeling aptitudes, discovered by Panksepp. These and other capacities were increasingly coordinated by a central executive function in the cerebral cortex.

Further, in hominid precursors to modern Homo sapiens, advantages to this coordination driving ever more ego integration would have included improved abilities to forage and obtain food. Certain discoveries would be recognized as not just novel but as having meaning relative to goals and aspirations. Ancient "ah ha" moments would be associated with ongoing pressures and efforts. These would have included group strategies associated with nourishment, environmental challenges, predators and competing tribes. Group bonding increased because, over time, certain members of groups with more "wego" tended to survive and produce offspring.

No one can possibly debate that Buddha's "being on earth was actually a help to"[302] Subhuti on the occasion that resulted in the Diamond Sutra. The help proffered by Buddha's presence (rather than absence and silence) just as clearly extended to the monks in attendance and to future Buddhists, now in the hundreds of millions. But the fact of attachment-as-help, as skillful means, has not been fully appreciated. Subhuti, in fact, was no stranger to Buddha. He was one of Buddha's Ten Great Śrāvakas or disciples. We can behold the Diamond Sutra as a most sacred we-space. Subhuti and Buddha must have been in an intimate dialog for many hours, perhaps days. Buddha was intensively devoted to the task of expressing to Subhuti this precious approach to realization. Surely Buddha's own words flowed, if analyzed from the relative side of the street, buoyed atop an emotional vitality and an attachment-love transmitted/born of all we have called Buddha's Mom. In her, we can more fully honor such intimate dialogs and teachings, thematic of Buddha and his monk, Jesus and his disciples, and Teresa of Avila and those fortunate to have known her.

The teacher-disciple "adult attachment" or we-space should be considered an important element in its own right, alongside the content and concepts of the teachings. The wego concept might help in this regard. If we allow that Jesus' and Buddha's realization included (was integrated with) attendant love and kindness, then we can infer that lovingkindness, metta, God's love, and related frames (such as attachment-love) have phylogenetic roots in our ancestors' social attachment capacities. By inference, this factor (or vessel) only becomes more relevant, more beautiful and profound at the highest reaches of consciousness.

Teresa of Avila unapologetically restores the role of attachment within the vastness. One wonders if only a woman can do so with such eloquence and parsimony. She speaks through the lens of the mother and her attachment to the son. For her, conveying the ultimate spiritual realities are not harmed, and in fact, are helped by a love large enough for the fullness of humanity and earthly existence and the emptiness of the beloved's fate, death and ending. Were any of us to have known Jesus or Buddha, we would likely have experienced a love for them. Prajapati's struggle to accept her son's greatness on the one hand, and grounding in nibbana, in emptiness on the other, parallels that of Teresa. Any of us would have to experience the other side of our devotion, the inevitable limitation of our ability to cross over and fully inhabit their brilliance. The disciples and monks are forever asking for one more booster shot. With Jesus, the emptiness or void took a different form. He not only had to die and lose his reputation, to be outcast, but he had to first psychologically die to his own faith. In being forsaken, abandoned, and left to die by the source of his own ultimate spiritual-parental attachment, he encountered emptiness.

Perhaps this form-emptiness dance parallels the ultimate portrayals that physicists ascribe to a universe born in a flash from complete emptiness, with particles decaying into ever lessening existences and others emerging from complete vacuity. Form-emptiness seems in concert with black holes in the center of galaxies where mass collapses endlessly into a smaller space. That this something-nothing dance permeates physics itself seems relevant. Might everyday consciousness not be in sync with this co-arising that Buddhists refer to as form-emptiness?

Another important sutra is based upon dialog between Buddha and Sudatta. Sudatta was a very wealthy man, a major patron of Buddha, and more to the point, someone who asked Buddha whether it was possible to be, in effect, both materialistic and enlightened. Sudatta was known for his concern for those in need. Before meeting Buddha, he had a reputation for caring and generosity and for helping orphans and the poor.

Upon meeting Sudatta, Buddha "saw at once the sterling quality" of Sudatta's heart.[303] This set up is quite tender. Sudatta expresses his longing to do anything Buddha tells him to do. He was very financially successful in his role as treasurer to the King and noble but relayed that it held no emotional bonds. He was good at it, and many in his employment relied upon him. Moreover, as a wealthy householder, he likely had servants, good food and drink, probably had sexual relations, and routinely participated in aspects of life prohibited in monkhood. But the larger point was clear. Sudatta was equally willing to continue as a householder engaged in the world of money, sex and things or leave behind his way of life and be an ascetic. His heart was open and Buddha saw its purity.

The fact that he had long helped orphans and those in poverty is significant. He had done so of his own accord, prior to meeting Buddha. In this, he demonstrates that he is not materialistic, but also not non-materialistic. Buddha clarified that anyone who has wealth but does not cling to it and instead uses their money and power correctly has the same access to realization as anyone else. According to Buddha, "It is not life and wealth and power that enslave"[304] but an over-attachment to these.

Several exquisite strands come together here. Buddha and his sangha would spend nineteen rainy seasons at land donated by Sudatta called Jeta's Grove. There he would give the majority of his major discourses, including the Ākankheyya Sutra.[305] The mother-matter and father-space pairing radiates. In this, "the two attachments" corresponding to Bowlby and Buddha respectively cross over to an integral attachment. That this unfolds in a we-space, finally, cannot be overlooked.

Buddha rhythmically relayed a series of nineteen assertions. Each of these uses this form: Should a monk express a wish, "May I..." and proceeds to list various sublime potentials that a monk seeking enlightenment might envision for himself. These then end with, "Let him fulfill the precepts." The gist is that anything, even what appears to be surreal, supernatural, or miraculous, is possible if one devotes himself to practice. In the fourteenth of these, Buddha gives a resplendent description of the potential to transcend form and emptiness. This speaks to a synthesis beyond matter-spirit duality impregnated with an ever-deepening sentience.

> If a bhikku should wish... "may I appear and vanish; may I go unhindered through a wall, through an enclosure, through a mountain as though through space; may I dive in and out of the earth as though it were water; may I walk on water without sinking as though it were earth; seated cross-legged, may I travel in space like a bird; with my hand may I touch and stroke the moon and sun so powerful and mighty"...let him fulfill the precepts.[306]

Thus Buddha rhythmically implores his listeners to place themselves, immediately, in the first person in scenarios wherein self/ego/mind becomes incoherent and beyond measure. Ego this connotes more than declares is other than just a conduit of suffering and illusion. The same medium somehow involves liberation. Ego's craving, desires, and wishes are more than fetters and do more than portend anguish. The full message and context of these sutras show how the crossing of an attachment-nonattachment bridge involves features of attachment. These include elements seen in all human attachment, for example, unconditional regard, love, playfulness, creativity, and joy.

Walking on water brings to mind Christ's miracles, and like flying or turning invisible, it can be understood as an inmap (a term we previously suggested as similar to archetype). Unlike Buddha, some stress, Jesus engaged in miracles involving healing. Relatedly, Jesus is more associated with claims of being a deity and unified with God.

A transcendent view notes the shared basis in an inmap associated with superhuman potential. It honors differences while recognizing intrinsic similarities. To heal means to make whole. In both traditions, the suffering of devoted followers is a central focus. Then, based on their response to the teacher, devotees may or may not be healed, that is to say, made whole. In both cases, such a process entails a fuller embedding in ultimate realities. Sinners are children of God who need to confess their desire to be separated no longer. Those in samsara are similarly not aware or awakened to their true nature.

The Wisdom traditions use contrasting language which obscures an important, shared essence. But a divine/awakened marriage is possible. In relative attachment terms, Jesus called for attaching to an extant, supreme, divine loving source. For his part, Buddha mostly emphasized a detaching from all that is limiting. The potential for a *something more* generally takes a back seat to the emphasis on renunciation. In the Diamond Sutra, there is some softening of this hard edge, where all-things-attachment must be vanquished. It seems plausible to feel one's way into a balance of the hard edge with the interpersonal sentience pervading this remarkable text. Buddha was devoted to helping the oh-so-earnest, but not-quite-there-yet Subhuti to open his heart. This seems as palpable as the concern Jesus had for the many he encountered and helped who had physical diseases.

Buddhism's parallel to a divinity accessible through the son shimmers forth in the Diamond Sutra. Looking directly at Subhuti, one can speculate, Buddha rhythmically addressed Subhuti's self/ego/mind. "You or it," he intoned, "are actually an ineffable, vast reality here and now, as am I." "We are immediately present but not what we see or name." Where a Christian accesses divinity through Christ, self/ego/mind in Buddhism find portals in Buddha as the Tathagata, not to mention the other two gems, dharma and Sangha. The Diamond Sutra steps out in the direction of the supernatural and divine more than most sutras. It describes an incalculable, immeasurable vastness and such an abundance of treasure and merit that concepts do not do it justice. One will not find the words love, miracle, or healing but "gods" are referred to eight times.

To regroup for a moment, we have described our humanity as at least partially mappable as a vessel. In and through this, I have contended, sentience is transmitted. I have attempted to anchor this model in biological, social, and emotional attachment processes. At this point, we can add that integral love connects attachment with Buddha's metta and Christ's agape. Such a love explains how disciples, followers, family, and friends of both Jesus and Buddha benefited from the relationship.

In total, these ideas give us Buddha as an awakened member of our species, as richly engaged, across his lifetime in relationships with other humans. These we-spaces became filled with and formed of an integral love. This love, along with wisdom, comprises the vessel and dynamic we have referred to mainly as Buddha's Mom.

We see this symbolically in the following: Buddha's wife Yasodhara, biological mother Mahamaya, stepmother Prajapati, father Suddhodana, son Rahula, half-brother Nanda, and first cousin Ananda all received our species' lineage transmission. All became arahants. Arahants are highly realized beings freed of suffering. They have transcended worldly cravings, a form of sin that separates beings from their true and blissful nature. In this, all achieved nibbana (or in Pali, nirvana). They were made whole, united with their true nature and therefore healed.

Let us return one last time to the we-space described in the Diamond Sutra. Near the close of this extended, intimate exchange that would become one of Buddhism's most revered sutras, Buddha addressed Subhuti yet again by name. By this point, he had done so more than 100 times. This is recorded as follows, "This so-called 'idea of a dharma,' Subhuti, has been preached by the Tathagata…"[307]

Perhaps this is Buddhism's "I am the truth and the light…" moment. Buddha again refers to himself in the third person, as the Tathagata, and thereby as in alignment with the endless references to immeasurable "its" throughout the sutra. In this marathon of intimacy and kindness, we can almost feel Buddha's essence. This brilliant, hard-working, devoted man and enlightened being was engaged in a we-space, was giving his all to yet another hungry listener.

Buddha, it seems fair to say, was attempting nothing less than a nuclear download of himself, as a trigalactic megagalactic worldsystem, as dharma, as vastness and emptiness into an other, who was not and could never actually be separate. Naturally Buddha was well aware and much accustomed to the immediate paradox of the mindset of the eager seeker. All of us are swept up in this illusion to perceive ourselves as separate, as missing out, as not "it". A seeker, it follows, is one who longs to be reunited but, in longing, creates separation and suffering. We have explored these givens sufficiently, I hope, so we can recognize how Subhuti's deep respect and earnest questions were the very same ones we all have and which consist of, at bottom, desire. Subhuti was attached to the possibility of grasping more, understanding more, and seeing reality more clearly.

Elsewhere in the Canon, we are told that Buddha was handsome, that he had a resonant voice and deep blue eyes. We all might dare to consider being present that day and being seen by the "lovely-eyed son of Suddhodana."[308] A starting point is to recall any exceptionally poignant encounters one has had in the past. Most would probably agree that the attendant words and ideas paled next to qualities of the other that are, to make this point more precisely, hard to put into words or to formulate as an idea. We left the encounter freer, moved, not dismissed but deeply understood. In a sense, we retain access to this wego experience ever after. Immediate contact fades but we remain a better, larger spirit still connected to the experience. This, we have tried earnestly to articulate, is our species' transmission. Subhuti had his day to be sure. As if talking to a beloved child, Buddha summed up the entire teaching in the last sentence.

> "This so-called 'idea of a dharma…' Subhuti has been preached by the
> Tathagata as idealess. That is why it is called the 'idea of a dharma.'"[309]

Buddha declares one last time that reality, freedom, and enlightenment are not ideas. With a gentle, rolling thunder, the universe itself seems to express, we, you, and I, that this reality and love here and now are not ideas. We exist, we are here, talking, listening, learning, and awakening together—already awake actually, simply together, just talking…

Dogen

Perhaps "Buddhist Invasion" could be an appropriate term to refer to the spiritual influx from the east coinciding with the sex, drugs, rock and roll phenomenon, the so-called "British Invasion" from the other side of the pond. No small part of Buddhism's influx can be attributed to a Japanese monk who lived from 1200 to 1253 and whose teachings have recently become significant. The much-adored Zen Master Dogen lived out a "mega-galactic" life. As with Siddhartha, a fuller picture of Dogen's spiritual quest calls upon his mother.

In his time, Dogen founded the Soto school of Zen Buddhism. He left behind a large body of scholarly writing and poetry. In the modern era, Dogen's impact has gained momentum. His life and work has been exalted by one of one of the Buddhist Invasion's biggest stars, Suzuki Roshi. Suzuki was a modern Soto Zen master who played a major role in introducing Zen Buddhism to America in the 1960s. In addition to the Hippies, many of whom became great teachers in their own right, Suzuki Roshi was revered by other Eastern practitioners. Chögyam Trungpa is said to have been deeply moved by his relationship with Suzuki Roshi, calling him his "accidental father". The Upaya Center is deeply involved in the translation of Dogen's works. Next to the Dharma Ocean shrine for Chögyam Trungpa is one for Suzuki Roshi.

Unlike Siddhartha, Dogen's mother is acknowledged as having influenced his enlightenment. This credit stems from the fact that Dogen himself chronicled an early epiphany. As he sat by his mother's cold body, it is said, he watched a wisp of smoke from a burning stick of incense. In an instant, the truth of transiency, impermanence opened wide. As Suzuki Roshi described this:

> When he saw the smoke from the incense stick and felt the evanescence of
> life, he felt very lonely. But that lonely feeling became stronger and stronger,
> and flowered into enlightenment when he was twenty-eight years old.[310]

Like Siddhartha, Dogen came from nobility. He was about eight when his mother died and may have been adopted at that point by his mother's brother. Scholars are in debate about whether his father had died earlier, and none endorse the presence and care of a stepmother figure. [311] At some point, perhaps around age 10, Dogen left his home and became a novice monk at a local Tendai Buddhist center. He dove into the deep end of the detachment pool (and this relative attachment pole) practicing intensively. He struggled with the basic Tendai claim that all sentient beings are intrinsically, innately enlightened. He would come to ask his teachers, "Why do all the buddhas in the past, present, and future arouse the wish and seek enlightenment?"[312] Feeling dissatisfied with the answers provided, he and another novice monk, Myōzen, left the monastery.

Thus began what has been chronicled as Dogen's lifelong search for a spiritual teacher and a spiritual home. This took him to several local centers in Japan and eventually to China. Because Dogen wrote so prodigiously and was so intelligent and articulate, much is recorded regarding these mentor relationships and training experiences. These sometimes turned from hope to despair, but what stands out is how the largess of the initial spiritual infatuations persisted in its absence. The original allure and heartfelt allegiance survived in the shadowy remnants as the relationship ended.

An opposing, complimentary and more tantric-based view goes as follows—the deepest conveyance of realization flows through awareness of life obtained relationally, through attachment-love and its loss. Structurally, great insights push ego to first become stronger and more elaborate and then to the verge of disintegration, wherein wego holds on to the thread, the transmission of Buddha-nature. Dogen's courage, intelligence, discipline, and study accomplished the former. Then as his innate capacities engaged with local masters, and he attempted to work out ever greater mysteries through these mentor wegos, his former bases or holds on reality crumbled.

These spiritual crises, as we have discussed, have enormous potential. Dogen's life at such times was likely a clash between his sense of intuiting that there were reaches vaster than even great teachers were capable of conveying. Here, we have tied these to our species' innate sentience and through attachment to Buddha's Mom. Similarly, the path to such insights, biographers have suggested, has its headwaters in the death of Dogen's mother. According to Suzuki Roshi, Dogen's mother herself understood the "teaching of transiency" and was concerned with passing this along to her son. In other words, she was grounded in Buddhism's basic tenet, enshrined in the Four Noble Truths, regarding the impermanence of all phenomena. She desired that her son would also come to fully know this truth for himself.

> She had full experience of the teaching of transiency, and she wanted Dogen
> to be a priest of great sincerity. He decided to follow her will.[313]

Perhaps her life, love, and attachment, as much as her death and detachment, should be credited with her transmission of this central tenet. His mother may have heard sermons or similarly have come to an abstract acceptance of life's fleeting nature. One can speculate that for this mother of a beautiful, intelligent son, she was forced to grapple with this when she became ill. As they say, "nothing so focuses the mind like a hanging in the morning." In confronting death, she faced not just her own death but the loss of her young child. From a modern perspective, she may very well have possessed the characteristics attributed to Dogen. Being also brilliant, strong, and courageous, she may have suffered a spiritual crises years before he did. Broken open, facing the obliteration of an intense attachment-love, an ego-less source of love and sentience may have been born and transmitted, albeit in an inchoate form.

The standard view touches on this but might go further. Biographers credit Dogen's mother's death with his early encountering of annica, impermanence. Apparently, while at her funeral, he came to realize this quintessentially Buddhist idea, one of the three "facts of existence." History records no Prajapati figure at hand as his mother's health worsened. Was there anyone holding this child as he ventured up to his mother's corpse? Dogen's access to Buddha's Mom (as a source of sentience via maternal and social-emotional attachment) may have gone from hearty to this abrupt ending. On the human scale, she may have been able to listen and love him until near the end. On the spiritual scale, "she" may have shifted suddenly from an implicit, eternal, ubiquitous, that is to say, an emotional cosmos for Dogen, to a wisp of smoke. A once healthy we-space was abruptly lanced.

Any psychological analysis of Dogen would do well to transcend the human realm. Lone, downriver attributions, for example, that Dogen's attainment was a function of his heroic hard work and unique aptitude should be balanced with one that looks to evolution and the rich, complex ways that our species' sentience is transmitted. To begin with, most mortals are products of nature and nurture and do not suddenly become brilliant or accomplish masterful leaps in character. As discussed, these also tend to call upon early, rich, consistent doses of mother-love to be catalyzed. A conservative assessment would suggest that by virtue of his genetics and specific early-life attachment, Dogen was blessed with a formidable access to Buddha's Mom and this undergirded his epiphany at age eight. Having been passed the keys, Dogen's life unfolded as a series of intensive efforts to unlock ever more doors.

At age 23, he and Myōzen set out on an arduous trek to meet great Chan Buddhist teachers in China. Undoubtedly, this called for courage and involved great hardship. But one might also appreciate that these healthy young friends were immersed in the experience. Young people are always striking out, choosing, it seems, the most impossible odds to satisfy their hunger for raw experience. But always that which one hungers for is shaped by the givens of one's karmic situation.

In our time, the Star Trek call "to go where no man has gone before" and the massive appeal of all the films and iconography touches the same soulful longing. Dogen delved into all that was available to him, all the pre-scientific, cultural givens of his era. He knew deep in his being that something majestic was missing, so he persevered with amazing courage.

The same quest for raw and transcendent experience may be the "force" within both Star Trek creators and fans. Ours is a time of "secular humanism" and a rational, materialistic zeitgeist. But spirit is timeless. A longing for transcendence and majesty is ultimately spiritual, but for many, there is no viable religion or deity to complete its expression.

The passion for Star Trek sometimes stems from so-called nerds' insecurities. They may fear that they are missing a gene for normal emotional expression. They find no depth of meaning in organized religion at one extreme and no emotional connection to romantic comedy movies and other cultural outlets at the other. Yet their hearts pound as they live vicariously through Star Trek adventures. In these, a beloved crew of interstellar explorers encounters exotic worlds and alien lifeforms. Through these exploits, logic and so-called normal consciousness meets with plausible but exotic variants. Material possibility and transpersonal experiences co-arise. No wonder that countless scientists, Buddhists, and Buddhist scientists are unabashed fans.

Along with fantasy and escapism, Star Trek provides the potential for freedom and liberation. Scientifically-minded and often gifted, Trekkies may experience an expanded sense of being and belonging through stunning and creative-but-credible extensions of science. The adventures feature the magic of material reality. Buddha's Mom (with a basis in evolution, affective neuroscience, attachment-love) is also a celebration of material reality, which bridges to the exotic emanations of reality described in Vajrayana and Tantric Buddhism. Through science, the oceanic sentience arising from "just being" in this outrageous universe of ours is glimpsed. The crew's curiosity, hardships, crises and courage are portals of meaning that Trekkies can inhabit without judgment. Fans' sense of connection and belonging speaks to science as a path of transmission.

Similarly, Dogen's search parameters pushed on the outer limits of that established in his era. In China, he and his friend "traveled on foot, donkey, boat, and cart from monastery to monastery without finding a Ch'an master who impressed him as the right teacher." On the verge of giving up and returning to Japan, he would finally meet Ju-ching, the new head of the T'ien-t'ung Monastery.

> The decisive moment for Dogen, as recorded in Kenzeiki, came during a session of intensive meditation when Ju-ching thunderously reprimanded another monk for falling asleep after countless hours of zazen: "In zazen it is imperative to cast off body and mind! How could you indulge in sleeping at such a critical point?" Dogen was suddenly awakened upon hearing this remark."[314]

Dogen, at the age of 28, had finally achieved enlightenment. While sitting in the fashion credited to him, called shikantaza, Dogen experienced "a flashing into the vast phenomenal world, a flashing which included everything, which covered everything, and which had immense quality in it; all the phenomenal world was included within it, an absolute independent existence."[315] Immediately afterwards, Dogen went to Ju-ching and offered burning incense to Buddha. We will never know but can be forgiven for wondering whether this particular incense had another special meaning for Dogen hearkening back to his mother's funeral. In time, Dogen would come to feel a profound kinship with the "ancient Buddha", Hongzhi, who had been abbot of T'ien-t'ung Monastery before his visit there. We will consider the implications of this connection in the last chapter when we delve into "modern attachment theory".[316]

Up to this point, Dogen had engaged in a series of teacher relationships alongside very intensive practice. He sought mentors to co-discover and co-articulate his inchoate mega-galactic view. As each failed to blossom, Dogen must have felt an intolerable burden. Try as he might, he could not construct a wego of what he knew to be imminently simple, accessible, and beautiful.

Disenchantment and depression and spiritual crises are important turning points. Often behind these is a latent sense of vastness, beauty, joy, and kindness. All one senses intimately, firsthand as real and freeing is as yet unrequited. One needs a teacher, friend, or life partner to form a we-space that can bear the beauty. There is shame in being given a gift and not knowing how to say thanks. Maybe in dark moments with a flagging wego, Dogen found himself doubting what he knew to be beyond stunning.

Finally, he found all this with Ju-ching. Once engulfed by joy, this would not turn out to be a permanent state. Dogen soon returned to Japan. Over the next decade, he attempted to communicate his vision for Buddhism. There were political tensions and turf wars with the Tendai stakeholders who sought to suppress Dogen's claims. At age 42, he collapsed in a depression.[317] Perhaps he had been prone to such episodes. These may have contributed to his sporadic disenchantments with teachers over his lifetime, and indeed, may have stemmed from a deep grief over his mother.

What is recorded concerns how Dogen strove to share his vision with Buddhist luminaries of the time. His cries landed on deaf ears. He sometimes criticized those who rejected him for what he perceived as their misunderstanding of the dharma.[318]

As any sensitive person knows, being angry or disappointed in another person simply hurts, often with sadness below anger. Depression sometimes results as a function of becoming worn down. This is something like a hose turned down to a slow drip. One forgets how it is capable of an intense torrent. One feels cut off from, held down by all she is missing, not loving, not witnessing. We might understand the spiritually mature Dogen's depression as a subjective sense of threat to all he fervently knew to be so.

From the current view, his soul was crying out, "Mother, why has thou forsaken me?" What makes Dogen so timeless and forceful is how he lived out this question at the heart of human nature, and how, over and again, he came up with penetrating answers. His original burning question, (why already enlightened Buddhas seek enlightenment) was itself an answer to the deep mystery embedded in suffering in the form of a kōan. Even after becoming fully liberated, he seemed to continuously walk the thinnest line. Psychologically speaking, he trusted the shadow's tug as this disrupted his most revered relationships. Applying Chögyam Trungpa's language, Dogen could "stay in hell." He could be the stillness within confusion and pain. On an absolute side of the street he had awakened to the mega-galactic response in which the self is no more, depression lifts and life expands.

> To be enlightened by all things of the universe is to cast off the body and
> mind of the self as well as those of others. Even the traces of enlightenment
> are wiped out, and life with traceless enlightenment goes on forever and
> ever.[319]

One finds upheaval and renewal to be the norm with many geniuses. They are propelled by the majesty of their penetrating glimpses into reality and bless us with pioneering scholarly, philosophical, and artistic vessels for these. In the West, such persons have been called "renaissance" men, and more recently, polymaths. Contributing to the enlightenment (historical pun noted) virtuosos such as Blaise Pascal manifested their realizations as inventions and breakthrough scientific models. Perhaps great minds who had no opportunity to pursue Buddhist practice nonetheless demonstrate their Buddha-nature by way of the humanities and science. Pascal's words echo themes we have suggested as consistent with Buddha's Mom and a less religious, more spiritual Buddhism. These include the integral nature of reality, expressible both/neither as fullness and emptiness.

> For after all what is man in nature? A nothing in relation to infinity, all in
> relation to nothing, a central point between nothing and all and infinitely far
> from understanding either. The ends of things and their beginnings are
> impregnably concealed from him in an impenetrable secret. He is equally
> incapable of seeing the nothingness out of which he was drawn and the
> infinite in which he is engulfed.[320]

Here Pascal references an ultimate as "impregnably concealed." In this, yet again, the feminine is rediscovered at the very edge of the knowable and describable. Like Dogen, Pascal employed artistic writing to get at what is concealed. He is famous for declaring, "Le cœur a ses raisons que la raison ne connaît point" — the heart has its reasons that reason knows nothing of. The other side of mind and reason is the point to be taken. With the great chain, body-mind-spirit, heart reasoning and mind reasoning co-exist. As Dogen wrote: "Body, like the mountain. Heart, like the ocean. Mind, like the sky." Space surrounds and runs through and holds all these. All these disappear in space. In this way, mega-galactic space corresponds to the mother inmap or, to be more precise, the mother-child inmap. Awareness, stillness, is a mother to its children, its subtle arisings including confusion, heartbreak, and pain.

> You should study not only that you become a mother when your child is
> born, but also that you become a child.[321]

Through intimacy with mind's offspring, one is on the awakened path. The feminine and the mother are ever present at these most sublime altitudes. Jesus is not just the son of God, but the "son of man." This is yet another implicit Buddha's Mom reference where the divine parents of evolution's child merge. In persevering, the mother field yields to its own offspring. Nothing is separate and "Enlightenment is just intimacy with all things."[322]

For Dogen, intimacy smoothes the path to stillness. Dogen's most essential call is to sit zazen in a certain erect, motionless posture called shikantaza. In this posture, one is in immediate and intimate, nonconceptual contact with reality. Egoless and limitless, one experiences expansive, transcendent stillness. To sit shikantaza is all, Dogen declared in another reference to the absolute. Practice as enlightenment is a core Soto tenet.[323]

At the same time, presumably many Zen monks practice for years, and a relatively small proportion achieve enlightenment. Few, at least, awaken instantly. Perhaps the conundrum of shikantaza can only be understood through shikantaza. In this, the body is very still. The urge to move itself highlights the what-it-is-not formulation. The shikantaza/enlightenment oneness is not the pain of joints and muscles—it is not the breath or thoughts arising because it is just life itself before perception and interpretation.

The motion in emotion is another inverse signal of the vast, perfect stillness. In Dogen's call to "become a mother," we would then speculate that the true, still maternal source that he referenced is the "transcept" at the heart of this book. Her stillness is ever so close always and more so when awareness seems replete with surging and upheaval. We must usher this stillness to the fore; that is to say, accept the mother and make space for these upheavals and attachments. We must be "windless, waveless."[324] Stillness of mind is likened to water so clear that "even the waves, breaking, are reflecting its light."[325]

> Dogen said, "I can walk on the edge of a white blade. I can do without food
> and drink, but it is not possible for me to forget my mother's last words.[326]

As another face of Buddha's Mom, Dogen's mom is neither a fetter nor a historical point of interest. Dogen does not seek reunion with his mother's love nor does he seek to detach from her own realization and desire for him. These present no conflict. Through writing emerging from his illumination, we see how the deep, living mother-child attachment is not a hindrance but a vessel of enlightenment. The pain-space associated with Dogen's mother's death was huge. But within this acorn is the tree of life. Dogen pioneered a way to make this life-shaping experience to continue as a positive influence. From this flowed a superseding, positive experience of the truth of the transient nature of life. Such is the correct understanding of impermanence as a "fact of existence".

A larger, tri-megalactic embrace of reality transformed the raw experience engraved in a young boy's soul into his still flourishing legacy. This love and loss, and search for a spiritual home, would write his life across his years on earth. The search became like rings on a pond, expanding outward, larger and more faint, never fully disappearing.

We have made a case for Buddha's Mom as a living, changing, tantric fact of existence born of attachment. Often both invisible and irrepressible, her truth flows through the ecstasy and agony of close relationships. Relative attachment, both the pull towards and away from intimacy powerfully shaped Dogen's life. At the very end of his life, he seemed intent on conveying the tenderness, the vulnerability, the irrepressibility, and the sheer sweetness of all he lived out and came to know.

> To what indeed shall I liken
> The world and human life?
> Ah, the shadow of the moon,
> When it touches in a dewdrop
> The beak of the waterfowl.[327]

Sixth Realm

In an earlier section, we discussed the University of Wisconsin's collaborative work with the Dalai Lama involving the neuroscientific study of the brains of hundreds of advanced practitioners. Out of this came the declaration that French genetic scientist turned Tibetan monk and confidant of the Dalai Lama, Matthieu Ricard, was the "happiest man alive." His "abnormally large capacity for joy" corresponded to abnormally great brain scan results.

At this point, we can add to this perspective what Buddhism identifies as the sixth realm. There are, accordingly, six realms of existence ranging from hell, hungry ghosts to animals and gods, with the human realm defined as the most favorable. Only from the human realm may a being escape samsara. Few of us realize this profoundly blessed reality, leaving samsara at the helm. Our review of deep self disturbance underscored some of the inherent challenges associated with the prospect of climbing out of this hole. But for all the inherent blessing of being born human, the small number of six in the face of an enormous span of sentience, across inanimate objects, bacteria, and so on, is an endorsement of the severe unlikelihood of evolving past this realm, of as the Noble Truths frame it, the cessation of suffering.

In the few who manage to stably awaken to the profound meaning implicit in human beings (in simply, only being, with no level of accomplishment required), various realization flows: compassion for others who are not awakened, the fortune and joy of an existence that bridges to non-returning, and the cessation of suffering. Such is the quick smile, giddiness, easy laughter one sees in the Dalai Lama and his friend Matthieu Ricard.

They are examples of dharma in flow, vitally and energetically alive within a vessel. We have suggested this can richly be described in a variety of ways, for example, as practice, journey, the word dharma itself and verbs such as hold, bear, and carry, and the feminine principle. As seen in Subhuti as well as the etymology of the word, ego itself is a portal to this ridiculously vast primordial nature. As a major hallmark of evolution, ego implicitly points to an obstacle/opportunity to transcending human realm.

For ego, the "trigalactic" enormity is naturally, appropriately terrifying and traumatizing. But being a doorway, our challenge is to cultivate an inner, friendly, most intimate immediacy. And for this to never wane. In doing so we soon discern how self/ego/mind is an exquisitely sensitive touchstone. Microscopic aggressions and slights are like butterflies whose ripples manifest in hurricanes, as described by Chaos theory.

As if this world is not overwhelming enough, five others compete to push through. It is almost impossible not to falter and be grotesque, to kill, to be destructive and hateful. Metaphorically if not actually, all the lifetimes replete with trauma and heinous acts compete to push through. Just a little, ever so gentle breath and noticing goes a long way. We too can at least glimpse the perfection of a higher desire, the non-returning, constant Buddha-nature. The sixth realm, Manusya-gati is referred to as the realm of desire, the Vajrayana is referred to as the path of desire, and indeed a higher, unrecognizable desire is yet another possible phrase for our species' lineage.

While it is tempting to continually anchor our species' indigenous lineage, in evolution, a fuller and more accurate view is based in a present tense, collaborative, and deliberate modeling. For example, biological, maternal attachment was never adequate to prevent deep self disturbance and the psychological platform of a Matthieu Ricard. Primitive, indigenous peoples were very attached, and capable of keeping their children alive. However, the degree of spiritual maturation, articulated as possible in Buddhism and seen in advanced practitioners, is the result of the co-evolution of the deep feminine and self/ego/mind.

Dharma

Reggie Ray speaks of cells having desire, of clouds and rivers and galaxies having sentience, and of our bodies being comprised of disparate centers, each "a living force, an individual galaxy unto itself."[328] According to Deepak Chopra, the universe "mirrors itself in you and me and everything that is alive." Sentience occurs as the universe sees itself through your brain and my brain/mind. The same goes for bats, dolphins, lions, and mosquitos. "So," says Chopra, "...when a mosquito looks at the universe, it's a mosquito universe."[329]

Forms of panpsychism, the metaphysical premise that all matter is conscious, are nothing new. Indigenous peoples, going back to the dawn of time, ascribed sentience to inanimate objects. A 2014 TED Talk by philosopher David Chalmers lays out the case for panpsychism as a solution to what he famously coined the "hard problem of consciousness."[330] This is the age-old mystery of how subjective, phenomenological qualities such as taste and color are derived from merely physical properties. According to Chalmers, there is no hard problem if, in addition to physical properties, all matter has a corresponding internal, subjective, and mental aspect.

With respect to sentience, most of us draw a line between inanimate objects, such as clouds and mountains, and if not plants, certainly animals. We also tend to view consciousness as having verticality, as more elaborate in more complex life-forms. Such a cozy consensus, however, is suspicious. It fails to challenge what may be just the latest version of Homo sapiens' narcissism which Galileo and later Darwin pierced. We humans get to presume superior sentience. Consequently, we can continue to dismiss and miss the actuality before us, not taste the critical urgency of transcending the self and awakening while incarnate and sentient.

Some of us inadvertently maintain a status quo by dressing up Buddha-nature and the like as just prettier versions of the self we have been dealt. We read books, attend retreats, make progress, but never shake the prison of incrementalism. Some go a different but ultimately identical direction.

We view primordial ground, transcendence, and awakening as real but just reserved for someone else. Perhaps for those more daring or brilliant, mystical superstars, "just not me." In other words, as I look up to a great teacher, I look down on myself.

We forestall our own personal transformation in so many ways. Presently, there is a movement in mainstream science to search for signs of life elsewhere in the universe. At first glance, this appears exciting and highly related to the ultimate questions of meaning and of our place in the universe. NASA's Kepler telescope has recently verified over 1000 "Goldilocks", earth-sized, potentially habitable planets among the estimated 8.8 billion just in our galaxy, so this number could increase by 100 billion.

This all seems destined to follow a familiar track. Fantastical possibilities often begin as irrelevant if not unsubstantiated "woo." We wait around for some news from somewhere to bowl us over. Eventually, when new methodologies, new data, new discoveries arrive, however, what seemed to hold such promise becomes run-of-the-mill, the new normal.

This seems to be the way of the world. The threshold for the unimaginably exotic resets, perpetually re-establishing a buffer of the mundane. We humans continually need the ordinary to catch our breath. The truth of our wondrous brief moment here on our rock is already too destabilizing and intoxicating. Lama Surya Das says that meditation translates as "getting used to" life, to "things as they are" being nothing more or less than primordial perfection.[331] According to Dzogchen, awakening need not be incremental or take long at all. As Lama Surya Das explains, "Whether the mind is tied up in knots of confusion and identification or free, open and clear, it is still primordially perfect."[332]

By inference, we should not wait for some evidence of microbes on a distant planet or radio waves from deep space or the next best anything. The tendency to perpetually reset a buffer between life as we know it and primordial perfection reflects a stuckness in a bottom-up/top-down linearity. The evolution of consciousness, itself the spear tip of an expanding universe, is a common bottom-up accounting of reality. Even signs of life elsewhere in the universe would likely fall prey to a confirmation bias, e.g., that it was simply an inevitable result of the elemental forces and primitive matter originating in the aftermath of the Big Bang.

Top-down, in this context, refers to something like the universe itself having sentience and somehow transmuting this into a chosen people. More liberal, similar views hold that an omniscient deity or power goes further, perhaps transmitting sentience into all life forms, or further still into dust, gasses, and raw materials. Religions are inherently top-down. In this sense, Buddhism is referred to as a religion for good reason. Dharma is universal truth, not a philosophy or science built from bottom-up reasoning. Siddhartha's birth, the reader will recall, is steeped in top-down, heaven-to-earth, supernatural symbolism.

Worth further reflection, a sublime melding of top-down and bottom-up dynamics guided Siddhartha's entire adult life. This took the form, "I don't know what I'm after, but I'll know when I see it." He would empirically try, experience, check out everything in front of him, and one by one, move on. Not materialism, not the love of his family, not the local versions of asceticism, not the extremes of the austerities—none would prove to be the elusive something he would know when he saw it, when he experienced it.

At the close of his thirty-five years of this pre-awakening pull, Siddhartha-cum-Buddha referred to the paramitas as the sheath which allowed him a final release of all previous attachments. Once awakened, he often referred to himself and "the Tathagata," one beyond coming and going, beyond ascending and descending.[333] The essential notion was that the dependent origination, the co-arising of bottom-up and top-down processes, and (yes) all duality, is transcended and negated, manifesting as non-dual, primordial awareness, Buddha-nature, and awakening, among its many names.

Great teachers speak comfortably of top-down truths and processes. They move between the rarified and the ordinary so very fluidly. They calmly tell us of the paramitas, galactic sentience, mosquito universes, and how every wisp of awareness now and forever anywhere whatsoever is the universe giving birth to itself with certitude. Significantly, many such teachers agree that a path to these heights of wisdom and bliss was uniquely practiced and conveyed by a holy man from India long ago. They re-assert ways that this path is available to each of us right now. Small wonder small minds, bounded by bottom-up explanations, cannot make sense of it all. Jack Kornfield advises, "After the ecstasy, the laundry."[334] This is a great teaching. If I may, with inspiration from Ray and Chopra, this translates as, *Yes, I am human. Yes, the universe is awakening in me. So there is no me separate from the universe. And now, the laundry.*

Hopefully, the ideas we have considered, what could be called biological Buddhism, helps with this bottom-up/top-down crisis-opportunity. My sense is that the power and elegance of science, of evolution and of bottom-up realities are inadvertently entrapping unless one has had some sort of very personal, direct experience of countervailing, top-down forces. Without this, a bulwark persists. And, paradoxically, this pushes back against pure splendor. We are just flies abiding in fly-minds, buzzing about as Einstein fills the blackboard with equations. The real risk of a great book or teaching is that these just make us slightly smarter flies. I have tried hard to write with an allegiance and alignment to these countervailing, top-down forces being what they may in me.

Such is my understanding and hope for any chance of bottom-up and top-down to disappear in the Tathagata's beyond coming and going, ascending and descending. And for getting used to wonder and splendor, for the fly-and-Einstein-mind to find common ground in a (literally) universal sentience. Siddhartha felt its inverse even in the dissatisfaction and longing which propelled him before awakening. Perhaps that is why we read and attend dharma talks. We are comfortable accepting that we seek transcendence. But what of the prospect that transcendence, something more, is leaning down to give us a hand? Einstein, one of history's most brilliant bottom-up analysts, seems to state that anything less is delusional. Toward the end of his life, he made a famous and, one would have to agree, also deeply Buddhist and integral proclamation.

> A human being is part of the whole called by us "universe," a part limited in time and space. We experience ourselves, our thoughts and feelings as something separate from the rest, a kind of optical delusion of consciousness. This delusion represents a prison for us, restricting us to our personal desires and to affection for the few persons nearest to us. Our task must be to free ourselves from the prison by widening our circle of compassion to embrace all living creatures and the whole of nature in its beauty... The true value of a human being is determined primarily by the measure and the sense in which they have obtained liberation from the self... We shall require a substantially new manner of thinking if humanity is to survive.[335]

All around us is evidence that we do not so much have to rally and transcend ourselves as notice the transcendence at hand. We transcend states of consciousness cyclically, waking, daydreaming, sleeping deeply, dreaming consistently. While in one sense, we are unconscious, in another, our substrate self is never even close to being deleted. My me permeates these comings and goings without thought. Across another dimension, we can sense how our particular flavoring of sentience dependently co-arises with others in our lives. Their face tells us how we feel. Our pets sense and verify and shift our mood.

Consider a species few of us will get to befriend in a direct sense: priodontes maximus, the giant armadillo. What we have called attachment-love and what Buddhism refers to as metta is not unrecognizable in this elusive species. Priodontes maximus may be the longest-lived, super-attachment species on the planet. They have very few offspring. Until recently, little was known about the mother-offspring attachment of this elusive, nocturnal creature. Biologist Dr. Arnaud Desbiez and his team observed one mother and son whom they named Alex.

"I have just returned from the field... and Alex is still in his mother's territory.
Although they do not share a burrow every night, at 17 months old he still
uses the burrows his mother has dug and they continue occasionally sharing
a burrow… We were surprised to learn how high parental investment was.
This new information is extremely important and demonstrates how rare,
and how much care each baby giant armadillo requires."[336]

Priodontes maximus dates back to the Paleocene, 56 million years ago, a big chunk of the 200 million years since mammals first evolved. By contrast, Homo sapiens are thought to be about 200,000 years old. One can make a case for all of the following: similarities between priodontes' and human love are illusory, due to anthropomorphism; simply due to the fact that we share a common ancestor; to attachment-love as a random epi-phenomenon occurring in some and not all complex life-forms. So are we just picking and choosing, and overstating correlations?

Similarly, one can claim that this attachment-love only occurs on our planet, or that any occurrence on other planets is also based in bottom-up evolution, from simple proteins via random mutations. Even if forms of love have randomly evolved in billions of other places, one can make a case for these never co-mingling and having no origin other than that of a materialist's version of the Big Bang or a bottom-up panpsychism.

Further, one can rest in the solipsism that the burden of proof for any claim of a transcendent metta, Buddha-nature, any form of panpsychism and any fly-Einstein scenario, falls upon the one making the claim. One can insist that any ultra-advanced force of love is thus far undetected and therefore irrelevant.

Buddhism teaches us to simply notice the one who doubts with such authority. Within wego, holding on to smallness is common fare. Delusional and proud of it, the small self/ego/mind denies love's beckoning, the pulsing interplay and the immediate experience of self and other. Arising others, objects of a soft witnessing, can include the breath, a child, friend, animal, or the Milky Way. An insistence of a proof of this obvious, ever-present more reveals a stubborn reductionism and desperation. To be sure, this has a discursive purchase, one dismal moment at a time. A love of science denies its own inadvertent emphasis on the first of these two, love and science. A science of love, however, is what Einstein would call for. As cozy as it can seem in the moment, we all have to resist remaining the fly in the scenario, spending our precious time here telling Einstein that his equations make no sense.

If biological attachment evokes attachment-love, pair bonding and by way of spiritual practice, metta, compassion, and lovingkindness, then the body is implicated in Einstein's plea for a "new manner of thinking". Such a notion fits with Reggie Ray's portrayal of the path to attainment through the body. It makes sense that we cling to the little we think we know. If body-mind-spirit is somehow a vessel for universal metta, the scale of metta as a top-down dimension of reality is incomprehensible. Even middle-of-the-road astrophysicists speak of the universe as having seven to nine or more dimensions. Measurable matter is less than five percent of the total matter-energy in the universe. It seems there are plenty of places for a top-down Buddha-nature to lurk. A deeply personal curiosity, humility, and openness to top-down, yes, "supernatural" forces, may be the only antidote to fly-mind.

One side may argue that bug sentience cannot be proven. Increasingly, the other, panpsychism camp makes the case that no line exists demarcating the origins of awareness. A busy little silverfish's efforts to escape the bathtub may in fact intimate its sliver of tanhā, a proto-desire. By extension, germs, insects, and sharks want. The same extending process, however, need not arbitrarily stop with humans. A transcendent sentience, in fact, is to be found at least in the claim of Buddha-nature.

A continuation of this line of reasoning bears on morality. At no point in the arc of evolution, dating back to the Big Bang, do gasses, rocks, germs, sharks, or even human sociopaths cross some definitively clear line from bad to good or from good to evil. Boundaries can be defined reflecting biological complexity, affective and sentient complexity. Logical parallels to the notion of the depth or degree of suffering follow suit with implications for gender. Much of this book has been concerned with the feminine principle, maternal attachment, patriarchy, yin/yang, and other lines of research and theory directly or indirectly associated with gender. Before closing, we need to extend these explorations further. Through some of the darker dimensions of human nature, we land more fully at the doorstep of a trans-human, Buddha-nature.

In a bizarre evolutionary arms race, males of certain species have become prone to use rape to inseminate females, and females have co-evolved countermeasures. Forms of male gang rape of females have evolved in various duck species. Unprecedented in birds, male ducks have strange-shaped, elongated penises, which extend up to forty centimeters. Penis length has been shown to correspond to "the degree of vaginal elaboration" with "dead end sacs" and "clockwise coils". In this biological "arms race" female vaginal morphology appears "to function to exclude the intromission of the counter-clockwise spiraling male phallus without female cooperation."[337]

These sorts of gender-specific phenomena initially eluded Darwin. Only three of 500 pages of *On the Origin of Species by Means of Natural Selection* were dedicated to what would be a central theme of his subsequent 900-page work, eleven years later, *The Descent of Man and Selection in Relation to Sex*. Initially Darwin viewed gender specific phenomena as driven by "survival of the fittest". As almost any modern person would know, this is the essential "struggle for existence", where animals eke out an environmental niche based, for many, in a kill-or-be-killed battle to eat and fend off prey.

Later Darwin would propose a sexual selection theory. He had come to appreciate that gender-specific physical and behavioral traits depended "not on a struggle for existence, but on a struggle between the males for possession of the females; the result is not death to the unsuccessful competitor, but few or no offspring." Sexual selection, not natural selection, accounted for "wholly different habits of life in the two sexes."[338] He referred to this evolutionary force as "less rigorous" than survival of the fittest. We might translate this as sexual selection, accounting for subtler, internal and behaviorally complex gender distinctions. Generally, the most vigorous males, those best suited for their place in nature, will leave the most progeny. However, in many cases, victory will depend not on general vigor, but on having special weapons, confined to the male sex.[339] These special weapons include rape and infanticide. Such tools increase the probability of a male of a given species impregnating the females, often by preventing other males from doing so.

The "war between the sexes" has extremely deep roots as this cursory look at ducks, chimps, and the giant armadillo attests. Only in recent history has one human aspect of this weaponry even been named. This involves a perversion of love consistent with what Darwin elsewhere refers to as "the charms of males"[340] yet it goes by the gender-neutral term, "domestic violence". This form of abuse, which is by far mostly directed at women at the hands of men, was not even being defined, measured, or studied until very recently. The nominal disconnection from any identification with the male gender, and also with sexual selection theory, is very unfortunate but quite understandable. On the one hand, there are patriarchal cultural factors. On the other, our language regarding gender is so limited that there are no synonyms for yang. It is noteworthy that when females are the perpetrators, the relational dynamics are the same. The one in the alpha role is excessively controlling, belittling, emotionally and/or physically abusive. Perhaps the problem could be called Alpha Sexual Selection Syndrome or ASSS.

Women in Siddhartha's time, as in any other, suffered at the hands of such men. Much as today, misogyny was infused into the culture. A monk once approached Buddha and explained that he was "backsliding" because of a woman and he was considering leaving the order. Buddha counseled him that the problem was desire and that "womankind are ungrateful, treacherous, untrustworthy."[341] Perhaps this never happened or was originally taken out of context but the main point holds. Misogyny, the deriding of love and intimacy—what I suggest is sourced in maternal attachment—was the norm and may have even older roots.

Papua New Guinea offers the best examples remaining of primitive, indigenous, tribal life. A study of women there found that two-thirds experienced domestic violence and one-half had been forced to have sex. Another of any number of such statistics associated with the so-called modern world is that 97% of rapists never spend day in jail.[342] The ASSS includes male-on-male aggression and can be framed as an imbalance of attachment-love that shows up as child abuse, racial, social, economic oppression, regime change and CIA subterfuge, not to mention in the exploitation of Mother Earth. Now understood through polyvagal theory (just ahead), these pervasive, attendant, yang neurobiological processes should be understood as implicated in the everyday political venom that hides in Trojan horses such as "conservative principles", where strength, leadership, and decisiveness actually bow to authoritarianism. In all instances, an inter-being based in love is too weak to prevent aggression.

Soma's integral, freeing lineage calls for a return to Earth. The body syncs when pre-linguistic senses are reset in the woods, forest, jungle and ocean. When asked certain forms of questions, Buddha's practiced and modeled noble silence. These question forms are too yang-heavy, driving for demarcations between existence and nonexistence, eternal and temporal, past life, current and future life, whether the soul dies with the body or lives on. To respond with words to these fourteen question forms would be unedifying. He made this point with yang precision, wisdom and yin lovingkindness at other times.[343]

Balance calls for transformation. As metaphor and model for the deep feminine in Buddhism, Buddha's Mom provides comes ever more into being across the three turnings. The weight of evidence takes this arc even further, as found in the work of Reggie Ray, to a human lineage that is technically post-Buddhism. Fits and starts are the rule for the feminine's transformative integration. The life of Prajapati, a palpable, concrete expression of the feminine in Buddhism, is illustrative. Over and again Ananda encouraged Buddha to allow her (women, this beginning aspect of the feminine) into the sangha. Finally, the Holy One declared that women and men are equal in the eyes of the dharma.

Three months after Buddha died, his disciple Mahakasyapa convened 500 followers for what would be called the First Council. The goal was to preserve Buddha's teachings. There is no record of the inclusion of nuns in this important meeting.[344] The absence of the feminine is conspicuous in light of Ananda's central role and his direct advocacy for inclusion. The First Council's silence on the matter indirectly suggests a political swing back in the direction of patriarchy. The feminine's slow unfolding across the three turnings, and the need for a recognition of integral attachment as a science of love, speaks to the same slow meandering course.

One related factor is that patriarchy seems intrinsic to reality itself, and therefore not in need of any further elucidation. Men are bigger, stronger and "better armed" than their victims, be these women, children, or the nations armies invade. Bob Marley's Sheriff Brown was too eager to use his badge and gun, power, and control. "Every time I plant a seed, he said kill it before it grows." In humans, relentless alpha violence seen in male ducks and chimps seems to co-exist alongside those of priodontes (the armadillos) and human attachment-love. But co-exist does not equate to balance and can mask the disproportionality. Female ducks are, to put it mildly, forced to become mothers but then go on to protect and nurture their young.

Evolutionary hacks have contributed to the polarization of yin and yang in Homo sapiens. In his Pulitzer-winning bestseller, Jared Diamond documented in gruesome detail the overthrow of a peaceful indigenous tribe, which valued harmony and cooperation, by an ASSS tribe.[345] By inference, this dynamic occurred repeatedly over time as disparate peoples encountered one another. As Diamond shows, the globe was "civilized" over the last fifteen thousand years by aggressive cultures with worse germs and bigger guns.

Corresponding evidence of the advanced status of Buddha's Mom (attachment-love, metta, Buddha-nature) leads to the conclusion that our species is undergoing its own yin-yang arms race. Issues ranging from global warming, the death penalty, affirmative action, gun control to "regime change" are polarized accordingly. This view of our psychospiritual, sentient lineage supports a secular interpretation of karma. Canonical theory holds that each of us was brutish and violent in some of our past lives and spiritual and kind in others. Perhaps this explanation is metaphorical and captures something very core regarding our psychospiritual inheritance.

The same war of the sexes plays out across trans-tribal scales. Bodies such as the United Nations attempt to intervene when governments fail to provide their citizens basic attachment needs (safety, food, shelter). Efforts to curtail ethnic cleansing in Bosnia and Rwanda, for example. At least in theory, well-armed peacekeepers are ready to kill, if necessary, to keep or forge peace. This paradoxical use of power and violence to prevent abuses of the same fits with the transcend-and-include model.

The Vajrayana has much to teach in this regard. Tibetan Buddhism's protector deities, the dharmapāla, are defenders of the dharma. For the not-yet-enlightened, they appear hideous, extremish and beyond categorization. The dharmapāla have roots in pre-Shakyamuni, Hindu iconography and deeper still in indigenous, tribal life dating back to the origins of sentience. This is often referred to as the dawn of time and could be more precisely rendered, the dawn of time, space, emotion, and sentience. Their wild, unconfined protective stance finds a home within a trans-religious, trans-cultural Buddha's Mom. If necessary, she will kill to protect her offspring. Terrorists' effigies of their sworn enemies tap into this yang essence. This essence arises the split-second we judge another for we have just distanced the tributary of the self from its flowing bodhisattva source.

Vajrayana Buddhism refers to these bodhisattvas as wrathful deities. Their malevolent manifestations are faces of an unending compassion. For the sake of sentient beings, they arise in violence and terror and are portrayed as bloodthirsty and murderous. Their eternal truth is reflected in the gentle Jesus's controversial proclamation, "Whoever does not hate his father and his mother as I do cannot become a disciple to me."[346] Wrathful deities' seemingly wicked powers are used purely for good. Hatred and violence are transcended and included for a higher calling much as a river flowing to the sea destroys mountains in its path.

Perpetrators of domestic violence, terrorists, and racists may portray their enemies in similarly grotesque ways and make similarly grotesque claims of superiority. They are only hurting, oppressing, and murdering because they follow a higher call. In all such poisonous affairs, the full breadth of the feminine—as metta, attachment-love, Buddha-nature, Christ consciousness, and intrinsic to the potential for liberation—is conspicuously marginalized. Only in this tender largess does the negating of attachments serve the release and realization that Buddha achieved and symbolizes.

The wrathful deity, Palden Lhamo, would seem to have nothing in common with Prajapati or Buddha's Mom more generally. But she also reveals the yin-yang arms race within our species at its relevance to enlightenment. Married to a warrior king, her love was never enough to quell his desire to destroy Buddhism. Their father-like son was destined to carry out the deed. Palden Llamo would channel a higher attachment-love and kill her son in order to protect the dharma. She transcended and included her love for both through violence that a transcendent, species-wide love (dharma's metta) would live on.

The embodiment of this divine, transcend-include task is portrayed in resplendent, wretched imagery. Palden Llamo flayed her son's body and drank his blood from a cup fashioned from her son's skull. His skullcap, or kapala, is typical of the protector deities. A "gesticulating shaman figure," she has with three blue eyes, dark blue skin, riding a white mule or steed across a sea of blood.[347] She sits on the recently flayed skin of her son. This drips with blood, providing sustenance for a throng of undulating snakes![348]

Palden Lhamo is a co-arising shadow of Buddha's Mom. The latter pours herself into and is released in her son. The former kills him. Prajapati's selfsame son is bottom-up evolutionary transmission who lives on. Palden Lhamo's son symbolizes inherited vessels that must be destroyed to touch the spiritually descendent dharma, to ensure the top-down Tantra flows uninterrupted.

While it is tempting to try and stuff this sick, ugly, fascinating genie back into some culturally bound bottle, an updated, United Nations' version of Palden Lhamo might not be impressed with modernity's ability to stop patriarchal carnage. Unfortunately, orthodox Buddhism has limited its forays into the mess and madness of modernity. The Dalai Lama's *Mind and Life Project* has mainly focused on the neuroscience of meditation. A focus has been the brains and minds of practitioners with tens of thousands of hours of meditation on their resumes.

However, Palden Lhamo reminds us that dharma needs to descend on mass murderers as well as those who practice peace and happiness. The world needs more of the courageous, creative sort of work that Roshi Joan Halifax does with prisoners and dying patients. Siddhartha-Buddha touched many lives. Of these none (Prajapati, Rahula, Kisa, Ananda, and Patacara, for example) seemed to have suffered from early life attachment wounding resulting in deep self disturbance and the sort of psychopathology that gives rise to domestic violence, oppression, and terrorism. None of what we could loosely call Buddha's patients demonstrated what today is termed borderline personality disorder. Even these many years later, Buddhism tends to supply something of a one-size-fits-all definition of suffering.

It would be helpful to see experts in the full embodiment of the paramitas move beyond dharma talks and the neuroscience of high functioning individuals, into for example, genocide, psychopathology, politics, education, and parenting. Ricard himself is said to be dedicating proceeds from his books and his energies into supporting orphanages and schools in Asia. The insights of such an advanced mind, working directly with abandoned children—precisely those sentient beings suffering from attachment wounding—would be invaluable from the perspective of Buddha's Mom.

Another metric along these less travelled roads is the United Nations' Declaration of Human Rights.[349] The combination of Buddhism's discoveries of our species' natural state and associated findings from neuroscience should be the foundation of such noble efforts. Perhaps one day this document will say much more than, "Motherhood and childhood are entitled to special care and assistance." If Buddha's Mom is close to the mark, the role of maternal, biological attachment in the cultivation of a sound self/ego/mind would be encoded into proclamation of human rights. Buddhist concepts and moral codes would be translated into modern, secular equivalents strengthening an ever-evolving spirit-science bridge. Principles already present in various moral, indigenous, and spiritual traditions would be incorporated. These, the paramitas, Buddha-nature and the reality and bounty of what we have framed as the human lineage would increasingly translate into policy and action. Perhaps one day the U.N.'s blue helmeted peacekeepers and other authorities will strive to answer the bodhisattva call, proactively disrupt "ethnic cleansing" and identify and reverse the *before* of famine, poverty, global warming, corporate abuse, pollution, and systemic oppression of girls, women, and minorities.

The counsel and consensus of the world's most advanced practitioners could be the critical source of policy and intergovernmental action. For any chance of legitimacy, persons charged with this function would have to be free of narrow religious identifications. Tantric doctrine and rituals were secretive for a reason. Chants focused on protector deities, for example, and concepts concerning our species' sexual and violent propensities were and are, naturally, ripe for misinterpretation. Palden Lhamo and her cohorts are intended to assist with the most sublime levels of psychospiritual realization. From the relative side of the street, that which is perpetually paradoxical can even appear grotesque and violent. These hate-your-mother and kill-the-Buddha forces pulverize and destroy the impurities of mind. Hopefully in the near future, integrations of

Buddhism and science will better channel such potentials and intervene wherever small minds with big weapons restrict humans' access to buddhadharma.

While we are dreaming of a brighter now, a flowering of an indigenous Buddhism is at hand for any awake enough to experience the dream, where integrations far beyond those alluded to in this book will continually renew and astonish. These would include the other side of sitting and stillness and ever-deeper returns to body, skin, muscle, emotion, movement, and desire. We have considered tantric connections to therapeutic modalities such as somatic experiencing and ecstatic traditions involving shaking and quaking. The most ancient, indigenous taproot available for direct study and synthesis is that of the African Bushman. This includes skin-to-skin and "skinship" rituals with no small echoes of the world of moms and babies on one side and Tibetan yab-yum practice on another. Surely the future will be flooded with indigenous, endogenous, naturally arising complementary forms of ecstatic meditation. It seems abundantly clear that these will take thousands of forms and reflect—perhaps a better word is channel—the thousand-armed bodhisattvas of Tibetan Buddhism.

The flood of ideas, techniques, recommendations, endless flow of books such as this, all the teachers and dharma talks are not unrelated to what children do outside of schools and churches indigenously and endogenously: play. The tanhā tenet which anchors Buddhism captures how our species is prone to boredom, novelty-seeking, play, and innovation. The explosion of yoga and other ancient and traditional practices in the West, including the many sweaty and sensuous dance and movement forms—so many paths are ripe for connecting participants to deeper spiritual threads. The eruption of experimental, secular sanghas seems inevitable. While an evaluation of their depth vis-à-vis transmitting the dharma is obviously important, "primitive" passages should not be overlooked.

The Bushmen have a universal non-word sound, "njom", that they use in the throes of ecstasy to express the sublime, delicious joy of life.[350] This is similar to the "mmm" sound we all make when eating something amazingly tasty, and it has the same basis as "ohm" and "mama" as we discussed. Appreciated at a level of tantric, sensual transcendence, this may be the sound of Siddhartha partaking of Sujata's milk, and can be the sound of any one of us drinking of the feminine's golden vessel.

Integral Wonder

Kids play a game that has probably been played for eons. This involves the repeating of a common word ad nauseam. Try and repeat, for example, "gear" way too many times. This simple word game inevitably results in an experience where an everyday, totally normal word is instantly bizarre and hilarious. The possibility of such a release, according to advanced Buddhist practitioners, is always close at hand—even for complex mental phenomena.

Strings of sounds fluidly form words, thoughts, and express ideas. Few of us notice each distinct phoneme any more than we are aware of separate photons smashing into our retina. Upon forced reflection, presumed, familiar experience is suddenly murky and odd, and then ordinary once again. The implicit, naive hilarity that kids spontaneously experience in such mental play is the same coy humor that runs through the thousands of pithy Zen sayings.

Even the big, hefty "I" upon reflection turns out to be a fleeting, internal-external, consensual contrivance. This aggregation, masking as a whole, is merely the sum of parts that themselves are ultimately beyond any stable distinction. It (you, me, I) gives way. But with no alternative resting place, the "I" insidiously, persistently snaps back in place. Spiritual practices engender skillful means that can be applied to such larger expanses of mental territory. Another realm is fear itself. As in the normal-to-odd-to-normal word game, we feel we know fear before it hits consciousness. Fear and "I", e.g., self/ego/mind are ancient, evolutionary co-travellers. These co-arise in an ongoing, ever-present mist. We are already engaged in a combative stance or have darted far away "before we know it", with it being the surface flow of experience. We cognize this "it" before we re-cognize it. And this *before* can be nearly impenetrable.

The little secret revealed by the word game is that we live the before. We live the *prior to* the expansive, freeing feeling of seeing the true reality that is unconstrained by mind. Self/ego/mind is revealed by such peeks for what it is, a mass of mental artifice that keeps reality at bay. We live out much of this precious life in this *before*, before some sort of clarity and opening into our true nature. Before now.

Kids catch on immediately and find delight that their world is not what it seems. What seemed to be a whole is somehow constructed and thinly consensual. We all go about as if this bit of mouth-moving and sound-making is a thing. But it is bizarrely random and contrived, is no thing per se — and *this* nondual open, immediate otherness is joyous.

This access, this opening and ever-present potential freedom may not answer the *why* but makes decent stab at *how* there is something rather than nothing. What is unveiled may be the one corner of the larger fractal patterns that neuroscientist Antonio Damasio refers to in his books, *Self Comes to Mind* and *The Feeling of What Happens*. Contrivances and consensual agreements about self, other and world snap together across vast fields of mental experience. Words, thoughts, fears come to (be) mind within a field of awareness. We can touch and navigate this living unfolding ever more mindfully with practice. One has heard and said the word, felt the fear, with less mindfulness, less freshness, ten thousand times. But in leaving the before for the now, *this* time something is different. Something implicit and not initially comprehensible occurs. One little bit of life is entirely both old and new at once, both ordinary and extraordinary. All this offers some everyday wiggle room around the paradox of mind as a hindrance versus the call to be more mindful.

Fear is experienced as fear precisely because of this quality of bearing down on mind unbidden, unwelcome. At least in concept, we have the potential to see this very, very old and repetitive pattern afresh — and to taste some freedom and release alongside this. As with this simple kids' game, the surprise of fear can turn out positive. Not threatening, confining or marginalizing but enlarging. The sensitive, open self/ego/mind here encounters and releases into a larger internal field.

As discussed in the previous chapter, Buddhists talk about an inner vastness that is life-affirming, an empty space that is surprisingly full. Experientially, we can and should, these insights show, remain earthy and real even as we free-fall. On the cusp of the ordinary and extraordinary, where the Zen monk continues to chop wood and carry water, she becomes more rooted in the already, always right-here-within-me-all-along. Such is the promise and feel of implicit witnessing of "everyday" experience. A miracle beckons when one manages to experience—*to know* is a much better description—fear as surprisingly unsurprising.

If some enlightened and friendly relationship with fear (stress, anxiety, worry) is not yet fully accomplished, one can take some solace from the fact that another opportunity at practice is just around the mind bend. The intervals between such "opportunities" are seldom long. And the trainings may last for days when we would so prefer they be seconds. By the very definition of not enlightened (not realizing one is realized) one has either no awareness of these dynamics or some dawning awareness after the fact. As the "oops I did it again" feeling sets in, one is still slimed, rattled, hurt, and angry. Note how this unwelcome, unsurprising surprise first arises. At bottom, there is the generic, comprehensive rattling of the mind-body cage. This is the human plight, the baby's cry before it has the concept of hunger or milk. *Hair on fire! Do something!* Demanding, attention-grabbing, yet mind-numbingly the same over and over again; fear is the proverbial good ol' hammer that reduces everything experiential to a nail.

Fear is no word game. It saturates human consciousness because it permeates our genus, Mammalia. Whales, wombats, and we humans have managed to forge our respective niches because of this unsung skillful modality. And in our case, this niche was and is built upon self/ego/mind. Claims of ways to manage or overcome fear need to be taken with many, many grains of salt. Many are sleight of hand and partial truths rather than anything leading to lasting transformation. My takeaway from many years of clinical work is that whatever one might experience as confronting and overcoming fear is nine times out of ten both very important and very illusory. Fear is so fused with our familial and cultural neurobiological programming that there is almost always more to the story.

Generic, substrate fear is the opposite side of the same coin as Panksepp's *seeking*. Given that *seeking* is the master emotion, fear and cousins such as anxiety and panic could hardly be more of a ground zero. When anything at all arose in the field of awareness, our species' deepest evolutionary programming favored fight/flight and anxiety, panic, and the like over parasympathetic calm. Fight-flight's rarer alternative, freezing, is clearly also triggered by fear. Where there is a life instinct, fear is not far.

We have already linked the fundamental Buddhist tenet of clinging and attachment—tanhā of the Noble Truths—to *seeking*. The substrate of fear fits as an iteration of tanhā's partner dukkha, co-arising in relative conscious realms. It's hardly surprising that there are multitudes of words and models for the two sides of human nature. Most would be in concert with fear and derivatives co-arising with *seeking* and its derivatives. We have already considered how neurobiological *seeking* resonates with experiential states higher up the "great chain", such as expectation. These sync on one side with anxiety, dread, and on the other with satiation, homeostasis, and satisfaction.

We have also argued for the useful concept of relative attachment. As we consider these many layers, relative attachment seems to only become clearer. It arises as fear, dukkha (etc.) on one side and as tanhā, hope, and expectation (etc.) on the other. Such is the human plight commonly associated with self/ego/mind. In a recent impromptu response, the Dalai Lama gave perhaps the ultimate pithy summation of these ideas. He had been asked about his decades-long interest in neuroscience. He was asked what led him to develop a mind so eager to understand itself.

> Since my childhood I think I... kind of person or boy (sic) who always
> curiosity whenever I come cross something new. I always raise question why
> how why how always (laughter) so I think that may because of the

plasticity...I feel because of my mother very, very kind mother, very, very affectionate compassionate, so therefore my brain...no fear, no kind of anxiety so that some help. I think the problems of development my brain so I think one of the nature of brain the human brain not animal the human brain is the ability to inquire. Because of kindness I think really helped I think the proper development of my brain. I'm quite sure if I grow in the atmosphere of fear anxiety I think the natural proper develop of brain I think some difficulties...And then because of neurodevelopment...start study.[351]

Biotensegrity & Fascia

Biotensegrity is an emerging science of the human soma with parallels to Buddha's Mom. The term stems from the work of R. Buckminster Fuller, designer of the geodesic dome. An iconic example is the huge golf ball looking "Spaceship Earth" at Disney World Florida. Smaller, domestic versions and "yurts" can be found all over the world. Fuller coined *tensegrity* to describe engineering applications in which *tension* throughout a structure produces its *integrity*. Biotensegrity refers to the biological extensions of tensegrity seen in biological forms, most notably in the human body. It takes tensegrity further on the great chain, from inorganic and mechanical to organic and biological. Intersections with the themes associated with Buddha's Mom suggest confluences at even higher echelons, in essence, psychological, spiritual, and possibly, Tantric tensegrity. The work of one of Fuller's early admirers offers an invitation.

After spending the summer of 1948, sculptor Kenneth Snelson began experimenting with building tensegrity-based structures. Twenty years later, he built a 60-foot-high "Needle Tower" for the Hirshhorn Museum in Washington DC. At once unassuming and basic, made of only short metal tubes and lengths of cable, the tower nonetheless seems to defy logic. None of the linear, rigid elements (analogous to skeletal bones in biotensegrity) touches another. None is more than a few feet long and there is nothing at the top holding the entire tower up.

Snelson's tower provides a visual depiction of tensegrity. The tower provides a mechanical representation of the push-pull of attachment-detachment. The same engineering could support a much smaller or larger form. As the theory proposes, a continuous, inter-connecting tension provides a scalable structural integrity. The self-contained, buoyant aesthetic arises from the fact that,

> ...the compression-resistant struts do not touch but instead are individually lifted, each embraced and interconnected by a system of continuously tensed cables, a condition that Snelson and Fuller called "continuous tension, discontinuous compression."[352]

From the simplest level and scaling up components "interact to bring out each other's essential nature"[353] Snelson's tower dramatically portrays the combination of rigidity and flex, "cables pull in on both ends of the struts, while the struts push out and stretch the cables."[354] In the human body, of course, bones are rigid and muscles pliant. The load or tension is distributed evenly across great spans. Component elements are said to be "prestressed", evoking structural integrity but also to be responsive to external forces. For example, spider's webs are continuously reshaped, within limits, as the wind blows.

> While they are stabilized by prestress, tensegrity structures are also
> exquisitely responsive to outside perturbation. Their components
> immediately reorient when the structure is deformed, and they do so
> reversibly and without breaking.[355]

According to Snelson, there is nothing all that special or dramatic at hand. Kids' kites formed of two sticks and string operate on the same principles, as do spider webs (in two dimensional space). But this only begins the journey toward biotensegrity. Any given component is a mix of subcomponents providing its overall rigidity/flexibility. More pliant elements (corresponding to muscles, tendons, ligaments and fascia or kite string) work in conjunction with more rigid ones (bones and joints or a kite's dowels) yielding overall integrity. Fully scalable, the whole of the body complies with tensegrity principles, as do endless subcomponents. Each conforms to the simple kite design but in three-dimensions. Spatially, the components and tension forces exist as polyhedrons. This emerging area within material science is referred to as the study of soft matter.

The polyhedrons are theorized to be formed of multiple triangles with hinged sides capable of enclosing spaces, interlocking in scalable chains from cells up to the entire soma. Stevin Levin, MD, who introduced the term biotensegrity, asserts that the most important of the polyhedrons is the icosahedron, a spheroid made up of 20 triangles. This structure resembles a simplistic, symmetrical geodesic sphere made of the least number of triangles capable of fully enclosing space and forming a rigid, ball-like unit.

> Tensegrity icosahedrons are used to model biologic organisms from viruses
> to vertebrates, their cells, systems and subsystems. There are only tension
> and compression elements in tensegrity systems. There are no shears,
> bending moments or levers, just simple tension and compression, in a self-
> organizing, hierarchical, load distributing, low energy consuming
> structure.[356]

Just as a spider web has a multiple of independent points in space, so too does the body. But in the human body, the points are in relationship to one another and not an outside referent, such as a tree branch. Accordingly, the body is a self-enclosing, self-unfolding, self-sustaining web of tension-integrity with no need for a fixed external reference. Points within somatic space "press outwardly against..." one another "...in the tension network to form a firm, triangulated, prestressed, tension and compression unit." From atoms to molecules to cells to body "parts", these units fit what Wilber calls holons (whole-parts). And also to comport with the Russian doll form.

All biological life forms, for example, is comprised of cells. Despite their outlandish heterogeneity in shape and size, all cells have an outer membrane with organelles inside. A pliable "cytoskeleton" creates the inner space. *Compressional support* is provided by relatively large microtubules, similar to the rigid struts in Snelson's tower. Countervailing *tensional support*, corresponding to the tensed cables, is provided by microfilaments.

A living integration of these fractal-like, holonic structures manifests in strength, flexion and motion. Accordingly, biotensegrity accounts for the grandeur of Cirque de Soleil acrobatics, mixed martial arts' fearsome moves, and the supreme athleticism and artistry of über surfer, Kelly Slater, Ashtanga yogis, and ballet dancers. Superhuman feats of normal people lifting cars off of crushed loved one come to mind. The overlapping of ordinary and extraordinary is of course a deeply Buddhist insight. In line with Zen's washing dishes, the astonishing truth of biotensegrity (and as I will consider just below) extends into psychological and spiritual realms. Levin places all of these amazing-and-ordinary somatic capacities squarely within inherited animals' musculoskeletal architecture. He came to this realization when considering how none of the discoveries of dinosaur tracks were accompanied by evidence that they dragged their tails on the ground.

> The Diplodocus had a tail that was over 100 bones long and was held up in
> the air. It didn't drag on the ground. It used to whip around. There's no way
> that that could have functioned unless it was in a tensegrity structure. The
> muscles are adjacent to the bone. There's no lever that you can possibly make
> out of it, so it has to function as a tensegrity.[357]

Fascia enthusiasts denounce orthodox formulations of fascia as passive sheets of connective tissue. The emerging view is one of an interactive, spongy foam or gel, perhaps something like a 3-D trampoline in which our skeleton is suspended. These "discoveries" are not new for Tai Chi and Qigong teachers and correspond to the beauty and fluidity of movement. The body is formed and remains under tension or biotensegrity. There is no separation of muscles, tendons, ligaments, joint spaces and there are no pins or levers. In conjunction with the skeleton, these interconnected elements evoke somatic tensegrity. Conventional part-based views of the body are giving way to the new integrative paradigm.

> Histologists classify muscle cells separately from the "connective tissues"
> (bones, ligaments, tendons, and fascia), but muscles and connective tissues
> are all derived from mesoderm and are anatomically continuous with one
> another. Muscle cells simply have some properties, such as contractility, that
> are not found in the true connective tissues, so from a cellular perspective,
> they earn their own category.[358]

Fascia is a heroine. Descriptions of it redefine, for example, sitting upright in meditation or walking meditation as any sort of passive enterprise. Postures and movements are an exaltation of being. In sitting and walking meditation, in yoga asanas, the body is celebrated in a most direct manner. In reaching for the sky, lengthening the spine, and breathing into areas that so easily live unnoticed of somatic compression, we engage fascia.

> …fascia offers a unifying medium, a structure which literally ties everything
> together from the soles of the feet to the meninges which surround the brain.
> This ubiquitous material offers support, separation and structure to all other
> soft tissues and because of this produces distant effects whenever
> dysfunction occurs in it.[359]

Classical anatomy is mechanical, based in levers and pulleys. Muscles were believed to apply force through hundreds of ligament cables. Avison, however, asserts that only six of the body's supposed 900 ligaments actually fit the criteria. The old view is based in artifacts derived from the dissection of dead tissue.

> Anatomically, muscles are wrapped into fascial bags containing the fibres in which contractions take place. Although the fibres are only located within the belly, or pastor, of a muscle the connective tissue, that is the fascia, continues on to become the tendon. It then continues on to become the outer covering of bone known as the periosteum. Periosteum continues along the shaft of a bone and will rise up to become a tendon of another muscle. This way of learning about muscles will, for many, be in stark contrast to the way medical students are encouraged to think of muscles.[360]

Fascia plays a critical role in what we have already explored as psyche's substrate. This emerging model places connective tissue on the great chain, spanning from physical and physiological upward toward mind yet downward toward body, with implications for somatic sentience. Fascia invites a journey of body-mind-spirit-mind-body and so on, a tantric encircling. Known to be key in proprioception (perception of body in space), research has also linked fascia to interoception (bodily self-sense). Interoceptive receptors in fascia, for example, outnumber proprioceptive receptors seven to one. Interoceptive signals are processed in different brain regions than those giving rise to proprioception. As I will discuss just ahead, there is yet another sentient pathway referred to as neuroception. This pertains to an evaluation of and response to somatic safety and threat that normally occurs outside of awareness. Neuroception forms its own circle. Through compilations of meaning-structuring processes, fascia has much to offer with respect to philosophy's hard problem, the brain-mind divide on one hand and concepts of the soma as the ultimate substrate of sentience on the other.

> It is now recognized that fascia network is one of the richest sensory organs. The surface area of this network is endowed with millions of endomysial sacs and other membranous pockets with a total surface area that by far surpasses that of the skin or any other body tissues.[361]

The body's living, fluid, sensorial mapping of itself is synthesized in the subcortical areas that Panksepp identified. These affective touchstones provide evidence of the pipeline, or more grandly and inclusively, of the transmission of our innate species' lineage. Fascia highways account for the felt sense of one's heartbeat, for temperature, pain, tickle and itch, positive affectionate touch, hug and caress, also hunger/thirst. As discussed, Panksepp has shown how affective inputs catalyze fear, grief, lust, and other emotional bases of the human sentience. As the sad stories of feral kids demonstrate, these substrates of psyche do not pop out of thin air.

Their attachment soil is somatic. The indigenous neonate and infant are commonly "worn". Much of their first weeks and months, they ride about in contraptions attached to their mother and are drenched in sensory input. Multi-channel somatic inputs include skin-to-skin contact, exposure to varying temperature and not just gravity but acceleration and deceleration as their beast of burden walked, sat, gathered berries, rocked and bounced them. These would bridge forward from earlier, in-utero impressions toward ever richer bodily maps. The many channels, homeostatic, sensory, proprioceptive, interoceptive and affective, by design are not experientially distinct but tributaries leading to streams to rivers to the oceanic soma. A cogent, somatic sentience and "that which observes that which arises" give wego its most essential form. To be human is to receive this lineage.

We do not create or earn this gift. As Buddhism teaches, it comes gift wrapped in suffering, only more so where these earliest substrates are sparse and jumbled.

Thankfully, vasovagal theory lights the way back to the body. Deep emotions are often the conduit. Consider the infant's experience as its mother snatches it out of harm's way. Within seconds, the baby might experience some vague and sudden visual change, loud sound, proprioceptive disruption, racing heart, breath and fear. When maternal attachment goes well, it would follow, the somatic ground of being would marry such moments with a host of inputs, warmth, soothing feelings, sounds and positive affect. The sense of "we" would hold the whole of such dips out of and back to a coherent affective flow, and translate as safety and refuge. The essence of the call to stillness and bare attention within Buddhism taps into the same dynamic. Fear, confusion, pain, noise, nonsense arise automatically and stress the sophistication of our ability to house these. Thoughts without a thinker refers to a degree of sophistication wherein one's personal, dysfunctional container is adequate enough to be transcended. As it sloughs off, a living emptiness remains. Vessel and contents, "me" co-arising in wego, the Vajra body, awareness itself holds the space and is the space.

Adding fascia to this dignified list is justified. Fascia's modularity and scalability parallels relative attachment as a sister "transcept". It also fits with integral theory's transcend and include dynamic. Fascia's added value comes from its direct associations to somatic awareness, maternal and social attachment. Successive regroupings push onward from biological to affective, evoking refinements in the same way any great painting is composed of primary colors. Fascia as a portal to somatic sentience is palpable, visible and inviting. To get there, we adults may need to move lower, earlier and more into direct experience. As the bible puts it, "unless you change and become like little CHILDREN, you will never ENTER the kingdom of HEAVEN."362

Children have more spring in their step than their adult editions ever will. They walk and move with more lift and bounce, reflecting a wider, softer range of biotensegrity's tension-compression balance. Just as wolf, leopard, and orangutan toddlers pounce, prance, leap, cavort, ambush, scream, and snuggle, more cognitively advanced human rompers overflow in affective extensions of their physicality. Emotion in toddlers flows more freely all day, everyday than it will in later years. These natural experiments bridge toward increasingly facile iterations of self/ego/mind.

Kids laugh, cry, fight, sleep, are heartbroken, lose control, giggle-scream, laugh-and-cry, have meltdowns, feel overwhelming guilt, say sorry, forgive all so much more dynamically, frequently, flexibly, in shorter bursts with more acuity, less stuckness, more release and freedom than they (we) ever will again in life. Securely attached kids are immersed in affective dialog. This constant current of texting and interacting in Instagram and Snapchat, all the checking in, responding with LOL and emoticons, are the stuff of everyday, we-space attachings and detachings. Obviously maturation of these body-mood-mind arcs is key to each species' success. Kids are not capable of raising kids. The best way out is through. They must transcend-include and recapitulate attachment-love across broader canvases so as to perpetuate species' transmission. For the millions of us who missed out on a robust download at the beginning of life, we would do well to re-awaken through the body, through play and emotion reconnecting to these tree roots.

At age 18, Mexican painter Frida Kahlo was impaled and nearly killed in a horrendous accident. A metal handrail entered her hip, pierced her uterus and exited her vagina destroying her ability to have a child.363 Her "Flower of Life" painting, like so many great works of art, flows with themes we have explored associated with the Tantric tradition. Elements and affects represented include male and female genitalia, blood and pain depicting terror, longing in juxtaposition with life's fervent, incessant pressing forth.

Such lives and works of art are celebrated because they touch a chord. We sense the courage of a being which refused to be crushed. What could be identified as Kahlo's sentient-tensegrity, the meaning in life she felt was actually what she felt actively, felt-into-being. Her spirit more than endured. It became, came to be, because of her immersion into psychologically devastating events and relationships. Kahlo's pain, early life attachment wounding and rigidities, the absence of suppleness, looseness, and play, all point toward the possibilities associated with fascia. *Discontinuous experience*, ignorance, attachment and aversion, self/ego/mind or any particular addiction, fixation and rigid take on life is both dead and deadly until its biotensegrity womb and somatic mother is re-engaged.

Anything proclaiming separation is actually uplifted and borne of less visible supports. Buddhism refers to this complex of supports in multiple lofty ways from Buddha-nature to the natural state, to unborn mind and pure awareness. Biotensegrity and fascia as spiritual matrix evokes a somatic appreciation of the three gems: dharma as a bodily conduit to truth; sangha as a self/ego/mind's we-space home; Buddha as being freed from all definition.

Understandably, much attention is paid to the falsity of anything less. Suffering flows from separateness. Dukkha equates to some chunk of the whole, in effect, of some subset of Snelson's tower declaring itself to independently exist. To owe nothing, to float free with no deeper essence. Buddhism's core teaching of dependent origination is also in sync with biotensegrity. That which arises co-arises in an interconnected matrix.

Culture offers another path home. We discover hidden discontinuities through encounters with anyone too quickly dismissed as weird, foreign, or exotic. Frida Kahlo took great pride in her maternal Mexican, indigenous genealogy. That she had so much to draw upon following her accident implies emotional depths preserved and strengthened across childhood. These resources would be essential for navigating both the enticing successes and pain she would suffer in adulthood. Having traveled quite a lot, I felt deeply moved by an offhand comment I once heard. A missionary described how every time he returned to Dallas-Fort Worth from South America, North Americans seemed like walking corpses.

A wacky only-in-America meme amplifies this insight. On May 23, 2005, Tom Cruise appeared on Oprah. Oprah had landed the interview where Cruise would, presumably, finally respond to the news and rumors of his romance with Katie Holmes. From the perspective of biotensegrity, his antics are worth revisiting. Somehow his affect and movement, motion and emotion, were offensive, astounding, enticing, and/or bewildering. His behavior was a superheated topic for weeks, and at the close of the year, would be replayed as one of the major events. We North American walking dead types were not sure how to metabolize what our eyes gobbled up. Was he trying to sell a movie, overcompensate, exploiting, unstable, grabbing the spotlight? Not too many saw a man overcome by the intensity of the expectations projected onto him, of true love, affectively integrated, and in excellent condition—though some mix of these was just as plausible.

Clients who successfully make deep dives into the pain of childhood and resurface in their here-now soma, awaken each time with more of its attendant surplus of motion/emotion. They complete stints in therapy not cured or rigidly happier but with a greater capacity for the lows and highs of feeling. They are more affectively pliable. Research on "posttraumatic growth" has tracked what the wisdom traditions have taught regarding the potential for good to come from suffering.[364] As multiple lines of evidence indicate, pain incurred in early life registered in the body often paves the way.

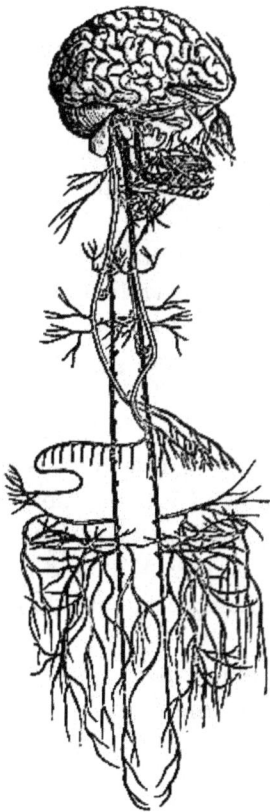

Polyvagal

The vasovagal cranial nerve can be added to the list of physical and physiological substrates that make up the architecture of sentience arcing from Bowlby to Buddha. The vagus, as it is referred to, deserves a place alongside biological attachment, attachment-love, inmaps, Panksepp's seven affective systems, fascia, and biotensegrity. Cranial nerves are neural tentacle-like extensions of the brain that pass through openings in the skull, for example, to the eyes, ears, and nose. Although referred to in the singular, the vagus is actually bifurcated with one branch on the left and one on the right side of the body.

A new model, called polyvagal theory both requires and invites some deep dives into the interface of soma and consciousness.[365] A good starting point is vasovagal syncope (temporary loss of consciousness), one of the most common forms of fainting. People who pass out at the sight of blood, injury or in anticipation of an injection do so because of the vagus. Animals which "play possum" due to a perceived threat are another example. Sometimes called, "death feigning", this strange innate capacity has not earned the "Darwin award". By definition, predators sometimes do not complete the killing of their suddenly dead-looking prey even when doing so would presumably be easy. This weird phenomenon has major implications for a somatic portal to some of the Vajrayana's major themes. Before considering these Bowlby-to-Buddha strands, let's examine the polyvagal model.

According to Porges, the vagus is a hierarchy of three viscerally-based levels. Each is a distinct phylogenetic sub-system.[366] In evolutionary order, from oldest to most recent, these are as follows. The ancient, vegetative or dorsal vagus associated with death feigning. This level modulates major muscles, the heart, lungs and blood pressure. Syncope may result from the slowing of the heart and drop in oxygenation. The second level is the familiar, combined sympathetic-parasympathetic nervous system. Fight-flight is counterbalanced by its "rest and digest" counterpart. Five cranial nerves to the face and head comprise the third and newest circuitry. These "special visceral efferents" are directly associated with adult attachment, which the author refers to the "social engagement system."[367]

With these insights, Porges disambiguates the whole of binary sympathetic-parasympathetic from that which preceded it and that which followed it in the evolution of the human form. Everyday emotional security is not just a matter of quelling fight-flight, but an exquisite three-level physiological dance. Mid-level, activating-relaxing circuitry works the ancient death feigning, collapsing response on one hand and emotional intimacy on another. This research adds fainting or folding to fight-flight. Freezing is sometimes also advocated as yet another innate, vasovagal defensive repertoire. Porges, however, clarifies that the iconic, deer-in-the-headlamps form of immobilization is distinct and requires further investigation.[368] Unlike fainting, freezing involves muscle tone (tensegrity) and emotional vigilance. Freezing may stem from an amalgam of the high alert, 'freak out' mode associated with the secondary level and the immobility associated with the third, ancient, death feigning level.

Genetic survival favored the right degree of emotional and muscular activation, which translates into caloric intake, contribution versus burden on the tribal unit. Too little or too much arousal would eventually not make the cut. Consider the soma of early humans (who would live to hunt another day) as they encountered a large, lethal mammal. In encountering a dangerous four-legged source of protein, they would be appropriately, highly activated. Tribe members would use their necks to orient, give and receive facial signals, use their ears to listen, mouths to utter intonation and words to coordinate the kill.

If one member was maimed or frightened off, the whole of the tribe would be impacted and its genetic maternal more at risk. The human capacity to surf the edge of death with cunning, confidence and bravado is celebrated in versions of war dances and chants. The Māori haka dance is especially breathtaking with exaggerated, edgy facial gestures and staring that, in theory, accompanies the overcoming of fears and channeling rage for the betterment of the tribe. To survive and be successful, aggressive capacities are informed rather than overwhelmed by fear and pain.

Porges work in combination with attachment theory is central to an exciting, research-based movement that seeks to put soma at the epicenter of psychotherapy. "Attachment" is in the subtitle of recent works by some of this movement's biggest names. In each of these, polyvagal theory looms large. These include recent books by Daniel Siegel, Stephen Porges, Bessel van der Kolk and Pat Ogden. Though Buddhism is scarcely mentioned in these great works there is ample emotional and somatic territory we have discussed associated with Buddha's Mom is.

> Psychology and psychiatry, as disciplines, have paid scant attention to the behavioral (i.e., muscular, organic) responses that are triggered by trauma reminders and, instead, have narrowly focused on either the neurochemistry or the emotional states associated with the reminders. They thereby may have lost sight of the forest for the trees: Both neurochemistry and emotions are activated in order to bring about certain bodily postures and physical movements that are meant to protect, engage, and defend. [369]

Pat Ogden, for example, has pioneered a somatic-based, professional training model.[370] Clinicians worldwide undergo training in her sensorimotor psychotherapy model in order to help their clients reset somatic posture, structure, movement, muscle tone that was negatively impacted, often, by dysfunctional early life attachment experiences. Ogden and Fisher have recently come out with an 832-page manual for therapists and clients to use collaboratively.[371] The exercises and approaches are implemented within the we-space of a trusting, caring, clinical relationship. This is, of course, in keeping with the essential idea of therapy as a corrective relational experience. Emotionally held, patients with trauma and attachment wounds, presumably including those with deep self disturbance, are guided in various ways to reset their nervous system.

With the therapist in the caring mother role, and witness placeholder, the sacred wego vessel conveys what we have called the human lineage. Within this architecture, the transmission of attachment-love is heightened. Clients become their own soma's expert witness. Intense attention is paid to the extremes of arousal in accordance with Daniel Siegel's "window of tolerance".[372] Too little is associated with the dorsal vagus and too much with mid-level sympathetic over-activation. The body's intelligence is center stage. Through both modeling and direct experience clients become attuned to their somatic inner life, tension, fidgeting, withdrawal and the noticing of any felt sense of danger. This is one side of the skillful means equation; another pertains to resources, joy, intimacy, support, and engagement with nature, music, and play.

The ideas comprising Buddha's Mom certainly seem to be aligned with this revolution within formal psychotherapy research and practice, and may even offer some important extensions in the direction of transcendence and realization. As just alluded to, the path to healing associated with these advances in body psychotherapy fits with the rendering of the two attachments' achievement of a transcend-include, negate-preserve ground of being that is one with love, with bodhicitta or what Zen refers to as one's Original Face.

When your mind is not dwelling on the dualism of good and evil, what is
your original face even before you were born?[373]

A couple of stories highlight this soma-spirit embrace. An eyewitness of an American slave auction described a mother's reaction to seeing her daughter being sold at auction. "When they sold her, her mother fainted or draped dead, she never knowed which." The person who witnessed this event added that heartbroken slave "wanted to go see her mother lying over there on the ground" but the man who bought her "drove her off like cattle" before she could.[374]

In my work as a consultant at a major hospital, I met with a mother who had found her 16-year-old daughter dead. At some point about a day and a half later, this woman attempted to kill herself and had been admitted for medical treatment. When I spoke with her, she was trying to piece things together. The timing of everything was still unclear. She was confused by images on her phone of an impromptu vigil they had held.

More often than not, humans confronted with extreme psychological trauma do not die but do dissociate. At the extremes, there is a drop in blood pressure and a possibility of dropping dead. Mobility and motility drop away. The bowels let loose. One is often both literally and figuratively scared shitless. Dropping dead in a single instant is rare in humans. Presumably evolution maintained the dorsal vagus in modern humans for other purposes. Beyond the scientific explanations of somatic psychotherapy models lies one based in the ultimate arc of sentience

Before enlightenment, during the austerities, Buddha flirted with bodily death. Getting by on one grain of rice each day, his human form (we can infer) moved well into the threat of starvation. His discipline, one can conjecture, then took him through the somatic fear and lunging for relief as he used honed parasympathetic resources to quell any emotional impediments. But an altogether somatic extreme, consistent with the polyvagal skillful means rounds out the somatic-spirit picture.

Buddha was born human to open a portal to spiritual awakening for all humans. As his body approached dorsal shutdown, an encounter with his own raison d'être, the story states, saved him. His experience of the meaning of his life, the current thesis suggests, to bring the dharma to all sentient beings, alone called him back from the edge. This *Bodhisattva* turn was away from a solo, somatic renunciation and a turn towards love, the nondual, his, your, and my original face. Stainless, unending metta. Here an important element arose. Precisely at this juncture of somatic-sentience extinction come the protector deities.

> The Bodhisattva concludes that the austere practices do not lead to
> awakening and, encouraged by some protective gods, he begins to eat a
> normal diet once again, and regains his health.[375]

"Some" gods show up. They *encourage* Shakyamuni. This detail fits with the Tibetan deity practice already discussed. Protector deities, with their gruesome, alluring, attention-grabbing faces shake soma-sentience as it plunges toward torpor. They embody the risk and the reward as both reach a breaking point. As somatic stopgaps, the protectors safeguard our species and thus, the flow and transmission of the lineage.

A contiguous passage attributed to Buddha (referred to previously on "breathless meditation") can also be reinterpreted from the polyvagal perspective. With respiration diminishing, the protector deities express outrage, reinstating the mid-level heart-lung machinery with their ultimately loving vengeance, restoring biotensegrity, feeling and emotion.[376]

> I stopped the in-breaths and out-breaths through my mouth, nose, and ears.
> While I did so, violent winds cut through my head. Just as if a strong man
> were splitting my head open with a sharp sword.[377]

The aforementioned slave's mother also, probably, physically survived her dorsal dive. With no chance of sensorimotor psychotherapy, she likely suffered from trauma for the rest of her days. Both she and the hospitalized mother I met made desperate efforts to employ the attachment-vagus, face gazing system to prevent fear, grief, and abandonment hyper-arousal. Looking back toward her daughter, the slave's mother was attempting to somatically and affectively stabilize. As their relationship eviscerated before her eyes, her dorsal vagus compensated and she fainted. The hospitalized mother showed me photos of her daughter on her phone. Having found her dead had led to her own suicide attempt. In both cases, the daughters looked back. One, still alive, was swept up in the trauma and humiliation of being sold. The other smiled sweetly from the screen of a smart phone.

These examples of trauma are more clearly mappable than that stemming from early life attachment wounds but provide an important outline. According to Porges, trauma is not simply a bruising of self/ego/mind, but more like shearing forces brought on outside of awareness by neuroception. This refers to a direct, one-to-one, soma-to-soma activation.

> The simple physiological fact, however, is that under threat embodied and
> conceptual self-awareness go off-line as the more primal parts of the brain
> activate an ancient trove of wisdom that has assured the continuation of life on
> earth for millions of years.[378]

This ancient trove of treasure is not limited to syncope and death feigning. Biotensegrity dropped to nil in the slave's mother. This momentary plummet was probably followed by dissociation and all that falls under umbrella of psychological trauma. Trauma, the emerging somatic psychotherapy models agree, is both somatically held and a function of fractured being. The more profound, the greater the severance of the traumatic, deeper sentience from the more superficial, daily vessel of the same, e.g., self/ego/mind.

The grieving mother that I encountered in the hospital was in a quasi-fugue state characterized by decreased sentient tensegrity. Other ways to describe this would be dissociation, diminished emotional cohesion, or psychological integrity. But the weight of the evidence points to the importance of her being allowed this betweenness. Touchingly, she used the present tense as she showed me photos of her daughter and talked about how beautiful she is, was.

People in shock are said to blanche and appear pale "as if they have seen a ghost". Some have a strangely flat face. In addition to looking at her daughter, my patient also wanted to talk about how she herself looked strange. She was referring to a particular photo of herself at an impromptu vigil they held within less than 24 hours after her daughter's suicide. She remembered telling someone how her ability to literally feel was altered. The sensation of an object pressing on her skin was diminished. She was looking for a face to remind her of the meaning in life that had slipped away.

For a child in a dysfunctional attachment context, all three levels of the vagus flicker in ongoing efforts to achieve homeostasis. Her attachment figure might be physically present but emotionally absent, or emotionally inconsistent. When things go well, neck muscles facilitate mutual, enjoyable face-to-face behavior, eye gazing and to support the larynx to use loving intonation and the neck to nod the head in support. For many kids, however, the mother's voice, empathic gaze and affection are woefully inadequate at critical times and/or consistently mediocre. Dissociation protects the psyche. The personality may land on anxious or avoidant as a norm, but both of these float atop a soma that longs for wholeness, vigor, wonder, power, and joy.

Buddha's Mom proposes that the transmission of our spiritual lineage and the potential for realization is through attachment. It follows that where the early life attachment context is severely wanting, all three vasovagal levels would shape the overall personality. From the newest branch to the oldest, the vasovagal might result in chronic variations on: a desire to find safety through attachment and mirroring; fear, panic, grief, depression; alongside disengagement and dissociation. A person raised in this somatic, affective planetary system may spend decades in their own skewed orbit.

Polyvagal theory offers a shorthand category for those relatively better and worse off. A modern, reasonably happy, not overly neurotic, or detached, dissociated and aloof person is said to have *high vagal tone*. Conversely, poor emotional adjustment is referred to as *low vagal tone*. Low vagal tone is associated with elevated stress hormones, higher rates of major illnesses, and an earlier death.[379] Those with especially high vagal tone tend to be more compassionate. Rather than detach and distance from images of suffering, they express empathic concern.

This research is relevant to our efforts to embrace Buddhism as a science. The bodhisattva heart expands rather than contracts when confronting dukkha. As a deeper reality, this second turning marked by Mahayana translates as a more accurate perception of ultimate meaning. Porges deemed study subjects with the highest vagal tone, "vagal superstars". Their natural reaction to upsetting images was one of empathy, compassion, and altruism.

In Buddhist terms, the vagal superstar overflows with bodhicitta, lovingkindness and characteristics which blossom in the bodhisattva.[380] Buddhism's emphasis on the bodhisattva's compassion as implicit, an embedded characteristic with no bounds, is notable in this context. They simply cannot bliss out on their attainment knowing suffering remains behind. Their compassion overflows.

The vagal superstar response also has a counterpart in Tonglen, the taking in another's pain into one's heart and sending of metta. Pain is mutated in metta for the benefit of both. Finally, research by Dr. Porges' wife, Dr. Sue Carter, points to how in the inverse, a freedom from more primitive somatic snares is directly associated with emotional bonding and to the brain's oxytocin system, the proverbial "cuddle hormone".

> The complex functions of the vagus facilitate social interactions, communication, and emotional regulation while inhibiting self-defense functions associated with the "vegetative" vagus and the sympathetic components of the ANS (autonomic nervous system). Both oxytocin and vasopressin are implicated in autonomic functions, providing important neurochemical substrates that could influence emotions.[381]

Many with deep self disturbance struggle unsuccessfully for decades to develop a high vagal tone. They may even find someone who listens, cares, is supportive but then bungle the invitation to show up in their life. Cutters go into a spaced-out deadness by way of pain. Razor in hand, they "look death in the eye", dissociate for just a few minutes and get some relief. Outsiders are quick to call these attention-seeking, sabotage or declare a person "needs to hit bottom", but these have the same logic as blaming individuals for systemic racism or misogyny. The Canon gives us Devadatta as an example not easily pigeon-holed. Similarly, many who knew Jesus firsthand did not accept the salvation he offered.

Thankfully, emerging somatic psychotherapies are increasingly in sync with ancient somatic based traditions. No doubt in the coming decades, empirically-based healing theories and modalities will continue to incorporate experimental and indigenous forms too easily dismissed and potentially misapplied making each the better for it.

Polyvagal theory further clarifies the nature of suffering and possibility of its ending. Fight-flight is easy to understand from the perspective of tanhā. One craves safety, wants to avoid pain. The same goes for longing to love and be loved, associated with the newest branch of the vasovagal system.

The dorsal, "vegetative" vagus, however, is activated by both extremes of danger and bliss, a familiar Buddhist pattern. This mystery leads back to the nature of desire, and this to pure desire and this to transmission. Worth repeating, Reggie Ray names the Vajrayana as the path of desire. The dorsal vagus' powers of dissociation are protective in this light. This source of bodily wisdom allays threats to suchness, to being itself. Paradoxically, such threats include both agony and ecstasy. To wit, neglected child dissociates not only because of emotional pain but in order to retain the possibility of a joyful liberation from all desire.

Here we have made the case for this attachment as desire, as love and lineage, and as consistent with both biological attachment and nonattachment. Suffering as such is a misalignment with desire. Buddha's Mom is nothing more than a compilation of evidence underpinning this expanded view of dukkha and realization, experienced directly and fully beyond all names and models.

An advanced meditator whom I'm delighted to call a friend, returned from back-to-back, extended silent retreats. These culminated with a deepening capacity to stably abide in bodhicitta. After telling me about many heart-openings, Reed shared that, during some long sits, he would sometimes suddenly run out of breath! Before he knew what was happening, he would gasp. This experience was intermittent, mysterious and sometimes accompanied by a sense of embarrassment. He felt exposed and worried he might be bothering others in the group.

While meditating or between sits, nothing in particular came to mind. Reed's sense was one of a peacefulness interrupted by his own gasping and grasping for air. During a one-to-one interview with the meditation teacher, Reed raised this topic and soon found himself talking about an experience when he was five years old. Walking down the sidewalk ahead of his parents, he encountered a dog as tall as he was. Reed recalled how the whole situation was confusing. Was this huge, powerful, beautiful dog simply marvelous or a threat? As fear of the latter set in, he glanced back at his parents. He vividly recalled their faces. They were laughing at Reed's confusion and worry.

Everything Reed had compiled in life suggested screwy mirroring was the norm, probably repeated thousands of times prior to the dog encounter and long thereafter. For some reason, this moment was emblematic and dense with meaning. As Reed put it, something more dangerous than the dog broke through the veil. When he saw his parents laughing, Reed knew that he was profoundly alone. Whatever he might have assumed or hoped in any other direction was simply not to be.

At this juncture (at least in theory) the tri-parte polyvagal response kicked in. Encountering the dog, this heart-lung, "flight" response was deployed evoking rapid inhalations. After years of courageous personal development, this fearful gasp resurfaced. The ambiguous, possibly dangerous stimulus prompted Reed's head-turning, face-to-face orienting. An instantaneous repeat of the same followed his sudden gasping during meditation. He was prompted internally to connect to others in the room. Per evolution, this innate capacity elicits immediate nonverbal, also often verbal attachment information, a telling term.

As a child, in place of a coherent reply, Reed received a message too large to land: emotional disengagement, mocking, and laughter from would-be protectors. In place of attachment-love was something more dangerous than the dog. For Reed, as we have suggested, the transmission of sentience through natural species-typical channels was snarled and failing him. With nowhere to turn, the ancient vagus came online as a stopgap. Deep somatic continuity was sacrificed and paradoxically safeguarded via dissociation, such that the upper ranges of the psyche, of self/ego/mind, could survive.

Reed's psychological death instinct arose in the mirror of a somatic survival instinct. In life, Reed would gravitate into cerebral, left-brained pursuits well into his 40s. He then veered off course into the most immediate shadows and emotional pain. This path led ever backwards and inwards and deeper into the core of his attachment trauma. Along the way, he came to have the bearing and skillful means to navigate these sorts of openings to nowhere, to void. The path of desire has protectors and teachers who show up in the oddest ways. Even when Reed did not know he was accepting their help, he was. He dropped more fully into the flow of his spiritual inheritance as he gazed at the face of the teacher and discussed his gasping. This seemingly silly irritant was not assumed to be anything more, nor less. As Reed explained, while simply slowing and talking a river of bodhicitta flowed. Bowlby-Buddha is a koan which evokes the species' lineage in fullness. Reed's "rude awakening" was a re-marrying of soma and self/ego/mind.

The breadth of Reed's journey is revealed in research on "disorganized attachment". Early attachment researchers, as we have explored in depth, proposed a causal chain resulting in three forms of attachment (secure, anxious and avoidant) which tend to have stability across the lifespan. Those who did not fit into any of these categories were identified as having disorganized attachment. Giovanni Liotti described the character of their attachment experience in these haunting words, "early, multiple, incoherent, reciprocity incompatible."[382] He determined that survivors of sexual abuse suffered less than those not sexually abused but with disorganized attachment.[383]

A logical extension would frame such disturbances of personality as suffering arising from a jumbled, incoherent somatic and psychospiritual tensegrity. Polyvagal theory shines a light on these mini-traumas that may accumulate as somatic-sentient fissures. At the interface of psychological death, meaning, caring, desire and reason along with respiration and blood pressure drop towards zero. Surviving trauma requires dissociation to tolerate the torment of meaninglessness.

But exactly here, if we are to believe the great sages, is the door to perfect clarity, peace, and infinite meaning. Through extremis came the middle way. The same soma-denying principle runs through all first turning, renunciate, ascetic forms. Spirit is freed in turning away from turning away from greed, lust, and overindulgence. With the Mahayana, there is no separate peace. Profound compassion pours through the fissures. The Vajrayana extends the understanding of somatic openings to the bardo, the transitional realm between bodily death and rebirth. It also views lust and sexual desire as doorways. Research on the vasovagal cranial nerve is, at least theoretically, consistent with all these.

Ecstatic music fans may pass out when their beloved star walks out on stage. Overcome by the "holy spirit", Christians are "slain in the spirit". They lose consciousness, tensegrity and droop to the ground with tears of delight streaming down their cheeks. Implicit knowledge of this interface of death feigning and ecstatic fainting that shows up in everyday language. "I thought I was going to pass out" refers to either joy or fear at the extremes. Somatic dis-association is, potentially, spiritual re-association. Shamanic and indigenous rituals commonly assert the possibility of transcendent spiritual states just this side of bodily death. There's no sunlight between death awareness and realization of the true nature of life. Life is death, life as death. The entire Diamond-cutting Sutra spills over with Buddha patiently describing the nature of such conundrums to Subhuti.

> "Subhuti, do not maintain that the Buddha has this thought: 'I have spoken
> spiritual truths.' Do not think that way. Why? If someone says the Buddha
> has spoken spiritual truths, he slanders the Buddha due to his inability to
> understand what the Buddha teaches. Subhuti, as to speaking truth, no truth
> can be spoken. Therefore it is called 'speaking truth'."[384]

There is tenderness and compassion at this interface where life and death manifest in miniature, in joy and pain, hope and fear, ecstasy and trauma. Perhaps spiritual transcendence is psychological projection born of fear and wishful thinking. Perhaps the dorsal vasovagal response is a wash. The small subset of animals who actually die under its control, from the point of evolution, may have anyway. Death feigning may simply convey a last ditch chance of survival. Perhaps this enhanced the viability of survivors. Animals that feign death and are not mauled to death or eaten may pass on their genes because they survive both physically and emotionally. Animals may shake off the physiological tension or alternatively fold. They employ mechanisms so as not to somatically register the arousal response. As a result, they are not hobbled by a traumatized nervous system and are able to function, respond to future threats, and mate.

Each of us can come to his or her own conclusion. To presume material death is indistinct from sentient death is the conclusion of many but not of those humans who have looked into this in the most rigorous and direct manner. Tibetan deity worship is at least partially atheistic. Everyone trained in this knows in advance these deities only play God. Worship of the protector deities is two-fold. First to foster a breakthrough during life, and second, in case this does not come to pass, to assist in the transition to the next. Hopefully, having trained well, one does not leap at the first opportunity to be reborn. The protectors' various qualities are inculcated as placeholders in the tumult. Recognizable characteristics include hyper-sexuality, fierceness, aggression, sweet compassion, and the promise of protection. These figures aggregate the most intense sentient forces running through human nature. As transcept forms, they shield and buffer the mayhem of losing one's body, loved ones, name, and whatever else dies at death.

Just as awakening is possible now, so too great spiritual teachers tell us it is possible at death. The prospect of what Buddha refers to as egoless and deathless accelerates with the dissolving and disintegrating of smaller vessels of sentience, advancing the potential for a fuller realization and awakening. In line with this, Reggie Ray's focus on meditating with the body is framed as a path through the soma to its very essence as a mirror of the universe. The universe is the ocean of the body; the body is the ocean of the self/ego/mind; but from the relative side we are but a droplet in a droplet in a droplet. Death is one-side fixation. The living, flowing, blinding, perfect dharma is too much to handle without death, gods, soma, emotion, and self and the beautiful illusory shells surrounding our Vajra body.

Elizabeth Kübler-Ross said no one is confronted with more than they can handle. Beauty and terror may have the same mother. Family and friends at the bedside of a dying loved one often describe their beloved as having peace or refer to death as beautiful. Pet owners say something similar. A transcendent peace is a core facet of near death experiences, which are surprising common. That these can be induced and have neurological correlates seems to me just another relative truth.

Neuroscientists estimate human "just noticeable" perception of time at one-tenth of a second. At least conceptually, this might explain the potential junction of the two attachments and how letting go is possible even at the extremes somatic demise. If so, the relative proximity of measureless love and infinite sentience is encouraging.

I had no notion at the time but have surfing to thank for whatever bio-psycho-spiritual tensegrity I have cobbled together. From age 18 and for twenty years thereafter, I lived in Hawaii and had thousands of experiences I now appreciate in a new way. One thing about being so blessed is the trail of tanhā, the longing for more. My dreams are filled with exhausting efforts to get to the beach and in the waves. Some seem to last all night and I awake with dukkha, glimpses and almosts, but no surf. Buddha's Mom has helped me understand the beauty of this longing. The spirit longs to be more not less awake than its brightest day.

Probably the most powerful biotensegrity-building experiences occurred in some of the less traveled spots or in conditions where I skirted the limits of my skillful means. There's no describing being held under massive, shifting planes of water and not knowing which way is up. These undulating caverns have their own autonomy and their own sense of time. Seconds can feel like minutes. As huge sets come through, when diving after a wipe out or exhilarating ride, one returns to these haunted paradises below the passing birds, air, fellow surfers, and sunshine. There is a sudden absence of the waking world, replaced with whooshing sensations and deep, distant thunder, and a sense of time that could stretch forever. Sometimes I hit the reef, got cut or twisted in hilarious ways. This is exactly when to trust one's body, to seriously release any unnecessary worry even if one cannot tell which way to get back to the surface because if one does not, panic and an urge to inhale can be lethal.

Reading about the vasovagal, I would guess that the dorsal branch boosted my ability to replace panic with peace. Even if statistically negligible, the soma's felt proximity to death, to distensegrity, seemed to race about in the backdrop. Obviously, even sophisticated models are hackneyed relative to the billions of neural connections making up the inner somatic cosmos. Somehow, I'd bet instant, intensive cellular conversations were raging in me as they did in the slave woman, the hospitalized mother, and Reed. In the case of surfing, I'd been held under a thousand times. Familiarity bolstered parasympathetic peace. But some experiences were stretching. Side by side, panic and vegetative torpor beckoned as the world seemed to slip away. At the same time, attachment to my beloved mother ocean helped me retain focus.

There's no small hint of Buddhism's beauty and the word, awakening, in these variations on learning not to die by letting go of life as anything containable. Everything is "this too". One has to be hyper-alert and calm at the same time. Mind must love and trust its muscular and somatic extensions. This was the strange-but-true paradox during the craziest wipe outs, when I did not get adequate air or lost too much hitting the water. The only way out is through, through the peace, slowing down. Awareness listens for some echo within. An inner assurance of safety associated with countless similar experiences. This is the living witness, heightening, expanding, deeply appreciative for raw experience.

Otherness is also a gigantic piece. The ocean was profoundly other, and yes, mother. Her authority and majesty were objectively factual. The felt-sense is one of a long awaited, terrifying, deeply recognizable taste of the absolute. One wonders sometimes how someone can do the same thing every day, woodworking, surfing, meditating. For them it's not the same, as they bow deeply and reverently to otherness and its mystery. The whole of surfing is a familiar place to which I somehow owe my being and sanity. Surfing was an ongoing process of corrections to my spirit's proprioception, my place in the ocean as womb—I can see this a little more clearly now.

The sheer beauty, feel, taste of the ocean was there before humans evolved, as was this living, accessible witness, this delight in some divine mirror. My body is an experiential moment, and this a silent, flawless drop in some pan-Hawaiian watery womb, and so on to all that Buddha transmits to Subhuti. Awareness as a dancing space in the ocean, a holding, basket, and further, again in mud, earth, depths, in turn a drop in the galaxy—something like this. Each unto the next, mother to child and child to mother. Flowing arms of light giving form, being held. Naked love. Each anything is a cosmic whisper, a direct expression with its own tension-integrity, channeling brilliance. Tantric transmission through soma.

Biohacking

"Biohacking" offers a unique, D-I-Y angle on somatic transformation, and has some surprising alignments with Buddha's Mom. Two of its major proponents, Dave Asprey and Ray Kurzweil, are obsessed with biohacks—shortcuts, based in science, to boosting health, longevity, and well-being. They and many of their ilk take scores, perhaps hundreds of supplements daily. Through specialized lab work, they track droves of biomarkers. Kurzweil plans to "live long enough to live forever". By this, he means long enough for technological advances to enable human consciousness to be uploaded to a computer. He calls this point future when man and machine merge, the singularity. Asprey aims to live to be 180 years old and has bestsellers and a line of supplements to help others do the same.

Despite obvious signs of self/ego/mind as a driver, biohackers' passion deserves reflection in the vastness of the Vajrayana. They too view life as a desperately precious opportunity, albeit in ways which translate into marketing campaigns. But demand rather than supply is the point. Biohacking reflects a cultural meme, a self-help genie with no interest in returning to the bottle. Many of the millions who buy books, supplements and do cross-fit to optimize their health, also do yoga, and also are consumers of Buddhism, or soon will be. They do online retreats and use apps to sync up and meditate with friends around the globe.

Ego's skewing of life as opportunity cuts multiple ways. The focus on ultimate health stokes the great, perennial quest for meaning and happiness. Increasingly, the same consumers buying Pema Chödrön's books purchase supplements from Asprey's "Bulletproof" products. Leading biohackers have a big, unabashedly *seeking* orientation to life. In his podcast series, Dave Asprey interviewed Stephen Porges, providing his listeners a portal into polyvagal theory for help with trauma.[385] During this show, Asprey expressed how he himself had PTSD since birth due to the umbilical cord being wrapped around his neck. He asked Porges about polyvagal hacks to bring about healing. Biohackers are quick to describe the suffering that propelled their search, and how this has manifested in a combination of practices and products.

Tony Robbins is another major figure in this arena, though more of a self/ego/mind hacker. His goods and services are less oriented toward diet and supplements and more mental and motivational in nature. He uses the words *decision, mission,* and *passion* a lot and advocates taking *action* to achieve one's potential. Heads of state, Hollywood and sports elite succeed based on his motivation and action hacks, as well as hundreds of thousands not so famous. So much so that he has been to 100 countries which he can now afford to visit using his own airplane. He has also, "partnered with Feeding America to provide 100 million meals to families in need".[386]

Through the largess of ego, an even larger force surges. In light of Buddha's Mom, a reverse, upriver notion has weight: these hackers, their millions of followers, everyone concerned with diet and exercise and work-life balance is being hacked by Spirit. Hackers' radical embrace of the gift of life may border on obsession with its physicality yet makes way for their unique, authentic gifts. But through body, the fruits of the Vajrayana, such "gifts differing" as the bible says are ever nearer. Biohackers' unique remolding and intensification of the self-help industry may be the disruptive force that finally breaks up modernity's love-hate relationship with ego. Ego seems to be both everywhere and nowhere. Biohackers' narratives move with authenticity from a confessional, highly personal tales of suffering into stories of those they have helped achieve transformation. Does not both the bodhisattva cry both sad and joyful tears?

Asprey, for example, claims to have discovered a sort of supercharged form of meditation based in neurofeedback. One week of this hacked, intensified retreat, according to its proponents, is equal to forty years of Zen practice—and is priced and marketed accordingly. Few, says Asprey, go through this without a profound somatic response, often vomiting and weeping. In particular, he has learned to deeply forgive others. The human lineage flows wherever vessels allow. It is stymied and smothered wherever vessels purport to be loving mothers but actually have crossed into clinging and grasping. In shaking off previous cultural confines, in learning English and adapting to the West, Chögyam Trungpa's was a similarly disruptive force. In this sense, he hacked both East and West givens and provided shortcuts to the depths of the Vajrayana as an unbounded reality. His passion, the Tantric trail to Passion itself awaits—the path of desire, our linage and true nature—awaits hacks of every color.

Asprey's landing on the power of forgiveness in transformation is interesting. The ultimate hack, one might say, for this is embodied in Jesus' path to liberation through forgiveness. Forgiveness in this light is one with compassion and mercy. We have discussed at length how a Jesus is consistent with Buddha's Mom. Worth adding is the fact that compassion and mercy have etymological roots in the Hebrew, *rachamim*, which translates as womb and mother love.[387]

Regulation

Proclaimed the "American Bowlby", clinician, researcher and author of multiple seminal texts, Allan Schore, has forged a comprehensive updating of Bowlby's model.[388, 389] Over the past couple of decades and in conjunction with multiple collaborators, Schore has expanded on what was already "the broadest, most profound, and most creative lines of research in the 20th century and 21st century psychology."[390] His "modern attachment theory" incorporates Panksepp's discoveries and Porges' polyvagal theory and highlights the central role of regulation. Schore views the breadth, cohesion and force of this massive cross-fertilization as a "paradigm shift".[391] He envisions alignments across multiple disciplines including pediatrics, family law, developmental, clinical psychology and psychoanalysis and psychiatry. Affective dysregulation, for example, is common to virtually all psychiatric disorders and is also critical for optimal functioning.[392]

Schore's extended, more integral model of human psychological functioning seems only to embolden the psychospiritual truths expressed within Vajrayana.[393, 394] Atop the list of its riches is a refined understanding of the development of the implicit self. This would appear to be synonymous with psyche's sentient substrate and an implicit self/ego/mind. On the side of applied science, Schore and colleagues are marrying the neuroscience of attachment with rich, creative psychotherapeutic applications (including those mentioned previously). By definition, this information is significant for those with attachment trauma resulting in hypo- and hyper-arousal. Connections to attachment, as we have explored in depth, have no upper limit given the compelling evidence for enlightenment as species' lineage by way of attachment. "Realization" is synonymous with the experiential reality of attachment's fullest expression and release. A richer resolution of this innate, inherited bounty is now possible.

For starters, Schore has clarified that the critical period begins in the last trimester of pregnancy and runs through second year of life and that the most salient brain structures and processes are associated with the right orbitofrontal cortex (OFC). Functioning as the "senior executive", the OFC shares extensive connections with primary sensory and association cortices, limbic system, and subcortical areas mapped out by Panksepp. These modulate input from the vagus nerve in keeping with Porges' polyvagal model. The OFC supervises the complex, massive fire together/wire together process that, for better or worse, results in the affective foundations of the human psyche.

These findings further validate early attachment's lifelong impact, and they concur with research I did twenty years ago on the extensive reach of early attachment in adult functioning.[395] I found insecure attachment to negatively impact multiple, general areas of coping, health, and well-being. Insecure attachment correlated with diminished awareness of bodily tension build-up, of situations which were "stressful and caused dysfunctional arousal" of a person's "optimal stimulation range".[396] Those with insecure attachment demonstrated poor skills at lowering tension through relaxation or other means. They had trouble organizing and managing basic resources such as time and energy and related deficits. They were poorer at planning, setting goals and limits, and were less likely to actualize priorities and pace themselves. Attachment-related difficulties impacted the use of financial resources to cope with stress and/or poor management of such resources caused them stress. Those with a fearful attachment orientation correlated with worse physical health in comparison to their secure peers. This factor included overall health and wellness factors such as the absence of chronic disease, freedom from pain and worry about health matters, energy for daily demands, and perceived physical appearance.

Multiple associated areas of behavior and functioning showed relationships in the same direction. Those reporting attachment issues such as ambiguous feelings toward intimacy, fear of abandonment, and a sense of being unlovable were more likely to report dissociative tendencies. As already discussed, dissociation is a symptom of dorsal vagus activation. In my research, this corresponded to a variety of adult attachment factors such as discomfort with closeness, ambivalence, anger and uncertainty in intimate relationships and low lovability, or romantic self-esteem. Inattention correlated with a variety of similar attachment issues such as trust, ambiguous orientation toward intimacy and lovability. The latter two attachment variables were also more pronounced in those with drug and alcohol addiction.[397, 398]

In total, evidence in support of a combined affect regulation/modern attachment model is persuasive and cohesive. As covered, dorsal vagus activation corresponds to the "hypo-arousal" seen in depression and dissociation. Hyper-aroused adults under the influence of the sympathetic, fight-flight branch of the vagus have corresponding anger and anxiety issues. In both cases, the arousal orientation is out of sync with actual, personal and environmental stressors. It therefore potentially interferes with functioning in general. In my research, far-flung areas were not immune to the impact of dysfunctional attachment (and therefore, per this updated model, dysregulation). For example, I found that people who reported fearful and preoccupied forms of insecure attachment used more cigarettes, caffeine, alcohol, sleeping pills, and were more likely to engage in crash diets. Attachment wounding also correlated with obesity, eating disorders, headaches, sleeping and breathing problems.[399] Schore's expanded model can account for broad-ranging phenomena such as dysfunctional lifestyles and "self-medicating" behaviors as based in a maintenance of an implicit self/ego/mind through regulation.

These myriad efforts to manage the implicit self's suffering fits the tānha-dukkha formulation at the heart of Buddhism. Practically speaking, mindfulness, equanimity, vitality, joy, and a wonder for life only have a fighting chance when one's attachment wounds are healed. This brings us back to questions we raised early in this book and framed as "the two attachments". Should one attach lovingly to earth, animals, people and life, or does attachment lead to suffering? Modern attachment theory in combination with spiritual concepts already explored evokes some surprising answers.

Schore (in line with Bowlby) unreservedly places the responsibility for early life regulation on the neonate's major attachment figure. In a nutshell, the mother is the regulator of the baby and simply has to be. Per polyvagal theory, the mother's role and power comes by way of the ventral vagus (which could be called the attachment vagus). This guides all the lovey-dovey cooing, gazing and much more. The baby's innocence in this dance underscores the truth that shines through the sometimes maddeningly simplistic spiritual proclamation, "do not judge". The latest, best science demonstrates that a neonate can no more get a driver's license than regulate itself. By extension, it cannot mother itself or love itself. Then, given that the baby's implicit self/ego/mind becomes that of the adult, this yields: the implicit self/ego/mind cannot love itself in any genuine, meaningful manner.

Self-loathing, elaborate, self-reinforcing judgments of one's mother and intricate convictions of her collateral damage across the years are all built on implicit codes of fairness. The implicit self/ego/mind tends to be very invested in such matters. But the aggregate neuroscience of sentience points elsewhere. That which we use to determine the cardinal points of right and wrong, of significance and meaning itself, has a taproot that disappears in darkness, in the affective, somatic and sentient substrates of consciousness.

Naturally and paradoxically, for adults with a severely wounded implicit self the drumbeat, "do not judge" and "love unconditionally" becomes tortuously self-defeating. Just as the baby (and corresponding implicit substrate of the walking, waking implicit me) cannot mother or love itself, the Buddha and Jesus tenet to be above the fray and endlessly forgiving and compassionate just re-enters the stream of self-loathing and related negativity. The facts on the ground, possibly horrible abuse, personality disorders, extreme emotional neglect, deep self disturbance keep knocking. The notion of non-judgment seems to imply non-differentiation, no up, no down, e.g., nonsense.

The Vajrayana clarifies this in an outrageous way: we are neither stuck with what we did not receive nor without all we did not receive. The absence of fault actually refers to the independent fact of unconditional love. This turns "unfair" on its head. The attachment-love tantric bridge from mom-baby care to emptying of the self in an ocean of metta, all we have explored in Buddha's Mom, is birthright. It has no possible association to fault or fairness, no more wrongness than breastmilk. Judgments concerning fairness pertaining to abuse and dysfunction, damage to the fledgling self, trauma are real. But their reality is relative and unreal in terms of ultimatums or separateness from Buddha-nature.

These crumpled, hemorrhaging entities co-arise in a shared birthing process. The implications of this living, moment-shaping, unconscious practice is greatest where the implicit self is subtlest. By the time this reaches a torrent, we are in arousal states that push the gifts of the attachment vagus offline. Sadly, at these distances, decades can fly by without radical transformation. The thread of such renewal, the already awakened essence within, runs through highs and lows of arousal and all the colors of our emotional days. Where dependent origination arises in the implicit self, we tap into prajñā. Embodied wisdom is not affectively detached nor as gleeful, sad, or angry as close-up emotions feel. A rich quiet abides the betweens. Very nearby, closer in fact than even the biggest storms—inside these actually—is a constancy, a tingling, a pre-affective, pre-sentience shimmering. This is easy to miss and remains invisible as we cycle through good days, bad days—not meditating because we feel good and not meditating because we feel bad.

Another way to miss the forest for the trees is to exalt the right brain and the call to feel, feel, feel. For the deeply wounded, feeling too quickly evokes degrees of arousal and suffering impervious to left-brained interventions. We do well to notice the humming of our living soma as it walks on this earth between emotional dramas. Otherwise, the amazing language-proficient, conscious, adult mind is at the mercy of moods, judgments, and pain. It bounces atop waves like a boat that should have never left its harbor. Below, there is just darkness, mystery, energies that elude conceptual lassos.

The both/and, good/bad, tattered tension is the way and truth and light to the same, to wholeness and healing. Sharon Stanley, a major collaborator of Schore's, has developed therapeutic rituals and practices aimed at detecting associated somatic cues. She refers to subtle rhythms, tensions and vibrations throughout her recent work on *somatic transformation*.[400] She and her trainees are sensitized to notice micro-movements and micro-sensations, and they guide clients to an internal, interoceptive awareness of these. This is done collaboratively, in a caring, supportive wego space that relies heavily on the attachment vagus.

By invoking attachment-love, recovery from trauma proceeds through a "fear-based conversation with safety".[401] This evokes a "new flow of information and energy".[402] Positive shifts occur when bodily feeling syncs with emotional feeling, when "we feel what we know and know what we feel". In a form recognizable within Buddha's Mom, her trained therapists are interoceptively-attuned as they attune to their clients, guiding their clients to attune inwardly to their lost worlds and wounded implicit selves. The medium is the message and purpose is the meaning: love, healing, wholeness, recovery, and freedom. Such therapeutic extensions of Buddha's Mom specifically follow a soma-sentient path, upriver and down. From angst, meaninglessness, confusion, desperation, and all flavors of dysregulation to something more than non-dysfunction, something each of us may frame in their own way—often as 'spiritual not religious', often involving love.

Science-spirit breakthroughs at this time are breathtaking. Literally, scientifically, adult humans are pre-programmed with no choice or responsibility for the living, unfolding superstructure that undergirds arms, legs, physical, affective, and sentient self/ego/mind. Un-love, dis-union, anger, tightness, avoidance, all forms of subtle, pre-verbal emotion, behavioral and somatic wrinkles keep re-setting, keep arising even, and even/especially in those referred to as enlightened. An embodied karmic foundation of "me" was and is continually reformulated. A karmic load is embedded in—and reinforced through—countless, pre-verbal, pre-conscious neural processes. As Jung clarified, feeling is an exquisite emotional agency. Feeling provides rich perceptual valuations, colorations of like and dislike. Judgment co-arises in relative, often implicit formulations. Emotion as a vessel of judgment is allowed, nonjudgmentally, in the ultimate map we are calling Buddha's Mom, and traditionally referred to as enlightenment.

Cosmos wants through us. In sublime, somatic feeling and perceiving, we discern a divine yet entirely human love. Awakened teachers tap into and transmit a somatically innate yet cosmic love free of judgment. They speak of loving desire as that which seeks and as accessible and alive in the soma. "I am that" is the seeking of individuation, the pulse to express oneself as a unique expression of the universe, a pulse that simply is. In Buddha's Mom, we have endeavored to articulate this somatic-universal, evolutionary desire, with attachment-love as a touchstone, as our species' lineage.

Realized persons demonstrate the elusive call "do not judge" in everyday, simple ways. The love that holds a mother and son, two dear friends, and loving wego forms, imperfect as they are common, are not hard to spot. Such moments are consistent with religious creeds, tenets, and instructions to love unconditionally, to reach out to another in pain, and to let go and forgive those who harm us. Let's turn to some of the emerging insights at the threshold of science and spirit, and look for ways to meet life with love.

One area is an expansion of mom-baby attachment based on advances in the associated science centered in (what could be called) *regulation theory*. When an infant is hyper-aroused, be this crying, terrified, or even in an overly elevated, manic mood, the mother draws from her evolutionary repertoire. She vocalizes in a matching then guiding, down-regulating cadence, "OH, Oh, oh…. THERE, There, there." Immediately, a mystery opens. Those of us hobbled in early-life are quick to run scripts regarding our damaged self. But is it actually possible to enter into such judgment about what we did not receive without some backdrop of love, of a loving, nonjudgmental, attentive, devoted parent figure? As a plant bends toward light, the implicit self also recognizes attachment signals that feed the soul.

As discussed, the most recent, attachment vagus nerve branch that enervates the throat, vocal apparatus, face, and ears. Our fears and freak outs around needing love but feeling unloved can be met with a YES, Yes, yes, with LOVE, Love, love as we catch glimpses of this extraordinary-to-ordinary in nature, teachers, friends anytime. Just as the mom is impaled by that universal baby screech (that eerie, skin-tingling cat-like cry) so too we know the actual nature of being pierced by unrelenting pain, loneliness, wide-eyed helplessness. Her attachment-attuned senses spike her own arousal. Being self-regulated, she uses this to attend, empathize, and socially engage her little one. Her movement, voice, and face initially match the upset. Where is this mother when we see only a cage? She is in the midst of our mood, fear and hope co-arise. Buddha's and Jesus' compassion is ours, our inheritance. The upside and immediacy of this birthright, call it absolute bodhicitta, basic goodness or another name, naturally takes time to get used to. Few are ready for such joy and clarity. We even run back to old habits after experiences where such doors of perception open.

Mom's employ fast-to-slow, decelerating regulation kinesthetically as well. Related, soothing and invigorating forms of affection are both powerful and lacking in the histories of those with deep self disturbance forms of hyper-arousal. As a baby escalates, the adept, well-attached mother may rush in, grab, hug, lift, and rock. She engages in state-shifting kinesthetic acrobatics. Her movement and touch meet the intensity, proceeding from an initial surge to a slowing in line with the infant or toddler's emotional alignment.

Regulation theory has much to offer anyone inclined toward meditation and spiritual practice. Consider the exemplar of a cave-dwelling, always-meditating sage juxtaposed with a day in the life in modernity. It is not uncommon to see variations of voluntary complexity. Everyday equations are everywhere, with variables such as facebooking, driving, smoking, eating, sharing (pics of) our food, listening to music, complaining, bragging, empathizing, and sincere caring too. Such an unforced, outpouring of energy occupies the time and space of life.

Consider how much of this involves the attachment vagus' mouth, voice, eyes, and interpersonal emotions. Efforts to sync, pace, and modulate under- and over-arousal are one of many explanations for the other side of the equal sign. Others are more in line with the proverbial dog-chasing-its-tail, half fun, half delusional, half folly. We fumble for our smartphone to "capture the moment". A protective vagus mechanism fuels self-stimulating, frenetic activity. Better to shake it up and enter into here-now intensity than dissociate or miss out, slowed by depression. Better to amp up, join the anxiety as mothers do and then down-regulate. Voluntary complexity compensates for dissociation from our somatic-affective immediacy. In countless ways, we attempt regulation but have misinterpreted soma's longing for reunion. We over-react to her pains. We run from what seems an intolerable, eerie quiet, or we sink into this, confusing it for depression.

Many people with deep sources of affective dysregulation race headlong into love with old longings as fuel. Love, as they say, sweeps us off our feet. People with hypomania classically decide they are cured and no longer need their medication. But such times are precisely when we need third party objectivity. Some children, when tired, laugh to the point of tears, or roughhouse and end up surprised by their own aggression. Our OFC, inner designated driver can help us find a threshold of danger and learn a new level of confidence with respect to that universal human dream to fly. A baby may be gurgling, amused, and self-pleased. In response, Mom smiles, nods, agrees, and extends, "weeeeee…" (an attachment term of endearment indeed). She prolongs the play and laughter going. Rick Hanson advocates specific ways to enrich positive affect. These include ways of expanding all major characteristics, including the duration, intensity, a curiosity regarding new variants and new ways the positive emotion may be optimized and bring about a deepening of meaning.[403]

Moms work with the medium arousal zones as well. As a baby finds then loses interest in a toy and dips between engagement and boredom, she grabs her car keys, changes the baby's position and modulates her little one's sensory engagement. A multimodal affair, she may also cluck her tongue against the roof of her mouth in that universal maternal staccato, that decelerating auditory exchange that parents do with their offspring. Adults use television or wine to force a filter over the day's intensity. The human mom-baby frame is instructive. She does not need anything from formal Buddhism or Ikea as she fires on all cylinders. In clucking her tongue, she mimics the rhythmic sucking of breastfeeding—the suck and release as a vacuum is created then discharged.

Micro-movements in meditation may parallel such rhythms. A "good mom" node becomes an accessible, embodied potential through meditation practices. This healthy, living somatic feminine serves to up-regulate, down-regulate, and sync the eternal soma to the here-now mess. This parallels, is the attachment basis of being, wherein the totality of the sound, touch, and movement, the baby's or monkey minds' raging internal state is forced to share the stage with this other intense field of stimuli. An overly aroused implicit self/ego/mind is allowed and interrupted. Awareness is thereby invited or forced (yin-yang) into alignment with the breath, or slow to and fro of the spine. Adroit mothers engender their offspring's emotional de-escalation while breastfeeding another child and stirring a pot of food. A good starting point is demystification, an acknowledgement of this internal wego as already occurring and entirely ordinary. With practice, one can hold conversations at the grocery store and remain "in" their lower belly at the same time. A baby may continue to scream while staring at its mom, while soaking up the many safety cues. Our stormy inner life may rage even as we feel gravity's warm, constant embrace.

Our bodies go everywhere with us throughout the day. The old, inherited attachment echo extends across the lifespan and through the soma by design. All über dominant species exploit redundancies to get multiple bangs with one buck. The clinician-client, guru-disciple, pastor-parishioner, and BFF inmaps are examples of correlates of mom-baby attachment relationships with the potential to provide the selfsame right-brain to right-brain regulation. Generally, one being operates at a richer mode (of grounding, metta, chi) as another receives, incorporates, and embodies. The helper uses their ventral/attachment vagus as they listen, gaze caringly, speak intimately, and empathize. The core attachment formula is regulation (helper to helpee) to co-regulation (helper/helpee) to self-regulation (intra-helpee-regulation). Interpersonal, emotional factors influence intrapersonal, physiological functioning. Relatedly, some researchers purport that women's menstrual cycles become synchronized under certain conditions. "Emotional attachment" and social factors, they suggest, influences physiological regulation.[404, 405]

As Buddhists and pet lovers all emphasize, actual teachers may appear lower on an intellectual, sentient or moral continuum. In fact, the more we are in need of healing, the more constrained our concept of an appropriate healer. People with borderline personality manage to both feel victimized and reject legitimate, sincere offers of help. Paranoid forms of psychosis go a step further, convincing the mind that others are plotting murder.

Recently, one woman in my hospital practice was in such a regressive state that even fleeting eye contact was impossible. The psychiatrist's sedatives and benzodiazepines barely slowed her. She had chewed the insides of her cheeks and had blood stained teeth. I tried to stay grounded, in touch with my lower belly and to come from love as she thrashed about. I did not know what to do and slowly whistled a children's song. I tried to hold her hand and rub her back. Perhaps just coincidentally, she slowed down for a minute. Then three of us got her back in bed as she began flail again and decisions were made regarding the use of restraints.

Additionally, what we know of some of Buddha's actual relationships is not only consistent with modern attachment and regulation theory but offers insights regarding liberation. Kisa, Prajapati, and Devadatta, for example, each coped, according to canonical sources, with varying degrees and forms of emotional dysregulation. For each, interactions with Buddha appear to have mediated (regulated) untoward emotion, and this process preceded each of them achieving some form of awakening. Kisa's encounter with Buddha occurred following the death of her toddler. Prajapati and Devadatta knew Siddhartha-Buddha for decades.

Kisa, as discussed, was way off-kilter. She was hyper-aroused, carrying around her dead baby in sheer, raw agony and grief. She was likely also half checked out, suffering from hypo-arousal, yielding a combinatory disabling-protective psychological state of dissociation. Descriptions have her completely unreachable by all but the Buddha. These days, she would have been deemed psychotic and placed in an inpatient psychiatric unit against her will. Kisa's dysregulation evoked Buddha's deep concern. As covered previously, the transformative power of Kisa's encounter with Buddha at least in theory fits the general outlines of Buddha's Mom. In her case, the shifts in regulation and arousal were dramatic and long lasting.

Prajapati, of course, raised Siddhartha and presumably was one of his major attachment figures. By inference, her right OFC guided and refined her attachment repertoire when he was a baby and across the whole of decades-long relationship. In the early months and years, she facilitated his foundational, internal, intrinsic capacities for affective regulation. Presumably, she had adequate and possibly extraordinary skills as a mother figure, as I have suggested throughout this book. These would have something to do with his affective development and the basis from which he would discover penetrating, transcendent truths regarding consciousness and human potential.

What is written about Prajapati's later life would be consistent with her having emotional intensity, range, and capacity as a baseline, across many decades. Shortly after Siddhartha was born, she stepped into a situation that required chutzpah. She must have had doubts. She may have wondered if people were only kind to her because of her association with Suddhodana? The biography suggests, like most of us, she coped with horrific lows and highs and forms of dysregulation. Self-doubt, jealousies often are counterweights to emotional inflations that go along with getting what you think you want. The gods took her sister's life, as was meant to be, because she alone was called to raise this golden child. As time passed, her non-biological baby became a gifted child, handsome young man, and eventually a profound, baffling sage with a huge following. She may have been proud, even too proud; she may have had felt left aside, unappreciated—and in general had a life filled with variations of arousal.

Prajapati provides both an ordinary and extraordinary example of our species' affective and sentient inheritance. She was human and, for most of her life, striving and falling short of enlightenment. She likely experienced variations on familiar themes. She may have felt like an imposter in the whole affair, deserving no credit for her son's achievement yet craving praise. Like almost everyone, she probably hit walls as she tried to meditate and jealously compared herself to others who worked less and achieved more. Maybe she was self-loathing or felt cheated because she could not come close to her son's skills. The gods robbed her! Perhaps she (instead or also) felt shame for wanting more accolades. She adjusted and, from all we know, found ever deeper reservoirs from which to love in non-possessive ways.

In all, Prajapati demonstrated not just affective range and capacities for regulation but also aptitude. Her affective muscles enabled her not just to cope with hardship but to learn from it. Her wisdom grew and spirit deepened, enabling an ever more meaningful relationship with her son. In her maturity, she transformed herself in his image. She discovered a deeper, tantric desire not to return to the human emotional love and war zone and became Buddhism's first nun.

Prajapati more than coped with dysfunctional arousal. She and others must have navigated various so-called positive emotions. These would have included expansive affects based in their inside track, emotions stemming from feeling utterly understood, special and loved. Their stories demonstrate that how a modern, integrative attachment model supersedes (transcends and includes) capacities for affective regulation and trauma resolution.

For these contemporaries, rather than achieve affective stabilization and stop, the finish line was continually resetting itself. Awakening appears to be more process than event, more verb than noun. One becomes ever more emotionally free and expansive and ever more keyed in on the same. Said another way, even so-called enlightened masters suffer, hurt, and keep evolving in a relative sense. They fully welcome, if not go after, theirs and others' suffering with an ever more expansive bodhisattva heart. Nothing takes away from their freedom; conversely, suffering seems to open ever more doors of non-possessive love and compassion.

The journey of the securely attached infant, toddler, child, adolescent, and adult provides an outline for this essential feature of human nature. As peek-a-boo, scary movies, rollercoasters, and sad songs prove, so-called negative emotions actually defy a single plus/minus valence. The full functioning elephant and human both grieve the loss of loved ones. Love infers the capacity for loss. Buddha did not simply assist Kisa to regulate and overcome trauma. He helped her to open her being to the depths of love which includes loss. She could gather no mustard seeds; every home she visited had lost someone they loved. In this, her love (and affective capacity for intra- and interpersonal empathy for even profound loss) was restored and expanded, superseding itself.

Buddha helped Kisa, Prajapati and Ananda penetrate the darkness of their various "negative" emotions and discover the gems these protect. The wrathful deities in Tibetan Buddhism represent this very truth. For Kisa, what would eventually result in realization was masked by raw heartbreak and grief. For Prajapati, less acute but longer lasting emotional struggles marked her zigzag, slow process of awakening.

The even-keeled Ananda, renowned for his devotion, suffered a subtler emotional fetter. His devotional love was continually getting snagged on the relative rocks this side of freedom and bliss. He was, for example, dearly attached to Sāriputta (another disciple) and had trouble accepting his death. This was repeated after the death of Buddha.

Ananda stands out in another way. Despite his close proximity and protracted relationship with Buddha (across most of the Holy One's lifetime), Ananda almost died without achieving liberation. Buddha even left a teaching regarding this possibility. Ananda's journey speaks to the maddening tenet of non-judgment and the mysterious inter-relationship of so-called negativity and enlightenment. Consider the interplay of Ananda's emotional stickiness and his great achievement as guardian of the dharma. Further, it was Ananda who persisted and finally (from outward appearances) persuaded Buddha to allow women into the sangha.

Buddha, we can speculate, was in the position of the loving mother who delights in his child's wobbles and foibles. She never views development as lacking. Ananda's intense, selfless, obsessive flavor of love fueled his remarkable achievements. Perhaps there would be no Pali Canon had he achieved enlightenment sooner. He drove himself to the brink, as a practice in itself, to catch every single word, every subtle intention and meaning, every molecule of the Master's transmission.

Siddhartha's father, Suddhodana, also wrestled with relative love's sticky side, and this too eventually led to healing and realization. Most will recall his decades long effort to control every aspect of Siddhartha's existence. When Siddhartha was born, the wise men were summoned. They inadvertently upended Suddhodana's identification with legacy as a source of identification and meaning. They predicted, based on the baby's body markings, that it would either be a great ruler or great spiritual teacher. Thereafter Suddhodana was hell-bent on convincing his son of the superiority of the ruler's path of riches and comforts. This theme echoed in the story of Jesus and the devil's temptations. Suddhodana so wanted Siddhartha to follow in his footsteps and veer from the hardship of the world outside the palace. Famously, the King ordered that his son never glimpse even withering flowers, much less old age, sickness, and death. Most interpretations recognize Suddhodana's psychology as exactly that which Buddha declared problematic. In this light, he symbolizes power and control and a doomed effort to achieve a sort of permanence through legacy and happiness through riches.

The full breadth of attachment theory combined with what we have referred to as Buddha's Mom expands on this. The King's obsessiveness corresponds to a form of affective dysregulation. We can add that though his fatherly love is genuine, it is disembodied. He was not grounded enough in his love to empathize with his son's unique, brilliant spirit. Siddhartha, of course eventually shakes off the shackles. In leaving the palace, he dispatches any possibility of fulfilling the King's hopes. This move also puts to rest which of the wise men's predictions will come to pass.

The relative, messy side of love is further highlighted, as we have discussed, in Rahula. Siddhartha named his only child based on the word for impediment or fetter. Rahula's innocent, species-based pull for attachment heats up the unvarnished, pre-enlightenment, attachment-detachment tug-o-war that nearly prevented Siddhartha from fulfilling his destiny. Ray tells the most moving story of Chögyam Trungpa once staring at him in sheer helplessness, asking, "Why me?" Why was he chosen?

Siddhartha was similarly called by the lineage. In his case, he was to reject a legacy already forged by his father and take the ascetic path. It is safe to say, I think, that Siddhartha's heart was broken, that his father loved him and he loved his father, and that the same bond was shared with Rahula. His sacrifice was not simply power and riches. He was called to forsake attachment-love and leave his son, wife, mother, and father, possibly never to be able to hug them again. As we will return to below, *this* Buddha would be one or the other of two extremes.

This book has focused on Buddha's enlightenment as an awakening through and into our species' attachment lineage. The stories of these contemporaries of Buddha offer additional perspectives. Where Kisa was highly dysregulated and in modern diagnostic terms probably both traumatized and temporarily psychotic, others such as Prajapati were far more "high functioning". Yet the degree of Kisa's dysfunction did not restrict the speed or fullness of her healing. In fact, the person who had the most direct, sustained relationship with the enlightened Buddha, Ananda, took perhaps the longest of all to achieve liberation. What accounts for these variations in regulation and awakening?

As discussed in the section on Pandita, the Buddha was an advocate of evidence and expertise. From an ultimate, absolute perspective, Vajrayana views all humans as traumatized.[406] The ubiquitous suffering of humanity is consistent with the Noble Truths. Thankfully, at this time in history, the evidence is building from both extremes toward (what might be) a new middle way. On the science side, developmental trauma rather than single-incident, shock trauma correlates with more complex forms of wounding and a longer journey to affective regulation. On the spirit side, Buddhism's greatest hits validate the test of time. These include Hinayana discipline, hours and intensity of practice; Shamatha focused mindfulness; Vipaśyanā openness, insight into suchness; and Shikantaza perfecting, bliss and nonmeditation.

Work on attachment's role in the healing of developmental trauma affirms the importance of firsthand, interpersonal encounters as critical and potentially transformative. Superimposing the stories of some of those who knew Buddha only reinforces these discoveries. With help from perhaps the world's leading researcher of this subject matter, we can dare to imagine the nature of the regulating moments that transformed Kisa and the others. In theory at least, the Buddha's face would have communicated a living, interactional sea of empathic attunement and safety cues, and what Buddhists refer to as the co-arising perfect dyad of compassion and wisdom.

> Human beings are astoundingly attuned to subtle emotional shifts in the people (and animals) around them. Slight changes in the tension of the brow, wrinkles around the eyes, curvature of the lips, and angle of the neck quickly signal to how comfortable, suspicious, relaxed or frightened someone is. Our mirror neurons register their inner experience, and our own bodies make internal adjustments to whatever we notice.[407]

The flavor of the above passage along with the massive data on the associated neurobiology of attuned, empathic encounters, however, reflects a residual science-spirit schism. Scientists are understandably reticent to speak of realization and enlightenment. In this regard, the vignette of the visiting wise men in the biography of Buddha may deserve a second look. Their input not only set up Suddhodana's great turmoil but possibly speaks to an incomprehensibly greater rift at the very root of the dharma.

Anthropologists would be familiar with the so-called wise men who shared their vision with the King. Their ecstatic practices and claims of clairvoyance are recognizable forms running in indigenous cultures. These wise men, sages, mystics, soothsayers, seers, hermits, shamans—by whatever name—lived outside of Kapilavastu, outside of "civilization". They wandered Earth's forests, jungles and lived in her caves

Jesus' birth has a similar motif in the three kings, also called wise men, who followed the Star of Bethlehem to the nativity scene. With their sky-god orientation, the baby Jesus' stargazers differ from Siddhartha's seers. Theirs was a paternal, Heavenly Father, an iteration of Zeus and Yahweh. Jesus' biblical magi looked up toward heavenly bodies for divination in contrast to Asita and his co-travelers who peered into the human form itself.

This distinction is both important and partial. Both Christian and Buddhist orthodoxy view the human body as more than mere flesh and bone. Both have scores of passages disparaging the body, many with misogynistic overtones. The body's cravings, drives, and enticements, goes the drumbeat, lead to sin and suffering. Christianity, however, goes further, ultimately associating the body to evil itself and, all gloves off, to the very center of the *earth* where evil's overlord resides.

The Vajrayana reverses this vitriolic judgment and, as we have seen, upholds the spiritual essence of body and earth as sacred. Buddhism has no need of a devil or god. Soma's vastness mitigates any requirement for outside authorities. Although Jesus is embodied divinity, even he leaves both earth's dark lord and heaven's perfected deity untouched. These disembodied forms are included in his realization but not entirely transcended. They are preserved but not negated, certainly not by what becomes a mass religion in his name, wherein spirit and matter (god and man, heaven and earth, spirit and flesh, etc.) remain alienated.

Immersed in the extremes of this cultural, historical dissociation, Jesus' (attachment-love's) tantric leap was a suicidal mission. His is a pre-turning, a vessel born of a Mother so detached that she is named for her inability to conceive. A cosmic bodhisattva, Jesus might have continued wandering his mother's earth with his ragtag followers. Instead, he flung himself at our species' murderous, yang instincts. We did not know better, did not love better, so he would die showing us the way. His lovingkindness was irrepressible, bigger than life. His only sanity was in obeying this higher rule of law, this universal dharma—that we have associated with evolution and therein, Buddha's Mom.

The same essential dissociation, spirit versus flesh, yin and yang and so on, continues in endless forms of spiritual materialism. Chögyam Trungpa's Vajrayana lineage is a living, chaotic cutting through accessible through soma. This undertaking entails a fearsome negating and transcending of dualities. Nondual, heaven-and-earth, yin-yang, and soma-as-cosmos merely await a seer. A witness.

Where to begin? The word *ecstatic* offers a hint. This term is often applied to the traditional, to the seers and shamans. These indigenous members of our species manage their tribe's ultimate existential, cosmic relationships. In this wego, self/ego/mind grapples with gods, evil, meaning, and all existential ultimatums. Ecstatic means to "stand outside of". Shamanic ways of perceiving and knowing are by definition outside of established tribal customs. The word *esoteric* offers another clue. This is also used to describe these same ancient, earth-based traditions. Esoteric refers to a special, extra degree of *inside* positioning. Esoteric was originally used to describe Greek philosophers' insider knowledge—a topic we addressed with Diotima. Tantra is commonly referred to as ecstatic and esoteric, as well as specialized, secretive and mystical. All are true.

It follows then that indigenous, shamanic, earth-based spiritual practices pulse within the heart of the Vajrayana and Tantra. Reggie Ray has referred to his and Chögyam Trungpa's lineage as "an ancient, esoteric, "primordial" tradition".[408] In the Vajrayana, Buddhism very distinctively goes against the stream of the world's 'high religions' and their skyward, disembodied truth claims.

> Chögyam Trungpa in his Shambhala teachings said more or less the same thing: there is within each person, irrespective of his or her historical period, culture, tradition, or orientation, an inherent human spirituality that lies at the very heart of the human being as such. My own practice of Tibetan yoga (Vajrayana)—carried out in dialogue with the study of earth-based spiritualities, as mentioned—has confirmed this fact on an experiential and practical level.[409]

In his scholarship and as a spiritual teacher, Ray has produced an immense set of somatic meditation and earth-based, Vajrayana practices along with multiple, associated scholarly works. I would conjecture that Ray has articulated how soma is both the ultimate veil of spiritual materialism (one of his teacher's major themes) and the definitive portal to liberation. Soma and body are terms for the material self. As discussed in depth, the word matter is derived from *mater* and refers to mother, origin, and source.

Despite immense efforts to find such a self in the brain, the amassing, associated evidence points to an implicit, somatic, affective, relational, sentient, integral, and co-arising ground of being. Such marks ultimate reality, the human realm of consciousness and sentience and a path to affective regulation and ever higher states of realization. Spiritual materialist leaves us prone to making idols of ideas, people, experiences and getting stymied. But as Ray underscores in practices directed at a seeming nexus of materialism, the body and earth, cut through. These involve, for example, opening the back of the body and descending into earth's infinity. Transformation through relationship with our material essence is doable. Interoception opens doors to the a 'natural state' that defies any final definition, that is both universal and unique, eternal and changing. Schore's synthesis model provides new, precise, empirical paths to the door of ecstatic and esoteric insights at the heart of the Vajrayana.

In a recent conference, Ray (2016) spoke fondly of Hongzhi Zhengjue, the Ch'an Buddhist sage who lived from 1091 to 1157.[410] As I understood Ray's teaching, Hongzhi brilliantly synthesized various streams: the Indian roots of the Vajrayana, Taoism, and indigenous, earth-based spirituality. In Hongzhi's "silent illumination", Shakyamuni's lineage achieves an advanced, sublime translation. Echoes of indigenous spirituality, the same infinite relationship to earth, the same ultimate, endless somatic home—all found in Ray's work—run through Hongzhi's writings. Note, for example, the spiritual cutting through of materialism in Hongzhi's "mind ground dharma field". May Buddha's Mom deserve a place in this sage's "unwithered fertility".[411]

> The field of bright spirit is an ancient wilderness that does not change. With boundless eagerness wander around this immaculate wide plain... Directly arriving here you will be able to recognize the mind ground dharma field that is the root source of the ten thousand forms germinating with unwithered fertility. These flowers and leaves are the whole world. So we are

told that a single seed is an uncultivated field. Do not weed out the new
shoots and the self will flower.[412]

Ultimately with its "striking similarities to the Tibetan Mahamudra and Dzogchen",
Hongzhi's synthesis became part of the Tibetan Vajrayana stream.[413] Remarkably, this ancient Ch'an
master was also one of Dōgen's major influences and therein comes to us in Soto Zen. For the last
three decades of his life, Hongzhi was the beloved abbot of T'ien-t'ung Monastery. Seventy years
later Dōgen practiced there with Ju-ching. As mentioned, one day Ju-ching was scolding a drowsy
monk causing Dogen to suddenly cast off mind and body. Dōgen's "just sitting" shikantaza is an
iteration of Hongzhi's "silent illumination", and as one measure of his affection, scholars not that
Dōgen quotes Hongzhi more than any other Zen master.[414]

The Buddhist complement to modern attachment theory helps bridge trauma and
transformation. Tracing this, the original Hinayana calls for renunciation and practice forms
involving leaving the household, silence and removal of stimulation. These and many other forms
such as the Vajrayana dark retreat practice can only partially be understood as negating. Such
practices (recall Wilber's "negate and preserve" as half of "transcend and include") set up and force
opportunities to engage and savor the silence of being—a being that simply is bodily and of this
earth. The Vajrayana in particular picks up where a framing of regulation as a reduction or repair of
dysfunction ends. The wounded implicit self/ego/mind is reset in interoception, in the many somatic
meditation forms, as a portal to soma; soma is a home to be discovered, a transfiguring, embodied,
living belonging—vibrant, free, and without reference to space or time.

Sharon Stanley's somatic transformation model abides in this betweenness. In this,
indigenous sources are seamlessly integrated providing a unique expansion of Schore's modern
attachment paradigm.[415] Stanley has a wealth of direct experience stemming from time spent with
native peoples and healers. These include members of Afro-Brazilian, first nations tribes and the
Chammoro peoples of the Mariana Islands. Stanley's practitioner-scientist paradigm emphasizes the
healing power of ceremony and ritual. Common, effective elements include: healthy intention,
communal gathering, strong leadership, bodily movement, and use of natural, landscape, and earth
elements.

> In many ways, the encounter of the new paradigm in Western healing
> practices, right-brain-to-right-brain affective embodied experience that
> Schore (2012) advocates, are ceremonies that bring essential elements
> together for healing trauma... The elements that make it a ceremony
> included and embodied intersubjective relationships, the rituals of sacred,
> uninterrupted time, the development of bodily-based rhythm and
> movement, and somatic relational exploration of internal and environmental
> influences on human experiences.[416]

With this, we can reflect further on the shamans who came to view baby Siddhartha. In their
ritual viewing, they very well may have entered into a shamanic, ecstatic trance state enabling them
to visualize what goes by "Vajra body", "subtle body", and "energy body". In line with Buddha's
Mom, these seers (as they are also called) are embedded in the feminine principle. They belong to
the earth. Their prophecy could be thought of as a Himalayan oracle. These four specifically saw
bodily signs, marks or markings; they translated these to mean that this baby would be a Buddha of
one or another great realm. Of the four seers, Asita is famously noted as having the highest

precognitive powers. But this story element may be very secondary next to the larger fact of their shared vision, their consensus message regarding *this* Buddha.

This event, involving special somatic signs and markings which only shamanic seers detect, possibly pertaining to Siddhartha's Vajra body, invites consideration of related Buddhist concepts. The wise men may have "seen" Siddhartha's nadis. According to ancient Hindu sources, as well as Tibetan Medicine, nadis are the pipes, vessels, fibrous and energetic lines that form the soma. Nadis have vibrant intersections along the central channel at each of the chakras, perhaps even forming the chakras. There are tens of thousands, possibly millions or billions of these. Some of Ray's Mahamudra practices (which he fully credits to the Vajrayana and Chögyam Trungpa) guide participants to bring the nadis into alignment through a synchronization of soma and (the essential, energetic) earth.[417, 418]

Maybe we have been wrong to leave these seer-hermits with only their cameo appearance. Maybe they are true masters, mediums, and mystical intuitives, and others across history have been and even now are the same. Perhaps their counsel remains profound. The shared consensus that this Buddha will be one of two forms trumps the reinforcing detail regarding Asita. Yes, he could see the baby's subtle, energetic body in a slightly higher resolution as history would prove. But the more significant message concerns the collective, ecstatic consensus of a bifurcated buddhadharma.

Perhaps the world was only ready for one half or aspect of dharma. Perhaps one flowering had to come first before the other, or before a new age wherein both come into being. For now, the earth awaits a compassionate order overseen by a Buddhist monarch whether this means a "new world order" or some sort of bureaucratic-savior and vast form of governance based in lovingkindness. Certainly, the extent of fixable starvation, stoppable war and preventable disease cry out for an earth-based, pragmatic healing. The earth needs a declaration of Interdependence, based in our exploitation of her and destruction on one another. Although absurd on the one hand, the emerging work on regulation suggests that the upside of attachment theory is without limit. The seers at Siddhartha's birth may have communicated that Shakyamuni would be one Buddha and, beautifully, that another ruler or regulator or regulation was yet to come. The etymology of *ruler* or monarch, which the seers identified (possibly) as another Buddha, another dharma, an enlightened road yet to come, is intriguing.

> Old English borrowed Latin regula and nativized it as regol "rule, regulation, canon, law, standard, pattern;" hence regolsticca "ruler" (instrument); regollic (adj.) "canonical, regular."[419]

The grand potential of Shakyamuni that was partially seen, partially obscured, might yet prove to be a turning of the wheel of dharma, a societal enlightenment. In this, the earth-based, primordial enlightenment of pre-history, pre-civilization would come into fullness and be available to modernity. Dharma and regulation both refer to a body of law, canon, and ordering principles. The seers communicated not that a fuller reach of canonical law and principle would never come, but simply that such a form of regulation would not manifest in the first turning. The breadth of the initial Shakyamunian regulatory transformation would be of a spiritual form, not a new age of governance, not one associated with the "world monarch".

The regulation or concordance between Chögyam Trungpa, Reggie Ray, and the Vajrayana (and others with similar realization) and the modern attachment paradigm may be the foundation of love as international law, as policy, as the ordering principle for our species existence on this earth. If such a Buddha or turning is in-utero, ideas considered in Buddha's Mom suggests the importance of a fierce mother or feminine to prepare the way. We might find her in daring to ask, what is love? At least part of this grand, perennial mystery is now locatable map big enough for the best of both science and spirit.

Any effort to marry love and regulation would have to reconcile what looks like chaos and order from the outside. The trickster energy that characterized the shaman inmap is often attributed to Chögyam Trungpa. These associations suggest that where there is love, there is earth-based sorcery and mysticism. That other-worldly powers living in the soma, demanding attention *regularly* upend the status quo and bring about transformation, and in this more and more love. Love spills out of an energetic soma visible perhaps only those steeped in our species' ancient, earth-based spiritual roots. Through earth, a love-soma, energy body, or Vajra body may be liberated. This non-suffering, cosmic vessel for a physical and emotional body that suffers may be one's ever-present state. So-called negative emotion, if encountered without judgment, is radically transformative. The seemingly negative is actually unencumbered, seeking only expression. It is encumbering only from the perspective of the personality's status quo. Non-judgment forces/allows an endlessly deepening empathy. This actually is not just transformative but a 'transcend-include' portal on an intrapersonal and interpersonal bodhisattva path. The open, welcoming space where non-judgment abides is soma, and in turn, earth. And so, what is negative is protective, creative and positive. We have also heralded this architecture as Buddha's Mom, and as Witness in wego.

No surprise then that so many of these elements collide in one of the greatest poets of love ever—full stop. Like Socrates' Diotima (his "instructress of love" as discussed earlier), the great Rumi too channeled (what we have portrayed as) a tantric source of metta. His source muse was a Sufi mystic, trickster, and scholar was named Shamsi Tabrizi. Shamsi was also, notably, a whirling dervish. Ecstatic dance channels the same visceral, unstoppable, direct expression of the energy body as it is fluidly mapped across the physical body. We touched on the Maori's Haka warrior dance previously and would note echoes in the revelry of the Greek symposium and the dance of desire that animates Tibetan consort practices. All are living, moving embodied forms of transmission and transformation.[420]

Rumi's mysterious consort, Shamsi, is variously referred to as wild haired, charismatic, a "wandering dervish", and very learned. Through him flows "immense kindness but at the same time great severity". What we can recognize as a potent metta transmission occurred over an intensive two-year period. This began when Rumi was 37 with a "massive outpouring of poetry" following.[421]

> Learn the alchemy true human beings know: the moment you accept what
> troubles you've been given, the door will open. Welcome difficulty as a
> familiar comrade. Joke with torment brought by the friend. Sorrows are the
> rags of old clothes and jackets that serve to cover, then are taken off. That
> undressing, and the naked body underneath, is the sweetness that comes
> after grief.[422]

Diotima, Shamsi Tabriz as well as, in the case of Buddha, Asita and the wise men, all were oracles and mediums of the lost world of our ancestors. The rise of small city-states at the beginnings of modernity marked a drastic turning point in the human journey. The whole of human's animal life, built atop Panksepp's mammalian nervous system and base sentience, was on the brink. Our one and only, our ultimate tantric tap root, was getting ripped out by an acceleration of our own yang-based brilliance. An intimacy with earth's water, plants, animals, weather, seasons marks the surfaces. Below this, our emotional way of life had always been richly tenuous and vibrant because of the immediacy of cold, hunger, risk of attack—a dependency that naturally was steeped in vigilance and mystery. Tribes prayed for protection, rain, and made sacrifices directly, intuitively out of this fierce embedding, this belonging to an other on whom we slept, upon whom we walked, climbed. We picked her berries, hunted her creatures and never knew anything else except her yin-envelopment.

The shamanic realm is an earth-human bridge still accessible through the implicit self-ego-mind. Traditionally hallucinogens, trance, exhaustion, isolation, pilgrimages, and other means opened doors of perception to Gaia.[423] She is the majestic, fearsome, life-giving, life-taking other inseparable from the ascent of consciousness. As mediums and changelings, medicine men and women were charged with regulating the tribe's relationship to earth. Their rituals helped the tribe deal with existential terror and life tenuously dependent upon her. The shaman-trickster, with necklaces of bones and shrunken skulls, mediates what appear from this side to be mysterious, dark powers. Like all inmaps, shamanic earth-based rituals facilitate self/ego/mind's relationship with the unconscious. Modern attachment/regulation theory provides a more nuanced model. The sentient space entrusted to the shaman, potentially, is available via interoception and the implicit self.

Paradoxically, that which once assisted tribes to survive on earth led to a disconnection from her. With the rise of civilization, our species' instinctual spiritual lineage based in attachment was in jeopardy. Dysregulated rulers, those not transformed by the first spiritual turning (the first regulatory epoch) and their bureaucracies and armies distanced us from our own tantric essence in shifts from hunter-gatherer to the first city-states. The extra-inside, extra-outside realm of the seer, sorcerer and shaman remained vivid in the wild-haired crones, hermits and dervishes. These names for the old, indigenous, and realized speak to ways the new insiders, the moderns, existed in a tension with the whole of attachment-love as lineage. The most exceptional of these new, brilliant men (mostly, given the shift to patriarchy) were impregnated by and embodied the old.

In various ways, as we have explored, Socrates, Dogen, Rumi, and Buddha (recall Siddhartha's many years walking and meditating in the forest and jungle) received earth-based, yin transmissions. According to Reggie Ray, interwoven Buddhist and earth-based practices were passed along, marking the Vajrayana lineage. Succession of realized male and female masters have managed to convey earth-based wisdom to Dogen, Chögyam, and others. This tantric essence was at great risk of being severed with the close of the Pleistocene and the accelerating rise of modernity.

Safe moderns living far from the dangers of the wilderness need this same connection, especially for deep healing or spiritual transformation. Hope may begin as imagination and proceed in embodied, wordless memory. Consider the terrifying yet reassuring power of trickster-shamans. They summoned the gods, demanded sacrifice and otherwise transmuted confusion and paranoia. They oversaw rites of passage, received and communicated wisdom from ancestors who had crossed over. Loved ones we so longed to reattach to. They healed with herbs and, like many modern correlates, were adept at what at present is called the placebo effect. They assuaged hyper-aroused tribe members who, for example, like Kisa decompensated in grief and the same embodied source that was indeed theirs is ours, as lineage. We frequently reach out to others with modern variants of these powers, and can reach within for a more direct connection and transmission.

In closing, the short-lived shamanic element at the beginning of the biography of Lord Buddha may have more significance than typically portrayed. The turnings beginning with Shakyamuni Buddha may one day extend tantric rule, taking the dharma from the caves and forests not just to the monastery, not just to the household but further, into the village, city, government, into education, law, medicine, and military arenas, to wherever beings suffer from dysregulation.

Chögyam Trungpa and Reginald (Reggie) Ray are lucid echoes of the repeated blend of shamanism, scholarly genius and love seen in Buddha's Mom-Buddha, in Diotima-Socrates and Shamsi-Rumi. Ray, for me, is Buddhism's unstoppable, prolific Rumi. Here we have celebrated evidence of love-as-lineage within regulation theory and can now even more deeply appreciate dharma as an evolutionary law of love. As mentioned, regulation and dharma, canon and law have a shared root meaning with regulation. Maybe coincidental, maybe serendipitous is the etymology of the name, *Reginald*. This name is derived of three elements: queen, advise, rule/ruler. *Ray* in turn comes from terms for the spoke of a wheel, ray of sun and evokes images of the thousand-armed bodhisattva.

Bioneurology

The term *neurobiology* reverses the emphasis taken in this book on *biological* attachment as the substrate of sentience and spiritual awakening. As we have reviewed, Bowlby's work now undergirds a broad, integrated field incorporating Panksepp's affective neuroscience[424], Porges' polyvagal model[425] and achieves fruition in Allan Schore's paradigm-shifting, "modern attachment theory".[426] To be sure, *neurobiology* inserts body/biology, and therefore resonates with mammalian and maternal attachment as a major source of sentience. This terminology is, thankfully, far less constrained than "cognitive neuroscience" which enjoyed too long a run. But the accent on brain and neurons as the bricks of being remains. Even the Great Chain, rendered as body-mind-spirit, sets spirit distal to body and closer to mind. Both reflect modernity's obsession with brain and neurons as the basis of consciousness, and by extension, spiritual experience.

Perhaps the inverse, *bioneurology*, is more in line with an inquiry into the full expanse of sentience and human potential. Hints of this reversed evolutionary inflection are rooted in the Pali Canon. Famously, Siddhartha went not from cave and forest to civilization but in the opposite direction. Similarly, Chögyam Trungpa abandoned Tibetan hierarchy. He cast off his robe and walked away from his commanding status as the eleventh generation of the Trungpa Tulkus. Somatic practices are the very heart of the Vajrayana lineage he inherited and the Shambhala lineage he forged.[427] His protégé, Reggie Ray, has no end of passion or creativity in this regard.[428]

Similarly, Jesus confronted Judaism's cleaving of the profane and sacred realms, proclaiming the body as the temple of God. Jesus descended from heaven, and was made *flesh*. These realized beings challenged patriarchal, hierarchal givens. Led were they by divine, disruptive, intuitive winds which no one in their time could have possibly predicted. Jesus upended the tax collectors' tables, much as these geniuses of the human heart upended expectations and cultural norms. For Jesus, the sacred was not mediated by any ruthless, hyper-masculized, sky-god such as Yahweh.

As we will explore, wrath gets resituated in the service of the perfection, love and bliss these realized men sought to convey. Like Rinpoche Chögyam Trungpa, Jesus too derided spiritual materialism, for example, calling out hypocrites who "shamelessly cheat widows out of their property and then pretend to be pious by making long prayers in public".[429]

The architecture of the Middle Way fits nicely with the emphasis in *bioneurology*. As much discussed, Siddhartha's breakthrough came on the heels of the austerities, the term given to his rigorous exploration of the ultimate sentient implications of biological existence. Indeed, for six years leading up to this, he had wandered and survived essentially as a human animal in his local, biological ecosystem. With the austerities, he was in search of the ultimate biological roots of consciousness. Moving in reverse of body-mind-spirit, his drive was to test body/biology as ultimate a portal to enlightenment. Ultimately the Middle Way demonstrates the disruptive nexus of biology and spirit.

Siddhartha's somatic research was as unrelenting as it was grim. It is written that he lost such weight that he could push his hand into his stomach and curl his fingers around his backbone.[430] His legs were like bamboo sticks and his eyes dropped like stones into their sockets. Nothing worked until everything did. In failing, he succeeded. Emaciated, exhausted, our wizened Siddhartha finally concluded, "I have not attained any superhuman states."[420] Denial of basic bodily needs was not the way. Rather than extremes, the path to liberation, the path-fruition, opened from the middle. The Middle Way refers to body-mind/mind-body transcendence.

Especially in light of polyvagal theory, some intriguing, tentative conclusions are now possible. As mentioned, the vagus and closely associated nerve networks correspond to three phases of evolution and three domains within the human body. In phylogenetic order, these begin with the ancient, dorsal vagus. This causes immobility, including folding, fainting, and feigning death. Second is the mid-level, the familiar, 'fight-flight' system. Third is the most recently evolved, and the focus of this book: the maternal, social attachment system. Danger and threat trigger fight-flight-fold and safety-seeking through social attachment. Porges summarizes these three domains as immobilization, mobilization and socialization.[431]

Relatedly, Mary Ainsworth (Bowlby's student) pioneered one of psychology's most elegant and revealing experiments. The 'stranger situation' demonstrates the fluid interplay between threat detection and safety seeking. In this, a baby and mom are in a room when an unknown person enters. Normal, e.g., securely attached babies (as we have suggested Siddhartha would have been) looked to their mothers for safety cues. They responded appropriately to her nonverbal signals. If her face, eyes, voice indicated the stranger was not a threat, they might continue to explore the room or check out the stranger. If mom displayed concern, the securely attached baby would orient or move in her direction. Intermittent, nonverbal and verbal communication would calibrate the push-pull between safety-seeking on one side and curiosity and play on the other.

During the austerities, in barely breathing, in starving and isolating himself, Siddhartha's three-way polyvagal system was (in theory) engaged. Taking some license here, his sympathetic nervous system cascaded with fight-flight terror. His self/ego/mind would have perceived corresponding drives and attachments to breathe, eat, drink, snap out of it.

Affect is evolution's elegant, singular answer to the multiplicity of threats and needs faced by our brilliant, sensitive, complex species. Like a switchboard operator, the brain eventually connects given demands with a fitting response. But whole of the process is mediated by global affects when need be. The risk of anoxia triggers anxiety and the drive to inhale, trumping all other motivations. And so on for cold, hunger, loud noise or predator attack. Somehow in Siddhartha, these somatic calls even screams, for air, food, warmth, sleep, safety, normalcy, and social connection were met an even greater love and acceptance. It is written that he would hold his own breath so long that he fell senseless to the ground—a dorsal vagal response. He persisted despite (what clinicians would likely call a panic attack): feeling violent pain in his ears, head and whole body.

Thus, a beginning map of how such somatic states inform Buddhism comes into view with polyvagal theory. The physical extremes associated with the austerities would naturally activate a 'fight-flight', sympathetic response. Presumably, in his six years since leaving the comforts of home and hearth, Siddhartha had made working with anxiety, fear, terror and pain a devotional practice. Where most of us feel the density in fear and respond accordingly, he permeated and found room within its heaviness and affective demands.

The years in the forest, letting the forest be his mother, his extended body, makes deeper sense from a modern lens. Siddhartha, on the cusp of becoming the Buddha, could let go because the living world all around him was not just a mental or abstract notion. Somehow his body, the air it breathed, the ground it sat on, the rice seed in his mouth and his mouth, the cold, his skin, merged, forming a loving, sustaining somatic shell. This is the stillness gateway that penetrates pain, found in the severity of Zen shikantaza (perfect stillness while in sitting meditation). Others find different pain doors to the same new pain-free soma. These include Shaolin monks' who melt snow off their bare backs, and self-immolating Vietnamese monks. They protested with a fierce inner peace against the insanity all around them.

Recently 'the iceman' Im Hof has made an art of teaching anyone interested various, some related skills. To handle freezing cold temperatures, he guides people in breathing techniques recognizable from a polyvagal perspective. These involve the activation of seemingly opposing bodily forces, for example, of sympathetic arousal and parasympathetic relaxation. Though he did become emaciated over time, Siddhartha achieved a level of metabolic efficiency that parallels various species' in torpor and hibernation. He thus heeded the parasympathetic, 'rest-digest' call to some extent while benefiting from the dorsal vagus' cardiopulmonary brake (decreased heartrate, blood pressure and respiration).

In total, Siddhartha as a mere mortal persevered ultimately giving us one of history's most iconic examples of seemingly, impossibly brutal self-punishment while resting in a profound state of samadhi. A warrior (e.g., activated aggression and wrath) for the dharma, he simultaneously fought with peace in his heart. No flailing, no unnecessary movements. In giving into pain, he received. Ever less self-ego-mind, ever more a refined, nondual experience of what co-arises as self and pain in a larger housing, not reducible to its parts.

Like Jesus on the cross, he may have yelled out but truly he never broke. Tears likely flowed at times from the hardship and for the sheer beauty of our being, our earth—his container. Awe and gratitude co-arising with disease, agony and endings. This must have entailed an unfathomable somatic intensity, such that the relevance and authority of distinctions dissolved in a bigger hold, a bigger vessel, and fuller dharma. Self/ego/mind and other disappeared. Siddhartha's being opened to all beings, to all phenomenological arisings. His love proceeded, stainless, indistinguishable, an all-inclusive emptiness. As a fully freed Bodhisattva, his essence permeates suffering anywhere.

He would later assert that one risks slander in claiming any authority on what he did or experience in awakening.[432] This comment is at once a great teaching. Everything here is informed speculation, nothing less or more. In somatic extremis, Siddhartha's oceanic expansion, this choice of new life over physical death (in theory), was and is bolstered by the ancient dorsal vagus. Under its control, mammals and humans sometimes literally drop dead. This most ancient inheritance would appear to be involved when, as so many spiritual masters teach, we must die that we may live. Enlightenment, the Middle Way implies, is possible for the supplest of body-mind, and perhaps only for such. But Buddhism's good news and kingdom on earth need not be the stuff of sermons. Where there is suffering, there is invitation. And the invitation is from the body. The universal appeal to commit suicide, I believe—having met with many who have tried, speaks to this very bodily bidding—albeit misinterpreted by self/ego/mind.

Close to this ultimate biological precipice (again, taking much license), Siddhartha-cum-Buddha's heart, breathing, digestion, and blood pressure may have dropped just as occurs in animals that pass out, play dead or drop dead. Perhaps his heart and organ functioning actually stopped. Perhaps he looked over the ledge, tasted the peace of ultimate, nondual bodily surrender, but returned to teach that such peace need not wait for death. After all, according to orthodoxy, he chose his parents and incarnation that he might achieve this very moment. Also worth noting, he himself did not demonstrate such omniscience or psychic aptitude prior to enlightenment. Having transcended all disparate pulls, having turned away from common death, he forged or discovered (in yang and yin terms respectively) an ultimate reality.

What he would then spend decades teaching is also consistent with the ancient, mysterious, dorsal vagus. The proverbial *letting go* is an invitation to spill into an abyss. There mind and body waystations drop away. Rather than dissociation and hypo-arousal, Buddhist letting go is simultaneously replete with the mid-level, vagal intensity, physical discipline and courage. Letting go is also characteristic of the parasympathetic side of the autonomic nervous system. Its message, in effect, to the activated stress-response in 'fight-flight' is to chill, let go.

Vipassana meditation calls for a balance that leans toward letting go while calling for passive vigilance and witnessing. Mindfulness meditation reverses the accent, placing an emphasis on a gentle but persistent focal point, usually the breath. Buddha's full-body awakening was a vital, energetic encompassing of his biological totality. Whole, beyond words, and ever-emanating, the teaching of masters is often described as an energetic transmission.

But, finally, what can be said of the ventral vagus, the attachment vagus system? This, of course, is the main topic at hand. With respect to the austerities and the Middle Way, somehow, Siddhartha's loneliness and isolation, day after week after year, did not spur any crippling paranoia. The absence of human contact did not cause him to seek rescue or return home. As with the oldest, dorsal system, and the mid-level, fight-flight system, Siddhartha exceeded the demands of this third, newest vagus' system. He did not heed the call for social attachment nor did he fully reject it. A closer look at this in juxtaposition to his awakening deserves further consideration.

Polyvagal theory while tripartite is also, obviously, an embedded somatic system. The miracle of the soma is that every element is a vessel contained by yet another. Consider simply the notion of 'freeze', deer-in-headlights, compared to 'fold'. Both have dorsal correlates to fainting and playing possum. But in freeze, there's sympathetic tension, vigilance and autonomic arousal, halfway in a sense between fight and flight, and also halfway between autonomic freaking and dorsal folding. Between freeze and fold, perhaps, is the door to Buddhist stillness.

We have considered these many *betweennesses* before (e.g., Diotima-Socrates, Shamsi Tabrizi-Rumi, Prajapati-Siddhartha) and will soon consider another: Siddhartha and Sujata. As suggested, "wego" offers a conceptual, between and so relief to all that ego has come to connote. Between has no opposite or equal.

Polyvagal theory sheds more light on stillness as betweenness. In threat scenarios, rabbits are commonly semi-still, calm but twitchy and vigilant at the same time. A deer may behave identically or move toward vipassana calm, chewing slightly more slowly to take in a distant sound. Predators lying in wait are in similar, barely moving states between hypoarousal and vigilance. These capacities are clearly gifts of evolution, prized for their caloric efficiency and survival prognostics. The crocodile uses very little energy while lying in wait for his protein morsel. By definition, antelope gain more from eating than they use through all other activities including those involving cardiopulmonary paranoia.

Another betweenness deserves note. In Mahayana Buddhism, two nuns achieve status of high ranking female disciples. Both are, in the eyes of men, problematically beautiful. Both Khema and Uppalavana are said to wrestle with this until Buddha teaches them about impermanence and aging. Uppalavana accepts aging and bodily death metaphorically in standing up to Mara. He had been "desiring to arouse fear, trepidation and terror… and make her fall away from concentration". But she fluidly achieved sublime betweens, thus remaining in peace.

> I can make myself disappear
> Or I can enter inside your belly.
> I can stand between your eyebrows
> Yet you won't catch a glimpse of me.[433]

Nature's Goldilock's levels of physiological activation contain this imagistic, spiritual seed. The science of caloric efficiency and evolutionary advantage do not account for the spirit therein. It's acorn to tree (which includes acorn-to-tree). Blissed out house cats purr in a state of somnolent glee, surrounded by safety cues—their big house, food, toys, as some large mother figure caresses them. Owner-dog carousing and juvenile romping seen in mammals in the wild—the whole world of play suggests that there is much more at hand than survival. Or that Darwin's concept of survival should no longer be denuded of its thrills. To be sure, animals use play to develop agility and skill at wrath and aggression, to calibrate bluffing and the micro-skills in hunting and killing. And play is intrinsic to socialization and the negotiating of pecking-order battles and alliances. But a bottom-up only view discounts play as purpose unto itself. One teleology over others is possible. But so is both/and. Buddhist sages consistently affirm (based in extensive, introspective empiricism) that joy just is. That delight is characteristic of that in which we are embedded, cosmos.

Neuronal building blocks and their correlates—neural circuits, polyvagal components, base affects—are, Buddha would teach, not to be disputed. Such an enterprise is not skillful. His point cuts both ways. Those searching and reporting on such matters are doing as they deem right. Their efforts may absolutely be 'right speech', and ethical and meaningful. But to devote oneself to disputing them *or* joining them as such—as raison d'être, is not the path to liberation. This not-path imprisons the political oppositionist. An integral look at play fits the Pandita teaching (discussed previously). To be sure, there is much to play that experts understand. But the more one seeks an ultimate evolutionary, neurological, biological building block, the more the finish line recedes.

For example, "PLAY" is one of Panksepp's seven primary emotional colors. These form the core of his affective neuroscience paradigm.[434] As with the three polyvagal levels, related blends and betweennesses abound. Five of the seven affects occur in succession in mom-baby peek-a-boo. Separation distress (part of PANIC) spikes FEAR and SEEKING (mom's face). Her CARE (ventral vagal, attachment) response evokes joyful relief (indicative of PLAY). A sixth base affect, RAGE, is also intrinsic in play, in numerous sports, in the often humorous British parliament. A pet dog may growl and bark thunderously while wagging its tail. So play too is another betweenness, sometimes a marriage of vigorous, sympathetic pseudo-aggression and parasympathetic and ventral trust. Seeming hostility within a context of joy. Rounding out Panksepp's seven, lust (SEX) and play are, of course, common bedfellows, and the main fare at Hollywood rom-com movies. Play merges and remains, is transcended and included. Not to mention, that social attachment in Panksepp's model does not reflect a primary affect in the first place, not even CARE.

Play-betweennesses, just sticking with this, may be either or both sequential and simultaneous. Accustomed to peek-a-boo, a baby both seeks and fears even separation distress within limits. Dark, intense feelings are tied to light, joyful ones. This has parallels to the popularity of murder mysteries and how excitement over attacking another country is excused as patriotic. Everyone has seen admixtures of affect in babies playing peek-a-boo. They become energized and animated, with blends of varying emotion washing over them. Imagine what a great sage might accomplish in this regard, taking deep dives into affective havoc while cultivating another betweenness, a distance between the emotional chaos and stillness.

A flow of affect can even be inferred as the secure toddler in Ainsworth's Strange Situation experiments is momentarily worried about the new person entering the room.[435] Fear arousal is quelled by the ventral vagus through mom's reassuring facial gestures and "motherese" prosody. When all goes well, the child's natural curiosity and joy (affective branches of SEEKING and PLAY) return. Attachment types, secure, anxious and avoidant, simply stem from their experience and development of skillful means to date. The secure child has been fortunate to have the parallel of a great somatic meditation teacher in their mother.

Other somatic between-forms entail different sorts of physical arousal and the joy intrinsic to play. Many involve movement and chanting. We touched upon Sufi whirling and Maori Haka previously. These sorts of cultural forms are vigorous, energetic expressions of I:Thou. The dancer seeks to become aligned with (what seems to outsiders to be) mystical forces. Through this, they communicate something that transcends and includes play and pleasure. With the Maori, the dance and chant incorporates wrath. With the Sufi, there's purposeful overloading of proprioception, pushes the somatic sense of self in space to new limits.

In advanced meditators, the terrifying and tender can arise side by side. They observe bodily and emotional dramas over and over. They sit through somatic storms from an ever more neutral vantage. Affective bursts are not repressed but silently, instantly let pass. Their unique moment-to-moment features flow through with no impediments, no judgment or response. The work is hard, but not with the goal to be hardened. Rather the work is to be softened by life, ever simpler, more porous, welcoming and nurturing.

Meditation is supreme pattern recognition. A 'been there done that' that naturally induces a smile. Siddhartha famously began his life in pseudo-softness. His every need was met. Not only were shelter, food, family and safety cues in abundance, threat and risk stimuli were hidden. But six years prior to the Sujata-moment, he found his way into the densest pain. He had declared that old age, disease and death were everyone's fate, and determined to embrace such realities as he entered ascetic life and searched for a lasting bliss.

By the end of the austerities, we can conjecture he was a seasoned sailor of all somatic and affective storms—including those Jungians call the dark night of the soul. Siddhartha was civilized before he was de-civilized. As a student, he mastered debates. As a new ascetic, he mastered existing practices. By this point, he had no time for conversation and mental gymnastics. He invoked bodily suffering that he might come to fully know this side of human existence. A world leader in trauma, van der Kolk, concurs. Healing must first be somatic not cognitive, that 'the body keeps the score'.[436]

> Our research did not support the idea that language can substitute for action. Most of our study participants could tell a coherent story and also experience the pain associated with those stories, but they kept being haunted by unbearable images and physical sensations.[437]

Siddhartha had tracked such somatic scores with great care. He'd worked his way through so many hell realms that he finally learned to abide betwixt and between without effort. Neither forgetting nor dwelling nor suppressing. He was free, residing in a separate peace.

These various bioneurological-Buddhist leaping-off points also inform what happens next: Siddhartha's encounter with Sujata at the close of the austerities. That she spoke to him, and he to her, puts us in the territory of social attachment. Polyvagal and attachment theory would view this through the lens of safety-seeking, a secure base and physiological regulation. To appreciate this, we should go back a bit, and ask, what can be said of Siddhartha's rejection of home and hearth in the first place. On the outside he left comfort for hardship. But finally, his ultimate teachings put this on its head. He was not hardened by the austerities but softened. He became more tender, caring and sensitive and would soon dedicate himself to helping others to find their own way to the same.

Perhaps his experiential world began to overflow with lovingkindness and free-wheeling ecstasy, while to an outsider he was simply more emaciated and closer to death. If he 'let go' of the need for (recognizable) social attachment, e.g., companionship and family (parasympathetic and dorsal over ventral—so to speak), maybe he did so because the ultimate source of compassion and wisdom *and* bliss surged even larger.

While no one can possibly know, at least we have the coincidence of the encounter with Sujata to assist in informed speculation. The scientific and spiritual meaning of this turn in the story is informed by modern neurobiology. Ventral vagal support occurs when attachment cues from other members of an animals', primates' or human tribe signal safety. As in the baby assured all is well by mother, trust and curiosity are restored. We are freed to explore, hunt and gather, rest-and-digest and also play.

For Buddha, these evolutionary basics, including any rudimentary form of play, were transcended by the oceans containing these. After his encounter with Sujata, he did not reject love but became love. From this point on, his devotion to other—to all sentient beings, even the evil Mara—was beyond delineation. All we have developed as 'Buddha's Mom' therefore suggests that Sujata is another representative of the deep feminine marginalized and overlooked by his-tory. The next section is devoted to her.

First, more from polyvagal theory and its neurobiological matrix deserves mention. The Middle Way's somatic trail transcends and includes related concepts of *interoception* and *neuroception*. Interoception is bodysense, "arm-ness" or "toe-ness", for instance, and is a staple of somatic meditation practice and somatic psychotherapy. One might feel tension and enter, for example, into the field of the chest, into the heart chakra or similarly into the lower belly, into the perineum. Any given neighborhood has subtle, living character. In the lower belly, one may feel and implicitly know humanity's relationship to the mother inmap, to Mother Earth's nurturing presence, robust yet not locatable.[438]

Neuroception, according to Porges' polyvagal theory, is a *subconscious* process of monitoring possible situational threats to biological safety.[439] By design, we are often not aware of the cues that trigger a somatic response, only the response itself. As we have considered, Siddhartha's fierce efforts, his self-starvation, physical stress, anoxia and the like would have resulted in somatic cues associated with danger. His outrageous perseverance stemmed from his ability to penetrate or inter-penetrate intense neuroceptive impasses. These otherwise trigger polyvagal defenses, whether fight, flight, fold or social attachment. Working both sides, being both sides, he dissolved ever subtler self/ego/mind holds and abided in an ever-widening flow of equanimity and happiness. Described variously as skillful means, buddhanature, the natural state, new ground is broken with the discovery of the Middle Way.

A variety of Buddhist practices can be articulated from a bioneurological perspective. For example, the ancient charnel grounds' practice found in Vajrayana purposefully confronts bodily death and therefore somatic defenses and safety-seeking. Practitioners meditate alongside rotting corpses, permeating their senses with the reality of bodily death. Many in the West have some familiarity with the concept of charnel grounds' practice through the Tibetan Book of the Dead. In theory, meditators develop awareness of subtle states which supersede bodily death and doing so prepare for death and rebirth.

During the austerities, Siddhartha engaged in this very practice. It is said he wore rags from the cadavers while wild animals loomed about. The presence of flesh-eating predators in the middle of the night, in a crude graveyard, captures much of what neuroception is designed to detect, e.g., existential, somatic threats.

Siddhartha's upriver, backwards against the grain of evolution, toward the origins of our somatic beginnings. His mission to him into neurobiological (bioneurological) drives we have inherited from our animal ancestors. To eat, breathe, maintain warmth, avoid the gnashing teeth of predators, for example. Over and over, he walked up to these precipices and leapt, eyes open.

Classically, charnel grounds' practice is framed from the perspective of being with the ultimate, the cusp of existence and nonexistence, with death itself while very much alive. It's one of several ancient Buddhist portals to streams of consciousness outside of the normal, waking state. Other practice forms we can infer he also pursued weave through dreaming and deep sleep.

Death-focused forms are focused on the bardo, on life after death, on rebirths and other lifetimes. Neuroception, as an evidence-based, scientific construct, proposes a bio-neuro waystation. Here, self/ego/mind normally dissolves, as it encounters subconscious, somatic knowing, knowledge not of its own making. But as Siddhartha resisted normal (normal sleeping, eating, breathing, and any exit from discomfort, fear or pain whatsoever, awareness persisted.

Where charnel grounds' work spikes death-related affects, e.g., fear and safety-seeking, other forms place the accent on rage, care and sexual desire. In Tibetan deity practice or *yidam* the meditator cultivates certain deity's trans-human wrath—a fierce resolve to safeguard the dharma, or summons another's heart-melting compassion for all of mother earth's creatures including oneself. Alternatively, in tantric yab-yum practices, the advanced practitioner pursues sacred transformation sensually and sexually.

Deities exemplifying this potential include Chakrasamvara and Vajravarahi (whom we first discussed in a section on "Tantric Evolution"). The iconic, blue, twelve-armed Chakrasamvara (also called Heruka) is often depicted in a highly charged vision of love-making with his consort, Vajravarahi, on his lap. One beckons the transformational potential of Chakrasamvara-Vajravarahi. Theirs is an ecstatic eruption of cosmic union. In concert with one's partner (or consort), boundaries dissolve gently, or perhaps oneness erupts. Distinctions may both burst and drop away, for example, between emptiness and bliss, masculine and feminine, and human and divine. These experiences mobilize the bodhisattva potential. There is no separation between enlightenment and samsara. Such an enlightened Buddha remains fully, freely immersed in the world of old age, disease and death.

Tantra refers to this same practice space, once again with distinct bioneurological overtones. In Buddhism's most courageous, encompassing approach to working with attachment and desire, carnal drives and animal urges are uniquely transcended and included. Lower torrents and ancient affects (such as discovered by Panksepp or associated with Porges' polyvagal model) meet with sophisticated, intensive study and universal ethics. Affective regulation and discipline are required for delayed gratification. Recruitment of social attachment capacities and more recently evolved language and reasoning capacities are necessary but not sufficient for the transformation Tantra invites.

The ventral vagus (attachment vagus) is clearly implicated. This recruits mirroring circuits and, presumably, attachment-love and lovingkindness capacities. Sympathetic activation of the large muscle groups involved in fighting and fleeing coincides with expansive, blissful dissociation supported by the dorsal vagus. Mental formulations regarding one's own physiology, perceived and expressed in sexual desire and orgasm, give way to direct experience of expansive meaning and joy. Focus lives alongside happy disorientation and the loss of one's bearings. The soma dances in discovery, with no one polyvagal or affective state dominant.

These redefine pleasure as the goal of desire and satisfaction as the goal of attachment in line with bodhicitta. Desire is lost and found within the vastness of the bodhisattva who longs for all beings to share her lasting bliss arising from the cessation of all suffering. Rather than sin, the opposite of right speech and right action, or the breaking of holy commandments and precepts concerning defilement, sex can be a somatic song of praise. It can rise to a living appreciation for the gift of life. Enlightened sex, presumably, is not abusive, dull or predictable—but is also spiritual.

Tibetan (so-called) deities are not fixed beings. They find no parallel in the deities of ancient Greece or the world's major religions. Rather they are dimensions of and portals to realities discoverable through the journey Siddhartha had taken since leaving home six years before enlightenment. Deity practice is a form of playing God that facilitates an undoing of the inverse. That is to say, this helps dis-integrate unskillful, entrenched identifications, e.g., playing human. These practices stretch consciousness to breaking points, whereupon a new sentience awaits. Vajravarahi is, for example, a *wrathful* aspect of the female Vajrayogini. She's in sexual union, achieving cosmic union with Chakrasamvara—himself a vessel of oceanic compassion.

These practices are said to help us humans when we find ourselves overwhelmed and disoriented when dying. We will be profoundly scared and confused during the bardo phase. The singular major risk, according to Tibetan tantric orthodoxy, is rebirth. This can be viewed through the polyvagal model. A neuroceptive-like paranoia may leave one lurching for misinterpreted cues of safety. One may confuse any opportunity to be reborn as rescue. This includes social attachment and sexual enticements. If these are not passed over, rebirth occurs and common attachment themes, linking gender, longing and belonging, affection, sex and safety-seeking repeat. Jesus (I believe) is referring to this same sweet, frightening challenge in his call to hate one's mother and father.

Tibetan Buddhists use deity worship to cultivate a sort of spiritual armor not so much for earthly achievement but to protect them in the bardo. These practices bolster their transition into the vast dharma as surroundings, bearings, identity and attachments dissolve. While specifics are few, Siddhartha-Buddha is said to have cultivated his readiness for awakening across countless lifetimes and, by implication, much experience in the bardo. In awakening, he entered/became a living-knowing that he would then spend the rest of his life teaching and transmitting. He was/is the love and wisdom available to all of us. Such source and ground is unchanged by the coming and going of incarnations and the quantum ebb and flow of being of all forms of sentience. Yet each form is a manifestation of this source and ground. So, all this is indescribable and also not not-describable and so on.

At life's most sublime, trying and courageous fronts, our fragility and tenderness is mirrored by cosmos. If we have encircled this territory adequately in this lifetime and others, something profound and enduring coalesces, a sort of nonself abiding. A wealth of practice, said otherwise, ample familiarity with so-called emptiness translates as a used-to-it-enoughness. At key points or when beckoned, a seaworthy-enough vessel may present herself as compassion, out of compassion. This is the view from the mature, loosened self/ego/mind. Survival and safety drives, and ego holding patterns, are no longer prioritized.

There's emptiness and nonexistence on one hand and, as so many Buddhist lists suggest, specific, often numerated, characteristics on the other. Truths, perfections, kayas, gems, kleshas, jhanas. In all this, we do well to keep in mind the place of verbal language and abstract, conceptual reasoning on the Great Chain. Our species' capacity for these falls at the evolutionary ending of the grand vasovagal and neural architecture that forms our somatic being and informs awareness. Names and concepts, by inference, should seek balance with experience. They should bow to the authority and precision of the living, bioneurological truth of the Middle Way, wired-and-alive within each of us.

The emerging, *bioneurological* model expands nicely within the Buddhist perspective. Advanced meditators gain facility at steadying their awareness. An ability to rest in stillness precisely in the flux of betweennesses goes to the very heart of practice. As Panksepp, Porges and Schore's work demonstrates, the human realm spans great distances.[440] Nodal points include organism-environment drives related to taste, touch, pain and temperature regulation to in-brain, homeostatic drives such as thirst, hunger and thermoregulation. Up the scale in complexity and experiential sentience are the seven core affects, the consolidation of a self/ego/mind complex, the world of we and attachment-love. Other frames include classical continuum of psychological functioning (psychotic-borderline-neurotic-normal), inmaps and yin-yang.

Meditators enter this flux informed by Buddhism's basic formulation of drive-and-suffering, or expectation-and-disappointment. They are increasingly able to find stillness in chaos by way of a third or 'witness position'. This fosters a direct experience of impermanence. The more skillful, the more one can sit with the expanse and its contents.

Moments are born and die needing no judgment. Before this, any somatically-informed being-in-the-moment is covered over by a mental notion of the same. Anyone alive and familiar with meditation or Oprah is prone to a substrate of judgment. "Hey, I'm in the moment" or "I need to let this go". But with practice, such arising-fading dynamics are but mosquitos, tolerated with ever less swatting about and distraction. A dying-while-being-born present loosens the existential dread and background preoccupation with body death as a detached, fixed, future moment.

Overthinking death is (paradoxically) a common mental escape from the ego death that 'just sitting' invites. Dying becomes a dimension of the present moment, a characteristic of suchness, 'just so'. Again, impermanence as a given. Death gets closer and clearer than ever, an impossibly, intrinsic what is. Finally indistinguishable from this moment, death becomes more workable and less deadly.

Siddhartha came to discern this everyday flux and impermanence as the essence of life. All this might be better framed for us mere mortals as edgeless overabundance. And in the very same, this space of being must be empty because there's no possible edge, boundary or fixed points. As Siddhartha would finally discover, the flame of desire-for-asceticism is extinguished in this void because there is more than any desire can fathom. Desire keeps expanding and dissolving.

Critically, emptiness and impermanence are not without *meaning*. The culmination of his six years of intensive practice was not nihilism but the precious dharma! Both the exotic claim of void and the gush of teachings regarding its character embolden scientific models and psychological findings. Consider one of the most iconic self-help books ever, The Road Less Traveled.[441] Psychiatrist, M. Scott Peck, described how in romantic love, one may experience boundless joy, a loss of self, bliss and oneness with their beloved. Peck explains that this grand love is illusory and due to temporary egoic inflation. Real love calls for delayed gratification and discipline. For Buddhists ego's dissolution as the result of disciplined practice is standard fare. But the Vajrayana goes further in articulating means for transpersonal, living encounters with cosmic bliss (metta) and other gateways to realization.

Another unearned gift is that a coherent, glorious dharma can be communicated through teachings and achieved through practice. From the Buddhist perspective, there truly is no way to organize or properly exalt the very heart of what it means to have a human lifetime. After dedicating his first 36 years on earth to exploring every possible aspect of this inheritance, Siddhartha was at the brink of starvation, collapse and death. The purity of his intent and his devotion to discovery carried him to the verge of a defeat that earned total freedom. An eviscerating nihilism descended as a new somatic temple arose.

Somehow at this juncture, he came to know that the living imprint in him, the lifeforce that transcends death, was/is accessible. This cosmic pulse is shared by all beings and at the same time always uniquely experienced. Here, the master explains, maps dissolve in nibbana. In transcending his own being, a Buddha's heart broke wild and open. There was finally nothing to prove, attain or investigate. Like stars suspended in the darkness of night, just boundless, majestic void.

Some refer to the "diamond fire" that does not burn or scar. It does not destroy self/ego/mind outright as much as inter-penetrate. Self/ego/mind loses its errant, centrist positioning. A love-mind happily loosens its grasp. In my 20s, I came to a beginning, naive sense of this ultimate territory though the work of Elizabeth Kübler-Ross—a pioneer in death and dying. Decades later, I would briefly meet Reggie Ray after a talk he gave. Out of the blue, I found myself asking him if he had known her. He said though they had not met, he felt affection and affinity for her and her work.

A baby's, a mother's, a body's, and a spirit's wailing, according to Kübler-Ross, is always heard. No one is ever given more than they can bear. A cosmic love knows every wound with depth and precision, meets it fully and seeks its return to the fold. Every hair on one's head is enumerated and known by God. Kübler-Ross was as tough as she was compassionate. She had been a physician in Austria after World War II. As a scientist, she dove into the trauma, pain and death before her.

She transcended and included the medical model, pioneering what today informs palliative care and hospice. Her declaration of a supernatural, cosmic wisdom and compassion grew from the grit of her firsthand, bedside, practitioner-scientist experience of the dying—because at this juncture, over and again, she encountered a universal, living metta. Kübler-Ross' view is consistent with the Middle Way. In war, there's no end to the sort of somatic hells Siddhartha faced. Kübler-Ross gives us the stages of grief culminating in acceptance. The mystery begins with there always being a greater peace, more open stillness.

Our species has achieved the potential to *embody* these ever vaster expanses. As much as we share with other species, plants, insects, reptiles, birds, fish and other mammals may not have the neurobiology required for an existential fear of death or post traumatic disorder. Presumably, few Woody Allen, non-human lifeforms live in the seas, forests and fields. As Siddhartha would encode the noble truths, worry and worse, dread and terror, are part of something all too human.

There's a knock at the door. It's the cosmos. And the key that opens the door is suffering. Our suffering then is sacred. An evolutionary bridge to spirit. As Buddha said, yes, this stems from attachment. We now know more about the neurobiology of what opens and opens and opens, while remaining vivid, palpable and embodied.

Chögyam Trungpa trusted his ragtag, hippie groupies with the highest teachings, in this regard. He chose them over those who would want to dole out the dharma based on rank and insider positioning. So-called hippies felt the hypocrisy of Western culture. They were broken open enough to question 'the establishment' and want something better. Their ignorance, confusion and seeking was fertile soil. In not knowing, there was space and the chance that some would see all he was.

A modern shaman dubbed 'the Ice Man' offers yet another vital channel. Wim Hof is adamant that he's just a regular person. More accurately, he insists that any regular person can achieve superhuman prowess. Through a set of skillful means, involving hyperventilation and meditation, he has achieved multiple world records. He has climbed the better part of Mount Everest in shorts, been immersed in ice water for nearly two hours and run a marathon in a desert with no training and no water. Perhaps even more impressively, Hof *and* his trainees have undergone double-blind, scientific research; the results indicate his and others' have the capacity to alter somatic factors thought to be beyond conscious reach, e.g., portals to the autonomic nervous system.

For Wim Hof, as with Siddhartha and many we have considered, attachment-love spurred heartbreak followed by seeking and eventually awakening. Hof lost his wife and the love of his life to (what used to be called) madness and finally suicide. After years of study and training in various philosophies and practices, he transcended and included what he calls "lost love".[442] We can recognize this as the inherent suffering in relative attachment just the same as Siddhartha felt leaving his wife and son, and as Kisa felt holding her lifeless baby.

In his journey, Wim Hof came into contact with this wound-portal to our shared, human lineage in ever more profound ways. (The word *profound* stems from before-bottom, a deeper depth.) Through cold, Hof's *lost love* returns. Cold may restore the same disconnection that we all have to "Buddha's Mom". After decades of intense practice, he has come to identify an ultimate tantric strand that readers will recognize. As he explains, "While waiting to be transferred to the OR my mother delivered me in the freezing hallway of the hospital. I can't shake the belief that this connects to the cold that runs like a red thread through my life."[443]

Perhaps in leaving the womb's warmth (and variants of this, over and over, as we cross into infancy and subsequent stages), there are ruptures in the transmission of our human lineage. The thread of cosmic, integral attachment gets frayed. These sources of suffering, Hof seems able to prove, are invitation to a natural state of power and clarity. Hof, for me, is a somatic bodhisattva. For him, ultimate love is physical, and is one with strength and health.

> Final stage is go back the grief, go back to the love, the lost love. I want to
> bring back love to the world. Love is compiled by happiness, strength and
> health. If you radiate good energy because you are healthy, happy and
> strong, that's love. So love is my mission.[444]

Hof's methods involve vagal factors discussed in the section on bioneurology. For example, he trains students to hyperventilate, exhale fully and then hold. After a minute to two, the body launches lifesaving inner measures. When the panicky urge to gasp for air is not acted upon, the dorsal shut down system is initiated. There is an actual danger of passing out, hence this should not be done while in an ice bath. The moment beckons the possibility of a new level of somatic witnessing supported by corresponding physiological changes. These include hyper-oxygenation, increased heart rate, adrenaline and blood alkalinity--stabilizing .[445] These somatic changes support a steady, calm witnessing.

Wim Hof works with people of all ages, many with illnesses. Within a couple of days of training, they are able to practice while submerging their body in ice water or hiking in freezing temperatures in only shorts. The risk of hyperthermia triggers both fight-flight fear and faint-overwhelm. But their ability to use his tummo-like breathing meditation techniques turns the key. Able to control one's body temperature, while at somatic extremis, one feels more alive, more true to one's innate nature. This proffers a sense of *control*, e.g., an actionable wisdom, regarding of our shared, mystical, human lineage.

Siddhartha's awakening story refracts the same neurobiological encounter with cosmic love — as no other story ever will. Upon meeting Sujata, Siddhartha recognized that he neither needed to survive on one grain of rice nor adopt any extreme in the other direction. What was true for base drives for air, food and water was true for attachment and love. His body's longing for more than he had been allowing it gave way. His intense hunger to awaken was droplet to ocean. The puzzle needed no further analysis. One sees a pure *other* in a vast mirror, then suddenly *re-members*, sees *one*'s self, one-self.

In *entering* vastness (yang) and *becoming* vastness (yin), all that arose was unfettered and nondual. Impersonal and empty yet unique, personal and tender. In the Mahasakuludayi Sutta, Buddha would teach his disciples technique he discovered during the austerities. In these, a pain-ridden soma was superseded by another soma of sorts.

> Again, Udayin, I have proclaimed to my disciples the way to create [through
> trance states] from this body another body having form, mind-made with all its
> limbs, lacking no faculty… And thereby many disciples of mine abide having
> reached the consummation and perfection of direct knowledge.

It's time to take a closer at the fruition of this new body. Now 36 years hence, Siddhartha would enter the dharma as no other human ever has. With the Sujata-moment, a cosmic lovingkindness would pacify hellish, Mara hallucinations. The same, sweet compassion would forever characterize Buddha's path and teaching.

In the past, the same force flowed through Prajapati, soothing baby Siddhartha's every need — the initial focus of this book. Post-enlightenment, Siddhartha-now-Buddha would soon return home. As caring father to Rahula and later as the deeply empathic father figure to Kisa, this river of compassion and awakening would continue. Kisa was the distraught, grieving mother compelling the famous mustard seed parable. An aging Buddha would rhythmically lull Subhuti into the same river of abundance. To a lovingkindness that transmits wisdom concerning suffering and impermanence—giving the world the Vajracchedikā Prajñāpāramitā, the Diamond-Cutter Sūtra.[446]

This transformative potential would inspire hundreds of millions over the next 2500 years. Kisa, Rahula, Subhuti nor the many hundreds of millions would starve themselves nearly to death or meditate in a graveyard. Yet vast numbers would take refuge and find safety in this new vessel, making it their own. The miracle here is that this compassionate love knows all pain, and flows to all the suffering created by desire and attachments. And it does so somatically.

Milk

At this iconic point of transcendence, the eccentric, brilliant, courageous monk—nearly dead from starvation—accepted the rice-milk offering of the young Sujata. And here we meet Hongzhi's *unwithered fertility* in person, in food and in ritual. Would the Buddha-to-be, she asked, accept her "poor gifts of snowy curds, fresh-made, with milk as white as new-carved ivory?"[421] Sujata's rice-milk, the stories and legends make clear, was hardly ordinary. Sujata first drove a thousand cows into a meadow of rich grass. With their milk, she fed five hundred cows, with their milk she fed 250, and so on, all the way down to eight special cows. The calves of these eight moved away as from their mothers' udders flowed streams of milk. These multiple, successive "transcend and include" stages will be familiar to the reader by this point. With each, something ordinary is transcended and negated (detached from) and something very special is preserved (attached to).

> Seeing this miracle, Sujata, with her own hands, took the milk and poured it into new pans; and with her own hands made the fire and began to cook it. When that rice-milk was boiling, huge bubbles rising, turned to the right and ran round together; not a drop fell or was lost; not the least smoke rose from the fireplace.[447]

Let us allow the power of these beautiful moments to carry us forth while pausing to note associated, neurobiological underpinnings. The Middle Way reflects mind-body transcendence. In barely breathing, in starving and also in isolating oneself—from severing ties, in this case the love of his stepmother, father, wife, child, half-siblings, cousin, close friends, any normal person's sympathetic nervous system would cascade into an interior cacophony of fight-flight, terror signaling. The body's effort to alert its interpersonal, environmental agency, via the self/ego/mind, would mimic that of a response to an outward predatory attack.

In Siddhartha's hard-earned, majestic synthesis, last ditch torment was met with an ever greater love and acceptance. We can speculate based in overlapping lines of evidence, old and new, that in the years leading up to the Sujata moment—and in the moment itself—his practice had become so advanced, so rigorous and sublime, that sitting was at one the hardest and simplest imaginable action/inaction. His was a somatic meditation supported neurobiologically. He cultivated the ventral (attachment) vagus' warmth, kindness and wego-drive toward connection.

To put it mildly, he transcended any mere restoration of physical safety or restoration of socialization to achieve physiological homeostais and affective regulation. His concern for self and other—for all sentient beings, for his own inner screams, all that was arising abided neither factions or boundaries. Siddhartha-cum-Buddha did not split off his self/ego/mind as an other nor give it any more centrality than any other arising, falling point of reference. Rather he ever-opened to all inward, outward, moods, images, cognitive content as just more phenomenological beings, and did so with such intensity that these dissolved. They achieved their dignity, their cosmic expression and were liberated in the vast expanse of his dharma consciousness.

During the extremis of the austerities, this oceanic expansion, this limitless living out, this including, transcending mode of being manifested in a shift, from an outsider perspective at least. The Buddha, much suggests, was transformed. The outward and inward trending toward physical death turned toward life. This turn, a modern analysis would indicate, was bolstered by the ancient dorsal vagus' maternal, protective character—and so too for Jesus on the cross, who surpassed the fear and agony, and 'went to heaven'.

And actually so too, for the supplest of mind, for all of us, swept up by the sea of our own pain. The dorsal vagus is ultimately an integral, life-promoting, ancient resource. It conserves the flow of biological-spiritual lineage in extremis, even as we feel tears and overwhelm at life's sheer, expansive preciousness, at the singular chance to be alive ever, at all. Somatically-assisted by the dorsal vagus, Siddhartha-cum-Buddha's heart, breathing, and digestion slowed, as it does in animals that "drop dead" and in spiritual devotees 'slain in the spirit'. But strong of heart, with ventral vagus' warm connectivity, he looked over this edge and survived. Perhaps his heart and organ functioning stopped? So spiritually talented and gifted, he tasted the peace of ultimate, nondual bodily surrender. Having transcended all disparate pulls, he turned away from common death and forged or discovered (in yang and yin terms, respectively) a new, ultimately human reality.

This journey to a higher love, which now inspires hundreds of millions, calls upon each of our own, now recognizable, polyvagal pillars. From oldest to newest, a somatic space is forged via letting go, dissociation and hypo-arousal. In life, or on the out-breath. At the mid-level, a transcendent synthesis stabilized. Letting go potentiates the possibility of transformation. A blending of the sympathetic nervous system's intensity, clarity, and discipline (associated with arousal and vigilance) and its parasympathetic, rest-digest equanimity is achieved—then transcended.

In partaking of Sujata's nurturing and nourishment, Buddha became one with the totality of his somatic being. He allowed it air, food, and even emotional attachment having found a path back that encompassed all he saw and now knew of death, sickness and old age, of tanhā, craving and needing. In accepting her offering, he was surfing a wave of attachment-love, yet he was not constrained by our species' most recent "attachment vagus". His acceptance of her love and milk reflects all this, as does his reintegration of his "rest and digest" system.

Classically, this occurs in animals when there are appropriate attachment safety cues from other members of their group. The Sujata tale could hardly be plainer. Symbolically speaking, of course, where there is milk, there is Mother. In fact, in a parallel version of the Sujata tale, Siddhartha's biological mother makes a cameo appearance. Mahamaya's earthly life ended when her baby was seven days old. In this version, she returns from heaven to deliver the unambiguously divine rice-milk. Nineteenth century Buddhist scholar David Rhys likens this to the "bread of heaven" described in Christian theology. Rice, of course, was the indigenous grain of Asia just as wheat was in Mesopotamia. With supreme simplicity, the metaphor bridges the spirit-flesh chasm. Said Jesus, "I am the living bread which came down from heaven: if any man eat of this bread, he shall live forever: and the bread that I will give is my flesh, which I will give for the life of the world."[448]

So divinely potent, this rice-milk would be Siddhartha's only food for the next seven weeks. As possibly Mahamaya, quite likely Prajapati, and nameless nursemaids had earlier, Sujata assumed the flesh-spirit milk-giving mantle. Socrates' Diotima reminds us, "many names, one path". One oracle, one vessel, one dharma. In accord with transcend-and-include, this special milk does not simply morph from physical to spiritual, but is both and neither.

But the story does not want us to overlook the mystical and spiritual. After drinking this milk, Siddhartha "drank no water, nor did he relieve himself."[449] Here, Sujata is briefly, delicately, yet another female lineage bearer, another Buddha's Mom. Much as Prajapati had 35 years earlier, Sujata arrives on the scene just in time to provide sustenance to Siddhartha who is once again physically vulnerable and in need. The possibility of greatness is captured here but delimited as usual. Whether cast as Nature, Mother Earth, Goddess, this fleeting face of Buddha's Mom is the ever-present, life-giving feminine principle. "She" is source and sustenance. There are echoes with the Sujata motif of relative attachment as an extension of biological attachment: a female's life-preserving milk restores the body so that mind and spirit might flourish. Bowlby's and Buddha's attachments once again converge as Siddhartha enters into all that he will forever be known for.

The interplay of images associated with biology — with rice and milk, with breastfeeding and the Great Mother, with Mother Earth, Buddha's Mom, ground, source (any of these are fitting) — will reach an ultimate inflection point seven weeks after Siddhartha awakens as Buddha. This moment is said to occur at the moment Siddhartha reaches down and touches the earth with his finger. There are a couple of lovely hints foreshadowing this. As Sujata is "tremblingly nigh" (close in both time and space) to giving Siddhartha the rice milk, some resources have her first ceremoniously kissing the earth.[450] Other sources have Sujata washing Siddhartha's feet with sweet scented water. These gestures illustrate a reverence and love for earth and, it seems fair to add, for this very unique child of hers.

A point that can be easy to overlook when one flows with the narrative stream is that Buddha's enlightenment was not his alone. There would be no Buddhism were his enlightenment not to also point to the "always, already" Buddha-nature in all sentient beings. With Buddha's Mom, we can increasingly appreciate the depths of sentience, of our shared, unbounded lineage, as integrated with all we have sketched as Buddha's Mom. With his reaching and touching the earth, our species is awakened. This child of Nature, of Mother Earth, of Homo sapiens, Suddhodana, Mahamaya, and also Prajapati, reached beyond time, beyond biological attachment and stages of development to achieve Awakening itself. Later Buddhist orthodoxy would move from an individual interpretation of Buddha-nature to one embedded in these interconnections, e.g., the Bodhisattva.

The point worth repeating here is that there is no before and after, no duality, no lineage bearer conveying the lineage until there is an Awakening. With this, all is awakened. This context reinforces why Sujata deserves a place alongside Prajapati, Kisa, Patacara, and others as another incredible face of the Buddha's Mom. Her name, in fact, means "of happy birth". As Prajapati had done, providing tender care and milk at the beginning of Siddhartha's earthly life, she of happy birth does so at this

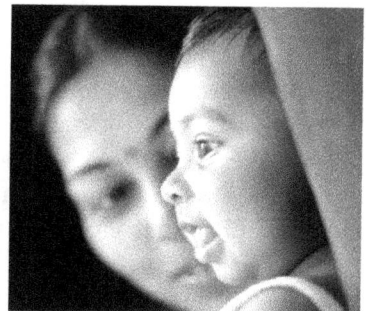

point, and this quite plainly translates as a scaffolding for Siddhartha's coming rebirth as the Buddha.[451]

One more motif is added to this rich collection of earth-based, indigenous, sacred feminine symbols. Siddhartha was ready to accept the rice milk that Sujata had to offer—but, alas, he had no bowl of his own. Recall that Siddhartha had been surviving on single grains of rice. He had renounced materialism when he left home six years before, and at that time had strived to discover the very bare minimum needed to remain alive. This running opposite of desire and dependency, as mentioned, has the deepest of roots. At the age of seven days, Siddhartha had walked and declared his independence. Here with Sujata, he was making a turn, ready for something more than the bare minimum for existence. He was ready to receive milk but owned no vessel. This can be interpreted as having no way to receive, to hold, and to contain. Recall that dharma translates as bear, hold, carry, and that the Pali Canon is comprised of the tripitaka, the three baskets. Without a container, there is no life-giving milk, no transmission, and no continuity. Without this, death looms.

So, Sujata gave him a golden bowl. Such a special vessel is very prominent in the literature on the feminine principle. As Jungians and scholars such as Joseph Campbell have written, the vessel is an archetypal symbol of the womb. The vessel in myth and literature is often associated with the sacred feminine, the goddess, and the feminine principle. Sailing vessels are routinely given feminine names. This symbol, in fact, is associated with the proverbial Holy Grail of the Arthurian literature. This has been shown to refer to the sacred feminine in Christendom. The feminine as vessel is the holding, supporting container or space. That which is held, supported, and conveyed is the active component associated with the masculine. The vagina as container for the phallus is another iteration. She is being to his becoming. Through being comes forth life.[452]

Buddha's Mom, we have suggested, is unsung because of the patriarchy's wont to marginalize and objectify the feminine. As a mere mother, she is downgraded as biological baby-maker and milk-supplier. Corresponding to womb and breastfeeding, the bowl and the milk in this story, however, are rendered extraordinary. The bowl is golden; the milk is the perfected culmination of a magical, alchemical process. This signals the presence of the sacred feminine.

Having introduced this mixed association to the feminine—a young maiden bearing milk as well as a container—to deeper feminine spirituality, some accounts set out to ensure that the former is bracketed. Siddhartha constructed his entire philosophy on pushing back against the stuff of physical life: clothing, food, and physical contact. Even his own son had been declared an impediment. Relationships with his mother and wife had long been forfeited. His sudden decision to partake of Sujata's milk must not be mistaken for something undignified.

> Gotama partook of the gruel from Sujata without desiring or shying away
> from her or her beauty or her sexual presence, for in that realm too he had
> experienced every possible variation regarding sex, from indulgence to
> abstinence.[453]

Similarly, in response to the unnecessarily ostentatious bowl, the story provides another protective measure. Buddha is not materialistically interested in gold, itself a symbol of the riches he had long ago disinherited. Therefore, shortly after drinking the milk, Siddhartha tosses the bowl into the river. He then declares, "If I am to become Buddha this very day, may the bowl go upstream; if not, may it go with the current."[454]

The golden bowl flows upstream conveying the good news. Siddhartha will not die and indeed will awaken as a Buddha. Not only does the bowl float upstream, but it submerges downward in a whirlpool. A whirlpool circuitously rotates towards the center of Mother Earth. Not dying, the end of constant rebirth and samsara, is again linked to the feminine. This time, the association is to her face as terra firma, Mother Earth. After being magically drawn upstream, the golden bowl "disappeared in a whirlpool, and the hero heard the muffled ring as it landed, in the subterranean world, among those other bowls the former Buddhas had emptied and thrown away."[455]

Not to put too fine a point on it, milk symbolizes Buddha's Mom, herself both symbol and living lineage. Tens of thousands of hours of early life, loving attachment translated in Siddhartha into what trauma researchers refer to as resources. More tens of thousands of hours of what would today pass for a robust sense of self and good self-esteem would have catalyzed via multiple channels. Across countless hours of play, healthy competition, friendship, relaxation—all scaffolded atop the simple luxury of being loved, safe, smart and in a stable home where loving interactions, Bowlby's mirroring, were the norm.

Such resources are easily overlooked and indeed simply forgotten much as one forgets how they once learned to ride a bike, all the while having the knowledge and skill just so, as "suchness". For contrast, one might spend a decade watching how children of loving parents unfold. This offers some possibility of truly appreciating how children-turned-adults are commonly wounded, simply left without implicit bike-riding wisdom.

Where the milk barely flows, the wellsprings of emotionality are not broadly tapped; the art of friendship is not honed; peaceful, aimless wandering and innocent reverie are undernourished, back-and-forth empathic depths with parents and friends are not plumbed. Attachment and detachment are just sides of the same coin. You have to have something in order to let go of it. Siddhartha's twenty-nine years blessed him with inner resources. This fueled the raw, single-minded six years of deeply personal searching for / letting go. Same coin. A superbly advanced mind survived the severities of the austerities. All this led to the vicious encounter with, and renunciation of, Mara.

As we move through these final moments, let us notice how certain advanced resources quietly take center stage. Our bedraggled, serene monk will face an onslaught of supernatural forces aimed to derail his transformation. Inversely, these call for superhuman fortitude, concentration, equanimity, and that which, if overt, might be referred to as character. These smack of the paramitas. They show off a wondrous self/ego/mind at the brink of accepting this as just so, as flowing milk, as the somewhat quiet, somewhat astounding suchness. A man alone, merely sitting.

Per usual, the emphasis is less on something, more on nothing. Less on what is, more about fending off. By now, we are accustomed to this lopsidedness and distortion of the feminine principle. She is not the opposite of detachment; mothers pass on their milk and transmit our species' genius through relative attachment. Mothers who do not love and mothers who "love too much" do not tend to remain in the gene pool. As we have seen, conflating the feminine and the attaching side of relative attachment is an old standby. Other tactics include silence, marginalization, and hyperbole.

Although technically male, Mara embodies the patriarchy's negativistic packaging of the feminine. His name means death as in *death, rebirth, and samsara*. He kills with desire. By enticing minds to want, materially or sexually, he trips up the earnest efforts of mortals to renunciate. He would have us lust, binge, leap for illusions of permanence and get pulled in by the allure of youth, love, power. Mara is the imbalanced, over-attaching side of relative attachment, the half-truth of clinging and tanhā gone mad. Never mind that Siddhartha is only the exquisite human that he is because of his journey, his character, his resources, his own self/ego/mind, albeit on the precipice of a radically sweet "transcend and include" experience.

To convey this, the biography returns to a heavy dose of archetypal and supernatural symbolism. We first encountered this with the divine pregnancy dream of Buddha's biological mom, followed by her death seven days later. With Mara's arrival, the sweet, nurturing, life-promoting side of the feminine principle—the lovely Sujata, her precious milk and golden vessel—also comes to an abrupt stop. Where does this leave yin, soma, mother earth, and attachment-love?

Bhumisparsha

With the "earth touching mudra", the Bhumisparsha mudra, these many feminine symbols reach a crescendo. These culminate in an evocative moment without which there would be no Buddhism. Back from the brink of death, Siddhartha has sipped from the golden bowl of milk lovingly prepared by Sujata.

As the golden vessel moves upstream, the reversal of samsara is at hand. The end of death and rebirth, freedom from attachments, from suffering, old age, sickness and death, the Third Noble Truth, the truth which declares the cessation of suffering—*dukkha nirodha ariya dacca*—all come by way of the feminine. Sinking under the water, Siddhartha's golden bowl knocks into those of others who have achieved liberation. The stillness of the river basin and the movement of the river are as inseparable as mud and lotus.

Afterwards, sitting on a throne of grass under the Bodhi tree, Siddhartha is a picture of serenity. This is more than the jealous Mara can bear. Mara throws everything imaginable at Siddhartha. These last ditch attempts to elicit illusion, confusion, temptation, and exhaustion are legion. Mara tries everything to prevent the transmission of all that previous Buddhas have achieved—our species' lineage as we have suggested. As Mara's armies escalate efforts to jostle the lone monk, Siddhartha sits. He will meditate as a seeker just once more before becoming a fully realized, awakened being—a Buddha.

The arrival of Mara and his evil hosts marks a shift toward shadow. Where selfless Sujata, her milk and golden vessel symbolize the feminine principle, Mara represents the opposing side, the shadow of these. Male in gender, Mara is the negative pole of the patriarchal take on the feminine. The bright-shadow split in a bifurcated rendering of Buddha's Mom. Her earthly essence is divided.

For Sujata's part, her first cows fed from earth's grasses which fed from her soil. The feminine undergoes a transcend-and-include developmental sequence, as mentioned, from soil to milk and from milk to finer milk. This is served not in the usual earthen clay bowl but in a golden one. Siddhartha accepts Her (Sujata, milk, earth, the feminine) and drinks, restoring him physically, bodily and thus, more.

In Mara, earth and body are rendered in the typical, established, negative ways. The golden light shines on Siddhartha, its shadow on Mara. This shadow feminine is the same as the Bible's spirit and flesh, all the hostile connotations projected onto matter, the evils of lust, greed, and materialism. An iconic form of this occurs in one of Buddhism's hell realms where hungry ghosts are tormented by base cravings. All of this shapes the higher philosophy of the four noble truths and precepts concerning attachments, cravings, how tanhā drives dukkha and samsaric suffering. Thankfully, the trail does not just end with the feminine, earth, body, attachment, split down the middle. In fact, as Jung reminds us, the shadows portend transformation, greatness beyond the constraints at hand.

> Jung said the truth of the matter is that the shadow is ninety percent pure
> gold. Whatever has been repressed holds a tremendous amount of energy,
> with a great positive potential. So the shadow, no matter how troublesome it
> may be, is not intrinsically evil. The ego, in its refusal of insight and its refusal
> to accept the entire personality, contributes much more to evil than the
> shadow.[456]

Ken Wilber has endorsed the seminal role of shadow in his "integral life practice" model, rendered as body-mind-spirit-shadow. Very loosely speaking, these translate as exercise, yoga, mindful embodiment, creativity, intelligence, seeking, meditation, lovingkindness, prajna—and then shadow! With Mara, we arrive at a critical and ultimate developmental juncture. Shadow has a way of upending everything else—all that seems good and reasonable. As Siddhartha nears enlightenment, shadow's dark and light potentials loom large.

Re-entering the story, we find Mara bearing down, backed by armies of angels, with great terror. At instinctual animal levels, these "hosts of Mara"[457] are a supernatural parallel to animal displays of power and might. At higher realms, the Mara-shadow moment is a supernatural echo of the grueling physical hardship of the austerities. Mara's hosts serve to echo and inflate, like some sort of monkey-see monkey-do dance in a house of mirrors. These capture that definition of insanity: the inescapability of doing the same thing with the same hapless result: samsara on steroids, the pathos of repeated existences, immeasurable suffering flowing from the Big Bang on through endless lifeforms.

At this juncture, light and shadow, yin and yang, life and death dart back and forth, in and out of one another. The well-armed Mara and all his "armies" is also, and more accurately, an echo of the many thousand-armed bodhisattvas and protector deities. These are also equipped with what on a lower evolutionary rung fit Darwin's descriptions of male charms and weaponry. Siddhartha's moment of realization connects him with the depths of biology and a spirituality that predates his own time in history. Among the well-armed tantric deities is the Vajrayana version of Hinduism's über deity, the elephant-headed Ganesha, Maha Rakta. He has twelve hands in order to hold, to name a few, an axe, arrow, hook, sword, and spear.

Like Palden Llamo, Maha Rakta also holds a kapala, a "skullcup", filled with human blood. We can see with some clarity, then, how the kapala is the golden bowl's shadow. Statues and images of Vajrayogini depict her drinking blood from this. Distinctions between the golden bowl of milk and the skullcup filled with blood are transcended in the Bhumisparsha. Siddhartha will drink of the feminine, Buddhism's Holy Grail, reach and touch Mother Earth.

In the next narrative turn, Mara's hosts attempt to undo Siddhartha's newfound reconnection to the feminine. His embrace of this earthly life, symbolized in his partaking of Sujata's nurturing and nourishment, is thrust back at him with a vengeance. Mara's hosts pelt him with earth forms of all types, with driving rain, rocks, ash, charcoal, sand, and mud. When these fail, the attacks escalate into (manmade) flaming, smoking swords and spears. Time and again, Siddhartha empties these attacks of their power to harm. Form and emptiness dance. Evil intentions and weapons are transmuted. A lethal javelin loses its power. A discus transforms into a garland of flowers. Finally,

Mara launches a "fourfold darkness" intended to terrify. But, the story continues, all fear dissipates as darkness does with a sunrise.

These exchanges move up the great chain of earth-animal, and in the human sphere, up the ladder of body-mind-spirit. When physical and bodily threats do not derail Siddhartha, Mara attempts to emotionally overwhelm him with the fearsome darkness and alienation. He soon engages in a mind game and attempts to outwit Siddhartha.

We should pause and consider our story's hero at this moment. Having evolved to the brink of full realization, he now sits in deep meditation. If we grant that he is not suffering incoherent, tortured hallucinations, then these battles with Mara reflect an advanced, sublime spiritual process.

Next, the contest shifts. Siddhartha and Mara are briefly ensnarled in a strange competition for the higher moral high ground. There is some back and forth concerning almsgiving codified as being "perfect in all goodness". Almsgiving reflects the bodhisattva insight, that being concerned only about one's own enlightenment is inherently a lesser vehicle. As householders, we give of our labor, placing what we can in bowls to feed the body and nourish the spirit of future Buddhas. Sujata has just done so, the deep importance noted by the golden bowl.

At this stage, Siddhartha-Mara co-arise in a debate about love and authenticity. A priest might call this spiritual warfare. Who has given truly of their heart, without an eye toward their own betterment? As Mara accuses Siddhartha of not deserving enlightenment, the future Buddha counters:

> Mara! It is not by you that the Ten Cardinal Virtues have been perfected, nor
> the lesser Virtues, nor the higher Virtues. It is not you who have sacrificed
> your-self in the five great Acts of Self-renunciation, who have diligently
> sought after Knowledge, and the Salvation of the world, and the attainment
> of Wisdom. This seat does not belong to thee, it is to me that it belongs.[458]

Buddhism would hence declare, that the almsgiver and monastic "in mutual dependence both reach the true dharma."[459] Almsgiving by householders to monastics runs parallel to the release of relative attachment in nonattachment, this resplendent emptiness. Siddhartha-as-Buddha needs no more of Sujata's milk offering. With enlightenment, the bowl is always empty, always filled by the dharma. Integral spiritual resplendency is hard-earned. The path is seldom predictable and commonly chaotic, dark, and deadly, as we considered previously with Jesus.

In yet another turning point, Siddhartha is tortured by demons. Of these evil multitudes, one great and terrifying being orchestrates and speaks. Psychiatrists might diagnose this element as an auditory hallucination. We should not be too quick to dismiss all this as ancient, cultural hyperbole. Where there are eyes to see, this biography continues to enchant. Consider the similarities between Mara and what will not be for another thousand years, Tibetan Buddhism's wrathful deities. They protect the dharma and, in death, help beings who find themselves flung into the bardo.

Mara's power and cleverness calls for further consideration. At this precise juncture, the seasoned, worn, wise Siddhartha is alone—and he is talking to some sort of demon. Strangely, the highly realized son of Buddha's Mom even here finds himself in a regressed, terrifying state—but able to enter this relationship with shadow on an even playing field *because of* his accomplishments. The entire biographical arc, leaving home, wandering, nearly dying, drinking of Nature's milk, brings him to this juncture. The flow of sentience through biological attachment, into mammalian seeking, humans' clinging, expecting life force, manifesting in wego consciousness, helps reset the proportions at hand.

As Siddhartha and Mara co-arise in this wego moment, the stunning formulations of Tantra's psychotic, seemingly wrathful deities proffer a new sheath of understanding. Again, this begins with an appreciation of Mara as the ultimate wrathful deity, that is to say, protector of the dharma. Why is such a regressive, hostile image co-arising with Siddhartha at this advanced point? Why this precise something and not another thing, or no thing? Perhaps because, trite but true, there is actually no time like the present. None. And the present is wrapped in such a veil, carried in such a vessel.

Why specifically a wrathful deity, a dharma protector? That this moment deserves nothing less is a reasonable hypothesis. A great, highly realized being is on the brink. The entire universe could witness the lotus open, or not. Mara as dharma cheerleader, enforcer, jester, and villain bursts on to the scene to test, prod, and hold all that is in play. Siddhartha is a spiritual spear tip, a leading edge of the dharma, the living lotus opening, our species' lineage here, now—so advanced, so rare, so vulnerable. Commonplace self-doubt has atomic proportions. On the edge of the freeing void, at great risk of clinging to lesser angels, fears, and small-mindedness only intensify.

Without Mara and all that the Vajrayana fills out in time, without these bizarre wrathful forces and what the Jungians call shadow, we remain fractured and lost to ourselves. So why something rather than nothing? Because even Siddhartha-Buddha almost does not see the perfection that permeates. As he sits, the forces of love, wisdom, and freedom in evolution will not take less than perfection for an answer. Any conceptions still arising as distances yet to be traversed are axiomatically impediments, relative attachments, a clutching to a smaller reality. Mara is here to help, deep in the upper reaches of human potential.

As mentioned, the impediment seemingly gains traction at this point as the story concerns almsgiving. Mara chides Siddhartha for not having what it takes to awaken. He accuses Siddhartha of not measuring up in this department, implying that he has not been selfless enough in the giving of alms or simply has not given enough alms. Mara then proclaims that he himself has witnesses to the fact that he personally excelled at almsgiving. He asks his mirroring multitudes to endorse his claim of moral superiority. They do so with glee.

Householders give alms to support monks' realization. The emphasis here is on what the bible calls works, more on earning merit more than on awakening. Mara is speaking up for relative reality. Where is Siddhartha's evidence of ethical behavior? Where are his witnesses? Again, beautifully, Siddhartha speaks to higher law. He refers to vessels he has to leave aside, and to others that carry him not just further but from a relative vantage, in reverse, upriver. Properly understood, a wrathful Mara is the dharma's sword and shield and the perfections are a new mother, father, and brother.

> Here is this multitude exerting all their strength and power against me alone.
> My mother and father are not here, nor my brother, nor any relative. But I
> have these Ten Perfections, like old retainers long cherished at my board. It
> therefore behooves me to make the Ten Perfections my shield and my sword,
> and to strike a blow with them that shall destroy this strong array.[460]

There is no mother or father in this trying moment—"against me alone." There are overtones here of Jesus', "Father why has thou forsaken me?", and more generally between Siddhartha's austerities and Jesus' forty days in the wilderness, fasting, followed by his own Mara moment. From the current perspective of an indigenous, secular, evolutionary lineage, one can easily see these events, riddled with torment and testing, through an understanding enhanced by shadow. The more one strips away religion and understands the supernatural as archetypal and psychological, the more one's heart pounds in gratitude and humility for the lives and legacy of such rare, advanced beings. Why make the distance so vast, with devils and hell realms, when the more parsimonious alternative is so welcoming? These great, wide-open expressions of humanity, these figuratively naked, flailing, daring, courageous beings are "alone in the wilderness". As we may now understand this, they are deeply embodied. They have abandoned all distinctions between their nature and Nature.

Worth noting, Jesus' call to "Love thy neighbor as thyself" offers a lucid, enlightened definition of an advanced wego. Here we would simply fine-tune love, in light of Buddha's Mom, to attachment-as-love and view this precept as a pointing out that other is a co-arising evolutionary flow of sentience, metta, goodness, and wisdom with no separation to be found. Love thy neighbor and enemy too, these are statements of suchness. Love is that which knows no alteration. One simply sees the perfection of the second person as a co-arising reflection of one's first person. This statement is the same as "I am that," just replacing subject and object with love, or to be consistent, with Buddha's Mom as attachment-as-love.

For the neurobiologically-oriented, Mara represents neuroceptive panic. So too does Lucifer, who was seemingly defeated by Jesus' love expressed through his attachment to God the Father. This supreme, numinous attachment had to then leave all imprints of duality behind. This divine space opened as Jesus' embraced doubt, "Why has thou forsaken me?"

These are the visions and voices of death throes as organs begin to shut down, but more to the point, of uniquely mature beings as they remained aware and intent on awakening. In these raw, animal bases of perception become one with the advanced, much practiced spirit. Hard-earned grounding in attachment-love arcs towards its cosmic, limitless expanse. The entire point of spiritual practice is made clear by these events. For the most realized of beings, ultimate awakening was a most tenuous prospect. The rest of us would do well to practice in the face of everyday glory, fear and tenuousness. The path is not linear, not necessarily ever steepening. That is another gift of these ancient tales. Masters have gone on before us, have lit the way. These forces include the Mara/Lucifer-like protectors, there when we feel forsaken. A Tantric line pulls us into her flow. One can empty, be emptied into her river.

At the Mara/Lucifer precipice, the bodhisattva realization presses hard. They are sentient beings too, emblematic in fact of samsara and sin. Not too "remain in hell", as Rinpoche Chögyam Trungpa alluded, is just so, is sin, separation, death, samsara, rebirth—is hell. For Buddha, for humanity, this time there could not biological survival or biological death. There could not be a winner and loser. The gate was open.

One more lovely gesture awaits us as Siddhartha holds forth. Mara has tried to score points by ridiculing Buddha for being alone, having no witness to his claims of having left mother and father and entered into some sort of abiding perfectionism. As the ultimate bodhisattva, Siddhartha-Mara co-arises on the brink of a higher vibration. Siddhartha cannot leave if Mara suffers. If Mara is attached to his domains of influence, harbors jealousy of Siddhartha's gifts, or put the other way, fails to see himself mirrored in the brilliant supreme peace before his eyes, then a last tentacle clings. Mara is that which is threatened by Buddha's beauty and perfection.

Recalling that Mara represents earthly attachments, we may recognize the next movement as a longing abiding in our very own heart. Siddhartha-becoming-Buddha "holds his ground and reaches his hand over his knee to touch the earth." He holds his ground *with* Mara by enjoining Mother Earth. She is the remainder and completion of his nature because she completes his own rejected shadow that would otherwise just go on forever claiming separation from our full earthly, evolutionary inheritance. For Christians, the separation is sin and is a given fact of the fall. Ego has been sullied with much of this historicity. But in Buddha's Mom, many such distortions are reset.

This gesture—when Siddhartha-now-Buddha touches earth—marks the achievement of Buddha-nature through Nature. This anchoring is the eternal and deepest meaning of "grounding". At this precise point, Siddhartha-Buddha re-collects their shared story, the ever-larger field of consciousness between breaths and words, that which bears and carries us. She is perennial Witness, co-arising in perfect oneness. Co-arising with our species' development and with the rise of Buddha consciousness across evolution. The sentience, the suchness, formed from upriver influences is always, already, ever present. Buddha's Mom is the witness that remains across fits and starts. The "I am that" which both waits for *the day when* and celebrates all those in between—as moms do. She is that which traversed, transcended/included, attached, and detached across vast expanses of time and space, a river, realizing oceans of life-giving milk, an unstoppable dharma.

On the eternal day of the Bhumisparsha, through Buddha's Mom, we transcend illusions of evil, death, and impermanence. These are but more faces of fear. Through earth's transcendent witness, "directly arriving here…" we recognize, "the mind ground dharma field" just as fear escalates.[461] We enter the eye of the storm and therein silence. In the middle of pain, we reconnect with our deepest essence as humans; by attaching to this transcendent source, we detach from all that came the moment and lifetime before and are liberated. By letting go, dropping mind, descending into body, we are no longer partial, small, and dislocated. Love for all earth's orphans becomes source and presence.

Bibliography

[1] Porges, S. (Jan 22, 2001). The polyvagal theory: Phylogenetic substrates of a social nervous system. International Journal of Psychophysiology, 123-146.

[2] De Waal, Franz, (2014). *The Bonobo and the Atheist: In Search of Humanism among the Primates*, New York: W. W. Norton & Company.

[3] Moore, D. (1880). Buddhism. The British and Foreign Evangelical Review, Volume 29 (p 482). Nisbet, London.

[4] Siegel, D. (1999). The developing mind: Toward a neurobiology of interpersonal experience (p. 263). New York: Guilford Press.

[5] Cohen, A. (2002). Living enlightenment: A call for evolution beyond ego. Lenox, Mass.: Moksha Press, p. xiv.

[6] Salzberg, S. (1999). Voices of Insight (p. 65). Boston: Shambhala.

[7] Garfield. J. L. (1995). The Fundamental Wisdom of the Middle Way Nāgāriuna's Mūlamadhyamakakārikā (p.99). New York: Oxford University Press.

[8] Wilson, L. (1996). Charming Cadavers: Horrific Figurations of the Feminine in Indian Buddhist Hagiographic Literature (p. 142). University of Chicago Press.

[9] Walker, B. (1988), Crone (p. 177). New York: Harper Collins.

[10] McWilliams, L.A., Bailey, S.J. (July 2010). Associations between adult attachment ratings and health conditions: Evidence from the National Comorbidity Survey Replication. Health Psychology, 29(4), 446-453.

[11] Mikulincer, M. & Shaver, P. (2010). Attachment in Adulthood: Structure, Dynamics, and Change (p. 481). New York: Guilford.

[12] Ibid., p. 248.

[13] Seigel, D.J. (2012). Pocket Guide to Interpersonal Neurobiology: An Integrative Handbook of the Mind. New York: Norton, 6-4.

[14] Suomi, S. J., Collins, M. L., Harlow, H. F., & Ruppenthal, G. C. (1976). Effects of maternal and peer separations on young monkeys. Journal of Child Psychology and Psychiatry. 17. 101-112.

[15] Newton, M. (2003). Savage Girls and Wild Boys: A History of Feral Children (p. 16). New York: Thomas Dunne.

[16] Lane, H. (1979). The Wild Boy of Aveyron (p. 4). Boston: Harvard University Press.

[17] Ibid., p. 42.

[18] Ibid., p 160.

[19] Hood, B. (2012). The Self Illusion: How the Social Brain Creates Identity. New York: Oxford.

[20] Thorpe, W.H. (1974). Animal Nature and Human Nature (p. 232), London, UK: Methuen.

[21] Bancroft, A. (2000). The Buddha Speaks (p. 71). Boston: Shambhala.

[22] Changizi, M., Zhang, Q. & Simnojo, S. (2006). Bare skin, blood and the evolution of primate colour vision. Biology Letters, Jun 22, 2006; 2(2): 217-221.

23 Mikulincer, M. & Shaver, P. (2010). Attachment in Adulthood: Structure, Dynamics, and Change (p. 481). New York: Guilford.

24 Ibid.

[25] Ibid., p. 482.

26 Aronson, H. (2004). Buddhist Practice on Western Ground: Reconciling Eastern Ideals and Western Psychology, (p. 153). Boston: Shambhala.

27 Ibid., p. 162.

28 Bhikku, T. (2004). Handful of Leaves V2: An Anthology from the Samyutta Nikaya (p. 41). (G. DeGraff, Trans). Redwood City, CA, USA: Sati Center for Buddhist Studies & Metta Forest Monastery.

29 Buswell, R. & Lopez, D. (2013). The Princeton Dictionary of Buddhism (p. 1023). Princeton, NJ: Princeton UP.

30 Davids, T. (1878). Buddhist birth-stories; Jataka tales. The commentarial introduction entitled Nidanakatha the story of the lineage (p. 169). Translated from V. Fausböll's ed. of the Pali text. London: G. Routledge.

31 Bhikku, T. (2004). Handful of Leaves V2: An Anthology from the Samyutta Nikaya (p. 527). (G. DeGraff, Trans). Redwood City, CA, USA: Sati Center for Buddhist Studies & Metta Forest Monastery.

32 Illustrated History of Buddhism (1954) (p. 27). Rangoon, Burma: Young Men's Buddhist Association.

33 The Fruit of the Homeless Life: The Sāmaññaphala Sutta in the Pāli Canon Digha Nikaya. Sīlāchāra Ed. (Bhikkhu) (p. 23) (1917). London: Buddhist Society of Great Britain and Ireland.

34 SarDesai, D.R. (2007). India: The Definitive History (p. 53). Boulder, CO: Westview Press.

35 Boslooper, T.D. (1962). The Virgin Birth (p 141). London: Westminster Press.

36 Thudy, Z.P. (1993). Buddha and Christ: Nativity Stories and Indian Traditions (p 124). Leiden, Netherlands: E.J. Brill.

37 Glover, M. (2006, Oct 14). Bill Clinton Rallies Activists in Iowa. Retrieved from http://www.washingtonpost.com/wp-dyn/content/article/2006/10/14/AR2006101401338_pf.html

38 Schumann, H.W. (1989). The Historical Buddha: The Times, Life & Teachings of the Founder of Buddhism (p. 99). Maurice O'C. Walshe (Translator). New York: Arkana.

39 Müller, F.M. (1952). Sacred books of the Buddhists, Vol 18. (p 139). London: Oxford Press.

40 Fâ-hian (1886). A record of Buddhistic kingdoms being an account by the Chinese monk Fâ-hian (p. 48). (J. Legge Trans). Oxford: Clarendon.

41 Beer, R. (2003). The handbook of Tibetan Buddhist symbols (p 37). Boston: Shambhala.

42 Turnbull, C. & Thubten, J.N. (1970). Tibet (p 154). New York: Touchstone.

43 Nelson, W.H. (2000). Buddha: His life and his teaching. New York: Tarcher.

44 Beer, R. (2003). The handbook of Tibetan Buddhist symbols (p 37). Boston: Shambhala.

45 Kishen, S. (2014). Kingdom of Shiva (p 262). New York: Partridge.

46 Ashvaghosha (2008). Life of the Buddha: Clay Sanskrit Library (p. 11). New York: NYU Press.

47 Ibid.

48 Shostak, M (1990). Nisa: The life and words of a !Kung woman (p. 9). London: Earthscan.

49 Müller, F.M. (1952). Sacred books of the Buddhists, Vol 18. (p 221). London: Oxford Press.

50 Martin, K. (1999). Women of courage: Inspiring stories of courage by the women who lived them (p 285). Novato, CA: New World Library.

51 Morelli, M., & Wilber, K. (2006). Integral life practice starter kit: Version 1.0 ; the simplest practice you can do to wake up. S.l.: Integral Institute.

52 Wilber, K. (2001). The eye of spirit: An integral vision for a world gone slightly mad (p. xiv). Boston: Shambhala.

53 Andrews, R. (1993). The Columbia dictionary of quotations (p. 805). New York: Columbia University Press.

54 Wilber, K. (2000). Sex, ecology, spirituality (p 223). Boston: Shambhala.

55 Ray, R. (Winter Dathun. 2011). Episode 57: Space gives birth to love. Retrieved from http://www.dharmaocean.org/

[56] Thera, S. (1999, July 06). Satipatthana Sutta: The Discourse on the Arousing of Mindfulness. Retrieved from http://www.accesstoinsight.org/tipitaka/mn/mn.010.soma.html

[57] Cohen, A. (2002). Living Enlightenment: A Call for Evolution Beyond Ego. Introduction by Ken Wilber. EnlightenNext Inc., Amazon Digital Services.

[58] Ricard, M. (2011). The art of happiness (p. 328). London: Atlantic.

[59] Wilber, K. (1981). No boundary: Eastern and Western approaches to personal growth (p. 19). Boulder, Colo.: Shambhala.

[60] White, D. (2000). Tantra in practice (p. 9). Princeton, NJ: Princeton University Press.

[61] Sharma. S. (2002). Life profile & biography of Buddha (Rev. ed., p. 32). New Delhi: Diamond Pocket Books.

[62] Campbell, J. (1972). The hero with a thousand faces (2d ed., p. 131). Princeton, N.J.: Princeton University Press.

[63] Ibid.

[64] Nhat Hahn, T. (1998). The heart of the Buddha's teaching: Transforming suffering into peace, joy & liberation: The four noble truths, the noble eightfold path, and other basic Buddhist teachings, (p. 206). New York: Broadway Books.

[65] Shaw, S. (2006). Buddhist meditation an anthology of texts from the Pali canon. London: Routledge.

[66] Gupta, K. (2005). The Aryan path of the Buddha (p. 446). New Delhi: Sundeep Prakashan.

[67] Wilber, K. (2000). One taste (p. 15). Boston: Shambhala.

[68] Rogers, C. (1961). On becoming a person: A therapist's view of psychotherapy. Buena Vista, VA: Mariner.

[69] Wilber, K. (2006). Integral spirituality (p. 253). Boston: Shambhala.

[70] Pandita. B.. & Gomes. I. (2007). Introducing Buddhism (p. 4). Taipei: Corporate Body of the Buddha Educational Foundation.

[71] Gowans, C. (2003). Philosophy of the Buddha: An introduction (p. 20). London: Routledge.

[72] In the Buddha's words: An anthology of discourses from the Pāli canon: translated from the Pāli by Bhikkhu Bodhi. (p. 62). (2005). Boston, Mass.: Wisdom Publications.

[73] Gowans, C. (2003). Philosophy of the Buddha: An introduction (p. 20). London: Routledge.

[74] The middle length discourses of the Buddha: A new translation of the Majihima Nikaya: translated from the Pāli by Bhikkhu Bodhi. (1995) (p. 264). Boston: Wisdom Publications in association with the Barre Center for Buddhist Studies.

[75] Ibid.

[76] Wishes for Toni. (2013. August 12). Retrieved from: http://www.existentialbuddhist.com/tag/tonipacker/

[77] Wilber, K. (1996). A brief history of everything (p. 11). Boston: Shambhala.

[78] Well-connected hemispheres of Einstein's brain may have sparked his brilliance. (2013. October 13). Retrieved from: http://www.sciencedaily.com/releases/2013/10/131004104754.htm

[79] "The Guru and the Pandit: The Evolution of Enlightenment", Andrew Cohen and Ken Wilber in Dialogue," What is Enlightenment? Spring/Summer 2002, 38-49, 136-143.

[80] Ibid., p. 140.

[81] Ibid.

[82] Wilber, K.. & Palmer. M. (2004). The simple feeling of being: Embracing your true nature (p. 101). Boston: Shambhala.

[83] Wilber, K. (1996). A brief history of everything (p. 59). Boston: Shambhala.

[84] Woodman. M. (1990). The ravaged bridegroom masculinity in women (p. 126). Toronto, Canada: Inner City Books.

[85] Wilber, K. (2000). Sex, ecology, spirituality (p 6). Boston: Shambhala.

[86] Pinker, S. (2002). The blank slate: The modern denial of human nature (p. 236). New York: Viking.

[87] Chödrön, P. (2002). Comfortable with uncertainty: 108 teachings (pp. 91-92). Boston: Shambhala.

[88] Ibid.

[89] Sayadaw, M. (n.d.). Discourse on Ariyavasa Sutta. Retrieved from: http://www.mahasiusa.org/ariyavasa.html

[90] Salomon, R. (2000). A Gāndhārī Version of the Rhinoceros Sūtra: Gāndhāran Buddhist texts 1 (p 12). Seattle: University of Washington Press.

[91] Diamond, J. (1998). Guns, germs, and steel: The fates of human societies. New York: W.W. Norton & Co.

[92] Saul, H. (2014, October 14). Orphaned baby rhino Gertjie refuses to sleep alone after witnessing his mother's death at the hands of poachers. Retrieved July 24, 2015. http://www.independent.co.uk/news/world/africa/baby-rhino-gertjie-refuses-to-sleep-alone-after-witnessing-his-mothers-death-at-the-hands-of-9518603.html

[93] Brewster, E. (2013) The Life of Gotama the Buddha Compiled exclusively from the Pali Canon (p. 147). Hoboken: Taylor and Francis.

[94] Thomas, E. (2013). The life of Buddha as legend and history, (p. 133). New York: Routledge.

[95] Olson, C. (2005). Original Buddhist sources: A reader (p. 135). New Brunswick, NJ: Rutgers Univ. Press.

[96] Thomas, E. (2013). The life of Buddha as legend and history, (p. 133). New York: Routledge.

[97] Ray, R. (1999). Buddhist saints in India a study in Buddhist values and orientations (p. 63). New York: Oxford University Press.

[98] Ibid., p. 171.

[99] Olson, C. (2005). Original Buddhist sources: A reader (p. 135). New Brunswick, NJ: Rutgers Univ. Press.

[100] Snyder, D. (2006). Complete book of Buddhist lists: Explained (p. 30). Las Vegas: Vipassana Foundation; First Edition (2006).

[101] Clark, A. (2016). Surfing uncertainty: Prediction, action, and the embodied mind. Oxford: Oxford University Press.

[102] Gautam, N. (2009). The essence of Buddhism (p. 89). New Delhi: Mahaveer & Sons.

[103] Keown, D. (1996). Buddhism: A very short introduction (p. 72). Oxford: Oxford University Press.

[104] McDougall, G. (2005). The four noble truths (p. 120). Boston, Mass.: Wisdom Publications.

[105] Ray, R. (Winter Dathun, 2011). Episode 57: Space gives birth to love. Retrieved from http://www.dharmaocean.org/

[106] Wilber, K. (2000). Sex, ecology, spirituality (p 6). Boston: Shambhala.

[107] Ibid., p. xii.

[108] Wilber, K. (1998). The marriage of sense and soul: Integrating science and religion, Boston: Shambhala.

[109] Moffitt, P. (2008). Dancing with life: Finding meaning and joy in the face of suffering (p. 85). Emmaus, Pa.: Rodale.

[110] Pickering, J. (1997). The authority of experience: Readings on Buddhism and psychology (p. 58). Richmond: Curzon.

[111] Kirk, G. (1970). The Bacchae (p. 136). Englewood Cliffs, N.J.: Prentice-Hall.

[112] Rehm, R., & Harrison, R. (2011, March 15). Greek tragedy. Podcast retrieved from http://itunes.apple.com

[113] Bucknell, R., & Fox, M. (1986). The twilight language: Explorations in Buddhist meditation and symbolism (p. 165). London: Curzon Press.

[114] Maurice, D. (1961). The greatest adventure (p. 83). Kandy, Ceylon: Buddhist Publication Society.

[115] Khenpo, R. (1995). Natural great perfection: Dzogchen teachings and Vajra songs (p. 95). Ithaca, N.Y., USA: Snow Lion Publications.

[116] Moore, J. (1908). Sayings of Buddha, the Iti-Vuttaka (p. 70). New York: The Columbia University Press.

[117] Batchelor, S. (2010). Confession of a Buddhist atheist (p. 4). New York: Spiegel & Grau.

[118] Ibid.

[119] Ibid., p. 18.

[120] Blass, T. (2000). Obedience to authority current perspectives on the Milgram paradigm (p. 10). Mahwah, N.J.: Lawrence Erlbaum Associates.

[121] Buswell, R., & Lopez, D. (2013). The Princeton dictionary of Buddhism (p. 304). Princeton: Princeton University Press.

[122] Wiltshire, M. (1990). Ascetic figures before and in early Buddhism: The emergence of Gautama as the Buddha. Berlin: Mouton de Gruyter.

[123] Dhammika, S. (2010, March 25). Of Aryans, Nazis and Buddhists. Retrieved from http://sdhammika.blogspot.com/2010/03/of-aryans-nazis-and-buddhists.html

[124] Dhammasaavaka, A Buddhism Primer: An Introduction To Buddhism, Ltilu.coni, 2005, 35.

[125] Salzberg, S. (1999). Voices of Insight (p. 65). Boston: Shambhala.

[126] The connected discourses of the Buddha a new translation of the Samvutta Nikāya; translated from the Pāli by Bhikkhu Bodhi. (Vol. 94(2)). Boston: Wisdom Publications.

[127] Ibid.

[128] Tanahashi, K. (1985). Moon in a dewdrop (p. 99). San Francisco: North Point Press.

[129] Damasio, A. (2010). Self comes to mind: Constructing the conscious brain. New York: Pantheon Books.

[130] Mipham, S. (2003, January 1). Shambhala Sun, 14-14.

[131] Hardy, R. (1967). A manual of Buddhism in its modern development (p. 152). Varanasi, India: Chowkhamba Sanskrit Series Off.

[132] Johnson, M. (2002). The Virgin of Guadalupe: Theological reflections of an Anglo-Lutheran liturgist (p. 78). Lanham, Md.: Rowman & Littlefield.

[133] Salzberg, S. (1999). Voices of Insight (p. 65). Boston: Shambhala.

[134] Mitchell, R.A. (1991). The Buddha: His Life Retold. Paragon House.

[135] Krishnamurti, J. (Ed.). (1920). The Herald of the Star, 9, 166-166.

[136] Nyanaponika, H. (1997). Great disciples of the Buddha: Their lives, their works, their legacy (p. 155). Boston: Wisdom Publications.

[137] Walters, J. (1994). A Voice from the Silence: The Buddha's Mother's Story. In History of Religions, 358-358.

[138] Melnyk, J. (1998). Women's theology in nineteenth-century Britain: Transfiguring the faith of their fathers (p. 221). New York: Garland.

[139] Walters, J. (1994). A Voice from the Silence: The Buddha's Mother's Story. In History of Religions, 358-358.

[140] Wilson, L. (1996).Charming Cadavers: Horrific Figurations of the Feminine in Indian Buddhist Hagiographic Literature (p. 142). University of Chicago Press.

[141] Ibid.

[142] Rochholz, L. (2004, November 16). Gotami's story: reading analysis. Retrieved from http://www.csus.edu.

[143] Faure, B. (2003). The power of denial: Buddhism, purity, and gender (p. 184). Princeton, N.J.: Princeton University Press.

[144] Wilber, K. (1998). The essential Ken Wilber: An introductory reader. (p. 129). Boston: Shambhala.

[145] Merton, T. (1973). The Asian journal of Thomas Merton (p. 287). New York: New Directions Pub.

[146] It's a girl: The three deadliest words in the world [Motion picture]. (2012).

[147] Webster, I. (2003). Merriam-Webster's collegiate dictionary (11th ed., p. 279). Springfield, MA: Merriam-Webster.

[148] Bible Gateway, Matthew 25:40, Holy Bible, New International Version®, NIV® Copyright ©1973, 1978, 1984, 2011

[149] Mila Grubum: The One Hundred Thousand Songs of Milarepa, Tibetan Buddhist Hermit. (n.d.). Retrieved October 24, 2012, from: http://www.hermitary.com/articles/milarepa.html

[150] Sacks D, Stevenson B, Wolfers J. (Dec, 2012). The new stylized facts about income and subjective well-being. Emotion 12(6),1181-7.

[151] Klotz, N. (1999). The hidden Gospel: Decoding the spiritual message of the Aramaic Jesus (p. 65). Wheaton, Ill.: Quest Books, Theosophical Pub. House.

[152] DeHaan, M. (2007). Been thinking about: Coming together around the ideas and issues that divide us (p. 246). Grand Rapids, MI: Discovery House.

[153] Ray, R (2014). When lightning strikes [Audio]. Boulder: Sounds True.

[154] Bloom, S. (2013). Creating sanctuary: Toward the evolution of sane societies (p. 80). New York: Routledge.

[155] Campbell, G. (2012, November 30). An Interview with Jaak Panksepp: The Origins of Emotions, Episode 65. Retrieved from http://brainsciencepodcast.com/

[156] Panksepp, J. (2004). Affective consciousness: Core emotional feelings in animals and humans. Consciousness and Cognition, p. 32.

[157] Ibid.

[158] Panksepp, J. (1998). Affective neuroscience: The foundations of human and animal emotions. New York: Oxford University Press.

[159] Siegel, D. (1999). The developing mind: Toward a neurobiology of interpersonal experience (p. 265). New York: Guilford Press.

[160] National Human Genome Research Institute, Knockout Mice, (2015), Retrieved from: http://www.genome.gov/12514551

[161] Panksepp, J. (2012, November 30). Interview with Ginger Campbell, MD. Retrieved from http://brainsciencepodcast.com/

[162] Batchelor, S. (1997). Buddhism without beliefs: A contemporary guide to awakening. New York: Riverhead Books.

[163] Kramer, G. (2007). Insight dialogue: Interpersonal path to freedom. Boston: Shambhala.

[164] Steiner, H. (2010). Handbook of basal ganglia structure and function (p. xxiii). Amsterdam: Elsevier/Academic Press.

[165] Jacobson, M. (1993). Foundations of neuroscience (p. 6). New York: Plenum Press.

[166] Schore, A. (August 8, 2009). The paradigm shift the right brain and the relational unconscious. Speech presented at 2009 APA Annual Conference. Toronto, Canada.

[167] Ibid., p. 159.

[168] Graziano, M. (2013). Consciousness and the social brain (p. 85,103,159). London: Oxford University Press.

[169] Ibid., p. 103.

[170] Ibid., p. 159.

[171] Bowlby, J. (1973). Attachment and loss (Vol. 3, p. 45) (word added). London: Hogarth Press.

[172] Graziano, M. (2013). Consciousness and the social brain (p. 165). London: Oxford University Press.

[173] Diamond, J. (1998). Guns, germs, and steel: The fates of human societies. New York: W.W. Norton.

[174] Graziano, M. (2013). Consciousness and the social brain. New York: Oxford UP.

[175] Wilber, K. (2000). Sex, ecology, spirituality (p 223). Boston: Shambhala.

[176] Kübler-Ross, E. (1969). On death and dying. New York: Macmillan.

[177] Howlett, P. (2011). How well do facts travel? The dissemination of reliable knowledge (M. Morgan, Ed.). Cambridge [England: Cambridge University Press.

[178] Snyder, D. (2006). Complete book of Buddhist lists: Explained (p. 30). Las Vegas: Vipassana Foundation; First Edition (2006).

[179] Snyder, D. (2006). Complete book of Buddhist lists: Explained (p. 30). Las Vegas: Vipassana Foundation; First Edition (2006).

[180] Panksepp, J., & Biven, L. (2012). The archaeology of mind: Neuroevolutionary origins of human emotions (p 101). New York: W. W Norton.

[181] Ibid. p. 101.

[182] Ibid. p. 98.

[183] Ibid. p. 399.

[184] Ibid. p. 98

[185] Ibid. p. 373

[186] The man who makes rats laugh. [Interview of J. Panksepp]. (2012, May). Retrieved from http://www2.centralcatholichs.com/copied articles to review/Neuro/rat humor interview DISC.pdf

[187] Ibid., Panksepp, J., & Biven, L. (2012). The archaeology of mind: Neuroevolutionary origins of human emotions (p 96). New York: W. W Norton.

[188] Boorstein, S. (1996). Don't just do something, sit there: A mindfulness retreat. New York: Harper One.

[189] Snyder, D. (2006). Complete book of Buddhist lists: Explained (p. 30). Las Vegas: Vipassana Foundation; First Edition (2006).

[190] Lopez, S. (2009). Encyclopedia of positive psychology. Malden, MA: Wiley-Blackwell.

[191] Mineka, S., & Kihlstrom, J. (April, 1978). Unpredictable and uncontrollable events: A new perspective on experimental neurosis. Journal of Abnormal Psychology, 256-271.s

[192] Wolman, B. (1988). Psychosomatic disorders (p. 63). New York: Plenum Medical Book.

[193] Craig, A. (2015). How do you feel? An interoceptive moment with your neurobiological self (p. 52). Princeton: Princeton University Press.

[194] Campbell, G. (2015, July 28). Interview with Dr. Bud Craig, Author of How Do You Feel? An Interoceptive Moment with Your Biological Self (p. 14). Retrieved from http://brainsciencepodcast.com/

[195] Craig, A. (2015). How do you feel? An interoceptive moment with your neurobiological self (p. 3). Princeton: Princeton University Press.

[196] Ibid.

[197] Ibid., p. 209.

[198] Ibid., p. 52.

[199] Ray, R. (2008). Touching enlightenment: Finding realization in the body (p. 97). Boulder: Sounds True.

[200] Ray, R. (2008). Touching enlightenment: Finding realization in the body (p. 97). Boulder: Sounds True.

[201] Frowde, H. (1999). Sacred books of the Buddhists (Vol. 47, p. 301). London: Oxford University Press.

[202] Carus, P. (1915). The gospel of Buddha, Chicago (p. 125): Open Court Pub.

[203] Ibid., p. 127.

[204] Ibid.

[205] Ibid.

[206] Ashvaghosha; Tice, P (2003). Life of the Buddha: Clay Sanskrit Library (p. 125). New York: NYU Press.

[207] Tripāṭhī, Ś. (2008). Encyclopaedia of Pali literature (p. 150). New Delhi: Anmol Publications.

[208] Newshour interview with Judy Woodruff.

[209] Webster, I. (2003). Merriam-Webster's collegiate dictionary (11th ed., p. 613). Springfield, MA: Merriam-Webster.

[210] Wilber, K. (2000). Sex, ecology, spirituality (p 223). Boston: Shambhala.

[211] Levine, P. (1997). Waking the tiger: Healing trauma: The innate capacity to transform overwhelming experiences (p. 18). Berkeley, Calif.: North Atlantic Books.

[212] Levine, P. (n.d.). Trauma and the Science Behind the SE Approach. Retrieved September 10, 2014.

[213] Peter Levine. Waking the Tiger: Healing the Trauma. the innate capacity to transform overwhelming experiences (p. 18). Berkeley, Calif.: North Atlantic Books. p.18.

[214] Morey, J. (2014, October 23). BG 337: Relational Mindfulness - Buddhist Geeks. Retrieved from http://www.buddhistgeeks.com

[215215] Walker, B. (1988), Crone (p. 21). New York: Harper Collins.

[216] Masson, J. (1984). The assault on truth: Freud's suppression of the seduction theory (p. 27). New York: Farrar, Straus and Giroux.

[217] Ibid.

[218] Jowett, B. (1996). Symposium: The Benjamin Jowett translation (p. 39). New York: Modern Library.

[219] Ibid.

[220] Ibid.

[221] Cobb, W. (1993). The Symposium and, the Phaedrus; Plato's erotic dialogues (p. 147). Albany: State University of New York Press.

[222] Ross, S. (1984). Art and its significance: An anthology of aesthetic theory (p. 61). Albany: State University of New York Press.

[223] Ibid.

[224] Jowett, B. (2010). Dialogues of Plato (Simon & Schuster paperback ed., p. 314). New York, NY: Simon & Schuster Paperbacks.

[225] Ibid.

[226] Ibid.

[227] Morris, D. (2005). The Naked Ape: A zoologist's study of the human animal (p. 49). London: Vintage.

[228] Ibid.

[229] Ibid., p. 51.

[230] Howatson, M. (2008). Plato, the Symposium (p. 24). Cambridge, UK: Cambridge University Press.

[231] Ibid.

[232] Allen, R. (1991). The dialogues of Plato. New Haven: Yale University Press.

[233] Jowett, B. (2010). The works of Plato (Vol. 3, p. 281). New York: Cosimo Classics.

[234] Ibid.

[235] Cobb, W. (1993). The Symposium and, the Phaedrus; Plato's erotic dialogues (p. 45). Albany: State University of New York Press.

[236] Arora, V. (2013, June 28). Bhutan's Buddhist monks accused of sexually molesting boys. Washington Post.

[237] Benardete, S. (2001). Plato's Symposium (p. 38). Chicago: University of Chicago Press.

[238] Jowett, B. (1996). Symposium: The Benjamin Jowett translation (p. 10). New York: Modern Library.

[239] Jowett, B. (1951). Dialogues of Plato (p. 196). New York: Washington Square Press.

[240] Jowett, B. (2010). The works of Plato (Vol. 3, p. 281). New York: Cosimo Classics.

[241] Ibid., p. 280.

[242] Bible, New International Version, John 1:1.

[243] Rinpoche, T., & Kunsang, E. (1999). As it is (p. 59). Hong Kong: Rangjung Yeshe Publications.

[244] Bible, New International Version, John 9:25.

[245] Evola, J. (1991). The metaphysics of sex: Eros and the mysteries of love (p. 59). Rochester, Vt.: Inner Traditions International.

[246] Robinson, J. (Ed.). (n.d.). The Nag Hammadi library in English (Revised ed., p. 179).

[247] Walker, B. (1988), Crone (p. 177). New York: Harper Collins.

[248] Neusner, J., Frerichs, , & Levine, A. (1989). Religious writings and religious systems: Systemic analysis of holy books in Christianity, Islam, Buddhism, Greco-Roman religions, ancient Israel, and Judaism (p. 71). Atlanta, Ga.: Scholars Press.

[249] Herbermann, C. (Ed.). (1907). The Catholic encyclopedia: An international work of reference on the constitution, doctrine, discipline, and history of the Catholic Church (Vol. 6, p. 597). New York: Robert Appleton.

[250] Wallace, V. (2001). The inner kālacakratantra a Buddhist tantric view of the individual (p. 7). New York: Oxford University Press.

[251] Herbermann, C. (Ed.). (1907). The Catholic encyclopedia: An international work of reference on the constitution, doctrine, discipline, and history of the Catholic Church (Vol. 6, p. 597). New York: Robert Appleton.

[252] Robinson, J. (Ed.). (n.d.). The Nag Hammadi library in English (Revised ed., p. 231).

[253] Sedley, D. & Wilson, A (2010). Ancient models of mind: Studies in human and divine rationality, (p 16). Cambridge: Cambridge University Press.

[254] Blocker, H. (1974). The meaning of meaninglessness (p. 132). The Hague: Martinus Nijhoff.

[255] Wilber. K. (2013. July 13). Integral Semiotics (p. 21). Retrieved from https://www.integrallife.com/integral-post/integral-semiotics

[256] Ibid.

[257] Bodhi, B. (2011). The Noble Eightfold Path Way to the End of Suffering. (p. 54). Chicago: Pariyatti Publishing.

[258] Caputo, J. (1997). The prayers and tears of Jacques Derrida religion without religion. Bloomington, Ind.: Indiana University Press.

[259] Gautama, N. (2009). Buddhism A Faith of World (p. 129). New Delhi: Mahaveer & Sons.

[260] Burlingame. E., & Lanman. C. (Eds.). (1921). Buddhist Legends: Translation of books 3-12 of the Dhammapada, Vol. 28 p. 106. Buddhaghosa Trans. Boston: Harvard University.

[261] Burlingame. E., & Lanman. C. (Eds.). (1921). Buddhist Legends: Translation of books 3-12 of the Dhammapada, Vol. 29 p. 253. Buddhaghosa Trans. Boston: Harvard University.

[262] Gautama, N. (2009). Buddhism A Faith of World (p. 129). New Delhi: Mahaveer & Sons.

[263] Burlingame. E., & Lanman. C. (Eds.). (1921). Buddhist Legends: Translation of books 3-12 of the Dhammapada, Vol. 29 p. 254. Buddhaghosa Trans. Boston: Harvard University.

[264] The Buddha [Motion picture]. (2010). PBS Distribution.

[265] Ohnuma. R. (2012). Ties that bind: Maternal imagery and discourse in Indian Buddhism (p. 89). Oxford: Oxford University Press.

[266] Wangyal. T., & Lukianowicz, A. (1993). Wonders of the natural mind: The essence of Dzogchen in the native Bon tradition of Tibet (p. 159). Barrytown, N.Y.: Station Hill.

[267] Neel, A. (1971). Magic and mystery in Tibet (p. 199). New York: Dover Publications.

[268] The Camillians Celebrate Sister Candida. (2014, February 20). Retrieved from http://www.camilliani.org/en/the-camillians-celebrate-sister-candida/

[269] Ibid.

[270] Ibid.

[271] Hanh, T. (1996). Be still and know: Reflections from Living Buddha, living Christ (p. 95). New York: Riverhead Books.

[272] Wilber, K. (2006). Integral spirituality (p. 34). Boston: Shambhala.

[273] Hanh, T. (Ed.). (2007). Chanting from the heart: Buddhist ceremonies and daily practices (p. 25). Berkeley, Calif.: Parallax Press.

[274] Thurman, R. (2005). The jewel tree of Tibet: The enlightenment engine of Tibetan Buddhism (p. 122). New York: Free Press.

[275] Nyanaponika, H. (1997). Great disciples of the Buddha: Their lives, their works, their legacy (p. 155). Boston: Wisdom Publications.

[276] Saddhatissa, H. (2013). The Sutta-Nipata: A New Translation from the Pali Canon (p 16). London: Routledge.

[277] Wilson, A. (1995). World scripture: A comparative anthology of sacred texts (Part 2) (p. 571). St. Paul, Minn.: Paragon House.

[278] Sutherland, E. (2013, October 13). Prehistoric cave artists were likely women, not men. Retrieved from http://www.examiner.com/article/prehistoric-cave-artists-were-likely-women-not-men

[279] Damasio, A. (1999). The feeling of what happens: Body and emotion in the making of consciousness (p. 52). New York: Harcourt Brace.

[280] Kegan, R. (1994). In over our heads: The mental demands of modern life (p. 32). Cambridge, Mass.: Harvard University Press.

[281] Wilber, K. (2000). Integral psychology: Consciousness, spirit, psychology, therapy (p. 126). Boston: Shambhala.

[282] Schireson, G. (n.d.). Zen women: Beyond tea ladies, iron maidens, and macho masters (p. 50).

[283] Ray, R. (Winter Dathun, 2011). Episode 57: Space gives birth to love. Retrieved from http://www.dharmaocean.org/

[284] Ibid.

[285] Beer, R. (2003). The handbook of Tibetan Buddhist symbols. Boston: Shambhala.

[286] Panksepp, J. (1998). Affective neuroscience: The foundations of human and animal emotions. New York: Oxford University Press.

[287] Shrestha, R., & Chopra, D. (2006). Goddesses of the celestial gallery (Special ed., p. 3). San Rafael, Calif.: Mandala Pub.

[288] Gyatso, G. (2000). Guide to Dakini land: The highest yoga tantra practice of Buddha Vajrayogini (2nd ed., p. 343). London: Tharpa.

[289] Ibid.

[290] Shrestha, R., & Chopra, D. (2006). Goddesses of the celestial gallery (Special ed., p. 3). San Rafael, Calif.: Mandala Pub.

[291] Gutschow, K. (2004). Being a Buddhist nun the struggle for enlightenment in the Himalayas (p. 227). Cambridge, Mass.: Harvard University Press.

[292] Baker, I (author) in Shrestha, R., & Chopra, D. (2006). Goddesses of the celestial gallery (Special ed., p. 10). San Rafael, Calif.: Mandala Pub.

[293] Tripāṭhī, Ś. (2008). Encyclopaedia of Pali literature (p. 89). New Delhi: Anmol Publications.

[294] Batchelor, S. (Director) (2014, May 28). A Culture of Awakening (Part 1). Talk given at Upaya Zen Center, Santa Fe, NM, 87501.

[295] Harrison, P. (2009, August 2). Vajracchedika Prajñaparamita Diamond Cutting Transcendent Wisdom (p. 1). Retrieved from: http://www.nczencenter.org/Garfield Docs/Diamond Cutter Sutra.pdf.

[296] Braarvig, J. (2000). Buddhist manuscripts (p. 153). Oslo: Hermes Pub.

[297] Harrison. P. (2009. August 2). Vairacchedika Praiñaparamita Diamond Cutting Transcendent Wisdom (p. 1). Retrieved from http://www.nczencenter.org/Garfield Docs/Diamond Cutter Sutra.pdf

[298] Ibid., p. 9.

[299] Harrison. P. (2009. August 2). Vairacchedika Praiñaparamita Diamond Cutting Transcendent Wisdom (p. 9). Retrieved from http://www.nczencenter.org/Garfield Docs/ Diamond Cutter Sutra.pdf

[300] Teresa of Avila. (2007). Interior castle (p. 126) (E. Peers, Ed.). New York: Dover.

[301] Ibid.

[302] Ibid.

[303] Ambedkar, B. (2006). The Buddha and his Dharma (p. 147). New Delhi: Siddhartha Books.

[304] Ibid.

[305] Burlingame. E.. & Lanman. C. (Eds.). (1921). Buddhist Legends: Translation of books 3-12 of the Dhammapada, Vol. 28 p. 8. Buddhaghosa Trans. Boston: Harvard University.

[306] Nanamoli. B.. & Bodhi. B. (1995). The middle length discourses of the Buddha: A translation of the Majjhima Nikāya (p. 116). Boston: Wisdom Publications.

[307] Harrison. P. (2009, August 2). Vairacchedika Praiñaparamita Diamond Cutting Transcendent Wisdom (p. 9). Retrieved from http://www.nczencenter.org/Garfield Docs/Diamond Cutter Sutra.pdf

[308] Müller, F.M. (1952). Sacred books of the Buddhists, Vol 18. (p 131). London: Oxford Press.

[309] Harrison. P. (2009, August 2). Vairacchedika Praiñaparamita Diamond Cutting Transcendent Wisdom (p. 9). Retrieved from: http://www.nczencenter.org/Garfield Docs/Diamond Cutter Sutra.pdf

[310] Suzuki, S., & Dixon, T. (1970). Zen mind, beginner's mind (p. 129). New York: Weatherhill.

[311] Realizing Genjokoan: The Key to Dogen's Shobogenzo.

[312] Tanahashi, K. (1985). Moon in a dewdrop (p. 4). San Francisco: North Point Press

[313] Roshi, S. (1962, December 1). Suzuki Roshi Transcripts. Retrieved from http://suzukiroshi.sfzc.org/

[314] Heine, Steven (1985). Existential and Ontological Dimensions of Time in Heidegger and Dōgen, p. 27. Albany: State U of New York.

[315] Ibid.

[316] Ray, R. (March 9, 2016). Working with Trauma in the Non-dual Body: An Experiential. Speech presented at 2016 CIIS Nondual and Psychotherapy Conference. San Francisco.

[317] Dumoulin, Heinrich (2005b). Zen Buddhism: A History. Volume 2: Japan. World Wisdom Books.

[318] Ibid.

[319] Kim, H., & Leighton, T. (2004). Eihei Dōgen: Mystical realist (p. 125). Boston: Wisdom Publications.

[320] Pascal, B., & Eliot, T. (1958). Pascal's Pensées (p. 18). New York: E.P. Dutton.

[321] Tanahashi, K. (1985). Moon in a dewdrop (p. 99). San Francisco: North Point Press.

[322] Rubin, J. (1996). Psychotherapy and Buddhism: Toward an integration (p. 83). New York: Plenum Press.

[323] Loori, J. (2004). The art of just sitting: Essential writings on the Zen practice of shikantaza (2nd ed., p. 167). Boston: Wisdom Publications.

[324] Anderson, R. (2001). Being upright: Zen meditation and the bodhisattva precepts (p. 117). Berkeley: Rodmell Press.

[325] Heine, S. (1997). The Zen poetry of Dōgen: Verses from the Mountain of Eternal Peace (p. 117). Boston: Tuttle.

[326] Leighton, T. (2004). Dogen's extensive record: A translation of the Eihei koroku (p. 286). Somerville, MA.: Wisdom Publications.

[327] Dumoulin, Heinrich (2005b). Zen Buddhism: A History. Volume 2: Japan (p. 72). World Wisdom Books.

[328] Ray, R. (2008). Touching enlightenment: Finding realization in the body (p. 97). Boulder: Sounds True.

[329] Chopra, D. (July 23, 2014). You made it weird podcast.

[330] Chalmers, D. (2014) TED Talk.

[331] Lumiere, L., & Lumiere-Wins, J. (2003). The awakening West: Conversations with today's new Western spiritual leaders (p. 85). Gloucester, Mass.: Fair Winds.).

[332] Ibid.

[333] Chalmers, R. (1898) Tathāgata (p 103). Journal of the Royal Asiatic Society Great Britain and Ireland.

[334] Kornfield, J. (2000). After the ecstasy, the laundry: How the heart grows wise on the spiritual path. New York: Bantam Books.

[335] Rucker, R. (1977). Geometry, relativity, and the fourth dimension (p. 118). New York: Dover Publications.

[336] New giant armadillo behaviours caught on camera and win awards. (December 3, 2014). Retrieved from http://www.pressreleasepoint.com/new-giant-armadillo-behaviours-caught-camera-and-win-awards

[337] Brennan, P., Prum, R., Mccracken, K., Sorenson, M., Wilson, R., Birkhead, T., & Pizzari, T. (2007). Coevolution of Male and Female Genital Morphology in Waterfowl. PLoS ONE, 418-418.

[338] Darwin, C. (1902). On the origin of species by means of natural selection (p. 80 & 481). London: Grant Richards.

[339] Ibid. p. 481.

[340] Darwin, C., & Peckham, M. (2004). The origin of species: A variorum text (p. 732). Philadelphia: University of Pennsylvania Press.

[341] Chatterjee, R. (1925). The Modern Review (37), p 538. Prabasi Press Private, Limited: India.

[342] Papua New Guinea | Oxfam Australia. (2011, October 13). Retrieved from https://www.oxfam.org.au/about-us/countries-where-we-work/papua-new-guinea/

[343] Buswell, R. & Lopez, D. (2013). The Princeton Dictionary of Buddhism (p. 87). Princeton, NJ: Princeton UP.

[344] Mills, L. (1979). Banner of the Arahants: Buddhist monks and nuns from the Buddha's time till now (p. 151). Kandy, Sri Lanka: Buddhist Publication Society.

[345] Diamond, J. (1998). Guns, germs, and steel: The fates of human societies. New York: Norton.

[346] Chesbro, D. (2012). The Gospel of Thomas A Spiritual Interpretation for the Aquarian Age (p. 101). Chicago: Findhorn Press.

[347] Dimand, M., Mailey, J., & York, N. (1973). Oriental rugs in the Metropolitan Museum of Art (p. 313). New York: Metropolitan Museum of Art.

[348] Landon, P., Younghusband, F., Walton, H., & O'Conner, W. (1905). Lhasa: An account of the country and people of central Tibet and of the progress of the mission sent there by the English government in the year 1903-4 (p. 357). London: Hurst & Blackett.

[349] The Universal Declaration of Human Rights. (1948, December 10). Retrieved from http://www.un.org/en/documents/udhr/

[350] Keeney, B. (2010). The bushman way of tracking God: The original spirituality of the Kalahari people (p. 17). New York: Atria Books

[351] Dalai Lama (2014, November 26). Neuroplasticity and healing (University of Alabama conference). Retrieved from http://brainsciencepodcast.com/

[352] D. E. Ingber, M. Landau (2012). Tensegrity. Scholarpedia, 7(2):8344.

[353] Ibid

[354] Ibid.

[355] Ibid.

[356] Levin, S. M. Biotensegrity: A new way of modeling biologic forms. http://www. biotensegrity.com/

[357] Levin, S. (2015, February 2). Dr. Stephen Levin: Biotensegrity (LBP 035) - Liberated Body. Retrieved from http://www.liberatedbody.com/stephen-levin-lbp-035/

[358] Hartwig, W. (2008). Fundamental anatomy (p. 259). Philadelphia: Wolters Kluwer Health/Lippincott Williams & Wilkins.

[359] Chaitow (1997). (IN) Sharkey, J. (2008). The concise book of neuromuscular therapy: A trigger point manual (p. 48). Chichester, England: Lotus Pub.

[360] Sharkey, J. (2008). The concise book of neuromuscular therapy: A trigger point manual (p. 53). Chichester, England: Lotus Pub.

[361] Pinto, H., & Shea, M. (2014). Myofascial release therapy a visual guide to clinical applications (p. 30). Berkeley, Calif.: North Atlantic Books.

[362] The Gospel according to Matthew 18:3: New International Version. (1973). Grand Rapids, MI: Zondervan.

[363] Zamora, M. (1990). Frida Kahlo: The brush of anguish (p. 26). San Francisco: Chronicle Books.

[364] Calhoun, L., & Tedeschi, R. (2013). Posttraumatic growth in clinical practice (p. 6). New York, NY: Routledge.

[365] Porges, S. (2011). The polyvagal theory: Neurophysiological foundations of emotions, attachment, communication, and self-regulation. New York: W. W. Norton.

[366] Porges SW. Orienting in a defensive world: Mammalian modifications of our evolutionary heritage: A Polyvagal Theory. Psychophysiology. 1995; 32:301–318.

[367] Porges, S. (2011). The polyvagal theory: Neurophysiological foundations of emotions, attachment, communication, and self-regulation (p. 287). New York: W. W. Norton.

[368] Porges, S. (2015, Dec 15). The Polyvagal Theory & the Vagal Nerve (D. Asprey, Ed.). Retrieved from https://www.bulletproofexec.com/?s=264

[369] van der Kolk, B. (2015). Introduction. In P. Ogden & J. Fisher, Trauma and the body: A sensorimotor approach to psychotherapy (p. xxi). New York: W.W. Norton.

[370] Ogden, P., Minton, K., & Pain, C. (2006). Trauma and the body: A sensorimotor approach to psychotherapy. New York: W.W. Norton.

[371] Ogden, P., Fisher J. (2015). Sensorimotor psychotherapy: Interventions for trauma and attachment. New York: W.W. Norton.

[372] Siegel, D. (1999). The Developing Mind: Toward a Neurobiology of Interpersonal Experience (New York: Guilford Press, 1999)

[373] Ingram, P. O., & Streng, F. J. (1986). Buddhist-Christian dialogue: Mutual renewal and transformation (p. 150). Honolulu: University of Hawaii Press.

[374] Born in Slavery: Slave Narratives from the Federal Writers' Project, 1936-1938. Library of Congress, Manuscript Division. Washington: Library of Congress.

[375] In the Buddha's words: An anthology of discourses from the Pāli canon: translated from the Pāli by Bhikkhu Bodhi. (p. 62). (2005). Boston, Mass.: Wisdom Publications.

[376] Gowans, C. (2003). Philosophy of the Buddha: An introduction (p. 20). London: Routledge.

[377] In the Buddha's words: An anthology of discourses from the Pāli canon: translated from the Pāli by Bhikkhu Bodhi. (p. 62). (2005). Boston, Mass.: Wisdom Publications.

[378] Fogel, A. (2013). Body sense: The science and practice of embodied self-awareness (p. 152). New York: W. W Norton.

[379] Porges, S. (2015, Dec 15). The Polyvagal Theory & the Vagal Nerve (D. Asprey, Ed.). Retrieved from https://www.bulletproofexec.com/?s=264

[380] Keltner, D. (2009). Born to be good: The science of a meaningful life (p. 241). New York: W.W. Norton.

[381] Carter, C. (1999). The integrative neurobiology of affiliation (p. xii). Cambridge, Mass.: MIT Press.

[382] Liotti, G. (1999). Disorganization of attachment as a model for understanding dissociative psychopathology. In Solomon, J. & George, C. (Eds), Attachment disorganization (pp. 291-317). New York: Guilford Press.

[383] Stephen Porges: The Polyvagal Theory. (2015, January 2). Retrieved from https://www.youtube.com/watch?v=-EqT8p5X908

[384] Diamond Sutra - A New Translation. Chapter 21. (2005, June). Retrieved from http://www.diamond-sutra.com/diamond_sutra_text/page21.html

[385] Asprey, D. (2015, December 1). Stephen Porges: The Polyvagal Theory & The Vagal Nerve, Episode 264. Retrieved from http://bulletproofexec.com.

[386] Asprey, D. (2016, May 3). Tony Robbins & Peter Diamandis: Special Podcast, Live From The Genius Network, Episode 306. Retrieved from http://bulletproofexec.com.

[387] Gross, A. S. (2014). The question of the animal and religion: Theoretical stakes, practical implications, (p. 208). Columbia University Press: New York.

[388] Schore, A. N. (2003). Affect regulation and the repair of the self. New York: Norton.

[389] Schore, A. N. (2015). Affect regulation and origin of the self. New York: Norton.

[390] Cassidy, J., & Shaver, P. R. (2008). Handbook of attachment: Theory, research, and clinical applications. New York: Guilford Press.

[391] Schore, A. (August 8, 2009). The paradigm shift the right brain and the relational unconscious. Speech presented at 2009 APA Annual Conference. Toronto, Canada.

[392] Schore, A. N. (2015). Affect regulation and origin of the self. New York: Norton.

[393] Schore, J.R. & Schore, A.N. (2008) Modern attachment theory: the central role of affect regulation in development and treatment. Clinical Social Work Journal, 36:9-20

[394] Hill, D. & Schore, A. N. (2015). Affect regulation theory. New York: Norton.

[395] Schroder, V (1996). Attachment and Coping. ProQuest Digital Dissertations. (Pub. number pending).

[396] Matheny KB, Aycock DW, Curlette WL, Junker GN (1993). The coping resources inventory for stress: a measure of perceived resourcefulness. Journal of Clinical Psychology 49(6), 815-30.

[397] Schroder, V (1996). Attachment and Coping. ProQuest Digital Dissertations. (Pub. number 10154986)

[398] Matheny KB, Aycock DW, Curlette WL, Junker GN (1993). The coping resources inventory for stress: a measure of perceived resourcefulness. Journal of Clinical Psychology 49(6), 815-30.

[399] Schroder, V (1996). Attachment and Coping. ProQuest Digital Dissertations. (Pub. number 10154986).

[400] Stanley, S. (2016). Relational and body-centered practices for healing trauma: Lifting the burdens of the past, p. 41. Routledge: London.

[401] Ibid.

[402] Ibid.

[403] Hanson, R. (2013). Hardwiring happiness: The new brain science of contentment, calm, and confidence. New York: Harmony.

[404] Barbieri, A. (1996, September 14). Girls, we're in this together. Retrieved from http://www.independent.co.uk/life-style/girls-were-in-this-together-1363360.html

[405] Gosline, A. (2007, December 7). Do women who live together menstruate together? Retrieved from http://www.scientificamerican.com/article/do-women-who-live-together-menstruate-together/

[406] Ray, R. (March 9, 2016). Working with Trauma in the Non-dual Body: An Experiential. Speech presented at 2016 CIIS Nondual and Psychotherapy Conference. San Francisco.

[407] van der Kolk, B. (2015). The Body keeps the score brain, mind and body in the healing of trauma, p. 80. New York: Penguin Books.

[408] Ray, Reginald A. (2008). Touching Enlightenment: Finding Realization in the Body, p. 112. Boulder, CO: Sounds True.

[409] Ibid., p. 108.

[410] Ray, R. (March 9, 2016). Working with Trauma in the Non-dual Body: An Experiential. Speech presented at 2016 CIIS Nondual and Psychotherapy Conference. San Francisco.

[411] Zhengjue, Leighton, T. D., & Wu, Y. (1991). Cultivating the empty field: The silent illumination of Zen Master Hongzhi, p. 26. San Francisco: North Point Press.

[412] Ibid.

[413] Zhengjue, Leighton, T. D., & Wu, Y. (1991). Cultivating the empty field: The silent illumination of Zen Master Hongzhi, p. xii. San Francisco: North Point Press.

[414] Heine, Steven (2015). Dogen and Soto Zen. London: Oxford, 2015. Print.

[415] Stanley, S. (2016). Relational and body-centered practices for healing trauma: Lifting the burdens of the past. Routledge: London.

[416] Stanley, S. (2016). Relational and body-centered practices for healing trauma: Lifting the burdens of the past, p. 77. Routledge: London.

[417] Ray, Reginald A. (2008). Touching Enlightenment: Finding Realization in the Body. Boulder, CO: Sounds True.

[418] Ray, Reginald A. (2002). Secrets of the Vajra world: the tantric Buddhism of Tibet. Boston: Shambhala.

[419] Harper, D. (n.d.). Online Etymology Dictionary. Retrieved from http://www.etymonline.com/index.php?term=regular

[420] BBC Radio 4 - In Our Time, Rumi's Poetry. (2016, February 11). Retrieved from http://www.bbc.co.uk/programmes/b06ztx2w

[421] Ibid.

[422] Jalāl, R., & Barks, C. (2010). Rumi: The big red book : the great masterpiece celebrating mystical love and friendship, p. 126. New York: HarperOne.

[423] Child, A. B., & Child, I. L. (1993). Religion and magic in the life of traditional peoples. Englewood Cliffs, NJ: Prentice Hall.

[424] Panksepp, J., & Biven, L. (2012). The archaeology of mind: Neuroevolutionary origins of human emotions (p 101). New York: W. W Norton.

[425] Porges, S. (2011). The polyvagal theory: Neurophysiological foundations of emotions, attachment, communication, and self-regulation. New York: W. W. Norton.

[426] Asprey, D. (2015, December 1). Stephen Porges: The Polyvagal Theory & The Vagal Nerve, Episode 264. Retrieved from http://bulletproofexec.com.

[427] Ray, R. A. (2014). Touching enlightenment: finding realization in the body. Boulder, CO: Sounds True.

[428] Ray, R. A. (2016). Awakening the body: somatic meditation for discovering our deepest life. Boulder, CO: Sounds True.

[429] Bible, New International Version, Mark 12:40.

[430] Obeyesekere, G. (2012). The awakened ones: phenomenology of visionary experience, p. 26. New York: Columbia University Press.

[431] Porges, S. (2011). The polyvagal theory: Neurophysiological foundations of emotions, attachment, communication, and self-regulation. New York: W. W. Norton.

[432] Diamond Sutra - A New Translation. Chapter 21. (2005, June). Retrieved from http://www.diamond-sutra.com/diamond_sutra_text/page21.html

[433] The connected discourses of the Buddha a new translation of the Samvutta Nikāva, p. 225; translated from the Pāli by Bhikkhu Bodhi. (Vol. 94(2)). Boston: Wisdom Publications.

[434] Dr. Jaak Panksepp – The Importance Of Play. (2010, December 7). Retrieved from http://brainworldmagazine.com/dr-jaak-panksepp-the-importance-of-play/

[435] Ainsworth, M. D. & Bell, S. M. (1970). Attachment, exploration, and separation: Illustrated by the behavior of one-year-olds in a strange situation. Child Development, 41:49-67

[436] Van der Kolk, B. A. (2014). The body keeps the score: Brain, mind, and body in the healing of trauma. New York: Viking.

[437] Ibid., p. 194.

[438] Ray, R. A. (2016). Awakening the body: somatic meditation for discovering our deepest life. Boulder, CO: Sounds True.

[439] Porges, S. W. (2015). Clinical insights from the polyvagal theory. London: Norton.

[440] Fosha, Diana., Siegel, Daniel J.,Solomon, Marion Fried. (Eds.) (2009). The healing power of emotion: affective neuroscience, development, and clinical practice New York: W.W. Norton & Co.

[441] Peck, M. S. (2012). The road less travelled. London: Rider.

[442] Inside the Superhuman World of the Iceman. (2015, July 16). Retrieved from http://www.youtube.com/watch?v=VaMjhwFE1Zw

[443] The Iceman – Up Close with Wim Hof. (2016, August 22). Retrieved from http://www.enjoythemomentrituals.com/the-iceman/

[444] Ibid.

[445] Kox, M., Eijk, L. V., Zwaag, J., Wildenberg, J. V., Sweep, F., Hoeven, J. V., & Pickkers, P. (2014). Voluntary activation of the sympathetic nervous system and attenuation of the innate immune response in humans. Intensive Care Medicine Experimental, 2 (Suppl 1).

[446] Diamond Sutra - A New Translation. Chapter 21. (2005, June). Retrieved from http://www.diamond-sutra.com/diamond_sutra_text/page21.html

[447] Davids, T. (1880). Buddhist birth stories; or, Jātaka tales. The oldest collection of folklore extant: Being the Jātakatthavaṇṇanā (p. 92). Boston: Houghton & Mifflin.

[448] John 6:51, King James Bible.

[449] Full text of "Back Copies of Buddhist Studies Review." Retrieved from http://archive.org/stream/BackCopiesOfBuddhistStudiesReview/Bsr4.11987_djvu.txt

[450] Arnold, E. (1885). The light of Asia; or, The Great Renunciation (Mahabhinishkramana), p. 121. London: Tuübner.

[451] Lillie, A. (1883). The popular life of Buddha, containing an answer to the "Hibbert lectures" of 1881 (p. 81). London: K. Paul, Trench & Trbner.

[452] Jung, E., & Franz, M. (1998). The grail legend (2nd ed.). Princeton, N.J.: Princeton University Press.

[453] The future Buddha receiving the milk-porridge offered by Sujata. Retrieved February 6, 2013, from http://wanderling.tripod.com/sujata.html

[454] Herold, A. (1929). The life of Buddha according to the legends of ancient India, n.p. London: Thornton Butterworth.

[455] Ibid.

[456] Zweig, C. & Abrams, J. (1991). Meeting the shadow: the hidden power of the dark side of human nature (p. 21). Los Angeles: J.P. Tarcher.

[457] Führer, Alois Anton Monograph on Buddha Sakyamuni's birth-place in the Nepalese Tarei (Volume 26, Part 1) (p 14). London: WH Allen.

[458] Davids, T. (2000). Buddhist birth stories: The oldest collection of folklore extant (p. 100). London: Routledge. Reprint Trübner & Co. Ltd. 1880.

[459] Bhikku, T. (2004). Handful of Leaves V2: An Anthology from the Samyutta Nikaya (p. 173) (G. DeGraff, Trans). Redwood City, CA, USA: Sati Center for Buddhist Studies & Metta Forest Monastery.

[460] Elliot, C. (Ed.). (1910). Sacred writings in two volumes: Volume 2: Christian (part 2), Buddhist, Hindu, Mohammedan (Vol. 45, p. 633). New York: P.F. Collier.

[460] Zhengjue, Leighton, T. D., & Wu, Y. (1991). Cultivating the empty field: The silent illumination of Zen Master Hongzhi, p. 26. San Francisco: North Point Press.

I grew up in Florida. When I was a kid, many of my father's international students wove in out of our lives and sometimes lived with us. My mom loved opening our home to people of all persuasions and was intent on her children opening their hearts in the same manner. Sylvie (from France) and Yuriko (from Japan) lived with us. They remained very close to my mom and dad over the years, eventually sending photos of husbands and babies. Preecha (from Thailand) was often at our house working on my dad's Renault Carravelle and remained in close touch. A Canadian Christian monk once lived with us while working on a massive book on saints. Despite being homeless and having no money, he was selected to be my godfather. He and my mom practiced contemplative prayer/meditation. They were big fans of Thomas Merton. As far as I could tell, their god and spirituality was bigger than any one religion.

Because of my parents' love of travel and cultures as well as my passion for surfing, I set off for Hawaii at age 18. I attended the University of Hawaii and remained in Hawaii for the next 20 years. I had many harrowing ocean encounters similar to those described in early sections of "Saltwater Buddha", which I recently read with delight. Having been to and lived in Europe, my father, brother, and I eventually traveled the other direction. Preecha met us in Bangkok and took us all over Thailand. Thai Buddhism and Thai culture made a huge impression on me. I would end up going back many times. In the 1990s, I finally met HER—my wife, Ni. She and I were married in Florida and also in her village in Thailand where Preecha represented me in a traditional Buddhist ceremony. Ni and I have since been blessed with three children.

As a clinical psychologist, I've worked with kids, families, couples, Hospice patients, and in a variety of settings in addition to private practice. For a long time, leading up to writing *Buddha's Mom*, I carved out a niche with what I call, "underperforming gifted" adults, including many people outwardly successful and inwardly tormented. I have increasingly come to view deep self disturbance, "affective dysregulation", trauma—whatever frame might be applied—through spiritual eyes: as mappable, perfect in its own expression, and thus perfectly workable. Many of the ideas and enthusiasms I've written about here welled up and were tested for muster while working with some of the most incredible people one could ever hope to know. Over the years, I've also loved giving talks at universities in Thailand, though sometimes I would discover that I was about the only English speaker in the room. More recently, I have been functioning as a medical psychologist at a major hospital. In close connection with amazing nurses and doctors, I assist in assessing and brief treatment of patients often "in extremis". This book has been a labor of love, calling for mountains of each labor and love. Please read it and/or thank you for doing so! Feedback is welcome: winyahn@gmail.com.

www.ingramcontent.com/pod-product-compliance
Lightning Source LLC
Chambersburg PA
CBHW080617030426
42336CB00018B/2996

9780999812840 5